THE

WAR CORRESPONDENCE

OF

THE 'DAILY NEWS'

1877

WITH A CONNECTING NARRATIVE
FORMING A CONTINUOUS HISTORY OF THE
WAR BETWEEN RUSSIA AND TURKEY
TO THE FALL OF KARS

Elibron Classics
www.elibron.com

Elibron Classics series.

ISBN 1-4021-7760-7 (paperback)
ISBN 1-4021-2542-9 (hardcover)

This Elibron Classics Replica Edition is an unabridged facsimile of the edition published in 1878 by Macmillan and Co., London.

THE WAR CORRESPONDENCE OF THE "DAILY NEWS" 1877

WITH A CONNECTING NARRATIVE

FORMING A CONTINUOUS HISTORY OF THE

WAR BETWEEN RUSSIA AND TURKEY

TO THE FALL OF KARS

INCLUDING THE LETTERS OF

MR. ARCHIBALD FORBES, MR. J. A. MACGAHAN AND MANY OTHER SPECIAL CORRESPONDENTS IN EUROPE AND ASIA

London
MACMILLAN AND CO.
1878

LONDON:
WOODFALL AND KINDER, PRINTERS,
MILFORD LANE, STRAND, W.C.

PREFACE.

THIS volume has been issued to meet the wishes of those who desire to possess, in a permanent form, letters which once yielded them pleasure and instruction. On their first publication these letters were reprinted by daily and weekly Journals throughout the kingdom, and may, without exaggeration, be affirmed to have been more widely reproduced than any communications ever despatched from fields of battle. Of a large proportion of them, it may be said, that they were welcomed by the public as affording the earliest, fullest, and most specific information at critical moments of the campaign, and if it should further be found that these same letters, hastily written in the bivouac, on the field of victory, or in some hovel on the line of retreat, have at the same time the merit of being among the most vivid and truthful pictures of war that have at any time been offered to the public, the popularity they have attained would be accounted for.

Owing to the large number of the Special Correspondents whose letters are now republished, and in order that each of them may have credit for his own labours, a conventional sign has been appropriated to each correspondent and prefixed to his letters, by which his writings may be distinguished.

"DAILY NEWS" OFFICE, BOUVERIE STREET,
December, 1877.

CONTENTS.

CHAPTER V.

THE ASIATIC CAMPAIGN.

CHAPTER VI.

THE EVE OF THE CROSSING.

CHAPTER VII.

THE FIRST PASSAGE OF THE DANUBE.

CHAPTER VIII.

THE CROSSING AT SIMNITZA.

CHAPTER IX.

THE ADVANCE INTO BULGARIA.

CHAPTER X.

RUSSIAN OCCUPATION OF TIRNOVA.

CHAPTER XI.

GENERAL GOURKO'S EXPEDITION.

CHAPTER XII.

THE FIRST CHECK AT PLEVNA.

CHAPTER XIII.

THE GREAT RUSSIAN REPULSE BEFORE PLEVNA.

CHAPTER XIV.

SECOND PERIOD OF THE CAMPAIGN IN ASIA.

CHAPTER XV.

THE RUSSIAN DEADLOCK.

CHAPTER XVI.

THE FIGHTING IN THE SHIPKA PASS.

CHAPTER XVII.

THE THIRD ATTACK ON PLEVNA.

CHAPTER XVIII.

THE SECOND DEADLOCK IN BULGARIA.

CHAPTER XIX.

CRISIS OF THE CAMPAIGN IN ASIA.

CHAPTER XX.

INVESTMENT OF PLEVNA AND FALL OF KARS.

CHRONOLOGY OF THE WAR.

APRIL 24, TO NOVEMBER 18, 1877.

Apr. 24, 1877.

Russian declaration of war, and immediate entrance of the Czar's troops into Roumania and Turkish Armenia.

Apr. 25.

Seizure of the Barbosch Bridge, and occupation of Galatz by a Russian division.

Apr. 26.

Abandonment of Bayazid to the Russians.

Apr. 30.

The Queen's proclamation of neutrality.

May 1.

Lord Derby's despatch to Lord A. Loftus, conveying disapproval of the war begun by Russia.

May 6.

Lord Derby's despatch to Count Schouvaloff, enumerating the British interests which the war might imperil.

May 11.

A Turkish three-masted turret-ship blown up near Braila, by a shell fired from a Russian battery. Serious repulse of the Russian Rion detachment by the Turks near Batoum. Bombardment by the Turks of towns on the Russian coast of the Black Sea.

May 13.

Capture of Sukhum Kaleh by a Turkish squadron, and landing of troops and Circassians in Great Abhasia.

May 14.

Great revolt of the Mussulman population in Trans-Caucasia.

May 17.

Capture of Ardahan by assault.

May 26.

Destruction of a second Turkish monitor between Matchin and Braila by Russian officers with torpedoes.

May 30.

Reply of Prince Gortschakoff to Lord Derby's letter of May 6: "the Russian Government will respect the British interests mentioned by Lord Derby, as long as England remains neutral."

June 2.

Investment of Kars.

June 8.

Sudden evacuation of Olti by the Russians.

June 14.

Investment of Bayazid by Faik Pacha.

June 16.

Battle of Taghir and defeat of the right wing of the Turkish Army in Asia.

June 19.

Surrender of 1,200 Cossacks to Faik Pacha at Bayazid, and instant slaughter of the whole body by Kurdish irregular troops.

June 21.

Battle of Eshki Khaliass and defeat of the left wing of the Russian Army in Asia.

June 22.

Passage of the Lower Danube by the Russians, and landing at Matchin.

June 25.

Defeat of the centre of the Russian Army in Asia at Zevin.

June 27.

Passage of the Danube by the main body of the Russian Army at Simnitza.

July 2.

Russian bridge completed at Sistova. Retreat of Russian Army in Asia to Kuruk-Dere.

July 4.

Occupation of Bjela by the Russians. Relief of Kars by Mukhtar Pasha.

July 8.

Capture of Tirnova by General Gourko.

July 10.

Relief of the garrison of Bayazid by General Tergukasoff.

July 14.

General Gourko debouches into the Tundja Valley beyond the Balkans.

July 15.

Capture of Nicopolis by the Russians.

July 16.

General Gourko defeats a Turkish force after a sharp engagement.

July 17.

General Gourko enters Kezanlik.

July 18.

General Gourko attacks the Shipka Pass in the rear.

July 19.

Occupation of the Pass by the Russians. Abdul Kerim Pacha, commander-in-chief of the Ottoman Army in Europe, dismissed. Mehemet Ali Pacha appointed his successor. General Krüdener, with part of the 9th Russian Corps attacks Plevna and is repulsed; is attacked in turn and defeated.

July 20.

Sulieman Pacha at Adrianople with 20,000 regular troops.

July 21.

General Krüdener, having received reinforcements, renews his attack on Plevna, and is again defeated.

July 28.

Capture of Loftcha by Osman Pacha.

July 30.

Defeat of the Turks by General Gourko at Yeni Zagra.

July 31.

Decisive defeat of the right wing of General Gourko's force at Eski Zagra. General Gourko, menaced by the whole force of Suleiman Pacha, returns to the Balkan Passes. The Russians, under General Krüdener and Prince Schahofskoy, attack Osman Pacha at Plevna with 32,000 men, and are defeated with heavy loss.

Aug. 2.

Retreat of General Gourko into the Shipka Pass.

Aug. 19.

Suleiman Pacha occupies the village of Shipka.

Aug. 21.

Suleiman Pacha attacks the Russian position in the Shipka Pass, held by 3,000 men with 40 guns, but only gains the outer lines.

Aug. 22.

Repulse of a Turkish attack on Selvi.

Aug. 23.

Determined and prolonged attack on the Shipka Pass by Suleiman Pacha, which is repulsed late in the evening, when the Russians receive timely reinforcements. Turkish attack on Jaslar, retreat of the Russians to Sultankoi.

Aug. 24.

Renewed and desperate fighting.

Aug. 25.

Turkish attack on the Russian position near Kuruk Dere in Asia, with heavy loss on both sides. Passage of the Danube by the main body of the Roumanian Army.

Aug. 27.

Suleiman Pacha having failed to take the Shipka position, telegraphs for reinforcements.

Aug. 29.

Turkish attack on Karahassankoi, the Russians driven over the Lom to Popkoi.

Aug. 31.

Osman Pacha, making a sortie from Plevna, is severely repulsed.

Sept. 3.

Capture of Loftcha by General Prince Imeritinsky.

Sept. 5.

The Russians defeated by Ahmed Eyoub Pacha at Kaceljevo on the Lom. Turkish attacks rapulsed at Ablava, and Popkoi.

Sept. 7.

A heavy fire opened upon Plevna from the Russian siege guns, and continued for four days.

Sept. 11.

Great infantry attack by the Russo-Roumanian Army: capture of two redoubts by Skobeleff and of the Grivica redoubts by the Roumanians. Repulse of the attack at all other points with enormous loss.

Sept. 12.

Loss by Skobeleff of the two redoubts captured the day before.

Sept. 17.

Suleiman Pacha makes another desperate attack on the Russian position in the Shipka Pass, and telegraphs to Constantinople that he has taken Fort St. Nicholas. He is repulsed with great loss, and Fort St. Nicholas remains in Russian possession.

Sept. 18.

First detachment of the Russian guards passed through Bucharest to the front. Unsuccessful attempt of the Roumanians upon the second Grivica redoubt.

Sept. 21.

Mehemet Ali attacks the Russians near Cairkoi, and is defeated.

Sept. 22.

Entry of Chefket Pacha's reinforcements and convoy into Plevna.

Sept. 24.

Mehemet Ali's retreat to the line of the Lom.

Oct. 2.

Capture of the Great Yagni position by the Russians in Asia.

Oct. 3.

Mehemet Ali succeeded by Suleiman Pacha.

Oct. 9.

Bombardment of Sulina by the Russians.

Oct. 12.

The bridge at Nicopolis carried away by a storm.

Oct. 15.

Great battle at Aladja Dagh between Kars and Alexandropol; overwhelming defeat of Mukhtar Pacha's Army, and large capture of guns and prisoners.

Oct. 24.

Capture of the Gorny Dubnik position on the Plevna-Orkanieh road, by General Gourko.

Oct. 28.

Capture of Teliche by the same.

Oct. 31.

Capture of Tetewen by the Russians.

Nov. 1.

Occupation by the Russians of the Dolny Dubnik positions, from which the Turks had withdrawn during the previous night

Nov. 4.

The Deve-Boyun position before Erzeroum stormed by the Russians, the Turks losing 42 guns.

Nov. 5.

Sortie of Turks from Kars, repulsed by the Russians, and eight guns spiked in Fort Hafiz Pacha.

Nov. 8.

Russian attack on the outworks of Erzeroum.

Nov. 9.

Retreat of the Russians from the position gained before Erzeroum.

Nov. 12.

Second unsuccessful Russian attack upon the forts before Erzeroum.

Nov. 17-18.

Kars carried by assault, 300 guns and 10,000 prisoners taken.

THE WAR CORRESPONDENCE

OF THE

"DAILY NEWS."

CHAPTER I.

THE DIPLOMATIC PERIOD.

The Insurrection in the Herzegovina—The Consular Commission—The Andrassy Note—The Berlin Memorandum—The Bulgarian Massacres—The Servian War—The Conference—The Protocol—The Russian Declaration of War—Lord Derby's Protest.

On the 24th of April, 1877, Prince Gortschakoff addressed to Tavfek Bey, Turkish Chargé d'Affaires at St. Petersburg, a short note, in which was the following passage :—" The earnest negotiations between the Imperial Government and the Porte for a durable pacification of the East not having led to the desired accord, his Majesty, my august master, sees himself compelled, to his regret, to have recourse to force of arms. Be therefore so kind as to inform your Government that from to-day Russia considers herself in a state of war with the Porte." At the same time a Circular Note was addressed by the Chancellor of the Russian Empire to its Ambassadors at the principal courts of Europe, stating that, for reasons assigned, the Emperor had resolved to undertake that which he had invited the Great Powers to do in common with him, and had given his armies the order to cross the frontiers of Turkey.

By this announcement the Emperor closed a memorable period of active and anxious negotiations between the Great Powers, which had extended over more than a year and a half. The insurrection in the Herzegovina and Bosnia, which had assumed serious proportions in July, 1875, had led, in the following month, to the appointment by the Great Powers of a Consular Commission to inquire into the state of the disturbed districts of European Turkey; a step which was met by the Porte with a profuse issue of Firmans and Proclamations full of admissions of shortcomings and promises of reform. These, however, failed to inspire the Sultan's revolted subjects with confidence, and the Austrian, German, and Russian Governments agreed in declaring that the internal disorders of Turkey constituted a permanent source of danger to Europe, and resolved to take into their serious consideration the means of removing them. Their deliberations led to the preparation of a letter to the Porte, since known as the Andrassy Note, in which the reforms rendered necessary by the condition of European Turkey were set forth. The principal demands made in this Note were the establishment of complete religious liberty, the abolition of the system of farming the taxes, the granting of facilities to Christian agriculturists to acquire land, the application of direct taxes to local purposes, the indirect taxes going as before into the Imperial Exchequer, and the appointment of a mixed commission of Mussulmans and Christians to ensure the execution of these reforms. This Note, to which the assent of the English Government had been given, was presented on the 3rd day of January, 1876, and on the 13th of February the Porte issued a circular to the Powers agreeing to all the demands except that which limited the application of the direct taxes, promising, however, that a certain sum out of the Imperial revenue should be devoted to Bosnia and Herzegovina. The insurgents were not, however, assured by the action of the Powers or the promises of the Porte, unguaranteed as were the latter by Europe, and the Note remained without effect. Bands of armed men from Montenegro and Servia crossed the Turkish frontier to aid the insurgents, and the Porte prepared to make war upon the former State, but desisted when its intentions became the subject of joint deliberation on the part of the Great Powers. At the beginning of May, 1876, the Governments of Germany, Austria, and Russia were deliberating upon the further steps necessary to be taken to obtain the pacification of the Christian provinces of Turkey, when an outbreak of Moslem fanaticism at Salonica resulted in the murder of the French and German consuls. The excitement spread to Constantinople, and Sir Henry Elliot, the Queen's ambassador to the Sultan, telegraphed for the English squadron to move to Besika Bay for the protection of the Christians. On the 13th of the same month Prince Bismarck, Count Andrassy, and Prince Gortschakoff, who had assembled at Berlin, agreed upon a Memorandum on the affairs of Turkey. It pledged the Governments adhering to it, to urge the Sultan to execute the reforms suggested in the Andrassy Note, and to demand a suspension of hostilities for two months, and it concluded with the declaration that, if the armistice should fail to secure peace, "other and more effectual means" would be resorted to in order to prevent the development of the war. The Berlin Memorandum received the support of Italy and France, but on the 19th of May Lord Derby informed the other Powers that the English Cabinet declined to agree to it. The French Government expressed their surprise and grief at this decision, and their opinion that the attitude of the English Government was a "public calamity." But before the five assenting Powers could act upon the Berlin Memorandum, the Sultan, Abdul Aziz, had been dethroned, and the diplomatic Note in which it was to have been embodied was not presented at Constantinople.

Early in May troubles, which seemed serious, were heard of in Bulgaria: but, on the 14th of that month, the Ottoman ambassador here received from the Turkish Minister for Foreign Affairs, a telegram, informing him that, although in the district of Philippopolis disturbances had taken place, they were "far from having the importance which malevolence had tried to attribute to them, by representing them as forming a veritable Bulgarian insurrection," and that, the Government having taken "suitable measures" to suppress them, the disturbances were tending to subside. Gradually the facts concerning the massacres and outrages in Bulgaria became known, and four hundred public meetings were held in this country to protest against the Turkish atrocities. On the 5th of September Lord Derby wrote to Sir Henry Elliot that "the outrages and excesses committed by the Turkish troops" in Bulgaria had roused a "universal feeling of indignation in all classes of English society," and that, "in the extreme case of Russia declaring war against Turkey, her Majesty's Government would find it practically impossible to interfere in defence of the Ottoman Empire." On the 21st of the same month Lord Derby directed Sir H. Elliot to demand an audience of the Sultan, and in the name of the Queen to denounce the Turkish atrocities in Bulgaria, and to call for justice on their perpetrators, and for reparation to be made to their surviving victims.

At the beginning of July the Government of Servia commenced hostilities against Turkey, but by the 24th of August it was reduced to ask for the mediation of the Six Powers; Montenegro joined in the same request, to which the Powers assented. On the 14th of September the Porte, objecting to any armistice, proposed six conditions of peace with Servia, and suspended its hostilities until the 25th of the same month. The Powers at once declared the Turkish terms to be inadmissible, and at the end of September hostilities were resumed, a large number of Russian volunteers coming to the aid of the Servians. But notwithstanding this foreign assistance, at the end of October, Alexinatz, the great stronghold of the Servians, fell into the power of the enemy.

In the meantime diplomacy had not been inactive. On the 26th of September, Count Schouvaloff had informed Lord Derby that in the opinion of the Czar the misrule in Turkey could only be terminated by the interposition of foreign Powers. He proposed that Russian troops should occupy Bulgaria, that Austrian soldiers should be sent into Bosnia, and that the united fleets of the Powers should enter the Bosphorus, adding, however, that the Czar was willing to abandon the idea of military occupation if the naval demonstration should be considered sufficient by her Majesty's Government. Lord Derby declined to support the plan of an armed demonstration, but proposed an armistice which Sir H. Elliot was instructed to press upon the Porte, being likewise directed in case of its rejection to leave Constantinople, "as it would then be evident that all further exertions to save the Porte from ruin would be useless." Lord

Derby also proposed the meeting of a Conference as soon as the armistice should be agreed to. The Turkish Government replied by offering a six months' armistice, and by promulgating a scheme of reform for the whole Empire. The proposal of a six months' armistice was rejected by Russia supported by Italy, as a merely dilatory measure. The negotiations then lagged, until the Servian lines having been forced at Djunis, on the 30th of October, the Russian Ambassador at Constantinople demanded an armistice of six weeks, and an immediate suspension of hostilities. To this demand the Porte gave its consent. Lord Derby's proposals, which were to serve as the basis for the deliberations of the proposed Conference, were the maintenance of the integrity and independence of the Ottoman Empire, and the establishment of a system of local administrative autonomy.

Early in November Lord A. Loftus sent home an account of a remarkable interview which he had had with the Czar at Livadia. On this occasion his Majesty professed his extreme desire to preserve the good-will of England and "pledged his sacred word of honour, in the most serious and solemn manner, that he had no intention of acquiring Constantinople, and that if necessity should compel him to occupy a portion of Bulgaria it would only be provisionally, and until the peace and safety of the Christian population were secured." He earnestly requested the Ambassador to do his utmost to dispel the cloud of suspicion and distrust of Russia which had gathered in England. The next day Lord Derby telegraphed to Lord A. Loftus that his Majesty's assurances had been received by the Cabinet with the greatest satisfaction. At Moscow on the 10th of November, the Czar made a speech in which he said he hoped the Conference would bring peace, but should it fail to do so, and should it prove that no such guarantees as were necessary for carrying out what the Christian Governments had a right to demand from the Porte could be obtained, he was determined "to act independently," convinced that the whole of Russia would respond to his summons should the honour of Russia require it. On the previous day Lord Beaconsfield had made a speech at the Guildhall, in which, after blaming Russia for rejecting the offer of a six months' armistice, he said that, though England's policy was peace, no country was so well prepared for war. The Czar's Moscow speech was supposed to be an answer to that of the English Premier, but erroneously, as it has since been established that when the Czar spoke he had no knowledge of what had been said by Lord Beaconsfield. On the 17th of October the Czar had given orders for the mobilization of six corps d'armée.

The Conference proposed by the English Government was accepted by the Porte on the 20th of November. The Powers appointed their delegates as follows :—Turkey was represented by Safvet Pacha and Edhem Pacha, the former of whom occupied the position of President, the Conference being held in the Turkish capital. The French delegates were Comte François de Bourgoing, the resident Ambassador, and the Comte de Chaudordy. Germany had but one representative, Baron Werther. Austria sent Count Zichy, the resident Ambassador, and Baron Calice, Consul-General in Roumania; Count Corti represented Italy, and General Ignatieff was deputed by Russia, whilst the British delegates were Lord Salisbury and Sir Henry Elliot. The delegates of the Six Powers held a number of preliminary meetings, to which the Ottoman Plenipotentiaries were not invited, and in which they deliberated on the proposals which were to be subsequently made to the Porte. The last of these meetings was held on the 17th of December, and on the 21st of that month the Plenary Conferences began. In the preliminary meetings, the Russian Ambassador surprised his colleagues by the facility with which he made one concession after another. The proposal to occupy Bulgaria with Russian troops was at once abandoned, and only reforms and guarantees were included in the scheme which was finally prepared for recommendation to the Porte. On the day before the opening of the Plenary Conferences Midhat Pacha was raised to power, and when the Plenipotentiaries met, their deliberations were disturbed by salvoes of artillery; these, they were informed by the representatives of the Porte, celebrated a new Constitution freely granted by the Sultan to all his subjects, and which would bring in a new era of peace and good government throughout the empire. It soon appeared that the Turkish members of the Conference had instructions to resist all foreign interference with the affairs of Turkey, as both unnecessary and an encroachment upon the independence of the empire. The Pachas knew that the Powers were not agreed to coerce them. Count Andrassy, indeed, on seeing Lord Derby's proposals for the Conference, had suggested that the Powers should first agree on their terms, and then impose them if the Porte refused; which, he said, "could easily be done by a naval demonstration at Constantinople." "Conditions dictated by a combined fleet at Constantinople would be accepted." But as early as the 22nd of December, Lord Derby had made known the decision of the English Cabinet not to use any kind of coercion if the Porte should decline the proposals of the Conference; and on the 10th of January, 1877, when the attitude of the Turkish Government remained unchanged, he still objected to any kind of "ultimatum" being presented to the Porte. On the 18th of January, the Turkish Government having refused the minimized proposals of the Powers, the Conference broke up.

The Porte now showed itself solicitous to make peace with Servia and Montenegro, so as to exclude further foreign interference in the form of mediation; as far as Servia was concerned, it was successful, while Montenegro held out for terms which were not acceptable at Constantinople. Prince Gortschakoff informed Lord A. Loftus that he considered the result of the Conference to be an insult to Europe, and on the 31st of January issued a Circular despatch to the Great Powers, inquiring what they severally meant to do under the circumstances. All, however, hesitated to take any immediate measures against the Porte. On the 17th of February Prince Bismarck thought that the time had not come for replying to the Russian Circular, and on the 19th Count Schouvaloff informed Lord Derby, on behalf of his Government, that if the other Powers abstained from further action, Russia must act by herself. Lord Derby said he understood what the Russian Government wanted was to secure an honourable retreat from its present position, and was told, by Prince Gortschakoff's orders, that Russia was ready for action but desired peace. Subsequently, Russia proposed that the Powers should unite to sign a public declaration setting forth their demands on Turkey, and after much negotiation such a document was drawn up.

On the 31st of March a Protocol was signed in the Foreign Office by the Ambassadors of Russia, Germany, Austria, France, and Italy, and by Lord Derby on behalf of our own Government. In it the Powers re-affirmed their interest in the settlement of the difficulties in the Turkish provinces, and after announcing their intention to watch carefully over the manner in which the promises of the Ottoman Government were fulfilled, went on to declare that, should their hopes be again disappointed, they reserved to themselves the right "to consider, in common, as to the means best fitted to secure the well-being of the Christian population and the interests of the general peace." As if to show how little the different Powers believed in the efficacy of this proceeding, three of them made separate declarations before signing it. That of Lord Derby protested that, as regarded England, the Protocol should be null and void in the event of the non-attainment of the object proposed—*i.e.*, reciprocal disarmament on the part of Russia and Turkey, and peace between them. Count Schouvaloff stipulated that Turkey should send a special envoy to Russia to treat of disarmament, and added that a renewal of such massacres as those in Bulgaria would of necessity stop demobilisation; whilst Count de Menabrea insisted that Italy should only be bound by the Protocol so long as the agreement which it established between all the Powers was maintained. The Porte was informed of the nature of the Protocol the day after it was signed, and treated the whole transaction as highly inimical to its interests. On the 6th of April, Prince Gortschakoff conveyed to Lord Derby his regret that the English separate declaration had been made known to the Porte, which might be encouraged to resistance by its language, and stated further, that Russia would make no more concessions, and that, if the Porte should reply in unsatisfactory or evasive language, the time for military action would have arrived.

The following letter from the Own Correspondent of the *Daily News* at Constantinople, dated April 5th, treats of the political situation immediately after the signature of the Protocol:—

:: Amid the conflicting discussions concerning the Protocol between England and Russia, the great question of interest to the Christian populations of Turkey is—Are the Powers going to do anything to improve their condition? So far as we can see at present, almost every other consideration has been carefully discussed but this. How to avoid war; how to satisfy Austria; how to baffle Russian designs, have all demanded attention and have obtained it. But, meantime, the primary, fundamental question of all seems to have been lost sight of—how to make the Turkish government a tolerable one for the majority of its subjects. Statesmen who live only from hand to mouth may be content to make arrangements for peace at any price in the hope that meantime something will turn up to render their arrangements permanent; but if they are only covering up a sore, they may have before long to deal with the old disease in a worse form. It seems as if the fact has been forgotten by the English Government that the reason the Eastern Question forces itself upon them is that Turkish oppression had passed the point of human endurance, and that nothing short of the lessening of that oppression can allay that question. The great design to which England seems to have been directing her energies is—not to lessen this oppression, still less to abolish it—but to get rid as soon as possible of the turmoil which has been occasioned by it. To quiet Russia, and above all to take care that she shall not attempt to coerce Turkey into better government, has apparently been the principal business of our Government during the last three weeks. But assume that Russia, knowing that England will never allow her, and properly so, to seize an acre of European Turkey, and with the fear of Germany and of Austria before her, consents to disband her army, and consents for the hundredth time to trust the cause of the Christians of Turkey to the promises of the Turks—the Eastern Question is neither finished nor shelved for any considerable time. The results which will have been gained are not such as are likely to be satisfactory to the great bulk of the English nation. Peace will have been obtained, and may now be assumed to have been obtained for a short time; but on the other side of the account will have to be placed, first, the fact that all the sources of the present troubles are still in existence, and are likely to be more fruitful of mischief in the future than in the past; and, second, that Russia will have largely increased her prestige in Turkey, while England will have lessened hers. Although war is avoided, all the causes of the recent internal troubles out of which the external ones have grown remain. It would be bad enough if this were all. The half-starved peasants of Herzegovina and Bosnia, even when subdued, are not likely to be better treated. The relations and friends of the murdered thousands in Bulgaria are not likely to be better subjects than they were a year ago. But unless England and Russia are prepared to do much more than the telegrams which have arrived would lead us to believe, the evils of the future are likely to be much worse than those of the past. For eighteen months Turkey has had no European loans upon which to draw. Her war expenditure has been so great that she is heavily in debt to every banker and merchant in the country. Many of her soldiers and public servants are eighteen months in arrears of pay. Gold is rapidly disappearing from the country, to be replaced by a paper currency down to twopence. The expenditure of past years has been framed on the supposition that Turkey would be able to pay the interest on her debt and a portion of her expenditure out of borrowed capital. In order to float her paper money she has been compelled to allow a large portion of her taxes to be paid in this currency, so that with an expenditure greatly beyond that of former years she has a smaller revenue. To keep herself going she will therefore have to make still further drains upon an exhausted population. As before, this drain will fall most heavily on the Christian communities. It is impossible, therefore, not to conclude that from the financial position alone the situation of the population has become worse instead of better. But in addition, and worse than this, is the fact that the Turk has been induced to believe that he has beaten all Europe, and can do as he likes. From every part of the country at this moment are coming tales of disorder, lawlessness, and oppression. The Moslem population in Thessaly and Epirus believe that they have everything their own way, and are beginning to help themselves to everything to which they take a fancy in the possession of their Christian neighbours. The Government is entirely unable or unwilling to check the anarchy which reigns in Bulgaria. Gangs of robbers are beginning to infest all the chief districts of Asia Minor, and in large towns, such as Smyrna, Europeans, as well as the respectable part of the population, have taken to carrying revolvers. The condition of Armenia I am able to show by some extracts from letters I received a day or two ago.

Whether, with such a condition of things, the policy which

has for its sole programme that of being the friend of the Turkish Government, and neither coercing it nor allowing any other Power to coerce it into making reforms, is an expedient one, is easily answered. It is essentially the policy of weakness and folly, and, in the interests of England and of Turkey, the worst that could be adopted. It is far worse than the policy which prevailed in the time of the Crimean War. Under Lord Stratford de Redcliffe the Turks were told plainly that England meant to support them, but that the price of such support was a tolerably decent government. Now we are showing them that we are still their supporters, and that they may do as they like. What can the Turks think of the conduct of England, when, after writing a despatch like the famous one of Lord Derby's, demanding the trial and punishment of the leaders in the Bulgarian atrocities, England has taken no steps whatever to enforce the course she so emphatically enjoined? What but that either England was either hypocritical when she so wrote, and never intended that her words should be regarded, or that Turkey is so strong, and England so bound by her own interests to support her, that she dare not move a step towards carrying out her wishes. During the time of the Great Elchee, the Turkish Government would have been compelled, by the representative of England, to have brought the Bulgarian murderers to punishment—would have been told that the price of England's support was obedience to England's dictation in such a matter. Now, thanks to the vacillation and weakness which have characterized the dealings of the English Government with Turkey during the past year, though England even succeeded in obtaining an agreement among the Powers represented at the Conference, she has left the impression upon the Turks that the country dare not do otherwise than support them, and that Turks may massacre Christians to any extent, so far as England is concerned, without any danger of losing her friendship or support. The old policy of England was to support the Turk, as the ruler of this empire, without specially troubling about questions of internal government; but the right of intervention, exercised vigorously, kept things tolerably straight, and prevented the most gross forms of outrage. The new policy appears to be to support Turkey and her oppressions, and neither to interfere ourselves nor allow any one else to interfere with the ill-treatment of the subject races. If this official reading of the Treaty of Paris be maintained, then its principal effect is to condemn the Christian races to hopeless subjection; and as the negotiations, which our Government have been mainly responsible for, have brought this doctrine of non-intervention for the benefit of the Christians most prominently into notice, we are to some extent liable for the position which I have maintained—that the signing of peace, without the taking of guarantees for good government, will make the situation of the Christians of the empire worse than it was two years ago.

If Russia's object is to acquire Constantinople, and to that end to gain the sympathies of the Christian populations of Turkey, the situation for her is a satisfactory one. At the Conference she claimed good government and civil and religious equality for the Christians. Hers were the largest demands for reform—demands which history will say were not more than, in the justice of the case, ought to have been made on behalf of the Christians. Anxious to bring about these reforms by the help of Europe, she cut them down first to meet the wishes of England, and then piecemeal, so as, if possible, to ensure the assent of Turkey. When Turkey rejected what the united wisdom of Europe declared to be the minimum of reform which Turkey ought to concede, England refused to join with Russia in enforcing what were now as much England's demands as her own. Russia, still determined to insist upon them, though at a vast expense, increased her army, and made vast preparations for war. At every step she was checked by England, until at length finding that England would not only herself oppose, but would bring other nations to assist her, she consented to the present Protocol. Such, or something very much like it, will be the view which will be generally taken throughout Turkey of the history of the negotiations. Russia will still pose as the friend of the Christians; England as their enemy. Russia, thwarted at every step in her endeavours to secure justice for them, will have the sympathy which wise statesmanship at this rare opportunity could have obtained for England. Had we recognized the inevitable, that the Turks are disappearing, decreasing in numbers year by year, becoming poorer, side by side with Christians who are already richer, more intelligent, and better instructed than their Moslem neighbours, and who cannot be kept back except by massacre, who must become the inevitable future rulers of the country, we should have seen that the policy of England is to gain the support of the Christians, in order to keep Russia out of Turkey, and not to drive them into the arms of Russia.

Once more we have missed a great opportunity. The hand-to-mouth policy is merely to prevent the outbreak of insurrection and hostilities, without caring to remove the causes which cannot fail to reproduce insurrection. The statesmanlike policy, even from the Russophobist point of view, is to do our utmost to make a strong nation on the Bosphorus, and as that nation cannot be strong which has a majority of its own population hostile to the government, while the government itself is in the hands of an intellectually inferior race, such policy would indicate the expediency of not throwing in our lot with the effete minority against the rising majority, but of insisting on reforms which, while they would do justice to the Christians, would also tend towards the substitution of a strong government for a weak one.

On the 9th of April the Porte made its formal reply to the Protocol. It was a very angry rejection of that document, and was received by Lord Derby with a strong expression of regret. The Protocol was rejected with indignation, as "destitute of all equity;" and the clause referring to possible ulterior measures was "a measure of intimidation calculated to deprive the acts of the Porte of any merit of spontaneity." Finally, the Ottoman Government declared that, "strong in the justice of her cause, and trusting in her God, Turkey had determined to ignore what had been decided without her and against her."

A fortnight was allowed to elapse between the decisive reply of the Porte and the next move of the Russian Government, but on the 24th of April appeared "A Manifesto of the Emperor of Russia," addressed to his subjects. In this document the Emperor said,—

"Our faithful and beloved subjects know the strong interest which we have constantly felt in the destinies of the oppressed Christian population of Turkey. Our desire to ameliorate and assure their lot has been shared by the whole Russian nation, which now shows itself ready to bear fresh sacrifices to alleviate the position of the Christians of the Balkan Peninsula. The blood and the property of our faithful subjects have always been dear to us, and our whole reign attests our constant solicitude to preserve to Russia the benefits of peace. This solicitude never failed to actuate us during the deplorable events which occurred in Herzegovina, Bosnia, and Bulgaria. Our object before all was to effect an amelioration in the position of the Christians in the East by means of pacific negotiations, and in concert with the great European Powers, our allies and friends."

After a brief summary of the disinterested measures which had been taken by the Imperial Government, the Manifesto concluded,—

"Having exhausted our pacific efforts, we are compelled by the haughty obstinacy of the Porte to proceed to more decisive acts. A feeling of equity and of our own dignity enjoins it. By her refusal Turkey places us under the necessity of having recourse to arms. Profoundly convinced of the justice of our cause, and humbly committing ourselves to the grace and help of the Most High, we make known to our faithful subjects that the moment foreseen, when we pronounced words to which all Russia responded with such complete unanimity, has now arrived. We expressed the intention to act independently when we should deem it necessary, and when Russia's honour should demand it. In now invoking the blessing of God upon our valiant armies, we give the order to cross the Turkish frontier."

In a Circular Note to the Powers, bearing the same date, Prince Gortschakoff wrote that the rejection of the Protocol by the Porte, and the motives upon which that rejection was based, left no hope that the Porte would accede to the wishes and counsels of Europe, and excluded also every guarantee for the execution of the projected reforms for the improvement of the lot of the Christian population. The Emperor of Russia had therefore resolved to undertake that which his Majesty had invited the Great Powers to do in common with him, and had given his armies the order to cross the frontier of Turkey.

Thus, then, Russia was committed to one of the greatest military enterprises she had ever undertaken. The English Government, however, while determined to remain neutral, except as its own interests might require, did not allow the allegations in the Circular of Prince Gortschakoff to pass unchallenged. In a despatch dated May 1st Lord Derby wrote that her Majesty's Government had received the information communicated to it with deep regret, and could not accept Prince Gortschakoff's statements and conclusions as justifying the resolution adopted. The Porte, though protesting against the Protocol, had again affirmed its intention of carrying out the promised reforms, and the British Government could not, therefore, admit that its answer had removed all hope of deference on its part to the wishes and advice of Europe. The despatch then referred to Prince Gortschakoff's assertion of the belief that Russia's action was in accordance with the sentiments and interests of Europe, and pointed out that it was a contravention of the Treaty of Paris (1856), by which Russia and the other signatory Powers each engaged to respect the independence and territorial integrity of the Ottoman Empire. Lord Derby further declared that the Czar had separated himself from the European concord hitherto maintained, that it was impossible to foresee the consequences of such an act, and that the British Government felt bound to state that the decision of the Czar was not one which could have their concurrence or approval.

CHAPTER II.

PREPARATIONS FOR WAR.

The Ottoman Army—Fortresses of the Danube—Turkish Line of Defence—Abdul Kerim, the Ottoman Generalissimo—The Russians at Kischeneff—Naval Power of Turkey—The Russian Black Sea Fleet—The Emperor Alexander's Address to his Army—The Defences of Varna.

THE masters of armies had not been inactive while the diplomatists were devising their "solutions" of the Eastern difficulty. The order for the mobilization of six corps of the Russian army preceded, as we have seen, by six months the actual declaration of war, and on the side of the Turks a corresponding and perhaps greater activity had been displayed. The following letters, from a Special Correspondent at Rustchuk, show what was being done and hoped for by the Turks in the few weeks before war was declared :—

△ RUSTCHUK, *April 18th.*—The Turks here are in high spirits, and think it a mere trifle to vanquish within a few weeks not only the Russians, but the whole of Europe. The miraculous victory of Djunis, after their previous despondency, has impressed them with the idea that they are enjoying the special protection of Allah and his prophet, who will place them on the pinnacle of glory and prosperity. Unless the Great Powers earnestly and unanimously interfere and enforce peace, war will not fail to devastate the now flourishing fields of Bulgaria and Armenia. All the Turkish reserves in the Danubian provinces have been called to the colours, and are, as fast as they arrive, incorporated in various regiments, filling up the gaps which disease and bullets have made in the ranks. This measure, if strictly carried out, will produce salutary effects, inasmuch as the Roumelian Bashi-Bazouks, with the exception of some gangs of highwaymen and marauders, are likely to disappear. Only the horsemen, especially the terrible Circassians, about 30,000 strong, are to be allowed to follow their own fashions, in which they excel the most savage redskins: before them, anguish and horror; after them, death, ruin, and despair.

The health of the Turkish troops has very much improved since they camped under tents on the hills close to the entrenchments, at which they are still arduously working. Seven redoubts, with a central fort on the uppermost crest, able to protect each other by cross-fire, crown the ridge of heights around Rustchuk towards the land side, and four others defend the plain, stretching along the river side behind the railway station. The parapets of these earthworks, however, are not yet completed, nor are they provided with palisades or other artificial impediments. The number of battalions has increased here already to 26, representing a total of about 18,000 combatants; others arrive daily, or are on the way to Varna from Constantinople. The Turks intend to concentrate here gradually about 50,000 men, with the view to cross the Danube immediately after the declaration of war, and occupy Giurgevo. It is supposed that the Roumanians will offer no serious resistance, because they withdrew their troops from the banks and diminished the garrison to a few companies.

The Commander-in-Chief, the Serdar Abdul Kerim Pacha, arrived here yesterday evening, coming from Varna, accompanied by numerous staff officers. He is to proceed to Silistria and other fortified places, in order to inspect the various military positions actually held by the Ottoman troops. It appears that the Russians imagine themselves to be able to finish the struggle within a few weeks by throwing overwhelming forces into their enemy's country; but this idea, practicable where solid roads and railways and thickly sown towns and villages secure the supplies, is not easily realized in the Sultan's neglected dominions, where the Turks have already extorted everything the unhappy inhabitants possess. It is of no use employing large armies in places deprived of the means to sustain them. It is, moreover, obvious that no manœuvring of the best strategist in the world will dislodge the Turks from their strongholds on the Danube. Such a result is not to be obtained by storming with swarms of skirmishers, or in dense columns, the well defended parapets; but only by the military engineers' patient labour, and the heavy artillery, both requiring time to do their work. So it would be, for instance, impossible to force the entrenched camp here, when defended by, perhaps, 30,000 men, and assailed by 80,000 men, and the necessary artillery, in less than six weeks from the beginning of the siege, provided that the passage of the Danube had been previously effected, and an hermetical blockade established around the whole position. The main task consists especially in conquering the Sary Bair Fort, on the summit of a range of hills. It must be attacked, on account of its deep ditch and scarps in masonry, in a regular way, through a system of trenches, batteries, and mines, until its battlements crumble into pieces, and the storming columns can advance without encountering more substantial impediments than the bodies of the defenders. This fort once taken, the surrender of the remaining entrenchments, and the city itself, would be only a question of days, because the work just mentioned looks over and dominates them all. Reckoning, therefore, from the moment of the declaration of war to that of the final occupation, and supposing that no other obstacles prevent the progress of the operations, at least three months will elapse. Besides this, the other principal fortresses, especially Widdin and Silistria, the strength of which is superior to that of Rustchuk, have to be besieged and taken before a serious attack could be directed against the Balkan line. The supposition that the Russians will employ, at the least, about six months in conquering the Lower Danube, appears not exaggerated. In this persuasion one is at a loss to understand their continual tarrying; notwithstanding that the season is favourable, no sign indicates a determined movement on the left bank of the Pruth.

Nature is still favouring the Turks. They have, indeed, reasons to offer thanksgivings to the propitious Danube, as the Egyptians of old did to the Nile. The water was very high during the whole winter, and is still increasing, thus enabling men-of-war of considerable tonnage to cruise from the mouth of the river up to the Iron Gates, and to throw their shells with ease and effect over the Roumanian lowlands. A further important hindrance consists in the difficulties against which the Russians have to struggle before they can have an opportunity to build their bridges and put the heavy pieces in position for protecting them, so long as the banks are overflowed to a wide extent, or remain in a swampy condition. A hundred buffaloes could not drag a big gun through the mud, unless a dyke for that purpose were constructed beforehand. Fresh troops arrive here continually—Turks, Kurds, Arabs, and Gipsies; some of them remain in this fortress, others are conveyed by steamer to various other places on the Danube, denoting thus the Serdar's intention to cover the whole immense line with the 150,000 men actually at his disposal. Strategists of renown have a maxim, that he who tries to cover everything, covers nothing. The troops are busy here arming the detached works with heavy breech-loading cannon.

△ RUSTCHUK, *April* 21*st*.—The Turkish Commander-in-Chief, Abdul Kerim Pacha, accompanied by the General in command of this fortress, Ahmed Pacha, gave on the 19th instant a mere glance at the work of entrenching, started the same afternoon by steamer for Silistria, and returned hither yesterday morning. He will, it is said, proceed either to Shumla or to Widdin, pending instructions from the War Office. The Commander-in-Chief is a Turk of the good old time, about sixty-seven years old, with white hair and beard, lively round brown eyes, and dark complexion. His jovial face and corpulent body do not at all indicate a soldier of nervous disposition, consumed by arduous activity and ambition, but one of passive energy, capable of stubborn resistance. To a man of his stamp, war does not seem to be a complicated game, wherein the lives of hundreds and thousands and the destinies of empires are at stake, but only a disagreeable incident of ordinary life, against which dauntless courage and unshaken equanimity are the best remedies. So we must not expect a brilliant campaign and pitched battles from the Turks, but an obstinate resistance behind parapets and natural bulwarks.

On the Russian side, the preparations for war had been carried on with much secrecy, and for months before the declaration of war, the most unfavourable rumours were current in Europe as to the health and organization of their troops. The headquarters of the Army of the South, as that intended for the invasion of Turkey was styled, were at Kischeneff.

† KISCHENEFF, *April 17th.*—I found Kischeneff a very different-looking place from what it was when I paid a visit here in February. Then we were still apparently in the middle of winter. The country was covered with snow, the air was sharp and frosty, the cold severe, and the streets covered with a solid pavement of frozen snow and mud, in lieu of a better. As the greater part of the army was distributed throughout the towns and villages of Bessarabia in comfortable winter quarters, comparatively few troops were seen here, although the place was full of officers, and the town of Kischeneff wore nearly its ordinary aspect of sleepy dulness. Now I find everything changed. In the first place, the country has exchanged its winter clothing of white for a summer costume of the freshest green; and instead of the severe cold and bracing atmosphere of winter, we have the soft, perfumed air of welcome spring. I passed through a violent snow-storm in Moscow on my way to this place, and here I find the peach trees and plum trees already in bloom. There are the snow and ice of winter in St. Petersburg and Moscow; the warm breath of summer here and in the Crimea. Russia is an outstretched giant, whose head is covered with Arctic snows, and whose feet are overgrown with summer flowers.

Kischeneff besides is swarming with soldiers, who have been assembled for the grand review, and who are in part lodged in the town, and in part camped in the fields outside the town, where the review is to be held. Kischeneff has put on its holiday attire, and a very gay attire it is. Decorations, Chinese lanterns, and transparencies with the letter "A," surmounted by the Imperial crown, abound in untold quantities, flags and streamers flying from the houses by the hundred, and by the thousand. The place is adorned, if not with flowers, at least with flags and ribbons that, flying in the wind and the brilliant sunshine, give this homely, ungainly, ill-looking Kischeneff the appearance of a bride on her wedding-day. And the people are all in a flurry of excitement and enthusiasm at the long-looked-for arrival of the Emperor, and the grand review, and the expected declaration of war—the greatest events ever known in the history of Kischeneff.

I cannot imagine how people got it into their heads, as they seem to have done, that Bessarabia was only one great marsh, in which the Russian army was encamped, under conditions which insured something like its complete destruction by fever and other dreadful epidemics. I have never heard that the health of the people of Bessarabia was in such a fearful state, and it is certain that the health of the army has been exceptionally good all through the winter, and that the troops are now in excellent condition. Not more than the fourth of the beds provided in the hospitals that were established at the time the army was mobilized have been used, and the fact is, as was natural under the circumstances, that the soldiers distributed throughout the villages of Bessarabia, lodged in warm, comfortable houses, well clothed and well fed, were in better health than when housed in barracks. There will undoubtedly be a great increase of sickness as soon as the army begins to move. The weather is still uncertain, and if a spell of rainy weather should set in, as is very possible, the roads for a couple of weeks will be very bad, and the health of the troops obliged to camp on the wet ground will undoubtedly suffer. But this cannot last more than two or three weeks, and by the time the army reaches the Danube the fine weather will have permanently set in, and the conditions under which the campaign will then progress will be very favourable.

The following letter from the resident Correspondent at Constantinople presents an estimate of the forces of Russia and Turkey formed on the eve of war:—

: : CONSTANTINOPLE, *April* 17*th.*—People here are carefully counting up the forces which can be brought together in hostility, and the preparations which have been made on both sides for attack and defence. It is noted that, if the Russians possess an overwhelming force with which to take the field, Turkey has the superiority at sea, and the Turks hope much from attacks upon the southern shores of Russia. As far as can be understood from the disposition of her forces, Russia intends to attack the Ottoman Empire simultaneously in Europe and Asia, whilst the Turks will endeavour to hold their own on land, and create a diversion in their favour by means of the fleet, which will attack the fortified ports along the Russian shore, and harass the enemy in every manner possible. Russia, as well as Turkey, has had to think of defensive measures, though hardly from fear of invasion. All through the winter she has been steadily at work along the Black Sea shores building forts, throwing up earthworks, laying down torpedoes, and training men to the use of submarine weapons. The Russians are trusting to torpedoes and heavy guns, and hope the dread which the former inspire will keep the Turkish commanders from venturing with their vessels too near the shore.

The first question for the Russians after a declaration of war will be, how to overcome Turkey's first line of defence; in fact, how to cross the Danube. Turkey possesses a strong flotilla of armoured gunboats on the river, which, if properly handled, ought to considerably impede any operations carried on for the purpose of constructing a bridge, and to inflict great loss by shelling the enemy from a distance. These vessels will also facilitate the landing of Turkish troops on the Roumanian shore, should it be decided to have a trial of strength on what may be termed enemy's territory, in a fight with the Russian advance guard. The difficulty of crossing the river owing to these gunboats has not been under-estimated by the Russian Government, and with a view of paralyzing their action, and protecting the operations for throwing over a bridge, a number of small torpedo boats have been added to the equipment of the invading army. These boats are steam launches about thirty feet long, constructed, with the exception of one, which is of steel, of thin iron plating. They are fitted with engines of 8-horse power and possess great speed. Being specially built with a view to transport by rail, they are exceedingly light for their size, and do not weigh, with their engines and fittings all complete, more than 3½ tons. They will probably be fitted with the spar torpedo, and the crews will trust to their speed to carry them alongside an enemy's gunboat and away from it again, before the Turks will have sufficiently recovered their presence of mind to point a gun correctly or even fire one. As a protection against rifle-fire, these boats carry shields at each end, but there is nothing to prevent their being sunk by the fire of a great gun. Well manœuvred, under the command of bold and enterprising officers, these launches might become very dangerous to the Turks, and, in any case, are likely to prove a valuable auxiliary force, as they may be used amongst other purposes for carrying over the advance guard. Once at the river, the Russian army will be delayed until the bridge is constructed for the passage of the main body. Materials for a bridge have been collected in abundance at the town of Ismail, on the Kilia branch of the delta, and include both pontoons and boats, as well as the necessary timber. All these, however, will have to be transported to the point fixed upon for attempting the passage, and here again the Turkish gunboats will come into play unless the torpedo boats can drive them away. The Russians, apparently, are feeling their naval inferiority, and would like to get a few larger craft than these launches on the Danube. They have a number of heavily armed gunboats at Nicholaieff all prepared, and ready for sea at a moment's notice. It is probably the intention of the Russian Government to try and slip them into one of the mouths of the Danube immediately it is decided to send the declaration of war. Should this design be carried out it would materially alter the state of affairs; but the Turks are taking their measures in time, and to-day a well-chosen squadron of small ironclads has left for the north, with orders to keep the strictest and closest watch possible over the delta. This squadron, which is under the command of Mustapha Pacha, consists of two heavily armoured iron corvettes, splendid craft in their way, mounting guns of the heaviest description, 12½-ton muzzle-loading Armstrongs, in a battery so arranged as to admit of a fire being delivered almost in a line with the keel. These craft are the *Mukademieh Hhair*, or Happy Beginning, and the *Fethi Bulend*, or Great Victory, and in addition to them are the *Hiftzi Rahman*, or Divine Protector, and the *Lutfi-Djelil*, twin screw ironclad sea-going turret vessels, carrying each of them four 150-pounder Armstrong guns.

For the moment, then, this is the naval force outside the river, and now a few words may be said about the squadron inside, which is under the command of Mustapha Pacha, an officer who has generally obtained credit for energy. The squadron on the river consists of some seven armoured gunboats and a few small wooden steam vessels armed with light guns. The ironclad gunboats are all about 115 feet in length, carry each of them two breech-loading Armstrong guns (80-pounders) in a battery placed on the fore part of the deck, and are protected with 2-inch armour. The remaining two are of very superior construction, carrying their two guns (80-pounder Krupps) in a turret placed forward. They were built at Constantinople, and only launched a few months ago, and are now on their way to join the force under Mustapha Pacha, in company with the squadron which sailed yesterday. The armour of these boats is sufficient to prevent the penetration of projectiles from field pieces, and they will be able, therefore, to move up and down the river, delivering a galling fire at any point almost with impunity, unless the measures taken by the Russians to destroy them or keep them at a distance prove successful. Nothing is known as to whether the Roumanian authorities have connived at the placing of torpedoes in the river on the part of the Russians, though doubtless the latter will have thought of it, seeing how much the Federal gunboats were hampered in the southern rivers during the great war in America by the torpedoes placed by the Confederates. The Turks at one time thought of having recourse to these weapons, and placing them at every point on the Danube at all suitable for crossing, but there is reason to believe the idea has been abandoned.

The Russian troops are concentrated at Kischeneff, and in view of the great superiority of force on their side, the invading army will probably attempt to cross the Danube at two points. Let us examine, then, the disposition of the Turkish troops made to receive them. The numerical strength of the Turkish army, as I have before explained, has been greatly overstated, purposely so on the part of the authorities, and by the European press almost of necessity, from there being few other sources of information on the subject than the local newspapers. From one of the best authorities, however, I gather that the whole force for the defence of the Danube cannot possibly exceed 100,000 men, in addition to a force of 34,000 south of the Balkans, between Nisch and Sophia. These troops but a very short time ago were distributed between the various fortresses on the river, half the force stationed in about equal numbers at Silistria and Rustchuk; and the remainder, with the exception of a small reserve force at Shumla, concentrated at Widdin. The Turks have made the mistake, according to the best military authorities on the subject, of attempting too great a line of defence. They will be too weak to offer a successful resistance at any point where the Russians may attempt to cross. The bulk of the Turkish army will be shut up within fortresses which the Russians will only blockade, and not regularly besiege. There will thus be nothing to stop the march of the invaders to the plains south of the Balkans, and it may be to the gates of Constantinople. As far as one can judge, the Turks have an idea of commencing resistance before the Russians shall have reached the Danube, of fighting a battle on Roumanian soil, for it has been given out that the moment the advance guard of the Russians reach the Pruth the Turks will cross over in face of Silistria and intrench themselves at Kalarash; whilst the army at Widdin will also take the offensive. The fortresses on the Danube have been repaired lately, and a few new earthworks erected at Silistria, Widdin, and Rustchuk, as well as at one or two places in the Dobrudscha. Their armament has been changed within the last few months, and most of the batteries on the Danube now mount Krupp guns of considerable calibre. The best chance for the Turks, according to foreign military authorities, would be to let the Russians cross over, while they themselves concentrated all efforts on the defence of the Balkans; but in their pride the Turks will not believe in the possibility of the enemy ever reaching the passes, and so there is reason to imagine that not so much attention has been given to the gates of the Roumelian plains as, from a Turkish point of view, ought to have been given.

Returning to the Black Sea, the same necessity does not exist for the Turks to defend their ports as is imposed upon Russia, owing to the former having the command of the Black Sea. They have a fine ironclad fleet, sufficient in number, possibly, when supplemented with their wooden vessels, to blockade, if necessary, the whole of the Russian coast. Properly watched, not a vessel ought to be allowed to escape out of a Russian port; and though there is a fine fleet of merchant steamers at its disposal, the Turks ought to be able to prevent the Russian Government from sending any supplies to its various corps d'armée except overland. With enemy's vessels stationed here and there, and a squadron of fast-steaming ironclads sweeping round the shore, threatening the sea-coast towns, attacking the fortified posts, and destroying the Government depôts, as the Turks if they understand the value of their fleet will certainly do, the Russians will have to retain considerable forces in the south for their own defence. Recent intelligence from Odessa declares that the army destined for this work consists of at least 270,000 men, of which 200,000 at the present time are in quarters near that town, the remainder being distributed in detachments along the shore to the northward and eastward, as far as the mainland on the other side of the Crimea. This is a large force certainly, but ships have the advantage, in the present day, of steam, and can move about with far greater celerity than troops. Feints and threatened attacks upon certain positions with small portions of the fleet will serve to draw off the troops from other places whilst the main body of war vessels is preparing for a descent upon the towns thus left only partially defended. This is the sort of work which would be undertaken by a British fleet in similar circumstances, and the Turks are supposed to have studied in the same school. They possess amongst the vessels of the ironclad fleet just the sort of craft to suit a dashing commander—vessels of light draught, heavily armoured, mounting guns of large calibre, and steaming well. Two of the vessels in question, as previously mentioned, have already left for the mouth of the Danube, and there are two others of precisely the same description lying at Batoum, the *Avni Illah* and *Mouni Zaffir*. In addition to these vessels there are four other armoured corvettes, called respectively the *Idjlalieh*, *Athar Tefyk*, *Athar Shefket*, and *Nedjim Shefket*, which carry on the average eight heavy guns each, two of which, as a rule, are mounted on revolving platforms on the upper decks, for the delivery of "all-round fire." These ships, lying off a battery end on, could pour in a very destructive fire against a battery or other object as a target, whilst from their small size and absence of heavy masts and sailing gear they would present but a very small mark for the enemy. These eight vessels do not form the whole of the strength of the ironclad fleet, as there are lying at the present moment at the mouth of the Bosphorus five large broadside ironclad frigates, one of which is one of the most formidable vessels of her class afloat. She is called the *Messoudieh*, and having left the building-yard of the Thames Ironworks Company only within the last two years, has had every recent improvement, and is even a finer vessel than our own *Sultan*, which she closely resembles. She is protected by a belt of 14-inch armour, and carries fourteen 12½-ton guns, with two indented ports on either side, for firing fore and aft. The guns are protected by armour-plated bulkheads, and a double bottom; division into watertight compartments reduces considerably the risk of her total destruction by the explosion of the enemy's torpedoes. Unfortunately, she consumes an enormous quantity of coal, and so is hardly the ship for such active operations as I have sketched, though she would answer admirably for an attack upon a fortress or the blockade of a port. Another vessel of precisely the same description and size is expected shortly from England; she is called the *Hamidie*, in compliment to the Sultan; and as there are now but a very few thousand pounds to be paid to complete the contract price, she will probably be delivered into the hands of the Turkish authorities in a few days. The four other ironclad frigates I have mentioned are of an old type, and only protected by plates of 4½ inches in thickness. They are the *Mahmoudieh* (now stationed at Batoum), the *Azizieh*, the *Orchanieh*, and *Osmanieh*. They carry each of them sixteen heavy Armstrong muzzle-loaders, and possess very good steaming qualities. The whole strength of the Ottoman navy consists of fifteen ironclads, five wooden steam frigates, eleven wooden corvettes, two wooden gun vessels, and eleven gunboats, of which seven are armoured, and form the Danube flotilla previously described. There are thirteen large transports, six fast despatch vessels, and two Imperial yachts, besides a number of small steamers and wooden hulks. The official report places the total number of vessels of all descriptions at 132, manned by some 18,292 officers, seamen, and marines. Turkey, then, has, numerically speaking, one of the finest fleets in the world, and this naval force in other respects also is now not so deficient as it was some months ago. The ships are fully manned, armed, and provisioned. The captains handle their vessels fairly, and the crews work the guns in a smart manner. The weak point of the fleet is in manœuvring together, but this would only tell in an action with an enemy of anything like equal force, and need enter into no calculation with regard to operations against the enemy's coasts, for there it is rather judgment in placing the vessels for attack, and cool courage and endurance on the part of the officers and men, which are required.

The Russian navy cannot compare favourably with the Turkish, for though their official list contains the names of a large number of ironclads, by far the greater portion of them are small turret vessels and monitors, designed for coast defence, and hardly fit for a voyage to the Mediterranean. They have five large frigates, it is true, but there is not one of them to be compared to the *Messoudieh;* and in all probability any one of the Turkish corvettes of the *Fethi Bulend* class would be a match for a Russian ironclad frigate. According to the list in question there are five frigates, one of which is building—one breastwork monitor building, three sea-going batteries, seven turret vessels, ten monitors, and two Popoffkas (circular ironclads). At the present moment the Russians have but one ironclad in the Mediterranean, two wooden frigates, and two gunboats. In case of war, however, this force would doubtless receive considerable additions, not with a view of giving battle to the Turkish fleet, but in order to draw off some of the ironclads from the Black Sea, and thus afford a better chance for the transports to move about. The Turks, in fact, will have to send some vessels to the Mediterranean in order to protect their own transports and merchant steamers, amongst which may be classed the Egyptian mail vessels, as they will of course acquire an enemy's character as far as Russia is concerned, from Egypt's connection with the Ottoman Empire. It has been proposed to divide the fleet into two portions, the one to consist of all the large broadside ironclads, together with a couple of wooden frigates, and a corvette or so, and the other of all the armoured corvettes and smaller ironclads; the first to cruise in the Levant, with the Dardanelles as headquarters, and the other to operate under the command of Hobart Pacha in the Black Sea. It is not likely that the Russian fleet will attempt to meet the Turkish, though if they could do so, and accomplish a victory, there would then be nothing much to prevent their forcing the Dardanelles and appearing at Constantinople. It is true that there are some very respectable forts about the narrows of the

Dardanelles, built upon modern principles, and mounting Krupp guns of heavy calibre; but the American war showed plainly enough that batteries alone would never stop ironclads. During that memorable struggle the Federal vessels ran past batteries designed to protect channels, with great success on several occasions, and even set the torpedoes at defiance. The forts at the entrance to the Dardanelles are not of much account, being of somewhat ancient type, and though constructed of masonry, would soon be knocked to pieces by the fire of modern artillery. These batteries contain no very heavy guns, most of the pieces being smooth-bores of an old pattern; and though of late a few Krupp guns have been added there is nothing which would do much damage to an ironclad passing at a distance. From the entrance to the narrows there is nothing in the way of defences; but here two well planned and constructed forts, the one called the Namazieh battery, at Kilid Bahar, and the other, the Medjidieh, a little to the northward of the town of Chanak, can deliver a cross fire that would make it very warm for a few minutes for any vessels attempting to pass against the will of the Turks. In Fort Medjidieh there are two 12½-ton Armstrong guns, besides some ten 15-centimetre Krupp guns. The Namazieh battery's armament, too, is very heavy, consisting as it does of some eight 22-centimetre Krupps. These are the strongest forts about the Dardanelles, and the only ones likely to inflict much damage upon a hostile fleet, although there are three others which would still have to be passed. One of them, like the Namazieh, is of modern construction, and mounts a few Krupps of small calibre; but the others are like those at the entrance, and not much to be feared. The forts of the Bosphorus are in much the same condition as those of the Dardanelles. From the Black Sea to the two Kavaks, although there is a battery on almost every point on either side, no great damage could be inflicted upon ironclads forcing a passage, as their armament is not of much value. At the two Kavaks, however, where the channel of the Bosphorus begins to narrow, is a very formidable array of batteries, well arranged for cross fire. Two of them are of quite recent construction, and mount fourteen very heavy Krupp guns each, quite capable of piercing the armour-plating of most ironclads. As far as torpedoes are concerned, the Turks do not appear to have done much, although the Imperial arsenal at Tophaneh has turned out within the last four months a number of large cases intended for submarine mines. It is said that a number have been placed both in the Bosphorus and at the Dardanelles, and a notice was issued some time ago respecting torpedoes at Batoum. The torpedoes used by Turkey consist of large iron cases cylindrical in shape, filled with some 1,000 lb. of large grain powder, and so arranged as to float within thirty-five feet of the surface of the water. They are intended to be fired by electricity from the shore.

With regard to the defences of the towns along the southern shore of the Black Sea, the Turks are behindhand, as it is only at Batoum that the batteries are in anything like an efficient condition. At Trebizond there is nothing, and this large town, the most important as far as commerce is concerned along the whole southern shore, the port of Erzeroum, and the landing place of goods for the Persian market, is completely at the mercy of any bold naval commander who with a ship or two, even armed merchant steamers, can manage to slip past the Turkish fleet. At Sinope batteries for the defence of the harbour have been in the course of construction for years past. They were so far from complete, however, in February last, that not a single gun could be mounted, and it is not likely that they will be finished for months yet. The positions of the batteries have been well chosen with regard to cross fire, and every part of the harbour is well commanded. Batoum is the point to which the Turks have given their greatest attention, for they know how ardently the Russians covet its possession. Lying close to the Russian frontier, it presents such a tempting prize that to acquire it alone the Russians might almost risk a war. It is undoubtedly the natural port of the Caucasus, for there is no other harbour for miles around where vessels can lie in all weathers. Under ordinary circumstances the place presents much more the appearance of a Russian seaport than a Turkish harbour, for, as a rule, there are seven or eight Russian steamers always lying in the port. All goods for the Caucasus have to be transhipped at Batoum into small steamers to be taken inside the bar of the river at Poti, and it is naturally very galling to the Russians that the place should be in the hands of the Turks.

Not many years ago they offered a very large sum for its cession, but the Turks would not entertain the proposal to sell it, so the idea was taken up of creating a port at Poti. Vast sums of money have already been spent, and still the moles of Poti are not complete, as each succeeding winter destroys a large portion of the summer's work. The defences of Batoum consist of a battery on the point, mounting 25 guns of various calibre, ranging from 12 to 22-centimetre Krupps, and two other smaller earthworks arranged to fire across the bay. The one to the northward mounts four guns, 15 and 22-

centimetre Krupps, whilst the one at the head of the bay is armed with seven, three of which, however, are smooth-bores of heavy calibre. Although the defences of Batoum seaward are formidable enough, no provision has been made for its protection against an attack in the rear. The Russians would have, however, a tremendous task to come down upon Batoum from behind, for there are high mountain ranges and thick forests to be traversed, and numerous streams to be passed, necessitating months of pioneer work before the army could advance. There is another approach to Batoum, however, from the northward, and if the Russians had the command of the Black Sea it would not be very difficult to capture the place by advancing with a sufficient force from Poti. The extensive plain of Poti is terminated by a spur from the mountain chain at a point about half-way between that town and Batoum. Here at this place, which is called Tsikinzir, the Turks have thrown up a number of redoubts, and armed them with 24-pounder howitzers and mountain guns of small calibre. Their position is, in fact, exceedingly strong, and the redoubts could not be carried but at a great sacrifice of men, for not only would the invading army have to face their fire, but in advancing they would also be exposed to the fire of the Turkish squadron stationed at Batoum for its protection. The Turkish troops at Batoum at the present moment amount to something like 12,000 men, but preparations have been made for enrolling the Circassians as light cavalry, so that in case of need a very large auxiliary force can be added. It is quite likely that the Turks will, in the event of war, advance upon Poti, resting their left wing upon the fleet. There are no difficulties in the way, as the intervening streams are all fordable and the distance not great. By capturing Poti the Turks could inflict a heavy blow, as the railway to Tiflis would be in their hands, and they could destroy it as well as the harbour works. For the defence of Poti, three earthwork batteries have been thrown up, one near the southern mole mounting four large Krupp guns, another a little south of it mounting two Krupps and twenty mortars, and a third four Krupps and thirty mortars. There is also a long intrenchment for riflemen, and a few torpedoes have been laid down as a "scare" for the Turkish ships. The Russian troops for the invasion of Asiatic Turkey are concentrated at Alexandropol, a large town on the frontier, but a very few hours' march from Kars. They are said to have something like 150,000 men, with all the transport arrangements ready for making an advance. Kars is now very strongly fortified, new batteries having been constructed.

From Poti round to the Crimea there are a few small fortified posts, as at Anapa, Sukhum Kaleh, and Redout Kaleh; but they would offer very slight opposition to the Turkish fleet, as the guns are of no great calibre, and the Russians are trusting not so much to driving off the ironclads with a heavy fire, as to giving a warm reception to any landing parties by having detachments of Cossacks stationed along the coasts, assisted by batteries of light field pieces. It is said also that a very large number of torpedoes have been laid down along the coast, some of them far out at sea. How much has been really done in this way can hardly be known, except to the Russian officers immediately concerned, as the successful use of submarine weapons depends more than anything else upon the secrecy with which the operations have been conducted. One thing, however, is known for certain, that the Russians throughout the winter have been most actively employed in manufacturing torpedoes in the arsenal at Nicholaieff, and that a great number have already been laid down in the harbour of Odessa, and the estuary of the Bug River. Odessa is naturally the point to which the greatest attention has been given by the Russian authorities, for they have there so much to lose. It is their great commercial port in the Black Sea, and vast sums of money have been spent upon harbour works. Batteries have been constructed all round the bay, but according to the best judges their sites might have been better chosen, for it is quite possible, under existing circumstances, for a hostile ship to enter the bay and shell the town without being exposed herself to the fire of more than two batteries. Some of the earthworks might even be enfiladed by taking up positions close to the shore, and the depth of the water will allow of the approach of vessels up to a draught of 25 feet. About 70 guns, large and small, are in position, and probably some 400 torpedoes have been placed in the bay. The latest addition to the defence is a battery of light guns on the outer mole intended for the protection of the inner lines of torpedoes. Some of the batteries are placed on the top of the cliff, and others about halfway down. It is said that some of the torpedoes have been laid down as far out at sea as five miles, but if so they are far beyond the range of any of the batteries, and might either be picked up or destroyed by an adventurous enemy not afraid to risk his men. Towards the end of the American war the Federals became so used to the work that they regularly swept the rivers, and picked up hundreds of the Confederate torpedoes with, comparatively speaking, little loss in the way of men. It is true that the torpedoes of that date were different from those of the present day, in that their explosion depended upon mechanical action, and not upon electricity. The necessity for the employment of conducting cables renders it easier, however, to destroy electrical torpedoes, as by creeping with grapnels from boats it is possible to pick up the wires, and when once the latter are cut the mine is useless. The boats naturally run the risk of being destroyed, as the torpedoes being laid down in groups and lines "en échelon," they must at times be hovering over some one or other of them; but then a torpedo can be used but once, and if fired for the destruction of a boat, a gap will be formed for the passage of the ships. Nicholaieff, where the Russians have their arsenal, is most strongly defended by torpedoes. From the estuary to the town the whole channel is mined, and there is little probability of the Turks attempting to force a passage. The Russian torpedoes are made of thin sheet copper, filled with dynamite, and are to be fired by electricity from the shore. They have been laid down off all the seacoast towns, and the Straits of Kertch are full of them, for the Russians have a lively recollection of what was done by our gunboats round the shores of the Azof during the Crimean war.

So far I have spoken of the Turks only as acting upon the offensive in the Black Sea, but it is quite possible that the Russians, who have many enterprising officers in their navy, will in their turn try to do what injury they can to the Turks by sea. They have in the fleet of the Black Sea Navigation Company some very fast steamers, which, slipping out of the blockaded ports at night, might run past the Turkish fleet and capture or destroy the Turkish transports. They are all at the disposal of the Government, and most of the officers have served in the navy. Armed with one or two breech-loading rifled guns, and fitted with the Harvey torpedo, they would make famous cruisers for any sort of work, short of encountering regularly armed men-of-war. There is reason to believe that both at Odessa and in the mouth of the Bug River, as well as at Kertch, the Russians have small torpedo boats, intended to operate against blockading ships, and there is little doubt but that this war, if it take place, will exhibit a new phase of torpedo warfare. Before concluding, it should be said that one great advantage possessed by the Turks, which will facilitate considerably the intended operations of their fleet in the Black Sea, is the coal mines of Heraclea. An abundant supply of this most necessary material can be easily obtained, as the distance from any part of the Black Sea to the port of shipment is inconsiderable.

Such, so far as I can learn, are the means of offence and defence possessed by the two Powers now face to face with each other. I have limited myself to giving facts. Those who have followed the course of Turkish history for the last twelve months, or even years, will have little doubt on which side their sympathy ought to lie.

War having been declared, and the Russian military preparations having, as was supposed, been completed, the Emperor Alexander had only to give the word to his troops to cross the frontier. This he did in person and in a somewhat imperial manner at Kischeneff, on the 24th of April.

† KISCHENEFF, *April 23rd.*—The Emperor reviewed the troops yesterday (Sunday) at Zineringra and Birzala. After the review he addressed the troops in a speech, in which he said: "I have done everything in my power to avoid war and bloodshed. Nobody can say we have not been patient, or that the war has been of our seeking. We have practised patience to the last degree, but there comes a time when even patience must end. When that time comes I know that the young Russian army of to-day will not show itself unworthy of the fame which the old army won in days gone by." The excitement and enthusiasm of the soldiers were very great.

The Emperor passed through here to-day without stopping, on his way to Ungheni, which is situated on the frontier where the railway crosses the Pruth. He will review the troops there, and return here to-night. He is accompanied by the Grand Duke Nicholas and the staff which went yesterday to meet him at Tiraspol, where he passed the night. He is, besides, accompanied by the Czarewitch, General Ignatieff, M. Milutin, the Minister of War, and many other dignitaries of the Empire. There are great preparations here for the reception of his Majesty at the grand review, which will probably be held the day after to-morrow. There is no considerable movement of troops towards the frontier yet, except light cavalry and Cossacks. The weather is fine, and the roads are rapidly drying. According to all appearances, they will be in very good condition within a week. The enthusiasm here is immense. The feeling is real, deep, and universal after a long period of suspense, which has been far more trying than an actual state of war.

April 25th.—The Emperor passed through Kischeneff on Monday morning, but without stopping, as he was on his way to

Ungheni, on the Roumanian frontier, where the railway crosses the Pruth, and where a considerable portion of the army was quartered, impatiently awaiting the signal to advance. He reviewed the troops, addressed them in very nearly the same language as the manifesto, which was only read the next day, and then returned to Kischeneff, where he arrived at twelve o'clock at night, and where an enthusiastic reception awaited him. As the next day was the anniversary of the death of the late Czarewitch, his eldest son, it was thought that, as he never receives visits on that day nor transacts any business, the review would not be held and the manifesto would not be read.

Tuesday, the 24th, had however already been fixed upon, as I telegraphed you from St. Petersburg some time ago, and in the morning news soon spread that the review was to be held after all, and soon nearly the whole population of Kischeneff was pouring out of the narrow, filthy, muddy streets of the Jewish quarter, across the little valley of the Briskhova, to the slopes and the fields on the other side, where part of the troops were camped, and where the review was to be held. The spot was well chosen, on a gentle undulating hillside, which enabled the spectators to see the whole army at once, as the lines rose behind each other higher and higher up the slope. It was a beautiful sunny morning, and the bright colours of the uniforms, the glitter of thousands of bayonets flashing in the sunshine, and the broad blaze of light reflected from a long line of polished field-pieces, and all set in a frame of brilliant green that covered the surrounding hills, made a beautiful and striking picture. It was all the more impressive that this was no mere holiday review arranged for show, but a review which everybody knew was the prelude to war. These uniforms, now so bright and fresh-looking, would soon be soiled with mud and dust, blackened and begrimed with the smoke of powder, and bespattered with blood. And those guns, with their brand-new look, whose voices had never yet been heard, would soon be speaking in tones of thunder, and their fiery throats vomiting destruction and death. A review under such circumstances is a solemn sight; and so the great crowds of people who had assembled to witness it seemed to feel. The troops were already under arms by nine o'clock, and they stood there in long lines and masses, never moving in the slightest, motionless as statues, and as silent too, for an hour and a half, until the arrival of the Emperor. There was something strangely impressive and awful in this prolonged silence and immobility. The crowds looking upon the serried lines so silent and motionless, became themselves silent, and gazed with wonder and awe. Those masses of men, and horses, and cannon, with the power of causing such a hideous uproar as to make the very earth tremble, were now so still and silent that they seemed to be held petrified by some mighty spell, and they inspired in the crowd feelings of vague dread. There was none of the laughing, or joking, or chaff of which one usually hears so much in a crowd assembled for a holiday sight. They spoke to each other in hushed voices, and every face wore a serious, earnest look. Nor was the silence broken upon the arrival of the Emperor. The crowd only swayed and opened a passage, taking off their hats as he passed, and not till he mounted his horse, and, accompanied by his brother the Grand Duke Nicholas and followed by an immense staff of more than a hundred officers, began to ride slowly along the lines, was the silence broken by the sound of music and cheers.

The review proper lasted nearly an hour, and was over about half-past eleven. Then, when the music ceased, there was silence again; the soldiers took off their caps, and their example was followed by the crowd. The voice of one man was heard, it was that of the Bishop of Kischeneff, saying a grand military mass. This lasted about three-quarters of an hour, during which time everybody, spectators as well as soldiers, remained uncovered, with composed but expectant faces. Finally this came to an end, and then an anxious murmur ran through the crowd. If the Manifesto were to be launched, if war were to be declared, now was the moment when it would be done. In fact, the long-expected, long-hoped-for moment had come. There was a dead silence for an instant, during which I could hear the ticking of my watch; then a clear strong voice broke the stillness. It was not the voice of the Emperor, but of the Bishop of Kischeneff, who was reading the manifesto; and, strange to say, he had not read more than half way through it, when sobs were heard, and people looking about to see whence they proceeded perceived that they were from the Emperor Alexander, and that he was weeping like a child. It had been the pride and glory of his reign that it was one of peace; it had been his boast and his hope that he would finish it without a war; and now, in spite of everything he had done to avoid it, the step was at last taken, and a war was declared, the consequences of which no man can foresee. When they saw how much the Emperor was affected by it, there was probably not a dry eye within the range of the reader's voice; but no sooner had the Bishop finished than there went up a wild and universal shout, such as I never heard before, and scarcely expect to ever hear again. It was a shout of exultation, of triumph, and of relief, as though a great weight of suspense were lifted from the heart of the multitude. It spread through the army with the rapidity of sound itself, and was instantly taken up by the crowd outside, and repeated over and over again, until the very sky was full of it. The soldiers tossed their caps high in the air and caught them on their bayonets, and twirled them round and round, shouting and yelling as though they would burst their throats. This continued for several minutes, and when silence was again restored the Bishop of Kischeneff addressed the army. His discourse was very effective and telling, and was received very much in the same way as the manifesto itself, with shouts and cheers. Then the *ordre du jour* of the Grand Duke Nicholas, Commander-in-Chief of this army, was read to every battalion, squadron, and battery. The Emperor and his staff retired, and work for the day was over. A part of the army, I believe, started directly from the review to the frontier, without a moment's pause, and the rest began rapidly preparing for the march.

The following letter relates to the defence of the Turkish territory north of the Balkans :—

△ RUSTCHUK, *April 28th.*—I wrote my last letter from on board the mail steamer lying off Varna. Since then I have been over the fortifications of that town; and, thanks to the courtesy of the English Consul, have had an opportunity of inspecting the various details of defensive preparation. The Turks have been, ever since their intrusion into Europe, an essentially military nation; and, however apathetic they may have shown themselves in the work of progress and reform, in all justice it must be said they have not lost a tithe of their quondam military ardour. They have set themselves to work with a will, and the main line of defence, from Varna to Rustchuk and Widdin, bristles with the result of their energy. Varna, as fortified at present, is, if only decently defended, impregnable. The old line of bastioned wall has been put in a thorough state of repair. The embrasures have been opened, and freshly revetted, and guns of heavy calibre put in position, principally in the batteries looking seaward. The six lunettes constructed as advanced works during the memorable defence of 1828-9 are fitted up anew, and, in consonance with the necessities accruing from modern long-range artillery, fourteen forts and redoubts have been constructed on the heights dominating the town at some three miles distance. Turks have always fought well behind fortifications; and masters of the Black Sea littoral for the moment, thus securing water communications with the base of supply, they will probably give a warm reception to any force attempting the capture or investment of Varna. At this moment seventeen battalions are camped in and about the town. Of these six are of the Egyptian contingent, which latter is accompanied by two batteries of Krupp 8-centimetre field guns. The various forts and lines mount over three hundred guns, varying from 10 to 15 centimetres calibre, and all of the latest model. The supply of ammunition seems unlimited; and all day long the troops toil unloading the barges crammed with shell and cartridge boxes brought up by the transports. The general military command is in the hands of Ruchdi Pacha, an Egyptian by birth. The artillery is directed by Streker Pacha, a brigade-general, a Prussian officer, who entered the Turkish service many years ago. Everything is conducted with the greatest order; and though so many thousand troops are accumulated in the place, not a single act of violence or irregularity has hitherto occurred as a consequence. The defensive preparations may be said to be completed; and events would seem to prove that it was not a moment too soon. I can well understand the importance the Turks attach to Varna. It is the true base of operations in the defence of the Danube lines; the way by which the supplies of the defending army arrive. Once in the hands of an enemy victorious on sea, not only would the army supplies have to be conveyed by a long and difficult land route, but also a hostile expedition could at any moment be launched against the rear of the army of the Danube. This consideration makes the defence of the coast line a consideration of the last importance; and, apart from the dangers threatening Turkey from the land side, she has also to think of the possibilities of a naval reverse, which would speedily end the struggle. Hobart Pacha, who left Rustchuk yesterday to join his fleet, seems thoroughly impressed with the necessity of keeping the Russian ships at home. Despite the efforts made in certain quarters to prevent the bombardment of Odessa, the Admiral, I understand, vows that, orders or no orders, he will do his best to leave the place in ruins, and I believe he is a man of his word. But as Odessa is quite as strongly fortified as Varna, it may be he will come away less confident than he arrived.

The train by which I left Varna was crowded with troops bound for Shumla, the head-quarters of the Danube army. The soldiers seemed in good spirits, and most anxious to come to blows with the enemy.

CHAPTER III.

CROSSING THE FRONTIERS.

Entry of the Russians into Roumania—Advance of the Army of the Caucasus—Seizure of the Barbosch Bridge—Occupation of Galatz—Compulsory Departure of Foreign Shipping—The Cossack of the Don—Special Character of the Campaign—Composition of the Army of Occupation—General Nepokoitchitsky, Chief of the Russian Staff.

IMMEDIATELY after the issue of the Imperial Manifesto of April 24th, the Russian troops in Europe and Asia crossed the Turkish frontiers. The principal échelons of the European army crossed the frontier at Leovo, Beshtamach, and Kubea, and marched into Moldavia. On April 25th Reni, Galatz, Braila, and the railway bridge over the Sereth at Barbosch were occupied. Fresh échelons coming up, Ismail and Kilia, on the Lower Danube, were taken possession of. The Russian troops thus anticipated the Turks in garrisoning Galatz, the key to the railways of Roumania—a circumstance of the first importance for the concentration of the army, and the transport of its baggage and train. For a few days some difficulty was experienced in crossing the Pruth, in consequence of the inundation at Leovo. The Turks undertook no offensive operations, except that on the night of May 3rd two Turkish ironclads exchanged a few shots with the Russian field artillery at Braila.

Simultaneously with these movements, the Russian Caucasian army crossed the Asiatic frontier of Turkey in three columns. The main force, advancing from Alexandropol, marched upon Kars; the Rion detachment marched upon Batoum; and the Erivan detachment upon Bayazid. The Alexandropol corps, under the command of Adjutant-General Loris Melikoff, entered Turkish territory in two columns, and, taking the Turkish outposts prisoners, on the same day reached

Molla Musa and Bash Shuragel. On April 27th the greater part of the corps crossed the River Kars Tchai, and passed the night at Kuruk Dara, Hadshi Veli, and Subatan. On the 29th the corps reached Zaim and Angi Keff, despatching twenty-seven squadrons and sotnias, with sixteen guns, to cut off the communication between Kars and Erzeroum. This cavalry, in their successful reconnoitring on the 28th, 29th, and 30th, destroyed the telegraph between Kars and Erzeroum, and pursued a Turkish detachment of eight battalions marching from Kars to Erzeroum, and commanded by Mukhtar Pacha himself. To support the cavalry, General Loris Melikoff ordered twelve battalions of grenadiers, without knapsacks, accompanied by forty guns and five sotnias, to turn the flank of the enemy at Kars, and proceed rapidly to Vesinkoi. At the same time eight Turkish battalions sallied forth from Kars, and, with some artillery, took up a position under cover of the fortress guns. The artillery which accompanied the Russian cavalry, opening fire, dismounted a Turkish cannon. After this engagement, General Loris Melikoff left the cavalry at Vesinkoi, and, with his remaining forces, returned, on May 1st, to his former camp at Zaim. The troops of the Rion detachment, under the command of Lieutenant-General Oklobjio, marched upon Batoum in two columns. The left column, under the command of Major-General Denibekoff, made for Muchastir, while the other, under General Scheremtieff, proceeded along by the Atchmarum road. On April 25th the left column, after a serious engagement, took the camp of Muchastir, and, on the 26th, fortified this strong position. The other column marched by the Atchmarum road, and likewise had an engagement with the enemy. The troops of the Erivan detachment, under the command of General Tergukassoff, on the morning of April 30th, reached Bayazid, and occupied the town and citadel. The Turkish garrison, 1,700 strong, hastily withdrew to the Allah Dagh hills when the Russian troops approached the place.

The neglect of the Turkish military and naval authorities to destroy the bridge over the Pruth was one of many proofs of incapacity which marked the direction of the war for the first three months of the campaign, and did much to produce those impressions under the influence of which the campaign was judged, until the gallant stand made by Osman Pacha at Plevna. On the 8th of May the special correspondent with the Russians in Roumania thus noticed the events of the first ten days of war:—

† The campaign is proceeding slowly on this side of the Black Sea, whatever it may be doing on the other. The weather has decidedly made common cause with the Turks. So late a spring has not been known here for years, and the amount of rain that has fallen since the break-up of winter is something exceptional. It rains every day, sometimes all day long, sometimes for an hour or two, as if persistently to undo all that the sun may have done towards drying the country during the few hours in which it gets a chance to shine. The roads, therefore, remain in a fearful condition, and the progress of that part of the army which is moving forward on foot is but slow. Nevertheless, the Russians have, by their energy and rapid marching, won the first move in the game just opened, or rather the two first moves—first, in preventing the destruction of the railway bridge near Galatz by a wonderful march; and secondly, in throwing forward a sufficient number of troops to prevent the occupation of Roumania by the Turks. It was evidently so clearly the proper move of the Turks to cross the Danube, destroy the railways and the bridges of all kinds, skirmish with the advance guard, and retard and harass the march of the army, that the Russians were quite convinced they would do this. The moral effect would have been great, the dissatisfaction of the Roumanians very emphatic, and the consequent loss of prestige to the Russians, unable to prevent the invasion of a friend and ally, a very serious matter. Instead of this, the Turks have remained supinely inactive, and allowed the Russians to occupy Roumania without firing a shot.

The expectations of great rapidity of movement on the part of the Russian army, which had been raised by the crossing of the Pruth and the prompt seizure of the Barbosch bridge, were not fulfilled, and the subsequent movements of the Imperial forces were made in a manner which led to the belief that the Russians were not so well prepared for war as had been supposed.

Two months were to elapse before the Russian army which was to cross the Danube into Bulgaria, would be ready for that operation. There were marches of many hundred miles to be performed by thousands of the troops, for whom the railways were not available. Stores and supplies were to be conveyed over roads and bridges that were constantly breaking down. It was a time of uneasiness and suspense for Europe, of commencing discredit for the Russians, and of active defensive preparation for the Turks.

One of the first objects of Russian solicitude was to get entire command of the Danube, and first of its lower section. The earlier measures taken for this purpose are the subject of the two following letters :—

* GALATZ, *April 27th.*—About half-past two o'clock this morning the passengers from Bucharest to Galatz were left standing on the broad platform of the Barbosch junction, some six miles from the latter place. For a mile at least before reaching the station we had seen the watch-fires of the Russian picquets to the north of us on either side of the Sereth River; and close to the railway bridge, the timbers piled on either bank marked preparations for the construction of a road bridge just alongside the iron structure on which the railway crosses the now flooded Sereth. It was natural to expect some bustle, if not confusion, in a railway station which was in the immediate proximity of a camp, and which was for the time the terminus of the Russian advance in this neighbourhood; but all was quiet and methodical. Perhaps there were a few more goods trucks than usual in the sidings, and the platform was here and there encumbered by accumulations of stores, while three sentries tramped up and down among the passengers; but the refreshment-room waiter was ready with his invitation to hot coffee, and his recommendation of a Galatz hotel, with as much *sangfroid* as if there had not been a Russian outside Bessarabia. A few Russian officers were drinking tea in the restaurant while they waited for the train for Bucharest, and at the other end of the long table was a fussy but puny Roumanian major, who could not succeed in his obvious desire to get on terms of comradeship with the Russian gentlemen. In the darkness it was not possible, as the train journeyed onward to Galatz, to see anything of the Russian dispositions flanking the route of the railway. Among our travelling companions between Barbosch and

Galatz were several Russian officers, who on arrival at the latter hurried off to the Concordia, which from its proximity to the Russian headquarters in a large private house in the town, is the hostelry chiefly affected by the Russian officers. The leading features of Galatz, as impressed on the traveller arriving at the railway station, are bad smells and amphibiousness. But although the former characteristic cleaves obstinately to Galatz on further acquaintance, one finds himself at least high and dry on reaching the upper town on the low continuous bluff lying inland from the comparatively small strip of town on the edge of the Danube. I take leave to opine that if all street pavement was like that in Galatz, creation generally would rise in rampant rebellion against the institution, and strenuously demand instead soft mud, if no improvement which did not involve miscellaneous masses of chance-shaped blocks of rock, alternated with water holes capable of drowning a horse, could be contrived.

Mercantile Galatz had a rough and busy time of it to-day. It appears that when the Russians first came into the place it was intimated that, although all the merchant vessels here and at Braila would have to leave, a reasonable time would be allowed to enable them to load up and effect a clearance. But this morning there burst on the mercantile community a thunder-clap in the shape of a peremptory edict, transmitted through the Russian Consul, that all ships must be clear of Galatz by six o'clock this evening, no matter whether loaded or not. The blow told perhaps most severely on our countrymen, for there are several British firms here, and a large portion of the trade from the Lower Danube is carried on in British bottoms. It was determined to request the Consuls of the various nationalities interested to use their offices with the Russian general commanding here, from whom the order had emanated, to beg that he would reconsider it, and allow reasonable extension of time. A number of merchants accompanied the Consuls to an interview with Prince Schahofskoy, who received his visitors with great courtesy. But courtesy, as a merchant plaintively remarked to me, will not freight ships. The Prince stated that he had his orders from Kischeneff, and that he had no option in the matter. In reply to one remonstrant he pointed out that the shipping people had been in as good a position as any for reading the signs of the times, which had for some time indicated the imminence of such a step as that which his instructions have compelled him to take. He allowed that a hardship was involved, but, then, did not war always bring hardship and precariousness to mercantile interests? Finally, he said, he himself could do nothing, but would telegraph to Kischeneff to ask whether an extension of time was permissible, warning, however, the deputation not to expect any consideration, and going so closely into detail as to compare the time on his watch to that shown by the watch of one of the deputation.

One after another the steamers, ready or not, loosed their moorings, and steamed down the river. Nothing had actually been said on the subject, but it was felt that, in the intimation of the General, there was a latent flavour of torpedoes, and that torpedoes are not affairs to be trifled with. One stubborn Irish captain, whose ship lay at Braila, got his back up, refused to go till he had his cargo aboard—say in the course of a couple of days—and went so far in the *civis Romanus sum* direction as to snap his fingers at torpedoes. But he ultimately succumbed to persuasion, and his steamer passed down the Danube opposite Galatz within a few minutes of the hour specified in the notification. On the broad open space of the Galatz jetty, by the side of the Bourse, had congregated a large proportion of the mercantile people of Galatz to watch the departure of the shipping, which was felt as the stamping upon them of the seal of the coming war. Square-set honest-faced Britons, sallow-faced soft-eyed Turks, Jews of all types of feature, from the aquiline Arabian to the thick-lipped sensual-faced Austrian Jew, here and there an Armenian, a group of Italians, voluble and gesticulatory, a little knot of Frenchmen disposed to cynical humour, even under what in the northern portion of our island would be termed a "dispensation," Germans in fair abundance, with the interstices of the gathering filled up by dark-eyed Roumanians, whom it was difficult to distinguish from the Italians—stood by the brown water as its wavelets washed the quay, and gossiped about cargoes, and charters, and torpedoes, and Turkish gunboats, as the *Farnley Hall* and the *Mary Coverdale* came swiftly gliding down stream with their figure-heads pointed for Sulina. Over the marsh land across the river was visible the spread sails of canvas of the sailing craft as they stood the reach of the river that bends away south-east below Galatz. A few still remained clinging to the jetty, whether in a hope of the relenting of the Russians, or that their skippers for some reason or other did not care to go, I know not. The Consuls at night handed in to their Russian confrere a formal protest against the shortness of notice accorded, but this measure was felt to be a pure formality; so the shipbrokers and grain agents of Galatz may close their offices and take a holiday till the dogs of war are muzzled again, and Galatz has the distinction of being the first mercantile place to feel the incidence of war in the total arrestment of its water-borne traffic. The holders of grain may indeed find customers in the Russians for some portion of their vast stock, the accumulated produce of last year; but their purchases cannot compensate for to-day's arrestment of export; and it is little to be wondered at that this evening the spirits of Galatz are not exuberant. Omelettes, of course, cannot be made without the breaking of eggs, and it is no fault of the Russians that the first eggs to suffer are the interests of the merchants of Galatz. The bridging of the Danube below Galatz might not, indeed, of itself altogether arrest navigation, but it is necessary to cover the work both from above and below by flanking protection and outlying picquets in the shape of torpedoes, since the Turks have craft both higher up and lower down, which could impede if not altogether hinder the construction of the bridge, and which could destroy it even if built without their interference. The Russians have made all their preparations for the construction and protection of the bridge which they design to throw across the Danube on this section of their advance. At Ismail a mass of timber and pontooning appliances has been collected. Two days ago there arrived by train at Galatz, and have since been launched, two steam launches, with a full complement of torpedoes—the craft which were described in my colleague's letter from Constantinople, which you published on one of the early days of the present week. Three more of the same craft are, I understand, already in the Sereth at Barbosch, and yet two others, conveyed thither in carts, are inside the mouth of the Pruth. These vessels will doubtless be used for the double purpose of laying down torpedoes, to cover the bridge or bridges, and of attempting the destruction of the enemy's vessels in case of an effort on their part to interfere with the work. A hundred timber pontoons have been ordered to be made with all speed in Galatz, probably in view of the construction of a second bridge. Lighters have arrived in the Pruth, towed up stream by a Roumanian gunboat, laden—the lighters, I mean—with punts or row-boats, manifestly to be used in the construction of the bridge. That the commencement of this work will be immediate is proved by the short and peremptory notice given to the shipping at Galatz and Braila. It remains to specify the point at which that work is to be undertaken. I cannot claim to have received any authoritative information on this head, but indications are not wanting to serve as guides to what I anticipate will prove an accurate speculation. The Russian military dispositions, so far as they are known, point with what seems unmistakable precision to the conclusion that the force which will cross the Danube to the east of Braila will not be the main body, but only the left flank. With our huge modern armies, marching on a broad front is an imperious necessity, and this all the more so when the march will be through territories where the roads are few and bad. The left flank then here, let us say, between Braila and Ismail, commences its operations earliest, because it has practically the furthest distance to go, and must go to work early to get up in line, or thereabout, with the rest of the invading army, which, wherever it crosses the river, will have the advantage and greater celerity of railway transport for a more or less great proportion of its journey through Roumania. The whole of the Dobrudscha to the north of the little railway running athwart it from Tchernavoda on the Danube to Kustendjie on the Black Sea, is a promontory running northward, and the Russian left flank must tramp along this promontory, south at least as far as the railway I have named, to get on a front approximately in line with the rest of the army reaching the Danube further west. Then its route would lie on Bazardjik, and so south to the Pravadi Pass; or, in the alternative of a concentration on Shumla, it would turn to the right and follow the Varna-Shumla highway.

With this extra work before it, the left flank must be across the Danube betimes, and ought not to delay an hour in crossing. But a man standing on the heights of Galatz and looking southward over the Danube may ask himself in vain the question—Where is it possible for the crossing to be effected? In the distance, on the Turkish side, no doubt, is high and dry country, a low, broken spur of the Balkans indeed; but how to reach it across that swamp of bulrushes struggling up through inundation, broken only by casual islets on which a few sheep are grazing, the whole expanse being intersected by deep lagoons of the nature of backwaters? That broad swamp, in which neither to east nor to west seems there any break, could be traversed neither by a Cossack pony nor the garron of a border moss-trooper—it is folly to think of it affording foothold for an army. A month's drought, apparently, could scarcely make *terra firma* of it. But if the reader has a good map, and will look at it, he will see marked on the Turkish side, about midway between Galatz and Braila, a place called Isatchia. At this point the upland of the Dobrudscha comes very near to the river, and there is a hard strand and a sound road all the way from the water's edge. Nor is this all. From Isatchia there are two very tolerable roads leading southward through the whole length of this

Dobrudscha promontory. One road bends away toward the west, and, without touching Matchin, presently gets on the shoulders of the Balkan spur, where they trend down into the Danube valley, and so goes on southward till the isthmus is reached, across which is drawn the Tchernavoda-Kustendjie Railway. The other road from Isatchia bends away south-eastward on Babadagh, and then holds a course almost due south, somewhat inland of the coast marshes. On the Roumanian side opposite Isatchia the conditions are as favourable as can be expected. There are two roads direct from Bolgrad, one on either side of the Lake Jalpuch, and there are also two roads from Ismail, only one of which, however, I believe, is out of the water at present. A crossing here would turn both Tulcha and Matchin, both of which have, at least nominally, batteries and guns, but that consideration, of so little account are the defences of these places, is of no moment. In fine, I venture to express the anticipation that the first bridge at least made by the Russians on this section of the Danube will have its end on the Turkish side at Isatchia.

In the construction of other bridges the Russians are working hard. They are widening and improving the new bridge near the mouth of the Pruth, which on Sunday last took the place of the old ramshackle structure by which the road crossed the river, and which was used by the first detachment of Cossacks who came over. Another bridge is in course of erection higher up. Two bridges are being made on the Sereth. No further troops in any numbers have come for the last two days over the Pruth through Galatz. Braila was occupied yesterday by a regiment of Cossacks with two field-gun batteries.

I this afternoon visited the Pruth, which is distant twelve kilometres east of Galatz. In crossing the chaussée, which alone shows above water between the Danube and Lake Brattich, one realizes how easy it would have been for the Turkish turret ship which was cruising off it with ports open on Tuesday evening, when the Russian troops were crossing, to have arrested their progress by its fire. A few guns are in position on a knoll commanding the mouth of the Pruth. Cossacks are picqueted at the Galatz end of the bridge, and on the further slopes Russian infantry are encamped under canvas. The officer on duty on the bridge was very civil—civility is the *mot d'ordre* of the Russian officers in Roumania—and allowed our carriage to pass without hesitation. Time did not permit us to go further than just the other side of the bridge. The road toward Galatz from the bridge was lined by infantry sentries and Cossack vedettes. All the troops I saw seemed in excellent physical case, hard as nails, warmly clad; indeed, I wondered how in the heat they tramped along so sturdily in their long heavy boots and thick overcoats of duffle blanketing.

Later in the afternoon I paid my respects to Prince Schahofskoy at his headquarters in the town. His Excellency appears charged with administrative functions as well as with the chief command of the advance army. He is a rather thick-set man, with strong shrewd face and iron-grey hair and beard. He possesses no little humour of a dry, sententious character, has a very courteous and genial manner, and speaks English with singular fluency and precision. "I come here," said he, "with the most pacific intentions." "Towards the Roumanians, of course, your Excellency," I ventured to reply; "but how about the Turks?" "Oh, they are different, I admit," was the rejoinder, with a quaint glance from under the grizzled eyebrows. I should have been glad to know where the General was to lay his bridge, but the subject was not touched upon. It was a pleasant coincidence to find on duty, as Prince Schahofskoy's officer of the day, Count Keller, a young officer of German birth, who had been one of the best men on General Tchernaieff's staff in the Servian war, and who distinguished himself in the command of a separate column in the operations against the Turks in the vicinity of Saitchar immediately before the final catastrophe of Djunis.

GALATZ, *May 5th*.—Yesterday afternoon I went again out to where the road from Galatz to Reni crosses the Pruth and enters Bessarabia. There passed me on the chaussée carried along between the waters of Lake Brattich and the Danube a couple of battalions of Russian infantry, proceeding to Galatz in heavy marching order. The regiment was the 44th of the line, and belonged, as all the troops now hereabouts do, to the 11th Army Corps, commanded by Prince Schahofskoy. They came along in loose order, straggling all over the chaussée, at a pace of close on four miles an hour—a long, dogged, steady tramp, clumsy to look at, but undeniably lasting. The rank and file in but few cases were tall men, but were burly, square-set fellows, broad in the shoulders, deep in the chest, but clean in the flanks, as I have noticed most Russians are. They wore a kepi of French shape, blue with red band round it, blue tunic, longer and looser in the skirts than ours or the German tunic, and had their loose blue trousers shoved into long boots, reaching over the calf of the leg quite up to the knee. The knapsack was of the German pattern, neatskin with the hair left on, badly carried by cross-belts over the chest. The rifle was the Kranke, and the men marched with fixed bayonets, although they carried bayonet scabbards. The Russian infantry man carries no sword, as does his German comrade. His belts are of black leather, and so he escapes being a chronic victim to pipeclay. The *tente d'abri* was carried in three pieces, and every man carried his own kettle on the back of his knapsack. A certain proportion of the men carried entrenching tools, and nearly every one had some extra weight dangling about him. One a pair of new boots strapped on his knapsack; another a bundle containing who knows what? a third a billet of wood for the camp fire, and so on. They carried their heavy brown great-coats rolled over the left shoulder, in the same manner as the Germans do theirs. The detachment had marched some fifteen miles in heavy marching order, as I have described, with three days' rations in their haversacks, and not a man had fallen out. Lord Albemarle says that in Diebitsch's campaign every Russian officer had his caleche, and journeyed luxuriously. With other times it is clearly different habits with the Russian officers now. Each battalion was followed by two large waggons, drawn by four horses harnessed abreast, containing the baggage of the officers. There was an ambulance waggon, or rather a carriage, conveying the battalion surgeons' stores, instruments, and medical appliances, a couple of forage-carts, and this was all the train of two battalions marching to commence a campaign that, put the time as low as you will, must be measured by months. Of course, I don't include ammunition-waggons in the train in this sense. The men looked hard, brown, and healthy. As they swung along with those great strides of theirs, they made light of their heavy kit, and sang with wonderful taste and great vivacity. In fine, I never saw soldiers in better condition and better heart for the varied phases of a campaign—marching, campaigning, and fighting.

A little way further along the road we met a detachment of Cossacks ambling along, one of their number making a noise on a whistle, while the others sang to the not wholly satisfactory accompaniment which this instrument produced. All the Cossacks hereabout until to-day, when a "polk" of Circassian Cossacks marched in, are Cossacks of the Don, descendants of the fellows who in the early years of the century followed the white moustaches of Hetman Platoff into Western Europe, and hobbled their shambling ponies in the glades of the Bois de Boulogne. One Don Cossack is so like another that the idea is difficult to get rid of that they have all been made to order in one mould, and that in case of accident their heads, arms, or legs are interchangeable. The

Cossack is not a very savoury gentleman, but Galatz is a fine place for taking the edge off one's sensibilities regarding smells, and we can get to windward of the Cossack we wish to inspect, which is more than we can do in regard to the Galatz drains. Friend Cossack is a little chap, about five feet five, even on his high heels, but at once sturdy and wiry. His weather-beaten face is shrewd, knowing, and merry. His eyes are small, but keen; his mouth large, and between it and his pug nose—rather redder than the rest of his face—is a tuft or wisp of straw-coloured moustache. His long, thick, straight hair matches his moustache in colour, and is cut sheer round by the nape of his neck. He wears a round oilskin peakless shako with a knowing cock to the right, to maintain which angle there is a strap round his chubby chin. Below the neck the Cossack is all boots and great-coat exteriorly. The great-coat, which is of thick grey blanketing, comes down below his knees; his boots come up to them. He is more armed than any man of his inches in Europe, is our little Cossack friend, and could afford to lose a weapon or two and yet be a very dangerous customer. Weapon number one is the long black flagless lance, with its venomous head that seems itching to make daylight through somebody. He carries a carbine, slung in an oilcloth cover, on his back, the stock downwards. In his belt is a long and well-made revolver in a leather case, and from the belt hangs a curved sword with no guard over its hilt. Through the chinks in his great-coat are visible glimpses of a sheepskin undercoat with the hair worn inside (to-day at noon the thermometer was over 70 in the sun). His whip completes his personal appurtenances; he wears no spurs. He rides, cocked up on a high saddle with a leathern band strapped over it, a wiry little rat of a pony, with no middle-piece to speak of, with an ewe neck and a gaunt, projecting head, with ragged flanks, loose hocks, limp fetlocks, shelly feet, and a general aspect of knackerism—the sort of animal, in fine, for which a costermonger would think twice before he offered "three quid" for it at the northern Tattersall's on the outskirts of the Metropolitan Cattle Market on a Friday afternoon. But the screw is of indomitable gameness and toughness—lives where most other horses would starve—is fresh when most other horses are knocked up—and is fit to carry its rider across Europe, as Cossack ponies have done before to-day. The Cossacks seem to be used indiscriminately for all sorts of work. They were the first to enter Roumania, they ride about alone with despatches, they escort suspected spies, keeping the head of their lance carefully within easy distance of the small of the suspect's back, to be handy for skewering him if he would attempt escape; and Cossacks are placed on guard over the ships at the Galatz quay, to prevent their attempting departure. Dismounting and shackling his pony by a hobble on each fore-leg, connected by a leather strap with another hobble around the left hind leg above the hock, the Cossack takes up a position on the extreme edge of the jetty, with his lance pointed in the direction of the ship, as if he would transfix it should it attempt to escape, and there he stands, self-contained, affable, alert, and with a general aspect conveying the idea that he is patronizing that section of Christendom within his purview. He will accept a cigarette, and tender you a light from his in the friendliest manner, but you will never coax him to take his eye for a single minute off the ship which he has in custody. The Circassian Cossacks who marched in to-day differ in some respects from the Don Cossacks. They ride larger ponies, they wear busbies of Astrachan fur with a scarlet busby bag, and their great-coat is black, having its bosom slashed with a receptacle for cartridges, while they carry their carbine in a cover of Astrachan fur.

At the bridge over the Pruth—to return to our drive—I found a very busy scene. Quite a dozen craft of one kind or other were lying below the bridge, and were being swiftly loaded with torpedoes and their appliances. Detachments of sailors, working with a will, unloaded the waggons, which one at a time were brought across the bridge, and with a cheer and a pull slung their contents down the bank to the water's edge, where small boats were conveying the torpedoes to the larger craft in the stream. Coils of wire cable, electric batteries, red-painted buoys, followed the drum-like cylinders of the torpedoes, while groups of officers stood around and directed the progress of the operations. Already a batch of torpedoes had been laid down, and every night for some time will see their number added to. The chain crosses, I understand, just below the mouth of the Pruth, where the river passage is further guarded by several batteries on the fringe of the low bluff overhanging the spot where the Pruth joins the Danube. Beyond the bridge, in a vineyard under the shelter of some clay cliffs, was the camp of the sailors and torpedo engineers—a couple of rows of *tentes d'abri*, each holding three men, with the cooking-places in rear and the baggage in front. The officers are quartered in the fewcottages about the bridge.

I drove on by an excellent road till close on Reni, about twelve miles below Galatz. On the right lay the still available remains of a large earthwork thrown up by the Russians in

1853 to cover the points at which they then crossed the river. One of their bridges was at Isatchia, another at Galatz, the hither end resting on the town quay, and a third at Braila. On the homeward journey I met Prince Schahofskoy, the general commanding the Russian troops in and about Galatz, driving out in one of the common birzas of the town, accompanied by a single aide-de-camp and without any escort, to inspect the progress of the work at the Pruth.

This morning some Cossacks were sent across the Danube in boats to patrol through the villages on the Turkish bank. On the river edge of the marsh land there are some two or three of these villages, little squalid nests of smugglers, containing rather a mixed handful of inhabitants. There are some Bulgarians, some Roumanians, some Roumanian renegades, deserters from the army, who have fled, and professed Islamism, and some Turks proper. It appears that the crew of a Turkish vessel intercepted by the Russians opposite one of these villages went ashore, and, probably having got drunk, began abusing and assaulting some of the Christian inhabitants of the place. In this conduct they were, it is said, abetted and assisted by the Mohammedan residents, and the trouble continued till some Christian women, escaping, got into a boat, rowed across the river, and reported the ill-usage to the Russian officer on the other side. It was reported here last night that there had been some firing, but there is, I am assured, no truth in the statement.

The Russian troops are now on the Danube from Kilia, near the mouth of the northernmost arm of the river, to west of Braila. Here there must be—that is, between here and Barbosch—quite 15,000 men. Six thousand are now beyond Barbosch toward Braila; 8,000, with heavy siege guns, are in Ismail; and at Kilia some 2,000 are reported. To stop the Sulina mouth of the Danube is, however, of more importance than to stop the Kilia mouth.

The following letter describes the marching of the Russian soldiers and the composition of the army :—

KISCHENEFF, *May 10th.*—Although the Bessarabian roads still continue sloughs of despond, owing to the heavy downpours of rain which alternate with warm and dry weather, the Russian advance into the Principalities is further advanced to-day than was anticipated by the less sanguine of the Russian leaders before the declaration of war. The young infantry soldiers, notwithstanding the heavy weight they carry, and the thick mud through which occasionally they have to tramp, are vindicating the marching reputation of the Russian peasant soldier. Few finer marches have been executed in our time than that long, steady, unbroken tramp of the advance-guard of the 11th corps from the frontier across the Pruth, over the Reni-Galatz chaussée, and so onward to the Barbosch bridge; and men who saw the Russian subdivisions tramp through Galatz tell that, although the Cossacks who preceded the infantry men were in many cases asleep in their saddles, the foot soldiers closed up gallantly at the sound of the music, and strode on singing lustily, as if the day's march had only just begun, leaving scarcely a single straggler to bring up the rear. The first infantry troops who marched into Jassy, having moved along worse roads, evinced, it is said, more symptoms of distress, and men were reduced to the necessity of sitting down in the streets from actual exhaustion. But this was the first day's march; and men who remember how some of our best regiments fell temporarily to pieces on the comparatively short stretch from Devonport to Dartmoor at the commencement of the manœuvres which were mainly memorable for the vacillation of Sir Charles Staveley, and for the continuous rainfall, which made a dismal swamp of the theatre of mimic war, will hardly be surprised to learn that at the end of a long first day's march in heavy marching order, some of the weaker vessels should show symptoms of distress. Marching mostly by road, the mass of the Russian twelfth army corps is already in the immediate vicinity of Bucharest, in the neighbourhood of which capital, although not within the precincts of the city itself, a preliminary concentration of considerable magnitude will in all probability take place. With the advance of the mass of the army, Kischeneff ceases to have eligibilities as the headquarters, and accordingly on Sunday next the Grand Duke Nicholas is to take his departure for Bucharest. His Highness will be accompanied by Generals Nepokoitchitsky and Levitsky, the chief and second chief of his staff, his own personal staff, the generals on the staff commanding the cavalry, artillery, engineers, intendance, &c.; but the bulk of the head-quarter staff will be located in Ployesti. The dispositions which will ensue on this change cannot for the present be dealt with, but soldiers who have acquainted themselves with the military topography of the valley of the Danube, and with the history of previous wars between the Russians and the Turks, will not find material difficulty in drawing their own conclusions.

Without venturing to indicate in advance what may be the intentions of the Russian strategists in regard to the crossing of the Danube, and without being in possession of any definite, far less communicable, information respecting the subsequent movements they may have so far decided on as the plan of the campaign, it may nevertheless not be unseasonable to make a few remarks regarding the initial differences which make themselves apparent between the obstacles which the Russians have had to overcome in previous offensive operations against Turkey, and those which now confront them. It will, I think, be abundantly apparent that the prospects of the campaign now commencing are infinitely more favourable than those to which Wittgenstein had to look forward, when he led his army across the Pruth in May, 1828. Wittgenstein had under his command three army corps, having a total strength, on the maximum reckoning, of 84,000 men. The Grand Duke Nicholas crosses the Pruth in May, 1877, in command of six army corps, having an effective strength of 216,000 soldiers already seasoned by a winter and spring spent practically in the field. Sickness was decimating Wittgenstein's army while as yet it was in the Principalities—sickness, the germs of which it had carried from Bessarabia—and his sanitary arrangements were of the most feeble and rudimentary character. The Grand Duke's army of to-day underwent a special inspection before the frontier was crossed, and the weak and sickly were strictly weeded out. The health of the marching army is reported excellent; surgeons are in full complement, ambulance trains and hospital equipments have taken precedence in the railway, even of munitions of war, and the Roumanian civil and military hospitals open their doors to receive the Russian sick. Wittgenstein's men had to tramp every verst of the way through a country practically roadless, from far in the interior of Russia, down to the pontoon bridges on the Danube; and every pound of supplies, every load of munitions of war, had to be conveyed by road-transport—if the word is applicable to a region where, at that time, the roads were mere tracks. To-day the Russian battalions may travel from the place of their mobilization to the bank of the Danube by railway; those who march find in Moldavia and Wallachia, on the main routes, chaussées which will compare with our best turnpike roads in England; on the side routes, roads which are, it is true, deep in mud in wet weather, but afford excellent travelling in dry; and the railway, which has conveyed such of the troops as do not march, is available for the conveyance of provisions and munitions of war, solving, in a great measure, the hardest problem of every offensive war—the difficulty of maintaining that steady current of supplies which is necessary for the subsistence of an army in an enemy's country. In 1828, Wittgenstein had to cross the Danube in the face of eleven Turkish fortresses more or less formidable—Widdin, Nicopolis, Rustchuk, Giurgevo, Turtukai, Silistria, Hirsova, Matchin, Braila, Isatchia, and Tulcha, not to mention Turnan, and the tête-du-pont of Kalafat. One of these fortresses, Braila, delayed one of his corps before it from May 11th to June 18th; but Braila is now a peaceful trading city of Roumania, rather nervous just at present on the subject of shells from Turkish gun-boats. Giurgevo is no longer of Turkey, but of Roumania, and is an open town. To-day at Kalafat no Kuchuk Pacha as in 1828, no Omar Pacha as in 1854, sits watching for his chances on the flank and rear of a force essaying to cross the Danube. Nicopolis, Turtukai, Hirsova, and Isatchia, are fortresses no longer, even of the Turkish type, but practically open places having stuck about them a few crumbling batteries armed with honey-combed guns; Silistria, till three months ago, stood as when the Russians, repulsed by the efforts mainly of Butler and Glyn, recoiled in 1854 from before its battered ramparts and yawning breaches; Widdin is a piece of patchwork; Rustchuk is indeed formidable if adequately armed, not as a fortress, for the fortress of Rustchuk proper is rotten and obsolete, but as an intrenched camp, on a fine site, commanding, if not indeed forbidding, the crossing of the river on its frontier. Matchin was a place of strength only until rifled cannon came to be used in sieges. Wittgenstein had no siege train, and his men sickened and died waiting in the trenches, while the weary work of mining was sluggishly proceeding. There has gone toward the Danube already, not one, but several siege trains, such as would do credit to any army in Europe. The Turks have a fine and a deserved reputation for the desperate defence of fortified places, and history tells us how at Braila, Varna, and Silistria, the "peaceful inhabitants" manned and fought the breach regarded as defenceless by the "professional soldier." Rifled arms of offence are sad foes to unscientific heroism. A maid of Saragossa is incompatible with Krupp and Armstrong as contemporaries; and I do not think it would be rash to hazard the prediction that never more in civilized warfare shall we have occasion to witness the *ultima ratio* of the storming of a breach. The history of the Franco-German war is studded with sieges, but the student of it will search in vain for the story of the mustering of a forlorn hope.

Time is everything in such a campaign, for even under the most favourable circumstances it would be a severe strain on Russia that the mass of her army should have to winter in Bulgaria. Wittgenstein indeed crossed the Pruth in the early part of May; but he did not find himself in condition to cross the Danube till the 9th of June. It was not until the 11th that the whole of his third corps—constituting his army of invasion—was across the great river. Impeded by the resistance of Braila, Rudjevitsch marched slowly, and had only got seventy-five miles down the Dobrudscha on the 25th of June. There he waited eight days for the fall of Braila, stayed another week at Bazardjik for the seventh corps, which had been besieging that fortress, to come, and finally was in a position near Varna only in the middle of July. It took him thus thirty-four days to march the 180 miles between Isatchia and Varna, but, deducting the halts I have named, he did the distance in twenty days; which is at the rate of nine miles a day, very good marching under the circumstances. But I wish more particularly to contrast the time made in 1828 with that on which we may count in 1877. There can be no doubt that if the Russian left determines to cross at Isatchia, with intent to march down through the Dobrudscha, Schahofskoy will be across at the latest before the 1st of June. He will have no occasion to make the halts which were enforced on Rudjevitsch till Braila should have fallen and the reinforcements released from its siege should have come up. Sherman on that famous march of his from Atlanta to the sea averaged sixteen miles a day *de die in diem.* But assuming that Schahofskoy marches in 1877 at no faster rate than Rudjevitsch in 1828, he would have reached the vicinity of Varna in twenty days, or at the latest about the 20th of June. By all accounts there is little prospect of his encountering serious opposition from the Turks *en route.* In twenty days from now, that is by the 1st of June, there can be no doubt that the centre and left of the Russian army will be on the Danube, if not across it. From no point between Kalarash and Giurgevo is the Danube distant so much as a hundred miles from Schumla. There seems no reason apparently why the Russian main body, having left investing forces to deal with Silistria and Rustchuk, if needed, should not be in front of Schumla by the same time that the left is in the neighbourhood of Varna. There would remain then the alternatives of a concentration of centre and left against Schumla, or of the left operating separately, while the centre should "hold" the Turkish army in Schumla, or actively proceed against that intrenched camp, as might be resolved on. Such a position attained by the beginning of July leaves at the command of the Russians four available months for subsequent operations, and the withdrawal across the Danube before winter time of such troops as the exigencies of the situation might not render it expedient to winter in Bulgaria. There is no reason, so far as I can see—for I have no expectation that the Turks will stand up for a day against the Russians in the open field if they ever meet them there—why the Russians in 1877 should not do as did the Russians under Diebitsch in 1829, and concentrate their columns south of the Balkans on the 27th of July. Before then circumstances may have occurred which will materially alter the intentions which they now express respecting their line of action subsequent to the crossing of the Balkans.

General Fadéeff holds, in his "Opinions on the Eastern Question," that for 150,000 Russians to reach Constantinople, the number he considers capable of accomplishing that feat, it would be necessary for 250,000 men to cross the Danube. The Russians do not aim at reaching Constantinople, but it seems quite certain that the strength Fadéeff names for crossing the Danube is available for that purpose. Six corps are already within reach of the Grand Duke Nicholas's hand, viz., four which constitute the army bearing the technical name of "the army of operation," and two more constituting the army of Odessa. The total strength of these six corps is 216,000 men, 49,200 horses, and 648 cannon. In addition to this great force three more corps are reported fully mobilized, and being drawn down into Bessarabia as the troops of the army of operation march out. This represents a further strength of 108,000 men, so that the Russian army now mobilized available for the invasion of Turkey reaches a total nominal strength of 324,000 men. I am not in possession of particulars respecting the composition of the three corps last named, but the following are the details of the composition of the six corps constituting the army of occupation and the army of Odessa:

I.—ARMY OF OPERATION (ROUMANIA).

Commander-in-Chief—Archduke Nicholas Nicolaieff.
Chief of Staff—General Adjutant Nepokoitchitsky.
Sous Chef—Major General Levitsky.

8th CORPS.

Commander—Lieutenant-General Radetsky. | Chief of Staff—Colonel Dmitrowsky.

9th Infantry Division.

1st Brigade—33rd and 34th Regiments. | 2nd Brigade—35th and 36th Regiments.

14th Infantry Division.

1st Brigade—53rd and 54th Regiments. | 2nd Brigade—55th and 56th Regiments.

8th Cavalry Division.

1st Brigade—8th Dragoons, 8th Uhlans.
2nd Brigade—8th Hussars, 8th Don Cossacks.
14th Brigade—Field Artillery.
9th Brigade—Field Artillery.

9th CORPS.

Commander—Lieutenant-General Baron Krüdener.
Chief of Staff—Major-General Schnitnikow.

5th Infantry Division.

1st Brigade—17th and 18th Regiments. | 2nd Brigade—19th and 20th Regiments.

31st Infantry Division.

1st Brigade—121st and 122nd Regiments. | 2nd Brigade—123rd and 124th Regiments.

9th Cavalry Division.

1st Brigade—9th Dragoons and 9th Uhlans.
2nd Brigade—9th Hussars and 9th Don Cossacks.
5th Brigade—Field Artillery.
31st Brigade—Field Artillery.

11th CORPS.

Commander—Lieut.-General Prince Schahofskoy.
Chief of Staff—Colonel Biskupsky.

11th Infantry Division.

1st Brigade—41st and 42nd Regiments. | 2nd Brigade—43rd and 44th Regiments.

32nd Infantry Division.

1st Brigade—125th and 126th Regiments. | 2nd Brigade—127th and 128th Regiments.

11th Cavalry Division.

1st Brigade—11th Dragoons, 11th Uhlans.
2nd Brigade—11th Hussars, 11th Don Cossacks.
11th Brigade—Field Artillery.
32nd Brigade—Field Artillery.

12th CORPS.

Commander—Lieutenant-General Vannoffski.
Chief of Staff—Major-General Duckmasson.

12th Infantry Division.

1st Brigade—45th and 46th Regiments. | 2nd Brigade—47th and 48th Regiments.

33rd Infantry Division.

1st Brigade—129th and 130th Regiments. | 2nd Brigade—131st and 132nd Regiments.

12th Cavalry Division.

1st Brigade—12th Dragoons, 12th Uhlans. 2nd Brigade—12th Hussars, 12th Don Cossacks.	12th Brigade—Field Artillery. 33rd Brigade—Field Artillery.

ARMY OF BLACK SEA.

Commander-in-Chief—General-Adjutant Temecko.	Chief of Staff—Major-General Goremykin.

7th CORPS.

Commander—Lieutenant-General Prince Barclay de Tolly-Weimarn.	Chief of Staff—Major-General Janobbsky.

15th Infantry Division.

1st Brigade—57th and 58th Regiments.	2nd Brigade—59th and 60th Regiments.

36th Infantry Division.

1st Brigade—141st and 142nd Regiments.	2nd Brigade—143rd and 144th Regiments.

7th Cavalry Division.

1st Brigade—7th Dragoons and 7th Uhlans. 2nd Brigade—7th Hussars and 7th Don Cossacks.	15th Brigade—Field Artillery. 36th Brigade—Field Artillery.

10th CORPS.

Commander—Lieutenant-GeneralPrince Woronsow.	Chief of Staff—Baron Wolski.

13th Infantry Division.

1st Brigade—49th and 50th Regiments.	2nd Brigade—51st and 52nd Regiments.

34th Infantry Division.

1st Brigade—133rd and 134th Regiments.	2nd Brigade—155th and 156th Regiments.

10th Cavalry Division.

1st Brigade—10th Dragoons, 10th Uhlans. 2nd Brigade—10th Hussars, 10th Don Cossacks.	13th Brigade—Field Artillery. 34th Brigade—Field Artillery.

An Infantry Division consists of four regiments, each having three battalions, and of three batteries of nine-pounders and three of six-pounders, each of eight guns.

A Division is equal to 16,000 men, forty-eight guns.

A Cavalry Division consists of three regiments regulars and one of Don Cossacks.

The 7th Cavalry Division has two batteries of regular horse artillery of six guns each, every other division one battery regular horse artillery, and one battery of Don Cossacks (horse) of six pieces each.

	Men.	Horses.	Guns
Army of operation (4 Corps)	144,000	32,800	432
2nd Army (2 Corps)	72,000	16,400	216
	216,000	49,200	648

There are in addition four battalions of sappers, three battalions of pontoniers, ten regiments of Cossacks of the Caucasus and Ural, one brigade of rifles, one battery of mitrailleuses, three batteries of mountain guns, one company of Marines of the Guard, and two companies of railway artificers.

The following letter introduces us to a very important personage, the Chief of the Russian Staff:—

† KISCHENEFF, *May 10th.*—Kischeneff is the place *par excellence* for toiling all day, and perchance, after all the toil, gaining nothing. It beats Washington for "magnificent distances," and it seems as if everybody one wants lives away on the confines of civilization, where the streets merge into the steppes. The military bureaux are separated from one another by a mile or two of mud or dust, as the case may be. Colonel Romanoff, who lives on the eastern margin of the place, is extremely civil when at last you find him at home, after calling three times in as many hours. He does what he can for you, but the particular business in hand cannot be completed without the assistance of General Nicolaieff, whose office is in a garden on the extreme western edge of the town. The General is at Ungheni for the day, or is breakfasting with the Grand Duke, or has gone out for a ride. You may spend the afternoon in calling at his office at intervals, and are lucky if you catch him before he sits down to supper. If he is at home, no matter whether at supper or not, the General is most courteous and solicitous to be of service. I believe he would get out of bed if your business was at all urgent. But circumstances are too strong for him or for you; there is yet another place to be visited, and another officer to be seen, before what the Hindoos call the "bunderbust" is complete. Another day is spent in riding backward and forward in a rattletrap droscki from one bureau to another.

But this delay does not arise from any want of punctuality on the part of Russian officers. If you secure the promise of an appointment, you may rely on its being fulfilled, unless indeed very important concerns intervene. Having been the bearer of a letter of introduction to General Nepokoitchitsky, the chief of the Archduke Nicholas's staff, I received an intimation that the General would receive me at half-past two this afternoon, and punctually at the time the chief of the artillery on the general staff quitted his room, and I was summoned to enter. The General is a short, square-set, but active-looking man, hale and hearty, in spite of his seventy years; he looks as fit to make a campaign as if he were twenty years younger. He is of Polish extraction, and his name signifies "the unquiet or restless man," and is singularly inappropriate, for General Nepokoitchitsky is a man of the most placid manner, and the equanimity of his temper is proverbial among the officers who have served under him. A classical captain told me yesterday that he very felicitously combined the *suaviter in modo* with the *fortiter in re*. The *sous-chef* of the general staff, General Levitsky, is a man of much more bustling and excitable temperament, and the two officers are happily chosen, as the idiosyncrasy of the one seems to be the complement of that of the other. General Nepokoitschitsky's hair, whiskers, and moustache are snow-white; but there is a flush of hale colour on his cheek; his eye is not dim, neither is his natural force abated. He wore a simple undress uniform, with the aiguillettes which distinguish the staff officer, and his only decoration was the cross of St. George.

The General has seen more service than most of the Russian leaders, and his experience of staff duty in particular has been long and continuous. He joined the army as an infantry officer, and first saw active service in the Caucasus, where his merit was so conspicuous that he speedily received a staff appointment. He held an important and responsible office on the general staff in the army which Russia sent to co-operate with Austria in quelling the Austrian insurrection of 1849. In the Crimean war, or rather in the war which we know conventionally by that name, he was chief of staff to one of the corps composing the army with which Gortschakoff occupied the Principalities, and took part, under Paskiewitz, in the memorable siege of Silistria. Since 1855 the General has seen no active service, but has been continually in military employment of one sort or other. Although chief of the staff of the Army of the South, for which position he was chosen because of his acquaintance with the region of the Danubian Valley derived from his experience in the campaign of 1854, he is not the head of the great general staff of Russia. That high office is filled by Count Heiden. Before his appointment to the office he now holds, General

Nepokoitchitsky was at the head of the Commission for the reorganization of the army on the new system which has replaced the old Russian system, and the operation of which, although its institution is so recent that its full value is as yet not realized, has done much in all respects to improve the Russian army. Although then in years and service the General is unquestionably an old soldier, his position as President of this Commission sufficiently indicates that he is a disciple of the modern school of military organization, and of strategy and tactics. General Levitsky, the sous-chef of the general staff, has, I believe, been a professor in the Military Academy of St. Petersburg, and has also commanded one of the cavalry regiments of the Guards. He has not seen active service. I believe that, without exception, the generals commanding the army corps of the Army of Operation saw service in the Crimean war.

General Nepokoitchitsky commenced the conversation by hoping that all the formalities needful for my authorization to accompany the advance of the army had been carried through without difficulty, in accordance with his instructions. He then dilated at some length on the excellent appearance made by the army when recently reviewed by the Emperor, a spectacle which I did not reach Kischeneff in time to witness. He remarked how fortunate it was that the day of the review should have been the only wholly fine day of all this exceptionally rainy spring, and then proceeded to observe that the qualities displayed by the troops in their advance into the Principalities were on a par with the thoroughly serviceable appearance they had presented on the grand parade. All, he said, was progressing quite as favourably and as rapidly as had been anticipated previous to the commencement of the operations; and this, notwithstanding obstacles which might fairly be regarded as unexpected, produced as they were by unfavourable weather of an exceptional, and indeed almost unprecedented, character.

You have already been advised by telegraph of the mobilization of yet another army corps, making up the strength of the Russian army in the field to ten corps, or, in other words, to 360,000 men, exclusive of the army operating in Asia. In order that a comparatively unseasoned and recently mobilized corps should not be hurried into the field, but should have time for thorough consolidation, the 7th Corps, commanded by Prince Barclay de Tolly-Weimarn, and hitherto forming part of the Army of the Black Sea, has been sent forward to join the "Army of Operation," and form its extreme left flank, while its place in the Army of the

Black Sea is taken by one of the more recently mobilized corps, the 15th. The Russian army corps now mobilized on a war footing are as follows:—4th, 5th, 7th, 8th, 9th, 10th, 11th, 12th, 13th, 14th, and 15th, eleven in all, exclusive of the Guards and the Army of the Caucasus.

CHAPTER IV.

THE RUSSIANS IN ROUMANIA.

Destruction of a Turkish Turret Ship on the Danube—A Torpedo Expedition—Destruction of another Turkish Ship of War—Narrative of the Russian Officers concerned—Speedy Reward of Merit in the Russian Army—Braila in War-time—Facilities for a Crossing at Braila—A Tour with Prince Charles of Roumania—Russian Regimental Singers—A Military Improvvisatore—A Dancing Corporal—Break-down of; a Bridge—General Skobeleff and his Extraordinary Career—A Prince in the Ranks—The Fortress of Rustchuk—Character of the Turkish Common Soldier.

THE period of expectation and suspense which lasted throughout the months of May and the greater part of June was not unrelieved by feats of war, from which the ingenious attempted to draw inferences as to the military efficiency to be expected of the belligerents.

Among these feats was the destruction of two powerful ironclad Turkish ships of war in the Danube. The circumstances in which the first of these vessels was lost to the Ottoman navy on the 11th of May are described in the following letter:—

* GALATZ, *May 13th.*—The branch of the Danube known as the Old Danube extends from Hirsova to opposite Braila. On this branch is situated the Turkish fortress of Matchin, and in it is penned by the Russian batteries at both ends a portion of the Turkish flotilla. On Friday afternoon the Turkish turret ship, the same whose passage up the stream recently terrified Galatz, steamed out from Matchin, followed by two gunboats, and at half-past three was stationary under cover of the wooded end of the island, with its three masts visible above the trees. The Russian gunners from the batteries close to Braila, below the Roumanian barracks, opened fire from their light guns, the range being about four kilometres, but without effect. The general officer present

gave directions for two eight-inch guns of position, mounted in the battery, to come into action. The first shot had no effect. The second shot, fired at a high elevation with a low charge, dropped on the deck of the turret ship, and must have crushed down into the powder magazine. Immediately a tremendous flash and glare shot up from the interior of the doomed craft, followed by a heavy white smoke which hung like a pall. Through this white cloud there shot up to a great height a spurt of black fragments of all shapes and sizes. When the smoke drifted away all that was visible of the turret ship was her stern, with the mizen-mast standing, whence still fluttered the Turkish flag. The ship had gone down by the head in shallow water. The fore and main masts were blown out at once. Two Russian steam launches put off from Braila, boarded the wreck, gained the flag, gathered some of the *débris*, and picked up two men, the fireman and the engineer, both severely injured. One has since died. The other is still alive in the hospital. He reports the turret ship to have had a crew of 200 men, under the command of Kezim Bey. Fragments of the wreckage were picked up down the stream at Galatz. The Russian enthusiasm in the battery was intense, and the officers embraced each other. The Turkish gunboats hurried away abruptly on the explosion of the turret ship, but returned an hour later, and fired on the Russian launches engaged in the work of humanity.

The name of the turret-ship was the *Lutfi Djelil.* Its armament was five guns, of which two were nine-inch and two five-inch. The captain, a pacha, was on shore. Spies report that the intention was for the turret-ship to lie quiet till next morning, and then bombard Braila.

On the 26th of May a second Turkish monitor was destroyed by torpedoes. The following narrative of the exploit was drawn up from the statements of the Russian officers who accomplished it:—

† PLOYESTI, *May* 31*st.*—The destruction of a Turkish monitor the other night by torpedoes seems to have been a most brilliant and daring exploit. Two steam launches, with a handful of men, steamed boldly into the midst of the Turkish flotilla, placed two torpedoes under one of the monitors, and succeeded in blowing it up and completely destroying it. This feat, accomplished with impunity, without the loss of a single man, is a very remarkable one, and if it can be shown that it

can be repeated with success, monitors and gunboats on inland rivers will be rendered completely useless, and even the modern monster ironclad, built at such expense, will likewise be rendered practically of no avail for any kind of service near an enemy's coasts. An ironclad will not even be safe at sea, for any kind of ship, even a wooden one, can send out half a dozen steam launches in the night, surround an ironclad, and destroy it with impunity.

The little expedition which succeeded in blowing up the Turkish monitor was composed of four small steam launches, two of which were to make the attack and the two others to hold themselves in readiness to render assistance in case, as was probable, of an accident to either of the attacking ones. The two launches which were to make the attack were commanded by Lieutenants Dubasoff and Shestakoff, and manned, one by fourteen, the other by nine men. The crews were protected by an iron screen or awning, which covered the boat completely over from stem to stern, and which was sufficiently thick to stop a bullet. This screen, as well as the boat, was painted black, so as to be scarcely distinguishable at night, and the crew were thus protected against the fire of small arms, except the man at the wheel, who directed the movements of the boat, and who was necessarily exposed. The crews embarked in the boats a little after twelve o'clock on Friday night, at a distance of about seven miles from where the Turkish monitors were lying. The night was dark and rainy, and the clouds completely obscured the moon, which nevertheless prevented the night from being one of complete pitchy darkness. There was just enough light to enable them to distinguish the dark masses of the Turkish gunboats without themselves being easily seen. After an hour's steaming they came within the immediate neighbourhood of the enemy's flotilla. The engines of the launches were so constructed as to make very little noise, and when they were slowed down all the sound they made was a low dull kind of throbbing noise that was almost drowned by the continual croaking of the frogs, which are very large and very numerous along the marshes of the Danube. Nevertheless, the quick ear of a Turkish sentinel caught the unusual sound, and he cried out, "Who goes there?" in Turkish. The boats advanced without replying. The sentinel again called out and again remained without an answer. He called out the third time, and as it was becoming evident that the ship would be alarmed Lieutenant Dubasoff replied in Turkish, "Friends!" and continued to advance. The sentinel, however, was by no means satisfied, and after calling out again two or three times, he finally fired.

Then the Russians, who were by that time very near the doomed monitor, heard a noise in the ship. There was a scuffling of feet, the rushing about of sailors, cries and shouts, and the voice of an officer commanding them to prepare the guns for action. They heard the order given for the gun in the bow to be fired. They heard it given three times, and three times they heard the click of the hammer, showing that an attempt had been made to fire, and that the gun had refused to go off. Finally, the third time the order was given, a globe of flame leaped over the side of the gunboat, and a shell went whistling over their heads. They were evidently seen by the Turks. One of the boats, that of Shestakoff, now drew off, while that of Dubasoff continued to advance. Each boat was armed with two torpedoes, attached to the end of a long spar that projected from the bow. These spars were arranged to move on pivots, and could be swung round so as to describe a half-circle. The torpedoes were so placed that they could be detached from the spars at any moment, and, in addition to this, long light chains were attached to them by which they were to be tied on to any projecting part of the attacked ship, and they were connected with the boat by a fine flexible wire about 100 yards long. The officer in command carried a small electric battery fastened round his chest. A lively fusilade had now been opened upon the boat by the Turks, but in spite of this, the launch of Dubasoff shot under the bow of the monitor, the chain which was fastened to the torpedo was flung round a chain or rope that was hanging from the bow of the ship, the torpedo was dropped from the spar, and the current of the river carried it against the bottom of the ship. The launch then shot away again until the full length of the electric wire had been reached. The officer applied it to the battery round his chest, and at the same instant a huge volume of water rose up into the air, which half filled and nearly swamped Dubasoff's launch, and a fearful explosion was heard, which completely drowned the shouts and cries and firing of the Turks. In the meantime the other monitors became alarmed, and without knowing the cause fired at random, and a fearful scene of terror and confusion ensued. They not only fired on the Russian launches, that still kept dodging about like mosquitoes, but in their panic and confusion fired into each other. The bullets rattled over the iron awnings of the launches, but did them no harm. They were not once struck, although the bow of one was pierced and sunk by a piece of a shell that exploded near it. The two launches were now on opposite sides of the doomed ship. Dubasoff perceived that the monitor was sinking down before, but very slowly; while the Turks continued to fire away blindly, but incessantly, both with small arms and cannon. Dubasoff cried out to Shestakoff to try and place another torpedo in order to make sure of the ship, and the latter slipped in under the stern and put down another torpedo in the same manner as the previous one. He then shot off until he was at a safe distance, applied the electric battery in the same manner, and a still more terrible explosion followed. Parts of the ship were blown into the air, as was very soon perceived when a large plank a few seconds later came down endways, driving its way through the iron screen into the boat between two of the sailors who were back to back close to each other, without injuring either of them. Then the monitor sank rapidly, and after a few moments nothing but her masts were visible above water. The crew had all either been drowned or had escaped by swimming. Day now began to break, and the position of the two little launches within the near range of two other Turkish monitors became very critical. To add to the danger of the situation, the screw of one of them got fouled, and the boat became unmanageable; while they perceived a Turkish launch from one of the other monitors bearing down on them. They opened a fire of small arms on the Turkish launch, which veered off and showed no disposition to come any closer. One of the sailors got out into the water, and after several minutes' exertion succeeded in clearing the screw, and the two launches, having accomplished their mission of destruction, darted off, passed under the fire of the two other Turkish gunboats, escaped unharmed, and, rejoining their two consorts, returned in triumph to their place of starting. The Grand Duke received the news within two or three hours after, and the rejoicing among the Russians was very great. The two officers and the crews of the two boats have all received the Cross of St. George.

This is the first instance, I believe, in which a vessel has been destroyed in time of war by an enemy's torpedoes, and the ease with which this was accomplished makes it a most important event in naval warfare. What gives it more significance is that the Turks apparently were not taken by surprise. They had as much warning as a man-of-war could expect under the circumstances, and they found it utterly impossible to arrest or injure the swift and terrible instruments of destruction that were flitting about them in the darkness. The Turks are notoriously bad sailors, but it does not appear that even good sailors under such circumstances could have done any better. It is almost impossible to hit such a small and rapidly moving object as one of these torpedo boats with a shell, especially in the darkness, while the fire of small arms was useless. It does not even seem that the torpedo netting which has been lately invented would have protected a ship against an attack of this kind. It should be remembered that unless the netting was so high as to prevent the torpedo at the end of the spar from being hoisted over it and considerably lower than the keel of the ship, it would be practically useless. The torpedo was carried to its place, it should be remembered, by the current, and it could be as easily attached to the netting as to the fore chains, or any other part of the ship. Once the torpedo should be hoisted or thrown over the netting, even were this netting so high as to prevent the torpedo being thrown over it, and so low as to prevent it from reaching the keel, the men on board the launch would apparently have time to cut a hole in it and put the torpedo through. The netting might be a defence against the Whitehead torpedo. It does not appear that it would serve against a bold and daring attack from a torpedo boat. It only remains to be seen whether the exploit can be repeated with equal impunity and success, to enable us to decide whether our whole system of shipbuilding is not radically wrong.

As soon as the news arrived the Grand Duke sent for the two officers who had performed the feat, as he wished to hear the story from their own lips and judge for himself how much was to be attributed to luck, how much to skill and science, and whether it would be possible to repeat the experiment under like circumstances. The two officers soon arrived, and were lionized to an extent that completely overpowered them. They are both young men, both very modest and very unassuming. It is from their own lips that I have this story.

In the third week in May a report was published, in circumstances which obtained for it ready acceptance, that the Russians had crossed the Danube into the Dobrudscha. What really had happened was that, under cover of their batteries at Braila, they had taken possession of an island on the Danube and planted their first guns upon the enemy's soil. The following letter shows the military importance of Braila at this time:—

* Braila, *May* 21*st*.—Braila, as we call it nowadays—Ibrailow, I believe, is its correct name—is a historic place. Before the Russians threw up their earthworks on its flanks the

other day the visitor might have searched in vain around the precincts of Braila for so much as the relic of a bastion or a curtain, and its inhabitants of to-day, till the Russians came, probably only knew what a cannon was like because of occasional trips across the water. But Braila was once one of the principal fortresses on the Lower Danube; and there is a man yet alive—a man who many long years later had gazed from Meudon on the bombardment of Paris—who, when the second quarter of this present century was hardly yet begun, heard the sing of the round shot as they sped on to crumble the breaches in the walls of Braila. In 1827, when the Russians swarmed into the Principalities—which were then, by the way, not principalities—there were Turkish fortresses on the north as well as on the south bank of the Danube, and of these Braila was one. Around that city fortress a whole Russian army corps, 24,000 strong, stood, and dug, and mined, and fought from May 11th to June 18th. Its commander tried a premature *coup de main*, with the untoward result that of his river face attacking column there came back but a solitary man, a sergeant, who saved himself by swimming. Then he took to mining as well as battering, and by-and-by his engineers reported several practicable breaches. But in those old days, when a man's strong arm and stout heart went for something, when war was not a thing of cold science, and when the reduction of a place was not a question of mathematical calculation, the Turk had a fine noble habit of ignoring the abstract practicability of a breach, and of beginning strenuously to defend a place just at the moment when, according to the cut-and-dry rules of the warfare of the period, the place ceased to be defensible. Braila, before the Pacha consented to march out, cost the Russians well on to 5,000 men. Of the slaughter among their predecessors in the ranks of the army of the Czar, the Russian soldiers of to-day are reminded by the huge monument over the great grave which stands in the middle of a pretty garden where the blossoms of the locust tree dangle close to where the Russians of to-day have their camp on the environs of the town.

Braila, although smaller, is a much handsomer town than its neighbour Galatz, and has a snug, prosperous aspect, which tells of good commissions earned by the sale of Moldavian grain. Trade cannot be called lively at present, for ruthless edicts block the Danube, and not even stout merchant Captain Murphy, the Hibernian skipper, who roundly cursed the Russians when all foreign vessels were warned to quit at a notice of six hours, and who swore by St. Patrick that he would not slack a hawser till he got his cargo aboard, dares now to attempt the enterprise of dropping down the Danube. There is still a show of shipping alongside the quay on the water-side. Some twenty schooners and brigs lie there, but they lie there not to load cargoes and be off down to Sulina and through the Bosphorus, but because they cannot help themselves. They are the victims of war, and here they must forlornly remain till the fell dogs are muzzled again. Another cause may possibly tend to detract from the light-heartedness of Braila. Turkish shells now and then come tumbling into the place, and ever and anon there echoes through the streets and squares the din of the Russian cannon hard by, making the windows rattle in their frames and the spoons jump in the cups on the tables outside the café under the locust trees. The shell fire cannot be called ruthless, for the missiles seldom explode, and the casualties have been trivial; the hotel waiter speaks of cannon fire as he might of the arrival of an extra train on the railway. "Yesterday there came none, day before one or two. On most days there is some shooting. Red or white wine, Sir?" But to all is not given the insouciance of the hotel waiter. Ladies' nerves go wrong under the strain of cannon thunder, even although there is scarcely any lightning to speak about in connection with that thunder; and so it comes to pass that most of the gentlemen one meets are living *en garçon*, having sent away their wives and children. The place seems to me more than quite one half empty; and except for the casual rattle of a vehicle containing a Russian officer on his way from the camp to the Hotel Restaurant, or for the muffled clatter of Cossack pony hoofs, there reigns in the place a strange, weird silence that is very depressing.

Apart from its historic associations, there attaches to Braila not a little interest of to-day. In sight of it befell the Turks the first of the many catastrophes with which this war is pregnant for them—the explosion of the corvette *Lutfi Djelil.* Many believe that the Russians intend to follow the precedents of 1827, 1828, and 1853, and throw one of their bridges across the Danube at Braila. Specific predictions are always rash, and they are sometimes dangerous; but previous events give an amount of weight to an anticipation of the kind which may justify me in asking your readers to bear with me while I describe Braila and its vicinity somewhat in detail.

Suppose I ask the reader to accompany me to the roof of the house of Mr. Brown, the British Vice-Consul, near the centre of the town. Hence we look down on Braila, and across at Matchin. At our feet in front and to right and left is the town. That red-cross flag half a mile to the left waves over the hospital. A little distance further east is a Russian battery containing two large 8-inch guns and several smaller pieces. This battery is called the Northern Battery. Somewhat further to our right, and actually within the barrier of the town, is the Russian Southern Battery, containing four 8-inch cannon, besides smaller 12-pounders. It is made on a wooden bluff of some elevation, which gives it some dominance; but its position within the town exposes Braila to bombardment, as it nullifies its character of an open town. Hobart Pacha promised Mr. Sanderson, the English Consul at Galatz, that his vessels would not interfere with Galatz, Braila, or Reni so long as batteries were not made within them or in their immediate proximity; but this battery renders it allowable for Turkish cannon to burn Braila without violating Hobart Pacha's word. Allowable, no doubt; but I imagine the Russian view is that it is impossible now that their big guns sweep the Danube, and there is force in the argument. Only a chance shell might questionless fire Braila, and it must be said that the Russians have acted with some recklessness in exposing the place to this chance. Before lies the Danube, sweeping in towards the Black Sea with that steady, swift, ceaseless current which seems the embodiment of power. Opposite the Northern Russian Battery you may see the smoke still rising from the battered and burnt ruins of Getchet, otherwise Port Bender. There was a custom-house here, where the lighters coming down the Old Danube paid toll, and there was a guard house and a khan, and a few cottages—a mean place, all of a tremble with ague and river fever, and not to be chosen as a habitation by any one save of amphibious predilections. The Russians ten days ago battered it about and half burnt it, and sent across and ferried over the coal that had been deposited there for the use of the Turkish gunboats; but some irregulars had taken up a precarious position in the ruins, and kept popping away at the Russians on the Braila side in a troublesome manner. What other ultimate motive may have actuated the Russians in sending a detachment over, and keeping it there where it now is, I do not venture to ask; only if they have it in mind to cross here, I venture to think that it would have been better policy to have left the few houses standing, as they would furnish the nucleus at least of a tête-de-pont, and give some cover to a force thrown over to guard the pontoniers from molestation. Anyhow, yesterday Getchet was first battered by shell fired from the smaller guns of the Northern Battery, and then occupied by 600 Cossacks, who still remain in occupation. Let us finish off Getchet when we are about it. Practically the place is isolated. Behind it is a wide expanse of swamp, interspersed with lagoons and backwaters, which render the traversing of it impossible. This expanse is about two miles wide, and beyond it rises the broken picturesque hill country—the tail of that spur of the Balkans which runs northward through the Dobrudscha, and forms its backbone. The Danube seems in heavier flood than when I first looked down on it from the Belvedere in Galatz nearly a month ago; and so continuous are the backwaters that I am assured it is possible to go by water from Matchin to Isatchia without ever touching the Danube proper at all. From Getchet a precarious footpath skirts the bank of the Old Danube to Matchin; but for long distances it is now under water, and it never is anything but a footpath. Wherefore, applying the test of common sense, a crossing in force from Braila to Getchet would seem purposeless, at least for the present, while the waters are out. It is eminently practicable, for the Turks have nothing to interfere with the enterprise; the Danube is wholly under the sweep of the Russian cannon, and at the point named is not above one thousand metres wide. Pontoons abound; they are being manufactured in the vicinity by the hundred; but it is essential for an army corps safely landed at Getchet, if indeed about that juicy locality there be terra firma for an army corps, to find standing room on. The making of a raised chaussée to the upland, such as the Russians made in 1827 on the Bessarabian side from Salunevo to the water's edge opposite Isatchia, would be a labour which, if its accomplishment were practicable at all, would employ a division for a month, by which time the falling water would render it a useless superfluity. No doubt the Russians crossed here in 1853, but that was in July-August, when the river falls to its summer level.

A few hundred yards above Getchet there ends an island which begins at Hirsova, sixty miles higher up the river, and divides it for all this distance into two great branches. Of these the right branch, which flows more or less close to the foot of the hill country of the Dobrudscha, and on which stands the town of Matchin, is known as the "Old Danube;" the left branch, which spreads and ramifies over the flat Wallachian meadow land, is the Danube proper, of the present day at least. The island formed by these branches belongs to Roumania; it is low, flat, and intersected with water-courses. Perhaps at this season quite one-half of it is swamp. The tail of it here opposite to us as we look out from the roof of the Consul's house is partly bare, partly covered with low scrubby wood, alders and willows. The Old Danube beyond these alders and willows trends away sharply to the southward, almost, but not quite, at right angles to the main branch which lies at our feet between us and the island. Follow with the eye the course of the Old Danube. About half way up between the bifurcation and Matchin notice that tall bare spar rising in its nakedness high above the foliage. That is the still-standing mizenmast of the ill-fated *Lutfi Djelil*, the Turkish corvette which three weeks ago so proudly passed up stream opposite Galatz with ports open and fighting deck cleared, while the burghers glowered on her trim grimness with their hearts in their mouths. I have told in your columns the tragic story of her fate. In the hospital under the red-cross flag their lies torn and mangled the sole survivor of the 200 men who formed her crew. No flag now waves from that spar; the crescent and star hung there for two hours after the tragedy, but no Turkish craft put out from Matchin so that it might be possible to repeat the words of the chivalrous Francis after the catastrophe of Pavia. All was lost, and honour was not saved; for a Russian officer, boarding the wreck from one of the steam launches, climbed the mast and took the trophy. Some distance higher up are visible more spars above the trees; but these are not so lofty as the mournful relic of the corvette. Here, under what shelter the island-bank may afford, lie three Turkish gunboats. It is their masts we see. Their fate does not promise brightly. There is not sufficient water for them, it appears, to emerge from the Old Danube branch upward at the point where it quits the main river. They might indeed pass downward but for these Russian batteries which form across the stream, and which have already wrought the ruin of the fine craft alongside which they were mere cock-boats. They are penned, snared, imprisoned; their fate is either to be grounding here on their beef bones, while slowly the waters recede from under them and render exit down stream also impossible, or to strike their flag to the Russian gunners. Yesterday the great guns of the Southern Battery west of Galatz were trying the range in their direction, and with satisfactory results; they may be the targets of a crushing cannonade to-morrow.

Looking a little to the right of the topmasts of the gunboats, we trace the outlines of the principal buildings in Matchin. The distance is eight miles, so that even with the glass not a great deal is to be made out, save that in a slope near the centre stands a mosque, with an imposing front, flanked by two minarets. Matchin is said to be fortified after a fashion—that is, the old walls and peppercorn flanking turrets, and crenellated curtains, have not wholly crumbled into the moat; but it has no pretension to be a place of strength in the modern acceptation of the term. There are a few batteries about it, which were armed with large but obsolete small-bore cannon; but it is reported in Braila that some Krupps have reached Matchin, and been placed in position. If this be the case they have given no sign; but except when the Russian launches came up about the foundered corvette nothing hostile has been as yet within their range. On that occasion, not the Matchin cannon, but a battery on the edge of the hill country to the proper right of Matchin and almost immediately behind Getchet, came into action. Matchin slopes up on the hill-side, and is very pretty from the distance at which we look on it, while the sun is dancing on the housetops, and lighting up the sombreness of the woods on the ridge behind it. Growing gradually paler till it fades away into a faint blue, that ridge recedes in a south-westerly direction towards Hirsova, sixty miles off at the head of the great island.

I don't know that there is much more to describe. The Russians have attempted to effect no footing on the island, and from this side of the river their cannon, large as they are, cannot reach to Matchin. Likely enough, that place may wake up some fine morning and find itself in the hands of a Russian force, which, marching by the footpath from Getchet, may haply carry the place by surprise under cover of night, taking advantage of the notoriously bad night watch which the Turks keep. If we turn our backs on the Danube and look inland beyond the town, we see the *tentes d'abri* of the Russian camps half encircling Braila. There are camps of two kinds, standing camps and flying camps. In the former abide a division of the 11th Corps, under the command of General Staloff; the other division of the same corps (Prince Schahofskoy's) being in Galatz. This was the first corps to enter Roumania, and it has penetrated the least into that territory. After one day's march from the Pruth it sat down to hold the exposed left, while the rest of the Army of Operation marched through it, or by it, or round it. The inhabitants of the flying camps are there to-day and gone to-morrow. Now a regiment of Skobeleff's Cossacks put up for a day and ask for rations, on their way to Bucharest, Kalarash, Braila, Turna Magurelle, or Kalafat, who can tell? Now it is a brigade of Dragomiroff's stout fellows of the 8th Corps, with the mud of the Birlat Valley fresh on their long boots; now the dragoons of Prince Manueloff, surely the finest heavy cavalry of the line in all broad Europe. As the detachments march, the mass passes outside Braila, but a battalion, or a squadron, or a sotnia always makes its way through the town with what bravery of appearance is possible, with band playing or drums beating, or leading files thumping the cymbals or obeying the old genial command that has lightened so many a long day's march—"Singers to the front!" Rations are waiting for the in-marching troops, and the out-marching have their haversacks made up. At first the intendance contracted with the bakers in Braila for loaves; now they buy flour—only wheat and rye flour, they will have no other grain—and military bakers bake the bread in the field ovens in the camp. Right good bread it is. I speak from experience, for to-day I lunched mainly off it.

Whither do all the pontoons disappear? They are being turned out here in numbers, and also on the Sereth, but as soon as they are finished they disappear mysteriously under cover of night, some in carts, some by rail. All the world knows that pontoons are required for the crossing of the Danube, but, through me, for the present, no part of the world must know what is the destination of these pontoons.

Towards the end of May it became known that the Emperor Alexander was about to visit the army, although at that time no one imagined that he was likely to stay throughout the summer campaign.

The subjoined letter describes a tour of inspection in Wallachia made by Prince Charles of Roumania:—

* POIANO, near KALAFAT, *May 27th.*—Born a Hohenzollern and reared an officer in the Prussian army, it is little wonder that Prince Charles of Roumania is above all things a soldier. Since his election to the headship of the Principalities, he has sedulously devoted a large share of his energies to the improvement, or rather, indeed, in the first instance, to the creation of a Roumanian army, and that his labour has not been lost is apparent to any man having any conversance with military matters who has spent the last few weeks in the territory over which Prince Charles holds sway. Two corps of the Roumanian army, each numbering 28,000 men, are now in the field, fully equipped, and ready for immediate action, while the militia, whose strength is close on 100,000 men, is ready for mobilization at the shortest notice. The first army corps is now in position in Little Wallachia, chiefly in its more westerly section, and having previously visited other points at which detachments of his troops were on duty, Prince Charles and his military advisers arranged a tour of inspection of that corps, impelled the more to this course because of the near approach to completion of sundry pre-

parations which for some time past have been in progress at Kalafat, over against the Turkish fortress of Widdin. It was settled that his Highness should leave Bucharest yesterday morning, journeying on that day as far as Krajova, and, through the kindness of an old Servian friend, whose good offices we have experienced in not a few awkward places in the district between Saitchar and Djunis, an invitation to accompany the Prince on this excursion was given to Mr. Villiers, of the *Graphic*, and myself. We were strictly non-official. The official members of the party accompanying his Highness were the following:—the Minister of War, Colonel Cernat; the chief of the headquarters staff of the Roumanian army, Colonel Staniceana; the Maréchal of the Court, Colonel Vacaresco; Staff Major Lahovari, aide-de-camp of the Prince and commandant of headquarters; Colonel Greceanu, aide-de-camp of the War Minister; Captain Maurocordato; Colonel Dochtouroff, the Russian Military Commissioner with the Roumanian army; and Colonel Gaillard, the French military attaché with the headquarters of the Commander-in-Chief of the Russian army. The party quitted Bucharest at eight o'clock yesterday morning, in carriages attached to the ordinary day train running to Krajova, and on to Turn Severin and the Austrian frontier. This train conveyed also Commodore Demetrescu Maican, the commander of the Roumanian flotilla, with several other naval officers and a number of sailors, on their way to do duty as gunners in the batteries bordering the north bank of the Danube in Little Wallachia.

It rained furiously until after midday, and the country for a long distance was perfectly flat and dull, so that this portion of the journey was far from interesting. It was made apparent to me that it is not alone in England that mayors and other local dignitaries insist on asserting their own self-importance by the presentation of addresses whenever opportunity affords. The first gun of the running fire of addresses was fired in Gaesh, a station about half way to Pilesti, where a gentleman in a portentous white tie disregarded the rain and triumphantly read a document, concerning which all that I can say is, that its language was very sonorous. I had the pleasure of the companionship of a Russian colonel of engineers on his way to Slatina, and thence "to the Danube," which is a pleasant vague expression, which is very frequently in the mouths of the cautious and reticent Russian officers. The colonel gave me much very interesting and valuable information regarding the internal economy of the Russian army, which I must take another opportunity for recounting.

I found that it pleased him greatly that it was in my power to bear testimony to the orderly and decorous manner in which the Russian soldiers had conducted themselves during their march through Roumania, and casual confirmation on this head came, curiously enough, from a civilian gentleman who happened to share our carriage. It appeared from his narrative that a certain corporal of the Sapper battalion No. 6 chanced to break a glass on his billet in the little town of Remnik. His host, when he offered to pay for the damage, told him he would accept no recompense for what was a pure accident; but the corporal did not see the matter in this light. Failing to prevail on his host to accept payment for the damage, he went out and bought another glass, and, bringing that back to his billet, compelled the host to take it. The colonel also told me that the name of the officer in the Grand Duke's headquarters commanding the whole artillery of the Army of Operation is General Prince Masalski, and that of the officer commanding the whole engineer force, General Deebh—names which may be worth remembering as likely to recur in the story of the campaign. At Pilesti, where we halted for déjeûner, the station was very beautifully adorned with silvan and floral decorations; the vicinity of the station and the platform were thronged with masses of townspeople and peasants cheering the Prince with the warmest enthusiasm, and on the reverse side of the train a Russian infantry battalion, the contents of a military train which was halted in the station, paraded without arms, and showed to great advantage, the men being clean and neat in spite of their long journey, made under conditions unfavourable for opportunities of neatness and cleanliness, while their stalwart, soldierly forms excited the admiration of all capable of appreciating the physical good points of the soldier. While lunching, Prince Charles received from the Grand Duke Nicholas in Ployesti a telegram announcing the destruction by a torpedo of a Turkish gunboat near Braila, the particulars of which daring and successful attempt I sent you by telegraph last week. It was remarked that at the rate they are now disappearing no long time will elapse before the Turkish flotilla is wholly removed off the face of the Danube; and the exploit has a far wider significance in the lesson it teaches, or rather, perhaps, the contingencies which it suggests, than in its relation simply to the Turkish war craft on the Danube.

Until near Pilesti the train had traversed a region almost perfectly flat, but now we were in the vicinity of the higher ground, marking the commencement of the picturesquely gradual slope of the Carpathian Mountains, and the terrain became charmingly diversified with fertile swelling, rising grounds, covered with vineyards and broken by beautiful valleys in which pretty villages nestled among the oak trees by the margin of the wimpling brooks. Occasionally the line passes through deep cuttings—rare sights in Roumania—and these, I observed, are levelled by transverse bands of wattles fastened down by stakes, an expedient which seems an effectual, and must be a cheap, preventive of that tendency to fall in which is so common and so troublesome in a friable soil. Long stretches of oak copse alternated with fertile fields and vine-bergs; and no one could look on the land without acknowledging that it was fair. A country, surely, well worth fighting for, and calculated to stir the patriotism even of a people whose stomach for fighting has not hitherto been reputed to be very keen. The Roumanians themselves are conscious that this is the character generally ascribed to them, but the depreciatory estimate does not seem to be justified historically; and all I can say is, I have already twice seen Roumanian troops under fire without having observed any of the tremor which is not wholly unnatural in young and inexperienced soldiers.

At Corbu station, beyond Pilesti, we found paraded on the long platform an unarmed battalion of the 122nd Regiment, part of the 31st Division, now on its march in a westerly direction through Wallachia. The 31st is one of the divisions of the 9th Army Corps, its other division, the 5th, being in the line of march further in the rear. In every case the Russian troops paraded in the railway stations for the inspection of the Prince were unarmed, as they were travelling by military train, and their belts and arms when on such a journey are stowed away in separate carriages till the destination is reached. The Prince was received by the commandant of the battalion, the band playing the Roumanian national air as he alighted. He passed along the front of the battalion, and after exchanging a few words with the officers re-entered his carriage, the band playing the Russian Hymn, a beautiful and solemn melody, with a noble roll and sway in its stately measure. We have heard it often in England on the occasion of visits of members of the Russian Imperial family, but it is music which sounds most appropriate when performed at the head of serried ranks of soldiers. As the train left the station, the Russian soldiers gave his Highness three ringing rounds of real genuine "Hurrahs," which sounded to me strangely English, till I remembered that the "Hurrah" which we have come to regard as our own is really indigenous among the Cossacks of the Don steppes, and came to us across Europe from them. At Poleovo, which is the last station on the route westward to Slatina, we were detained for several hours. A little distance further forward, there had been an accident on the line the same morning, and the damage had not been made good sufficiently to admit of the passage of a train. There was no resource but patience. Here, too, was a battalion of the 122nd Regiment, with General Belokopiloff commanding the brigade to which it belongs, and after the Prince had inspected it, the General, to pass away the time, ordered the singing contingent of the battalion to gather on the platform and do their best to gratify the audience chance had sent them. A circle consisting of about two hundred strong-lunged yet sweet-voiced fellows—forming the chorus—was formed, and the open space in the centre of this circle was speedily occupied by the leading vocalist, a stalwart private, with a grin of curious humour, and a voice both strong and sweet. At a word he struck into a ditty, which evidently was highly comic in the estimation of his audience, among whom the bursts of laughter were frequent. I am unfortunately unacquainted with the Russian language, and could not follow the singer's meaning. The song was his own, and, I was told, an improvisation; but I could make out that there was a good deal in it about Turkey and about Asia, and several times the name of England was mentioned. I was told afterwards by my friend the engineer colonel that the vocalist was not complimentary to our native land, venturing freely on the assertion that England was taking the side of the Turks, but that this circumstance would not in the slightest degree interfere with the inevitable Russian triumph. The little colonel chuckled very wickedly as he replied to my question as to the tenor of the allusion, and I have no doubt it found sympathy in the bosoms of most of the officers, while all the privates clearly relished it entirely. "Disraeli," as the Russians still persist in styling my Lord Beaconsfield, is not a favourite in their army, and it is of no avail to attempt to persuade a Russian that England veritably means to be neutral unless events should occur which in the opinion of the more impartial Russians themselves would justify, nay compel, a departure from the line of neutrality. But to return to our military vocalists. At the end of each stanza of his song the solo performer demanded the chorus with a jerk of his arm and a nod of his head; and didn't the chorus just comply with the demand! The first tune was brisk and sprightly, robust and full of verve and go, but its music was by no means uncouth. At the chorus of the last verse a grizzled but lissom non-commissioned officer, a terpsichorean corporal, as a Russian officer anxious to display his proficiency in the English language called him, burst into a dance of galvanic wildness. Now he was down on his hams, jumping like a frog; now he was spinning high in air like a saraband. The fantasticality of his pirouettings forcibly reminded me of the weird performances of the Hill-men who danced their native dances before the Prince of Wales, as he and his suite and guests were sitting by the great camp fire out on the plain behind the historic Delhi ridge. Nor were there wholly wanting instruments to accompany and accentuate the voices of the soldiers. Whistles were heard on the outskirts of the throng, and the second song was accompanied by the dulcet melody of a tambourine. Later an accordion was produced, and a very creditable solo executed thereon by a grotesquely sentimental-looking private. But this was not lively enough for the general taste, so a jig was played on the accordion and tambourine in concert, while two privates enacted a break-down and cellar-flap performance in a style which would have secured them an immediate engagement from the proprietor of a London music-hall, if a gentleman of that enterprising order had been among the spectators. They maintained visages of the most preternaturally solemn, not to say lugubrious, aspect through the whole performance, to which one gave a pleasing variety by turning a series of somersaults backwards, while the other danced upon his hands, keeping time as with a pair of castanets with the heels of his boots, high in air. The finale was a plaintive song, sung with genuine feeling and good taste, and the pathos of the strain, although I could not know the meaning of the words, went far to supply the defect.

At length, after long and, spite of the singing, weary delay, the news came that the line was repaired, but that at the place of the accident it was yet unable to bear great weight. So the train was cut in two, and the Prince's special carriages went forward, leaving the rest to follow later. The scene of the accident was a steep slope, in the fall of which is cut the railway track, and it seems that under the weight of a heavy material train the outside edge of this had subsided. There had been a great smash, for three trucks lay on the slope more or less wrecked, and their contents had rolled to the little valley down the bottom. Among the massive chains and the bales of cordage were a number of torpedo frames. Had there been "live" torpedoes in the train, what a ghastly catastrophe would have occurred! We had to alight and walk past the scene of the damage, after which we rattled on merrily to Slatina. On the plateau across which that station is reached, a right pretty sight fixed our attention—the camp of the cavalry division of the 9th Corps. Alternately the horse-lines and the rows of little tents extended athwart the plain, and above the white tents of the Uhlans fluttered the red and white of their lance pennons. The quarter guard turned out and presented arms to the Prince as the train passed, and in a few minutes more we were in the station, where Baron Krüdener, commanding the 9th Corps, was waiting to receive his Highness in all the splendour of full uniform. The fine band of one of the Russian regiments of the division played on the platform while dinner was being eaten in the restaurant; after which the Prince took leave of the General, and the train proceeded on the way to Krajova. On the flat beyond the town of Slatina we passed large camps of Russian infantry soldiers, and nearer the crossing of the river Aluta there was a camp of Cossacks perched high on one of the bluffs overlooking the valley. This was the last of the Russian camps, but not yet the last of the Russians, for in the gathering twilight, just as, passing down a narrow ravine from the table-land, we descended into the broad valley of the Aluta, we saw, moving briskly along a narrow track winding down the same ravine, but far below the railway line, a polk of Cossacks riding forward to take up the forepost line for the night. The Aluta, thrice its ordinary size, came foaming down its bed in a brown flood, studded with ugly snags and dangerous drift timber, but the fine iron bridge was sturdily supporting the strain. Beyond the bridge we passed a series of battery emplacements and shelter trenches which the Roumanian troops had thrown up for its protection, in the apprehension of the crossing of the Danube by the Turks at Kalafat, and their advance eastward through the Principality. Fortunately these works are now but lost labour. Although the main bridge had withstood the flood, a lesser bridge on one of the many side currents of the swollen Aluta had gone down, its central pier having been undermined, and there lay in the mud and water below the débris of a train which fortunately carried no passengers, but materials. But the accident was very serious in its character, and still more so in its consequences, for it will take weeks to rebuild the bridge, and meanwhile a temporary line is being constructed, similar to that by which the Seine was crossed at Creil by the trains on the Northern Railway of France, before the stone bridge, blown up at the beginning of the war, had been rebuilt. Such a crossing, however, involves delay, and is always more or less troublesome. The Roumanian railway system has done its worst persistently to spite the Russians, and delay their advance. It is the creation of Dr. Strousberg, and cannot be called a triumph of good engineering or of conscientious construction. We found a train waiting on the other side of the ruined bridge, and were led to it by peasants brandishing great torches, for by this time it was quite dark. Soon afterwards we reached Krajova, where we were to halt for the night, and where the reception of the Prince was enthusiastic and hearty.

The morning rendezvous was the house occupied by the Prince for the night—the hour, eight. There is no railway beyond Krajova in the direction of Kalafat, and we were to make the journey in waggons, of which had been collected a very miscellaneous assortment, drawn by smart cobby ponies. The Prince journeyed in a caleche drawn by four horses abreast. Colonel Gaillard and a companion had a regular four-in-hand; our vehicle was a diligence with three horses abreast as wheelers, and a pair of very wicked leaders. From the rendezvous the party drove to the Greek church for morning prayers. Priests in robes of dazzling splendour stood before the gorgeous ikonostas. The church was filled with the sweet, solemn strains of sacred music, and the fragrance of the incense waved from a silver censer scented the air with its pungency. The Prince occupied a throne opposite the ikonostas; his suite formed a circle in the centre of the church, and the ornamented Grecian archways were thronged with the people of the place. On the conclusion of the service the priests escorted his Highness to his carriage, and the journey commenced in earnest. Our coachmen were peasants in white clothes, with round hats ornamented with long streamers of bright-coloured ribbons, and the vehemence with which they cracked their whips was a caution. I should like much to describe in detail the pleasing incidents of this drive through the pretty and fertile territory of Little Wallachia, but there is no time, for as it is I am stealing more than a few hours from the night to write this letter. I should have liked to speak of the statuesque beauty of the people, and the fantastic picturesqueness of their dresses, of their semi-subterranean dwellings, and of their simple enthusiastic delight at seeing their Prince. But there is no time. We galloped on through the beautiful oak glades, with charming glimpses of green sward interspersed, and now and then in a glade there would be waiting for us a picturesque group of peasant-horsemen, with banners flying above them, who with a cheer would fall in behind the Prince's carriage, and gallop on till the limits of their boyard's estate was reached, when they would give place to another civilian escort of a similar character; and at a wayside village the strains of music would greet us, and we would find a pretty bower, constructed on the road-side, of green oak branches, shading a cool carpet of new-mown grass strewn with roses and lilacs, and in this bower the Prince would be bidden to rest awhile in a chair whose back was of rosebuds, and whose arms were masses of locust-tree blossoms, and to partake of refreshments—preserved fruit, the dulczda of Roumania, the slafko of Servia—while the solemn fiddlers played a jig on their violins in the centre of a circle of lads and lasses, all in their gayest dresses, with flowers in their hands and wreaths of blossoms round their waists, who deftly footed the Chora—that dance which in name as in character is simply the χορεος of the ancient Greeks. Then the mayor's pretty daughter, the only damsel in the village possessed of shoon, presents her nosegay of roses to the Prince, and the cortége drives onward to a similar scene in the next village. It was Arcadia, but a precarious Arcadia indeed; for away across the far-stretching level flat on which sparkle in the sunshine the metal roofs of the churches, and yet a little further, beyond the broad flood of the Danube, whose gleam is visible here and there through the screen of willows, rises the low ridge of the Turkish bank, and behind that, faintly blue in the sunshine, the snow-streaked summits of the Balkan. Arcadia is not a day's ride of a squad of Bashi-Bazouks from that ridge yonder, and these blue mountains look down on a Turkish fortress and a Turkish army which lies between Arcadia and their hitherward slopes.

We had déjeûner under a shed near Bailesti—not strictly *déjeûner à la fourchette*, as some one remarked, because there was rather a scarcity of forks. Three hours further on we struck the Danube at Golenz, where the party alighted to inspect a very fine defensive position. Now we had quitted Arcadia, and were quite in a military atmosphere. On either side the road, troops were in camp or in bivouac—regulars, reserve, and militia, or, as they are styled in Roumanian, Dorobantzen. The broad plateau above Kalafat is encircled by the earthworks of generations of invaders and defenders; the profile of the works raised by Omar Pacha in 1853-4 is still almost perfect. At the entrance to the works the Prince was met by General Lupu, commanding the army corps, and by Colonel Tcherkess, commanding the division now in and about Kalafat, with their respective staffs, and escorted to the headquarters in the town. It is impossible for me now to describe in detail Kalafat, its defences, and its enemy—Widdin—opposite to it. Suffice it now to say that at present there are four batteries in all, armed, two with field guns on the edge of the bluff, and two with long 25-pounder 15-centimetre cannon on the water's edge. After an inspection of these, the Prince drove to the camp, where he found a brigade of infantry drawn up, presenting a most effective and soldierlike appearance. When it was near dusk the party returned to No. 1 Battery, and there witnessed the effect of a few shots which were thrown into Widdin for the purpose of getting the ranges, this having been the first time the heavy guns were brought into action. The results were all that was desired, and no damage was done by the warm—although tardy—fire which was poured in by the Turks, as well into the town as into the batteries. Three shells exploded in the battery whence the Prince and his party were viewing the practice, and I was struck by the admirable conduct at this time of the Roumanian gunners, who never flinched in the slightest degree under the trying ordeal.

Of the few Russian officers who have risen rapidly in reputation during this war, of none is the name now more familiar than that of General Skobeleff. The following letter is a description of him from personal knowledge acquired before he had an opportunity of distinguishing himself in Turkey :—

† PLOYESTI, *May 20th.*—Among the many officers on the Grand Duke's staff, there is one who would attract attention anywhere, and whose career has been curious and brilliant. He is a tall, handsome man, with a lithe, slender, active figure, a clear blue eye, and a large, prominent, but straight, well-shaped nose, the kind of nose it is said Napoleon used to look for among his officers when he wished to find a general, and a face young enough for a second lieutenant although he is a general—the youngest in the Russian army.

It is the famous General Skobeleff, the conqueror of Ferghana, or Khokand. The last time I saw him we were both standing on the banks of the Oxus, in the Khanate of Khiva. He was starting on his way to Tashkent; I on my return to St. Petersburg, in a boat which was to float me down to the mouth of the Oxus into the Aral Sea, where I was to find a Russian steamer. We were the last two who had seen the city of Khiva, for we were the last to leave it. He was then Colonel Skobeleff, and had just returned from a remarkable and daring expedition, for which he afterwards received the Cross of St. George. It will be remembered that of the five columns which marched on Khiva only four arrived, and that one, that of Markosoff, was obliged to turn back in the middle of the desert for want of water, after having incurred the most imminent danger of destruction from heat and thirst. Kauffmann wished to ascertain whether it would be possible for Markosoff to reach Khiva by that route, but the Turkomans whom we had just been fighting had all fled in that direction. To have explored the route with safety it would have been necessary to send a large column, which Kauffmann did not think the importance of the matter justified. The only other alternative was for a small party to make the attempt at the risk of falling into the hands of the exasperated Turkomans. This Colonel Skobeleff volunteered to do. He took three friendly Turkomans with him, disguised himself in the costume of a Turkoman, and started on his perilous enterprise. He did not return for ten days, and everybody had given him up for lost, when he finally appeared at Khiva the day before Kauffmann's evacuation of the capital. He had managed to elude the Turkomans and to reach the point where Markosoff had turned back; he explored the way, measured the depth of the wells and the amount of water they could supply, and returned safely, almost exhausted by his long ride. He wished, of course, to write his report immediately, but, as the army was moving next day, he determined to stay behind for that purpose in one of the Khan's palaces outside the city which had been Kauffmann's headquarters, and he asked me to keep him company, which I very willingly undertook to do. We remained there a day and a night after the departure of the army, and thus it came about that we were the last two of the invading expedition to look upon the Khivan capital.

Since that time I had followed his career in the Russian and other newspapers, and it has been a very extraordinary and brilliant one. First I heard of him as Colonel Skobeleff fighting with the Khokandians; then as General Skobeleff, to whom Kauffmann had entrusted the command of the forces sent against Khokand; afterwards as General Skobeleff, Governor of Ferghana, the new name of Khokand, the country which he himself conquered and annexed, and which contains a population of about two millions of inhabitants. Then I heard nothing more of him until I met him in the railway train on his way to Kischeneff to rejoin the Army of the Danube. I see that the papers are continually confounding him with his father, who is likewise in the Army of the Danube, in command of an independent division of Cossacks who were among the troops that made the famous march to Galatz on the day of the declaration of war, to protect the bridge of

Barbosch. The father is by no means an old man; father and son resemble each other as nearly as two peas, and the two together, both young and both generals, form a very curious instance of early success achieved without protection or favour. A parallel case is offered by that of General Ignatieff, the diplomatist, and his father, who is likewise a general in the Russian army.

The war resulting in the conquest of Khokand seems to have been altogether a very curious affair. The country of Khokand was very much in the same condition at that time as Turkey is at present. The people had been so oppressed and exasperated by the extortions of Khudoyar Khan that they had risen in insurrection against him in favour of his son, whom they at first succeeded in putting on the throne, forming a parallel case with the Bulgarian insurrection and the overthrow of Abdul Aziz. Curiously enough, this insurrection, which was altogether unexpected, broke out on the very day that a Russian Embassy arrived at the capital of Khokand. Within twenty-four hours the Khan was obliged to retreat towards the Russian frontier, and the Embassy was of course obliged to retreat with him. Skobeleff accompanied this Embassy, and his account is very amusing. Only about 200 men of the Khan's whole army remained faithful to him; all the rest went over to the insurgents and took part with the enraged population, who immediately began a pursuit of the retreating monarch. The Russians had about fifty Cossacks, who were obliged to take part in the defence, otherwise they would have all been killed. The Khan had started in the night with eighty cartloads of money and treasure, with which he had hoped to reach the Russian frontier. The hope was vain, but at the same time it probably served to save his life, and to prevent the retreating column from being completely cut to pieces, for every time that they were on the point of being overpowered by superior numbers, the Khan ordered a cartload of silver to be dropped, whereupon the whole insurgent army threw itself on the abandoned treasure, and fought for it among themselves, thus giving the retreating party a fresh start. This operation was repeated no fewer than sixty times before they reached the Russian frontier, when the Khan had only twenty carts left. The loss of life was comparatively small. The Khan submitted to his pecuniary losses with great equanimity, as he still had enough left, and he is now living in Orenburg on the débris of his fortune in a princely manner, still a very rich man. The insurgents succeeded in placing his son on the throne, and in spite of the fact that the Russian Embassy had been fired upon and had sustained some loss, Kauffmann informed the new Khan that he was willing to recognize his authority provided he would recognize and ratify the treaty which had been in existence for some years between Khokand and Russia. The people of Central Asia are much like the Turks, and every concession made with a view of avoiding difficulties is regarded by them as a sign of weakness. This very moderate proposition coming from Kauffmann after the Russian Embassy had been fired at was regarded as a proof that the Russians were afraid, and their reply to it was to cross the Russian frontier, burn two or three Russian post stations, and kill the post-masters. There was nothing for Kauffmann to do but to send a column to protect the frontier, and put a stop to these acts of lawlessness. This, of course, very soon resulted in a collision, and the Russians invaded the country. They marched to the town of Namangan, which they took by storm after a few hours' bombardment; but the detachment was a small one, while the enemy's forces were very numerous and very brave, with more or less discipline, and the Russians soon found that, although they had taken the town by storm, they would be unable to hold it. They withdrew from it therefore, and the next day began to retire towards the frontier, or, to put it more plainly, to retreat. They were immediately followed by the Khokandians, who attacked them with great violence and harassed them continually, keeping up a running fire all day long and making their position a very disagreeable one. On the third day of the retreat the Russian infantry had only fifteen cartridges left, the cavalry only three, and they still had three days' march before they could hope for reinforcements and supplies. The situation was a very critical one, and General Trotsky, who was in command of the detachment, decided that something would have to be done to put a stop to this incessant battle. The Russian detachment numbered only about eight hundred men, with three or four hundred Cossacks; while the forces of the enemy were some 6,000 or 7,000. The Khokandians had besides considerable experience in war. Their forces were regularly organized into companies and battalions; they had uniforms, standards, very good arms, and all the elements of a military organization. General Trotsky decided upon a night attack, and confided his plan to Colonel Skobeleff, then his chief of staff. The latter entered into the idea with great enthusiasm, and proposed to lead the attacking column himself; but, going upon the principle that a night attack should be rather with the view of striking terror into the heart of the enemy than with the hope of doing him any great deal of harm, he decided to take only 150 Cossacks for the attack. Skobeleff, having reconnoitred the ground, perceived that the Khokandians had encamped within a mile and a half of the Russians, in an open plain, which gave every facility for the manœuvring of cavalry. At midnight he took his 150 Cossacks, divided them into three parties, and cautiously surrounded the enemy's camp. The party led by Skobeleff himself managed to pass the enemy's outposts, who were sound asleep. Then he gave the signal for the attack by firing his pistol, and, followed by his 150 Cossacks, he rode headlong into the enemy's camp of six or seven thousand men, shouting and yelling like fiends, and cutting down everything in their passage.

The effect was tremendous. For a quarter of an hour the plain resounded with shrieks and yells, shots, the trampling of horses, shouts, and groans, and all the uproar of battle. Then all was silence. Skobeleff assembled his Cossacks, and when morning came he found that the whole army of the enemy had disappeared, leaving on the field about 40 dead, 37 standards, 2,000 turbans, 2,000 or 3,000 muskets and sabres, all their camp material and baggage. But what was his astonishment on calling the roll to discover that he had not lost a man either killed or wounded. For a small affair it was one of the most brilliant feats ever recorded, for it inflicted a most disastrous defeat on the enemy, saved the Russian detachment, and enabled it to reach the frontier and its base in safety. These kinds of exploits have obtained for Skobeleff the reputation, even among the Russians, of being a kind of madman, who would fling away his own life, and those of his troops, without the slightest regard to consequences. General Skobeleff is rather indignant at this view of his character, and I am convinced it does him a great injustice. There is method in his madness, or rather what at first appears madness; as, for instance, attacking 7,000 men with 150 was, as he explains it, not only not madness, but a reasonable, well-conceived plan, with the requisite number of chances on the side of the attacking party, and one that must have had the approval of all military men. His explanation is as follows:—Irregular troops, even of the very bravest and best, are peculiarly subject to panics when attacked unexpectedly or from an unlooked-for quarter. Now, anybody who has experienced it knows that a night attack is a most terrible and nerve-shaking thing for the army attacked, even when composed of regular troops. For irregular troops it is certain destruction and defeat, if the attacking party can penetrate their lines before they have time to get fairly awake, as in the present case. As to the small number of troops taken by Skobeleff for this attack, he says that the object of his attack was not so much the hope of cutting the enemy to pieces, as to strike terror among them and create a panic, and for this purpose 150 Cossacks in the night, when their number could not be seen, were quite sufficient, as they could make as much noise and produce as great an effect as ten times their number; while a small party was less liable to confusion, and to the danger of killing each other, the great danger of a night attack for the attacking party; and finally, if they did not succeed and should all be killed, an eventuality also to be taken into account, the loss would be small, and such as not to seriously weaken the detachment. It will be seen, therefore, it was not such a mad business after all; and the result proved Skobeleff had really calculated the chances as any prudent general would do, and simply found that they were on his side. Although the new Khan of Khokand, after this campaign, agreed to sign a new treaty of peace, the Russians had no sooner withdrawn from the country than he again opened hostilities, and Kauffmann found himself under the necessity of obtaining permission to conquer and annex the country, and this task he entrusted to Colonel Skobeleff, who, as commander of an independent army, was promoted to the rank of general. The task was accomplished with rapidity and skill, as may be readily understood when it is stated that when the Khan surrendered to General Skobeleff, after a three months' campaign, nearly his first words were, "Before we begin to talk, let me sleep, for I have not had a night's rest nor a sound sleep for more than a month."

I have given this sketch of Skobeleff because, although he has not yet received a command in the Army of the Danube, he will probably be heard of more than once before the present campaign is over.

The following letter presents a picture of another Russian soldier with no immediate pretension to military distinction, but who was certain to rise in the service of his Emperor :—

† PLOYESTI, *May 20th.*—I have just been surprised by a visit from Prince Tserteleff. The Prince will be remembered by many people in London society as the young and clever secretary who accompanied General Ignatieff on his trip to England, and his name is more or less familiar to the public as the second Secretary of the Russian Embassy at Constantinople.

It will be remembered that the Prince resigned his situation in the diplomatic service and volunteered for the war as a common soldier. He is now serving as a simple cavalry man in the Dragoons, although he expects soon to be transferred to the Circassian Cossacks under the command of General Skobeleff. He has been on outpost duty along the Danube ever since the beginning of the war, and is so changed by his uniform, by exposure to the weather, and his face is so sunburnt and so rough-looking, that I am afraid his own mother would hardly recognize him. He, in fact, resembles more a good-looking butcher-boy than anything else I can think of —a fact which, with the candour which should characterize friends, I did not hesitate to communicate to him. He was extremely flattered by the information. His great ambition is to look like a soldier, and this he considered as a preliminary accomplishment in the right direction. He is very proud of his uniform, in spite of its being about as ugly a one as could easily be imagined; and although there was no necessity for it, he put it on at St. Petersburg to make the trip to Kischeneff, in order, as he said, to get accustomed to it as soon as possible, and not to look as though he were masquerading. The uniform is dark blue, with light-blue facings, a grey overcoat of coarse, heavy cloth which a London groom would probably not consider respectable enough for a horse blanket, and which resembles somewhat the material used for convicts' clothes—a black, hideous-looking leather cap, with a brass double-headed eagle, with a visor or peak cocked up at a most ridiculous and ungainly angle. The sword is not worn attached to a belt, but to a strap slung over the shoulder.

Although the Prince was very proud of this costume, he found, when he got to Kischeneff, that it was a source of great embarrassment to him, and resulted in his getting nearly starved to death. According to the regulations then in existence, and which have only been relaxed since, a soldier cannot go into a theatre, restaurant, café, club, or any public place where he would be liable to meet an officer. He had not yet been attached to his regiment, and was not therefore drawing rations. The poor fellow consequently could not go anywhere to get anything to eat, except when he was invited to dinner in a private house. He went wandering about the streets, a kind of outcast and vagabond, without any visible means of existence, like a Constantinople dog, picking up a meal wherever he could find one. He finally found me, and from that time forward things went better, as he used to come to my hotel, order his breakfast or dinner, and eat it in my room. As I happened to be laid up with a sprained ankle at that time, the arrangement suited me very well, and being thus isolated, as it were, and cut off from society and the world, we might have been inclined to indulge in wild bacchanalian dissipation, had it not been for the fact that the Hôtel du Nord, in which I was stopping at Kischeneff, did not offer any materials for excess in the way of either eating or drinking. All we could get to eat was roast mutton and wild asparagus, while the only thing to drink consisted of some very stale beer, and a villanous kind of decoction, which they called champagne, and which no man in his senses would dream of drinking, unless he were bent upon a painful and lingering suicide. Now, beer and mutton are very good things in themselves, but they do not form a sufficient variety upon which to found a banquet, and although they are quite enough to sustain life, they are not calculated to tempt two young men, fresh from the restaurants of St. Petersburg, to any excess either in eating or drinking, and we were perforce obliged to remain temperate. At last the Prince got his papers enabling him to join his regiment, which had already gone forward, and one cold, wet, rainy morning he mounted his horse at the door of the hotel, and rode away without servant or guide, like G. P. R. James's solitary horseman, to overtake his regiment, which was already two or three days' march in advance. He succeeded in rejoining it, and since that time has been doing duty on the Danube. He said that he likes soldiering better even than he had expected, although he finds it pretty hard work to keep his arms and accoutrements clean; and he found it rather difficult at first to get on and off his horse, which, in addition to himself, carried behind the saddle part of a tent, a sack of oats, a blanket, a frying-pan, a tea-kettle, and a large bundle of hay, together with various other things that are considered useful in a soldier's life. He has been under fire three or four times already, and has been over the Danube once on a reconnoitring expedition.

Everything considered, the Prince may be esteemed as good a soldier, I think, as a diplomatist; but I hope for the sake of journalism that he will be more communicative in his new than he ever was in his old profession. There was never anything to be got out of him as a diplomatist. Never would he tell you anything that you did not know before, or, if he did, you would be pretty sure to find it in some newspaper a week old, that had escaped you. In my opinion, a diplomatist of this kind is utterly and entirely useless, and the sooner he exchanges it, as the Prince has done, for another profession, the better for all concerned. He has, I may remark, some pretensions to the literary profession besides, and has written a couple of novels, and was engaged, I believe, on an historical work of some kind, when the sudden cropping up of the Eastern Question interrupted it. He has hitherto kept his authorship a profound secret from his chiefs, because it would have created a great commotion in the service had it been known that he was dabbling in literature. A man with enough intellect to write anything more than a despatch, beginning with "I have the honour," and finishing, "I am, &c., &c.," would be regarded as a black sheep in any diplomatic service in the world, and be dealt with accordingly. But although the Prince may be a successful soldier, and reap multitudinous laurels on the field of battle, his hands and face have been completely spoiled, and will never, I fear, recover their pristine freshness.

The following letters from Rustchuk were written while the Russian advance was daily expected. The remarks they contain on the character of the Turkish soldiers are from the pen of one who has long known them well :—

△ RUSTCHUK, *May 18th.*—We are still lingering here, almost isolated from the rest of the world by the absence of regular postal and telegraphic communications. We are very quiet, too, not even being interrupted, as in time of peace, by the sharp whistling of the steamers on the river, or the railway engines. This situation, however, is only the calm before the storm. As the soldiers, moreover, who are on the average a mile out of the city, remain in their camps, stretching over the grassy plain, and among the vineyards on the hills, we hear and see very little of them, to the great satisfaction of the Bulgarians. Whatever may be said respecting their conduct when they are excited to commit outrages by their modern Byzantine rulers; it cannot be denied, on the other hand, that, when it is in the interest of their superiors to control them, they behave well enough, keep up good discipline, and very seldom infringe the regulations to which they are subjected. In consequence of their abstaining from the use of strong liquors, the prominent vice to which European soldiers and sailors are addicted, no brawls or scuffles in taverns take place. Atrocious deeds, due to drink, are committed here sometimes; but the authors are usually the so-called Krays, Turkish rowdies, who live by smuggling salt and tobacco from or to Roumania, and who are, on the whole, the worst set of rascals and ruffians that ever disgraced mankind. It is of them that the Christians are justly afraid. The troops are continually occupied in strengthening the intrenchments, in which they are instructed with remarkable zeal by the commanding officers. Their external aspect, it is true, cannot enter into comparison with that of European soldiers, on account of their ragged and slovenly dress. Instead of boots and shoes, for instance, most of them wear a nondescript foot covering, consisting of a piece of felt or coarse cloth, tied round the leg, and sandals of goatskin. Their attitude, moreover, denotes such a careless military spirit that, on parading them, an English sergeant or a German captain would grow exasperated, and declare that such troops could never stand against an enemy. Nevertheless, they are as solid as possible if properly commanded; and as their arms are excellent, of the latest and best systems, they are likely to prove more than a match for an enemy on equal terms. Their fare is as good as possible under the circumstances, but they have not been paid for many months. Their courage, however, has often been exaggerated by partial or inexperienced observers, and, if not stimulated by fanaticism and blows, has its well-traced limits. Their own officers acknowledge that at the beginning of the late Servian war, when the first shots were exchanged at Saitchar, three battalions threw themselves on the ground, frightened out of their senses. It was only when the Servians, in a similar state of nervousness, ran for their lives at the first onset of the Circassian horsemen, that their courage returned, and that their officers were enabled to move them ahead, exhorting them in the name of Allah and his prophet. When not on duty, the men cower down in their barracks, or conical tents, smoke, drink coffee, if they can afford it, and relate over and over again fantastical stories, which they have heard in their villages from wise old women and grave imaums, describing the achievements of bold highwaymen, or the doings of benevolent or malicious spirits in all shapes. Some always think of their families, parents, and relations in their far-off homes, which many of them have no hope of seeing again, and so gradually die of nostalgia. It is a general error prevailing in Europe to attribute to the Turks an inborn savageness of temper and character. Many examples show that this is not the case as a rule. When, as we witnessed last year, they fall on the Christians, and exult in massacre, rape, and plunder, they are solely actuated by religious hatred, and the fear of being murdered themselves. That feeling had been artfully instilled into their minds by their own ambitious and zealous leaders.

It is natural that a religion proclaiming the killing of infidels as a meritorious act should lead its adherents, without troubling their consciences, to the most abominable outrages against all who reject its doctrines. The proof that it is not the race but the religion that produces the inhuman crimes which the Turks are capable of committing, may be deduced from the fact that those here who adopt the mystical creed of Aaly, transfigured into a suffering god, distinguish themselves by exemplary behaviour in all their actions; and teaching tolerance, as well as claiming it, they never offend a Christian by haughty looks and words, and endure all the injuries and scornful treatment bestowed on them by their Mohammedan countrymen with astonishing self-control and stoic resignation.

The captain and some sailors of the ironclad *Lutfi Djelil*, which sank or was blown up off Potbashi, are here all badly bruised or burnt, in the naval hospital, under medical treatment. Their deposition throws only a certain light on the accident, inasmuch as it is ascertained by their testimony that the occurrence took place during an engagement with the enemy, and that the powder magazine did not explode, as stated in the official report, which also alleged that the vessel was at anchor, and not in action at the time. These men say that they found themselves suddenly in the water, where they recovered their senses; but that what happened before had entirely been wiped out of their memory. So the Russians alone can state how the vessel was destroyed.

The following letter contains a description of the greatest of the Turkish Danubian fortresses:—

△ RUSTCHUK, *May 25th*.—The water is getting higher and higher, and is already washing over the embankment, with the road on it, which borders the Danube. The fishes play in the cellars and yards of the passport office, and the lower parts of the quarter on the Lom River. This favourable state of things allows the Turks to complete their preparations in such a manner that the hope of overcoming their resistance in a single campaign must gradually vanish before the eyes of the most ardent Hotspur in the Emperor's staff. I have stated that the Russians, under the pressure of the advancing season, cannot hope to finish what they have not commenced yet—the uncontested occupation of Bulgaria—before winter. Each of the five principal strongholds, in which the Turks, well armed and provided, are waiting for the onset of their enemy, is in a state to endure a regular siege of more than three months. It may be admitted that one or the other of them might be carried at the point of the bayonet, as some examples, especially Otchakoff and Ismail, have shown; nevertheless, it is difficult to believe that a modern Russian general will ever engage his responsibility so far as to risk on one single chance the glory or the discomfiture of the army he is commanding. Now, supposing that the effective siege operations should begin in August, they are likely to be prolonged until November, when horrible weather is sure to prevail here; and when an alternation of mist, rain, and snow changes the ground into a tenacious cold mud, with which soldiers, without substantial fare and night shelter, are unable to struggle. Then it may come to pass, as was the case in 1827 before Silistria, that the besiegers will be constrained to leave all their heavy artillery behind them in the flooded trenches, and to retire as quickly as possible to more hospitable cantonments on the other side of the Danube.

Only one place affords a certain guarantee against such a mortifying emergency, and this is Rustchuk, on account of a metalled road, and, parallel to it, a railway running from Bucharest to Giurgevo, the terminus of which is situated on the Danube, permitting thus the transport of ammunition, provisions, and reinforcements to the besiegers, who, relying on this circumstance, can lodge themselves quietly in earth-huts, and may continue working and fighting in the trenches till the surrender of the city rewards their efforts. This course—which the Russians, if success is to be hoped for, are likely to follow—renders our fortress peculiarly interesting, and I think a brief description of its present means of defence may be acceptable to your readers.

The city is surrounded on the land side by a simple bastioned rampart and a dry ditch about ten feet in depth and thirty in width, with walled scarps and contrescarps, but without ravelins and coffers. On the Danube the defences are limited to some unconnected batteries on the edge of the natural clay steep, where the high ground drops down towards the water. At the north-eastern part of the bastioned inclosure, where a flat track facilitates the enemy's approach, a crown work was added, some fifty years ago, to the fortifications. It incloses a separate quarter which is inhabited by the poorest section of the Bulgarian population. As those ramparts are of no avail, or at all events not a match for modern rifled cannons, the plan was laid down and approved of transforming the environs into an intrenched camp, wherein the city itself was to figure as a secondary shelter for the garrison and the stores. Unhappily, as is always the case here, the project was well conceived upon paper, but as soon as it had to be carried out everything was wanting, especially the necessary money. At the end of last year the Turks had only just commenced the construction of the principal intrenchments on the Sary Bair, called the Levant Tabia, which crowns the uppermost summit of that elevation at a distance of 1,300 yards from the ramparts. It is formed of two pentagonal redoubts, shaped like a butterfly's wings, with a ravelin turned to the enemy's side before the open angle which they constitute there. It is said to be provided with barracks and casemates for the accommodation of three battalions, or 2,000 soldiers. The outside of the parapets, however, presents only simple earthworks consisting of clay and turf at an incline of 45 degrees, and the ten-feet deep ditches are neither studded with palisades nor flanked by caissonières. This fort is heavily armed with Krupp's breechloading cannons. Two lunettes, some 100 yards off, cover very judiciously the approach to it on the road to Rasgrad, which serpentines here over the hills, planted all over with vines and fruit trees. A series of four other redoubts on the ridge of these hills, almost in one line with the Levant Tabia, protect the city to the eastward, and outflank efficaciously the plain underneath, whereon the enemy might be tempted to establish himself and drive on his trenches. Three other intrenchments not yet completed and armed cover the fortress on its southern part, two of them being situated on the heights beyond the Lom River. Although they appear to be dominated by still higher ground behind them, this deficiency is not of such great importance now, because if the enemy were bent upon bombarding Rustchuk he could do so with ease already from the opposite bank of the Danube. The iron ring of the fortifications is closed on the flat towards the east by five redoubts of various shape and size, two of which, frowning well armed across the river, are ready to open their fire upon Giurgevo at the first signal.

I do not think it proper to give you a minute description of these earthworks, and will confine myself therefore to the remark that each of them is, as to its military position, strength, and armament, far below the aforesaid Levant Tabia. None of them is effectually secured against a surprise or an open assault by artificial obstacles, the want of which is to be pointed out as their cardinal defect. On the other hand, every military man will readily acknowledge that the dauntless courage of the soldiers called forth to defend them is, at all events, of a higher value than the solidity of a wall or the depth of a ditch. Had the Turks contented themselves with the described line of earthworks they would have done well, inasmuch as they would have been able to carry them out and arm them properly, which is in many instances not yet the case; but they have recently been inspired with a new, vast, and splendid idea, which, however, it seems too late to fully realize. It is obvious that the plateau behind the first range of hills on which the first series of intrenchments had been erected, being on the average considerably higher than those, commands them, and could be used by the aggressor for cannonading the troops and works with good effect. In the prevision of such an occurrence, it had been necessary to secure that plateau also by another series of pentagonal redoubts, of which the Mustapha Pacha and the Iswar Tabias are on the point of being completed. I have already alluded in my last letter to the difficulties which must arise, not only in constructing, but in no less degree in defending, such comprehensive and perfect, but at the same time extensive lines. However that may be, they are eagerly working at the execution of that plan. Near the Mustapha Pacha Tabia, where the Sary Bair plateau gradually slopes toward the distant Lom River, which the road crosses ten miles off in the village of Turlak, seven battalions under the command of a pacha are encamped, and busily occupied in drilling and digging. They form the vanguard, or rather the flying column, of our garrison, and are in consequence expected to repulse the first attack, in case the Russians should select the Shumla road for that purpose.

CHAPTER V.

THE ASIATIC CAMPAIGN.

Capture of Ardahan—Condition of Mukhtar Pacha's Army—Its Weakness and want of necessary Supplies—Want of Cavalry—Circassians and Kurds—State of the Turkish Fortifications—A Military Punishment—A Turkish Village—An unexpected Visit—Public Opinion on the War—Turkish Military Hospital—Mukhtar Pacha's Intelligence Department—Hairy Moses and his Assistants—Turkish Expedition to the Abbasian Coast—Destruction of Sukhum Kaleh—Landing of Troops—Insurrection of the Tribes—The Prince of Mingrelia.

WHILE the Russian Army of the South, under the Grand Duke Nicholas, was toiling across the breadth of Roumania, that of the Caucasus, under the Grand Duke Michael, ordered to operate in Asia Minor, or rather in Armenia, had already threatened Kars, and had had numerous minor encounters with the enemy. From the first the operations of this army, the strength of which had not only been enormously exaggerated, but was far below the work it had to perform, were slow and feeble. When the Russians crossed the Asiatic frontier it was believed that their army numbered 100,000 men, 200 guns, and 15,000 cavalry, that of the Turks being supposed to be about half that strength. This estimate of the Russian strength was framed upon an enumeration of the divisions composing the army, and it was not then known that some of those divisions were represented only by a single regiment. The order in which the Czar's forces entered upon the campaign has been stated in a previous chapter. The Turkish army was under the superior command of Mukhtar Pacha, who had, just before his appointment, been employed against the Montenegrins with small success. He had, however, the advantage of knowing the country and people of Armenia well, having been Governor of Erzeroum for several years. His Chief of the Staff was a most capable officer, a Hungarian named Kohlmann, who bore the title of Faizi Pacha.

The right Russian column, consisting of cavalry only, advanced from Akhaltsik, the centre or main body marching from Alexandropol, and the left from Erivan. This movement found the Turks unprepared, and Mukhtar Pacha, fearing that his retreat to Erzeroum would be cut off, left twenty-nine battalions and eight batteries in Kars, and fell back to a plateau on the Soghanli range. General Melikoff, commanding the Russian centre, did not follow Mukhtar Pacha, who had only nine battalions with him, but moved rapidly by Kars to Ardahan, which was captured after two days' bombardment. General Melikoff then returned to Kars, and began to erect siege batteries, Mukhtar Pacha employing himself in strengthening his position in the Soghanli range, and in collecting reinforcements. His right wing, under Mahomed Pacha, had been threatened by the Russian left, under General Tergukasoff, who had taken Bayazid without firing a shot, and pushed his opponent as far as Muli Suleiman. At the end of May a reconnaissance in force on Olti, made by the Russian force at Ardahan, so threatened Mukhtar Paçha's left wing that he ordered it to fall back upon his centre at Zevin, a position which grew stronger every day, and in which the Ottoman Commander remained until he found himself in a position to take the offensive. The fortified position of Batoum, guarding the important harbour below it, was attacked by a separate force, known as the Rion detachment, under General Oklobjio. For the first two months this force slowly gained some slight successes at a large cost of life, until it was compelled in June to join in the general retrograde movement of the Czar's forces.

The following letter describes the capture of Ardahan according to the report transmitted to the Emperor Alexander by courier:—

† PLOYESTI, *June 12th.*—An Imperial courier has just arrived here with full details of the capture of Ardahan. As I believe that nothing but a telegraphic summary has appeared up to the present, a detailed description of it may not be without interest.

Ardahan was captured on May 17th, twenty-three days after the declaration of war. The Russians marching from Alexandropol had already on May 10th or 12th arrived at Oltchek, near Kars, on the road between that place and Ardahan, and the communication between those two places was thus cut off. This detachment seems to have made a demonstration against Kars, and at the same time a real attack against Ardahan. In addition to this, Ardahan was attacked from the opposite side by a detachment marching from Akhaltsik on the frontier, which reached Ardahan at the same time as the column from Kars. They were before Ardahan on May 13th, and General Loris Melikoff immediately began making reconnaissances and combining a plan of attack. The column from Kars consisted of two regiments of grenadiers, three batteries of artillery, two regiments of cavalry, and a company of sappers, in all about 7,500 men, under the command of General Dewel. The column from Akhaltsik was composed of two regiments of infantry, two batteries of artillery, one battalion of sappers, half a battery of horse artillery, and three regiments of cavalry, in all about 8,500 men, under the command of General Gaiman. The Commander-in-Chief of the two columns was General Loris Melikoff, under whose direction the attack was made.

Ardahan is situated near the head waters of the river Kur, the same which runs through Tiflis and flows into the Caspian. The fortress is comparatively new, and did not exist in 1854. It was strongly fortified, defended by eleven forts constructed on modern plans, and one, it was said, on designs drawn up by an English engineer. On the south defending the road from Kars, distant two and a half miles from the town, was the fort of Guli-verdi, built upon a mountain and armed with nine guns, and near to it was another fort armed with three or four guns, on a hill dominated by Guli-verdi, from which it was separated by a valley only two or three hundred yards wide. Near the town, on the same side of the river, were three more forts, on the west Makhrab-tabia, in the centre Akhali-tabia, and on the east Singer-tabia. This latter is the one which was supposed to have been designed by an English engineer, and was of somewhat curious construction. There were three lines of defence, the escarpments were faced with stone, and they were built in a triangular shape, with the points towards the attack, and each line of defence rising terrace-like higher than the one before it. On the north side of the river there was another fort called Kai-tabia, which was connected with the southern side by two bridges, and on the north of the town, about two miles distant, was another strong fortress, called Ramazan-tabia, built like that of Guli-verdi, on a steep mountain which overlooks the town. The garrison, destined to defend all these forts, seems to have consisted of about 8,000 men, and all the forts together were armed with 92 guns. The greater part of these guns, however, were of small calibre, besides being old, and quite unable to compete with modern artillery. There seems to have been only two 24-pounders in all, the rest being principally 12-pounders, and there is every reason to believe that there was very little ammunition even for these guns, such as they were.

General Melikoff, after reconnoitring the place, decided to make his real attack on the south against Guli-verdi, while the Akhaltsik columns made a feigned attack against the fortress of Ramazan-tabia on the north. In the first place, the fortress of Guli-verdi seemed more accessible, and he besides discovered that Ramazan-tabia was not armed against the town, and that the guns of this fortress could not be directed against an attack from the south. On the night of May 16th he succeeded in planting four batteries, consisting altogether of sixteen guns, against Guli-verdi on three different points, and on the morning of the 17th the batteries opened on the fort, and poured a well-directed and destructive fire into the Turkish batteries. The Turks scarcely replied, either because the Russian fire dismounted their batteries, or because they had little or no ammunition, or it may have been in part owing to both these causes. However that may be, the whole Russian loss by the Turkish artillery was only six men wounded. About one o'clock the Russians began to perceive the Turks retreating in small parties from the fort to the town. In the evening General Dewel led three battalions to the assault of the heights of Guli-verdi, and carried them without losing a man and without firing a shot. The Turks offered little resistance, and, in fact, the fort seems to have been nearly abandoned when the assault was made. They found several of the guns dismounted, and the gunners lying dead beside them, and a considerable number of killed and wounded in the fort. As soon as Guli-verdi was taken, one of the Russian batteries which had been directed against that fortress was now turned towards the town, which was still defended by the forts, already mentioned, of Makhrab-tabia, Akhali-tabia, and Singer-tabia.

While this attack was being directed against Guli-verdi, several other batteries had been planted and directed against the three forts defending the town. By half-past five in the evening of the same day General Melikoff thought that the assault might be delivered, and General Gaiman, who was operating on the left, sent at about the same moment to ask if he should not make an attempt upon the works on his side. The assault was ordered all along the line at the same moment, and, although the fort of Singer-tabia was considered the strongest, it was the one which fell first. The others soon followed, although the Turks, as is usual with them, made a very desperate resistance on the walls, for they seem to have had plenty of ammunition for their small arms. After a desperate fight, in which the principal losses of the Russians occurred, the Turks were finally driven across the river by the two bridges already spoken of, and took refuge in the fort of Kai-tabia, everywhere hotly pursued by the Russians. When the latter, headed by General Gaiman, were a few yards from the opposite bank, the bridge gave way before them, but nothing daunted, the Russians sprang into the water, which, fortunately, was not very deep, and continued to cross by wading. General Gaiman himself was one of the first to leap into the water. The Russians had now possession of all the forts on the south side of the river; there remained only the fort of Kai-tabia and the fortress of Ramazan-tabia on the mountain. The Russians immediately attacked Kai-tabia, and the Turks were so discouraged by the Russian success that they scarcely made any resistance and fled. In fact, they had already begun to fly before the Russian attack began, so that by dark the town of Ardahan was in complete possession of the Russians. While this was going on General Dewel was occupying the attention of the garrison in the strong fortress of Ramazan-tabia on the north of the town. He soon succeeded in silencing the batteries in this fortress, which only fired three or four shots in all, and towards evening, about the time of the assault on the town, he likewise ordered an assault. But what was the surprise of the Russians, upon entering the fortress, to find that the Turks had all fled. They had evidently become panic-stricken when they perceived that the town was already in the hands of the Russians, and they had retreated to the west by the road towards Batoum.

The Russian losses in the whole affair were 67 killed and 293 wounded, besides one officer killed and ten officers wounded, making altogether 370 killed and wounded. The loss of the Turks, owing to the superiority of the Russian arms and the precision of the Russian firing, was immense. The account given by this Russian officer of the Turkish losses seems too absurd to be true. He says that the Russians buried 1,700 dead, and that 200 wounded were found in the hospital, besides which the Turks had carried off the greater part of their wounded, as many bodies were found along the roads on which the Turks had retreated, evidently the bodies of the wounded who had died on the way. Among the wounded in the hospital was the constructor of the fort of Singer-tabia. He was found by Colonel Boolmering, the constructor of the Russian batteries, who was anxious to see him and talk with him, but the poor fellow died almost as soon as he was discovered. The Russians captured ninety-two guns, an immense number of tents and camp material, also a large supply of flour and provisions, but they do not speak of any ammunition, and I suspect that the Turks had little or none. There were very few prisoners taken, and those of the Redifs, or reserves, who had been forced to come in from the surrounding villages, were immediately released and allowed to return to their homes; the Nizams, or regular troops only, were held as prisoners of war. Among the prisoners taken was General Ali Pacha, commander of the Turkish left wing, and several Turkish civil officials, besides many officers who had been wounded or otherwise disabled. The inhabitants, who had fled during the attack, upon being assured by the Russians that no harm should come to them, began to return, and in a very few days the town had resumed very nearly its ordinary aspect. The Turks taken prisoners had a feeble, half-starved look, which showed how long they had been on short rations, and this in spite of the large supply of stores and provisions which had been found in the town. The reason of this the Russians soon discovered.

The following letter deals with the condition of the Turkish army in Asia, at what was probably the lowest point to which it had been reduced by neglect, and shortly before it began to receive important assistance from Constantinople :—

HEADQUARTERS OF THE TURKISH ARMY OF ASIA, *May 28th.*—Since the capture of Ardahan by the Russians the belligerents have maintained an attitude of mutual observation. The Turkish forces abstain absolutely from any attempt to assume the offensive, and content themselves with watching the enemy's movements, occasionally shifting small bodies of troops, as the Russians seem to concentrate or change the position of theirs. There being absolutely no communications with Batoum, I am unable to say how matters stand in that direction. The Turkish army there is under a direction entirely apart from the main forces commanded by Mukhtar Pacha. Indeed, the only news we get from the coast is that sent to Constantinople, and thence telegraphed here.

When hostilities commenced, Ardahan, Kars, and Bayazid were the three main positions of the Turkish line. Two of these have fallen into the enemy's hands, while Kars still remains. At present the Turks occupy a triangle, of which Kars is the apex. Two days' march from that town, exactly half-way between it and Erzeroum, the centre is encamped. The right wing has its headquarters at Topra-Kaleh, a couple of battalions being advanced close to the Russians at Bayazid. The left wing, which was formerly at Ardahan, and which consisted of eleven battalions and six field guns, may be said practically to exist no longer. The greater portion of these battalions have been taken prisoners and the field guns captured. Even the Commander-in-Chief does not know where the remnant of the force which succeeded in escaping is at present. As the left wing consisted mainly of local forces, he is inclined to think that the survivors, on disbanding, immediately sought their respective homes. In any case we have no news of them; and it is more than likely that large numbers were picked up by the pursuing Cossacks. This unfortunate affair of Ardahan leaves the Bardes and Olti road entirely in the hands of the invading force, thus turning the position of Erzeroum, and menacing its communications with the base of operations at Trebizond. According to the latest intelligence, half of the sixty battalions which took part in the attack on Ardahan immediately directed their march before Kars with a view of forming a junction with the new Russian forces encamped at two hours' distance from its walls, in all probability with the design of commencing the investment of the place, or cutting off its communications with Mukhtar Pacha's army. Up to the present they have not succeeded in doing so. Probably they have not had time to arrive as yet, the distance between the two points being over one hundred and fourteen miles, and the execrable roads preventing the rapid passage of artillery and baggage. Only two days ago a brigadier-general, one of the Sultan's aides-de-camp, accompanied by two officers, arrived here from Kars, and reported the communications perfectly open, unmolested even by Cossacks. Telegraphic communication, too, still exists. The other half of the sixty Russian battalions have made a forward movement; but their whereabouts is not known as yet. On the side of Bayazid the Russians are confronted by a couple of battalions, who closely follow all their movements, and have instructions to resist to the last any forward movement. Another couple of battalions, stationed at Topra-Kaleh, form the support of the advanced force. Including the garrison of Kars (twenty-two battalions), the army of Mukhtar Pacha consisted, on the outbreak of hostilities, of fifty-two thousand men. Since the fall of Ardahan, eleven battalions must be deducted from this. With the limited force thus left him for the defence of a long line of frontier, and with a large portion of this shut up in Kars, I don't think the General himself entertains the slightest hope of being able to offer any serious opposition to the enemy's advance—at least in his present position. His left flank is already open, and the trifling force defending the road from Bayazid to Kuprikoi can make no resistance to a determined effort on the part of the enemy. Consequently, I believe that on the very first onward movement of the Russian forces, the Turkish army will fall back at once along the valley of the Araxes to the plain of Hassan Kaleh, within a day's march of Erzeroum, where a line of hills, closing the western extremity of the plain, has already been fortified. In thus retiring, Mukhtar Pacha can not only occupy the strong position capable of covering Erzeroum, but also concentrate his forces —picking up on the way the different detachments which guard the road, and being joined by the left wing retiring along the Bayazid road. This, I believe, is the only possible course of action under existing circumstances, and many days may not elapse before it will be put in execution. Should the Russian army succeed in penetrating by Olti to Baiburt, cutting off Erzeroum from the sea, it is impossible to foresee what course of action will be adopted. Should they feel themselves strong enough, the Turks will probably march northward and risk a decisive battle, or, fearing the issue of such an encounter, make a timely retreat to Trebizond, leaving Kars and Erzeroum to their fate.

It seems strange that Mukhtar Pacha should be left thus critically situated with so small a force and without any likelihood of reinforcement, and the more so as he seems convinced that the real attack will be made in Asia, not on the Danube. European jealousies are but too apt to bring the march of Russian conquest in the west to an abrupt halt, while in a remote corner of the empire like this, territorial acquisition would be but feebly protested against, if at all. As matters stand, and unless some of those unforeseen contingencies occur which sometimes set all calculation at nought, the Russians may be already looked upon as masters of Armenia from Kars to Erzingan and Trebizond.

I have had long conversations with Turkish general officers on the state of the army here. The two great wants they complain of are cavalry and transport service. As I mentioned in my last letter, Ahmed Mukhtar Pacha was obliged to make use of the services of a notorious brigand chief and his followers to obtain information about the enemy's movements, his only cavalry consisting of a few mounted troopers, who barely sufficed for orderly and *estafette* duty. The transport service is in an equally deplorable condition. A few mules and shaky carts of the locality convey to the front the commissariat and ammunition stores, and are miserably inadequate to the demands upon them. The traveller passing along the road from Erzeroum to the camp, and seeing it so silent and deserted, would never dream it was the main, indeed the only, line of communication between the army of Armenia and its base. I feel convinced that the necessary provisions are not transported to the camp by the straggling convoys I have met at long intervals struggling over miry roads and floundering in mountain quagmires on the line of march. Requisitions must be largely resorted to; and more than once I have heard peasants murmur as loud as they dared about the pressure thus brought to bear on them.

I know that there are many, very many, persons here who would hail the advent of the Russian troops with delight. That there are such in Erzeroum itself, I hear from the lips of the very highest authority. In view of the fact that a rapid and difficult retreat of the Turkish army seems inevitable, this lack of transport becomes a serious question. The Commander-in-Chief himself told me that, in order to be prepared for all contingencies, he had sent to the rear a portion of his tents, the number of horses and mules at his disposition being entirely inadequate for the transport of the proper number for his troops. As a consequence, the men are inconveniently crowded in the tents; though at the present moment I don't suppose they suffer much from this. The keen mountain wind whistling under the tent edges gives much more than the necessary ventilation, and I dare say the close proximity of the men when sleeping helps to neutralize to some extent the bitter coldness of the nights. For the past week we have had continued snow and rain storms, and each morning the mountains have been covered with a thick sheet of snow. Apart from this, great glacier-like snow beds remain since last winter, feeding by their gradual melting the already sufficiently swollen rivers. Within ten yards of my tent is one of these snow beds, and the wind passing over it is almost insupportable at night. If the same weather prevails higher up the country on the spurs of the Ararat chain, I am hardly surprised that the Russian advance is not more rapid, for to an ordinary European army, with its baggage and artillery trains, the country round the camp would be perfectly impassable.

The chief of the staff, Faizi Pacha, an old Hungarian officer who served in the same capacity under General Williams at the siege of Kars during the Crimean war, tells me that many departments of the Turkish military establishments are as backward as the transport service. Want of the necessary funds is one of the chief causes; but, besides, there was, he tells me, a singular want of activity for a considerable period preceding the declaration of war. It seems that up to the last moment the Government did not believe in the breaking out of actual hostilities, and neglected to push forward the necessary preparations. The Commander-in-Chief, too, tells me that he was despatched to the scene of action far too late to organize the necessary local supplies and prepare the frontier for a serious resistance. It is true, he says, that some years ago a military commission visited the frontier with a view of examining the points at which fortifications should be erected, and did actually fortify certain points, which at the time were, according to the best authorities, sufficient to hold an enemy in check; but this was in the days of old-fashioned smooth-bore artillery and muzzle-loading muskets; and before whole nations were put under arms, and colossal armies mobilized. All this work has gone for nothing. Kars and Erzeroum, the two principal strategic points, though almost impregnable twenty years ago, are now, from the want of the necessary outlying forts to keep the enemy's long-range artillery at arm's length, quite at the mercy of a hostile force, the moment the Turkish army in the field retires. Ardahan, said the General, affords an excellent example. Around it are a number of heights, dominating each other as they recede from the town; the nearer ones commanding the place itself. After the Crimean war it was deemed sufficient to fortify the nearer heights, and the redoubts of Emir Oghlu and Ramazan Oghlu were constructed as supplements to the actual enceinte. The Russians occupied the more distant heights dominating these forts, and speedily silencing their guns took them by assault. Master of these, the town itself was taken after a three days' cannonade, and with it half of the scanty field artillery of the main army. Erzeroum is in an exactly similar position; and, worse still, its artillery armament is entirely deficient, the hundred and fifty Krupps destined for its ramparts being yet at Trebizond, 180 miles distant, while the nature of the road and the steepness of the inclines precludes the possibility of a rapid transport.

It seems almost incredible that a nation like the Turks, once so renowned for their cavalry, should be now so entirely deficient in that arm. As I have already stated, Mukhtar Pacha finds himself sorely puzzled to conduct his reconnaissances on this account. He says the Russians have at least fifteen thousand regular cavalry along the frontier, covering their advance, and screening with an impenetrable curtain the movements of the main columns, so that he cannot discover the point at which they are massing for their main attack. A couple of days ago a regiment of five hundred mounted Circassians and a squadron of fifty Kurd horsemen were despatched from Erzeroum by way of mending matters to some extent. But these new troops are essentially irregulars, refusing absolutely to submit to the proper military organization and discipline, and, said the General-in-Chief, "every one knows what such troops are worth." Their main, indeed their only, use is for reconnaissance and vedette duty. In a regular combat they would be more in the way than otherwise. Besides, they are a lawless set of men, who deem the property of friend or foe equally welcome booty. A colony of these mountaineers has been established on the frontier of Greece, and the Sultan's subjects there complain that they are pillaged, both Mussulman and Christian, with the strictest impartiality, by these marauders. Whatever other qualities they may lack, picturesqueness is not one of them. I witnessed their entry into the camp. A battalion with military music was turned out to receive them. They came filing two deep in lengthy column over the hillside, each of the five squadrons having a crimson or parti-coloured red-and-white banner borne at its head, blazoned with white crescent and star. The horses were tolerably fair, but of diminutive stature. The men wore the long Circassian tunic, reaching to the middle calf, and confined at the waist by an embroidered belt, supporting the usual guardless scimitar and long dagger with primitive leaf-shaped blade, besides the accustomed supply of highly ornamented pistols, pipes, silver-mounted boxes, &c. The tunics were mostly black or dark olive, though there was a sprinkling of bright saffron, green, and crimson, especially among the chiefs and princes, for I understand there are several such in the regiment. They wore the usual Circassian headdress, a red or white tall cap surrounded by a mop-like covering of black or brown Astrachan fur, concealing all but the top of the inner cap. Both sides of the breast are covered by double horizontal rows of wooden or silver cartridge tubes, according to the social position of the individual. Each man carried at his back a sixteen-shooting Winchester rifle, and many, loth to part with their ancestral weapons, carried in addition the quaint-looking, straight-stocked, silver-ringed flint-lock of his native mountains. As a rule the physiognomies, especially of the older, white-bearded men, were handsome and dignified; but there was also a fair share of long upper lips, prognathous jaws, and lowering, murderous brows and eyes. They are commanded by Moussa Pacha (not Zulu Moussa the brigand), and have been sent on two hours in advance of the outposts. Next day came the Kurds, still more picturesque than the Circassians, with their huge bright-tinted turbans, and crimson and blue flowing garments showing through light muslin and silk mantles. Extravagantly wide trousers and red-leather boots turned up at the toe complete the attire. The armament consisted of the Winchester rifle, curved scimitar, and long reed-like lance, which they shook and brandished till it quivered like a vibrating string. They were much better mounted than the Circassians, each man's horse being his own property. For standard the leading horseman carried a piece of Manchester handkerchief stuff mottled red and green tied on to his lance. On the whole, their appearance was brilliant and dashing; and if their serviceable qualities are on a par with their warlike exterior great things may be expected of them.

It seems that on the 28th of April the Russians made a serious attempt to cut off the Turkish army from Erzeroum and shut it up in Kars. This was only defeated by the prompt action of Mukhtar Pacha in issuing from the town and retiring to the position on the Soghanli Dagh where I found him on my arrival. He was closely followed up by the Cossacks in large force, but as he retired in squares and posted his artillery advantageously, it appears the enemy did not think well to attack him, but withdrew after destroying a considerable portion of the telegraph line.

I have just had an opportunity of witnessing the roll call in camp, accompanied by the corporal punishment of a couple of military offenders. The camp is situated on the northern slopes of an oblong valley, closed to the east by a high ridge, terminating at either extremity in commanding heights overlooking the plain beyond. This ridge is the position to be defended in case of attack. The battalions were drawn up in columns of companies along the slope outside their tents. The report was made in the usual fashion, and then, just before the sun disappeared over the snowy sierras towards Erzeroum, the Imperial salute was rendered. The bands played a long-drawn-out wailing kind of air, the regimental bugles sounded a flourish, the drums rolled, and then simultaneously from the entire army burst the cry, "Long live my Padishah," while the troops presented arms. This ceremony was repeated three times, and then the offenders, two in number, were marched from their respective battalions to a point in front of the whole line. Each man placed himself on hands and knees, and by him stood a soldier holding a stout stick about a yard long. On a signal from the commanding officer the bands struck up a lively air, and the men with the sticks commenced belabouring the culprits, keeping time to the music with the greatest regularity. At a distance they had the appearance of men beating dust out of carpets. After each had received about fifty blows on the back the music ceased, and the offenders returned to the ranks, after which the ranks were broken.

KARAOURGAN, *May 29th.*—Since writing the preceding lines I left the camp and established myself at the above village two hours' march in rear of headquarters. It was impossible to remain in a windy tent during such weather. Besides, there was absolutely nothing to be bought, and the stock of eatables I had brought with me was long since consumed. But for the kindness of the staff I should have been without anything to eat. What they have for themselves is not much or very varied; but, under such circumstances, it appears quite regal. A person fresh from Europe would scarcely venture beyond the door of my present quarters; but to me, by contrast, it seems a very palace. As there is just now a total absence of military news, I shall try to give some idea of my surroundings and accommodation. The place is a type of a large class, for every village within a hundred miles exactly resembles it. Karaourgan is situated in a rocky gorge through which flows the torrent-like Chan See. The village occupies the right bank, and climbs to the summit of the rocky slope some three hundred feet high. Seen from a little distance, it resembles one of those scoria heaps one sees around iron-smelting works. Here and there a couple of feet of dry stone wall and a cave-like entrance suggest the possibility of the existence of human dwellings. Between these dwellings the spaces are carpeted with an elastic layer of dung and offal five or six feet thick. Huge ungainly buffaloes, with bodies like bisons and the eye of an octopus, low and moan, standing mid-leg deep in the filthy paths. Turbaned men are perched here and there like storks on the house-tops—pulling their beards, and giving the whole place a singular appearance. Calves, dogs, and fowls wander promiscuously among the chimney-pots, and now and then a dark-eyed, olive-faced woman comes stealing shyly by, her face, half averted from the gaze of the Giaour, partly concealed by the folds of her linen headdress. As the roof-tops have their share of dung and offal as well as the streets, and as their undulations are not more accentuated than the irregularities of the latter, it is well-nigh impossible to distinguish between them.

This morning I entered the village, descending the slope of the gorge. I knew from experience the difficulty of confining oneself to the pathway and kept a careful look-out for chimneys, the only beacons by which one can judge whether he is on a house-top or on a road. While thus vigilantly steering my way and believing that I was going all right, I felt my horse suddenly sink beneath me, and in another instant we were enveloped in a cloud of dust and splinters. We had both fallen through the roof of a house into an apartment where a family were at breakfast. Over and over again my horse had put his foot through the earthen roof of a house while I believed I was in the middle of the highway. My dwelling, seen from the outside, is a crude earthheap. You stoop low, enter the hole-like door, and find yourself in a gloomy interior some forty feet in length. It is divided into two compartments by a low boarded partition four feet high. That next the door is devoted to horses and buffaloes, the inner space affords accommodation to travellers. A little terrace of beaten earth, six inches above the floor, flanks both sides of the room. It is covered with coarse rush matting, and constitutes a seat by day, a bed by night. Two square holes in the roof admit light and air. The diet is eminently simple—honey, milk, and unleavened bread in the form and of the consistency of a shoemaker's apron, with an occasional egg, is all that the larder affords. There is another comestible greatly prized by the inhabitants, but which I could never appreciate. It is called "yaourt." It is thick sour milk, from which the watery portion has been strained. No coffee, no tea, no meat. The absence of meat surprises me, for there are immense herds of buffaloes, oxen, sheep, and goats feeding over pastures I have rarely seen equalled. There is no exportation of cattle, and I find it difficult to explain what is done with the vast surplus of kine.

I write this letter lying on the "divan." From time to time a melancholy ox walks in and looks at me with large mournful eyes. A playful buffalo calf is standing beside me, and I have just defeated him in an attempt to place his big, splay, muddy foot in the middle of my paper, as an initiatory step to settle down beside me on the divan. My attention is triply divided—first, by my work; secondly, by the cows and playful goats; thirdly, by the blackbeetles, who take advantage of an unguarded moment to walk into my inkstand. Then there is my host, who is essentially a praying man. Not content with the orthodox prayers four times a day, he takes advantage of every spare moment to repeat his orisons. A pot of water is put on the fire. While it is heating, out comes the praying carpet, and the red-turbaned, blue-trousered man is prostrating himself with unctuous groans. It is not easy to write under the circumstances; but I do my best. I don't speak Turkish fluently; but still I can carry on a conversation in a kind of way. For my host, I am the sole and only source of information as to what is going on at the front. He brings in a select circle of friends of an evening to hear the news. When I tell them that Ardahan has fallen, that Bayazid has long been in the hands of the "Muscovs," and that the Giaours are advancing swiftly on the road to Olti and Trebizond, there is a chorus of Mussulman expressions devoting the said "Muscovs" to "Shaitan," and murmured prayers for the army of true believers. These people seem to pin their faith to English succour. They will have it that an English army is advancing to their aid; and the presence of Sir Arthur Kemball and his staff officer confirm them in this belief. To do them justice, they seem to appreciate Englishmen—Englishmen and Hungarians. These two nationalities are for them the embodiment of friendship.

□ ERZEROUM, *May* 31*st*.—I rode into Erzeroum with my letter. I could not trust the ordinary modes of conveyance. I crossed so many rivers that I have lost count of the number. I have a vivid recollection of the Araxes—the "swift Araxes" of

Xenophon. Myself and horse fell in a hole, and I rescued the foregoing pages with the greatest difficulty. When I left headquarters all was tranquil. The Commander-in-Chief told me he was awaiting the Russian advance, and that his movements depended on theirs. Since I came in a rumour is spread abroad which I telegraph this evening—that the Russians advancing from Ardahan are within two hours of Olti on the road to Baiburt, threatening communications with Trebizond. If this be true, nothing is left us but a rapid retreat.

The following letter, from the headquarters of the Ottoman Commander-in-Chief, is dated from a position in which the Turks were able shortly afterwards to inflict on the enemy a serious defeat, which may be considered the turning point of the war in Asia. Although written under the impression left by a series of defeats, it contains clear intimations of the changing fortunes of the campaign:—

□ HEADQUARTERS OF AHMED MUKHTAR PACHA, ZEVIN, *June 12th.*—The retrograde movement of this army corps still continues. Little by little, but surely, it is shortening the distance between it and Erzeroum. From Kars it fell back rather precipitately to avoid being cut off by a formidable flank movement. It took up its position on the crests of the Soghanli mountains, a day and a half from Kars. Thence, on the fall of Ardahan, it fell back again to Yenikoi. During my absence on the left flank the Russian expedition to Olti and Nahriman caused a further withdrawal to the military position of Deli Baba. The six hundred Circassians and Kurds lately added to the Central Army Corps were kept well in front to prevent a surprise. A few days ago this body of irregular cavalry, on whose vigilance and activity such dependence was placed, allowed itself to be surprised at night by a couple of squadrons of Russian dragoons. In the conflict which ensued thirty Circassians were killed, and as many more wounded. The Turkish version states that the Russian loss was enormous, but the very significant fact remains that the Circassians at once retired on the main army at Deli Baba, and the main army in its turn hastily withdrew a day's march still further to the rear, two hours on this side of Zevin. The Circassians have not been again sent forward, but remain camped with the main force. The true secret of this continued retiring is to be found in the paucity of numbers of the main army.

Though now considerably swelled by reinforcements, the Turkish central force does not come up to thirty battalions, and many of these are at anything but their full complement. A solitary battery represents the artillery element; though another is at Hassan Kaleh, a day's march to the rear. The slightest flank movement of the enemy threatens to necessitate a general engagement, and is accompanied here by a rapid packing up and retiring to a new rearward position. One of the generals in command explained to me yesterday that the retreat from Deli Baba followed as a necessary consequence of the falling back of the Circassians. On the left flank, and parallel to the main line of communications of the army, is the Sarykamish road. This was covered by the vedettes of the irregular cavalry. These latter once retired, the army was more or less open to a flank attack, and adopted the system of falling back on the junction of these two roads at their present position in rear of Zevin. From all I can see, the Central Corps, under the command of Mukhtar Pacha, is for the present merely doing duty as a corps of observation, or at most retaining nominal possession of the ground, and preventing forays of Cossacks in search of provisions. Serious impediment to the advance of the Russian forces it certainly cannot, and does not, offer. Even as it is, the entire ground between Kars and the position of the Turkish army, three days' march, is entirely undefended, even by irregulars. I am told there are Russian troops in the intervening space, but this I can scarcely believe. There are, however, no means of ascertaining the truth from this side, it being almost certain death to attempt penetrating alone into the terra incognita intervening between the two armies. On the Olti side I am informed at headquarters that the Russian expedition of fifteen hundred Cossacks and three infantry battalions have retired before an equal Turkish force despatched against it. This may be so, but when I left that place the Turkish force was in the act of retiring. On the Bayazid side all seems inactive—at least no news has reached us, though a good deal of anxiety prevails as to the state of affairs there. I intend making an expedition in that direction shortly to see with my own eyes how matters stand. Up to the present I have refrained from doing so, the distance (a week's ride) making it an undertaking of no slight gravity.

The general opinion prevailing in non-official military circles here is that the Turkish army, while trying to keep up the appearance of holding its ground, is in reality merely temporizing to gain time till Erzeroum be in a state of defence, after which we shall have a final retreat on the fortified positions covering the place, and in all likelihood a couple of decisive battles. It is believed that the troubles in the Caucasus and the fighting on the Batoum flank, about which we know absolutely nothing certain, have a good deal to do with the slowness of the Russian advance. In all probability the difficult nature of the communications by which stores have to be conveyed to the frontier, and, up to a short time ago, the great severity of the weather, which prevented the accumulation of supplies necessary before an advance into an enemy's territory can be safely attempted, have all united to prevent decisive action. But, once these preparations completed, we may look forward to rapid and continuous action. The preparations at Erzeroum seem to be all that is being done to meet the coming storm; and these preparations are slow and miserably insufficient. People seem to lay great stress on the capacity of the Turks for defending fortresses, and build magnificent hopes on the supposed impregnability of Kars and Erzeroum. I scarcely think the Russians will put their defensive powers to the test, but will quietly isolate the strong places, and leave famine to do its work. By any one not actually on the ground the difficulty of learning what is going on at either flank or in the centre, if one be at either of the wings, can scarcely be realized. For instance, here at the centre, no one beside the Commander-in-Chief and his staff have the faintest notion of what is going on towards Olti, on the left; and as for the Bayazid flank, four days' march away, I think even the General is in a fog about the doings there.

Immediately on the despatch of this letter by special courier to Erzeroum, I shall post off to the right flank, if permitted, for that side seems to be a complete land of mystery just now. From a few European papers which have reached me here, I see that, as far as the campaign on the Danube is concerned, nearly all the correspondence is communicated by telegraph. Here, such a thing is out of the question. If, on an important occasion, one manages to get off a telegram, the briefest of the brief, after forty-eight hours' delay at the bureau, he may think himself fortunate. Between this and Constantinople there is but a single wire, and that is continuously engaged by Government messages. When last in Erzeroum I learned that for ten days previously the instruments had not stopped working night or day, transmitting military messages and instructions. In all that time, the inspector of international telegraphs could only obtain a few minutes, now and again, in all amounting to three-quarters of an hour, to forward the English and French despatches accumulated at the office. What hope, then, of getting off a couple of columns such as are being daily forwarded by our more fortunate colleagues in Europe?

The military doctors at Erzeroum and Hassan Kaleh are kept busily employed looking after the numerous invalids continuously pouring in from the army. Dysentery, typhoid fever, and affections of the foot consequent on the miserable condition of the soldiers' compound rag mocassins (I can't call them shoes), are the principal maladies, and the mortality, I am informed by the doctors, is very considerable. Want of hospital accommodation, necessitating the locating of large numbers of the sick in the miserable wigwams of the towns, increases the difficulty of properly attending to the patients, and contributes largely to increase the mortality. The doctors complain sadly, too, of "malingering." Soldiers present themselves for admission to hospital on the slightest pretence—"a pain on the top of the nose" being in one instance the claim for exemption from service. For the Circassians, especially the wounded proceeding from the late skirmish with the Russian cavalry, and most of whom suffer from sabre and lance wounds, a separate hospital has been established at Hassan Kaleh. The principal surgeon tells me he has the greatest difficulty in maintaining order among them, owing to their belonging to different tribes, and keeping up their old clan feuds with a persistency scarcely second to their aversion for the common enemy. These Circassians are steadily earning for themselves here the same unenviable reputation for violence and thievery which they enjoyed in Servia. Go where you will, your ears are filled with tales of their depredations. They quarter themselves on the inhabitants, take everything they fancy, and not only do not pay, but often savagely maltreat their hosts. In one village where I passed the night my host informed me, speaking under his breath, and looking fearfully around him, that only a few days previously they had assassinated a poor man in the place, at whose house four of them had lived free for a month, their host being often obliged to borrow money to meet their demands for tobacco and other extras. One is continually warned along the way to take care of meeting these Circassians, and even the authorities require one to take a mounted policeman as an escort. As bands of these marauders are continually passing and repassing to and from the front the villagers are kept in a constant state of dread for their flocks—all the property they possess. I have seen a Circassian horseman deliberately ride up to a flock of sheep, choose out the best-looking, and heartily curse the proprietor for not helping him to sling it before him on his horse. "Kaffir," "dog," "villain," were mild names for the poor Kurd who wouldn't aid the despoiler. The regular troops, the villagers tell me, aid in oppressing the population. They quarter themselves in the khans and private houses, eat and drink of the best, and then take their leave without even offering a halfpenny in payment. I have myself suffered more than once, indirectly, on account of this system of proceeding.

A few days ago I rode in from the camp to the village of Khorassan, some hours in the rear. A deluge of rain was falling, and I was thoroughly soaked through. I went from door to door for over an hour, asking for lodging for the night. The khans closed their doors, the proprietors telling me they were private houses; and at the private houses I was told there was nothing to eat. All this was because I was taken for a military man, and consequently either unable or unwilling to pay. At length, as I stood shivering in the midst of the mud hovels, an old man took pity on me, and, coming forward, asked if I had any money. On proving ocularly that I had, he brought me to his khan, from the door of which I had been turned previously. All necessaries were speedily forthcoming—that is, as necessaries go here—milk, unleavened bread, and a white stringy kind of cheese. Profuse apologies were offered for the first refusal, my being mistaken for a Turkish captain being considered ample justification for their inhospitable treatment of me. The irregular conduct on the part of the military, and the unpaid requisitions for the army generally, have produced a feeling among the population both Christian and Mussulman anything but favourable to the Government. There are many who recollect the Russian invasions of 1828–9 and during the Crimean war; and I have repeatedly heard the cash payments of the Russian army alluded to as a contrast to the present state of things. As I mentioned in a former letter, there are many, very many, who would welcome the invading army with open arms. No later than yesterday an old man, a Mohammedan, told me he had no intention of retiring with the army, but that on the contrary he would await the advent of the Russians, and willingly supply them with what they required. It may be that the Turkish Government is aware of this feeling. I know the local authorities, civil and military, are, and that they take no pains to conciliate the population, believing that the province is lost to Turkey—much as the Roumanians have been treated. That the Muscovite army will find itself at home here I am quite sure.

In a former letter (which I now find has miscarried on its way from the camp to Erzeroum) I made some mention of the great want of cavalry in the Turkish army of Armenia. The General-in-Chief repeatedly complained of this want, and told me he was unable to keep himself *au courant* of the enemy's movements. Fifteen thousand Cossacks, hovering like a cloud in advance of the main Russian columns, effectually screen the movements of these latter, and prevent their points of concentration from being known. Six hundred mounted Circassians and a squadron of Kurd lancers were hurriedly organized to supply the necessary reconnoitring element. Their vigilance and intelligence were counted on to compensate for their paucity of number. The very first time they came in contact with the enemy they proved quite inadequate to the mission assigned them. They were surprised, cut up, and retired on the main army, behind which they are now camped—a terror and a nuisance to all but the enemy. The marshal commanding has had to have recourse to another means to keep himself informed of the Russian movements. Upper Armenia has ever been, and to a certain extent is still, infested by bands of Kurd robbers, who, under various chiefs, and in detachments of from ten to twenty, lived upon the country, exacting blackmail from the villages, and pillaging travellers.

One of these men, popularly known as Tulu Moussa, or Hairy Moses, enjoyed an extensive renown for his successes in the brigand line. The General informed me that while governor of this province some years ago he had in vain tried to lay hands on this bandit. When the war broke out Tulu Moussa, stirred by patriotism, entered into negotiations with the military authorities, offering his services in return for a free pardon. His offers were accepted, and he is now the Pacha's main source of information as to the doings of the enemy. Accompanied by half a dozen followers, he scours the country in front, collects information, tracks out the Russian spies, and even ventures in disguise into the enemy's camp. I had the honour of dining with this redoubtable gentleman some days ago. He had just come in from a visit to the hostile lines, and laid before the Turkish General a sum of money given him by the Russian commander as earnest of larger payment for his espionage among the Turks. I believe he means honestly enough to his present employers, though for "a consideration" I daresay his Mussulman scruples might, at a given moment, succumb to the situation. He is a tall spare man of some forty years of age, sallow-faced and hollow-cheeked, his large black lustrous eyes sparkling with energy.

A heavy moustache scarce conceals a half-suppressed humorous expression about the corners of his mouth, and a dense growth of beard a fortnight old vindicated his title to the sobriquet of "hairy." His attire is brigandishly picturesque in the extreme. A long tunic resembling that of the Circassians, the skirt reaching to the middle calf, of a dark olive tint, and bound at the edges with broad silver lace, is confined round his slender waist by a belt of many silver pieces with pierced pattern. On either breast is a double row of silver cartridge tubes elaborately chased and ornamented with green enamel. His sabre and broad-bladed Circassian dagger are masterpieces of carving and enamel, the sheaths and hilts of massive silver set with coral and lapis lazuli. Wide dark trousers and high red-leather boots turning up at the toes complete his costume. His companions are attired much in the same manner, though less richly. They are quiet, resolute men, but with an unmistakably brigandish air.

Such are Mukhtar Pacha's chief of the "intelligence department" and his aides. The Pacha tells me Moussa is worth a whole regiment of cavalry to him, and the information he brings is thoroughly trustworthy. He partly apologized for employing a person of such peculiar antecedents; but though Moussa, he said, freely "took" whatever he could lay his hands on, he was believed to be free from the stain of blood. When I met him, he had just brought in four compatriots, caught in the act of dogging the retiring army as Russian spies. If appearance alone were sufficient to condemn, these people would have but little chance; for a more villanous-looking set I never laid eyes on—the foreheads low and compressed, the huge semi-Jewish nose out of all proportion to the small trumpet-shaped mouth and retiring chin, the large black eyes glittering with mingled cunning and ferocity. Huge red or blue turbans, the folds coming down in front and below the ears, left the face only partly visible, as they sat crouching on their haunches in a row, looking uneasily about them like newly captured wild beasts.

The following letter from a correspondent with the Russians relates to the attempts of the Turks to raise the tribes of the Caucasus against Russia:—

⊕ KUTAIS, MINGRELIA, *June 6th.*—Affairs are not going on very well hereabouts, in Mingrelia, where we are at present threatened at two opposite points, one near Batoum, the other towards Sukhum Kaleh. The low country of Mingrelia, *i.e.*, the Rion basin, will, on referring to the map, be found to constitute a sort of isosceles triangle, with its base on the sea, between two ranges of very high mountains. At the southern angle, that near Batoum, the Russians, unable to get at the latter place (in consequence of a fort and the fire of the numerous Turkish cruisers) by the road running along the sea-beach, are constructing another through the mountainous country in the interior, by which they propose to attack Batoum in the rear. This work, however, is one of considerable difficulty. Continual skirmishing goes on, and then there are the natural difficulties of the country—steep wooded mountain ranges, ravines and gorges clothed with dense masses of laurel, rhododendron, and azaleas, amongst which the wary Kabouletts, and other warlike Lazistanees, well supplied with arms and ammunition by the Turk, can lurk unseen, and by frequent attacks annoy the sappers, and disturb their operations. These Kabouletts are a Lazistanee tribe of the frontiers, originally Christians, but who, like the people round Akhaltsik, were forcibly converted to Islamism by the Turks in the seventeenth century. They were preparing to join the Russians, and had arranged to do so, but symptoms of this appearing, the Turks suddenly marched upon and occupied their villages, capturing the women and children of all the chiefs and principal people, whom they retain as hostages, only releasing them on the production of heads of Russian subjects by their relations, as proof of loyalty to the cause of the Padishah! In consequence of this policy, the able-bodied and effective fighting men of the tribe are compelled, *malgré* their tendencies to Christianity, to do a great deal of harm to their former friends and neighbours. On the Russian side, the men of Gouriel, being always, in consequence of their knowledge of the country, at the advanced posts, have to bear the brunt of the guerilla warfare which goes on. The Russian system is (while holding, of course, a strong force in reserve) to march with a nucleus of regulars and artillery, preceded by a cloud of frontier men, foot and horse, under their respective chiefs, all of whom are well acquainted with the language, country, manners, customs, &c., of the enemy. These are thrown out on all sides, at a considerable distance, on the front and flanks of the regulars, forming a great semicircular line of posts, connected by patrols and picquets with the same in advance.

Hassan Pacha, with the ironclads, is threatening the whole coast, cannonading the stations on the shore, and landing bodies of Circassians, who burn villages and devastate on an extended and effectual scale, causing not only alarm, but the detachment of a considerable force to check these operations. Sukhum Kaleh was burnt to the ground ten or twelve days ago in this way, and the Abhasians, who are in full revolt, have retaken the littoral between Sukhum and Pitsounda, and, in conjunction with the Circassians, are threatening Mingrelia along the line of the Kodor. Since then Ardler and Sochu, both open villages on the Circassian coast, have been destroyed, and probably all the estates thereabouts, as far as or beyond Tonapse, the telegraphs cut, &c. Hearing of these events, I left three days ago for Zugdidi, a large bourg some twenty miles from the coast (at Anaklia), between Poti and Sukhum Kaleh, which, if an advance in force should be contemplated by the Turks, combined with the insurgents and Circassians, would be an important centre of operations. Prince Nicholas, hereditary Dadian, or Prince of Mingrelia, has a country house here, and very large estates all round, shooting preserves, &c. He is constructing a handsome palace. I called soon after my arrival upon Count Rosmorduc, a veteran resident of the Caucasus, who has married into the Prince's family; and afterwards upon the Governor, where I saw Prince Mirsky, who has the command of all the reserved Caucasian forces. They were preparing for a move in advance, and two corps of Imeritian irregulars had been detailed to cross the river that afternoon as advanced guard, to be followed by three battalions of Russian infantry, the artillery, the militia, and the rest of the irregular cavalry and Cossacks—in all some 8,000 strong. This force is to repel the Turks, Circassians, and Abhasian insurgents, should they advance, by holding the line of the Kodor, and eventually to reduce the revolted province.

The general in command at Sukhum (Krachenkoff) has been making a "strategic movement to the rear," with undue precipitation, which, combined with the Abhasian revolt, has encouraged the invaders. Indeed, were it not for the difficulties of the line of route, three considerable rivers, and ten or twelve deep nullahs having to be crossed, it is probable the latter would by this have been near Zugdidi. As it is, had the Circassians, some 3,000 of whom are believed to have landed, possessed horses, it is probable that the panic here of a few days back would have turned out only too well justified. This alarm—one of those incidents common to the outbreak of hostilities anywhere—did not extend to the military, who, down to the latest raised levies, showed nothing but a commendable desire to come to close quarters with the supposed enemy. It was caused by the misinterpretation of a telegram from the general commanding at Azurget, on the Turkish frontier, who, having received a despatch advising that the Turks were landing at Anaklia (which they were cannonading), sent a message to Zugdidi, telling them to hold their ground as long as possible, and that he was sending reinforcements. This was interpreted as certain news that the latter position was about to be attacked by a superior force; and the civil and trading population, losing their heads, made a rush from the town, which, should the defenders be compelled to retreat, they of course imagined would speedily become another Batak. The alarm was aggravated tenfold by the local budmashes and loafers, who, foreseeing a rich harvest of loot, did their best by spreading all sorts of canards to precipitate events, so that the shopkeepers, after offering fabulous prices for arabas and conveyances for their goods, which in many cases were not to be had, finally bundled helter-skelter out of the town, leaving their half-emptied stores to the delicate attentions of the above gentlemen. By the time of my arrival, however, the commercial element had, after going half way to Novi-Sevok, and passing two or three nights "al fresco," returned to its senses, and resumed its ordinary course.

If the reports respecting the Turks having landed regular troops (Nizam) with artillery to match, and having armed the Abhasian insurgents with Martini-Peabodys and the Circassians with Winchesters, are correct, it is probable that some severe bush-whacking engagements, followed by a small general action, will shortly take place between the Kodor and Nighor; unless, indeed, the Turks are even stronger than is supposed, and while menacing an advance on the direct line by land between Sukhum and Zugdidi should suddenly descend in force at Anaklia—thus avoiding the passage of the rivers, and strike at the Russian base, in which case the advance of the latter towards Batoum would have to be completely suspended, and the greater part of the force at present employed on it have to be recalled for the defence of Kutais, which, as in Omar Pacha's expedition in 1856, would be the point aimed at.

There were about 600 irregulars (cavalry) in Zugdidi alone, besides militia and regular (Russian) soldiers, all, especially the irregulars, fine-looking men. The extraordinary thing was that the resources of the country did not seem in any way overtaxed to support them; there was no scarcity of anything, in spite of the recent panic. As an officer, who has served in the French army, observed, there was not enough in the place in the way of meat to satisfy two companies of English soldiers, yet here were 3,000 to 4,000 men, many of them of the upper classes. With a little millet boiled into a pudding, or "pasta," some goat's milk, cheese and onions, and a goblet of "vin du pays," the chiefs even are quite contented, while their retainers make good cheer over cake of Indian corn flour, some curds, a piece of dried fish, or a strip of tough beef among half a dozen. The Russian soldier is happy with his lump of black bread and glass of whisky, or tumbler of weak tea, with, in the evening, perhaps a basin of weak soup, something like the "black broth" of the Spartans.

CHAPTER VI.

THE EVE OF THE CROSSING.

Rustchuk and Giurgevo—Skobeleff's Straw-cannons—The Cossacks and their Customs—A War Observatory—A Reconnaissance on the Danube—Marching Powers of the Russian Soldiers—Life under Shell-Fire—A Hunt for a Spy—The Russian Artillery—Russian Light and Heavy Horse—The Russian Lines of Advance Compared—Osman Pacha at Widdin.

By the end of May the belief had become general that the long-suspended Russian blow was about to fall upon Turkey, and keen discussions were held as to the point at which it was most likely to be felt. But day by day it was reported that the Danube was still too high to permit of crossing. Either rain was falling and the river was swollen by the drainage of its vast basin, or the sun was melting the snow on the mountains, and so increasing the volume of the stream. There were those who said that the backward state of the Russian preparations was the sole cause of delay; but, for whatever reason, the passage of the river did not take place until a month after the time originally announced. In the meanwhile the Russian preparations were gradually approaching completeness. At Constantinople public feeling was turned rather to politics than to war, which everybody seemed inclined to leave to the complacent and all-assuring Abdul Kerim Pacha, who had his headquarters at Shumla. The following letter relates to the condition of the Russian army in Roumania:—

* BUCHAREST, *June 1st.*—It is hard to credit in gay and frivolous Bucharest that we are on the outskirts of war. It is almost possible to hear on the crest of Philarette the faint din of a heavy bombardment at Giurgevo or Oltenitza. And, indeed, along the Danube, although there has been as yet no heavy bombardment, the rattle of isolated cannon shots has rolled any day for a month back. But we cannot settle down to the realization that we are conventionally "in the midst of war," when not a wounded man has been dragged through the streets on his road to the hospital. An army stands around us with its sword indeed drawn and raised—we can see the bare blade flashing in the sunshine—but it has fallen nowhere as yet on an enemy, and the brightness of its edge is unsullied by the stain of blood. Russian officers swarm in Bucharest, making the most of the days of ease in the interval between a long march and an arduous campaign. The simple, honest fellows take their fill of well-earned enjoyment in a sedate decorous way which commands one's respect. They like to sit in the sunshine outside the café doors, or at the tables in some tree-shaded restaurant-garden, and as they drink tea to listen to music. They form a little *queue* outside the Turkish baths, waiting for that parboiling which they find so refreshing; they gather round a casual piano in the *salle à manger* of an hotel, and if they fight as well as they play and sing, a better army than that with which the Turks oppose them could have no chance against them. They are studiously polite and courteous when occasion calls for intercourse between them and the people of the land they have entered, or others; but withal, except in some exceptional instances, they do not court such intercourse, and through their courtesy there runs a vein of obvious reserve. The men of the ranks abide in their camps with a calm, sedate content, as if they had been used from their childhood to live under canvas, or crammed into little villages on the broad plains of Roumania, within sight of the spires of its capital. Nowhere is there evident any excitement, any confusion, any bustle, any swagger. But for the occasional clouds of dust in the suburban roads, the strings of troop horses watering in the pools and brooks, the provision trains defiling through the by-streets, and the strange officers in their white coats and caps pervading the town, the chance visitor to Bucharest would find it hard to recognize that his visit was not paid in the piping times of peace.

By the time this letter will be printed you will doubtless have heard by telegraph of the arrival of the Russian Emperor at his son's headquarters in Ployesti. The event is regarded throughout the Russian army as the immediate herald of active offensive operations on a large scale. No doubt the present apparent pause has been, if not absolutely necessary, at all events essentially wise; but it is well that it should come to a close as early as may be. There are some who argue that time compulsorily spent in inaction a few marches off the Danube has rather a beneficial effect than otherwise, since it is alleged the enemy is suffering from the tension of the strain. But I question whether time in one sense is not as valuable to the enemy as it is in another sense to the Russians. The Turks are always behindhand; but every day of respite they gain enables them to be less behindhand. They can reinforce points which seem threatened; they can throw up or strengthen batteries; they can drill their rawer troops; surely it is possible even for a Turkish intendance to accumulate stores faster than they are being consumed. To this I can at least testify that the Rustchuk of to-day is to the eye a very different place in its potentialities of defence from what it was five weeks ago, when I saw it first. The principle on which the Russians are acting is perfectly clear. They are determined to leave nothing to chance; they will run no rash risk of sustaining a reverse for want of preparation to avert such a reverse. Of course they might have been across the Danube a fortnight ago, if not sooner. Large as the river is, daring men might have crossed it in boats, made good a footing on the other side, and set themselves to cover the construction of bridges. Possibly, probably, all would have gone well. But then all might not have gone well; and although in itself a mischance might not have been of very serious import, yet the misfortune would have produced consequences which it would have been very unwise to risk. Steadily, really quickly, although seemingly slowly, are the masses gathering for the invasion. Every day brings its regiment, its brigade, its battery, up into the position chosen for the awaiting of the order to fall in in stern earnest. Gradually the huge wave is gathering. Its mass is slowly drifting rather than moving forward. But where the weight of it will fall in thunder, still remains concealed with a care and skill that evoke the sincerest admiration. I have visited most of the likely crossing points on the Danube. I have been to and fro among the Russian forces in the front line more than most people. I am almost singular in the possession of exceptional facilities for going in and out unimpeded about the Russian lines. I have not a few friends among Russian officers. But this I declare, that no specific indications are patent to me regarding the crossing points at which the serious attempts to pass the Danube will be made. I will not descend to the disingenuous subterfuge of averring that I am in possession of information which I am not at liberty to communicate; I frankly own myself wholly devoid of any information of the kind which, for my own guidance, I should like extremely well to possess. Inferences are open to me as to everybody, but of these inferences I must admit the comparative weakness; and there is a certain ruefulness in the sincerity with which I venture to congratulate the Russian military authorities on the admirable skill and finesse with which, down to a point necessarily so near the denouement, they have succeeded in concealing the details of their plans.

There exists a general belief that the Emperor means to be an eye-witness of the operation of the crossing of the main column of invasion, and it is averred, indeed, that he has the design of actually making the campaign. You will then, to all appearance, not have long to wait for more interesting tidings from the Danube than the petty details of skirmishing which have constituted hitherto the bulk of the intelligence. The difficulties of the crossing will be materially enhanced by the almost unprecedented height of the Danube at this season. It has been contended that these difficulties are insuperable, and that the Russian armies have no alternative but to remain quiescent until the abating of the waters. But this at least I can state with confidence, that the Russian engineers do not share this conviction. While admitting that the flooded state of the great river renders their task greatly more arduous, they profess their ability to overcome the difficulty in their way, if their orders are to make the attempt. The *modus operandi* of the crossing is a fair subject on which to speculate. It may be assumed that no bridge can be thrown across the Danube in the face of a hostile fire of any weight, nor is it easy to see how Russian artillery fire, however strong and steady, can wholly subdue a Turkish fire that should choose to ignore the Russian cannon and confine its attention exclusively to the pontoniers and their handiwork. If these assumptions are justifiable, it must be incumbent on the Russians, before throwing their bridge, to gain a footing on the Turkish bank, and carry and establish themselves on its crest, holding the points from which the river at the place about to be bridged can be commanded. In such an operation the Russians must obviously suffer more or less loss, according to the strength of the Turkish defensive forces and appliances at the respective points selected for crossing. The method which suggests itself to reduce this inevitable loss as low as possible is as follows:—The Russian artillery to come into action with great and sustained vigour, showering shells into the Turkish batteries and sweeping the whole face of the opposite slope. This to be maintained after the Turkish return fire should to all appearance have been in a great measure got under, when a detachment of infantry should cross the river in boats under the protecting fire of the batteries, and, having landed, advance to the attack. Simultaneously, or rather so long before as to admit of their attack being delivered simultaneously with that of the detachment designed for the direct attack, two other detachments should be ferried over, one higher up stream, the other lower down, their crossing to be also covered if need were by artillery fire, the mission of these two detachments being to assail the flanks of the Turkish position, while it is attacked in front by the first detachment. Perhaps it might be possible for the two flanking detachments to succeed without this co-operation. Perhaps indeed, as was the case at Isatchia in 1828, a single detachment might effect a surprise on the Turkish flank, although this is far more unlikely in 1877, looking at the assiduity with which the Turks are picqueting their bank of the Danube, than it was in 1828, when the successful enterprise was carried out by the co-operation of some renegade dwellers on the Dobrudscha shore. But what I desire now to make apparent is the necessity incumbent on the Russians of driving out the Turks from their river-bank positions and the occupation of these positions as the essential preliminary to the construction of their bridges. It is unlikely, indeed, that this indispensable task will be accompanied by very much bloodshed, since in all probability the points selected for crossing will hardly be those over against which the Turks are in strongest force.

Being desirous of paying my respects to General Radetsky, commanding the 8th Corps, who has been good enough to invite me to attach myself to that corps when active operations commence, I drove to Jilava, where his headquarters are for the present. Jilava is a village about eight miles from Bucharest, on the main road towards Giurgevo. The General is for the time leading a quiet rural life in a pretty villa situated in the midst of a large garden some distance from the road. The village is chiefly occupied by the staff and intendance officers of the corps; the mass of the troops being further distant from Bucharest in a southerly direction, disposed in temporary cantonments in the villages scattered over the face of the country. After some conversation with Colonel Dmitrowsky, the chief of the staff of the 8th Corps, I went on some miles further along the chaussée to visit General Dragomiroff, who commands a division (the 14th) of the 8th Corps, to which, with the General's kind permission, I mean more closely to attach myself. The division's headquarters are for the present in the pretty hamlet of Kerate, and General Dragomiroff abides in a beautiful and spacious chateau, which once belonged to a Briton. Being closely surrounded by trees and in the centre of a park, his quarters were not easy to find, and it became necessary to inquire the direction of some officers in a house at whose gate the green flag—token of the quarters of a "Polkovnik"—a colonel commanding a regiment—was flying. The colonel himself, Colonel Duhonin, chief of the 55th Regiment, was civil enough to answer my questions, and in a gossiping conversation which ensued to give me a quantity of very interesting information. He had open before him the regimental money chest, and he and the paymaster were counting out rouleaux of gold five-rouble pieces to pay for sundry current expenditure. He told me that the Russian officers draw their pay monthly, the rank and file being paid every quarter, at the rate of one silver rouble, or four shillings, per month. This is his pocket money, or, as the colonel put it, his "tobacco money," tobacco from his point of view being the only article of luxury on which the Russian soldier need have any call to expend money. This is about the same rate of free pay as accrues to the French soldier of the line, and considerably under the Prussian allowance, which, if I remember rightly, is 2½d. per diem. To illustrate the method of attack in the Russian army, which is as in the German army by the company column, the colonel called four of his orderlies, each one to represent a company, and stationed them in what is called the "cross" formation; that is, there stood a man representing a company at each of the four points of the figure of the cross. They moved forward maintaining these relative positions: they changed direction to right or to left, still maintaining the same; in the former case the company which had been the right flanking company becoming the leading company—in other words, marching at the head of the cross; in the latter case, the previous left flanking company taking the leading position. He told me that in each battalion there was one company of tirailleurs, or light infantry, whose duty it was more especially to skirmish. On occasion the tirailleur companies might be massed, if a rifle battalion or brigade were required; but this, in the nature of things, would be seldom. There is, he said, no cavalry attached to an infantry division of the Russian army, with the exception of a few Cossacks to act as orderlies and carry despatches; all the cavalry of each corps is massed into the cavalry division of that corps and operates independently. He pointed out that the different regiments are known—first, by the number of the regiment in front of the cap; and, secondly, by the facings, as with us, or rather it might be said by the colour of the collar patches. Thus the facings of his regiment, the 55th, are white—those of the twin regiment in the same brigade, the 56th, are blue.

The two following letters from Giurgevo, by different correspondents, exhibit the ways of life of soldiers waiting for the order to march against the enemy, and of a civil population hourly expecting bombardment:—

† GIURGEVO, *June 5th.*—Nothing could be more delightful than the view I have from my window here on the banks of the Danube. Immediately in front of me is a boulevard with gravel walks, green trees, benches, and little round tables—the boulevard made by the Russians when they were here in 1854—with a Russian sentinel now pacing up and down in front of it. Beyond, at a distance of twenty yards, are five or six small ships moored to the quay, and beyond them the Danube, more than a mile wide, rolling its swift muddy waters along, in a noisy, angry, threatening manner, as though determined to remain an impassable barrier for ever to the two armies waiting on its shores. On the other side are steep, abrupt banks, which here and there, however, melt away into glassy slopes that come down to the water's edge in a gentle incline, offering every facility for the landing of troops. Then a little higher up the river the tall slender minarets and gilded domes of Rustchuk, which glisten and burn in the sunshine in a wonderful way; and behind the town the green hills of Bulgaria, covered with orchards, vineyards, pasture-fields, and clumps of trees, among which may be seen here and there long lines and hillocks of fresh earth, the newly constructed earthworks and defences of the Turks. The hills rise up against the sky, where their summits are drawn in clear distinct lines; and along them may be seen thousands of white specks, that look about the size of eggs, that come out bright in the sunlight, and disappear when a cloud darkens the landscape, and which, seen through the field-glass, take the size and shape of tents. They are the tents of the Turkish army, which may be seen here and there all over the slopes half hidden among the gardens and trees, and may be counted by the hundred and the thousand. Far down below me the river widens out to the dimensions of a lake, and covers miles and miles of

land, which during ordinary seasons is never reached by the high waters. Here and there are little islands and clumps of trees standing in the water up to their waists, as if trying to keep cool, and looking in the distance like mirages I have seen in the desert of the Kizil Koum. The broad swiftly flowing river, the green hills rising behind to the sky, the white tents of the enemy, the slender minarets and glistening domes, the blue sky and the warm sunshine bathing it all in a glorious sea of light, make up a picture such as is rarely seen. There are few of the sights and still fewer of the sounds of war, and a man having heard nothing of the outbreak of hostilities, who should be dropped down here suddenly on the banks of the Danube in the midst of the peaceful picture, would probably see nothing to make him suspect that even amidst this beautiful scene armies are confronting each other, that the storm of battle may break over it and change this slumbering tranquillity into the fierce uproar and din of war. He might be astonished by a Cossack dashing madly through the streets from time to time, and if he looked more closely and knew the uniforms, he might be surprised by observing a post of Russian soldiers just below the town on the banks of the river; but he might remain here forty-eight hours, as I have done, without seeing anything further to excite his suspicions, and give him the idea that he was in the midst of war. What would seem most suspicious is the tranquillity and absence of ships and boats on the Danube. There are no steamers ploughing their way up and down its muddy waters, no rafts floating lazily down in the warm sunshine, no sailing boats, no fishing boats, no river ships, except three or four moored to the quay in front of the boulevard. The waters of the Danube are for once as untroubled by man as though no human being inhabited its banks and the art of navigation had never been invented. And then there is something suspicious in the mysterious tranquillity of the other shore; no sound is heard, no human being can be seen even through a magnifying glass. The green hills lie asleep in the golden sunshine, as dreamy and still as though no human being had ever trod their grassy slopes.

The town of Giurgevo is nearly deserted. All the people who were able left soon after the declaration of war; nearly all the shops are closed, and only those remain behind who have nowhere to go and no friends to receive them. The town is a dreary, deserted, lonely-looking place, which, but for an occasional Cossack dashing through the streets, reminds one of those dying cities of Belgium and Holland where there are more houses than people, and where one may walk about the streets for hours without meeting a single soul. But there is a circus here, and the circus remains in spite of the flight of the inhabitants and the threats of bombardment. This circus does not seem to have ever been in a very flourishing condition, which will appear from the assertion of the circus people themselves that they have not left the place for the simple reason that they had not enough money with which to go away. As there are very few soldiers in Giurgevo, the riders are naturally even worse off than in their most prosperous days, and the poor people are gradually undergoing extinction by slow starvation. As I believe in encouraging the arts, I have patronized this circus the two nights I have been here, and I may say that I was almost the only spectator. There were certainly not more than fifteen people in the house, and some of these I suspect had not paid for their admission. It was a sorry spectacle to see the poor people exerting themselves to please a handful of persons who had come to be amused. There were two clowns, two young girls who rode very well, and another one who could ride still better, it was said, but who stood by without taking any part in the performance, because she had been injured a few nights previously by a fall. There were a contortionist, a performing horse, a couple of gymnasts, and a ring master, and several other persons, besides half a dozen more horses. How they all managed to get a living out of the fifteen or twenty francs which they received for that night's performance I cannot imagine. The circus people, I am afraid, could imagine it far less than I could, brought as they were face to face with the necessity of the attempt. The laugh of the clown was but a hollow one, the old stale jokes were thrown off in a sad depressed voice which was anything but laughable, and the smile of the girls when we applauded them, for we did applaud them with all our hands, was but a weak and sickly one. Even the horses had begun to feel the effects of short commons, for their ribs were plainly visible, and their backs and hipbones stuck out in alarming prominence. What the poor people are to do if this state of things continues long it is difficult to foresee, for they do not take enough money to live upon, and they have not enough money to get away with.

Giurgevo and the banks of the Danube, both above and below, are occupied by the Cossacks of the Kuban, or Circassian Cossacks, under the command of General Skobeleff. These Cossacks, it may be stated, with the exception of one or two regiments, are not Circassians, although they wear the same uniform, the long coat reaching below the knees, with a row of cartridges across the breast, sheepskin cap, a dagger, and the shushka, or curved sword, without a guard. This costume was adopted, before the Caucasus was conquered, by the Cossacks who formed the line of outposts that guarded the frontier, and it seems to have been done in order more readily to deceive the enemy, and enable the Cossacks to employ all those ruses of war for which they are so famous, and which their regular organization and knowledge of the number and whereabouts of all their own troops, enabled them to do with comparative ease.

I have already spoken of the two General Skobeleffs in a previous letter, and predicted that we should hear of them again before the war was over. Since then a small and independent army corps, the strength and composition of which I am not allowed to state, has been formed and placed under the command of General Skobeleff, senior, with his son, the conqueror of Khokand, as his chief of staff, and it is they who just now are holding the Danube, near Giurgevo. It is a rather curious fact that these two officers, father and son, have distinguished themselves in almost exactly the same way, by attacking and putting to flight immensely superior numbers by means of cavalry charges, the one in Central Asia against the Khokandians, the other in Asia Minor in 1854, when he attacked with 800 men and completely routed about 5,000 Turks who had fallen upon him in a most unexpected manner.

I found them living in a small house just in front of the boulevard, which had been abandoned by its proprietors. All the furniture had been carried away, and they were encamped rather than lodged, with only their camp baggage to furnish the empty rooms. At the time of my arrival they were dining in a little garden attached to the house, in the shade of some fruit trees, and I was immediately invited to share their repast, after which General Skobeleff senior took me with him on a visit to the advanced post up the river. The road here passes within two or three hundred yards of the Danube through fields partly under cultivation, bits of wood, gardens, and orchards. Sometimes on the river bank we passed a post of from three to twenty Cossacks, to whom the General put a question or two or delivered an order as we drove by. All the houses along the road were abandoned, as the people living on the banks of the river have withdrawn into the interior, although they come down and cultivate the fields, and in many places we saw the peasants tilling the ground and preparing for the coming harvest.

After three miles' drive we were directly opposite Rustchuk. We got out of the carriage and walked down to the river banks. There were several fields here under the highest state of cultivation. They were planted with onions, beetroots, and garlic, exceedingly well cared for, and I was astonished to see there was here a system of irrigation, by means of water raised from the Danube. Little streams of water were running everywhere through the fields, and we soon came to a huge irrigation wheel, on the very brink of the water, at which two horses were working, attended by a lazy boy, who lay down in the shade of a shed, and threw stones at the horses when they stopped. We sat down by the side of a small haystack, and proceeded to reconnoitre Rustchuk. The river here was, I suppose, nearly a mile wide, and poured its waters along in a clear, heavy, and solid stream that filled the banks quite full. There were several small steamers moored along the water's edge, at the foot of the town, among which could be distinguished three monitors, lying in close to the shore. General Skobeleff expressed a longing for a steam launch and a few torpedoes, to try his hand at blowing them up. All was the most perfect stillness and quiet in Rustchuk, the only movement visible being that of three flags waving in the wind, on which we could distinguish, through our glasses, the crescent and the star, and three or four times I caught the faint sound of a trumpet borne across to us on the breeze, showing that beneath the calm exterior the Turks were alive and awake. Finally, another sign of life was manifested by one of the steamers getting under way, and moving slowly down towards Giurgevo, closely hugging the shore. She glided down, slipped round a point, and disappeared from our sight. We then proceeded higher up the river to a battery, which stood a couple of hundred yards from the water. The embankments, counterscarp, and every other part was completely overgrown with grass. It was an old earthwork, that had been constructed here in 1854, and had remained intact ever since. There were sentinels pacing up and down before it, and through the embrasures I could see, as we drove by, what appeared to be some very heavy cannon. I was considerably surprised and amused on being informed by General Skobeleff that these heavy guns, which seemed to be threatening Rustchuk, were made of straw, and that they had occupied this outwork fully two weeks. This was an idea of General Skobeleff junior, who, having occupied the position without any artillery, had determined to impose upon the Turks by mounting straw cannon. The ruse had succeeded apparently, for the Turks had not dared to open fire upon them, and, on looking over the English papers, I found telegrams from Rustchuk a day or two after these straw batteries were mounted, announcing that the Russians had occupied the positions about Giurgevo, and had mounted several batteries with very heavy siege guns. The fact is, that the real siege guns were only on their way from Galatz to Bucharest, and did not arrive until a few days later. They will already have arrived and been placed in position by the time this letter appears in print, so that there is no indiscretion in my informing the Turks of the trick that has been played upon them. A little higher up we came to a tête-de-pont, grown over with grass, quite green, which had also been constructed by the Turks in 1854. The Russians had not occupied it. Still higher up was a village, where was posted a large detachment of Cossacks. The inhabitants had all retired to the interior, taking their furniture and effects with them, and the Cossacks had the village all to themselves. Some had occupied the houses, while others preferred bivouacking in the shade of the trees. Some were asleep, some tending and feeding their horses, others cleaning their arms. Here and there, two or three gathered around a fire, cooking the afternoon meal, and others again, stretched out at full length in the shade, fast asleep. The latter were evidently those who had been on picquet duty during the night. We were received here by the colonel of the regiment, a very active and intelligent officer, who, although a full-bred Cossack, spoke French perfectly, and knew a little English. He further presented me to several of his officers, three or four more of whom I found spoke either French, English, or German, giving one a very different idea of the intelligence and education of the Cossacks from that which is generally entertained. The greater part of these Cossack officers are, in fact, rich men in their own country, have received a good education, and have travelled, and seen more or less of the world. The men themselves are tall and athletic, and have a very intelligent look, and they are far superior in this respect to the ordinary Russian soldier. As evening was now approaching, the colonel invited us to supper, which was spread in the shade of a large apple-tree in one of the gardens; and, although this was an extremely advanced post, the supper he gave us was certainly as good as any which could be obtained in any hotel, either in Ployesti or Giurgevo. The *pièce de résistance* was shashliks or kibobs, roasted on sticks over the fire, than which there is nothing better.

While eating and talking I heard of one or two curious incidents that occurred here when the Cossacks first came. In the course of reconnoitring the country, five Cossacks, with an under officer, came upon a post of twenty Roumanian soldiers, likewise under the command of an under officer. The five Cossacks immediately arrested the twenty Roumanians, brought them into headquarters, and reported them to General Skobeleff as prisoners of some unknown army. The Cossacks were not quite sure apparently whether they were Turks or not, so they thought that they had better bring them in, an operation to which the Roumanians, although vastly superior in numbers, consented with not a little murmuring.

These Cossacks have some very curious customs, one of which was described to me, and which just now is not without its interest. They are all comparatively young men, and nearly all married, of course to young wives. It often happens, as in the present instance, that they are away from home during a war for one, or even three or four years, and one unfortunate result is that some of the wives left behind do not prove to be Lucretias. The Cossacks are quite aware of this, and many of them, on returning home, buy a white scarf or handkerchief, which they take with them. Upon entering their villages, the whole population—women, girls, old men, and children—come out to meet them, including, of course, the wives of the returning wanderers. Now, those of the wives who have been unfaithful to their lords, of which there is usually a considerable sprinkling, go forward to their husbands, kneel down before them in the road, put their faces in the dust, and place their husband's foot upon their necks. This is a confession of guilt, and at the same time a prayer for forgiveness. If the husband then covers his wife's head with the white scarf, it means that he forgives her, asks no questions, and obliterates the past. In this case no one has a right ever to reproach the wife with her inconstancy; and if any one should be rash enough to do so, he would have to count with the husband, who is the protector of his wife's honour. If, on the contrary, the white handkerchief is not produced, the woman returns straight to her father's house without again entering her husband's dwelling, and a divorce is pronounced. Although, as I have heard, there is generally a considerable sprinkling of women who come forward to kneel down and put their faces in the dust, it rarely happens that they are not forgiven. A very tragical case, however, was related to me in which the reverse took place. A returning Cossack was informed by a malicious neighbour before he reached his home that his wife had been unfaithful, without waiting to see whether the guilty woman would come forward and confess her sins. The comrades of the Cossack perceived that he had all of a sudden taken to drink and dissipation, although he was not a man given to these vices. When he reached his village his wife, as he feared, came forward, knelt down, and put her face in the dust at his feet. The spectators saw him look at her as she lay in the dust for a long time. Two or three times he put his hand in his breast for the white handkerchief, as if he were going to cover the repentant woman's head—two or three times the movement was restrained. Finally, as if driven by a sudden impulse, he all at once drew his shushka, and with one stroke severed her head from her body! The punishment for the crime was two months' imprisonment; while the malicious neighbour, who had taken the trouble to inform him beforehand of his wife's misconduct, was sentenced to Siberia for three years.

By the time supper was over, darkness was already setting in, hastened by dark clouds that began to roll up from the west and threaten a stormy night. We started back to Giurgevo, where we arrived just in time to escape a severe drenching. The next morning I was called up early, and invited to go down the river to visit another Cossack detachment posted four or five miles below Giurgevo. The rain of the night before had cleared and cooled the atmosphere and laid the dust, and a drive down the banks of the Danube in the cool air of the early morning was an exceedingly pleasant one Less than an hour brought us to a spot on the river's bank where another detachment of Cossacks was bivouacking. The Russians had here erected a kind of observatory, about thirty feet high, on which two men were always placed with a field-glass, to watch everything that was going on. I ascended to the top of this observatory, and had a look at the surrounding country. The Danube had here spread out over several miles, and had formed two or three islands, or rather what appeared to be such by the trees, which were standing deep in the water; for the ground in which they were growing was completely submerged. We were here on a high piece of ground, and were as far down as we could go along the bank on account of the spread of the waters. To have gone further we should have been obliged to make a wide détour and pass round what appeared to be a large lake extending three or four miles inland, which encompassed and surrounded a whole forest of trees. The real channel of the Danube, however, was near the bank on which we were standing, and this channel was not more than 300 yards wide. Beyond this was an island completely submerged, and still beyond, an open lake extending to the foot of the hills on the other side; and along our shore, for two or three miles further down, was an island of brushwood, with a narrow channel between it and the mainland. Here were moored a number of boats and a large river sloop, which had been captured by the Russians and brought in. These boats were full of Cossacks, who were simply rowing them up and down the channel for the purpose of learning to row. There were evidently very few of them who had any skill in the management of a boat, but they were working away with heart and soul, and were learning rapidly. These Cossacks are capable of doing nearly everything, and there is no doubt they will soon be as much at home on these river boats as on their own little horses. Down the river two or three miles was a Turkish post situated on a high bank immediately overlooking the river. General Skobeleff, junior, was making a reconnaissance in this direction, and invited me, as well as two Russian gentlemen, who are now attached to the Diplomatic Chancery accompanying the army, to go with him. The General took fifteen or twenty Cossacks and three or four small boats, and we all started down the narrow channel leading inside the island of brushwood before mentioned. Proceeding down stream about two miles, we entered the brushwood by means of a narrow, tortuous channel, through which we worked our way with some difficulty, and finally emerged from the brushwood right in front of the Turkish post just mentioned, which was only six or seven hundred yards distant. We were within point-blank range of the Turkish sharpshooters, and the white coats of General Skobeleff and the officers in the first boat offered them a splendid target. The Turks were not long in perceiving us, and it was not many seconds before we began to see little puffs of smoke rising from the banks near the house, and soon after began to hear the reports, which were followed immediately by the whistle of bullets that passed over our heads, cut off bits of brushwood near us, or dropped into the water before us. The position began to grow rather warm, and we thought we saw once the gleam of the barrel of a cannon being brought to bear upon us, but it seems that we were mistaken, for no cannon was fired. The other boats now pushed their way through the brushwood, and began firing volleys at the Turkish sharpshooters, which soon put a stop to their fire. We saw a great commotion amongst the people about the house when we began firing, and one of the officers who was watching them closely through a field-glass, assured us that he saw one of a group stagger and fall, while the rest suddenly disappeared, and he believed that one of the Turks had either been killed or wounded. They disappeared from that moment and fired no more.

General Skobeleff, whose object was to see the state of the river, get as close a view as he could of the opposite shore, and observe the Turkish positions, continued the reconnaissance without being disturbed any more by the Turks; and having obtained all the information that it was possible to get, we put back, entered the brushwood, and worked our way back up the river to the camp. The detachment was commanded by Colonel Orloff, who, by our return, had prepared breakfast for us, which, as there were no trees in the immediate neighbourhood, we took in his tent. The whole length of the Danube through Roumania seems to be covered with earthworks, which have been erected during the numerous wars that have taken place between Russia and Turkey. The Colonel's tent was placed in a small one, which had been constructed in 1854 by the Russians, and it was completely sheltered from the shell fire of the Turks, had they been disposed to throw any in this direction; but they did not seem so disposed, and the rest of the day passed off tranquilly, without another shot being fired on either side. I do not suppose that up to the present time the Russians in and about Giurgevo have fired in all one hundred shots from their small arms, and they certainly have not fired a single cannon. This tranquillity will not last long, however. The Danube is, I believe, beginning slowly to subside, and probably ere this letter reaches you the stillness which has been reigning here for so many days will be broken by the roar of cannon and the din of battle.

* GIURGEVO, *June 5th.*—While these long, weary summer days —not of inaction, indeed, but of preparation—are hanging so heavily on the hands of those whose task it is to detail the incidents of the war, the smallest mercy in the way of powder-burning is a thing to be thankful for. Not that life in Roumania, even when there is no fighting, is wholly destitute of pleasure. We were making the best of the barren times, a little party of us, inhabiting that excellent hostelry the Hotel Brofft, in Bucharest. I may name its members. The tall, stalwart, fresh-coloured young man, looking so like an English squire, is General Skobeleff, the youngest of all the Russian generals, the youngest that is in years. But although to be a general at thirty-five is a thing almost unprecedented in the Russian army, outside members of the blood-royal, Skobeleff has owed nothing to what in Russia is known as "protection." He owes, indeed, something to luck—that good fortune which has placed him so often where opportunity offered to distinguish himself; nor has he omitted to make the most of every

opportunity. It is something for a man while yet in his young prime to have added to his country a territory larger than the whole of Great Britain—the Khanate of Khokand. It was but the other day that I met General Skobeleff for the first time, but another member of the little party and myself are old comrades, in that species of comradeship closer perhaps than any other, the origin of which dates back to dangers and privations shared together. Not once nor twice have Dochtouroff and myself lain in the same cheerless bivouac, and stood together while men were falling and dying around us. The third member of the party is—which descriptive appellation shall I put first?—a prince and a private soldier. This young Cossack private is probably better known throughout Europe than either of the officers I have named. The big house in Constantinople, the eagles on whose gateway were muffled up the other day as M. Nelidoff stepped forth from without its gates, knows well the young Cossack private who in the piping times of peace was the private secretary of General Ignatieff. It was but the other day that Prince Tzereteleff, visiting England in the same capacity, was Lord Salisbury's guest at Hatfield, and Lady Derby's at her reception in the State rooms of the Foreign Office. Another converse reading of the *cedant arma togæ* axiom. The young diplomat volunteered as a private into a Cossack regiment, and to-day, but that he is temporarily attached to General Skobeleff as an orderly, he might be cleaning his own horse and lying asleep in a swamp somewhere in the Danubian marshes.

Yesterday there reached us, as the party sat down at lunch, the tidings that there had been the same morning some heavy firing by the Turkish cannon into Giurgevo. Now an impression, rather than a belief, has prevailed among us that the Turks were about to display more offensive activity than they had hitherto manifested. The report went that Abdul Kerim Pacha had addressed strenuous representations to the authorities in Constantinople against the continuous inaction, or it may be the masterly inactivity, which has hitherto been the Turkish military attitude. Further, the story went that Abdul Kerim had received *carte blanche* to be as active as he pleased; as the result of which release from the bonds which had hitherto restrained him, he was now treading in the footsteps of Mr. Winkle—taking off his coat and announcing that he was about to begin. They had been expecting this beginning of his at Widdin for two days; now this shell-heaving of yesterday morning might be his commencement in the Rustchuk-Giurgevo position. Anyhow, the journey to

Giurgevo, as an alternative to vegetating in Bucharest, seemed worth making on the chance; and we arranged to rendezvous at the railway station for the start of the six p.m. train. You go to a bombardment by train now-a-days, and reach a battle-field in a first-class carriage, with a right to grumble if time is not kept. We all kept tryst, but later telegrams had brought tidings of the cessation of the Turkish fire. Abdul Kerim, if he had ever taken off his coat, which from previous experience of that General's inexplicably Fabian tactics, I take leave to doubt, had put it on again. Skobeleff wanted to buy a horse and would stay the night in Bucharest. Tzereteleff, as his orderly, would remain with him. Dochtouroff also determined to put off his journey to the morning, and evacuated the railway carriage after he had taken his seat in it. I had nothing to do in Bucharest; I had taken my ticket, and so I came on, not without a lurking hope that by not following the example of postponement I might be in the way of something in the early morning which would be missed by those spending the night at Bucharest.

My travelling companion was a fine soldierly warrior of the Caucasus, Major-General Yolchine, commanding the 1st Brigade of the 14th Division of the 8th Army Corps. He gave me statistics proving what I had already heard concerning the excellent health of the Russian soldiers. His division has marched the whole way from Kischeneff, after having been in cantonments near that horrible town all the winter. The men about the Pruth had to wade for miles together up to their waists in water, and there were occasions when officers had to strip with the men and give themselves to the task of extricating the waggons of the column from swampy sloughs of despond. Notwithstanding these hardships and the long march, the average of sick men in the regiments of the division—each regiment numbering close on 3,000 soldiers—was not above fifty men. The three prevalent causes of inefficiency are fevers—not infectious, but of an aguish type—sore eyes and footsoreness. Only the fever cases, and of these only the most severe, are left behind; the other cases come on with their respective regiments in the ambulance waggons, of which two, each conveying twelve men, are attached to each battalion. The General laughed as he gave me details respecting the spirit ration of the Russian army. On the march from Kischeneff, each man has received a dram four times in the week; when not marching the allowance is two drams of raki monthly. The food ration is three pounds of bread daily, with half a pound of meat, beans, &c., for making of the soup, of which the Russian soldiers partake twice a day, eating ever so many of them out of the same big camp kettle. As we came to a station a company of the General's brigade was encamped close by, acting as a picquet for the protection of the line, and most of the men were on the platform of the station. The General put his head out of carriage, and called out, "Good day, lads!" The soldiers responded, "Good day, father!" with one voice, and that a sufficiently loud one. The General left me at Fratesti, and pointed out to me his house, a little way across the plain, quite as if he had settled down there for good, expressing a hope that I would look in upon him should I happen to pass that way.

Giurgevo, of course, is in face of the enemy, a place of which every house is within easy range from the other side; a place which a day's heavy bombardment would probably lay in ashes; a place from which, when I landed in it six weeks ago, the inhabitants were flying pell-mell in a body. But threatened men live long, and Giurgevo's motto is *dum vivimus vivamus.* The birja drivers fought for me eagerly when I came outside the station. The air throbbed with the full-volumed sound of the chant of the Russian soldiers in their camp. In the streets light streamed from the windows of every house; groups of civilians gossiped at the street corners; women sat on the stoops outside the doors. I drove through the town to its extreme end, my destination being the Hotel Bellevue close to the headquarters of General Skobeleff the elder, who is in command of the place, which is mainly occupied by his Cossacks. As I turned the corner to the hotel I caught a glimpse of the Danube at my feet, and of the Turkish bivouac fires over the way. Rooms were ready for me, and supper; for accommodation had been telegraphed for for the whole party. "Oh, yes," said the chambermaid, as she showed me my bedroom, "there came lots of shells hereabouts this morning, quite close to the hotel. Why, there is nothing but the Danube between us and the Turkish batteries;" and then she desired to know whether I wanted slippers, and cared to buy a fragment of a shell which had fallen and burst in the back yard. I went out to call on the General, but I found that he was taking his evening siesta, and looked in upon the chief of his staff instead, who remarked in an incidental way that that morning about fifty shells had fallen about the place, in a tone which suggested that it might have been his habit from early childhood to take shells in his *café au lait* instead of sugar. He had not heard of anybody being hurt, and clearly regarded people in Bucharest as irrational alarmists. When I get up in the morning, the first thing I do is to look out of window, and beyond the few trees on which the birds are singing flows the broad even stream of the Danube, with the Turkish bank in clear view beyond. In the clear morning air it looks strangely near. With the naked eye I can see the sentries walking about on the parapets of the earthworks, the peasants driving their cattle to water, the women washing clothes on the edge of the stream. With the glass I can see into the mouths of the cannon frowning through the revetted embrasures. A train comes along the river face down into the terminus, which is half hidden by the trees of the intervening island. With the glass I can discern the profiles of the passengers as they show at the windows of the carriages. I wonder whether they know that they are actually within range of the rifle of the sentry walking to and fro on the little quay below me. It is so, for Turkish rifle bullets have reached as far as the quarters of the general staff, next door to the hotel, and one has broken a window in the pavilion in the garden. The waiter comes and tells me it is pleasanter to drink coffee in the garden in front than in the *salle à manger.* A sweet place is this public garden, with seats and walks overhung with the white blossoms of the locust trees, and the fresh, tender green of the sycamores. Most of it is on the flat summit of a little bluff, but it slopes down to the water's edge close by. In the garden I find officers and civilians sunning themselves and gossiping lazily. A little group at a table under the big tree are playing dominoes. Inside the pavilion is a buffet, and a girl from the hotel, who says that Turkish shells don't at all frighten her, is acting as *dame du comptoir.* She points out to you the pane broken by the Turkish bullet, and laughs if you suggest that what happened once may happen again. If you stroll round the garden among the roses and the acacia shrubs, you may chance on a few ugly holes with jagged edges, which are not in accord with the trimness of the surroundings. These are holes made by shells which fell yesterday; there is no reason in the world, seemingly, why others to-day should not follow those of yesterday; but it is time to think about them when they come. Meanwhile the coffee is ready, and the lady of the counter pours out a *petit verre* with as much insouciance as if big shells were bonbons. Later there come a few children into the garden, and two of them gather flowers and throw them into one of the shell-holes. Then the gardener comes and begins his task of watering: to-morrow the site of the garden may be required for a Russian battery, but the gardener has a fine sense of duty, and waters his plants as assiduously as if he were paid by a percentage on the number of bucketfuls of water he uses. The heat increases, but the shade is grateful, and loungers come in and fall asleep stretched on the benches under the trees. Presently there is a little bustle, and a crowd gathers on the garden esplanade overhanging the river. They are watching a Turkish monitor, which, with the white flag crescent-centred at its main, glides swiftly out from behind the island and heads down stream. What are to be its movements? If it bends across stream towards Giurgevo we may look out, we here on the esplanade, for yesterday these were the tactics of the monitor, which assisted with its fire that of the battery over the way. Are we to have a repetition of yesterday's performance? Have I gained an advantage by coming on last night while the others stayed behind? The monitor, it seems, is not bellicose this morning. She is bound on a cruise down stream, to have a look at our friends at Oltenitza no doubt, and make the attempt to find whether there are any big guns in the batteries thereabouts. She glides on behind another low bulrush-covered island, and we see no more of her. Ere she passes out of sight I have discerned through the glass her captain standing on the quarterdeck under the awning. Don't I wish there were an awning over the esplanade! As there is not, we go back to the seats under the shade of the trees, and sit there gossiping listlessly while the hours drag on. A boy comes round with bills of the circus which is nightly open somewhere in the centre of the town. What would the Russians say if a boat-load of Turks were to come from Rustchuk to attend it? Rustchuk, by all accounts, is not at present a very lively place. But shells are likely to be the only visitors from the Turkish side yet awhile, and the Russians will reverse the usual etiquette, and break the ice by paying the Turks the first call.

The languor of the afternoon is diversified by a little excitement, but of an internal character. Looking up from my book as I sit under a tree, I find that the garden is surrounded by a cordon of Russian infantrymen. I look across at the hotel and I observe that it too is in military occupation. Cossack sentries watch its various outlets, and permit neither ingress nor egress. It is amusing to watch people essaying in vain to go in to their dinner, or trying without success to get out in order to catch the train. But it is not quite so funny when all we people in the garden find that we are virtually prisoners for the time. The sentries are inexorable. A stout burgher, who might be the mayor, rolls pompously up to the gate, only to be turned back by a peremptory wave of the hand. I have no better success, and the sentry will not look at a "legitimation." At length a staff officer whom I know passes, and releases me. There had been a hunt for a spy.

The setting sun gilds the broad bosom of the Danube, and lights up the white-tented camps along the foliage on the gradually swelling slope of the other side. As the heat of the day wanes, some ladies come to promenade within the range of the bullet fire. Verestchagine, the Russian painter, who is here with the staff, leans against a tree on the esplanade, and watches the sun-tints on the water. Yesterday from the same spot he was sketching the aspect presented by the falling and occasional bursting of shells in the water. He came hither the other day direct from Paris, in obedience to a commission from the Emperor of Russia. Verestchagine has earned laurels in other fields than that in which the pencil and brush are the weapons; he wears the cross of St. George at his button-hole—the reward for an act of singular personal valour at Tashkend, in rallying beaten troops and retaking a captured cannon, although he himself then no longer wore the uniform of the Czar. As the twilight thickens a band of gipsies begin to play on the esplanade, the lamps are lit which dangle from the trees, beer-mugs glance on the little tables, officers and civilians fraternize; and so the evening glides away.

It is easily discernible by me that in the matter of earthworks Rustchuk is much stronger than it was when I saw it first six weeks ago. A great work near the extreme right of the Turkish position, which at the time I speak of was only begun, is now being finished, and it was from the guns in it that the shells came which fell in Rustchuk yesterday. The works on the lower ground, in the immediate vicinity of the town, are also evidently greatly strengthened, and on the slope of the bank, near the margin of the river, stretches an almost continuous line of shelter trenches for infantry. On the other hand, fewer troops seem visible, although I am well aware that the size of camps that can be seen from hostile positions is no serious criterion of the actual strength. But troops have been observed leaving Rustchuk, doubtless for the field army which Abdul Kerim Pacha is said to be organizing for operating between Shumla and Rustchuk, and this forenoon I saw two battalions quit Rustchuk marching along the river-side road which leads in the direction of Nicopolis. In Rustchuk as in Widdin, the hospital, denoted by the red cross or the red-crescent-flag, I know not which, is the most prominent building in the place—a large and lofty house in the heart of the town, and to all appearance immediately in the rear of a battery. It would seem as if the Turks chose such localities for their hospitals on purpose to gain pretexts for protests.

The following letter contains a description of Russian Cossack artillery, and a discussion of the qualities of the cavalry of the army generally:—

* BUCHAREST, *June 9th.*—It was nearly dark when I reached Turna Magurelle, a flourishing and well-built town of about seven thousand inhabitants, with a great deal of commerce, chiefly in fish and grain, which are exported by the Danube steamers touching at the landing-place connected with the town by a chaussée about two-and-a-half kilometres long. Like most Roumanian towns, Turna has several public gardens, and although the town is within range of the cannon in the Nicopolis batteries, I found quite a concourse of people of both sexes sitting under the trees and listening to the sprightly music of a Hungarian band. I found Prince Manueloff quartered in the house of an Englishman on the edge of the town nearest the Danube. He told me of the many uses to which he had had to put his troopers; how they were acting as infantrymen, had done a little sailor duty, and had served as engineers in the building of the batteries. There are hardly any infantry as yet in Turna, they remaining at present in reserve, and hence the variety of duties which has devolved upon Prince Manueloff's horsemen. His Highness, learning from me that I took a special interest in the cavalry arm of the service, was good enough to direct that a battery of Cossack horse artillery and a detachment of dragoons should parade next morning for my inspection, and I gratefully accepted the courteous offer. Accordingly, at ten o'clock yesterday morning, an officer of the Prince's staff came to me with the information that these representative detachments were in the square near the Prince's quarters. We first looked at the Cossack battery; explanations regarding it being given by its commanding officer, Lieutenant-Colonel Zotoff. The battery was the 9th battery Circassian Cossacks. The guns are bronze, of Russian make, fitted with range-finders; they are equivalent to our six-pounders; there are six guns in each horse battery, eight in each field battery, the pieces in the latter being equal in weight of projectile to our field twelve-pounders. The gun carriage is stout and well finished, the trail is rather shorter than with us, and considerably more weighty. The gun-team consists of six horses of medium size and quality; they are requisitioned for this purpose on the issue of the mobilization order, the

Cossack batteries being for the most part skeletons in peace time. As in every army except our own, in which shafts are used, the wheel horses are fastened to a pole, and thus divide the work of bearing back the gun going down hill, and the strain of pulling up. The rope traces are certainly too long, and even without kicking a horse must very often be over a trace when the gear is not taut. The harness is of black leather, strong, plain, and serviceable. There is not a bright buckle or link in the whole set, therefore there can be neither burnish nor rust. The splinter bars which the use of a pole renders necessary are of iron, somewhat heavy, and they must occasionally hit hocks pretty hard. The drivers, who wear the long black coat and the Astrachan busby of the Circassian Cossacks, are smart, well-set-up fellows, armed with sabres and revolvers; they drive with great expertness and plenty of dash. The detachment ride their own horses, the teams only being found by Government. They are armed in the same manner as the drivers. To each gun are two under officers—in action one is with the gun, the other with the team. Colonel Zotoff ordered one of the guns to unlimber, and come into "action front." With great quickness and precision the team wheeled and halted. There was no question as to the agility with which the detachment dismounted and unlimbered. Away to the rear went the team and the detachment horses, leaving standing beside the piece four men and the under officer ready to commence firing. I ought to have mentioned that one of the detachment rode with the sponge carried lancewise, an arrangement which does not seem a happy one. Altogether this Cossack battery, if it had not the dash and trim dexterity of one of our batteries of horse artillery, appeared perfectly up to its work, and had a wear and tear appearance calculated to commend it to the practical soldier. To each battery there are six officers—one lieutenant-colonel, one captain, two lieutenants, and two sub-lieutenants. The rank of major does not exist in the Russian artillery. Each cavalry division has two of these horse batteries—one battery being of regulars, the other of Cossacks.

The artillery moved off and the detachment of dragoons came up. The Russians do not claim to have any technically "heavy" cavalry of the line. There used to be a whole division of cuirassiers which were very heavy cavalry, but there remain of cuirassiers now but three regiments, and these belong to the Imperial Guard. But the dragoons I saw yesterday were virtually heavy cavalry—cavalry indeed as heavy as any in Europe. I am an old heavy cavalry man myself, and have naturally given special attention to this arm of the service. There was a time when I used to think there was no grander spectacle in the world than when good old General Parlby would bid his trumpeter sound "Gallop," and the Royals and the Greys abreast—Wardlaw at the head of one regiment, Darby Griffith in front of the other—would come sweeping over the springy green turf of the Curragh until the firm sod quaked again under the hoofs of the massive war horses. Were the glad chance given to me to participate in a cavalry charge in stern earnest I would ask no better place than on the flank of the leading squadron of the dear old Royals. But there came to me in 1870-71 the realization that there were heavier cavalry regiments in Europe than the Royals and the Greys. The cuirassiers and dragoons whom Bredow and Wedel led in that fierce ride on the French cannon on the red day of Vionville were, man for man, horse for horse, more massive than my own old fellow troopers; and now yesterday I realized that the Russian dragoons were heavier cavalry than the stout swordsmen of Bredow and Wedel. Horses seventeen hands high, neither clumsy nor weedy, strong-boned, close-coupled, powerful-quartered, noble-crested, with small well-bred heads, and the stamp of immense power and leonine courage pervading the whole frame. Men tall, square-shouldered, clean-flanked, rather heavy-limbed perhaps, but without clumsiness—men, in fine, of the stamp of our dalesmen, who furnish the best troopers to our household cavalry, only for the most part of greater breadth of shoulder and massiveness of limb. I will frankly aver that it has never yet befallen me to see troop horses so grand. Then I saw a handful of Uhlans—the men, take them as a whole, running a little smaller and lighter than the dragoons, but only a trifle so—the horses of equal substance; and another handful of hussars, the men perceptibly slighter and shorter than the dragoons, yet still big men, the horses scarcely so tall, but with almost as much power. The Russians, as they have technically no heavy cavalry of the line, so they have technically no light cavalry of the line; the Cossacks constitute their light cavalry. It is a fair question for discussion whether it is wise or the reverse to have all the regular cavalry thus massive, for really no other expression conveys so truthful an idea of their character. To my humble thinking it is merely a question of horse power. Some years ago we had a craze for light cavalry, and the expression "light men on light horses" was the watchword with many military reformers. Even in our heavy cavalry, which was cut down to four regiments, the maximum standard was 5 ft. 11 in., and in the hussars and "light bobs" the maximum height was 5 ft. 8 in. Now the tendency of our cavalry is to greater height and weight—weight of man I mean—and I think wisely so. A big horse, if he is well bred, is as active as a little one. Valentine Baker's smart lads of the 10th Hussars did not get much change out of the "tin bellies" in the autumn manœuvres, which unfortunately seem now to be memories of the past. It was sheer weight of man and horse that sent the Prussian dragoons crashing through the Austrian Hussars in that test-fight in the narrow street of Trautenau. It was in virtue of their weight giving pith to their impetuosity that the cuirassiers of Caulaincourt, smashing their indomitable way through and over masses of infantrymen, forced their way through the gorge of the great redoubt on the slope of Borodino. What but weight giving effect to impetus sent the Prussian cuirassier through the French Hussars, uphill though they charged, on the swell that rises from the north-east of Mars-la-Tour? Could "light men on light horses" have followed Scarlett and Elliot through that dense-packed mass of Russian horsemen that came lumbering down on our heavy cavalry on the day of Balaklava? The hunting man knows how useful it is when the going is heavy, that his mount is up to a stone or two more than his weight. And this is exactly what you bring about if you put men that are not too heavy and too heavily equipped on the most powerful horses that can be procured. I should say of these Russian Hussar horses that there is not one of them but is up to a lot more weight than he carries, having thus, in other words, a reserve fund of power. In the dragoon regiments the margin is smaller, in consequence of the greater weight of the men, yet by reason of the singular power of the horses a margin does exist. A big horse requires no more food to keep him in condition than does a small one; indeed the biggest feeder of the equine species I know is a twelve-hands high pony down Sydenham way. The Russian field ration for all cavalry horses alike are four "garnitz," *i.e.*, large double handfuls of grain, 10lb. of hay, and 5lb. straw; no doubt supplemented by pickings, for the Russian cavalrymen are admirable horsemasters. On this ration the Division Manueloff marched 700 versts in eighteen days, with several halt days. It rained most of the journey, and the roads were cruelly heavy. Nevertheless, I have never seen horses in better working condition, and at the end of the march barely five horses per squadron, or about 2½ per cent., were temporarily unfit for duty, the chief casualties being sore backs from the constant soaking rain. The artillery and waggon horses receive a larger ration than do the troop horses, on the ground that their work is considered harder. The Cossacks at home feed their horses themselves; they are now drawing the same ration as that supplied to the regular cavalry horses.

The Russian cavalry saddle is a very rudimentary, yet serviceable, article for practical work. It consists simply of a wooden frame raised on two wooden panels, which fit the horse's back lying lengthwise on either side of the backbone. The only leather about the saddle are the flaps, which come only a little way down, but extend the full length of the panels. Both pommel and cantle are high and cut out, so as to allow a current of air to circulate along the backbone between the panels. In front are a pair of immense wallets, which are stuffed with belongings of man and horse. Above the wallets is carried a sheepskin pea-coat, above that again the cloak neatly folded, not rolled, and the whole is covered by the horse-rug, which envelops the wallets and their superstructure, and, being carried backward to the cantle, furnishes also the seat of the saddle, there being no leather seat, as in our military saddles, above the wooden frame. Behind the wallets, or rather, perhaps, behind the top of the pommel, the dragoon carries rations for two days, bread, rice, salt, &c., in canvas bags made for the purpose. Behind him, across the cantle, hang also in canvas bags on either side his horse's ration of grain for two days, with two days' allowance of hay, packed very close in hay nets, hanging down on either flank. On the panel-ends behind the cantle is carried a small round valise, much of the same shape as that used by our cavalry, but without a flap. In this and in the wallets the dragoon carries the following kit:—One uniform tunic, one white tunic, three shirts, two pairs drawers, one sleeping comforter covering head and neck, one pair of boots, and one pair of leathers for making new legs to boots. Each third man carries a copper cooking-pot, which fits exactly over one end of his valise. Above the valise is half a *tente d'abri*, with one of the stakes. I should have said that above everything in front are strapped the picquet pegs and ropes, which, however, seemed to be very little used. Underneath the saddle frame is a felt blanket folded fourfold, which does duty for our numnah. It is re-folded daily, so that a fresh surface is always next the horse's back, an admirable preventive of chafing. A one-inch broad leather girth maintains the saddle in its place with the aid of another passing under the horse's belly some distance further back. A surcingle keeps the rug in position, and straps it down on to the frame. There is no breast-plate or crupper to the Russian saddle, but a leather band crosses the horse's chest to keep the saddle in position. The headstall is simple, strong, and eminently practicable; there is no gimcrackery of shiny buckles or brasses. The dragoon, who wears a kepi, a blue tunic, and pantaloons, with boots coming up to the knee, carries a breech-loading Kranke short rifle, not a carbine, in a leather case slung on his back, with the butt on the right side and the muzzle over the left shoulder. The non-commissioned officers carry no rifles, but are armed with revolvers. The private dragoon has no pistols. He carries a sabre, without a basket hilt, indeed in the Russian army there are few basket-hilted swords, in a leather scabbard lined with wood and tipped with brass, and bound by brass rings. On the sword scabbard is also the leathern sheath of a bayonet, for use with the rifle when the dragoon is fighting on foot. For the Russian dragoon is a dragoon proper, according to the original acceptation of the term. He is armed and trained to fight indifferently on foot or on horseback; you may call him a mounted infantryman when he is on horseback, but I should prefer to call him a dismounted cavalryman when he is on foot. The Russian dragoons march in sections of threes, and at the order to fight on foot, the centre of threes takes charge of the horses of his two comrades, the sous-capitaine of the squadron taking charge of the horse detachment, and while striving to avail himself of as much cover as possible, keeping also as near as possible to the force fighting dismounted. To sum up, the Russian dragoon has nothing about him that jingles as he rides—nothing that by sparkling could show his whereabouts afar off. He is a plainly dressed, workman-like, practical-looking soldier, with a genuine love for his horse, and, it appears, a real pride in his profession.

There are no studs as in Russia, for the supply of horses to the cavalry. Each regiment has a remount officer, who has the duty of buying young horses and of taking charge of the remount depôt, where thirty-six men of the regiment are stationed to look after the youngsters. The remount officer buys horses between the ages of one and three years. He has all Russia to select from; but the horses for the most part are brought by owners and dealers to the depôts, which are located chiefly in the governments of Tambof and Varonish, on the Volga, since in these governments horses suited for cavalry purposes are more plentiful than in other parts of Russia. The limit of price permitted to the remount officer is 133 roubles for horses destined for the cavalry of the line; for the Imperial Guards the limit rises to 300 roubles. At the age of four the young horses, which have previously been handled but not broken in, are drafted into the reserve squadron, where they remain for a year, during which time they are broken in; and at the age of five join the regiment for service. A horse is supposed to last seven years from the date of his joining the regiment, so that the remount officer has to furnish young horses yearly to the amount of one-seventh of the total service-strength. The reserve squadron in peace time is about one hundred strong, but in war time it is increased to twice or thrice this strength to meet the drafts made upon it to supply vacancies of men and horses in the field squadrons. Cavalry recruits who come from all parts of Russia, but are chiefly drawn from Little Russia, the people of which are extremely good horse-masters and fond of riding, are sent direct to their respective regiments, and are considered fit to be dismissed from recruit drill in three months. Formerly the period of training was nine months, but now they work harder, it seems, and are sent to duty sooner. I think a man is likelier to be a good duty-soldier at the end of nine months' fair training than at the end of three months' forcing; but then it appears tuition is sedulously kept up after the dragoon is sent into the ranks, and the accelerated training is of course a desideratum in war time, or when it is desired quickly to increase the strength of an army. The cavalry soldier's term of active service is nominally ten years, with five years in the reserve, but in practice he is sent home after having served four or five years, with liability to be recalled from this long furlough at a day's notice. Non-commissioned officers may go down or remain with the regiment at their option; if they engage for a second term of service they receive additional pay. Private soldiers are not allowed to re-engage.

I have left myself but little space to describe the Turna-Nicopolis position. The town of Turna Magurelle is on the edge of a low bank, just high enough to raise it out of the inundation. As I stood on the edge of this bank the inundation reached to my feet, spreading far and wide, so that it seemed "one water" all the way to the foot of the rock on the top of which is the fortress of Nicopolis. But it is not altogether so. From Turna Magurelle a chaussée runs across the inundation to a narrow strip of land which represents the true north bank of the Danube, all that is left of it sticking up out of the water, with a few houses on it, which are the buildings connected with the port and steamboat stopping station. The Danube proper is just now about one and a half kilometre broad, and the Turkish bank, almost as far as the eye can reach, is steep and in places precipitous. But just opposite

Turna is a little break in the crag, a narrow ravine, down the bottom of which comes a little stream to the Danube. Just at the mouth of this little stream is the port of Nicopolis. The town lies behind and stretches up the steep slope to the upper town, in front of which, on a semi-isolated rock, stands the citadel. A wall surrounds the area on which the town stands, and there are batteries, not only inside the space enclosed by this wall, but on and under the crags to right and to left. It is not a nice-looking place to carry by a *coup de main*, and if the Russians mean to cross here they will have to batter down the fortress and crush the batteries by the weight of superior fire from the lower ground, with the Turkish gunners able from their dominant position to look into the Russian batteries.

In the following letter the lines of advance of the entire Russian army south of the Danube are compared :—

* BUCHAREST, *June 19th.*—In one of my earlier letters, while as yet the plan of the Russian advance into the Principalities remained undeveloped, I ventured to foreshadow a scheme of strategical action on the part of the Russians which appeared to me to bear the impress of probability. Of that scheme the keynote was the value of time, or, to speak more explicitly, the wisdom of taking time by the forelock. That it was possible to cross the Danube a month ago at Isatchia, below Braila, cannot well be denied. A march through the Dobrudscha was scarcely perhaps a pleasant prospect, but it had obvious elements of advantage which I strove at the time to put forward. With their preponderance in cavalry the Russians might have by this time overrun the greater part of Bulgaria north of the Balkans, keeping clear of the fortresses and avoiding close quarters with such field force as the Turks were able to spare from their fortresses and standing camps, if such field force seemed too formidable to cope with. It would have been perfectly practicable that a large Russian force should have by this time swept the Dobrudscha, and be now in position about Bazardjik to accomplish whatever purpose it might have seemed expedient to assign to it. The question would have arisen, and the answer to that question would have depended on the strength of the force accumulated on the position I have named, whether Shumla should have been the first objective, or whether, one detachment having been detailed to watch Shumla, another to observe Varna, the main column should have pressed on through the Pravada Pass.

Doubtless there would have been risks attending the carrying out of such a scheme, although I venture to think they would have been smaller than at first sight might appear But, be this as it may, the Russian chiefs have chosen not to incur these risks; it remains to be seen whether in the doing so they may not have exposed themselves to greater. Their plan of campaign has been devised on the basis of leaving as little as possible to chance, and in view of this they have been compelled in a great measure to disregard the value of time. The swollen state of the Danube has had but little influence on the Russian dispositions. Had the Danube been going down, as is its normal wont in the month of June, no doubt they might have pressed on their preparations for the crossing of it; but looking to the magnitude of their arrangements, and their choice of crossing places, it is doubtful whether, even if the Danube had been practicable earlier, the preparations would have been sufficiently far advanced to admit of the crossing in force being accomplished sooner than now. Where that crossing is to take place, and when, of course it is not for me to anticipate, although, looking at the date at which this letter can be published, I imagine the revelation would do no harm to anybody. But one may localize the point within limits narrow enough for my present purpose. From the Aluta westwards the Russians have given the Danube line to the Roumanian army, therefore no Russians will cross higher up than the mouth of that river. Let us assume that the Russian main advance has effected its passage, and is disposed on the other bank of the Danube somewhere between Nicopolis and Rustchuk. What are likely to be its subsequent movements? The point might be discussed by a person writing in Fleet-street with to the full as many data for the consideration of the question as are at my disposal here; I confine myself to regarding the abstract possibilities and probabilities. Shumla cannot well be the preliminary objective of this main advance, because if such were the case, it is feasible to hold that the crossing would have been made at some point or points nearer to Shumla. Rustchuk is hardly a factor in the problem, because it is reasonable to suppose that it will be made safe, and the army there, unless it makes for the open, will be with all the greater nimbleness surrounded by a ring of iron. There remain three lines of advance to be considered. A march to Tirnova, and thence through the Balkans to Slievno, whence the descent in the great Roumelian valley is easy. Let me call this line of advance No. 1. Another more westerly route through the Balkans, conducts from Tirnova to Kezanlik, whence the great valley is yet more easily accessible than from Slievno. Let us call this line of advance No. 2. It may be stated that the pass through the Balkans by this route is perhaps the easiest of all the passes. There remains the manœuvre of turning the Balkans altogether, by taking the route to Sophia, which stands at the head of the great Roumelian valley. This let us call line of advance No. 3. The strategical conditions of each line of advance may be succinctly set forth.

Lines of advance Nos. 1 and 2 are chiefly influenced by the comparative proximity of Shumla, and the possible operations of the Turkish army understood to be concentrated in its vicinity. Were a Russian force operating in Central Bulgaria to advance from the Danube, and devote itself to the observation of the Shumla army, the influence of that army on the lines of advance open to the Russians would be sensibly diminished. In this case the routes Nos. 1 and 2, both of which, with a force so large as that which will probably constitute the Russian main advance, would be likely to be utilized, would have obvious advantages as involving a shorter march, a speedier passage through the dangerous mountain region, a more direct line of communication with the base on the Danube, and an earlier advent into the great Roumelian valley, whether to rest there in a comparatively hospitable region, or to go further, as the case might be. But the risks of such a movement are not to be ignored. If the Shumla army be not watched, or be insufficiently observed, there would be little to hinder it from falling on the flank and rear of the Russian advance on the Tirnova-Slievno road, after the column had committed itself to the mountainous regions, or, indeed, after the Balkans had been passed. The other seeming danger that the Shumla army, striking southward through the Shumla-Karnabat pass, might take in reverse the Russian army on its march towards Adrianople, may be disregarded, since the Russians would, no doubt, detail detachments to observe the debouchment of the passes.

Line of advance No. 3, *viâ* Sophia, affords many temptations. A march by it would avoid the difficulties of the Balkan passes, and once at Sophia the march down the great valley would present but few obstacles. But this route is greatly longer than any other, and the season is far advanced. And what about the Widdin army under Osman Pacha, whom the Servian campaign showed to be a capable man, if he had been allowed to prove his capacity? It is said that he chafes fiercely at not having been allowed to follow the footsteps of Omar Pacha in 1853, by crossing the river, and establishing himself in the commanding position of Kalafat, from which splendid strategic position Omar Pacha so long loomed out threateningly on the Russian flank, and menaced their communications in the Principalities. Although baulked in this aspiration, Osman Pacha at Widdin to-day holds a position only less commanding than that occupied at Kalafat in 1853-4 by Omar Pacha. While Osman Pacha remains there with a large and reputedly well-appointed force, leaning upon a fortress of respectable strength, there must, in the nature of things, be extreme danger to a Russian column marching from the Danube on Sophia. This column so marching must show a flank to the Widdin army, and must leave its communications seriously at its mercy. This constitutes the great complication of the Sophia line of advance. Large as is the Russian force, it cannot afford to detail columns of observation to every point, and pursue its march with a main body of overwhelming strength. The problem would be solved if Osman Pacha could be tempted away from under the guns of Widdin. If he chose, he might be at Sophia before the Russians could be there, and then they could fight him, and break him, and sweep him out of their way; but will he move? It may be that he will do so, under the apprehension of being cut off in the dead angle of Bulgaria, where he now is, and reaching Sophia before the Russians, not wait there to give them the chance of smashing him, but retire before them down the great Sophia-Philippopolis-Adrianople valley, in the hopes of effecting somewhere a concentration with the Shumla force, and in the event of the worst, holding himself available for the occupation of the "last ditch," the Kutchuk-Chekmedge line, across the throat of the Constantinople peninsula.

Assuming that the Russian main advance be by Sophia, it would then appear indispensable that the Widdin army should be decisively disposed of before the march through the hill country was entered upon. If Osman Pacha should not choose to come forth and fight the Russians, and in all probability he would not, there would remain no alternative but that the Russians should press in upon him where he harbours. True, the whole force of their main column would not be required; but at least the main column would have to wait while Osman Pacha and Widdin were being crushed. It has been suggested that the Widdin army might be left to the disposal of the Roumanians, strengthened by a detachment—perhaps a division—of Russians, and that the Bulgarian legion might also be utilized for this purpose. It is not for me to say that the Roumanians and Bulgarians so supported could not give a good account of Osman Pacha and his army. But I do not think a prudent general, with a sense of responsibility, would feel exactly easy with that army on his flank, and contingently on his rear, with the force in question as the only buffer. The military policy of the Russians will be no doubt directed keenly towards the opportunities of fighting the Turks whenever and wherever they can get the chance, knowing by past experience that the Turk is not good at standing before the Russian in the open field. And if this were so of yore, questionless it must be more so now, even if the martialism of the Turk may not have been deteriorated. There never in war has been so great a strain put upon men in the field as that to which it is possible now to subject them under a sustained converging fire of artillery. What says Moltke of the fighting characteristics of the Turks:—"An impetuous attack may be expected from the Turks, but not a lasting and obstinate defence. Against Orientals it is no use keeping troops in reserve. The best cards should be played out at once. A few hours always decide the fate of the engagement; and Turkish history affords no example of battles fought from sunrise to sunset, like those of the west of Europe."

But it is quite possible, perhaps I ought to say probable, that the Turks, if they can avoid it, will never give the Russians a chance to get grips of them in the open. It is known to me that in the Russian headquarters sagacious and far-seeing men looked forward to the contingency that the Turks, after making as stout a defence on the Danube as opportunity may offer, may draw off with their forces as little broken as possible, and leaving but mere garrisons in their fortresses, fall back uninterruptedly before the Russian advance till they gain the last shelter of the defensive position outside Constantinople, their design in this ignoble movement being the hope of forcing English armed intervention in the defence of Constantinople against a Russian attempt to take the capital. This idea will appear to most impartial persons as somewhat far-fetched, but without for a moment admitting it as worth considering, it is likely enough that the Turks will exercise extreme caution in giving battle in the open to, or accepting it from, their northern adversaries when the latter are in any respectable force.

The correspondents who have received permission to join the army are for the time detained in Bucharest by a vexatious change of the style of insignia by which they are indicated. We were, in the first instance, supplied with a huge brass brassard which was supremely ugly, but answered the purpose well enough. Some gentlemen of delicate sensibilities found, it appears, that this ticket imparted to the wearer a colourable resemblance to a railway porter, and suggested the alteration which is now being carried out. If I miss the crossing, what will it avail me that my arm be girt by a badge of gold lace with silver letters on it, and for the which I shall have myself to pay?

CHAPTER VII.

THE FIRST PASSAGE OF THE DANUBE.

Mystification of the Turks at Rustchuk—A Successful Torpedo-laying Expedition mistaken for a Repulsed Attack—Starting for the Campaign—A Field Equipage—A Search for the General—The Russian Soldier on the March—Brilliant Gathering at Alexandra—Crossing of the Danube at Galatz—The Bridge at Braila—The Departure from Galatz—Landing at Matchin—Fighting with Turks and Circassians—Inspection of a Torpedo-launch—A Visit to Matchin—Preparation for the Second Crossing—The Suite of an Emperor—A Princely Escort—Disappearance of the Commander-in-Chief.

THE period of mere preparation was now rapidly drawing to a close, and on all sides were apparent signs of movements, any one of which might issue in events of the first importance. As usual false alarms were raised, feints were taken seriously, and reconnaissances interpreted as attacks; meanwhile the Russian troops stood ready to advance to half a dozen points of crossing as they might be directed. The following letter from Rustchuk shows the kind of activity which was kept up by the Russians to the eve of the passage of the Danube:—

Δ RUSTCHUK, *June 23rd.*—The Russians have made an attempt this week to cross the Danube in the direction of Kiritach, above Pirgos, between the Ottoman picquets Nos. 6 and 8, at a distance of about two hours and a half from Rustchuk. Protected by the Wallachian forts at Parapan, the Russians advanced at seven o'clock on Wednesday morning upon the Roumanian island indicated on the map by the name of Gura-Kame. Their object was to fortify themselves on this island, in order to protect the invading column. In my opinion this movement was not a mere demonstration, or trap to draw on their adversary, but a serious attack upon a point which, compared with other defences upon or near the right bank, was certainly weak. The enemy aimed at a surprise, reckoning upon the skilful and effective fire of the batteries at Parapan, which, however, is very inferior to that of the Turks, whose guns, having a longer range, have caused terrible destruction, while the Russian shot scarcely reach the Turkish shore. Nevertheless, the struggle assumed larger proportions, and the situation was becoming extremely serious, for the Russian reinforcements were constantly arriving on the island, which it was the object of the Turks, by every means in their power, to prevent them occupying. Once fortified, the island of Gura-Kame would have commanded a strategical point of importance for the protection of their tête-de-pont and the passage of the Danube. The Turks quickly perceived the object of the movement, and were not slow in adopting measures which seriously impeded the enemy's advance. While awaiting reinforcements the Turkish artillery directed their batteries upon the fortifications of Parapan; at the same time the Ottoman monitors *Seareth* and *Haireddin*, and two armed tugs, attacked the enemy's flank upon the island, pouring in shell which almost all burst. At half-past ten a strong detachment of Circassians and frontier guards mingled their musketry fire with this artillery duel while advancing upon Gura-Kame, in order to take the island by assault and disperse the enemy. From this moment the combat became very brisk on each side, nor was either combatant wanting in dash or courage. Victory was for some time doubtful. The Turks, inferior in numbers, saw themselves exposed to the danger of a retreat; but, emboldened by their faith that they are fighting for a just cause, and encouraged by that verse of the Koran which promises them felicity in another world, they faced the enemy's fire with coolness. At noonday a reinforcement of regular troops took part in the struggle; and, protected still by the fire of the Turkish monitors, succeeded in triumphantly dislodging the Russians, who, notwithstanding that superiority in numbers to which I have already referred, precipitately evacuated the island of Gura-Kame, falling back under shelter of the forts of the village of Parapan, and carrying with them their dead and wounded.

In this encounter, which is certainly the most serious we have had upon the Danube since the commencement of hostilities, it would be unfair to omit to acknowledge the courage and audacity of the Turkish troops, who throughout this affair exhibited the utmost firmness. At four o'clock that afternoon the Russians, intending to make their enemy pay dearly for their defeat, suddenly directed five torpedo launches at full speed toward the Ottoman monitors, which had taken up a position not far from the island; but this enterprise failed, for once more the vigilance of the Turks baffled the terrible engines of their enemies. Having been an eye-witness of this incident, as well as of the combat in the morning, I was able to perceive that two of these torpedo vessels were seriously injured; one of them in particular had manifestly suffered some damage to her machinery. This struggle of a whole day, which marks the commencement of active hostilities on the part of the Turkish army on the Danube, may seem at first sight of trifling moment; but, on glancing at the map and noting the strategic importance to the enemy of this position on the right bank, it must be admitted that the Turks in repulsing their redoubtable enemy have achieved a not insignificant victory. The largest share in the triumph of this day belongs of right to Brigadier-General Hassan Tewfik Pacha, and to Lieutenant-Colonel Enim Bey, chief of the staff—the latter of whom in particular was enabled by his reconnaissances to choose the most favourable points for securing the success of the Ottoman troops.

At sunset the Turks, having perceived behind the Wallachian village of Slobosia a column of the enemy's troops, directed upon this point a heavy fire from the forts of Hizir-Baba, at Rustchuk, while one of the lunettes of this fort destroyed the fortifications of Slobosia. The steady aim of the Ottoman artillery, and the precipitate flight of the enemy, gave reason to suppose that the latter had sustained serious losses. At half-past seven that evening four Russian steam vessels, having been observed in the act of coming out of the channel at Giurgevo, were bombarded by the batteries of the fort of Inhudjuk and compelled to return. One of them was greatly damaged by two shells. At ten o'clock in the evening a torpedo boat, which had lain concealed during the day behind the scrubs of the great island opposite to Giurgevo, darted swiftly in the direction of a vessel of the Turkish flotilla; but the frontier guards and the sailors who were keeping strict watch received their assailants with a brisk fire of musketry, their efforts being seconded by a couple of cannon shot. The torpedo boat, thanks to the darkness, was not hit, and she succeeded in making her escape at full speed.

By the 23rd of June it was well understood that the Russian army was in movement with a view to the passage of the river, but correspondents were left to find out for themselves where the crossing of the Danube was most likely to take place.

* ALEXANDRIA (WALLACHIA), *June 23rd.*—On the afternoon of the 21st inst. my companion and myself finally cut adrift from the civilization of Bucharest, and set forth to join the army. It may be said we should have done so earlier; but it has been my invariable experience that a person belonging to or accompanying any part of an army, save its principal head-quarters, knows rather less of the doings of that army as a whole, and has less information concerning the general progress of events, than is at the disposal of any community in Europe who care to read. When, therefore, the specific section of an army to which one belongs or is attached is actively engaged in its portion of the task of making history, it is good to be with it, because you have first-hand knowledge—often the knowledge that eyesight brings—of what is going on, whereas the rest of the world can have at the best but secondhand knowledge. But while your division or army corps is doing nothing of importance, and when what of importance in reference to the future it may be engaged in the correspondent is prohibited from writing about, there is open to him only the rôle of vegetating, if he joins himself to it thus prematurely. It appeared that the crisis of action was so near that there would be little opportunity for vegetating to a correspondent now linking himself for the campaign to a specific section of the army in the field.

Our equipment may be worth a few words of description. I had found a carriage which, when covered with leather and fitted with sundry wells, makes a sufficient habitation for two men who can pack tight and can give and take one with the other. By a simple arrangement the floor of this vehicle becomes at night a bedplace, the cushions doing duty for a mattress. In case of rain, there is a projection from the tilt of the waggon which enables us to sleep perfectly dry; when the weather is fine our moveable bed-chamber is open to the front. In the wells is an assortment of provisions—tea, coffee, tinned meats, &c., with cooking appliances of extreme simplicity, for no inns are to be expected on the other side of the Danube, and it is not wise to trust wholly to hospitality, however generous you know it to be. With a covered receptacle for luggage behind, the waggon is complete. It is drawn by two sturdy grey horses, one of which is blind—a characteristic which his vendor cited as an important merit, since it made him steadier in a crowd. I have a riding-horse besides; a big, rather violent bay who has a will of his own, which yields only to *force majeure.* The horses are looked after by the coachman, a Roumanian Jew of exemplary stupidity, and we two are taken care of by Andreas, my old servant of the Servian campaign, who seems to speak a little of every known language, and has a wonderful faculty for finding fellow-countrymen in the most unlikely places. But the waggon I have described is not a waggon only. Cunningly contrived in a roll on the roof of it is a canvas house. All that one has to do is to unloose a couple of buckles and there unrolls itself a wide spread of canvas roofing. In the centre of the rolls are a couple of poles, and so when the contrivance is fixed there is a pleasant canvas drawing-room as a lateral appendage to the waggon. What does one want more than this for occupation by day, with a little table and a couple of stools, the waggon for a bed-chamber, and for kitchen a hole in the turf on the lee-side of the "eligible modern residence"? I think of taking the affair back to England with me after the war, and saving house rent during the summer months by inhabiting it, if only I could secure a good "pitch" for it—say the garden of Grosvenor Square, or in the inner circle of the Regent's Park.

My companion in the waggon, myself on horseback, we made our start, bidding farewell to friends military and civil, all bound later on the same errand, but probably along different paths, and jogged gently along the Giurgevo road. We passed Jilava, where three weeks ago General Radetsky, chief of the 8th Corps, had his headquarters, and a little further on Kerate, where at the same time abode General Dragomiroff, whose division, the 14th, we were on the way to join. Now Jilava and Kerate had lapsed into their wonted stillness, for the wave of the Russian advance had passed over the pretty villages, and Radetsky and Dragomiroff are—well where they are is just what I should like to know. A little beyond Kerate the road crosses the Argis River, and as we came round the turn to the bridge there came to us the sound of many voices joined in song. From the shadowy alluvial plain by the river's brink there was streaming on to the road the head of a column of Russian infantry—a brigade of the 32nd Division of the 11th Corps. I had made the acquaintance of this division and corps six weeks ago in Galatz, while they were lying there on the plateau above the bridge of Barbosch and on the broad plain behind Braila, deluged fifty years ago with the blood of Russian soldiers. The white caps showed in a dense mass among the willow trees of the Argis; it was as if a mighty host was pouring through the little plain, so far stretched the concourse of stalwart soldiers. This army is a white army now, white to the last shred, save facings and boots. Officers and men wear a loose white canvas blouse, which is the perfection of a campaigning garment for warm weather. The white of it is not so pronounced as to dazzle in the sunshine, nor do the dust of the road and the stains of the bivouac foul it into absolute dinginess. It can be washed and dried in an hour; it is loose enough to allow thick underclothing to be worn under it, when in this unaccountable climate burning heat turns suddenly into searching chilliness; it allows the freest ventilation, and withal is becoming, when once the conventional idea of military clothing is got rid of. I do not know whether it is an advantage or the reverse that when the soldier is thus clothed in white canvas it is impossible to tell to what regiment or division he belongs. The only indication of this is found in the number engraved on the gold or silver shoulder-straps of the officers, which they transfer from their cloth tunics to their canvas blouses. Since the hot weather set in, the marching of the Russian soldiers has been done as much as possible in the early mornings and late evenings, and frequently indeed in the dead of night. Bucharest people used to ride out in the afternoon to see a regiment or a brigade under canvas in the picturesque glade there behind the big unfinished chateau. Morning parties have been made up to go and visit the camp, reported so picturesque by the visitor of the previous day. But the excursionists found themselves disappointed of the spectacle they had got up to witness. There would be nothing left in the leafy glade but smouldering ashes, a few rags and bones, and a bad smell. These men of the 32nd Division had done a good march while the day was yet young, had halted to cook and sleep in the noonday heat on the bank of the Argis, and now in the cool of the after-day were recommencing a tramp of several miles more. The sun was yet very hot, and they were heavily laden, but they swung along with a brisk, long, firm pace in which there was no sign of falter or footsoreness. These Russian infantrymen, in the course of their long march from Russia and their camping in Roumania, have got into the very perfection of condition. Originally stout, hardy, well-built fellows, they have got rid of every ounce of superfluous flesh, are as hard as nails, and as brown as berries. Marching heavily laden at the rate of four miles an hour does not afford them sufficient vent for their energies; they must needs caper as they go when marching at ease, and when they halt there is always a dance. They sing the livelong day, and by night as well, when they are marching by night. Nor is their song a mincing, half-hearted strain. They sing as strongly as they march, as they dance, as they shout in social converse, as they indulge in horseplay, and as they will doubtless fight. They are physically a very masterful people, imbued with a vast force of energy that is neither fitful nor evanescent, yet withal, unlike most strong races, gifted with habitual patience, sweetness of temper and self-restraint, and their civility is as marked as is their sense of duty.

In front of the infantrymen we overtook several batteries of field artillery belonging to the same division. There is a want of finish in the aspect of the Russian artillery which probably interferes no whit with its practical efficiency. The traces are very long, so that the interval seems immense between the pairs of each team, and the pole almost trails on the ground when the draught is not on it. There is a cumbersome and heavy arrangement of swingle bars, and the attachments of the harness are clumsy. But the horses are good, and in tough, wiry condition, and the men seem smart enough. On each gun and waggon is carried a pile of hay, the evening's ration for the teams. The ammunition waggons are two-wheeled vehicles, drawn by three horses abreast, and on each is carried a bundle of branches lashed tightly together, doubtless to be used as impromptu fascines for filling up a rut or mending a bridge. At Kalugareni, on the banks of a little river about eight miles south of the Argis, we found already a large encampment of the same division, and an under-officer and two men from each company of the detachment still on the march, sent forward to take up ground for its camp for the night. These were already in position, waiting with little bannerets at the end of their bayonets. In this encampment no tents had been pitched; so fine was the weather that the men preferred to lie under the beautiful stars. Till the stars should come out they were cooking, bathing, mending their clothes, fetching their rations. The Russian soldier, contrary to received opinion, is a cleanly animal. He takes to the water like a duck. Sooner than not bathe at all, he will bathe in uninviting water. At the baths in Galatz there was constantly a long queue of Russian common soldiers waiting patiently for their turn to rid themselves of the dirt of the march and bivouac. In this little river the other night hundreds of naked men were splashing among the weeds and the frogs. Naked Cossacks were swimming about on their ponies, diving under them, hanging on by the tail, lying face upwards on their backs, and going through a series of antics that proved their aquatic expertness. Yet other Cossacks were coming in from the grass fields, their ponies laden with cut grass. In peace the Cossacks feed their own horses. Now this is not possible, and they draw supplies from the contractors; but the worst hay is thought good enough for Cossack horses, which are not the property of the State; and the patient fellows supplement the rations of their four-footed property by cutting grass in the fields and by the ditch-sides.

We should have been wiser to have gone on into Giurgevo for the night, but our way lay west of that town, and we were loth to go out of our road for the sake of a night's quarters. Near Fratesti we found a little wayside house, in the garden of which we located our waggon and horses, finding sleeping accommodation for ourselves in one of the two rooms of the cabin. Ere the night was out we heartily wished we had camped in the garden, for the mosquitoes made our lives temporarily miserable. We had other nocturnal visitors in the shape of the officers of a battalion of the 32nd Division, on its march into Giurgevo. The battalion had halted for an hour in a field close to us, and the officers thronged into the cabin for a short rest. Not a man of them could speak anything save Russian, so our conversational intercourse was limited, but we were able to give them some tea, and effusive handshaking was indulged in. Outside the cabin a private soldier accosted me in German; the subject of his query, whether the Turks or the Russians were the stronger. Like all, or nearly all, the private soldiers of the Russian army who speak German, he was a Polish Jew, and like all the Polish Jews with whom I have spoken, he did not fancy the prospect of fighting at all, still less of fighting with the Turks. I think the Russians would have done better to have left behind the Hebrews in their ranks. There has been much trouble with them in Roumania, for two reasons—their propensity to desert and their addiction to theft; they have no stomach for fighting, and will run when they can get a chance. With a chorus of farewells the officers took their departure, rousing the battalion with a few loud words of command, and away it went striding through the white moonlight, the stillness of the midnight air broken by the strains of its marching song.

Next morning at six o'clock we started on our search after General Dragomiroff, who had invited us to make the campaign in his headquarters. It is not easy in these times to gain information beforehand respecting the whereabouts of a Russian general who happens to be anywhere near the Danube. The general commanding an army corps hangs a red flag over the door of his headquarters, and a division general a blue flag. If you can only find the flag you have hit the general off, but one is reminded of Mrs. Glass's recipe, beginning: "First catch your hare." I had, from information received, a strong idea that Dragomiroff was to be found in some village of the angle between Giurgevo and the Vede River, but there are many villages in this flat, fertile, uninteresting angle, and it was like looking for a needle in a bottle of hay. We struck the Giurgevo-Alexandria road at the village of Vieru, about six miles west of Giurgevo, and there, in a charming little encampment, we found Colonel Orloff's regiment of Cossacks belonging to the division of General Skobeleff. It was Colonel Orloff's camp and regiment which, when it lay at Malarus, below Giurgevo, the Turks had shelled so persistently from the right flank of their Rustchuk position. He told me that some two hundred shells in all had fallen in his camp without hurt to man or beast. But although Orloff was delightful, dispensing his Cossack hospitality under a parti-coloured awning as he sat on Circassian matting, he was unsatisfactory on one point. He asked me if I knew where was Dragomiroff, before I had the opportunity to put the same question to him. He knew nothing save that he had been ordered to the village of Vieru to wait there for orders, and that there had been heavy firing the day before at a place called Parapan, on the Danube, due south from his position, and within sight of it. From what I have learned since, I incline to think that the firing at Parapan represented Dragomiroff's presence there, throwing dust into the eyes of the Turks with a flying reconnaissance. Orloff would fain we had stayed and witnessed some of the manœuvres of his gallant Cossacks, but I would not dally in my quest after Dragomiroff. After drawing in vain several villages further to the south-west, in which I found, indeed, men of Dragomiroff's division, but no Dragomiroff, we reached the village of Putinein, whence several roads radiate; and here it seemed, if anywhere, I could obtain tidings of the man I sought. We applied to the major of a battalion stationed there, who told us that he knew where Dragomiroff was; that he knew where Radetsky was; but that he was sorry he was compelled to decline imparting that knowledge to me or any one else. I knew the officer was simply doing his duty, and he certainly was as courteous as he could be. His advice was to go to Alexandria, where I might probably find some one in authority who would consider himself, under the circumstances, justified in giving me the information I desired.

Now, from Putinein to Alexandria there are two roads, one the main road, the other more direct, but not so good, along a valley whose entrance is close to Putinein, but, as it were, round a corner. I had previously travelled this latter road, and knew how much more near it was than by the former, besides which I had just seen a general officer with two ladies drive in a carriage into the mouth of the valley. It occurred to me that this might be the General, for I knew that his wife had been with him a short time before, and might be with him still—so I determined on the valley road. No sooner had we turned the corner and were inside the mouth of it than I found myself among the carriages of a huge pontoon train snugly stowed away in this well-chosen hiding-place. I may write of it now, for before these lines are in print the pontoons will be on the waters of the Danube. There was a road left open through the centre of the mass of waggons, and our vehicle was traversing this, when a soldier followed at a full gallop, and, riding in front, stopped it. We had to turn back, and the officer in command told us that the valley road was "défendu pour cause," nor had he any information to give of Dragomiroff. So with tired horses we disconsolately jogged on toward Alexandria. On the upland which overhangs the left bank of the little river Vede, on the right bank of which stands the town of Alexandria, we found a very large camp, containing the whole, or nearly the whole, of the 9th Division, the sister division of the 14th, Dragomiroff's, the two together making up the 8th Corps. As we came down the hill to the bridge we passed a number of officers belonging to the staff of the Emperor, and among them rode Count Schouvaloff, an aide-de-camp of the Emperor and the nephew of the Russian Ambassador to the Court of St. James's. The Count gave me some intelligence which has already gone forward by telegram, and added that, if circumstances rendered it impracticable for us to find General Dragomiroff at once, he would speak concerning us to Prince Mirsky, the general commanding the 9th Division. Later he was good enough to come to me with the information that General Dragomiroff was for the present engaged in a reconnaissance in which it was impossible that we could join him, but that Prince Mirsky would be glad to see us in the morning.

Alexandria swarms with troops of all arms. Its streets resound with the clank of sabres and the tramp of armed men. Here is the staff of the Emperor; here is the mass of the staff of the Grand Duke, the Commander-in-Chief; here are grand-dukes, excellencies, and the staffs of half a score of generals. Every house is billeted full to the doorstep—I had almost said to the garden gate. Cossacks cram the shops, and grumble good-humouredly at the bad exchange for their paper roubles. Waggon trains an inch thick with dust grind continually along the broad streets, heading to the south and south-west. There is no getting a seat at the principal—and I should say the worst—restaurant; and as for a hack-carriage, all in the place are engaged three deep. But withal, singular order and system prevail. There is the very acme of bustle, but it is not the convulsive bustle of confusion; the huge machine is working with wonderful smoothness, and, let me add, with wonderful quietude and secrecy. This morning, at eight o'clock, the 35th Division, constituting half of the 13th Corps, began its march through Alexandria. The most adverse critic could not take exception to the condition and appearance of the men and their equipment. Of some the boots were much worn and occasionally dilapidated, but then a second pair hung on the back of the knapsacks. Bands played and men sang, and the fellows marched with a swing and a swagger that were eloquent of conscious power and well-assured confidence. The division, which continued its march apparently by one road, took a south-westerly direction on leaving Alexandria, following the road which leads to Simnitza. But that does not imply that Simnitza is necessarily its objective.

Prince Mirsky, when we called on him, told us he was marching on Monday to a point thirty versts from Alexandria, there to rendezvous with the other division of the 8th Corps. Of that other division Dragomiroff is the commander. The Prince courteously invited us to march thus far with him, and then either join Dragomiroff or continue for the campaign with himself, adding that as the 8th Corps was to constitute the advance, it would be the pleasantest to campaign with for more than one reason. It would have the brunt of the fighting when that should occur; it would have the first fruits of what supplies the Turks might leave in the country. So we settled to start with him on Monday, only we don't in the least know where we are going.

After all, however, it was not the active and vigilant correspondent above Rustchuk who was to witness the first Russian passage of the Danube, but his colleague near Galatz, whose telegraphic letter is here subjoined:—

† BRAILA, *June 22nd.*—The Russians have at last begun to cross the Danube. Contrary to expectation, the great move commenced at Galatz. Everybody supposed that it would be somewhere between Giurgevo and Turna Magurelle. That the Turks were of the same opinion is shown by the fact that they had concentrated nearly their whole army between Rustchuk and Nicopolis, their line diminishing in strength towards Silistria, while the Dobrudscha was almost deprived of

troops. The manner of crossing was equally unexpected and unforeseen both by the Turks and the spectators. On this side of the river during the last four days the Russians have been industriously constructing a bridge near Braila, just below the confluence of the old and new channels of the Danube. This work has been done within sight of the Turkish forces at Matchin and on the heights beyond; yet the Russians have been allowed to construct the bridge in peace and quiet. It was finished last night except a narrow space left open for the passage of boats. The Danube is still very high here. A great part of the valley is still under water, which, however, is rapidly subsiding. The bridge was constructed from both sides of the river at once, for the Turks allowed the Russians to cross over and begin the bridge on the Turkish shore at the same time as it was begun on the Roumanian. A great part was constructed on trestles, and it is only in the real channel, where the water is swift and deep, consisting of a space of perhaps a thousand yards wide, that pontoons have been used. The pontoons had been floated to their places, anchored to trestle work constructed on both sides at the same time. The trestle work is continued along the old channel towards Matchin on the road to the latter place.

A glance at the map will show two channels of the Danube, running nearly parallel to each other, from Hirsova, where they first separate, to Braila, where they unite, the old channel making a sudden turn to the left just below Matchin, forming a right angle. It is along the north or right bank of this stream that the road runs from Matchin to Braila, and along this road, still submerged, the Russians are advancing by means of the trestle work. How deep the water is along here I am unable to say, but the Russians are evidently going to push a bridge along this road until they meet with serious resistance from the Turks. That resistance they have not yet encountered, and how far they will be allowed to continue without opposition from the Turks it is impossible to say; but the fact is it was expected last night that all would be ready for the passage. This seems to indicate that the Russians mean to take to the water, which cannot be more than a few inches deep, when they come to the end of their bridge. The Emperor and his staff, and the Grand Duke Nicholas and his staff, were to come here last night, and the passage was to begin this morning at daybreak; but, owing to news yesterday from Ployesti, the departure both of the Emperor and the Grand Duke was postponed until to-day, and it was understood that the passage of the river was likewise postponed owing to the fact that a large force of Turkish troops had been discovered lying in ambush not far from the end of the bridge, where they were waiting quietly for the Russians to advance.

However this may be, General Zimmerman, who is in command of the operations here, suddenly disappeared from Braila during the night, and this morning, a little after daybreak, the people of Braila were awakened by the sound of artillery and musketry fire on the other side of the river, showing that the Danube must have been crossed, and that a fight was proceeding on the other side. The Turks had for some time occupied the line of the heights where the battle was raging. General Zimmerman had gone to Galatz, and crossed the Danube with two regiments of infantry, and a proportionate amount of artillery and cavalry, in a number of boats towed over by steam launches. The distance traversed in the boats seems to have been over three miles. That he should have succeeded, and have effected a landing in the face of the Turkish troops, is not a little remarkable. He had immediately attacked the height in front of Garbina and Vakareni, and the battle had been raging along the summit of these heights since daylight until now, two o'clock, when the Russians seem to have advanced as far as Zizila, about five miles from Matchin.

The object evidently is to advance as near Matchin as possible in order to turn the Turkish positions and protect the long bridge and partly inundated road over which a larger Russian force will probably soon make the passage. They will undoubtedly fortify themselves near Zizila, maintain themselves in this kind of detached bridgehead, and protect the passage of the main body, which will of course rapidly move to their assistance. The Turks probably were taken by surprise as usual, and although there was a good deal of artillery and musketry fire they do not seem to have made a very stubborn resistance on these heights, a fact which may be easily appreciated when we remember that the Russians made an advance from daylight until two o'clock of twelve miles, crossing a wide river, fighting their way, carrying the Turkish positions, and occupying the heights. The view from this side of the river has been splendid. From an early hour the inhabitants gathered on the river bank to watch the progress of the conflict. It is a beautiful sunny day. Nothing could be finer than the landscape seen from the Russian batteries just below Braila.

Beneath us are a number of tall-masted ships and boats, among which are several Russian gunboats, and beyond is the low-lying valley of the Danube, half submerged, with islands of trees and brushwood rising out of the water all over it. Then beyond, the houses and minarets of Matchin are distinctly seen, and behind them rise the heights occupied by the Turkish forces, here and there along which a few tents may be seen. To the left of Zizila white clouds of smoke are suddenly leaping out from the hill-side, rolling away on the breeze, mixed here and there with the cloud of dust marking the rapid movements of the artillery or cavalry, while the heavy booming of the guns, and the sharp crashing musketry fire, come borne to us, softened by distance, on the still summer air. We could not distinguish the infantry, even with our glasses, though cavalry and artillery were easily made out, and we could only follow the progress of the Russians by the rising smoke which marked the line of the advance.

The battle seems over for the moment. I have just made out what appear to be two or three batteries of artillery, and perhaps a couple of regiments of cavalry, dashing rapidly down the heights from Zizila towards Matchin, raising immense clouds of dust. I suppose them to be part of the Turkish forces retreating to the latter place. We have no details of the fighting yet. General Zimmerman has not returned, and his chief of the staff here, who is expecting him momentarily, knows nothing more of the movement than what he has followed by means of a field-glass. As soon as the General arrives I hope to give you full details of the affair.

10 P.M.—I have not been able to ascertain the number of killed and wounded on either the Russian or Turkish side, but reports are flying about which say that the Russian loss is heavy. A Russian doctor who crossed with the first detachment of eight hundred men informs me that he does not believe out of this number twenty men are left who have not been either killed or wounded. The Turks do not seem to have been taken by surprise at all, and appear to have made a very desperate resistance. They were seen before the troops crossed to bring down towards the spot where the troops would land mountain guns on horseback, and seem to have been aware of the Russian movement almost as soon as it began. Refugees coming in from the other side of the river this evening say that the Turks have abandoned Matchin and withdrawn to the heights above it, and that the Circassians and Bashi-Bazouks have pillaged the place. As I write the troops are marching through the streets, evidently on their way to the bridge, in order to be ready for crossing at daybreak.

† Braila, *June 24th.*—The long-expected move upon the Danube has at last begun. The great barrier to the Russian advance—the first Turkish line of defence—has at last been crossed, and the campaign has fairly opened. Although the river has been falling very slowly, and is but a few inches lower than it was a month ago, it had been evident during the last eight or ten days that the Russians would wait no longer, and that the advance was about to begin. In spite of the secrecy with which the Russian staff has attempted to surround its movements, it was a secret for nobody here that the passage was soon to be made, and many people besides, including the Turks, seem to have known the exact spot, or spots, where the crossing was to be effected. The pretence of secrecy at the Russian head-quarters is, to say the least of it, amusing. No one on the staff would tell you a word regarding the intended movements and dispositions, and although a very clever officer, Colonel Hasenkampf, has been detached for the service of the press, for the purpose of giving information to journalists, the information obtained from him in the course of the last month might be written by a skilful caligraphist on his thumb-nail. This mattered little to the journalist, because you only had to go out into the street, and ask the first man you met for any information you wanted, about the movements of the Russian army, in order to be fully satisfied. The whole Roumanian people knows, and reports the movements of the troops with the most punctual exactitude, and Colonel Hasenkampf's caution in this respect was of little consequence. Besides, as correspondents were not allowed to telegraph anything they knew, it mattered still less whether they knew anything or not; but the amount of secrecy, caution, mystery, and obscurity in which everything relating to the army was enshrouded, was highly impressive. Everybody went about nodding and winking to everybody else, held whispering conversations in retired corners, giving mysterious glances of intelligence with an air of conscious knowledge of tremendous facts, that was highly edifying, no doubt. But, alas, our secrets are, I am afraid, stage secrets, and it is only the actors who go about oppressed by the mysterious knowledge we possess of the hidden things that are known to all the world, and especially to the Turks. Like the famous General Boum, in "The Duchess of Gerolstein," we stand aghast when the first ragamuffin in the street tells us the exact position of the army, where the crossings are to be made, and shows us that "the plan has been discovered."

It is difficult for an ordinary mortal to understand why this pretence of secrecy should be kept up any longer by the Russian headquarters. It is a great annoyance to correspondents not to be allowed to telegraph anything, even of the most harmless character, relating to the army, and it certainly makes not the slightest difference to the Turks, who, in the Roumanian people, have thousands upon thousands of conscious and unconscious spies. The Roumanian papers can say anything regarding the movements of the army, and a Turkish spy can send his information over the Austrian frontier, there to be telegraphed with impunity, with a delay of only one day, without speaking of those private telegrams which seem to be relating to business, weather, politics, and many other subjects, and which are really nothing but ciphered messages in disguise. The fact is, that as long as the Russian army remains in Roumania, and until it has crossed the Danube, it is simply impossible to keep its movements secret, and if General Nepokoitschitsky thinks the Turks are in any way deceived with respect to his plans and intentions, then the General will himself be greatly deceived. It had been imparted to me several days ago, as a dark and terrible secret, that the Emperor was going to Braila to be present at the passage of the river, as also the fact that the headquarters was to be transported to Alexandria; but within the next twenty-four hours after this dread information had been conveyed to me I met at least two hundred people, and among them the bitterest enemies of Russia, who were quite conversant with all the details. The amusing part of it is that Colonel Hasenkampf, in imparting no information to the correspondents, seems to be labouring under the delusion that he is preventing the correspondents from obtaining information. Colonel Hasenkampf is, I am sure, a most competent military man, but I am afraid he is not deep and subtle enough to deal with modern journalists, who are by no means the innocent, confiding persons for whom the Russian staff evidently take them. For the last ten days the Russians have been building a bridge at Braila in full view of the Turks, who watched the operation with that calmness and tranquillity for which they are so much admired and so much praised, without firing a single shot. Correspondents were requested not to mention the fact that the bridge was being built, for fear it would be giving information to the enemy, and, as far as I know, they all kept their word until the last moment, in spite of the fact that they would have been informing the European public of nothing that the Turks could not see with their own eyes. However this may be, whether the Turks were blind, asleep, or wide awake, it mattered little; the passage of the river has been effected in the most brilliant and successful manner, and the first great difficulty which the Russians had to encounter has been virtually overcome, for the passage of the river, which has been effected here, is of far greater importance than has generally been supposed.

When I arrived in Braila on Friday morning, I found that operations had already been begun. At five o'clock in the morning the inhabitants were already on the alert, gathering in crowds on the river bank, to watch the fight that was going on at the other side of the valley, which could be followed very distinctly by the smoke and the firing. The scene, when I arrived on the spot, was a most interesting and animated one. The left bank of the Danube, at Braila, is 30 or 40 feet high. Below us lay the river gleaming brightly in the sunshine, covered here with boats, ships, steamers, and barges, which were unable to escape during the time of grace that was allowed to them after the declaration of war, and which the Russians have seized and turned to account for military operations. Further down was the bridge, lying low upon the water, stretching far across the wide, swiftly rolling stream, and losing itself apparently among the marshes and reeds on the other side; beyond were marshes, trees, brushwood, tall grass, waving reeds, and rushes, through which could be seen everywhere the gleam of water, showing that the whole valley was still submerged; still further in the distance, and nearly ten miles away, was the town of Matchin, lying at the foot of a mountain slope, with a confused mass of houses, and two tall white minarets, rising from amongst them, and clearly defined against the low range of mountains beyond. Down the river, the water, growing broader and wider and deeper, spread over the entire valley, until it seemed to take the dimensions of a lake, where, in the far-off distance, lay Galatz, dim and indistinct in a luminous haze, looking like a mirage city in a mirage ocean. On that range of mountains running down from Matchin, in the direction of Galatz, puffs and long lines of white smoke rose up from the mountain side, and were borne away on the air in thin fleecy clouds. The dull, booming, heavy sound of cannon, a distant roar of artillery, and the continued and rattling crash of small arms were borne to us in a softened kind of roll on the still, sunny air. It was there that the battle was going on; the Russians were already on the other side, and were attacking the

Turks on those heights, and the long lines and fleeces of white smoke marked the progress of the conflict.

A battle fought under such circumstances—one army advancing and carrying successive positions, the other retreating but defending the ground inch by inch—is a long affair. Slowly the two lines of smoke advanced along the range of hills towards Matchin, one pursuing the other, and marking the progress of the battle. Slowly the Russians drove back the Turks, following them from rock to rock, from point to point, from summit to summit, from hill to valley, and from valley to hill, over the irregular and uneven ground; and the roll of musketry continued from daylight until two o'clock in the afternoon, until they had reached the heights above the village of Zizila, where the Russians halted, satisfied with their day's work and the ground already gained. The roar of cannon in the early morning was the first intimation that the people of Braila had that the Russians were already over the river, and the manner as well as the place of crossing was altogether unexpected and surprising. Everybody had been deceived by the construction of the bridge already spoken of. This bridge had been in process of construction for about ten days. It had been nearly completed on Thursday evening, and everybody supposed that the passage would be attempted on the bridge itself, and the idea of an army crossing over in boats was one which had not occurred to anybody but to the general in command. I do not know yet whether it was ever intended that the passage should be effected by this bridge. It does not seem probable that it should have been the case, unless it had been the intention of the Russians to wait several days or weeks longer for the water to subside, for the road to Matchin, with which it was connected, is still so deeply submerged that it would be very difficult to cross in the face of a determined resistance; in fact, the road is so deeply under water in some places that even a horse could not pass without swimming. All these places must necessarily have been bridged, while trestle-work must have been constructed nearly the whole way, a distance of nearly eight or nine miles. It seems probable, therefore, that the bridge was constructed partly with a view of attracting the attention of the Turks to this side, and partly in order to serve for the purpose of transport across the river later on, when the real crossing should have been effected. If it was begun in the hope that by the time it should be finished the river would have sufficiently fallen to allow the passage of troops over the road on the other side, this hope had been abandoned when it was seen that the water was falling so slowly that possibly weeks would have to elapse before the road would be in a passable condition, and another plan had to be adopted. It became necessary to effect the passage in boats, and possibly in the hope that the attention of the Turks would be attracted to the bridge, it was determined to make the attempt at Galatz, where, although a great distance had to be traversed, the water was deeper and more navigable, and less obstructed by bulrushes and reeds. General Zimmerman, having assembled a great number of boats of all kinds, shapes, and sizes at Galatz, suddenly left Braila, where he had hitherto kept his headquarters, and went to Galatz. He had a sufficient number of boats to carry over about 1,800 men at a time, and at daybreak on Friday morning that number of troops was embarked and started across on the perilous adventure. The distance to be traversed in boats was nearly three miles, and when land was finally reached it was not terra firma at all, for the ground here on the edge of the water was a mere marsh overgrown with reeds and rushes, with the water all over it, too shallow for boats, but deep enough to make the further progress most difficult on foot. It had been hoped that the boats might manage to cross two or three times before the Turks received warning, but the latter apparently had received correct information of the projected movement, and when the first boat-load of Russians arrived they met with a warm reception.

Although I have already given a description of the positions by telegraph, the transmission is so uncertain, and subject to so many errors, that I had better describe them again, at the risk of repeating some parts of my telegram. A glance at the map will show the Danube running in two separate channels from Hirsova to Braila. The old channel, the one on the right, makes a sharp turn just opposite Braila at Matchin, and runs at right angles with its former course, until it rejoins what is now the main stream, three or four hundred yards below Braila. It was just below the point where the two streams unite that the bridge had been constructed; the road from Matchin running along the lower banks of the old channel reaches the river at this point, and in fact the bridge has been built on the spot where the crossing is usually effected by means of a ferry. The whole valley of the Danube here, as well as this road, is still for the most part under water. Behind Matchin, supposing the observer to be standing at Braila, will be seen the range of low mountains or hills extending from Matchin in the direction of Galatz, opposite which place they diminish to a low narrow point, or promontory, which, rising out of the water, appears to be probably considerably higher than it really is. It was just opposite this point that the Russians landed, and the Turks were posted here on this narrow range of hills, in front of the very spot which the Russians had chosen, and as soon as they came within range the Turks opened upon them a well-directed fire. They had only two pieces of artillery, however, and the Russians were sufficiently well protected by thick plank bulwarks that had been constructed on the side of the boats, and it was not until they began to disembark, and wade through the water knee-deep, that the fire of the Turks commenced to tell. Then the fight became a close and desperate one. The first 1,800 Russians who arrived were obliged to maintain themselves against a very superior number of Turks until the return of the boats with a second lot, which they did by taking shelter wherever they could find it, by advancing part of the way up the heights and taking cover behind rocks, and otherwise availing themselves of every advantage which the ground offered. It is difficult to account for the fact that this inferior force of Russians was not overpowered and driven back into the water by the superior numbers of the Turks, but the fact is that they managed to hold their ground until they were reinforced by the return of the boats. When it is remembered that the distance to be traversed was something like three miles, that the only means of locomotion was rowing across the deep water, and using poles to push the boats along where the water is shallow, as it was for a great part of the distance, the courage and tenacity of the Russians will be thoroughly appreciated.

It seems that the hardest part of the fighting, and the greatest loss of the Russians, occurred at this time, and their position must have been a most critical and trying one, as they had absolutely no means of retreat; they had either to fight or to surrender. The Turks seem to have charged them with the bayonet, and the fight became a close and a hot one, though the small numbers engaged on both sides accounts for the small loss suffered by the Russians. Several Russians were killed and wounded by bayonets, and it is said that even the two or three hundred Turkish cavalry charged, or attempted to charge them, and some of the wounded had sabre cuts, to show how close had been the contact with the daring Turkish horsemen. These latter seem to have been Circassians, and the Russians say they fought like tigers. They succeeded in isolating and surrounding an advanced detachment of some fifteen or twenty Russians, and cutting them off to the last man, and in spite of a fire that was poured in upon them, and which caused them very severe losses, they got down from their horses in order to mutilate the dead by cutting off their noses and ears and hacking the bodies into as many pieces as they possibly could. Altogether the Russians say that the Turks behaved with the utmost bravery and resolution, but the fact that an inferior number of Russians was enabled to effect a landing and maintain its ground in the face of more than twice the number of Turks would not seem to confirm this assertion. At any rate, as soon as the boats arrived with a second lot the tide of battle began to turn, and the Turks from acting upon the offensive were soon obliged to defend themselves. Altogether two regiments, or about 6,000 Russians, crossed over in the morning with four pieces of artillery, and the Turks soon began to give way. The Russian artillery, however, proved to be useless, owing to the nature of the ground, which was so marshy that it was impossible to bring the cannon into action until it was no longer needed. As soon as the two regiments had landed they began to push the Turks hard, and, climbing up the heights on both sides, soon succeeded in carrying them. The Turks only retreated to the next hill, and again made a stand, and they were again pursued by the Russians, until, after driving them from hill to hill, they gained the heights above Zizila, where the combat ceased, the Russians having lost 200 men in killed and wounded.

The Turks seem to have had only 3,000 men here, with half a battery of artillery, and about 300 cavalry. The Russians advanced no further than Zizila on Friday, but it soon became evident that as soon as they wished to advance to Matchin they would meet with little or no resistance. About three o'clock I perceived the Turkish cavalry and artillery retreating from the last position, opposite the heights of Zizila, down the hillside towards Matchin, at full gallop, and I judged by the rate they were going that they would not stop even at Matchin. In the night, people coming over from that town informed the Russians that the Turks had abandoned the place, and during the night the Cossacks entered and took possession. Matchin was in the hands of the Russians, and the passage of the two army corps stationed about here was thus secured. Nothing further of any interest occurred during the night at Braila. The cafés and the restaurants, and the café concerts—for there is a café concert in every hotel—were full of people, Russian officers and inhabitants of the town, all discussing the events of the day in a most animated and lively manner. The streets were alive with people, the tread of troops marching through the town, as we believed, on their way to the bridge, to begin the crossing at daybreak. The people of Braila did not know that the road beyond the bridge was as yet quite impracticable for either cavalry, artillery, or infantry. A hard fight was looked for the next day, when the Russians should begin the passage, and everybody was on the alert at daylight to watch the splendid spectacle which would then be spread out before them. Daylight came, however, and no troops were seen about the bridge. The sun rose and grew hot; ten o'clock came, and there was no sign of troops. Then the arrival of the Emperor drew everybody's attention for a while in the opposite direction. He had passed through Braila at three o'clock in the morning, without stopping, had gone on to Galatz, visited the hospitals there, looked up the positions, assured himself that the detachment across the river was quite safe, and then came back to Braila to visit the positions there. He went away again at twelve o'clock, and people again began watching the bridge, and the river, and the boats. I had not been able to find General Zimmerman the whole of the previous day, and he did not return to Braila until about seven o'clock on the morning of Saturday. I managed to catch him about eleven, and was received in the most cordial manner. He immediately gave me permission to telegraph anything I chose about the events of the preceding day, for, owing to the obstinate stupidity of the Roumanian telegraph officials, no one was allowed to telegraph, even to announce a Russian victory, simply because they had received a general order, forbidding the transmission of anything about the movements of troops. I may remark that the stupidity of the Roumanian officials does not stop even here. No telegrams are allowed to be sent in the English language, although the English newspapers use the telegraph wires here more than all the other papers in the world put together. A correspondent is obliged not only to make a translation of his telegram, but to send the translation and not the original. The reason given is that there is nobody in the employ of the telegraphs who understands English. The idea of employing some man who does understand English is, of course, far beyond their intelligence.

The General informed me that he had not a moment to spare, as he was just going to start over to Matchin, whereupon I immediately asked permission, as a means of prolonging the interview, to accompany him. He laughed at the request, and observed that he suspected that it was rather to see Matchin than to see him that I wished to go; but he granted permission nevertheless, and put me in charge of an officer, Captain John Rogouly, of the Imperial Russian Navy, who conducted me down to the river-side, showed me everything that was to be seen there, and among others presented me to Lieutenants Shestakoff and Dubasoff, the two young officers who blew up the Turkish monitor with a torpedo. I was in luck that day, for Lieutenant Shestakoff invited me to go to Matchin with him in his torpedo launch, an invitation which I was very glad to accept, as I wished to see these famous boats, and observe their machinery and the manner of handling the torpedoes. I was soon on board, and Lieutenant Shestakoff, while swallowing a hurried dinner of roast mutton and salad, gave me an account of how the monitor had been destroyed. The launch was only about twenty-five feet long, with about four feet beam. The torpedo spars, of which each boat carried two, were about thirty feet long. They were placed one on each side of the boat in large iron rings fore and aft, which maintained them in a horizontal position when not being used. The torpedo is attached of course to the forward end of the spar. The torpedoes were taken off before we started, and I had no very great wish to look too closely into the mechanism of them, but I observed that they were about twenty inches in length by probably fifteen inches in diameter, covered apparently with wood. When used, the torpedo bar is thrust forward through the rings until it is only supported by one, and the torpedo on the end of the spar may then be hoisted up and down as on the end of a lever. As it would be difficult to steady it in this position, as soon as it enters the water, as it must do before it strikes the enemy's ship, there is a very simple contrivance arranged for this purpose. Across the bow of the boat, a couple of feet behind the stern, is placed a horizontal piece of wood, which projects about eighteen inches over the sides. Descending from this perpendicularly into the water nearly to the depth of the keel are two bars of wood placed just the distance apart to allow the torpedo spar to work freely up and down between them. These bars, with the aid of the forward ring, enable the operator to run the spar out at the proper moment to strike the bottom of an enemy's ship. It is well known that the force of a torpedo only acts within a radius of ten feet, and as the spar is thirty feet long the boat is thus at a safe distance from the explosion, except the danger of its being filled and swamped by the column of water which the torpedo inevitably throws up. The launch is an ordinary wooden one, covered over with a wooden deck, supported by very slight wooden or iron uprights. The sides from a little above the water are protected by plates of iron, a quarter of an inch thick, loosely fastened on to the uprights, and sufficient to stop a bullet, leaving exposed about four inches just below the deck for a crew to fire through in case of need. Neither the bow nor the stern, however, were protected in this way, and the launch coming end on would be exposed to be traversed from stem to stern by the enemy's bullets. As is well known, not a single bullet had ever penetrated the boat or wounded a man, although the launch must have been for several seconds within twenty feet of the monitor, and the Turks had fired probably more than 100 shots at her at that distance. The reason was that it had not occurred to them to fire down through the deck, which was only of wood, and all their bullets had been expended on the iron plates, which were of course impenetrable.

In the course of an interesting conversation with Lieutenant Dubasoff I found that a couple of errors had crept into the account which I have already given of the destruction of the Turkish monitor. In the first place the electric battery was not attached to a belt round the officer's body, but it was simply fixed in a little box in the stern of the boat. The system I have mentioned exists likewise, but it was not used upon this occasion by either Dubasoff or Shestakoff. In the next place, the torpedo was made to explode by contact, but it was arranged to be fired likewise by an electric battery in case the shock should not have been sufficient to explode the torpedo. The wire, too, which seems to have been used, was much larger than I had supposed to be necessary, being composed of a number of wires twisted together, forming a small cable more than a quarter of an inch thick. The first torpedo which was fired by Dubasoff was exploded by contact, while that of Shestakoff was fired by means of the electric battery. I find that the working of the engine made a great deal more noise than I had expected, and learned that it could be worked either at a very high rate of speed, or almost noiselessly, at a great expenditure, however, of steam. The expenditure of steam is so great that it cannot be kept up more than twenty minutes at a time, and as the time required to steam from Braila up to where the monitors were lying was nearly two hours, they had to stop several times to get up steam. The result was that daylight had almost come upon them before they had reached the vicinity of the monitors, and they finally decided not to attempt approaching silently, but to bear down with full head of steam, making as much noise as on ordinary occasions. This was the reason that their approach had been detected by the Turkish sentinel. Steaming round the point at the confluence of the two streams, which point looks like a green woody island, but is completely submerged, we were soon rushing gaily up the old channel of the Danube towards

Matchin. In an hour we came to the monitor which had been sunk first by the batteries at Braila. The mizenmast is still erect about twenty feet out of the water, and the mizen shrouds still retain their proper positions, which would seem to indicate that the stern of the ship at least had not gone to pieces. The only other part visible is the jibboom, which is broken back and projects eight or ten feet out of the water. A mile further on we came to the second monitor which had been blown up by the torpedo, with the mizenmast like the other one still standing, and no other part of the ship visible. We steamed gaily over the wreck, and I think that Lieutenant Shestakoff takes a grim delight in passing over it every time he goes by, as he does two or three times every day, and it seemed to me there was a thrill of exultation in the throb of the engines as the little boat glided over the body of the mighty monster that lay crushed and vanquished beneath.

General Zimmerman took with him three steamers loaded with men, each steamer towing two barges, which were lashed one on each side of it. These barges were protected on the side opposite the steamer by huge wooden bulwarks, built up to the height of a man, with loopholes through them, quite thick and strong enough for protection against a bullet. But a shell striking them would, I fear, have made sorry havoc among the men on board. Besides these three steamers and six barges, there were any number of small rowing boats which had started some hours before, and which we met near Matchin. In all General Zimmerman took over on this expedition about 2,000 men, with four pieces of artillery. No caution was used in coming up to the place, as Matchin was already full of Russian troops, and as we approached we saw the Russian sentinel on a little knoll overlooking the town and the river, where only twenty hours before had been seen a Turk. As soon as the inhabitants saw the boats coming they formed into a procession, and came down to the shore to meet us with banners, holy pictures taken from the churches, and various other religious emblems. They were led by three priests and some other Church dignitaries in full canonical robes, who met us chanting a hymn. General Zimmerman took off his cap and kissed the little wooden cross that was presented to him, while with a bunch of green leaves they splashed any amount of holy water over his head, and in fact almost drenched him. Each of those who followed were treated with the same copious shower-bath, and as the day was hot and we were all in a terrible perspiration, the ordeal, to which I submitted with as much grace as possible, was by no means an unpleasant one. The people then greeted us with loud hurrahs, and marched after us, manifesting the most extravagant joy, especially the boys, whose delight was as unbounded as it was troublesome. Nevertheless, in spite of something that was grotesque about it, all this reception of the conquerors by the conquered, of the invaders by the invaded, has a profound political significance which the Turcophiles, if there be any such people left, would do well to ponder. These people, instead of looking upon the Russians as enemies, and conquerors, and invaders, and oppressors, hail them with delight and satisfaction as their deliverers from a degrading and terrible bondage, which Europe has condoned and sustained too long. These same people would have hailed Englishmen with the same delight as the Russians, had English help but come in time.

To-day the inhabitants of Matchin are all Christians; the Turkish population, who were in a small minority, fled soon after the declaration of war, carrying away all their worldly goods. A great part of the inhabitants, too, are Russians, of the sect known as the Old Believers, who emigrated from their own country, and settled here on the banks of the Danube more than a hundred years ago. They still speak Russian, and wear the costume of the Russian peasant. The rest of the inhabitants are Bulgarians and Wallachians. We took a walk through the town. It had a strange, lonely, deserted, dilapidated look, partly owing to the fact that the houses formerly occupied by the Turkish population were quite untenanted, that the shops had not yet been opened after the previous day's scare, and partly because a Turkish town always has this dreary, tumble-down, unkempt appearance. We looked into the windows of many of the Turkish houses, and saw the empty, abandoned rooms which had so lately been inhabited, and which looked all the sadder and more melancholy because of the thought that came unconsciously into one's mind, that their owners would never come back again. We looked into the mosque. The doors were wide open as usual, and the floors strewn with dirty matting, dust, and litter, showing that it had not been used for many weeks; but there had been no desecration on the part of the Russian soldiers, no defilement of the house of worship, no insult flung at Allah. I remarked this particularly; I, who had seen so many Christian churches defiled and desecrated in Bulgaria. The verses of the Koran were still written on bits of board or paper, and hung round the walls as though they were expecting the Mussulman worshippers of Allah back again; but high up in the minaret beside it, whence the mullah was wont to call all good Mohammedans to prayer, stands a Russian sentinel—emblematic, perhaps, of the long struggle between Mohammedanism and Christianity, and ominous of the end.

From the mosque we went to the Konak, the residence of the Kaimakan of Matchin. It was rather a large, fine, well-looking house, one of the best Konaks of the Kaimakan that I remember ever having seen in Turkey. But not a stick of furniture of any kind had been left; all had been carried off in the hurried flight of the Turks. The floor of nearly every room was almost a foot deep with papers written in Turkish, torn to pieces and trampled about on the floor. They were the archives of Matchin, the records of titles and deeds of probably all the property in the district. The Turks, it is well known, keep their archives and records on scraps of paper which are tumbled promiscuously into bags that are hung on nails around the walls, and these papers may have been emptied out here on the floor and destroyed for the sake of getting the bags in which they were contained. Everything, in fact, about the place looks as though the Turks themselves had gone away never expecting to come back again.

The Russian soldiers found something which pleased them mightily here. This was a room filled half way up to the ceiling with tobacco, old, musty, and partly rotten, which they carried off in armfuls, like hay, with the greatest glee and satisfaction. The detachment here will now for some days have no lack of tobacco, such as it is. We walked about the streets, and finally sat down under the porch or pavilion belonging to one of the Russian inhabitants, who gave us excellent Turkish coffee, preserved rose-leaves, and Turkish tobacco, from which we rolled and smoked any number of cigarettes, and right glad I was to have once more the taste of real Turkish coffee, compared with which coffee in the European style is but a drug and a medicine. Then General Zimmerman held a review of all the troops there, and afterwards we got into a boat and steamed back to Braila. On the way back I was introduced to the young officer who had built the bridge, Captain Klemenka, and as he offered to take me over it and show it to me, I accepted the invitation. It is a splendid piece of work, strong enough to carry over the heaviest artillery, and is evidently made to last a long time. The first 1,600 feet from the Roumanian shore is trestle-work, built along over the railway, which before the inundation ran down to the edge of the river, where it was met by the ferry-boat. Part of the railway has been swept away, and even that which remains is still under water, and the bridge is now some five feet higher than the railway track under it. The bridge is made of immense wooden trestles on benches, exceedingly strong and solid, and they are put down on sleepers which lie along on the ground. Over this is laid a roadway of planks which is only wide enough for one waggon or cannon to pass. At the end of this trestle-work we come to the bridge proper, which is not constructed on pontoons, but on immense rafts. The length of this part of the bridge is 1,750 feet, and there are 50 rafts in all. These rafts are composed of long pieces of beautiful timber, whole trunks of trees from 60 to 80 feet long and from 15 to 20 inches in diameter at the large end. From eight to ten pieces compose each raft, and they are solidly bolted and fastened together, and anchored with strong hemp cables to heavy iron anchors dropped in the bottom of the river. The roadway is laid over this, as over the trestles. At the Turkish end we come to what was formerly the village of Getchet, which is a village no more. It was a place of probably 25 or 50 houses, not one of which is left standing. It was first demolished by the Russian batteries to drive away the Turkish outpost that was stationed there, and when Captain Klemenka began his bridge he found it necessary to continue the roadway to the other end, which was for the most part under water, in the best way he could. He simply used the débris and rubbish of these houses and walls to make a road, which is built right over the foundation of the houses. In no other way could he get a sufficiently solid foundation on which to build. The road, therefore, goes zigzagging about from house to house, with a piece of bridge here and a piece of trestle-work there, pieced into the chaussée in the most curious manner; but this new roadway has not been continued up over the old road for more than a mile, and there remain some five or six miles to be made yet before troops can pass over it. Altogether it is a most creditable piece of work so far, and does Captain Klemenka great honour. It will be ready, however, in four or five days probably, and then the 14th Corps, as well as the 4th, which is up in the direction of Reni, will perhaps cross over here. This crossing is of far more importance than it was at first supposed it would be. As the Turks have retreated to the Kustendjie Railway, the Russians are now in virtual possession of the whole of the Dobrudscha. It is impossible to understand Turkish strategy in thus leaving the Dobrudscha almost entirely unprotected. They do not seem to have had altogether more than 8,000 or 10,000 men here, and they must either have been convinced that the Russians would not attempt a passage at this place, or they must have decided to completely abandon the Dobrudscha, and allow the

Russians to cross with comparatively little opposition, in the hope of being able to crush them later when a Russian force, advancing from this side, should have reached the dangerous quadrilateral of Silistria, Rustchuk, Varna, and Shumla. A few more troops here would have made the passage of the Russians a most difficult matter, and although the great bulk of the Russian army is certainly between Giurgevo and Turna Magurelle, they still have two army corps about Galatz, Reni, and Braila, a force of about 70,000 men—an army quite large enough to make the Turkish positions about Rustchuk most critical, as soon as it should be able to get so far. It is, of course, impossible to say what the Turkish plan may be, but it certainly looks as though they had no plan at all, and that, as usual with the Turks, everything is left to the care of Allah.

It remains to be seen now what task will be set the 14th and 4th Corps—whether they will march on to Varna and Shumla, or whether they will begin the siege of Silistria. As it would take at least three weeks for those corps to march down and turn the positions of Rustchuk, it does not seem likely that the Russian armies between Giurgevo and Turna Magurelle would wait for the assistance that might thus be rendered to them. It is more likely that they will attempt the passage at once, and that ere this reaches you the telegraph will have recorded another passage of the Danube.

As soon as time for reflection had been allowed, it was perceived that, important as General Zimmerman's advance might be, it was not into the Dobrudscha that the Grand Duke Nicholas would be likely to lead the main body of his army, and attention was again therefore directed to the middle section of the Danube. Two days before the crossing the position of this force was described in the following letter:—

* LISSA, WALLACHIA, *June 25th.*—Our camp in Alexandria was in a garden nearly opposite the headquarters of Prince Mirsky, the general commanding the 9th Division of the 8th Corps. The *mot d'ordre* from his Highness, who had been so kind as to allow Mr. Villiers and myself to accompany his headquarters, was that we should be ready for a start early this morning. While we were striking the tent and packing the waggon, while as yet the sun was low in the sky, clouds of dust on the adjacent road told us that a great cortége was passing. This was by no means the first cloud of dust that had risen this morning on that much-trodden road. Long

before sunrise the cheering from the camp of the 9th Division, on the bluff over against the town, had told us that the regiments composing it were beginning their long day's march, and, as each marched out, that it was answering the kindly greeting of the general who was watching the outmarching in the chill grey dawn. Later the long column had defiled along the road through the town, bands playing and men singing with that fervour which the Russian soldier, no matter how heavily laden, always throws into the marching song. Behind the regiments or interspersed between them had rolled the heavy wheels of the cannon, and there had followed the column and the waggons of the telegraph train and the miscellaneous articles of the baggage and provision convoys. The division had passed on, bag and baggage, with no show or glitter, but with an appearance of genuine efficiency that betokened readiness for whatever fortune might send—a march across Europe, or a fight before the next meal. But this later cortége had a certain splendour and pretension. At its head rode staff officers gay with aiguillettes, horses prancing, and sword scabbards glittering in the sunshine. Then came an escort of mixed cavalry, Cossacks of the Guard in blue and gold; hussars, blue, brown, red, and green; lancers, with pennons of vivid hues; field gendarmes, and strange-visaged Asiatic servants. Behind the escort came a long cavalcade of handsome led horses, chargers of noble proportions and high mettle, and there were fourgons and caleches of wondrous size and multitudinous compartments, all designed to make campaigning a luxury instead of a hardship to which adventure gives the zest. Coachmen in plumes of peacocks' feathers; English grooms; valets, smiling sublimely from luxurious depth of cushions; cooks contemplating nature from the box seats of portable kitchens—all betokened something of much higher pretension than the headquarter equipage of a campaigning general. It was the suite of the Emperor on the march, but without the Emperor at its head. Now that actual war is imminent, the Imperial suite is a little forlorn. It does not belong to the field army, as does the less imposing suite of his Imperial Highness the Commander-in-Chief; in point of fact it does not seem to belong to anything in particular, but to be a cumbersome waif and stray. The Emperor is travelling with a modest personal accompaniment, consisting of Count Adlerberg and a practical general or two; his suite of Princes and Archdukes have been living for the last three days under canvas, in a wood somewhere on the environs of Alexandria, out of range of acquaintance with the progress of events. Now, they were on the road to take a similar camp nearer the Danube, whereabouts it was not my business to inquire. I have come to a resolution in relation to this war to ask no questions. What I see I shall try to describe, and with the description of what I see, I shall regard my work as done.

Presently Prince Mirsky sent a servant across to our garden to say that his little personal train was ready, and we fell in behind the waggon which contained the camp kit of his Highness. A soldier rode up to our carriage, and told us in excellent English that he was commanded by the general to serve as our escort. Russian private soldiers are not commonly conversant with English; yet this man, judging by his uniform, seemed nothing more than a "simple soldier"—an infantry man of the first regiment of the 9th Division, mounted on a nice little white horse. He wore the white blouse of the private soldier, with the red shoulder straps of the regiment; a bayonet hung from his waist belt. His loose trousers were tucked into his long boots. "Oh, yes, he had been in England several times; merely pleasure visits; he knew a number of people there, but was not good at remembering names; Lord Carington he had met several times." Here was a puzzling private soldier, truly. I left the carriage, mounted my horse, and joined him. We talked all the way to Piatra, and the more we talked the more I wondered to find in a private soldier a man who knew most of the capitals of Europe, who had seen in Berlin Count Seckendorff's water-colours, and who knew the details of the stampede of the troop horses of our Household Cavalry from their picquet pegs among the sands of Cove Common, who criticised the cookery of the Café Anglais, and whose brother is an aide-de-camp of the Emperor and the governor of a province. I am not good at asking people for their names, but as we rode down the hill into Piatra he casually mentioned that his name was Dolgorouki. I have had some strange experiences in my time, but never before has it fallen to my lot to have a Prince acting as the escort of my baggage waggon.

Our road lay at first down the right bank of the Vede River, and I imagined our destination was to be somewhere behind Simnitza. It must be understood that no information had been given to me respecting our halting-place, and that I had refrained from asking. All I was told was that the march was to be about eighteen miles long. But presently the Cossack, who was our guide, found himself slightly at fault, and there was a halt. Then I said that I knew the country, having made an excursion to Turna Magurelle, which I have described in a previous letter. So it was told to me that we were bound for Piatra. I had been to Piatra before, so I was able to supersede our guide. After leaving the river on our left rear, we reached a broad level plateau, cultivated to the last foot. Luxuriant crops of barley waved in the light breeze, already beginning to whiten unto harvest. To the south, beyond the verge of our green plateau, rose the shadowy dark blue of the high ground behind the Turkish bank of the great river. My companion gazed on it with interest, for it was his first view of the territory over which the Russian legions are soon to sweep. Journeying onward we overtook the rearguard of the division. It was high noon of a sweltering summer day, and the men had been marching since daybreak. We had passed but three men who had fallen out by the wayside, but it was clear that not a few were struggling hard not to fall out, and that nothing but pluck, and perhaps shame, kept them from succumbing. They trudged heavily along with bared throats, flushed faces, and parched lips. A few seemed on the point of having sunstroke, and were all but past replying to questions. Others, stronger and better inured, swung along more easily, and several carried the rifles of their less stalwart comrades in addition to their own. All the waggons were piled high with knapsacks, but there were few men in the ambulance waggons. There was quite a rush to a wayside well, and there was something almost terrible in the feverish eagerness with which the men drank. But there was no selfish struggling for the grateful water—no, the fellows took their turn contentedly, and some there were whose thirst was yet unquenched when the bugle sounded the "fall in," and who obeyed the signal wofully indeed, but without hesitation.

At length we had crossed the plateau, and there opened up at our feet the pretty valley in which lies so snugly the straggling village of Piatra. There were camps on every grassy slope, and in every meadow down in the green bottom. When I was last in Piatra a couple of dragoons sauntered leisurely up its broad street, and a village maid was washing linen at the fountain of clear water in the centre of its little Place. Now about the fountain was a concourse of thirsty soldiers; now dust filled the air raised by the tramp of a thousand men; now the throng in front of the little inn extended half across the road. There is but one house in Piatra, in our acceptation of the term; all the other habitations are mere huts, for the most part of wattle and mud. I had been looking forward to quarters in this one house, which belongs to a local boyard, and which is quite a palace in its way. When last in Piatra I had been courteously entreated in its dining-room, and had made the acquaintance of the ladies of the boyard's family. But, alas! as we neared the mansion, we saw that there waved from its gate the significant red flag. This betokened that the house was already occupied by a higher power, the general commanding the army corps. General Radetsky, as such, takes the precedence for quarters of General Prince Mirsky, who commands but a division, and we had to find our quarters further afield. We rode through the camps covering the green face of the plain that intervenes between Piatra and this village, our mark being the village church of Lissa, and hard by the church we found a little white farmhouse, surrounded by a wattled fence. Here were the headquarters of Prince Mirsky, who, indeed, travelling more swiftly by another route, had already arrived and taken possession. He occupies the only spare chamber of the little dwelling; his staff are in tents in the compound, in a snug corner of which also is our canvas habitation, under the shade of which I am now writing.

A great army lies around us. How great I am unable to tell. Serried batteries of artillery score the green slopes above us, the stoppered mouths of their cannon looking towards the Danube, the common objective of us all. Masses of white-bloused infantrymen are trampling up to the cooking places to eat their soup out of the huge camp kettles which hold each enough for half a company. The men have laid aside their arms, their fatigue has left them, their weapon now is but a spoon, they laugh and sing and gambol as they make for the steaming flesh-pots. "Let us taste the soup," says the Prince, and we go out of our inclosure, and down among the soldiers. The General has a kind word for his fellows, and they reply with frank, respectful manliness. The under-officer on duty over one of the kettles takes an extra suck at his wooden spoon by way of cleaning it, and hands it to me. The soup—well, I am not exactly sure that I shall send the recipe to my club and consider myself entitled to a vote of thanks from the committee. It is thick, and hot, and sour—and, what shall I say?—miscellaneous. It is not a dainty, but I suppose that many a time before the campaign is over we shall be glad to borrow the honest corporal's spoon, and take a turn with the others at the big camp kettle. In the meantime I prefer the recondite mess which Andreas has concocted over our little fire in the corner of the compound, and which amply consoles Villiers for the abandonment of the flesh-pots of Egypt, in the shape of the delicate, if costly, cookery of the Hotel Brofft in Bucharest. In Alexandria last night I met General Skobeleff the younger, who gave me a detailed account of the affair at Parapan some three days ago, to which I believe I cursorily referred in my last letter. Parapan is a village on the Roumanian shore about eight or ten miles west of Giurgevo. In view of the intention of pontooning the Danube still further west, it was thought expedient to set up a sunken hedge of torpedoes in the Danube to hinder the monitors which lie ordinarily at Rustchuk from interfering with the bridge. It was determined to lay down this hedge from Parapan to a point opposite on the Turkish bank. The night was spent in getting down through the marshes and bulrushes to the water's edge, and the real work of laying the torpedoes did not begin until daylight. It was a tedious process, for several islands at this point encumber the bed of the stream; but it was successfully carried out, and for a time Skobeleff and his little party stood on the Turkish bank. The work was interfered with by the Turkish gunboats which had steamed up from Rustchuk, and it was in dealing with one of them that Lieutenant Stridlin, in a tiny steam launch, displayed the conspicuous gallantry which I have already described in a telegram, in which however, owing to erroneous information, I laid the scene of his exploit at Rustchuk itself. After his dashing attempt the two gunboats sheered off, and the work was completed. But after it had been done, and when as yet Skobeleff's fellows had not got out of range, a couple of Turkish field batteries arrived at a trot from Rustchuk and opened fire on them. Their tardy arrival did not indicate much alertness; at the latest the alarm must have been given by daybreak, and they did not fire their first shot until after two. Owing to the presence of the gunboats on the watch lower down stream, it was thought well to get the little steam launch through the bulrushes to the bank, and to bring it away on an ox-cart. This operation had to be carried out under the fire of the Turkish field-guns, and the casualties were one officer killed and seven men wounded. Up to the present, even including the crossing of the Danube at Braila, the tidings of which reached us in Alexandria yesterday, the butcher's bill of the war is singularly light.

The problem of the day is, where can the Grand Duke be? I suppose Prince Mirsky knows, but it seems to me that nobody else does. The Commander-in-Chief of the Russian army, if his ability is only equal to his energy, ought to make himself a name among leaders. He is at once cunning and active. When he left Ployesti I came into Bucharest by the same train in which he travelled. He had not an ounce of baggage with him and drove away from the station in a hack carriage.

It was given out, as I telegraphed at the time, that he would return to Ployesti either that night or the following morning. He never did return. At three o'clock next morning, he started for Alexandria in a caleche with one companion. The four Roumanian ponies brought him the ninety miles without stopping, except for a drink twice on the road. He reached Alexandria at 1 P.M. of the following day, lunched with Prince Mirsky, and departed at 3 P.M. with a fresh team. Whither he went and where he is now are unsolved problems. But one problem is slowly but surely solving itself. It is certain now that the main column will cross to the west of the lake Jezeru, which projects into Roumania, and practically thus widens the stream of the Danube directly south of this place. Between the Bellona Picquet and the mouth of the Aluta is a distance of not greater than twelve miles, and between these two points it is now certain that the crossing must be made.

The Danube is said to have fallen very much. Some people are never content, and I heard a general complain that it was too small, and that the miasma which the drying marshes are evolving will poison the troops. He has, perhaps, got fever on the brain, for during a thirteen years' service in the Caucasus he had fever twenty-one times. But if it is not so now, I fear that later the Danube will take its revenge in its own way on the nation which essays to pass its broad stream. The people of Eastern Europe talk of the Danube fever in much the same strain as the planters of Northern Tirhoot speak of the "Terai" fever, which for months in the year isolates Nepaul from British India. The practice, which is irrepressible, of the Russian soldiers to plunge into cold water when heated is a provocative of fever in itself, and all the more so when the surface of that water has an impalpable layer of malarious emanations upon it. Of every war it is true that where battle slays its thousands, disease slays its tens of thousands, and there is no likelihood that in this campaign there will be any respite from the inexorable law.

26*th.*—Heavy rain all night; heavy cannon fire at Turna Magurelle against Nicopolis, and as heavy reply. We are just on the move; crossing probably to-night or, at all events, to-morrow night.

The following letter notices the reception of the news from Matchin at Constantinople :—

: : CONSTANTINOPLE, *June* 29*th.*—A vague rumour prevailed here for some days before the Russians crossed the Danube—namely, that they had renounced all intention of attempting the passage of the river. That the Czar had come all the way from St. Petersburg merely to go back as he came, was a story which could only find credence in a city like this, where the most extravagant statement finds many eager believers. The delay on the part of the Russians to pass over into Bulgaria was never attributed to the real cause—the high state of the water, and the determination of the Russian military authorities to have everything in the most perfect order before risking the passage. It was more convenient in Constantinople to say that the Muscovites were afraid, and shrank from the task they had set themselves to perform. When at length it was supposed concealment of the truth could no longer serve any purpose whatever, the Government thought fit to issue an official bulletin twenty hours after the Russians were on this side, as follows: "It is known that the Russians have for some time past been preparing to cross the Danube; and it is likewise known that the Ottoman military authorities attached no importance in a strategical point of view to the Dobrudscha, having only left there a small movable force, it having been impossible to concentrate a large body of troops in that part of the empire. From telegrams received here we learn that the Russians crossed the river on Friday night at Cara-Agatch—between Matchin and Isatchia. Although our troops did their duty, the Russians, regardless of the heavy losses inflicted on them, effected the passage in boats, coming over in successive groups, while our *corps de garde* retreated in good order." Such is the official version of this most important event, and since its publication the Government has followed its usual line of procedure—that is, to give no details whatever concerning the movement of the troops on the Danube. Brilliant victories are of course notified from Montenegro, and we are told of the recapture of Bayazid by the Ottoman forces, but of what most interests people here, whether the Russians are approaching this way or not, we are in complete ignorance.

The streets of Constantinople were surely never so full of strange faces and costumes as at this moment. Representatives of all the Mussulman tribes of Asia Minor, Arabia, and Egypt crowd the narrow streets and alarm timid visitors from Europe. Many of them are rascally looking fellows, and have already distinguished themselves by their cowardly behaviour. The police, however, keep a sharp look-out upon them, the Government knowing how dangerous it would be to have a repetition in the capital of the acts by which the Bashi-Bazouks are known in Bulgaria. That might offend the diplomatists of Pera. Therefore these men are sent off to the seat of war as rapidly as possible. The Egyptian contingent, comprising 6,000 infantry and 1,000 artillery men, arrived in the Bosphorus on Saturday. Eight steamers conveyed the men here from Alexandria, seven Turkish ironclads having acted on the voyage the part of protector as far as the Dardanelles to the Khedive's steamers and troops. Prince Hassan, who is the second son of the Viceroy, and who is also Egyptian Minister of War, is commander-in-chief of the contingent, and has for the time being taken up his abode in his father's palace on the Upper Bosphorus. In entering the straits from the Sea of Marmora the vessels were covered with flags, the sailors manned the yards, regimental bands struck up the Turkish Anthem, and considerable excitement prevailed amongst the Turks on shore as they continued for some time to shout, "Long life to the King of Kings!" When Prince Hassan stepped on shore he and his suite were at once conveyed in Court carriages to Yildiz-Kiosque, where the Sultan was awaiting his arrival. The Prince, it is said, will follow his troops to the field after a few days' rest here. He has already made one start, but has returned. If, however, his Highness be no more successful on this occasion than he was in the Abyssinian campaign, he might just as well have remained at home. A Minister of War at twenty-four years of age is hardly likely to make a brilliant display anywhere, even though he be a prince. If he had the genius of his ancestor, Mehemet Ali, much would naturally be expected from such exceptional gifts; but notwithstanding all the advantages he has derived from education and travel, he has up to the present moment displayed very little indeed of the military capacity of him to whom he owes his rank and fortune. The Abyssinian defeat is a sufficient measure of Prince Hassan's ability as a soldier. The Turks, too, at this moment are by no means rich in military talent, so far as commanders are concerned, and their friends ought rather to regret than behold with satisfaction another appointment which is exceedingly unlikely to enhance the military glory of the Ottomans. Along with the 7,000 auxiliaries, the Khedive sent 1,000 Remington rifles, 1,000,000 cartridges, one battery of cannon, and three steam launches for service on the Danube. With the exception of one vessel, all the others, with the contingent on board, left on Sunday for the Black Sea amidst a tremendous downpour of rain. Indeed, from the moment the vessels came to anchor in the Bosphorus, the rain hardly ceased coming down in torrents—a most unusual occurrence at this season. The Turks say the floods on the Danube have been caused by the Prophet's intercession, so that the enemy should not be able to cross. Whether the same agent sent thirty hours' continued rain here in honour of the Egyptians, it would, perhaps, be difficult for the most devoted adherent of the prophet to determine. The Sheik-ul-Islam, the Grand Vizier, the Minister of War, and others have been in constant attendance on Prince Hassan since his arrival.

CHAPTER VIII.

THE CROSSING AT SIMNITZA.

The Point of Passage—Banks of the Danube at Simnitza and Sistova—General Dragomiroff's Plan—The Turks on the Watch—Embarkation of General Yolchine's Troops—The Passage opposed—The Turkish Shell and Rifle Fire—Russian Losses—Landing of Yolchine's Brigade—Tenacity of the Turkish Artillery—Battle on the Slopes—Appearance of a Turkish Monitor—Continuance of the Crossing—An Hour's Fight of a Monitor with Four Torpedo Launches.

THE passage of the Danube by the advance guard of the main body of the Russian army was effected at Simnitza, on the 27th of June. The following letters describing this operation were transmitted by telegraph:—

* SIMNITZA, *June 27th.*—Returning yesterday evening to the headquarters of the 9th Division in Lissa, I received some information which led me to ride direct to Simnitza. I was told there would be two attempts at crossing the Danube, one at Turna Magurelle, the other from Simnitza to Sistova. The latter was understood to be more important, and I chose it. Reaching Simnitza, I found there the whole of the 14th Division, commanded by General Dragomiroff. The 14th is a division of the 8th Army Corps, commanded by General Radetsky. General Dragomiroff was in the midst of the preparations for crossing.

Let me first describe the locality. Simnitza is almost opposite the long straggling Turkish town of Sistova, which lies in a plateau above and in the hollows of a precipice overhanging the Danube. Below Sistova, for a distance of two miles, the Turkish bank is steep, in places quite precipitous, with here and there little hollows, and above the river-side are steep wooded slopes, covered with gardens and vineyards, leading to a bare ridge forming the sky-line. Two miles below Sistova is a narrow, marked depression in the Turkish bank, leading up from a little cove, formed by the affluents of a small stream. Above, and to the right of this cove was a small camp of Turkish soldiers, fixed there, doubtless, in consciousness of the weakness of the point; and above the camp on the sky-line was a battery of heavy guns. Between the cove and Sistova several cannon were disposed under cover of the trees, and immediately on the proper right of the town was a small open earthwork, armed with a few field guns. Sistova is an open town. Probably in and about it there was not more than a brigade of Turkish troops, but then it is not distant more than a long day's march from either Rustchuk or Nicopolis. So much for the Turkish side. About Simnitza the Roumanian bank is high; but between it and the Danube proper, which flows close to the Turkish bank, is a broad tract, partly of green meadow, partly of sand, partly of tenacious mud, the whole just emerging from inundation. This flat is cut off from Simnitza by a narrow arm of the Danube, so that it is really an island. A raised road and bridge leading from the town across the flats, to the landing-place on the Danube, have been wrecked by the floods. It was necessary, therefore, for the Russians to gain access to the flats by a short pontoon bridge. These flats are still in many places under water, are scored by intersecting streams, and studded with impracticable swamps, so that the road through them is now difficult and tortuous. They are quite bare, except that at the lower end, exactly opposite the cove on the Turkish side of which I have spoken, there is a wood of willows and alders of considerable extent, and capable of affording a good deal of cover. The Danube all along the Sistova position is about sixteen hundred paces wide, and flows very rapidly. There is a low island opposite Sistova, but it has no interest in the present narrative. The ground on the Roumanian side shows a sloping face to the higher Turkish bank, so that it is impossible to bring troops into Simnitza unobserved. Hence, probably, the Turkish preparedness, such as it was. The attempt was, as far as possible, to be of the nature of a surprise, and it was necessary, therefore, to postpone the dispositions till after nightfall. The Division Dragomiroff had the post of honour, and was expected to make a footing on the Turkish side by early morning. The Division Mirsky, in support, was to make a night march from Lissa, and be in position at Simnitza at seven A.M., to follow its sister division across in the event of the latter's success. In the event of failure, it was to take up the fighting, and force a passage at all sacrifices; for the Archduke Nicholas had announced that he would take no denial. The river had to be crossed at Simnitza, cost what it might. Other divisions stood within call if need were. The waters might be reddened, but they must be crossed.

With the darkness General Dragomiroff had begun his dispositions. The first work was to plant in made emplacements a row of field guns all along the edge of the flats, to sweep with fire the opposite banks. This was while his infantry was being marched over the flats down into the cover of the willow wood. The darkness and the obstructions were both so great that all was not ready till the first glimmer of grey dawn. There was no bridge, but a number of pontoon boats, capable of holding from fifteen to forty men each. These were dragged on carriages through the mud, and launched in the darkness from under the spreading boughs of the willow trees. The troops embarked, and pushed across as the craft arrived. Dragomiroff stood on the slimy margin to bid his gallant fellows "God speed." He would fain have shown the way, for he is a fighting as well as a scientific soldier, but it was his duty to remain till later. The grateful task devolved on Major-General Yolchine, whose brigade consisted of the regiments of Valnisk and Minsk, the 53rd and 54th of the line. The boats put off singly, rowing across for the little cove, and later the little steam-tug *Annette* was brought into requisition. For once, the Turks had not spent the night watches in heavy sleep. Their few cannon at once opened fire on the boats, on the hidden masses among the willows, and on the columns marching across the flat. Nor was this all. From the slopes above the cove there came at the boats a smart infantry fire. The Turkish riflemen were holding the landing-place. Yolchine has not gained experience and credit in Caucasian warfare for nothing. His boat was leading. The Turkish riflemen were in position about fifty yards from the shore. He landed his handful, and bade them lie down in the mud. Several were down previously with Turkish bullets. He opened a skirmishing fire to cover the landing of the boats that followed. One by one these landed their freights, who followed the example of the first boatload. At length enough had accumulated. Young Skobeleff was there, a host in himself. Yolchine bade his men fix bayonets, stand up, and follow their officers. There was a rush and a cheer that rang louder in the grey dawn than the Turkish volley that answered it. That volley was not fired in vain; but the Turks scarcely waited for cold steel. Yolchine's skirmishers followed them doggedly some distance up the slope, but for the time could not press on far from the base. Busily, yet slowly, the craft moved to and fro from shore to shore. The Russian guns had at once opened when the Turkish fire showed that there was no surprise; but however heavy a fire may be, it will not all at once crush another fire. The Turkish shells kept falling in the water, whistling through the willows, and bursting among the columns on the flat. One shell from a mountain gun fell into a boat containing two guns, their gunners, and the commandant of the battery. The boat was swamped at once, and all on board perished. This was the only serious casualty; but numerous Russian soldiers were falling on both sides of the river. Nevertheless, the work was going steadily on, and when, soon after seven, I returned to meet Prince Mirsky on the high ground before Simnitza, the report was, that already the whole brigade of Yolchine had reached the other side, that a Russian battery was there, and that Dragomiroff himself had crossed. We stood for some time surveying the scene.

Cast your eye down there to your left front, athwart the flats, and note the masses of troops waiting there, or marching on towards the cover of the willows. See the long row of guns in action there by the water's edge, covered by the battalions of infantry, in this case a mischievous conventionality, owing to the exposure, for the Turkish cannon will not just yet be wholly silenced. Note how deftly the Russian shells pitch into that earthwork on the verge of Sistova. But the gallant gunners stubbornly fight their guns under the rain of fire, and when one gun is quiet, another gives tongue. And what a mark! Half an army corps out there on the flat, with no speck of cover save that patch of willows down there. Hark to the crackle of musketry fire on the wooded slopes rising out from the cove. No wonder Yolchine's skirmishers are moving, for that Turkish battery on the sky-line is dropping shells with fell swiftness among the willow trees. Sistova seems stark empty. It might be a city of the dead. But the Turkish gunners cling to their posts and their guns with wonderful stanchness, amidst clouds of dust thrown up by the shells which burst around them. Nor are the single pieces among the trees wholly quiet. Shells are dropping among the troops on the flat, and the ambulance men are hurrying about with brancards, or plodding towards the Verbandplatz, with heavy blood-sodden burdens. You may watch the shells drop into the water, starring its surface as they fall, as if it had been glass. What a wonder that one and all should miss those clumsy, heavy-laden craft which stud the water so thickly! A shell in one of those boats would produce fearful results among the closely packed freight. Not less fell havoc would it work among those soldiers further on, massed there under the shelter of the clay-bank. One realizes how great would have been the Russian loss if the Turks had been in any great force in the Sistova position, and how, after all, the Commander-in-Chief might have been forced to take a denial, accepting the inevitable. But as the affair stands, the whole thing might have been a spectacle specially got up for the gratification of the people of Simnitza, enjoying the effect from the platform high ground overhanging the flats. The laughter and bustle there are in strange contrast with the apparent absence of human life in Sistova opposite. But then Sistova was a victim lashed to the stake. The spectators on Simnitza bluff knew their skins were safe.

Prince Mirsky has received his reports and final instructions. He gives word to his division to move down on to the flats, to be in readiness to cross. Previously, their march finished, they had been resting on the grassy uplands behind Simnitza. As we leave the plateau the cry rises that a Turkish monitor is coming down the Danube. Sure enough near the head of the island is visible what seems to be a large vessel with two funnels moving slowly down the stream. Now the ferry-boats may look out. Now is the opportunity for some dashing torpedo practice. But the Russian officers evince no alarm—rather, indeed, satisfaction. The fact is, as we presently discern with the glass, that the seeming monitor is really two large lighters lashed together, which the Russians are drifting down to assist in transporting the troops. No person is visible on board, yet some one must be steering, and the course held is a bold one. Slowly the lighters forge ahead past the very mouths of the Turkish cannon in the Sistova Battery, and are barely noticed by a couple of shells. They bring to at the Roumanian shore higher up than the crossing place, and wait there for their freight. Prince Mirsky takes his stand at the pontoon bridge to watch his division file past, and greet the regiments as they pass him. But in front of the 9th Division comes a regiment of the brigade of riflemen formed specially for this war, and attached to no army corps. This brigade is armed with Berdan rifles, and comprises the finest marksmen of the whole army. Prince Mirsky's division is made up of four historic regiments which suffered most heavily in Sebastopol during the great siege. They are the regiments of Yeletsk, of Sefsk, of Orloff, and of Brianski, the 33rd, 34th, 35th, and 36th of the Russian line. Very gallantly they march down the steep slope and across the bridge on to the swampy flats. Soon there greets them a scarcely enlivening spectacle, the Verbandplatz of the second line where the more serious cases were being dealt with before forwarding them to the house hospitals in Simnitza. As we passed, about twenty shattered creatures were lying there on blood-stained stretchers waiting their turn at the hands of the doctors. More than one I noticed required no further treatment than to be consigned to a soldier's grave. Beyond the first swamp we met a fine young officer of the Guards, carried on a stretcher with a shattered leg. But the plucky youngster raised himself jauntily on his elbow to salute the General, and wrote a telegram in my note-book to acquaint his friends that he was not much hurt. A little further on, as we were passing the rear of the guns, the Grand Duke Nicholas, the younger son of the Commander-in-Chief, rode out from the battery to greet our general. The members of the Imperial Family of Russia do not spare themselves when other subjects of the Czar are exposing themselves on the battle-field. In Russia it is not the fashion that lofty station gives exemption from the more dangerous tasks of patriotism. The young Grand Duke had been across the Danube, and was in high spirits at the success of the enterprise. Some distance further on we passed the second Verbandplatz whither many wounded had been brought. It was within range of the Turkish batteries about Sistova, and the mud around was pitted with shell-holes. But the Turkish fire by this time was nearly crushed by the steady cannonade of the Russians.

Here I may speak of the very efficient work of the Russian ambulance service belonging to the army. The ambulance force is strong, and the casualties were well within its compass, so that the work went like clockwork. The younger surgeons and the ambulance men were continually up among the fighting men, and the moment a soldier was struck he was attended to. If severely injured he was put upon a stretcher and carried off after simple bandaging. If lightly wounded he left the field on foot, assisted by one or two of the ambulance men. The first destination of all was the Verbandplatz of the first line, where the ambulance waggons were always waiting. The slighter cases went away sitting in the waggons. The severe cases were put on stretchers and taken to the Verbandplatz of the second line. The only hindrance was the deep sand and the deeper mud which impeded all movement and sorely distressed the wounded retiring on foot. Amateur help was present in plenty towards the end of the day, but, if not a nuisance, was at least a superfluity so far as concerned the work in the field. The wounds were severe in a large proportion. The Turkish shell practice was remarkably good.

Going still forward towards the willows we all but stuck, horses and all, in the deep holding mud. It was admirable to see the energy with which the heavily laden soldiers of the infantry-column battled on doggedly through obstruction. I should have said earlier that the troops were in complete marching order, and that for this day they had discarded their cool white clothing, and were crossing in heavy blue clothing. Two reasons were assigned for this. One, the greater warmth to the wounded in case of lying exposed to the night chills. The other, that white clothing was too conspicuous. The latter reason is rubbish. Blue on the light ground of the Danube sand is more conspicuous than white. Everywhere British scarlet is more conspicuous than any other. The true fighting colour is the dingy kharki of our Indian irregulars. After the mud we met a batch of prisoners under escort. Most were Turkish irregulars, defiant-looking, ruffianly, splendid fellows, a few were nizams of the Turkish regulars, gaunt-faced, but resolute-looking, and there was a squad of miscellaneous civilians, Turks and Bulgarians. Just outside the willows was a place where the dead who had fallen there had been collected. The bodies were already swelling and blackening under the fierce heat. The living soldiers stood around the corpses, looking at their dead comrades with concern, but with no fear or horror. The grass under the willows was littered with rags of the linen and bits of clothing, showing that the shells had not fallen thereabout for nothing among the masses of men gathered there in the early morning. One or two shells were still dropping as we reached the water's edge. All the Turkish opposition had seemed crushed, but it was not so. There was a regular little battle raging on the slopes above the cove where the landing had been made. The Turks, it appears, had rallied and concentrated on the upper slopes in front of their battery on the sky-line, and, gathering heart, had come down on the picquets of the brigade Yolchine, whose line had perhaps been scarcely sufficiently fed by reinforcements, as they landed at first. The Turks had made some headway and may have encouraged themselves with the hope of driving their northern foe into the Danube; but only for a moment. Men fell fast in Yolchine's skirmishing line, but it pressed upwards irresistibly. We saw the Turks falling back in trickling little streams, and the battery ceased to fire, and no doubt was removed for fear of capture. For soon after noon the Russian infantry had crowned the heights and settled themselves there, looking down into the interior of Bulgaria, with the Danube conquered in their rear. The Turkish infantry detachment tried to work round and down upon Sistova, but was thwarted by an intercepting skirmishing force, which got into position *à cheval* of the road from Sistova, and thus it would appear cut off the Turkish guns, which had been in the earthwork near the town. No attempt was made to occupy Sistova. That work is reserved for to-night.

And what of the Turkish monitor? She had been hemmed in by a cordon of torpedoes within the side channel to the south of the island of Vardim. Although she was puffing and blowing furiously in her circumscribed area, a Russian battery moving down the river bank on the Roumanian side shelled her into a melancholy victim of the acknowledged supremacy of the newest war machine. So the resistance terminated, and what followed is mere routine work. Iron pontoons began casually to make their appearance both from up stream and down stream, and accumulated about the crossing place, being used for the time as ferry-boats. A complete pontoon train is in reserve at Simnitza, and will be on the water's edge to-night and be laid to-morrow. Probably there will be two bridges, for this is the crossing place of the main column, and will be the great Russian thoroughfare to and from Turkey. Simultaneously with the pontoon boats appeared on the scene the Emperor's brother, the Grand Duke Nicholas, with General Nepokoitchitsky, and spoiled my prospects of dinner by requisitioning the whole hotel. The Emperor did not turn up.

The crossing has been effected by a *coup de main* with marvellous skill and finesse. Until the last moment no hint was given. The foreign attachés were nearly all abroad. The Emperor and suite were ostentatiously at Turna Magurelle, and yet further to promote the delusion, the Nicopolis position was assiduously bombarded the day before. The successful effort has probably cost only a thousand men killed and wounded. By to-night, or at furthest to-morrow morning, the whole of the 8th Corps will be across, and the brigade of riflemen as well. To-morrow follows the 35th Division, and later come the whole of the 12th Army Corps, the whole of the Cavalry Division of Skobeleff, the whole Cavalry Divisions of the 8th and 12th Corps, and probably the 13th Corps, to stand in reserve near the Danube, while the column pushes on over Tirnova. One hundred thousand men at the lowest computation will march in this column, practically an irresistible force. Nicopolis yesterday was laid in ashes. It is reported that an attempt was made at Turna simultaneously with that at Sistova, but I believe that the real attempt there was to be made last night by the 31st Division of the 9th Corps. The Grand

Duke Nicholas and General Nepokoitchitsky have received the Grand Cordon and Cross of St. George from the Emperor.

* SIMNITZA, *June 29th.*—I take up my narrative of the crossing operations at the time when my telegram of the 27th was despatched. During the whole afternoon, evening, and night, the troops kept crossing as quickly as circumstances would permit. The number of boats was augmented in the course of the day to about three hundred. General Dragomiroff followed up the retiring Turkish infantry, who fell back in the direction of Rustchuk. Their rear maintained a desultory skirmish till the summit of the heights was reached, and then they ran for it, pursued for a short distance by the Russians, both infantry and Cossacks, the latter being in but scanty numbers. Just as night fell General Dragomiroff brought up a battery of horse artillery in pursuit, which kept up a brisk fire for some little time. Since then perfect quietude has reigned. The great camp of the Russian troops is now on the plateau behind the sky-line of the heights. Up to the present time the following is the strength now across the Danube—three infantry divisions, the 8th, 14th, and 35th; the artillery of two divisions; one brigade of riflemen; two regiments of Cossacks, and miscellaneous detachments.

Sistova was occupied on the afternoon of the 27th. A detachment of Cossacks wound up the glen of Jerkir-Dere, at the mouth of which was the landing-place. It then inclined to the right, scouting along the footpaths, among the fields and gardens, poking its way cautiously along. The strongest detachment crept cautiously westward on Sistova. The leading files first peered into the shattered earthworks, where two dismounted field guns were found, and then gradually felt their way into the town, peering round the corners of the streets, and patrolling onward by twos and threes, until, with infinite patient circumspection, they had gone through the whole place. Some few houses which presented a suspicious aspect were entered. Sistova was found to be evacuated; scarcely any Turks were left. No cruelties had been perpetrated by the troops before withdrawing. The conduct of the Cossacks was most exemplary. No attempt was made at pillaging. Presently smoke began to rise from their little encampments in the gardens of the town, and they formed another camp on the slope over against Sistova. Some infantry followed the Cossacks into Sistova, but it remains with few troops quartered there. An infantry regiment is camped about midway between the town and the landing-cove to guard the Turkish end of the bridge which is being constructed further up the stream than the crossing-point of boats.

Yesterday about noon the proceedings of the crossing were temporarily interrupted by the sudden appearance of a monitor steaming slowly up the stream. It appears that she worked her way out through the lower end of the channel behind the island of Vardim, and had run the risk of torpedoes. Puffs of smoke rose from the Russian field battery opposite the western end of that island, and more distant reports betokened the return fire of the monitor. She passed the battery, taking its fire in so doing. This lasted about an hour and a half. There was a general rush back from the water's edge of the pontoon waggons. The infantry waiting to cross fell back for cover into the willows. The columns leaving Simnitza reversed their march, and there was something like a stampede of the baggage waggons. The bridge had already been begun, and it was felt that the monitor might do infinite harm. Her smoke drew nearer as she slowly steamed up the stream until at length she was in the same reach as the crossing place. There she stopped, and there she supinely waited for nearly two hours, neither moving nor firing a shot. The Russians made no attempt to dislodge her, so far as was apparent, but she inexplicably withdrew of her own accord, steaming away slowly down the river. All this arrested the crossing, the boats huddling up against either bank, and the construction of the bridge was also delayed, but it is just being finished as I write. The Emperor, with the Czarewitch, arrived yesterday morning, at eleven o'clock. His Majesty immediately visited the wounded, who number about 400, some in tents, some in houses. They are to be sent back by the Giurgevo and Bucharest Railway. At Fratesti two fully fitted-up sanitary trains are waiting, one from Dresden, the other from Moscow, under the charge of the Countess Orloff and a staff of trained lady nurses. The hospitals here are under the direction of Prince Tolstoi, working under Prince Tcherkasky, the head of the Red Cross organization. Several of the wounded died yesterday and to-day. In the afternoon the Emperor crossed the Danube, and went round the troops on Turkish soil, where he was received with tremendous enthusiasm. He visited Sistova, and returned at seven. He was urgent for the speedy completion of the bridge, and inspected the progress of construction both going and returning. In the evening he sent an aide-de-camp round the hospitals to distribute thirty crosses of St. George to the most valiant of the wounded. The Imperial head-quarters are in the chateau of the boyard of Simnitza, on the right of the town, and directly opposite Sistova. General Dragomiroff, who displayed skill and courage in no ordinary degree, will receive special distinction.

The eminent Russian painter Verestchagine, who was reported killed at Parapan, has only received a severe flesh wound, and is in the hospital at Fratesti. We are starving in Simnitza, but the Russian troops on this side are regularly rationed. Those crossing carried food for three days. A Cossack raid against the Bashi-Bazouks is said to be impending.

Some particulars respecting the visit of the Emperor to the trans-Danubian position may be interesting. He found the 9th Division on the left, the Rifle Brigade in the centre, the 8th Division to the right, and the 35th Division in reserve. He embraced General Dragomiroff, hailed him as the hero of the crossing, an honour shared by Yolchine and young Skobeleff, and gave him the 3rd Class Cross of St. George, the highest honour a division general can obtain. The Brigade Yolchine, as the first to cross, lined the Emperor's road into Sistova, and he addressed his valiant soldiers with a thankful greeting and warm praises of their valour. A Bulgarian priest received him at the entrance with a cross, and with bread and salt. The Czar kissed the cross, and tasted the bread and salt. He then went straight to the Bulgarian church, the Bulgarian women and children of Sistova strewing his path with flowers, and in the sacred edifice listened to a Te Deum and took the Sacrament. Much satisfaction is expressed at the pure Russian-hood of the Commanders of the crossing operations. General Radetsky, Prince Mirsky, and General Dragomiroff are of pure Russian birth. No crossing at Turna Magurelle was actually attempted, the resistance expected rendering the attempt unadvisable, but the plan obviously included the alternative. At Turna there was concentrated the same force as at Simnitza, one army corps and a half, and the Emperor, the Grand Duke, and the staff, were in the former neighbourhood. The weather is terribly hot.

Midnight.—I learn that a report has just arrived to the effect that a Turkish army has left Rustchuk, and is on its march towards Sistova, the position of the Russians. Prince Mirsky's division, which is on the flank next to Rustchuk, is intrenching itself as a precautionary measure, but it is the purpose and policy of the Russians to take the offensive and play out the bold game already begun by crossing the river midway between two armies, neither distant more than a long day's march.

† TURNA MAGURELLE, *June 29th*.—No crossing has taken place here, and probably none will take place. I always thought that the real attempt would not be made here. The report was so persistently spread that it must have come to the knowledge of the Turks, who concentrated a large number of troops at this point. The Russians, learning this, chose another way, made a serious demonstration against Turna, which they would have changed into a real attack had a fair chance of success offered, and up to the last moment it was, I believe, uncertain which point would be the real crossing—Simnitza or Turna Magurelle. The Emperor and his staff and the Grand Duke and his staff came here—a fact which soon became known to the Turks, who took it, together with other indications—the building of a bridge, collecting a great number of boats, &c.—as evidence that this would be the real point; but the Russian forces had been so placed in the villages in the neighbourhood that they could with equal ease fall upon Simnitza or Turna Magurelle. Before the astonished Turks could concentrate, the Russians had effected a landing at Sistova, and secured the passage. The Russians built a bridge here, as at Braila and Giurgevo. They had besides collected a large number of boats above the town at the mouth of the Aluta, and as there was a spot very favourable for passing by boats the feint would have been turned into a real attempt had it not been discovered that the Turks had already concentrated 30,000 men at this point, thereby necessarily weakening Sistova.

The Russian plan of action was this—to make a number of feints at crossing with sufficient material and number of men to turn each one of these feints into a real crossing should occasion offer. This forced the Turks to divide their forces to cover the whole line of the Danube, thereby rendering it weak at every point. They never really meant to cross in more than two or perhaps three places. The construction of the bridge was of very much the same kind of work as at Braila, with the exception that the trestle-work and road were constructed on the Roumanian side instead of on the Turkish. The materials for the bridge were collected, and on Wednesday night, at the same time as the passage at Simnitza, a demonstration was made which turned out to be only a demonstration, but it had all the appearance of a real attack. Hurrying from Braila, where I witnessed the passage, I arrived at Turna Magurelle about ten o'clock at night, and a strange terrible spectacle met my view as I came in sight of the town. When I began to descend into the valley of the Danube the first thing I perceived was the red flame of burning houses on the opposite shore at Nicopolis, of which there were several standing in a row, each looking in the distance like an angry burning coal, while there hung over the town of Turna what first appeared to be a monster comet with its head on the horizon, and its tail reaching to the zenith, extending across the sky in a broad flashy white light. It was an electric light employed by the Russians, or which was to have been employed by them, to light the other shore, show the positions of the Turks, and thus enable the Russian fire protecting the passage to be properly directed. Its pure white light formed a strange contrast with the red glare of the burning houses.

As we approached the town the roar of artillery and the boom of guns became more audible, until the whole valley of the Danube rang and echoed with the contending fire of the Russians and Turks. The hills on the Turkish side seemed to possess peculiar acoustic properties, for I observed that each report there seemed to be repeated a hundred times, growing in volume for several seconds, until even the report of small cannon produced an effect greater than the heaviest battery would under ordinary circumstances. My first impression on hearing this continuous roar, which seemed to be beyond the hills on the other side of the Danube, was that the Russians had already got across, and that a battle was going on on the other side of the river. It was not for some time that I perceived the real cause of this fearful uproar. The noise would have been deafening enough without this multiplication. The Russians were firing from three batteries above the town, composed two of mortars and one of heavy breech-loading 24-pounders. The Turks answered with might and main, supposing they were preventing the passage, while this passage was being quietly effected at Simnitza with scarcely more difficulty than at Braila. I believe some attempt was made to throw across a bridge to the right in front of Nicopolis, which bridge the Turks promptly destroyed. A move also was made above the town, as if to cross in number in the boats collected there. The corps marched down to the river-side. I myself was for the moment convinced that a crossing was really to be attempted. At twelve o'clock four batteries drove down to the road already made opposite Nicopolis, a considerable amount of infantry having preceded them earlier in the evening, and I thought a great effort was about to be made. But all resulted in nothing. The Turks showed in such force on the opposite side, and were evidently so well prepared there, that the risk was deemed too great, too serious a sacrifice of life being required to effect a passage. It was decided to wait the result of the affair at Simnitza. That having proved successful, the 9th Corps has received orders to march from this place to Simnitza, only a few troops remaining here to protect the positions and batteries. It is said that a real attempt will be made to effect a passage to-morrow night; but I do not believe it. The passage once secured at Simnitza, there is no necessity for another one here. Sistova is, in fact, an excellent point, as a road leads directly to the Tirnova Pass in the Balkans. The boats from the mouth of the river Aluta being floated down stream, under the Turkish guns, to Simnitza, to assist in the crossing there, the Turks fire upon them incessantly, but the great part succeed in getting through.

† TURNA MAGURELLE, *June 30th.*—A most interesting affair occurred on the Danube here during the operations attending the passage of the Danube—a fight between a Turkish monitor and four Russian torpedo boats. It was somewhere near the mouth of the Aluta. This monitor had been giving the Russians a good deal of trouble, and showed an amount of activity and energy very unusual with the Turks, continually shelling the Russian batteries, and destroying the boats. The Russians accordingly determined to destroy it.

Four torpedo boats were prepared, and sent against the monitor. Hiding behind an island, they laid in wait, and when the vessel was steaming past suddenly darted out from their hiding-place, and bore down on her in broad daylight. This monitor, it soon became evident, was handled and commanded in a very different manner from others with which the Russians have had to deal here. With wonderful quickness and skill she was prepared for action, and, nothing daunted by the fate of others, made a successful defence against her four terrible enemies, a defence of which the Russians speak with the greatest admiration. Her commander began by likewise thrusting out torpedoes on the end of long spars, thus threatening the boats with the danger of being blown into the air first, at the same time opening a terrible fire on them with small arms and mitrailleuse. He besides manœuvred his boat in a most skilful manner, with a dexterity and address which, with the torpedoes protecting, made it impossible for the Russian boats to approach sufficiently near. He besides tried to run them down, and very nearly succeeded in doing so. The reason soon became evident. The commander was a European, and, as the Russians believe, an Englishman, who directed the movements from the deck. He was plainly visible all the time, and was a tall man, with a long blonde beard parted in the middle. He stood with his hands in his pockets, giving orders in the calmest manner possible.

The torpedo boats continued their attempts for more than an hour, flitting round the monitor and seeking the opportunity to get at her, but without success. The monitor was equally active in trying to run them down, avoiding a collision by quick and skilful movements, backing and advancing, turning, and ploughing the water into foam as she pursued or avoided her tiny but dangerous adversaries—a lion attacked by rats. At one moment one launch, in rapid manœuvres, found itself between the monitor and the shore, with no great distance between them. The monitor's head was in the other direction, but her commander instantly began backing her down on the torpedo boat, with the intention of crushing it against the bank. Just at this moment the engineer of the launch was wounded. There was some confusion and delay in starting the engines, while the current carried her head aground in such a position as to render escape impossible. One of the crew sprang out into the water and pushed from the ground, while another started the engines just in time for her to escape, but the shave was very close. One Russian officer sprang ashore, and seeing the captain of the monitor coolly standing on the deck with his hands in his pockets, emptied his revolver at him, three shots, at a distance of not more than forty feet. The captain of the monitor, in answer, took off his hat and bowed, not having received even a scratch. Later, however, the gallant fellow seems to have been killed or wounded, for he suddenly disappeared from the deck. The monitor immediately afterwards retired precipitately from the scene of action.

Since that time she has kept out of the way like the others. The Russians suppose that she is no longer commanded by the same man. The fight was conducted with wonderful skill on both sides. The Russian boats were commanded by Lieutenant Niloff, and the attack was a most daring and tenacious one. His loss was only four or five wounded, in spite of the incessant fire of the small arms and mitrailleuse which poured into them. This shows how well-handled the boats were. They were, however, considerably damaged by the mitrailleuse fire. No attempt was made by the commander to use his guns, he evidently believing it impossible to hit such a small and rapidly moving object as a steam launch. That the boats should have suffered so little loss in one hour's fight shows how difficult it is to hit these launches. They were, I believe, fitted out in the same manner as those which blew up the monitor at Braila, but this attempt, as well as the one at Giurgevo, was made in broad daylight, neither of which succeeded. This monitor has since been surrounded by torpedoes, so that it is believed she cannot escape. All the monitors now on the Danube are surrounded by torpedoes. It is believed that those at Nicopolis have been abandoned by the Turks, as no sign of life has been seen on them for two or three days.

* SIMNITZA, *June 30th.*—Since my last despatch little of interest has occurred, although nothing has interfered with the work of the bridge, not yet completed. If three days are required to construct a bridge interrupted by no opposition, it may fairly be asked what would have been the Russian chances of crossing in face of a respectable resistance? I must own to much disappointment at the Russian tactics and methods of procedure since the morning of the crossing. That operation was indeed conducted with skill, but it was an imperative duty at all cost to keep sight of the retreating enemy, to ascertain their line of retreat, to learn whether they were receiving reinforcements, and what were the indications of their line of action. This course does not appear to have been pursued, and it is only to-day that young Skobeleff with a sotnia of Cossacks has gone on a scouting expedition to gather intelligence of the whereabouts of the Turks. This tardiness is all the more injudicious when it is remembered that the force now across the river has opposition on either flank, Rustchuk and Nicopolis. An advance is rendered precarious by the consequent threatening of communications, and in the absence of a completed bridge there is no line of retreat save by the hazardous recourse to boats. It is possible to despise an enemy too much. The minor arrangements, too, of the Russians are somewhat faulty. Access from Simnitza to the place of embarkation was and still is by a difficult track, which is not a road, down the bluff, over a single pontoon bridge, and by a tortuous sandy path through swamps and shallow patches of inundation on the flats. No attempt has been made to better these imperfect communications. The Germans would not have occupied a similar position for twenty-four hours without cutting half a dozen practicable roads down the face of the bluff, throwing at least two bridges over the branch of the stream, and making a good straight and firm track across the flats. They would have thrown up and fortified a bridge-head on the farther side. Their Uhlans would be within view of Rustchuk on the one side and Nicopolis on the other; their mass would have been on its march toward whatever objective

points might have been decided, instead of coquetting with time at a season of the year when every hour is valuable, if the campaign is to be triumphantly ended before the winter. The Germans would not have taken three days to build a bridge, the appliances for which were all prepared and at hand. Their troops on the other side would not be living from hand to mouth, so that a general's dinner has to be sent to him from his baggage waggon on this side. The Germans by this time would have accumulated in Sistova a depôt of provisions and ammunition, and surrounded this virtual base with a cordon of fortified redoubts.

To desist from comparisons, it may be said that in the Russian camps the sanitary arrangements are conspicuous by their absence. The atmosphere of this place is already poisonous. This neglect in a mere marching column might matter little, but when it is remembered that Simnitza, until Rustchuk falls, must be the leading point on the line of communications, that troops must succeed troops in the same camps here, and that a large resident staff must constantly occupy the place during the summer heat, to disregard rudimentary cleanliness is simply to tempt Providence. The water supply of Simnitza is abominable. The wells are sucked nearly dry, and the men are drinking now semi-fluid mud, but there are neither filters nor Abyssinian tube wells in the army. I have never seen a finer army, but the very fineness of it adds point to comment which candid criticism enforces. It is said that the interior of Bulgaria has been explored to a distance of 20 miles with a very trivial pretence at resistance, but I doubt the distance. Skobeleff's division of Cossacks, who ere now should have overrun a wide semicircle, are still on this side, except a comparative handful. The division is to be broken up into detachments, which are respectively to be entrusted to the command of officers illustrious for rank rather than military experience. The Czarewitch will have one; Prince Eugene of Leuchtenberg, who saw some fighting in Khiva, another; the Grand Duke Nicholas the younger, probably a third. An attempt to swim a detachment of Cossacks across the Danube resulted disastrously, and recourse must be had to a more certain method of crossing. Official returns give the number of the dead at 240, and of the wounded at 410, on Wednesday, very close to my hurried reckoning on the ground. The crossing of the Danube in 1827 cost 12,000 men! in 1853 it cost 15,000 men! a significant comment on the resisting capacity of the Turks.

Evening.—I have just learned that a detachment of Turkish infantry from Nicopolis has approached within six versts of

Sistova, and has there intrenched itself; but the movement is regarded as a diversion to distract the attention of the Russians from a supposed march of the Nicopolis force on Rustchuk by a circuitous route, penetrating into the interior. The Grand Duke Nicholas has to-day crossed the river to make arrangements for the extension of the Russian rayons.

* Sistova, *July* 1*st*.—This morning the Grand Duke Nicholas, with General Nepokoitchitsky and a portion of the staff, crossed the Danube on a visit of inspection of the troops. Where the bridge is made the river is divided into two nearly equal parts by a long island covered with low-growing trees. From the Roumanian bank to the island the bridge is finished, and the Grand Duke used it. The bridge is fairly made, partly of iron, partly of wooden pontoons. Five entire pontoon trains were used for the construction of this portion only. The reason of the delay is the high wind of yesterday and the previous day, when five of the pontoons broke loose and were lost. The freeboard of the iron pontoons was found to be too low, and the water entered them. The portion of the bridge over the Turkish arm of the river is not yet finished, and the Grand Duke crossed this branch in a boat. Communications from the water-side on the Turkish bank are extremely difficult, and the work of improving them is extremely tardy. The Grand Duke rode into Sistova, where are the headquarters of the 8th Corps, General Radetsky, and of the 14th Division, General Dragomiroff. Picking up these officers, his Imperial Highness rode out several miles to the camps of the 14th and 35th Divisions, south-west from Sistova, and thence rode on some distance into the interior, now overrun by the Cossacks. His Highness reached a point where a splendid view of the Balkan slopes was obtained, and returning through Sistova visited the battery on its eastern edge, whence the Turks so obstinately maintained their fire. The number of shell-holes in and about it proved how searching was the fire of the Russian batteries. The Grand Duke did not visit the headquarters of the 9th Division, Prince Mirsky, which are at Vardim, about seven versts due east from Sistova on the Rustchuk road. It is reported that the Cossacks are far into the interior, and I have been told they have already reached near Tirnova without seeing a Turkish soldier. General Skobeleff, junior, has returned from his reconnaissance.

Sistova is a charmingly situated little town of some eight thousand inhabitants, of whom the Bulgarians say one-half were Turks. Probably this is an exaggeration. Most of the houses are embowered in gardens. The ground on which the town stands is separated by abrupt ravines, which cut the place into several sections. The town standing on the slope is very clean. Its tortuous and narrow streets are hardly worthy of the name. The business part of the town is on a little flat by the edge of the Danube, where are the warehouses and buildings of the Danube Navigation Company. Business is almost exclusively in the hands of the Bulgarians. The doors and shutters of all their houses are marked with crosses of chalk, and over the portals of some are decorations of flowers and leaves. They afford a contrast to the houses inhabited by the Turkish population. Those Turks who had not previously left, fled on the night between Tuesday and Wednesday, a clear indication that the place and date of crossing were no secret to the Turks, and this knowledge makes all the more contemptible the Turkish dispositions to resist the crossing, the feebleness of which might have been excusable had the operation been a surprise, but which was unaccountably miserable as an outcome of foreknowledge. Between the period of the flight of the Turks and the entry of the Russian troops the Bulgarians sacked and wrecked the Turkish houses without a single exception. The pillage and destruction are as sweeping and universal as if the place had been sacked by a victorious army after storming. There is not a whole pane of glass in the window of any Turkish house in all Sistova. The wrecked interiors present an indescribable chaos of destruction. Cupboards are smashed, floors torn up, shelves torn down, stoves broken, in search of secreted money. The floors are strewn with miscellaneous débris and torn books printed in curious characters. Judging from the number of these in the better houses, the wealthier Turks of Sistova seem to have been a reading people. The furniture was broken in sheer wantonness, and the plaster shattered. The divans were broken up; in fine, the ruin is thorough and universal so far as the interiors of the houses are concerned. Nor has the destruction been confined to the habitations. There are eight mosques in Sistova, and all are wrecked. Their interiors are scenes of indescribable destruction. The very railings are broken into small pieces, as if in the keen zest and gloating enjoyment of laying waste. But they have not been defiled in the foul manner I have seen the Christian churches in Servia defiled by Turkish invaders. The few Turkish shops and stores in Sistova have been pillaged of everything valuable, and the fixtures of the interiors have been smashed into fragments and splinters. Nothing Turkish in the place has escaped wreck, and the aspect of uninjured dwellings intermingled with others reduced to the extremity of dilapidation is strange and significant.

It should be stated that no whit of this pillage and destruction lies at the door of the Russian soldiery. Their conduct has been exemplary in the highest degree. In the heat of fighting they gave quarter and took prisoners in the true spirit of civilized warfare. They protected the prisoners from the contumely of the rabble of Sistova. On entering the place they at once directed their efforts to stop the wreckage; but the Bulgarians had made the best use of their time, and desisted the readier because there was nothing more left to destroy. Still in quiet corners the Bulgarian youths of Sistova are slaying the slain. To-day I chanced on an outlying Turkish house, directed thereto by the crash of splintering timber, and found a gang of lads breaking up the doors and shutters with eager zeal. I have seen heaps of Turkish plunder in Bulgarian houses, but the Russian soldiers are wholly free from the stain. The Bulgarians have discarded red fezzes and taken to wearing white ones, wearing also white armlets, with a cross of gold-leaf fastened on them. They are naturally on the best terms with the Russian soldiers, and the Bulgarian and Russian languages are so near akin that they understand each other well enough.

The Turks of Sistova, to judge by the wrecks of their residences, appear to have been a thriving people in a lazy, easy-going way. The Bulgarians show few indications of having been materially oppressed, or perhaps have thriven wonderfully on oppression. Many of their houses are large and handsome. Paris fashions are not unknown to, or unstudied by, the Bulgarian ladies, whose beauty in many cases is as remarkable as their intelligence. The Konak of Sistova is a ramshackle structure, with a ruined harem behind over a stable. It is being swept and garnished for the occupation of the Russian local administrative functionaries. Prince Tcherkassky will presently cross the river, and commence the work of reorganization which has been entrusted to his able hands. There was no conflict between the departing Turks and the Bulgarians. The former, as the Bulgarians aver, tried hard to persuade the latter also to quit the place. Even the Turkish women resorted to unwonted blandishments to this end, but in vain. There is a story of two Turkish women having defended their houses against marauding Bulgarians, and having been found with muskets in their hands, but I cannot trace it to a reliable source. The Bulgarians assert that the Turks are committing atrocities in the interior as they retire, in which case Sistova is to be congratulated on its happy and certainly thorough escape. Sistova flows with milk and honey in comparison with Simnitza, where the people in the hotel are living on dry bread and bad water, and where a Mrs. Seacole is very badly wanted. With the completion of the bridge, supplies will stream across for the Russian army, and then doubtless the advance will at once begin. The flats are now black with waggons waiting to cross. Meanwhile the officers of the troops on the Turkish side have been pinched for supplies, having parted company from their stores. A general to-day sent across the Danube the modest request for a box of sardines and a clean shirt. The weather is fine, and a cool wind tempers the heat.

* SIMNITZA, *July 2nd.*—Rearrangements are in progress here prior to the general advance. An advanced division, to cover the front and lead the way, is being formed, under the command of General Gourko, who has not yet arrived. It will consist of a brigade of riflemen, the Bulgarian legion, and four cavalry brigades, made up of divisions formerly commanded by Prince Manueloff and General Skobeleff, senior, who have been attached to the Grand Duke's headquarters. The first cavalry brigade, consisting of dragoons, will be commanded by Prince Eugene of Leuchtenberg; the second brigade, of two regiments of Don Cossacks, commanded by General Cherkasof, himself a Cossack; the third brigade, of Circassian Cossacks, commanded by Colonel Tutolmin; the fourth brigade, of a regiment of Don Cossacks and a regiment of hussars, commanded by Duke Nicholas of Leuchtenberg, chief of staff to General Gourko. These brigades are now crossing the Danube.

To-day the Emperor visited the camp of the Circassian Cossacks. These troops, whether in camp or on the march, are the most picturesque in the army. Each sotnia, or squadron, has a large banner, variously emblazoned. All wear long black frocks, or tcherkesskas, for the sake of uniformity; but each regiment wears a different coloured silk under-frock, to which corresponds the colour of the top of the fur cap. In warm weather they habitually discard their black tcherkesskas. The effect of the varied bright colours is very picturesque. The Osetiny Cossacks, of which there are two squadrons, are the only Mussulmans now remaining with the Russian army of the Danube. Their banner is green. Originally they wore whatever colours they chose; now all wear a black tcherkesska to distinguish them from the Turkish Circassians. They inhabit the uplands of Cis-Caucasia. No Circassian Cossacks in the Russian army carry lances. Their arms are a sword, dagger, and carbine. Should Circassian meet Circassian in the Balkans, the contest will have special interest. The Russian Circassians will have the benefit of discipline and better arms, without, to all appearance, having sacrificed dash. The Russian regulars, with the recollection of the long struggle in the Caucasus against the indomitable Circassians, evince some nervousness at the prospect of their being found guarding the Balkan passes.

The better classes of the Bulgarians of Sistova profess shame and sorrow for the pillage and wreck of the Turkish houses of the place, and blame the Wallachs and gipsies, inhabiting the poorest quarter of the town, for most of the mischief. They plead in excuse the hatred following four centuries of ruthless oppression, and say that the wrecking was first commenced without any felonious intent. The pillage came afterwards. Steps are being taken to palliate the stigma. Yesterday in the churches an edict was read that all stolen property should be given into the hands of the police for eventual restitution to the owners. A committee has been formed, on which, by the way, are two women as experts, for the identification of the Turkish property and its complete restoration; and penal enactments are promulgated against all persons retaining it. A difficulty will probably present itself in inducing the Turks to return and claim their effects. It is believed that many of the Sistova Turks are still lingering in a village some twenty miles distant, and a deputation is being sent thither to beg them to return and resume their habitations on assurances of being unmolested, and having their property restored. This is not enough. Compensation should be forthcoming for the damage done to the houses. It is extremely problematical whether the Turks will return to dwell amid circumstances so altered, and perhaps the best thing would be to afford facilities to them for the most advantageous disposal of their effects and holdings. That the Turks deliberately meditated flight is proved by the fact that for many days before the blow fell, several hundred carts were in readiness to remove their families and movable effects. The Bulgarians say that had the Turks remained neither they nor their property would have suffered damage. Some colour to this assertion is given by the fact that the Turkish Cadi and his brother did remain, and were unmolested. The old gentleman was a popular man, and had exerted himself to protect the Christian refugees from recent massacres. He and his brother are free to walk about the town with a soldier in attendance, and it is hoped their influence may have the effect of reassuring their countrymen. The Bulgarians of

Sistova, in their penitence, express an eager hope that their example will not be followed in other towns under similar conditions, and profess an intention of notifying to their countrymen the wisdom of abstaining from lawless violence. It is impossible, however, not to apprehend that the occurrences at Sistova will be productive of evil, and afford a handle to the Turks for excesses prior to evacuation.

Colonel Wellesley has at length joined the army. He arrived to-day at the headquarters of the Emperor, to which he is attached, previous circumstances having too far strained relations to admit pleasantly of his joining the headquarters of the Grand Duke Nicholas. The whole of the Imperial equipage left behind by the Emperor at Ployesti in his recent rapid movements arrived here this evening. Its extent may be judged from the fact that the Emperor ordered sixty new carriages for the campaign. The bridge across the Danube was completed last night. Since then troops and vehicles have been passing in a continuous stream.

† SIMNITZA, *July 5th.*—The army is moving steadily across the river without intermission. Horses, ambulances, fourgons, caissons, infantry baggage waggons, are pouring down across the flats day and night, raising clouds of dust and making Simnitza scarcely habitable. The great number of cavalry accompanying the army, necessitating the transport of enormous quantities of forage, makes the train immense. The bridge, which is already spoken of as weak, does not seem equal to the strain. It has already given way twice, causing a delay of a few hours. I believe it is scarcely strong enough for the passage of the siege train without considerable strengthening. The Russian advance is about half-way to Tirnova, which the Turks seem to have abandoned and re-occupied. The report that the Russians have already occupied Tirnova is without foundation. It is impossible to push so far without cavalry. The Russians will not be there for some days. The Grand Duke Nicholas and Colonel Wellesley are now on excellent terms. Everybody here is treated in the most cordial manner by the Emperor. It is said here that his Majesty in conversation with Colonel Wellesley again touched on the political situation, and reiterated his promises with regard to Constantinople made in conversation with Lord Augustus Loftus.

CHAPTER IX.

THE ADVANCE INTO BULGARIA.

Order of the Advance—Negligent Outpost Service—Sarejar Pavlo—Plundering at Bjela—The Simnitza Bridge—From the Danube to the Jantra—Bjela and its Bridge—A Cross-Country Ride—Misbehaviour of Russian Soldiers—Climate of Bulgaria—Riches of the Country—Forbearance of the Turks.

† SAREVICA, *July 7th.*—The army is not all over the river yet. The bridge is continually giving way. The 9th Corps only crossed to-day. General Dragomiroff, with the 14th Division of the 8th Corps, is at Sistova, but he moves to-morrow. General Mirsky, of the 9th Division of the 8th Corps, is at Vardim. He moves in this direction to-morrow. The 5th Division of the 9th Corps marched through Sistova to-day towards Nicopolis or Plevna. There are indications that this corps, which, with the eighth, forms the army of the Grand Duke Nicholas, will march to Plevna, and thence to Loftcha, reaching that place about the same time as the eighth reaches Tirnova. The 35th Division is already at Batak, on the road to Tirnova. The advance guard of the cavalry is along the river Rusitza; the right wing is at Madrego, the left at Dragonova. The Turks still hold Nicopolis, but the Russians will probably take it with the 9th Corps before crossing the Balkans. It seems impossible to leave it untaken in the rear, especially as one column seems destined to march by Plevna. There will be a few shots between the advance posts, but probably no serious fighting, for a few days. The Grand Duke, with his staff, arrived this afternoon, but the baggage did not come till late at night, because the Grand Duke would not stop the passage of the troops that the baggage might pass. There were no cooking utensils and nothing to eat, and the whole party, including the Grand Duke himself, began cooking shashliks, or bits of mutton held on sticks over the fire. The Grand Duke enjoys roughing it. He is a true soldier. Carevica is a delightful place. The water is excellent. The health of the troops remains excellent. The cavalry finds plenty of hay and grass. The Turks in some places seem disposed to take the proclamation of the Emperor in good faith. At Batak, for instance, nearly the whole population, which is Turkish, remains at home unmolested. The Emperor remains at Simnitza, but

will probably not stay there long. Colonel Wellesley accompanies him. Their relations are most friendly. The Emperor treats him with the greatest distinction and consideration. It is not true that the Emperor ever informed Lord A. Loftus that if another officer but Colonel Wellesley were sent he would invite him to accompany the army. The Emperor did invite Colonel Wellesley in the most cordial terms.

* BJELA, *July 5th.*—Bjela, pronounced Biela, is a little straggling Turko-Bulgarian town on the river Jantra, about twenty miles south of the Danube, on the main road from Rustchuk to Tirnova, and nearly equidistant from Sistova and Rustchuk. It was occupied by a brigade of Russian cavalry this afternoon, and I think the narrative of the occupation may have some interest for the reader. I must begin a little way back.

I telegraphed yesterday to the *Daily News* nominally from Sarejar; the message was written there, some ten miles inland from Sistova, but I had to bring it myself across the Danube to Simnitza. Returning, I accompanied part of the way to Sarevica General Vannovsky, who commands the 12th Corps, and his headquarter staff. He was about to establish his headquarters for the night in Sarevica. I only hope he found cover somewhere. There was but one edifice in the village with any claims to the appellation of house, and that was already occupied by General Radetsky, commanding the 8th Corps, which remains in position, it appears, for the time, on the Danube, with Dragomiroff's headquarters in Sistova, and Prince Mirsky's in Vardim, so that the 12th Corps will have the *pas* of it in the advance. The Russian military authorities are singularly impartial in giving to respective commands the opportunity of distinguishing themselves. It is not with them always "The 42nd to the front!" as was the standing command in Ashantee. The 8th Corps had its innings at the crossing of the river, and now to all appearance other corps, the 12th, the 9th, and the 13th, will have openings to gain renown and earn decorations for their generals. At Sarejar there is, or was last night, encamped the 35th Division, and I am bound to say that it kept by no means a good watch. Outside every village occupied by troops during the Franco-German war, no matter how far from the front, there was always a double post at every exit, who demanded to know the business of every wayfarer not of their own nationality. There was a countersign which was rigorously exacted after sundown, and I have often known instances of German officers being prohibited from passing who were not in possession of it. I remember being myself prohibited from appearing at a dinner to which I had been bidden by the chief of an army, since the sentry would not allow me to enter the park gates of the château which he occupied because I was not in possession of the watchword. But anybody and everybody passed without challenge or interference along the road which traversed the centre of General Baranoff's camp. It is true that some distance on this road beyond the camp there were a couple of outlying picquets, each with a sentry, but there was no chain of posts round the camp, or even on the side of it next to the unexplored region, which was very near, as the sequel will show, and which might have been swarming with Turkish soldiers. Troops of any energy would certainly have found it no difficult task to surprise this camp; and even a few men could easily have caused an alarm which would have produced great confusion. The more I see of it, the more do I recognize that the Russian army, with its capital soldiers, its excellent equipment, and its thorough soldierly spirit, has much to learn even of the rudiments of the art military. It will readily be understood that I speak in no unkindly spirit, but I cannot conceal from myself, and therefore it is my duty not to conceal from your readers, that a surprising slackness seems to pervade the army in regard to the everyday duties of modern warfare. This was no paltry case of a captain and a couple of companies, where attention to the supreme duty of watchful alertness might be lax without demanding more than a passing comment. It was the camp of a whole division—a mass of men as large as we have been able to put into the field for the summer manœuvres at Aldershot, and a spy might have lounged through it without challenge; the Circassians might have been in its lines before the alarm had been given.

I did not wish to linger with the infantry, but to push on to overtake any one of the four brigades of cavalry which, as I have more than once mentioned, had been sent forward to constitute the advance. Only I did not know quite whereabouts any of them were. They were forward, and I could do no better than go forward in search of them. Now, Sarejar is on a main road—after a fashion—from Sistova to Tirnova. The Turkish recipe for a high road is apparently to level a section of ground, strew it with big stones, dig sundry trenches to serve as ruts, and powder the whole profusely with dust. This was the kind of road by which I had come from Sistova to Sarejar, and it ought to have been the road which I should have followed beyond Sarejar. But I lost it, or rather never found it, and set forth contentedly on a track going left from the direction of this main road at right angles—a track, in other words, leading due east instead of due south. I did not return from Simnitza till the afternoon, and so it was rather late before we started from Sarejar. In the first mile or two we travelled without company, but presently struck into the trail of a column of waggons preceding us on the same road. Its escort consisted of a mere handful of dragoons, mounted and on foot, and the column as a whole seemed in a very unhappy way. It was the train of Tutolmin's brigade of Circassian Cossacks, and on its way to find and join the brigade; but where Tutolmin was nobody had the remotest conception. Nor indeed was there any certainty that any force, any foreposts, any curtain of cavalry was between it and the enemy, or, at all events, the unexplored territory in which the enemy might be. At the foot of every little swell the waggons halted while the men escorting it on foot crept up and peered over the crest. At length, with darkness, this expedient was no more available, and so the convoy took its chance and did its own scouting, with not a few mutterings among the men about the Circassians, of whose prowess they have a mighty high opinion. At length some camp-fires were seen in the dark distance, and about eleven o'clock we found ourselves on the edge of a camp belonging to a regiment of Don Cossacks, forming part of the second brigade of the cavalry division of the 12th Corps. No outlying picquet challenged us, no sentry sang out the complicated Russian for "Who goes there?" the provision column simply formed up and halted for the night without a question from anybody in the Cossack camp. We pitched outside the line of waggons, and then, seeing a light in what was obviously an officer's tent, went to pay our respects to its occupant. I have occasionally been curtly, never uncivilly, treated by Russian staff officers, in whom the sense of responsibility no doubt had blunted innate courtesy, but from officers of the line I have uniformly experienced the most genial friendliness. The Cossack colonel proved to be an extremely pleasant fellow. He told me that he had one squadron in a hollow on in front, and that with this exception there was nothing Russian between him and Bjela, which he believed some Turks still occupied.

We remained overnight in his camp, which was close to the Bulgarian village of Pavlo. In the morning I went into the village, where I found a few inhabitants. The place, like all Bulgarian villages, is divided by a pronounced line of demarcation—on one side the Turkish portion of the village, on the other the Bulgarian. The Turkish side of Pavlo consists of about thirty mean cottages, surrounded by small tobacco gardens. Its inhabitants were Tartars, who, the Bulgarians report, chiefly lived on contributions from them, keeping a few horses on the grass-grown undulating country around, and cultivating but little except tobacco. The Bulgarian side has about a hundred and fifty houses, some of which are farmhouses, whose owners have quite a large stock of cattle and sheep. These had not been driven off by the Tartars, who left about ten days ago, regretting that they had no fire-arms with which to slay a few of the Bulgarians. Most of the latter had emigrated to Sistova when the Russians crossed, to be under their wing, and are only now returning to their homes, in the knowledge that the Russian cavalry has thus far overrun the territory. A convoy of them, men, women, and children, in waggons, came in when I was visiting the village, and heartily happy were they to find themselves again in their homes, and to find that these homes were undesolated by the retiring Turks. But when they saw how few were the Russian cavalry, they could not quell the expression of their fears that all was not yet safe, and I believe that one or two waggonloads actually returned.

The Cossack colonel had sent back to the division general for orders, which he hoped would instruct him to advance; and we waited on the chance that this would be so, intending in that case to accompany him. While we lay on the grass waiting, there came down the winding grassy road into the little hollow the dashing array of a regiment of Russian hussars. The front rank men of a Russian hussar regiment all carry lances; and the pink and yellow lance pennons fluttered gaily in the wind. The purple flag at the head of the gallant column denoted that there marched with it a general of brigade. In fact the hussar regiment was the sister regiment of our Don Cossacks, the two making up the second brigade of the cavalry division of the 12th Corps, commanded by General Baron Driezen. The brigade-general was General Stahl von Holstein. After a short talk with our colonel, the hussar regiment moved on, going down into the dip, and then winding up the steep green slope over which passed the country track to Bjela. Here I had the pleasure of making the acquaintance of the oldest lieutenant I have ever seen on active service. The age of this venerable subaltern is 73, and he does his duty with as much zeal and energy as the youngest of his brother officers. He bears an historic name. It was to his father, General Count Rastapchin, that the burning of Moscow was confided when Napoleon's legions were nearing the venerable capital. And how thoroughly he fulfilled his sad duty its smouldering ashes but too well testified. The present Count Rastapchin, the sprightly lieutenant of 73, is chamberlain to the Emperor, with the relative rank of general; but he has taken service in the Achtirski Regiment of Hussars, in the capacity I have mentioned, considering his military knowledge not compatible with a higher grade, but determined to serve in this veritable crusade. He sits his Cossack horse like a man of thirty, and has not ridden a yard in a carriage since the regiment crossed the Pruth.

Yet another column of cavalry came down the slope toward our Cossack camp. This time there were two flags in advance; one, the brigade purple, the other blue, denoting the presence of the general of division—Baron Driezen. He halted with the Cossacks, while the brigade general, General Arnoldi, went forward. He had invited us to accompany him. The brigade which this worthy old soldier commands consists of the Oldenburg Regiment of Dragoons, the finest dragoon regiment in the Russian service, and the regiment of Belgarski Uhlans; he had with him only the dragoon regiment, the Uhlans being a short distance behind. With the dragoons he had the divisional artillery, consisting of two horse batteries. The colonel of the dragoons, who rode with the General, is a very young man, barely thirty, and I was given to understand that Colonel Bilderling owes his early promotion entirely to merit. General Arnoldi had served many years, and had retired from active military employ, but came back in answer to the summons of the war.

We rode away up the green slope and over the breezy uplands, where the yellow barley waved ripe in the wind. The General told me that his commission was to occupy the town of Bjela, where it was believed there still remained some Turkish soldiers. The hussar regiment was still in front of us, but it was to halt in support at Kosna, while the dragoons and artillery went on against Bjela. The time passed swiftly, although the pace was slow and the route circuitous, for we were going along two sides of a triangle in order to strike as early as possible the chaussée between Rustchuk and Tirnova, on which Bjela stands. We passed the beautifully situated village of Burunli, lying in a deep grassy hollow, and the Bulgarian inhabitants crowded out with joy in their faces and words of welcome on their lips, carrying brimming pitchers of clear cold spring water, which in the boiling heat was preferable to nectar. Here in a camp, knee deep in natural grass, we left two squadrons of the hussars, and in half an hour more we were on the chaussée, and in sight of the swift flowing stream of the Jantra, overhung by dark umbrage. A patrol galloped out, and cut the wires of the telegraph line running along the chaussée, thereby interrupting telegraphic communication between Rustchuk and Tirnova, Nicopolis, Widdin, and indeed the whole north-western section of Bulgaria. If General Arnoldi had served in the American war, he might have learned to tap the wires instead of cutting them, and then perchance we might have gained some intelligence, which is wanted badly enough. But in all probability the Turks had abandoned the use of the line before the patrol cut the wires. At the junction with the chaussée we left all the hussars, except the advance guard, which still continued in front of us, and our way lay up the steep slope of a ridge which shut out from us the view beyond. As we topped it, the rich valley of the Jantra, waving with golden barley, lay at our feet, intersected by the sparkling river, and in the mouth of a little cross valley on the other side of the Jantra were the red-tiled roofs of Bjela, half hidden in foliage. But we were not yet in Bjela. It was a smooth slope down through the barley to the river brink from the ridge on which we stood. But beyond the river, flanking Bjela on its proper right, rose the steep marl heights, with abrupt grass-grown slopes beyond, of a position which at once arrested the eye of every trained soldier in the little band. If it were defended the carrying of it must cost dear. On our side, on the gentle slope, there was no greater cover than that afforded by a casual stook of barley. Then the river would have to be crossed—it would be necessary to search for a ford —and then these marl heights must be stormed, for there was no way of turning the position. It was a sight to stir the deepest interest—the loveliness of the scene, the gleaming river with the overshadowing masses of dark verdure above Bjela, the dusky red roofs recessed in the little valley, the golden slopes, the country village of Stirmana across the river on our left, where the marl steeps softened into green slopes—all this delighted the eye of him who looked at it in the spirit of the love of a sweet scene. And then how different the feeling of him who looked at it with a soldier's eye. If there be Turks on that crest opposite, ere it be taken the barley must wave over many a corpse; the silvery sheen of the Jantra must be dulled with blood; on the dazzling white marl must be dabbled many a red stain. The umbrage may hold sharpshooters; the pretty Stirmana may be a network of barricades; the bridge down there may be mined; among the red-roofed houses may be masses of infantrymen; behind these dark objects on the slopes, so like battery emplacements, may be lurking Krupp cannon.

We took a long steady look at it, all standing there on the little conical knoll on the ridge—a knoll on which a battery had begun to be built evidently not a week before, and a flanking shelter trench dug. General Stahl von Holstein had come on thus far with General Arnoldi, and the two held some talk apart, and then the former went off to have his hussars at hand for support if need should be. And so Arnoldi, taking his place at the head of the column, gave the word to march, and the dragoons began to descend the straight road leading through the barley-fields to the bridge. Till now it seemed to me that the duty of scouting had been very much neglected, looking at the fact that we were marching through a country presumedly hostile, and with an enemy known to be close. Arnoldi and his staff had constituted the advance guard; there were no flankers, and patrols were not thought of. But now the old soldier pulled himself together; out on the slopes to right and to left galloped flankers to peer down into the side valleys. A patrol trotted along the road in front. There was a cloud of dust, and three Cossacks came galloping up from the right front. They had poked their way across the river, but neither into the town nor on to the heights. The only information they brought was that some Turks were reported near Bjela, and their only capture was a Turkish pony. Who is this galloping *ventre à terre*, with a gun carried by the muzzle across his shoulder? A wild scared Bulgarian, with the intelligence that there are some Turks plundering in Stirmana, whence he had come; he could tell nothing about the heights or about Bjela. Half a dozen Cossacks are sent scouting away to the left toward Stirmana, and I accompany them—all of us led by the wild Bulgarian with the gun over his shoulder. He shouts and gesticulates with the maddest energy; he is in a paroxysm of furious rage and crazy terror, and yet he rides straight enough on his rat of a pony. We sweep down at a hand gallop, riding straight through the standing barley, and taking the banks and ditches in our stride. We lost no time, as my horse's heaving flanks testified; but the Cossacks were not quick enough for the light-heeled rascals of Bashi-Bazouks. As we dashed into the stream, I just caught sight of a very voluminous pair of blue unmentionables vanishing round the corner of a house, and that was all. The river turned out too deep to ford, and only one Cossack swam it; mine respectfully declined. So we went about, and as we were cantering back a single gun-shot sounded from above the village, as if in mockery.

I rode for the bridge, and struck the cavalry column close to it. It was reported that some Turks were prowling about the heights, but not in force, and the informants could not tell precisely of their whereabouts. Colonel Bilderling and myself rode forward to the bridge to find by the wayside there a company of Bulgarian people who had come out to welcome their deliverers. At their head stood their venerable priest. With streaming eyes the old man tendered the cross for Binderling to kiss as we stood there with bared heads in the presence of supreme emotion. Well might the old man weep in the glad agony of joy, and his primitive flock join their tears with his! I have known on the confines of Servia something of the feeling inspired by Turkish rule, but till now I have never realized how thoroughly a people can become sodden, as it were, with suffering and oppression, till they have come to look upon suffering and oppression as a matter of course—as things inevitable and to be accepted without remonstrance and almost without remark. They are cowards, these crouching Bulgars; but who shall reproach them for their cowardice? So terrible has been the crushing weight of the oppression that it has worked in them the saddest degradation that can overtake humanity. It has beaten them down so abjectly that the deepest extremity of cowardice has not found its recoil in the recklessness of despair. Oppression has so crushed them as to falsify the proverb that even a worm will turn.

Amidst sobbing and tears and kissing of hands, the attention of the General is not to be distracted from the work he has to do. He draws the back of his hand across his shaggy eyebrows, and the next moment his keen grey eye is scanning the white heights. He gives an order, and we ride across and stand at the feet of them and note how they rise steeply, yet in flaky strata, the crumbling of which gives a foothold to the climber. Suddenly there is heard the quick, steady tramp of armed men on foot marching across the bridge. Whence came they? No infantrymen followed our column of dragoons. But there is the gleam of bayonets! Surely infantrymen must have come up somehow. Listen narrowly a second, and the ear detects through the duller sound of the feet-fall the jingle of spurs. The Russian dragoons are dragoons proper in the original signification of the term, and as, when occasion might offer, they would show that they are heavy cavalrymen of the right stamp, now they were to show that they could act as infantrymen as well as the best foot soldiers who ever tramped. The outside men of threes in the first squadron had dismounted, giving over their horses to the centre men. They had drawn their short rifles from their leathern sheaths slung over their backs, and had taken their bayonets from the sheaths fastened on the sword scabbards. Their officers carry rifles like the men, all save the captain; and a fine, upstanding stalwart set of fellows they look, fit to go anywhere and do anything. Arnoldi points at the marl precipice, and they go at the face straight, extending to right and to left in skirmishing order as they climb. In splendid training, as hard as nails, and in the flower of agile youth, they climb up the cliff with a speed that winds me, unencumbered though I am with weight of rifle and sword. More follow the foremost. The top of the crag is reached, and we are on the steep green slopes. A moment's halt to get breath, and there is a run at the unfinished battery emplacements, which, to the great disappointment of the Russians, are found empty. The skirmishing line extends into the brushwood on the sky-line. A few snap shots are fired at skulking fugitives. There is hardly any reply. A prisoner is taken. Then I get tired of amateur skirmishing, and come down the marl cliff again. At the bottom I find the General some distance on the road towards the town, alone as regards his own people, and surrounded by a swarm of Bulgarians, male and female, greeting him with profuse humility of gladness. I do not know how often he has to kiss the cross tendered by different priests. The head of the column comes up, and he wheels it up the road leading towards Rustchuk, and not onward into the town, to the intense unhappiness of the Bulgarians, whose evident belief it is that they are to be left to the tender mercies of the Circassians, who are reported to be hovering on the other side of the town. The General goes on to the heights and detaches small parties in pursuit of the flying Turks, while he camps somewhere within convenient distance of the town. I accompanied him only a short distance, for I wished to see the town and the people before the Russians should enter the place; so, turning back along the chaussée, I reached the bend leading into the town, and followed the road which conducted into it. The whole population, to all appearance, accompanied me. They evidently regarded me as a Russian officer of high degree. Encountering a young Bulgarian who spoke French, I disabused them of this conception; but when I stated that I was a correspondent of the *Daily News*, they were more effusive than before. I was conducted to the best house in the town and given the best chamber in it, where I was compelled to hold a levée and shake hands with a large assortment of the principal inhabitants. Their great fear was that although the Russians had appeared, yet as they had passed without entering the place, a night incursion of the Circassians might still occur. They seemed to have little fear of the Turks proper, but to stand in terrible terror of the Circassians. I confess I did not myself greatly admire the situation, for, although the Russians had passed on one side of the town, the other was quite open, and fringed by woods, in which it was averred the Circassians were harbouring. However, I assured the people that the town would presently be full of Russians. I began as the day passed, however, to believe that the heading of this letter—"the occupation of Bjela"—would apply only to your correspondent; but as twilight began the clank of sabres was heard in the streets, and Arnoldi's dragoons swarmed into the place in the quiet, persistent search for schnapps. They further diverted themselves by hunting for hiding Turks, breaking open the shutters of suspected houses in these endeavours. Some four or five were thus captured. They were not at all maltreated, but simply conveyed as prisoners to the Konak, to be dealt with as superior authority shall dictate. In Bjela the Sistova example has been little followed. Few Turkish houses have been wrecked or plundered. There were comparatively few Turks in the place; the great mass of the population is pure Bulgarian. For the present they are a sufficiently abject people, but full of intelligence, and I do not know how to characterize the eagerness of their hospitality.

The cavalry of the 12th Division, followed by the infantry, are to pursue the chaussée route on Rustchuk. The cavalry of the four special brigades, the details of which I have already given, have not advanced very far on the road to Tirnova; some of their camps we saw to-day in the distance. The conduct of the Russian soldiers is most exemplary, but an example is made of the Turkish villages in which resistance has been made to the Russian advance. These are not numerous. One was burnt to-day on the right flank of our advance. It is impossible to understand why the Turks did not at least destroy the bridge over the Jantra. This would have retarded the Russian advance a couple of days. Three days ago the correspondent of a contemporary with the Turks was here from Rustchuk. It is a pity he did not leave a letter behind him; I should have had great pleasure in forwarding it.

* SIMNITZA, *July*] 6*th*.—I believe that there is as yet no postal organization of any kind in the Russian army on the

southern side of the Danube. In Roumania nominally there is a Russian post, but I have never known anybody to receive a letter by it. General Arnoldi told me yesterday that he had not received a letter from his wife for four months, while he knows for a certainty she writes every week. A correspondent without means of communication is a contradiction in terms. But in this war I foresee that correspondents will have to be couriers as well. It was under this conviction that I started this morning to ride the thirty miles from Bjela back to Simnitza with the above letter and a short telegram. I took a bee-line, holding a course nearer the Danube than the road by which we had travelled to Bjela, and I never saw a Russian soldier between the camp above Bjela and the fields beyond the ridge covering Sistova, where the foragers of the 9th and 14th Divisions were gathering hay for the horses. My route lay over alternate ridge and down into alternate hollow, through a solitude which was only interrupted by two or three villages passed on the way, and by a couple of very truculent gentlemen, who were marauders if not Bashi-Bazouks proper, and who had their quarters in an abandoned shepherd's hut in the throat of one of the loneliest villages. Never before in all my experience of war correspondence have I carried a revolver before this morning, when, as I left Bjela, I borrowed a weapon with which my servant has chosen to encumber himself, and I had some reason to be pleased that I had taken this precaution. One of the villages in my route I rode round, because of the information given me by Bulgarian peasants on its confines that a small party of plundering Circassians were in the place. I gathered that they had made booty of the wine-shop of the village, and owing to circumstances following thereon were not for the moment actively hostile. But the Russian troops sweep through this territory on their way to a given object, and, while they regard nothing to the right or left of their march, leave no posts in their rear to hold the villages and the country they have traversed. Now the glens and some villages hold Bashi-Bazouks, who lie quiet while the great wave passes over them, and start up to do a spell of looting after it has passed. The scoundrels are as protean as were the gentlemen whom it is the conventional duty of myself as a Scottish Highlander to reverence as chivalrous ancestors. When the brigade is passing they are peaceful agriculturists reaping the grain on the hillside—as like as not somebody else's grain, but who is to know? When it is passed, to a couple of stragglers or to a peaceful wayfarer like myself they are extremely dangerous and unpleasant. I foresee that in this war the danger to correspondents will be in keeping up communications, not in action.

* BJELA, *July 7th.*—When yesterday morning I left this place to ride to Simnitza, with the letter which I trust has safely reached you, I left my companion in the comfortable quarters of the town which he had taken up when General Arnoldi's cavalry spread themselves out on the crests of the ridge overhanging the place. In camp on that ridge I also left Arnoldi and his brigade when I rode out of Bjela in the early dawn. I returned to Bjela this morning, to find that during my absence occurrences had taken place the absence of my personal cognizance of which I have reason to regret.

Yesterday forenoon Mr. Villiers went up on to the heights to pay his respects to General Arnoldi, whom he expected to find in his tent in the midst of his men. Instead of this, the General was there indeed, but mounted and on the watchful outlook, his brigade was invisible, and only his outposts stood their ground in the position of the previous night. The General was not a little troubled. He had expected infantry to have arrived for his support before this time; the infantry had not come, and in his front the Turks were showing in very formidable force, and threatening an immediate attack. This, with a handful of cavalry, and his flank uncovered, he could not sustain, and he had withdrawn his camp and baggage and the mass of his brigade behind the Jantra River, which we had crossed the day before; maintaining a sort of attitude of defence on the heights, with a chain of picquets and vedettes, but having no other intention or alternative but to fall back immediately he should be attacked. He had definitely resolved, with perhaps an excess of caution, to withdraw altogether behind the Jantra for the night, if the supporting infantry should not have arrived by five in the afternoon. He blamed Villiers and myself very much for having slept in the town the previous night, seeing that it was quite unprotected from raids from the woods on its right, that he had not been able to send into it any force to cover it, and that some Turks must certainly have remained in it overnight, since one of his men who had remained in the town after dark as a straggler had been shot in the course of the night. He warned Villiers how precarious would be his position in the town should circumstances compel a retirement of the cavalry foreposts across the river, and advised him at once to quit the place and remove himself and our joint belongings into the camp. On this information and advice Villiers determined to quit the town at five o'clock, if before that hour the expected infantry should not have come up.

Comment on this cavalry advance on to the heights above Bjela cannot be of a favourable character. The advance of Arnoldi's brigade, unsupported by infantry, could effect no good purpose that was not open to half a dozen scouting parties, each consisting of an officer and a few men; and it might have been followed by very unpleasant consequences. The Russians complain of the advance of the British fleet to Besika Bay, as a direct encouragement to the Turks, and it is difficult not to agree with them; but there would have been scarcely less encouragement for them in the compulsory retreat of a brigade of Russian cavalry from a position deliberately taken up. The advance of Arnoldi, while his dispositions by no means included the protection of the town of Bjela, even while he camped on the heights close to it, compromised that place in a manner which its inhabitants would have had occasion bitterly to realize, if the retreat, which he regarded as almost inevitable, had actually been carried out. The Turks had quitted Bjela without working there any injury; but had they come back—and if their pressure had led Arnoldi to retire, they would of course have come back—they would hardly have practised the same moderation as before. They would have found some Turkish houses wrecked; they would have found the mosque not quite in the state in which they had left it; they would have learned that the Bulgarian inhabitants had hailed the Russian troops with enthusiasm, and guided Russian soldiers in their hunt after Turks who had remained behind. Turks are certainly human, and it would have demanded more than human self-restraint on their part if, under the circumstances, Bjela should not have had reason to mourn the hour that Arnoldi's cavalry rode over the bridge, without first making sure that infantry supports were within easy distance. I say then that their advance compromised unjustifiably the safety, if not the existence, of a friendly town.

But Bjela later had occasion to realize that in war-time friends are often nearly as cruel as foes. Indeed, a cynical inhabitant of Bjela might say that he had found friends more cruel than foes, for the Turks have left the place without doing any mischief. At five o'clock yesterday afternoon, some infantry of the 33rd Division arrived on the heights and relieved Arnoldi's mind. Leaving his forepost line standing, he withdrew to his camp on the Jantra, and the infantry and artillery took up the position on the heights he had occupied, and also on others covering the town. Bjela was thus safe from the Turks, at least until they should have defeated the Russian infantry on the heights in front, and having an easy mind on this score, Villiers serenely resolved to retain his comfortable quarters in the town. It is certain that he would have passed a pleasanter night in the camp; but it was a good thing for some of the people of Bjela that he remained in their midst. The infantry column began to pass through the town at six o'clock. The soldiers composing it did not break ranks, but marched through with that steadiness which characterizes the Russian soldier when under the eyes of his officers. But the march had been a long one, and there were many stragglers, who in straggling had escaped from under the eyes of the officers. What follows I relate as told me by Villiers and my servant, on whose word, through long experience of his truthfulness, I can implicitly rely, confirmed by the evidence furnished by the broken shop-fronts and the wrecked interiors. No doubt there are extenuating circumstances which may be urged. Guards should have been left in the place, and patrols should have been detailed to deal with stragglers, and protect the effects of the inhabitants from the instinctive impulse of unrestrained soldiery of any and every nationality to do a little plundering, when the chance offers of doing it with impunity. And it may be said for the plunderers themselves, that they found themselves in what is technically at least an enemy's country, and that they in their ignorance had few means of knowing—as doubtless as little care to know—whether the houses they were sacking were those of Bulgarians or Turks. I have read in one of your contemporaries, the assertion that no newspaper correspondent has been permitted to accompany the Russian army, except at the price of the sacrifice of his independence. Certainly I am aware of no such exaction having been attempted. It was definitely stated to me when my application to accompany the Russian army was granted, that correspondents were free to speak well or to speak ill of the Russians as might seem to them their duty, the only stipulation being that stipulation which does not require to be inculcated on a war correspondent who realizes his responsibilities, that pending events should not be prematurely written of. During some experience as a war correspondent, I have never submitted to the sacrifice of my independence, nor have I found that the maintenance on my part of an honest independence has injured me in the eyes of persons whose regard is worth having.

About eight o'clock yesterday evening a number of infantry stragglers were buying bread outside a shop near our quarters. They were not supplied with the quickness they desired, so they broke into and plundered the shop. This was witnessed by Villiers and a Russian cavalry officer who was sitting conversing with him at the window of our room. The officer at once went and drove away the plunderers, thrashing them soundly with the flat of his scabbard. Another cavalry officer joined the first, and the two, with my companion, walked down the street. A Bulgarian came up to them, wringing his hands, and complaining that his house was being robbed. They heard a tumult near, and shrieks of women, and as they approached a number of soldiers jumped out from windows, and through doors, laden with portable loot. The officers at once chastised these fellows with all imaginable vigour, and each took two soldiers prisoners; of the onlooking soldiers they organized an informal police patrol, and all plunderers subsequently caught they handed over to this body, after having previously thrashed them soundly. The officers took their prisoners, who were infantrymen, to the cavalry camp, whence, no doubt, they were forwarded to their regiment. The officers in the cavalry camp who were made aware of the circumstances, expressed great anger at the conduct of the soldiers; but the precaution was strangely neglected of sending protecting patrols into the town, probably because no cavalry soldiers were concerned in the mischief.

About one o'clock Villiers, sleeping in his room, was roused by the noise of woodwork being smashed in the street outside. Looking out, he saw by the light of the broken pieces of blazing wood carried torchwise by the soldiers that the work of plundering was going on apace to right and to left. Women were shrieking, not because of any violence offered to them, but because of the ruin to their property. Men were revelling in a liquor shop which had been broken open, and wine was running from the casks. On the other side of the way a butcher's shop was being cleared out, fellows tearing at the meat to make it part. The women of the house came into the room occupied by Villiers, and with tears besought his protection. But what could he do? There was no authority in the place—no man to whom appeal could be made. All was licence, and for the time the Russian soldier, ordinarily quiet, orderly, and respectful to superiors, was not himself. Villiers sat at the window, for a long time expectant of an attempt to break into the house we occupied. At length came the challenge, "Is that a Turkish or a Christian house?" My servant replied in Russian that it was a Christian house, and occupied by gentlemen accompanying the army. The soldiers no further attempted to gain an entrance, and apparently went away. But presently a knocking was heard below, and the people of the house said they were breaking into the cellar, which, as in most Bulgarian houses, has its opening direct into the street. Presently there was a wild tumult about the door and a hammering for admittance, which quickly brought Villiers and my servant down to the door. And now came the comic element in a scene that was surely grim and lurid enough. The proverb that ill-gotten goods never prosper had come home to the Russian soldiers with more than ordinary swiftness. As Villiers opened the door, there stood four of them in the torchlight, clamouring wildly, with bottles in their hands, a strange blackness about their lips, and a curious smell pervading the group which was certainly not the bouquet of any potable fluid known to my interesting young friend, who is not wholly destitute of experience in this department of practical knowledge.

The owner of the house had in his cellar a number of bottles full of vitriol used for the purification of wool in the manufacture and dyeing of woollen stuffs, which, it appears, is the man's business. These the Russian soldiers, who, although they did not invade the house, took the liberty of breaking into the cellar, promptly annexed, and having extracted the corks began to drink. The drink did not exactly meet their views; on the contrary, they must have had cast-iron mouths and throats, and the vitriol must have been greatly diluted, or they would have paid with their lives the penalty of their lawless conduct. As it was they had fared pretty badly. Their lips and mouths were burnt black, their clothes, hands, and boots were burnt, and they were half mad with rage and pain. They had rushed to the conclusion that the house must be a Turkish house, and the cellar a Turkish cellar, that the proprietor had purposely stored a quantity of devil's drink in wine-bottles, wherewithal to poison his Russian enemies, and that they were the victims. They insisted on regarding my servant as the Turkish proprietor, and strove to revenge themselves by forcing him to drink as they believed he had brewed. With wild cries and threats they forced bottles into his hands, and swore that he should drink. Now Andreas is always a sober man; he drinks only when he is thirsty; he has a will of his own, and would no doubt resent being made to drink under compulsion; still more recalcitrant would he questionless be if the proffered fluid were vitriol. He it appears objected to the beverage in the most emphatic manner. He imitated the unwilling horse in that they could not make him drink, but in the struggle he got his hands and clothes very much burnt with the vitriol. Villiers interfered physically in protection of one who is as much a comrade as a servant, and for the second time in this singular night he was in the hands of the Philistines. Still they had some sense of discipline and order left. They would not deal condignly with Villiers, although they professed to believe him a Turk and a spy. They whirled him up to a solitary under-officer who was addressed as the "Patrol," and who appeared to be serenely superintending the operations which I have attempted to describe. The patrol recognised the correspondent badge on Villiers's arm, and ordered the soldiers to unhand him, whereupon the victims of vitriol retired, probably in search of a less fiery fluid as an alterative.

After break of day the work of plundering flourished with greater vivacity than ever, and again our temporary residence was threatened. Now that there was daylight, and that he could see whither he was going, Villiers determined no longer to let the mischief continue without an effort to stop it. So he walked up to the infantry camp on the heights, found the colonel in command of the regiment, reported the proceedings to him, and asked for a guard to prevent further outrages. The colonel at once granted the request. He said he had already heard of the disgraceful conduct of the soldiery in the town, and was taking measures to stop it when Villiers came with confirmation of the discreditable fact. All his officers professed much disgust and regret. In a few minutes a strong guard was marching down into the little place with Villiers as guide. The officers commanding it at all events did their duty thoroughly. Every marauder met on his way to the camp from the town was searched. If his pannikin contained wine it was spilled upon the ground. The officer thrashed him, and then made him a prisoner. In the town a strategic movement bagged the plunderers of a whole street, some thirty-five in number, who were duly searched, thrashed, and made prisoners. The guard has ever since remained permanently on duty, a police officer has been appointed, as also a *commandant de place*, and now all is order and quietness. But the evil has been wrought, the scandal sticks like a blister. I believe there is an intention to give compensation for the damage done, but the *entente cordiale* between the Bulgarians and Russians has suffered. To descend to particulars, I will give the Russian soldier credit for being quite as expeditious and sweeping, if not so quiet and methodicala plunderer as the French "forager," as I believe he prefers to be termed. When I left there was in the place abundance of bread, meat, coffee, sugar, tobacco, cigarette paper, and writing paper, underclothing, boots, &c. When I came back there remained but the memory of these products of nature and art. The Russian officers feel deeply the discreditable conduct of a portion of their soldiers. The blame is not with the soldiers. It is in the nature of a soldier to plunder when he can see a chance to do so with impunity. The only soldiery I have ever seen who could be trusted to restrain this impulse are the North Germans proper.

* BJELA, *July 11th.*—We are, according to universal belief, bound for Rustchuk in the first instance, but we certainly are in no hurry to get there. This place was first reached by the cavalry advanced division on the 5th inst., and now on the 11th there has reached here, thus far on the road, but one infantry division, the 33rd, belonging to the 12th Corps. The 12th Division, belonging to the same corps, is behind a few versts at Pavlo with the Czarewitch, who is the Commander-in-Chief of the newly formed army, and the Grand Duke Vladimir, who is the new commander of the 12th Corps. Of the 13th Corps, which with the 12th makes up the army of Rustchuk, one division, the 35th, which was among the earliest troops to cross the river, was in the first instance sent on to Ovca Mojila, a village in a south-westerly direction from Sistova, has had to march across country, and will reach Kosna, which is close to Bjela, this afternoon. I believe that the 1st Division, the other division of the 13th Corps, is now in a valley to the south of Pavlo, so that the whole infantry of the army of Rustchuk is now within a few hours' march of Bjela. Bjela is two days' march from Rustchuk, but I have reason to believe that some days will elapse before the infantry will push onward from the present positions. As for the cavalry division, the headquarters of the division general, Baron Driezen, are at Monastir, about eight miles in advance of Bjela, on the road to Rustchuk, while the brigades Arnoldi and Stahl von Holstein are more forward and spread out over a considerable extent of country. Cossacks are also forward to the east and north-east of the Bjela position, sweeping the country, and driving in the scattered handfuls of Turks who have been lurking in the woods.

The delay may be attributed to several causes, but the principal reason is the necessity which is believed to exist for accumulating supplies to feed the troops before the advance shall begin in earnest. Precaution in this respect is wise, but it may be carried to an undue extent, and to cart supplies all the way round by the Simnitza bridge for an army beleaguering Rustchuk seems a needlessly circuitous process when a railway base is available at Fratesti, the station next Giurgevo, on the railway between that place and Bucharest, and when the Danube up to the margin of the range of the Rustchuk cannon, both above and below the fortress, must in a few days be free to be used by the Russians. The Simnitza route for the supplies as well as the troops having been chosen, inevitable delay would occur with but one bridge available for all purposes, even if that bridge were continuously available. But much as it has to do, the storm on the night of the 9th temporarily threw it out of working order, and the whole of yesterday was occupied in repairing it. The accident should impress the Russian military authorities with the necessity of having another string to their bow in the shape of another bridge. The strain on a single bridge is immense even with the best system, and General Richter, in whose charge is the traffic across the bridge, does his best to ensure that as little time as possible is lost in the crossing. Remember that it is not a bridge in the sense in which people accustomed to London Bridge and Westminster Bridge are wont to think of a bridge. The Simnitza bridge is considerably more than a mile long, and its traffic way is about seven feet wide. Troops marching in column of fours fill it from rail to rail. An ordinary vehicle leaves just space for a foot passenger coming the other way to scrape past at the risk of misfortune to his toes. Horses pass it by files; there is no room for three abreast. If an accident happens to a waggon in crossing, the stream is dammed till that accident is repaired. If you take your carriage or your horses over to the Sistova side, it is as yet *nulla vestigia retrorsum.* You may go back dodgingly to Simnitza on foot, but your equipage must remain on the further side. Try to imagine the difficulties and delays of taking across such a bridge a hundred and forty thousand men, with horses, with provision columns, with the multitudinous impedimenta of a great army. And imagine further the confusion and inconvenience which must arise from an accident which renders the bridge useless for a day. General Hastytemperovitz was across before the accident, but his tent, his baggage waggon, containing his personal supplies, and his servants were at the tail of the column, and while he is sheltering himself from the storm under the lee of the Sistova bank, they are fast among the sand on the Simnitza shore. The Onety-oneth Regiment has crossed under orders to push on as fast as possible to Tirnova to support the cavalry, who are waiting there for supports. The regiment has crossed, but its train, without which no regiment can march, is on the Roumanian bank, and a hundred yards of the bridge has foundered.

The 33rd Division, which is commanded by General Timofeieff, was visited yesterday by the Grand Duke Vladimir, the new commander of the corps of which it forms a part. A portion of the division is forward, occupying the heights beyond Bjela, but its mass is camped on the slope of a beautiful grassy down, at the foot of which flows the clear stream of the Jantra. One brigade is on a little grassy plain at the foot of the slope, and quite close to the river. All day long the soldiers are bathing in the broad expanse of water into which the stream is here dammed, or squatting under the lasher below the dam, enjoying a capital douche bath. In this part of Bulgaria there are great expanses of these delightful undulating grassy downs dipping into little intersecting valleys, in the bottom of which may lie a straggling agricultural village, fixed there by the presence of water which comes gushing forth from a rich spring, at the head of which there is always a massively built stone fountain, with a stretch of stone troughs for cattle and horses. I can find no warrant for the alleged unhealthiness of Bulgaria in the later summer months. It is all upland; there are no marshes; there is no standing water to breed miasma, and assuredly no fault can be found with the climate. The heat in the daytime, from nine till about five, is no doubt great, but it is not a relaxing heat like the heat of India. There is always a puff of wind from one quarter to another to fan the faces heated by the strong sun, and except in the vicinity of Sistova there is no dust, that pest and curse of marching in Roumania. The troops march along grassy paths over the downs and between the cornfields, and along paths which are not made roads at all, although quite practicable for vehicles, and indeed infinitely superior to the chaussées, but of which the surface has not been pulverized by the traffic of years. And the water is simply superb. It is not very plentiful—that is, there is not a brook in every valley, but it may be said that there is a spring and a watering place in every valley, and numerous wells dotted about the country. And the delight of a long drink of pure cold water from the gushing crystal stream of one of these springs is a joy unspeakable after the tepid, mud-thickened abomination which in Simnitza passed under the name of water. But I am wandering away from the visit of the Grand Duke Vladimir to the camp of one of his divisions. He found one battalion, with the divisional colours and his own banner, drawn up along the road leading down to the bridge of Bjela, and was received with that enthusiasm with which the Russian soldiers always receive any member of the blood Imperial. General Timofeieff inhabits the khan at the bridge-head, and here he met the Grand Duke and accompanied him in a ride through the camp on the slope and by the river-side. On the bridge across the Jantra the Grand Duke was met by a deputation of the inhabitants of Bjela, headed by the priests. His Highness alighted, kissed and was kissed by the priests, partook of bread, wine, and salt, the typical offering of the Bulgarian inhabitants, and escorted by the whole population of the place rode through the straggling town. Near the church a triumphal arch of green stuff had been erected, under the auspices mainly of my Servian servant Andreas, who has become quite a leading character in Bjela during the few days he has been in residence there. From the town the Grand Duke rode on to the heights to visit the battalions there, and after déjeûner in a tent outside General Timofeieff's quarters returned to Pavlo. The trouble of which I wrote three days ago between the Bulgarian inhabitants of Bjela and the Russian soldiers has passed away. Compensation was awarded by the General for the damage done, which after all was laid at the door of a comparative handful of men, who were severely punished. Since then, although the place is full of troops, the most perfect order has been maintained, and very genial relations exist between the townspeople and the troops. The latter are willing to pay for what they have, and the people of Bjela might drive an extensive trade if they only had any supplies worth speaking of to sell. They are harvesting serenely in the midst of the camping troops, who are very careful, whether on the march or in camp, not to injure crops on the ground, and whatever hay or grain they require the intendance pays for scrupulously.

My colleague with the Tirnova advance will speak in greater detail with regard to its object; but I may say that I have been given to understand its intended route across the Balkans is through the Gabrova Valley on to the Shipka Pass, and thence to Tatar Bazardjik, as well as by Kezanlik, and so into the Maritza Valley. The future of this army is somewhat indefinite. It is true that it is designated the Army of Rustchuk, and that Rustchuk is its immediate objective. But it is believed that Rustchuk contains now but a comparatively small garrison of from ten to thirteen thousand men, the rest of the troops which had been accumulated there having retired on Shumla. In this case a very large army employed in the reduction of Rustchuk would seem a waste of power. The mass of the 11th Corps I believe to be still at and about the

Giurgevo-Oltenitza position, and to be designed to co-operate against Rustchuk. The Russians here have the strongest belief that Rustchuk will hold out but a very short time. Judging from the strength of its natural position, from the pains which by all accounts have been taken in fortifying that position, and from what we know of the weight and extent of its armament; taking into account furthermore the traditional stanchness of the Turks in defensive positions—whatever this tradition may count for in the altered conditions of modern warfare, and after the experience of Ardahan—I should be inclined to set down this anticipation as sanguine, to say the least of it. But I am bound to say I have heard the opinion expressed with singular confidence in quarters not given to confidence without reason, and the Russians have in former times more than once found a golden key the easiest way to unlock the gates of a Turkish fortress, nor can it be said that the Turk of to-day is more incorruptible than the Turk of 1828. If, then, Rustchuk should fall after a short defence, this army would be free for further operations. If Rustchuk should hold out, there is no apparent reason why two out of the three corps—I include the 11th—after the parallels have been made and the batteries armed, should not equally be available for further operations, leaving a corps to devote its attention to Rustchuk. The objective in either case would be Shumla, if the Turkish army is to pursue the policy on which it appears at present acting, and decline any offensive in the open. An army marching against Shumla from the north-west would no doubt co-operate with Zimmerman's force coming southward from the Dobrudscha, and either the combined host might lay siege to Shumla, or one section of it mask Shumla, while another performed the same office for Varna, and a third struck southward through the Pravadi Pass and over Aidos in the direction of Adrianople. There certainly would seem a sufficiency of troops available for all three objects.

The era of "shaves" has set in already with considerable vigour. I own to some slight respect for shaves, on the principle that where there is smoke there must always be fire. So I am going to recount two of the current shaves, which you may take for what they are worth. I noticed in an English paper about the end of last month that a Council of War had met in Constantinople and had a conversation with Abdul Kerim Pacha as to the state of matters on the Danube. That venerable personage had reassured the sages of the Constantinople Council with the prospect of a battle of Bjela which would probably last several days. I have told the story of the "battle" of Bjela, in the course of which perhaps some twenty shots were fired. Now the story, gravely recounted to me by an aide-de-camp of the General, is this: that the Turkish troops retiring from about Bjela were met a long way off by the troops marching from Shumla. The troops marching from Shumla abused the troops marching from Bjela for not making a stand, and for falling back in such a pusillanimous manner without having spent more than a drop or two of blood. The troops from Bjela, on the other hand, objurgated the troops from Shumla for their tardiness in not coming to their support, so as to enable them to make a stand with some chance of success. The dispute grew into a quarrel, and, as the officer quaintly put it in his English, "a civil war was made." The other story is that the day after the Danube was crossed Prince Gortschakoff proposed to the Emperor that if the Turks should ask for peace then, they should have it on condition of granting autonomy to that portion of Bulgaria—strict geographers would call it Bulgaria proper—which lies to the north of the Balkans; but that the Great White Czar, having hardened his heart, and the initial difficulty overcome with so great comparative ease, declined utterly to listen to any such contingent terms, and avowed his determination not to conclude peace except on the basis of "freedom" for the whole of the Bulgarians on the south as well as on the north side of the Balkans.

The great problem of autonomy—the difficulty of bringing it about that Turk and Bulgarian should live together on equal terms—seems in swift course of solving itself in the manner which Mr. Gladstone's words "bag and baggage," construed literally, most accurately indicate. The "unspeakable" Turk is taking himself off "bag and baggage," self, wives, children, effects, flocks and herds, from before the advancing Russian. The instances that have come under my notice of Turks remaining to await events, or returning to their homes after a temporary abandonment, may be counted on the fingers of one hand. The old cadi of Sistova and his brother stayed behind; at Ovca Mojila a few families came in from the copses and begged to be allowed to resume the occupation of their dwelling-places. I have heard of no others. A number of Turkish families of the poorer classes are in the woods beyond this place, and keep shifting backwards as the troops push on. It is a pity that some assurance of safety on good behaviour should not somehow be conveyed to them. At present, so far as I can understand, they despair of good treatment, and act as if there were no hope. The men take up the rôle of Bashi-Bazouk—probably enough most of them were already Bashi-Bazouks, for your Bashi-Bazouk is nothing but an armed peasant, and the women are reported to have armed themselves. An unfortunate inhabitant of Bjela, going to a village beyond Monastir to discover whether the Turks had left it, and therefore whether its Bulgarian inhabitants were free to return to it, was killed in the woods, it is said by Turkish women. He was buried here to-day. All this is miserable work. The Russian chiefs, in compliance with the proclamation of the Emperor, are anxious to protect the Turkish civilian population if these would only remain to be protected, or, if already gone, if they would come back, and intimate their desire to live quietly and peaceably under whatever régime they may find themselves. I do not know what may be thought with you, but, speaking as a man who tries to the best of his power to disabuse himself of prejudices, it seems to me that the conduct of the Turks, as they evacuate Bulgaria step by step, has a claim to the admiration of the civilized world. We hear once and again of isolated acts of cruelty—there are two Bulgarians with broken heads in the hospital in Simnitza. But what did the world anticipate? Was it not that the retiring Turks would make Bulgaria a wilderness and a solitude? And how has this anticipation been justified? In Sistova no Turk touched the hair of the head of a Bulgarian, handled no scrap of the property of a Bulgarian. In the intervening villages the Bulgarian inhabitants abide under their unharmed roof-trees with their flocks and herds around them, fearful only in the apprehension of the visits from the Cossacks, which they have already learned are not simple visits of politeness. The crops, uninjured, wave rich and ripe in the fields; the hay stands in cocks in the fields; there is corn, and wine, and oil, and meal in the land. What the people of Bjela have suffered in property has been at the hands of lawless Russian straggling soldiers, not at the hands of the Turk, "unspeakable" though he may be. It is not my place to draw inferences, but it is my duty to state facts. It may be that the Turks simply went without doing damage or committing atrocities because of a consuming desire to get away without waste of time in any *divertissements* which might occasion delay. It may be that they went as they have done because they are not ferocious except under provocation, or fancied provocation, which they may have considered to justify ferocity. It may be that, being naturally ferocious, and having been guilty of fearful atrocities, they were determined to prove to Europe that for once, when they set themselves to it, they could practise self-restraint.

But waiving speculation on motives, I will aver this much, that whatever has been their sentiment or impulse, let what name soever be given to their actuating feeling, they have acted erroneously, speaking in a purely military sense. If their military policy has been that of retreat, the complement of that policy was to have left desolation behind them, not to leave a land flowing with milk and honey for the behoof of the invader. When Kutsoff and Barclay de Tolly retreated from Minsk to the Beresina, and from Beresina to Smolensk, and from Smolensk to Moscow, before the legions of Napoleon, did they leave behind them a fat land, villages teeming with flocks and herds, growing crops asking for the sickle, granaries for the replenishment of the provision trains? We all know that they left desolation and ashes, and that the desolation and the ashes have counted to Russia for heroism and patriotism, and, what is more to the purpose in my argument, for sound military strategy.

But let the Turk have his due. If he has been deficient in the legitimate resources of the military art, he has for once, and from whatever motive, erred on the side of humanity. And I cannot say that the Bulgarians have appreciated his forbearance. I have told the story of the wreck of the Turkish quarter of Sistova. Bulgarian Bjela has not been quite so rough on Turkish Bjela, but it has wrought not a little mischief on the latter nevertheless. The Turkish Bey here was a good man, held in high esteem among the Christians, for he consistently protected them from the lawless exactions of the Circassians to the best of his power. The Bulgarian inhabitants besought him to remain, assuring him that they would speak of him in such terms to the Russians that no evil could befall him. But the Bey did not relish the outlook, and departed with the people of his own nationality. One would have thought that the least the Bulgarians could have done would have been to have respected the good man's house. Well, it is not a pretty sight now. Not alone has it been sacked, the very floor has been wantonly broken through.

To-day was a fast-day, and the Russian soldiers have been going to church in batches all day long. He is a pious man, the Russian soldier, according to his lights. Before he dips his spoon into the big soup kettle, he chants a grace in chorus with his fellows. Fancy a grace in a British barrack-room! He says his prayers regularly in the morning, not in a corner, but *coram publico*. He doffs his cap and crosses himself when he enters a churchyard. He crosses himself before he bolts a dram of vodki. Every regiment has its field pastor with it, who commands as much respect among the soldiers as if he were an officer—more indeed, in a sense, for they salute the latter; they take off their caps to the priest.

CHAPTER X.

RUSSIAN OCCUPATION OF TIRNOVA.

Festive Reception of the Troops—Tardiness of the Russian Movements—The Three Armies of Operation—Rustchuk, Nicopolis, Tirnova—General Gourko's March on the Balkans—His Line of Route—Reported Russian Barbarities—The Army of Rustchuk—Impatience of the Officers—Hassan Pacha of Nicopolis, and the Emperor—A Scare at the Emperor's Headquarters—Gourko beyond the Balkans.

ONCE in Bulgaria the Russians divided their forces, turning both to the right and the left, and pushing onward. One of their columns was directed towards Nicopolis and Plevna, another towards Rustchuk, by Bjela and Pavlo, and a third southwards towards Tirnova and Gabrova, to prepare for the passage of the Balkans. The two following letters describe the occupation of Tirnova.

† SAREVICA, *July 8th.*—A courier has just arrived here from the front with news. The Russian advance has occupied Tirnova, with two brigades of cavalry and artillery, encountering little or no resistance. About 2,000 Redifs were there, who simply withdrew as the Russians advanced. Tirnova is a place of about 16,000 inhabitants, and is a convenient point for a base of operations in crossing the Balkans, but otherwise is not of great strategical importance, being too far away from the Balkans to give the command of the passes which converge upon it. It is not fortified, and would require immense works to render it tenable as a fortress. It is, however, beautifully situated. The Turkish population is about one-third. The infantry is pushing rapidly forward to support the cavalry. The plan of the Turks, probably, is to let the Russian army advance thus far, then marching from Shumla take it in flank and rear. The Russians hope for this, as they can then measure their strength with the Turks in the open field instead of behind fortifications. In presence of any other enemy but the Turks, the Russian advance on Tirnova before Rustchuk and Nicopolis had been taken would be a fearful blunder. It would simply be impossible; but with the Turks to deal

with, the Russians can do almost anything. If, for instance, the Turks were now to advance a column rapidly from Shumla, and take the Russian column now marching to Tirnova in flank, it might prove disastrous to the Russian column marching from the Danube to Tirnova. It would be impossible to concentrate at any particular spot where the Turks might strike in time. They could cut it in two in the middle without the slightest difficulty, and beat it in detail. But there is not the most remote probability that they will do so. The Russians extend their line with impunity over some forty miles in length.

† TIRNOVA, *July 12th*.—This has been a great day for Tirnova. The Grand Duke arrived to-day at noon, with the greater part of the 8th Corps, so that now the town may be considered really occupied by the Russians. The march from Sistova was rather like a military promenade or a triumphal procession than a forced march, which it really was. Everywhere the people came out to meet us, offering bread and salt and the most friendly greetings; while the women and girls offered fruit, and pelted us with flowers. At the entrance of many of the villages, arches were erected, covered with leaves and flowers. Processions, headed by priests, came out singing to meet us, with pictures from the churches, standards, and banners. There were deafening cheers, and the most extravagant joy. They insisted on shaking hands with us, would have kissed our hands had we allowed it, and sometimes they even shed tears. At the entrance of the village of Zavada, which is at the beginning of the gorge that leads to Tirnova, a rude arch was constructed of branches of trees. The whole population of the village gathered at the roadside near it. The soldiers, without orders from their officers, uncovered as they passed under, to the great delight of the people; while a huge bar of iron beaten by a mallet gave forth the first sound resembling a bell heard here for four hundred years. Just inside this gorge or hollow are two very ancient monasteries, built one on each side of a steep mountain side. The priests from these monasteries came down to meet us with banners and pictures, and a large beautiful Bible, which as many of the soldiers as could kissed as they passed, the people of these monasteries hoisting old bells which had lain hidden in the basements for four hundred years, and the voices of which will soon again be heard rolling up and down the hollows and gorges of the mountains.

The reception at Tirnova was splendid. The appearance of the town to-day presented a striking contrast with what I saw

R

when here last summer. Then, not a woman was to be seen in the streets nor at the windows of the houses, and men went about with a frightened, cringing air that showed the state of terror in which the people were kept. The zaptiehs were the only people who did not appear afraid of their own shadows. Now, all is changed. The zaptiehs are replaced by Russian soldiers. The streets are full of women, girls, and children, who mingle with the soldiers on the most friendly and sociable terms. The windows are teeming with the faces of pretty girls, flags, and streamers. The narrow, crooked streets are choked up by crowds of people, soldiers, horses, and waggons, and the town is ringing with excitement and joy. Such is the greeting the invaders receive at all hands. The Grand Duke arrived about noon. He was met at the usual entrance to the town by priests in robes chanting prayers in the old Sclavonic tongue, and by immense crowds of people. With deafening cheers he was conducted to the church, where he attended a short service, then passed through the streets, where several arches had been erected with the inscription upon them of "Welcome," followed by a crowd of girls singing. The women and girls at the windows literally covered him with flowers, while Christo Ignatieff with the enormous moustache was quite buried in the carriage under the leaves, flowers, and wreaths showered upon him. The Grand Duke then went to the quarters already prepared for him.

The people have opened their houses to the Russians. There is no trouble about getting billets. The officers have only to inquire at the first house, and if not already occupied they are sure to be received. I obtained a room in the first house I asked at. The people are all smiles and words of welcome. I can only hope that the Russians will not cause them to change their ideas before they go away. In only one village had we a cool reception. That was Akchair, where the people showed a disinclination to sell anything, either because they were afraid the Russians would go away and the Turks come back, or because some flying band of Russians had taken things without payment. The Turkish population fled everywhere. We passed through several villages which had been abandoned, the Turks carrying off all their effects that they had not been plundered of. I have been told that some of these villages had been fired by the Cossacks. I am inclined to think this a mistake. I saw myself an occasional outhouse or heap of straw burning that may have been fired by accident; but when I passed there was not the slightest indication of an intention to burn any village; nor do I think any has been burnt. The country along the road is very rich, but little under cultivation. Most of it is grass land, offering abundance of forage for horses. Nearly the whole Turkish population fled from Tirnova, carrying off their goods and chattels. The houses of those who fled were more or less damaged by the Bulgarian juvenile population. Windows and doors were smashed, as at Sistova. The most needy part of the population helped themselves to what the Turks left behind, which was not much. These acts were committed during the day or two of anarchy which followed the departure of the Turks and preceded Russian rule. They are repudiated by the better class of Bulgarians, who express great chagrin at them, but who are powerless to prevent them. There appears to be a disposition to attach more importance to these acts of Vandalism than they deserve. The breaking of a few doors and windows is, after all, but a slight vengeance for the oppression which culminated in the horrible massacres last May. These acts besides were not committed in the houses of Turks who remained at home. Fifty Turkish families have remained here quite undisturbed and unmolested. Had the Turkish population remained quietly at home none of these things would have happened. The conduct of the retreating Turks deserves mention. I have heard of isolated cases of outrage and murder and violence, but these are rare. They drive off all the Bulgarian live stock—sheep, horses, and cattle—they can lay their hands on, but do not go further. Several villages we passed through had not one four-footed beast left. This measure, however justifiable upon military grounds, naturally exasperates the Bulgarians greatly. As far as can be ascertained, very few troops are in the Balkans. I have just seen a young man from Elena whom I saw there last summer, who came here yesterday and goes back to-morrow. He tells me there are no Turks in the vicinity. Yet this place is on the direct road to Sliveno, from which point Yamboli on the railway is soon reached. General Gourko has gone forward in that direction to-day with cavalry and artillery and the Bulgarian legion.

It is not likely that the Grand Duke will leave here under a week or ten days. His march so far has been remarkable for its rapidity when once begun, and for the complete absence of opposition or even annoyance by the Turks. Not a single alarm, not a single shot fired. When we consider the distance penetrated into the enemy's country, it is remarkable. It is not easy to understand the plan of the Turks, if indeed they have a plan at all. I do not know how many troops there are before us, nor what force is destined for the defence of Constantinople; but unless they impede the march of this army more than hitherto it will be in sight of Saint Sophia within a month, whether Rustchuk falls or not. The Russian plan is very evident. They mean to imitate the Prussians in the Franco-German war, carry on the siege of a fortress, and attack the enemy's capital at the same time. Unless the Turks make a more stubborn defence than hitherto, this army may dictate peace at Constantinople possibly before Shumla and Varna have fallen. The Turks so far have shown themselves as incapable in war and as feeble against regular soldiers as they are savage and ferocious in fighting women and children.

Such is one view of the commencement of the Russian campaign. But there were observers on the spot who were by no means impressed with the military capacity it disclosed. A correspondent, dating from Simnitza on the 9th of July, wrote:—

* The Russians to-day celebrated here the taking of Tirnova by a Te Deum. Viewed as an isolated exploit no doubt the taking of Tirnova was a very fine thing, so far as we have yet information about it, and if a Te Deum was to the taste of the Russian headquarters nobody will grudge them the indulgence in the sacred triumphal music; but as a feat of expedition the advance of the Russians on Tirnova cannot take a high place. Let me review the position. The crossing occurred on Wednesday week, 27th ultimo. On the evening of that day the Grand Duke commanding in chief telegraphed that already an army corps, the 8th, was on the other side of the Danube. To-day is the 9th of July. Twelve days have elapsed since the day of the crossing. Tirnova is not more than fifty miles from Sistova. The Russian troops encountered no opposition between Sistova and the confines of Tirnova. Before crossing they had ample time to make their preparations, and a cavalry division might have crossed the day after the first crossing if the customary alacrity had been used in the construction of the pontoon bridge. That, however, was made good on the 30th, and cavalry crossed that night and the following morning. Tirnova has been taken by cavalry. It follows that it took a brigade of cavalry—a flying brigade be it remembered, a brigade specially designed to make a cavalry raid—no less than eight days to reach and occupy Tirnova, a place distant only fifty miles from the starting point of that brigade. This is marching at the rate of about six miles a day, allowing for no marching having been done on the day of the fighting against Tirnova.

The procedure of the Russian army in its march from the bridge-head at Sistova resembles the gradual unfolding of the flower which is the central figure of a transformation scene. The leaves fall to right and to left and reveal the heart of the blossom. The stamens projected earlier probably, but the corolla is only visible after the petals droop outward. Now this flower has been blossoming since the 27th ult., the day on the evening of which the 8th Corps stood on the Sistova side. But the progress of the blossoming has been wondrous slow. One petal droops toward Rustchuk, another toward Nicopolis. Now Rustchuk, even by the way the Russians are marching, is not more than fifty miles from Sistova. The petal that droops towards Rustchuk consists of the force on which has been conferred the name of the "Army of Rustchuk"—made up of the 12th and 13th Army Corps. The cavalry of the former has got three-fourths of the road, the 12th Corps itself is to-day behind Bjela, not half way on the road, the 13th Corps is yet further in the rear and only in part beyond Sistova. The Germans fought Gravelotte on the 18th of August and invested Metz on the 19th. Now Gravelotte is nearer Metz than is Rustchuk to Simnitza; but, on the other hand, there was a tremendous battle at Gravelotte and only a skirmish at Simnitza. It is not easy to see why Rustchuk should not have been invested in five days at the outside after the crossing of the Danube; instead of which the investing army is not yet half way on to the spot where its task of investment shall commence. The other petal drooped towards Nicopolis. The objective of the 9th Corps is that fortress. It marched from opposite Nicopolis round by Simnitza, and crossed the Danube on the 6th inst.; it has not yet commenced the investment of Nicopolis. From Turna Magurelle to Nicopolis, round by Simnitza, is a distance of about forty miles—that distance has not yet been traversed wholly, but twelve days have elapsed since the crossing of the Danube at Simnitza..

Now for the corolla. I have already spoken of the stamens—how one, the brigade Leuchtenberg, is already actually fifty miles away from its base after eight days' marching, and how the others, the remaining cavalry brigades, the tirailleur brigade, and the Bulgarian legion, are probably by this time nearly as far on. But the corolla proper consists of the head of the great infantry column—that is, the 8th Army Corps. That corps, as the Grand Duke has testified, crossed the Danube on the 27th ult. One division, the 9th, went east to Vardim, on the Danube bank; the other, the 14th, went west into Sistova. Both divisions quitted these positions to-day, to penetrate into the interior. In other words, they have remained within actual view of the point at which they crossed the Danube for the period of twelve days, exclusive of the day on which they crossed. I am not mathematician enough to calculate by what time at this rate of progress, and excluding all artificial obstacles, such as broken bridges and lions in the path, they are to reach Adrianople.

There was reason in the deliberation which the Russians exercised in their advance on the Danube and their preparations for crossing. Soldiers gave them credit for what is the best piece of soldiering after all—the determination to leave as little as possible to chance. But soldiers expected that, every precaution having been taken, every preparation elaborated, every button on every gaiter sewn firmly on, when the first blow was once struck, there should be no delay in striking home. But the delay in getting ready to strike home has been simply bewildering. There is forced upon us the apprehension that in their previous delay the Russians were exercising no option for the purpose of preparation and elaboration, but that they struck for the crossing of the Danube actually before they were ready to utilize the gain of the successful passage of it.

It is not easy to discern the cause of the delay. As for supplies the whole Russian army might live a month in Bulgaria without bringing an ounce of supplies across the Danube, if pre-organization were to be brought properly into effect, if intendants or contractors, or whoever they may be, who are charged with the furnishing of supplies, were simply to follow in rear of the advance and buy what they find on the spot. But supplies bear the blame, nevertheless. My own belief is that a great part of the reason is to be assigned to the pottering rearrangements of the commands in order that young gentlemen of the blood imperial may gain military fame and St. George's Crosses. But this is not all. There is a lack of go, of energy, of system, of purpose, about the direction of the army. The machine is a very fine one, the material is admirable, the workmanship is good, the finishing is fair—but there is not motive power sufficient to bring out its excellences and to do it justice. I do not know whether there is a reserve of steam power anywhere, but, if so, it is kept strictly in reserve, and is not turned on with sufficient pressure to bring nearly all the good out of the machine which it is capable of yielding.

* Obertenik, *July 15th.*—When I visited Tirnova on the 13th instant, General Gourko's advance command had gone forward forty-eight hours previously. A brigade was making a

reconnaissance on the Shumla road, where some Turks were reported in position, supported by some infantry and artillery of the 9th Division. Colonel Tutolmin's Circassian Cossacks were leading the advance of General Gourko's column, which has taken the bold, and perhaps even rash, course of marching direct on Kezanlik, whence Yamboli and the railway, as also the valley of the Tundja, leading straight down on Adrianople, are easily accessible. Of course, the march has its dangers. So bad are the tracks through the passes of the Elena Balkans that General Gourko's column of infantry, as well as cavalry, have resigned their waggon transport, and convey the baggage and provisions upon pack horses. Reports have come from Elena that there is not a Turkish soldier between Tirnova and that place, and that, indeed, no force bars the way over the Balkans. It is difficult to ascertain anything respecting the whereabouts of the Turkish troops in force; but some evidence exists that Abdul Kerim's field army, drawn from Rustchuk and Shumla, is echeloned on the line from Rasgrad over the Lom to Osman Bazar, apparently with the intent to cover the western face of the so-called quadrilateral. If this be so, General Gourko's daring crossing of the Balkans need apprehend no interruption, for Kezanlik is nearer to Tirnova, whence he started, than it is to Osman Bazar, whence the Turkish intercepting column might be expected to start. General Gourko need have no fear of the Turks breaking in upon the line of his communications, for he has cut himself adrift so far as regards the space between Elena and Kezanlik, and can operate nimbly as a detached force in the great Roumelian valley till joined there by the main force of the Russian invading column, marching by the more practicable, but more circuitous route through the Balkans, over Drenova, Gabrova, Shipka, and Eski Zagra. The head of this main column will consist of the 8th Corps, of which one division, the 9th, was already in Tirnova on the 13th inst., while the other, the 14th, was a day's march behind. The 8th Corps will be supported by the great bulk of the 11th Corps, now partly on the march on Tirnova, partly crossing the river, and probably the 9th Corps will spare one of its divisions, the 5th, to take part in the grand advance, which would thus consist of five divisions, or 80,000 men, not including General Gourko's advance contingent of some 15,000 more. There are, indeed, more troops to spare for this purpose. The 30th Division, belonging to the 4th Corps, the other half of which is reported with General Zimmermann in the Dobrudscha, is now on the road between Bucharest and Giurgevo. Its destination may be to co-operate in the siege of Rustchuk, wholly relieving the 11th

Corps at Giurgevo, or its rôle may be to march to Simnitza, and, advancing on Tirnova, act as a reserve to the main invading column. In any case, after muzzling the fortresses of the quadrilateral, and neutralizing Nicopolis and its troops, quite one hundred thousand men are immediately available for the crossing of the Balkans by the western line of invasion, over Tirnova, putting out of the calculation General Zimmerman's army on the eastern section of the theatre of war.

General Gourko's celerity is an exception to the general deliberation of the advance. It was not expected that the 8th Corps would move forward in force till about the 20th, and other portions of the advance would be later. So far as regards supplies, the Russians are determined to leave nothing to chance, with Bucharest as a great central depôt, where there are stores of meal, to which the supplies of rice for the relief of the Bengal famine were a mere bagatelle. Sistova will be an intermediate depôt, and Tirnova the advanced depôt. To facilitate the conveyance of stores another bridge of very substantial construction has been commenced between Simnitza and Sistova, higher up the stream than the one now existing. The key of the Balkans, Tirnova, is in Russian hands. Russian soldiers are climbing the Balkans. Russian cavalry have scoured Bulgaria till within sight of Rustchuk on the east, and up to Plevna on the west. All this has been done, not with dashing promptitude, but with prudent, careful deliberation, allowing full time for the concentration of opposition. Yet there has been no opposition worthy of the name.

Referring to the report of Russian barbarities practised on the Turkish inhabitants of Bulgaria, I may simply mention that about fifty Turkish families of Tirnova remained behind after the general exodus, and are living unharmed under the special protection of the Russian military authorities. The Bulgarians of Tirnova are drawing their supplies of firewood from abandoned Turkish houses. Speaking as a perfectly impartial man, who would have no hesitation in bearing testimony to the contrary, were the contrary true, and who has had exceptional opportunities for observation, I do not believe that in Bulgaria there has been a single instance of personal maltreatment of a Turkish civilian at the hands of Russian soldiers.

I turn now to the Army of Rustchuk. Activity hitherto has not been permitted to this force. It has simply stood fencing on one side of the broad lane along which the Balkan column has marched up the country to Tirnova. Of the 12th Corps, one division, the 12th, is at the confluence of the Jantra with the Danube. The other, the 33rd, remains still in position at Bjela. The 13th Corps has one of its divisions, the 35th, at Kosovo, a little distance higher up the Jantra than Bjela; while the other, the 1st Division, is at Pavlo, where still remain the headquarters of the Czarewitch and his brother Vladimir. I believe permission at last has been accorded to cross the Jantra, but a rapid advance on Rustchuk does not seem imminent. The front of this army is covered by three cavalry divisions, the 12th, the 13th, and the 8th, the latter not being needed with its own corps. The front of the three divisions extends from the Danube, about twelve miles west of Rustchuk, for some forty miles inland in a direction due south, their front facing the Turkish forepost position on the river Lom. The 12th Cavalry Division is on the left, with its headquarters here in Obertenik, the 13th in the centre, and the 8th on the right, with its headquarters in the village of Cairkoi. Small reconnaissances are pushed forward, but the mass of the divisions has been stationary for nearly a week.

Yesterday I accompanied a patrolling party along the road towards Rustchuk. At Trestenik we found a large abandoned camp, probably of the troops commanded by Ahmed Eyoub Pacha. Still nearer Rustchuk, within a few versts of the fortress and close to the Lom River, at a place called on the map Han Gol Cisme, we found an abandoned intrenched position which appeared to have been occupied by a body of from ten to fourteen thousand troops. Pushing on toward the Lom we were stopped by the Turks, and had a little brush; but there are no Turks between the Rustchuk road and the Danube so near to the fortress as Pirgos.

There crowd into the Russian camps the Bulgarian inhabitants of the villages along the River Lom, who report that their effects are despoiled by the Turkish soldiers, who are, doubtless, destitute of supplies, and take what they can find; but I hear no instance of personal violence, nor does smoke testify to the burning of villages. The Turks appear to be conveying supplies from their abandoned positions on the Rustchuk road along their front toward their left flank. Three days ago Prince Manueloff, commanding the 8th Cavalry Division, caught a Turkish convoy at the village of Cairkoi, in the act of executing this manœuvre, and at once fell upon it, met with resistance from the escort, and had to bring up artillery. He ultimately captured a mass of baggage, provisions, ammunition, and over a thousand head of cattle. But these things are mere *divertissements*. The Army of Rustchuk is burning for the opportunity of justifying its name.

*·PAVLO, *July 16th.*—The inactivity of the Rustchuk Army is naturally creating great dissatisfaction among the officers eager for an opportunity to distinguish themselves. Earnest entreaties have been persistently sent to the headquarters begging for a relaxation of the strict injunction that the infantry mass of the army was not to cross the Jantra for a long time, but without effect. Yet the Czarewitch and his brother Vladimir were among the supplicants. General Nepokoitchitsky—that silent, determined little man—was obdurate in the maintenance of the prohibition against anything save a defensive and preventive attitude. The policy of this attitude was obvious. While two corps stood lining the road of advance on Tirnova, no attempt to intercept that advance, or to disturb its communications, could be made. Nor was this all. The Turkish field army, reported to extend from Rasgrad to Osman Bazar, could not change its front and, marching to its left, move off into the Balkans to interfere with the passage of the Russians through the defiles without showing a flank, and, indeed, its rear, to this threatening mass of men, purposely motionless for the time, but ready to march quickly and far when the opportunity for doing good by so doing should offer. The policy was obvious, but it was cautious. It was not in accord with Prince Frederick Charles's standing orders—"Find your enemy, and fight him whenever and wherever you find him."

The restriction against crossing the Jantra has at length given way. The Army of Rustchuk is to move on towards Rustchuk, and in course of doing so its right flank should come into contact with the positions of the Turkish field army on the River Lom. Still, the advance will be a measured one. The headquarters move only to a village called Beleova, on the east bank of the Jantra, about midway between Bjela and the Danube, and the centre of the new position will be about Damogila, a village near Obertenik, the present headquarters of the cavalry division of the 12th Corps. Although the advance will be slow, to all appearance, yet I believe that the masking policy is abandoned, and that Rustchuk and Shumla will be besieged. We may expect a bridge across the Danube somewhere about Pirgos, to convey the siege train to a place where it can be of use. Then will be found some practical employment for that immense accumulation of large shells, weighing thousands of tons, collected at Banyasa, a station on the Bucharest and Giurgevo Railway, about ten miles north of Giurgevo. In the meantime the infantry advance will enable the cavalry to move forward and throw a circle of observation close around the rayon of the fortress, and thus isolate it from the rest of the world. It is of immense value to the Russians that they have obtained possession of Nicopolis thus early, setting free, as it does, quite a division, if not indeed a whole army corps.

* PAVLO, *July 18th.*—The staff of the Czarewitch has left here this morning, and crossed the Jantra in preparation for the advance on the Lom River and the investment of Rustchuk, with the army composed as already described. The Emperor and the Imperial headquarters, which arrived on Monday, remain until the 20th, and then proceed to Tirnova. The 4th Corps will cross the Danube at Simnitza, and advance towards the Balkans in support of the column crossing the mountains.

Yesterday was brought to the Imperial headquarters Hassan Pacha, the valiant Turkish defender of Nicopolis, of whose fighting prowess the Russians speak with generous appreciation. As he fought when free, so Hassan Pacha acted when a prisoner, bearing himself before the Great White Czar with true Turkish nonchalance. When asked why he capitulated, he said his ammunition was all gone, and he had been obliged to kill with his own hand three or four soldiers who left their duty. He said it was a stupid war, into which the Turks had been mainly led by the attitude of England, and the nation would be glad when it was over. He spoke as rank folly of the conduct of a Russian artillery officer who, when one position was barely carried, rode his guns in among the still undefeated Turks, and, unlimbering, came into action against other positions as yet uninjured. The Pacha left for Russia last night. The Russian losses at Nicopolis are not yet wholly ascertained. They are estimated at one thousand two hundred killed and wounded. The gain of the fortress frees the Russians from the threat of attack on their right flank. Of the 9th Corps which gained the success one division, the 31st, will, for the present, remain on the line of Plevna-Nicopolis to protect communications and guard against any trouble from the Widdin direction. The other, the 5th, will form a portion of the Balkan advance, which will comprise several columns operating in different directions.

On Sunday night, when the Emperor was camped at Sarevica, a few miles south of Sistova, there was a sudden alarm. A Cossack rode in with a hurriedly scribbled despatch from a telegraph clerk at the bridge across the Danube to the effect that the Turks were marching from Nicopolis on Sistova, and threatening to sever the Russian communications, destroy the bridge, and compromise the safety of the Emperor. Immediate steps had to be taken. One brigade of the 11th Corps was in Sarevica. The other brigades of the same corps were forwarded. Dispositions were made with the artillery and infantry covering the line of the heights protecting the line of approach from Nicopolis. The Emperor himself assumed the chief direction of affairs, and is said to have shown at once the most perfect coolness and competent military ability. The scouts sent out brought back the intelligence that the country in the direction of Nicopolis was quiet, and presently arrived intelligence from Baron Krüdener, commanding the 9th Corps, respecting his success at Nicopolis. It was ultimately discovered that the telegraph clerk had become confused and alarmed by the noise of firing at Nicopolis and concern for the Emperor's safety. The incident seems trivial, but shows on what thin ice the Russians have been treading with hostile forces left on both flanks.

The news of General Gourko having crossed the Balkans has been received with extreme satisfaction at headquarters, and at once produced a determination in favour of prompt action on the part of the Rustchuk Army. Rustchuk is to be at once invested, and if there is a Turkish army on the Lom River, it will have to fight or retreat.

* HEADQUARTERS, PAVLO, *July 18th.*—While half the world is speculating on the chances and method of its solution, the great problem of the war has already been solved. General Gourko has crossed the Balkans. He is in the valley of the Tundja; he has passed the difficulties of the main Balkan range, the passage of the lesser Balkans intervening between the valley of the Tundja and the great Roumelian valley through which flows the River Maritza. General Gourko's exploit is a romance of warfare. I can recall no expedition more brilliant, more successful. Stonewall Jackson's raids must henceforth resign their pride of place. Gourko has raided across the Balkans, but he has done more. He has burst open the lock of the door that closed Turkey against invasion. For the full details the reader must wait for the despatches from my colleague, who rides with General Gourko. The sketch I now give is compiled from General Gourko's own official despatch, a copy of which has been communicated to me, and from the narrative of officers who accompanied him and have brought back his accounts of his swift and successful progress.

General Gourko marched out from Tirnova on the morning of the 12th instant at the head of eight regiments of cavalry and six battalions of the tirailleur brigade. His main body marched upon Elena, a place south-east of Tirnova, but it was necessary to ascertain how far the Turkish concentration, said to exist about Osman Bazar, was in force, and whether the alignment of the enemy was prolonged from Osman Bazar in a southerly direction through the Balkans. Accordingly General Gourko led a cavalry reconnaissance on the Shumla road in the direction of Osman Bazar, and pushed it home with considerable determination. He suffered loss, and the Turks, no doubt, say they repulsed him. What concerned him was, that he found out what he wanted to know. He learned that there were some 6,000 Turks in the Osman Bazar district, which however constituted the left flank of the Turkish alignment between the Danube and the Balkans. Their position did not prolong itself into the mountains, so, leaving a detachment of the 8th Corps, which had followed him, to watch the Turkish position about Osman Bazar, he coolly turned his back on the Turks and headed due south for the Balkans.

About Elena he picked up the mass of his detachment, and in two forced marches, each of nearly thirty versts, he was in the heart of the Balkans, striking that section of the range known as the Elena Balkans. Through these there are three passes into the valley of the Tundja, nearly parallel with each other. One, which I believe is the central of the three, is called the Hainkoi Pass, from the name of the village at its southern exit. The most easterly pass of the three is called the Zupanci Mesari Pass. The name of the third I do not know. General Gourko had as guides the Christian inhabitants of the intricate valleys of the Balkan ranges, who have never wholly bowed to Turkish rule. Led by them, with long-extended and swiftly stretched-out arm, he clutched a grip of the throats of these three passes. Through each he passed a detachment, but he himself, and the mass of his command, penetrated the defile of the Hainkoi Pass, described as narrow, with precipitous rocks on either side in places, and somewhat tortuous. The gradients of the track are surprisingly easy, but the track was too narrow for the wheels of the gun carriages and mountain batteries which accompanied the column. In the most difficult part of the pass General Gourko's éclaireurs came on a fortified position held by a battalion of Turkish Nizams, who appeared taken utterly by surprise by the sudden appearance of the daring Cossacks. Many were killed and wounded, and the Nizams, who never had recovered from the confusion of the surprise, bolted precipitately.

Here, as in the two other passes, battery emplacements were found in judiciously chosen positions; but they had remained unarmed. General Gourko had been too nimble for the slow-paced, unmethodical Turks. When they were sitting still saying "Bismillah," he was riding through their unarmed earthworks. When General Gourko had traversed this Hainkoi Pass he found himself, as I have stated, in the valley of the Tundja, and he came out of the mountains into that valley at a singularly advantageous point, the village of Esekei, nearly equidistant from the three important places Kezanlik, Jeni Zagra, and Eski Zagra.

The importance of Kezanlik consists in its being at the mouth of the Shipka Pass, the main trans-Balkan thoroughfare between Gabrova and Kezanlik. Jeni Zagra is on the branch railway to Yamboli. Eski Zagra is quite beyond the Balkans, on the higher slopes of the Maritza Valley, and is the focus of good roads leading to all points of the valley. General Gourko knew that reinforcements were following him, and, seemingly believing in the axiom that nothing succeeds like success, struck at all three places. He sent a detachment of Cossacks to cut the railway at Jeni Zagra. He sent a small body of cavalry to occupy Eski Zagra, and collect transport materials. As for Kezanlik, information reached him that it and the Shipka Pass were strongly held by the Turkish troops. Assuming that these belonged to the same army he had already touched at Osman Bazar, his march had cut them off. He had traversed the line of communication between them and their main body. If so, they would the more easily be dealt with. If, on the other hand, they belonged to troops in force further west, or were simply an independent command, the daring wisdom of attacking them seemed to General Gourko equally obvious. So, instead of setting his face in a south-easterly direction down into the valley, with the glittering spires of Adrianople as his objective, he turned westward, and marched up the Tundja Valley on Kezanlik.

On the 16th he was one day's march on the road. To-day come reports that his advanced detachments are already in Kezanlik. He may be there by this time, but if so I do not believe there has been time for intelligence to reach Elena to that effect. By this time he certainly must be *aux prises* with the Turks in Kezanlik, if they have waited there for him. His intention was, as soon as Kezanlik was occupied, to strike the defenders of the Shipka Pass, and before marching he sent instructions that a column should march into the same pass from the northward and attack its defences in front. It is reported to be very strongly fortified and held.

Thus at present stands the position. The subtlety of the Turkish defence is a pricked bladder. The Turks have held the Balkan line no more firmly than they held the Danube line.

They have thrown away the chances and opportunities offered them with reckless and even contemptuous lavishness. The Russians earn few laurels in overcoming a foe thus unworthy. It remains untested whether the errors they commit arise from accurate gauging of Turkish imbecility, or are the result of shortcomings in military knowledge. It seems probable that General Gourko would have had a harder struggle in the Hainkoi Pass had it been held by Ashantees than with its defenders of the Turkish regulars. Numbers of pioneers are engaged in widening the Hainkoi Pass road, which will be practicable for the transport of vehicles in two days. Already the batteries of field artillery have gone through. General Gourko keeps his communications quite open with the base at Tirnova. The Emperor has sent him a message of warm congratulation.

We shall have an opportunity of tracing the march of General Gourko in the letters of the (†) correspondent who accompanied that officer. It will be seen in the sequel that the army of the Czarewitch on the left and that of General Krüdener on the right were intended to be used primarily to secure the advance across the Balkans to Adrianople, and that this was why the Czarewitch was temporarily hindered from committing himself to the investment of Rustchuk. It was when Krüdener's single corps proved itself too weak or too slow to secure the advance of the Tirnova column, and Plevna was occupied by Osman Pacha, that Gourko's advance was suddenly stopped, and the whole progress of the invasion arrested. This, however, is anticipating. In the following chapter we shall see the development of the movement south of the Balkans.

CHAPTER XI.

GENERAL GOURKO'S EXPEDITION.

Passage of the Balkans—The Roads and Scenery—A Mountain Solitude—Capture of Kezanlik—Prince Mirsky's Repulse in the Shipka Pass—General Gourko's Successful Attack—Turkish Treachery—Defeat of the Turks at Yeni Zagra—Decisive Defeat of the Bulgarian Column by the Turks at Eski Zagra—Retreat of General Gourko into the Shipka Pass—Suleiman Pacha the new Turkish Commander in the Balkans.

We have seen in what relation the advance upon Tirnova and the passage of the Balkans stood to the attitude of the Army of Rustchuk and the Western Corps, under General Krüdener. We now turn to the letters describing General Gourko's advance. The following is a summary view of that officer's operations, which are subsequently more fully described in the letters of the correspondent who accompanied him :—

* Bjela, *July* 23*rd*.—A recent telegram of mine recounted the progress of General Gourko through the Balkans into the valley of the Tundja, at the mouth of the Hainkoi Pass. I take up the narrative of subsequent events in the Balkans as communicated by the commanding officer to the Grand Duke Nicholas, and by him transmitted to the Imperial headquarters here. It was on the 14th that the Hainkoi Pass was forced. The Turks retreated westward on Konaro, but next day, having received reinforcements, they attacked General Gourko's vanguard, a rifle battalion, as the column marched on Konaro. After some sharp fighting the Turks were repulsed, Konaro occupied, and two of their camps taken. On the same day a column of Cossacks sent to Jeni Zagra successfully cut the telegraph and railway. Next day, the 16th, General Gourko marched on Maglish. His troops formed in three columns, one consisting of infantry, close to the mountains. The middle column was cavalry and infantry, and the left column cavalry only, with orders to cover the flank, and if possible to turn that of the enemy. At Uflami he was stopped by a strong position, and had to cope with the Turkish artillery, cavalry, and infantry. When he was pushing them hard, five battalions of Anatolian Nizams came up as reinforcements, and behaved very well. Their fire, begun as it

was at 2,000 paces, caused the Russians considerable loss. The Russian orders are not to open fire till within 600 paces of the enemy, and it was in the interval that the Russians suffered. But when their distance was reached they poured in a fire which soon compelled the Anatolians to give ground. The Russian direct attacking force was four battalions of rifles and two sotnias of infantry Cossacks, whom the Turks call "priests," because of the cross they wear to distinguish them from the Circassian Turks. While the direct attack was being delivered the Russian hussars and dragoons charged the Turkish flank. There was very hot fighting, sabre and bayonet both being used freely. The Turks were at length driven from their position with loss: 400 were left dead at one point. The Turks fought very hard here, but their defeat at Uflami seemed to destroy their morale, and subsequently they did not fight so stoutly.

On the 17th General Gourko approached Kezanlik. There was terrible heat, and it was fearfully severe marching. The infantry waded into little streams to become soaked and so gain coolness. There was fighting more or less all day. On the evening of the 17th General Gourko entered Kezanlik. The Turks had detailed from the force holding the Shipka Pass a column to occupy the heights flanking the entrance to Kezanlik and hinder General Gourko's advance; but his riflemen were beforehand in occupying these heights, and the Turks retired disappointed. It had been designed that Gourko should reach Kezanlik on the 16th, and on the 17th be free to assail in the rear the Turks holding the Shipka Pass, while Prince Mirsky with the 9th Division attacked them in front. But he was delayed by hard fighting, and the troops were too much fatigued to move further on the same day after the occupation of Kezanlik. So there was no co-operation between General Gourko and Prince Mirsky in attacking the Shipka Pass, but the latter nevertheless delivered an attack on that position marching southward from Gabrova. He sent against the Turks but one regiment, that of Orloff, which he divided into three columns. The pass was strongly fortified with six successive tiers of intrenchments and batteries, and defended by picked Turkish troops, Circassians and Egyptians. The latter fought very hard. Of Prince Mirsky's three columns, that on the right encountered little opposition and went on some distance, till it missed the support of the centre column, fought five or six hours, and then made good its lodgment in the hostile lines. The left column, consisting of two companies, missed its way, and was beset by twelve companies of Turkish soldiers.

It fought a retreating combat for four hours against terrible odds, losing eight officers killed and wounded and about 150 men. It was brought out of action by the only officer left standing, and he was wounded.

On the 18th General Gourko, his men refreshed, advanced to the attack of the Shipka position from the rear. Two battalions of rifles formed his advance. As they neared the rear of the position a flag of truce came out with a *parlementaire.* The rifles at once halted, and an officer acting as escort went forward to meet the *parlementaire.* While negotiations were going on, the Russian riflemen in their curiosity quitted their extended formation, and drew together into a mass behind where the officer was communing with the *parlementaire.* Suddenly volleys of rifle fire were poured in upon them from the Turkish position. The *parlementaire* took to his heels at a signal which the Russians heard but did not comprehend. So sudden and fierce was the fire that in their two battalions the Russians lost one hundred and forty-two men killed and wounded in a few minutes. The survivors in their fury waited for no order to attack, nor regarded any formation. With one common impulse and with yells of wrath they rushed on. It was a bad quarter of an hour for the Turks, but the riflemen, finding no signs of co-operation in the attack from the north by Prince Mirsky, contented themselves with driving back the Turks some distance, and occupied the abandoned Turkish camp in the rear of the fortifications. On the same night, in reply to General Gourko's summons to the Turks to surrender and abandon the further unavailing defence of the pass, there came a letter from the Turkish commander, Mehemet Pacha, offering to surrender. Negotiations were entered into, and the hour for the surrender of the Turks was fixed for twelve o'clock the next day. An armistice was arranged, and early on that morning the sanitary detachments went forward to bring in the wounded which the rifle battalions had been forced to leave behind. They sent back word that the Turks had fled and vacated the position. The offer of surrender was a ruse to gain time.

Meanwhile, on the 18th, Prince Mirsky had remained quiet, waiting for further information about Gourko's movements. But on the 19th, young Skobeleff, taking some troops of Mirsky's, had pushed forward a reconnaissance into the pass from the north. To his surprise he met with no opposition as he passed line after line of fortifications, and the hastily abandoned Turkish camps, with fires yet burning, rations half cooked, and half-written telegrams. At length he reached the crest of the pass, and the view to the south opened before him. In a hollow at his feet he saw troops in camp. Were they Turks or Russians? The tents seemed Turkish, but the soldiers looked like Russians. Skobeleff tried the Russian hurrah as a test, but it was not replied to. At length he saw the red-cross flag of the ambulance staff, and he knew that the men in the valley were his own people. A junction was immediately effected. All the Turkish camps and baggage, twelve cannon, four of them guns of position, and four hundred Turkish prisoners were taken.

The Shipka position is chiefly in a forest, and very difficult. The fortifications are very skilfully designed, and are alleged to have been constructed by an English engineer officer. General Gourko reports that all his wounded had been killed on the field where they fell, and the dead and wounded were found headless, and otherwise fearfully mutilated. There had been apparent deliberation, for the fallen Russians had been gathered together into groups. Some Turkish wounded were found who, in expectation of a similar fate, drew their daggers when the Russians approached, and prepared to sell their lives dearly. Their lives were spared, and they were attended to. General Gourko remains in Kezanlik till the 8th Corps, now occupying the defiles of the Balkans, shall have passed through them and massed, with supplies, for further progress. The road at present is only practicable for vehicles drawn by bullocks; but large numbers of men are engaged in improving it. Several days will elapse before the onward move is made. Even the cavalry expeditions are suspended for the moment. The Turks sacrificed their chances of defence by continually dribbling forward reinforcements of two or three battalions at a time, instead of either attacking in force, or keeping the bulk of their troops in hand for a strongly sustained defensive effort. Their treachery respecting the flag of truce and their mutilation of the wounded are barbarities which place them beyond the pale of civilized warfare.

The following letters are from the correspondent who rode with General Gourko:—

† PAROVCI, *July 15th.*—Deep in a gorge of the Balkans, in a dark, narrow little dell, whose sides are so steep that the dozen houses which make up the village seem to be holding on with hooks and claws, to keep from slipping down into the deep ravine beneath them, lies Parovci, from which this letter is written. It is night, and a thick veil of darkness

covers mountains, trees, rocks, and forests. Almost perfect silence reigns, and the occasional cry of some bird, startled in its slumbers, echoes fearfully distinct and alarming. Other sounds may be heard if one listens closely; an occasional hum of voices, the impatient stamp of a horse's hoof, and the rattle of harness. The fact is, that just beneath the little house where I have found refuge, stands a battery of artillery, and that extending two miles further up, and three or four miles further down the dark, crooked, rocky little hollow, lies an army asleep on its arms, without fire or supper, waiting the first ray of daylight to resume its march. It would be madness to attempt taking the artillery along this road in the darkness, and there are artillery and cavalry here trying to make their way over this almost impassable road, as well as infantry. We are in one of the most difficult defiles of the Balkans, at the entrance to a pass which the Turks have left unguarded, a pass which we hope to get through early in the morning, and this is the reason of our secrecy and silence, the absence of camp fires and supper, and the usual sights and sounds of a bivouac. The glare of camp fires reflected on the sky, and seen from the other side of the mountains, might give the alarm to the Turks, and a very small force, a very little thing, would stop the way, and even result in the destruction of the column. We are less than ten thousand men, and we are extended along this narrow, crooked defile a distance of probably seven or eight miles. Should the Turks get wind of our advance they could concentrate on the other side and cut us off in detail as we came out, as easily as you can catch water coming out of a bunghole. There are other dangers to be thought of too. One thunderstorm would render the road, already so difficult, quite impassable. Then should we succeed in getting out on the other side there is still the possibility, though a remote one, of the Turks rapidly concentrating twenty-five or thirty thousand men, and crushing us before we can get reinforcements. It is a hazardous undertaking, but one which, if successful, will ensure the passage of the Balkans to the main army, while, if we are lost, the loss after all is not very great. It is the detachment of General Gourko which left Tirnova yesterday for an unknown destination, and whose advance guard, after two days' march, has just reached and camped in the summit of the pass of Parovci. To-morrow the army will be over, and will pour out into the broad fertile valley of the Tundja like a torrent, to the great surprise of the Turks, who are watching for us in a very different place.

I left Tirnova the day after this detachment, and caught it up here in the night after a hard ride and search, during which I was astonished to find how completely so large a detachment could disappear in a single day, and leave no trace and no indication of the route it had taken. I knew, or thought I knew, it must have taken the direction of Elena or Gabrova, and it seemed at first a very easy matter to ascertain which it was. I first went out the road towards Elena, inquiring of the peasants coming from that direction whether they had seen the Russians, and where they were. I soon learned in this way, not only that the detachment of Gourko had not gone this road, but that the small Russian force in Elena had left that place, and gone across country in the direction of Gabrova. Very good, I thought, the detachment has gone to Gabrova, and I have only to take that road in order soon to overtake it. My disappointment and astonishment were great, however, upon turning back and trying the Gabrova road, to find the detachment I was in search of had not been over this road either. It seemed to me at first as though the whole detachment must have vanished into thin air, for it did not appear possible it could have taken any other road. I knew it could not have gone further to the right than Gabrova, which leads to Kezanlik, nor further to the left than Elena, which leads to Slievno. And as it must have gone somewhere, it occurred to me it might have gone by some road between the two places. I determined to try, and striking across country through the fields, pulled up after an hour's ride at the village of Aplakova, between the Elena and Gabrova roads. Here I soon learned that there was another road, leading over the Balkans between those of Gabrova and Elena, and that a strong Russian detachment—a large army, the peasants said—had passed through the village yesterday, going by this road. This was evidently my detachment; and having found the trail, I knew I should have no difficulty in following it. The road, I learned, led through the villages of Voinis, Raikovci, and Parovci, and the pass began at near the latter place. None of these places are marked on the Russian staff map, and although they are on the Austrian map, there are no indications of any road, which shows how little, after all, is known of the passes of the Balkans. The fact is, the road is a carriage road—if the lumbering wooden vehicles of the peasants drawn by oxen can be called carriages—and not a mere donkey path, as might be supposed. Now it is well known that light field artillery can always be taken over such roads, not to speak of mountain guns carried on horses or mules; and that consequently such a road is practicable for an army, although it may be difficult. That the Turks should have neglected such a road, supposing it impracticable, is only one more evidence of their incapacity. Leaving Aplakova, I found the road led through a narrow, crooked little hollow, shut in on both sides by low, steep, rocky hills, that were covered with a thick growth of wood, and offering the most wonderful positions for defence that could be imagined; and I thought what a curious thing it was that I—to all intents and purposes one of the invaders—should thus be passing through the enemy's country alone, unattended, and unarmed, by such a road without fear of molestation. This is, in fact, one of the characteristics of this war. I knew that if there had been a single Bashi-Bazouk, Circassian, or Turk in the vicinity, I should have immediate warning from the Bulgarian peasants whom I met every few minutes. The ordinary position of invaders and invaded in this war is reversed. The Russians are among friends who receive them everywhere with open arms, who bring them correct information, who tell them exactly where the Turks are, their numbers, where they go and whence they come, who do all the work of spies, as well as the service of outposts; while the Turks, who should be among friends, are among enemies, as much as the Prussians were in France; and thus, while playing the part of the invaded, have to fight at all the disadvantage of invaders.

Thus I pushed on without fear of meeting flying bands of the enemy, knowing well I should hear of them long before seeing them, and thus have time to avoid them. The road emerged from the crooked little hollow, led up over some hills that were covered with orchards and vineyards, then descended again into a wild narrow little hollow, down which poured a little stream over a rocky bed that just left room for the road beside it. A couple of miles of this, and I came to a very small house and a very small mill, where there was a single Cossack hobnobbing with the miller, his lance stuck in the ground, and his horse wandering about at will, filling himself with grass. Here the road again left the hollow and climbed over some low hills, through a dense dark oak forest, through which I pursued my way, finding nothing more alarming to startle me than three or four great heavy black vultures that arose at my approach with a great flapping of wings, and sailed off through the trees like a shadow. Then we emerged from the forest upon a high narrow ridge that seemed to be a watershed, where we had the most splendid view of the Balkans I have ever seen. There was first a low uneven hilly country, full of green little valleys and hollows, rich and luxuriant with orchards, trees, and growing grain, that almost hid the villages of fifteen or twenty houses which they surrounded. Then, beyond, the range of the great Balkans, their huge round forms rising up against the sky, in glorious robes of misty purple, and extending far away to the west until they mingled imperceptibly high up in the sky with the golden-edged, many-tinted clouds. Here and there they are still covered with snow, that gleams white in the sun, and brings out the purple with more beautiful effect, and seems to offer coolness, calm, and repose, high up there in the sky, far above the dust and heat and sweat of the earth. Now the road again descends into a delightful little valley, full of wheat-fields, and gardens, and fruit-trees, completely surrounded by high, steep mountains covered with forests, and we are in the village of Voinis, a cosy, isolated, primitive little place. Here we came upon the rear-guard of the detachment, and here we halted to bait our horses, and get something to eat. We went into the first house we came to, and had no difficulty in obtaining barley for our horses, milk, bread, and a roast chicken for ourselves. A tall, handsome peasant woman waited upon us, who wore a very curious headdress, such as I had never before seen in Bulgaria, and which I observed was worn by all the women in this village. A little round cylindrical cap set on top of the head, with a projecting brim on the top, to which was attached a long white veil that fell down over the shoulders and was wound about the neck and chin, and in the presence of Turks probably the lower part of the face. The cap itself is a thin brass shell set with some cheap kind of coloured stones.

From this village the road began to grow rough and wild, and we soon entered a deep narrow gorge, the sides of which were covered with short scraggy trees, and the bottom by a mass of stones and boulders, where no sign of a road was visible; a wild, desolate, forbidding-looking place, where there was no sign that the foot of man had ever trod. Here about sun-down we came upon the rear of the column, a regiment of hussars under the Grand Duke Nicholas of Leuchtenberg, moving slowly forward. I determined to reach the head of the column if possible, and I pushed on past as rapidly as I could. This was not fast. It is no easy thing to pass an army on a narrow road, and at ten o'clock at night when I drew rein here, not yet having reached further than the middle of the column, which had finally halted, the advance guard had already reached and crossed the pass, and was lying like ourselves without light and without fire, silently awaiting the first streak of day to pour out into the valley of the Tundja. This pass and this road I may say were discovered by Prince Tserteleff, to whom had been confided the whole business of obtaining information about the roads, the movements of the enemy, their numbers, dispositions, and so on. He soon ascertained that the Turks had fortified the Slievno and Gabrova Passes in such a way as to render the forcing of a passage at either of them a very difficult matter, and he determined to look for another. Count Moltke in his book refers to a pass between those of Gabrova and Slievno, but speaks of it as only a path not practicable for an army. Prince Tserteleff decided to investigate this pass, in the hope that it might lead to something. He soon ascertained that it had a very bad reputation—a place that was generally frequented by brigands, and rarely used either by Bulgarians or Turks. Among the Turks he found it had even a worse reputation than among the Bulgarians. It was a kind of tradition among them that this pass was in the clouds, that the defiles leading to it were so wild, so savage and barren, as to be unfrequented by either bird or beast—a kind of mountain desert where nothing could live. Pursuing his investigations, the Prince heard of a man who had been through this pass, and, finding him, he learned that he had been through in fact, but that was two years ago, and the road might have become impassable since then. But what made the information really important was that he had been through with one of the ox-carts of the country. If an ox-cart could go through, very probably a cannon might be got through somehow, and it was determined to reconnoitre and explore. Three days before the arrival of the Grand Duke at Tirnova, General Rauch went forward with 200 Cossacks for this purpose, taking with him Bulgarian guides. Without waiting to explore the road to the end, he immediately began preparing it for the passage of artillery, a task which, as far as the pass itself was concerned, turned out to be no very difficult matter, as the worst part of the road was on the south side. The most wonderful part of it though, which forcibly illustrates what I was saying about the Russians being among friends, was this: that, although these 200 Cossacks were working three days on this road, with the Bulgarian peasantry coming and going all the time freely, the Turks never got a whisper of their presence here, nor any intimation of the evident intention of the Russians to try this pass. They even sent three battalions from Kezanlik to Slievno to strengthen the positions before the latter place, and these three battalions passed by Khaini the day before the Russians issued out. These three battalions were just where they ought to have been had they known it, and they could have prevented the success of the movement. And yet, although the whole Bulgarian population of a dozen mountain villages knew the Russians were there, not one man was found among them to inform the Turks. Such is the advantage possessed by an army operating among a friendly population. The Turkish staff either did not know of this pass at all, or, knowing it, believed it to be so impracticable that they did not even think it worth while to place a corps of observation to watch it. The small body of troops mentioned in my telegram as being here turn out to have not been placed here, as I supposed, to watch the place. They were merely a small body whose retreat had been cut off by the Russians at Elena, and who had retreated by this road two or three days before the Russians came, without thinking it worth while to leave a single man to guard the pass.

The only danger, therefore, that the Russians had to fear was that some wandering party of Bashi-Bazouks or marauders should pass that way and discover what they were at, or that the noise made by the Cossacks in repairing the road should excite the curiosity of the small Turkish force which it was known was at Khaini, at the outlet of the defile. They did not dare to use powder for blasting the rocks, by which they might have made the road passable in several places where it could hardly be called so for artillery in the condition in which it was left by the Cossacks. Prince Tserteleff, who has greatly distinguished himself during the passage, and to whom must be given the honour not only of discovering the pass but of conducting and piloting the advance guard through it, went forward continually with one or two Bulgarians, reconnoitring the route far in advance of even the advance guard. He even disguised himself in a Bulgarian peasant's clothes, and went forward on foot, anxious to see if the road were really practicable, before the whole column should advance to what might, after all, be only a sheep-path over which it would be impossible to take artillery; and he was the first man of the Russian army and his the first horse to cross the summit, and the first to open out the defile at Khaini. For a diplomatist turned soldier, still a non-commissioned officer, the Prince is not doing badly.

† KEZANLIK, *July* 19*th*.—The road from Parovci to the top of the pass was not nearly so bad as I had supposed. Indeed, the road all the way up to this point has been much better than I could have imagined. It has been rough, to be sure,

full of holes and stones, in some places passing for a hundred yards at a time over mere heaps of stones that covered the whole bottom of the hollow; at other times through the fields by gates that we opened as we passed; but there have been but two or three places as far as Parovci where it has been at all steep. With help from the men in these two or three places, the horses have been able to draw the artillery through with ease. At Parovci the road began to grow steep, and from here to the summit, a distance of about two miles, the men had to help the horses nearly the whole way. But even here the great difficulty of mountain roads, their narrowness, does not seem to have been encountered at all. The road all the way to the summit was made wide enough for the wide-tracked artillery waggons without any difficulty. It leads up the side of the little hollow which is thickly wooded to the very top, and brings us out on a long narrow ridge, shaped like a saddle, and not more than fifty or sixty feet wide. This is the summit of the pass, and the descent on the south side is, we perceive, far more precipitous than the ascent has been. Here the men will have to help to hold the artillery back instead of pushing it forward.

We are 200 Cossacks drawn up on this ridge, with our horses' heads turned south, looking away over the interminable labyrinth of mountains, hills, ridges, valleys, hollows, and gorges, through which we still have to bore our way to the valley of the Tundja before our passage can be assured. The first streak of day is just growing visible in the east, and a long flash of rosy light is climbing slowly up the sky. Before and beneath us is a dark narrow gorge, still a pool of blackness, into which we slowly descend. We are soon down into the depths of the dark defile. The first three or four hundred yards are very steep; but at the end of that time we have come fairly into the little hollow, and the descent the rest of the way is gentle and easy, although the road is rough. The hollow is narrower even than the one on the other side, and the trees here are large, the branches completely uniting overhead, making it as dark as a cavern. We move on as silently as we can, for, to tell the truth, it is, for aught we know, a most perilous venture. The Turks might choose to lay an ambush for us—to let us pass, and place a small force on the road behind us—and a hundred or even fifty infantry would quite suffice to bar the way, and render retreat impossible. So we push on cautiously, watching for any indication of the presence of the enemy. Daylight soon begins to spread everywhere, even down in the bottom of this narrow gorge, in spite of the thickly overhanging trees that do their best to keep it out. General Rauch, who is in command, detaches here and there eight or ten men to repair the road where it appears necessary, and pushes on. This operation is repeated so often, that finally we have very few men left, and so we halt and wait for the detachment to come together again; and still there is no sign of the Turks. The little force at the end of the defile evidently does not dream of a Russian being nearer them than Tirnova.

Slowly we work down the hollow, repairing the road as we go, and by evening we have arrived at a place where the hollow spreads out into a little valley where there is plenty of grass for the horses, and here we camp for the night. As it turns out, we have made just half the distance between the pass and the outlet of the defile, and have likewise made the road passable for the army to this point. But we still have five or six miles before us to do to-morrow, and as the Turks are now so near no fires are lighted, no suppers are cooked, no tea is made. We eat a piece of hard bread and whatever bits of cold meat we have left about us, make shift to smoke a cigarette, wrap our blankets about us, and lie down on the ground for a sleep, expecting to hear the alarm sounded at any moment. But the night passes quietly without even a false alarm, and at break of day we are again in the saddle, without breakfast and without tea. We begin the work of the day before, pushing cautiously forward, repairing the road, watching for the enemy, who may appear at any moment, but who does not. The really most difficult and dangerous part of the road had still, as it turned out, to be discovered and repaired. The character of the country had quite changed since yesterday. Instead of the one high, steep, wooded mountain rising on either hand high above us, we were flanked on both sides by a labyrinth of low, sharp, rocky, steep hills and ridges, through which the road wound in the most tortuous manner, sometimes down deep in the bottoms of the gorge, sometimes skirting along the rocks two or three hundred feet from the bottom. It would have been a more dangerous place to meet an enemy even than higher up between the two great wooded mountains. A small force of infantry posted along these sharp rugged heights could have kept at bay almost any number of troops, for the reason that but a small number could advance at a time, and it was for the most part impossible to scale these rugged heights to turn the positions once they were occupied by a resolute enemy.

General Rauch paid less attention to the road here than hitherto, partly because of the necessity of pushing rapidly forward and seizing the outlet of the defile, partly because it would have required powder and blasting to repair the road in the places most needing it, and this would have given the Turks the alarm. We pushed cautiously forward, therefore, and about nine o'clock we turned sharp round a projecting bluff that a moment before seemed to completely bar the way, and found the defile suddenly open out to the width of half a mile and beheld beyond the valley of the Tundja, and here, not more than half a mile distant, we saw a Turkish camp. General Rauch had already learned from the Bulgarians that there were only a couple of companies here, and counting upon the effect of the surprise and the certainty that the Turks could not know that the whole Russian army was not at our heels, he determined to attack and clear the outlet at once. For two hundred Cossacks to attack two companies of infantry would be the height of absurdity in any other country in the world but Turkey. Here, however, it seems the most natural thing to do imaginable, and we accordingly began to advance, firing. We did not attempt to charge them, as our object was rather to drive them away than to come to close quarters, where we should certainly have got the worst of it. The Turks were, as usual, completely taken by surprise. It is not a little remarkable that outpost service should be often the very last thing learned, and that it should never be learned at all by some nations, as by the Spaniards and the Turks, in spite of their having everything else—arms, equipments, organization—appertaining to modern warfare. I have seen a Spanish army march boldly within the enemy's lines, billet the troops in a village in a little hollow surrounded by hills half a mile distant, without putting out a single picquet, with the usual result of surprise and defeat. The military history of Turkey is full of surprises and defeats caused by the neglect of the outpost service, and yet they have learned no more on this simple point during the last four hundred years than on any other. So the force here watching a most important point had put out no picquets, it was taken by surprise, thrown into consternation at the near approach of the Russians, and instantly began to retreat—two companies of infantry of the regular army before 200 Cossacks. I could hardly have believed it if I had not seen it. They fired upon us as they fled, and we pursued, firing upon them, but there was little harm done on either side, our loss being five or six wounded. We drove them out on the Slievno road beyond the village of Khaini and waited the approach of reinforcements. In the course of the day General Gourko arrived with six battalions of Russian sharpshooters numbering about 2,000 men, and towards evening the Bulgarian legion, the dragoons, the hussars, the rest of the Cossacks, and the artillery arrived, making up the whole detachment, and the outlet of the defile was made safe. The force under General Gourko's command now consisted of seven battalions of Bulgarians, about 5,000 men; six battalions of sharpshooters, about 2,000 men, the battalion of sharpshooters being very small; a brigade of dragoons, 1,000 men; a regiment of hussars, 500; and three regiments of Cossacks, 2,500 men; three batteries of field pieces of six, and a battery of mountain guns light enough to be carried on horses—in all about 11,000 men. With this force, half of which were raw recruits not yet four months under arms, and one-fourth more (the Cossacks) irregulars, the Russians made and secured the passage of the Balkans, one of the most formidable bulwarks ever raised by nature for the defence of a country. And they did it with a loss of six men wounded. For the passage was secured from this moment. Even had the attempt to force the pass at Kezanlik proved unsuccessful, the whole army could have crossed this pass with ease.

The next day there was some appearance of the Turks concentrating to attack us. The three battalions that had passed on the way to Slievno two days before seemed to have returned, and made a show as if they would attack. General Gourko took the dragoons and started to meet them, giving orders for the Bulgarian troops to follow, as he wished to try them once under fire. But the three battalions of Turks retired so rapidly before the two regiments of dragoons that the Bulgarians could not get up to them. The dragoons drove them some ten miles in the direction of Slievno, and then returned to Khaini. This retreat of three battalions of infantry, 2,000 to 3,000 men, before 1,000 cavalry, was almost as bad as the flight of two companies before 200 Cossacks.

The next day after this affair, or the third after the arrival at Khaini, General Gourko, leaving the Bulgarians to guard the place, took the rest of the detachment, and started for Kezanlik. We met a small force a short distance from Khaini, which fled before us firing a few shots. This force retreating before us proved to be a most unfortunate circumstance for four or five Turkish villages on the way to Kezanlik. They took refuge in these villages, and either they or the inhabitants fired on us from the houses. The result was that we set fire to every house from which we had been fired at, and, the fire spreading, these villages were for the most part destroyed. The Turks seem to have the faculty of always doing the wrong thing and never the right one. Had they fired at us from behind the rocks and trees in the defiles of the Balkans it would have annoyed us very considerably, delayed our progress, and have done the Turkish population no harm. Instead of that, they fire at us from villages in the plain in the most senseless and useless manner, where this kind of resistance could not delay our march an hour, with the natural result of getting these villages burned. They leave no mistake uncommitted that perversity, ignorance, and stupidity can commit.

In the meantime the news of our arrival had spread to Kezanlik, and the Turkish commander there detached three battalions from the force guarding the Shipka Pass, and sent them to meet us. We met this force near Maglis, when we had made about two-thirds of the distance to Kezanlik, and the fight began at once. The Turks had taken position in the gardens, and opened fire upon us as soon as we came within range. Without hesitating a moment, the Russians formed in order of battle, and advanced firing, and the Turks instantly began to withdraw. A running fight ensued, which was kept up all the way to Kezanlik, a distance of six or seven miles. That the resistance opposed by the Turks was not very stubborn may be judged by the fact that we made our usual march that day, and reached Kezanlik in the evening, having made the whole distance from Khaini in two days. The Russian loss in this running fight was some sixty killed and wounded, nearly the whole of which took place near Maglis, when the Turkish positions were first carried.

We got into Kezanlik in the evening, and were most enthusiastically greeted by the Bulgarian population. The Turkish inhabitants had withdrawn into their houses, frightened nearly to death. They had been kept in ignorance of the real progress of the Russians by the Turkish papers, which had been announcing a continued succession of victories for the Turkish arms. Their relief upon finding that the Russians passed through the town without molesting them was very great. But they still had the lower classes of their Bulgarian neighbours to deal with, and this proved to be a far more difficult matter than appeasing the Russians. These Bulgarians had many an old score to settle up, and they proceeded to call the Turks to account with a promptitude and decision which showed how firmly they believed that Turkish rule and Turkish domination were things of the past. Getting a Cossack or two, of whom there are always a number everywhere without any very absorbing occupation, to go along with them, they would go into a Turkish house and rifle it of as many valuables as they could conveniently carry off.

Money where it was to be obtained, jewellery, trinkets, ornaments, linen, clothing, carpets were the things that were seized. No house was, however, thoroughly pillaged and ruined, except a very few that had been abandoned by their owners, and those owners were men who, owing to their misdeeds of last year, did not dare to remain and allow themselves to fall into the hands of the Russians. One of these was a Sadoullah Bey, a namesake of the present Turkish Minister at Berlin, whose house was filled with plunder taken from the Bulgarians last year, and whose fields were likewise filled with cattle obtained from the same source. You may be very sure this man's house was thoroughly pillaged and wrecked, as were the houses of half a dozen others of the same class. The fault of it all must be fixed upon General Gourko, who for two days allowed the town to take care of itself, so intent was he upon carrying out the task which had been entrusted to him. Until the pass of Shipka was taken, his position was, of course, a most precarious and critical one. With a small force, completely cut off from the main army, and separated from it by the Balkans, against which the Turks might have rapidly concentrated their whole army south of the Balkans, he was, of course, justified in trying to get possession of the pass, and thus secure his own safety, before looking after the property of the Turks.

Nevertheless, I must say the Prussians managed things better. They did not appear in a village half an hour until there were proclamations on the walls, telling the inhabitants exactly what they were to do and not to do, with the penalty of disobedience printed in very large characters indeed. That penalty was usually Death. *Dura lex, sed lex*, and a hard law is, after all, perhaps better than no law at all. But to those people who may wish to prove by what occurred here that the Bulgarians are just as bad as the Turks—as I have no doubt there are people who will—I should like to observe that there were no houses burnt here, that there were no Turks murdered, that no Turkish women were outraged, that no Turk was roasted alive, and that no Turkish children were spitted on bayonets and carried about the streets. Let it further be remembered that many of the Turks living here now were engaged in the massacres of last year, and we have the measure of difference between the Turk and the Bulgarian. I should have been glad if the Bulgarians had shown themselves free from stain in this business, but I fear that perfection is not to be found in human nature, and the Bulgarians must take their chance with the rest. The greater part of the Russian officers did all in their power to put a stop to the looting, though the fact of there being no regular government organized, and that it was nobody's business, made it difficult. Among others I saw Prince Tseretleff laying about with his nagaika, or Cossack's whip, in the most unmerciful manner. Among others who had the misfortune to fall into his hands was the interpreter to one of the brigade commanders, a Greek or Italian, who had been received and treated as a gentleman. The Prince found him in a Turkish house dividing spoil with some Cossacks, and without any more ado, struck him a savage blow across the face with his riding whip, and ordered him under arrest, thus bringing his career as a gentleman interpreter to a close ; an undiplomatic measure, but just for that reason effective and necessary.

To return to the military operations. General Gourko, having reconnoitred the positions of the Turks in the Shipka Pass, determined upon an immediate attack. The village of Shipka is some six or seven miles north from Kezanlik, right at the foot of the mountains. A peculiarity of the Balkans is that, while on the north side there is a long series of hills, lesser mountains before you come to the main range, here on the south they stop off short, without any foothills at all, unless the other range south of the Tundja Valley may be considered such. As you ride along the valley of the Tundja you see those monster masses of earth and rock and forest rising abruptly out of the plain without any intermediate hills or irregularities, like a row of sugar-loaves placed along a floor and rounded off at the top. The pass is therefore only a couple of miles from the foot of the mountain on this side, and the road up to it is very steep and difficult. The Turks had fortified it in the most thorough and effective manner, and had the Russians been obliged to attack it from the other side it would have cost them a fearful loss of life. As it was, it has cost the Russians something like four hundred killed and wounded. But the Turks were discouraged when they found their positions were turned, and did not fight with any hope or chance of success. A Russian force had advanced on the Gabrova side, and it had been arranged that a combined attack was to be made on the pass from both sides at once; but, owing to the difficulty of communication, the combination failed. The attack from the Gabrova side was made a day earlier than it ought to have been, or the one from this side a day later, I do not know which, and both were repulsed. The Turks might have held out a long time had they but had a supply of water; but although they had victualled the fortress, they forgot what was more necessary than food and that was water. It soon became evident, therefore, that they would have to fly or surrender. Nevertheless, in spite of this necessity, which was self-evident, and of the certainty that a great many of them must inevitably fall into the hands of the Russians, they committed first an act of treachery and then acts of brutal atrocity, that would justify the Russians in putting them without the pale of civilized warfare. During the attack made by General Gourko they raised the white flag, and when the Russians ceased firing, and sent forward a flag of truce, they seized the bearer of the flag, murdered him, and opened fire upon the Russians without warning. The whole business is so barbarous and so savage that the story would probably not be believed if it rested on Russian authority alone. Fortunately it does not. There was a Prussian officer present, Major Liegnitz, on whose authority, as well as on that of many Russian officers, the truth of the story rests. The Russian sharpshooters were pushing up the heights, gradually approaching the batteries, when suddenly a number of white flags were seen, and the Turkish trumpets were heard ordering the cessation of the firing. The Russians immediately ceased firing, and the whole line uncovered itself in what proved to be a very careless manner. A large white flag was then waved from the Turkish batteries, and a Russian went forward with a white flag to parley. During this time there seems to have been a general relaxation of vigilance, and Major Liegnitz went near enough the Turkish lines to open a conversation with a Turkish soldier. No sooner had the bearer of the flag of truce gone into the fort than fire was opened by the Turks without warning of any kind; and it was opened, Major Liegnitz assures, not accidentally by the soldiers, but by the sound of the trumpet, showing the order was given by the commander of the fort.

The next day, when the Russians entered the fort, they found the body of the bearer of the flag of truce decapitated and horribly mutilated, together with the bodies of a number of other Russian soldiers who had fallen in the affair either killed or wounded, and whom their comrades had not been able to carry off. Most of the Russian loss in this affair was caused by the treacherous fire of the Turks after raising the white flag. What could have been the object of the Turkish commander in thus deliberately decoying a flag of truce into his lines and then murdering the bearer? Evidently a pure outburst of savage ferocity; the rage of the savage who finds himself beaten on all hands by a civilized enemy, and flings a deliberate defiance at civilized modes of warfare and revenges himself in the only way his barbarous nature can find satisfaction, by violating the most sacred law of civilized warfare—the inviolability of a flag of truce. It is even believed by those who have seen the body, from the marks of bleeding, that the bearer of the flag was first mutilated and afterwards killed.

* SISTOVA, *August 8th.*—The following is a narrative of General Gourko's advance from Kezanlik on Jeni-Zagra: His force consisted of three columns, with orders to converge on Jeni-Zagra as follows:—The right column, consisting of the Bulgarian Legion, two batteries of artillery, and three regiments of cavalry, were to march from Eski-Zagra; the central column, under Gourko himself, consisting of the Rifle Brigade, a regiment of Cossacks, and four batteries of artillery, marched from Kezanlik; the left column, of five battalions of infantry, two batteries, and some Cossacks, marched from Hainkoi, the objective of all three columns being Jeni-Zagra. Gourko marched from Kezanlik on the 29th July a terrible march of forty miles long. Nevertheless his troops came into action next morning on the left flank of the Turkish intrenchments in front of the railway station at Jeni-Zagra to support the attack of the left column on their right flank. The Turks fought desperately, and bayonet fighting was long and strenuous, but after midday the Russians forced the position, drove out the Turks, took Jeni-Zagra, captured three guns, blew up the railway station, and destroyed an immense mass of Turkish ammunition and stores. For want of cavalry, no pursuit was then possible; but next day the Cossacks fell on the retreating Turks. In the afternoon came tidings, by a circuitous route, that the right column was seriously compromised in an attempt to force its way from Eski-Zagra, and General Gourko determined to march westward to its succour. That night (the 30th) he reached Karabunar, where he arrived in darkness, but the whole valley was illuminated by blazing villages. Next morning he marched onward upon Dzuranli, on the road to Eski-Zagra, ignorant of the fact that some 30,000 Turks confronted him, and stopped the road into the latter place. The Turkish batteries swept the road with persistent fire; nevertheless General Gourko came into action, sending forward five battalions of infantry, covered by artillery. He had forty-eight horses killed in one battery, and eight in another. Later the Turkish masses strove to turn the Russian left. The operation was resisted by the Tirailleur Brigade, supported by two regiments of the 9th Division. The attack was repelled, but with heavy fighting. Still later a column of Circassian

cavalry strove to turn the Russian right on the mountain slopes, and the attack was succeeding, when there appeared on the scene Leuchtenberg's cavalry, which had cut its way from Eski-Zagra, and which repelled the movement of the Circassians and saved the right wing. General Gourko then bored on forward, and reached a position which afforded him a distant view of Eski-Zagra. Here there came to him an orderly who had evaded the Turks and brought him intelligence that his right column, consisting of the Bulgarian Legion, was beset in Eski-Zagra by a force of Turks estimated at twenty thousand men. General Gourko, small as was his force, resolved on an attempt to succour them, and in the meantime determined to maintain his position, but his resolution quailed before the appearance of two massive columns of Turks marching on his flank and rear. He had to leave the Bulgarians to shift for themselves, and make good his own retreat through the difficult and narrow Dalboka Pass, and thence through the Hainkoi Pass, accomplishing his retreat on Thursday, 2nd August, amid cruel hardships. In the retreat the wounded died like flies from jolting and exposure. Hale men succumbed from fatigue and sunstroke. As for the Bulgarian Legion composing Gourko's right column, they, after advancing from Eski-Zagra ten kilometres towards Karabunar, found the enemy and were driven in. On the 31st July, after very hard fighting, the Bulgarians had to retire into the defile north of Eski-Zagra, and thence effect their retreat through the Shipka Pass. Of the severity of the fighting a judgment may be formed from the fact that of the Bulgarian Legion, which began sixteen hundred strong, only between four and five hundred reached Shipka.

The Russian cavalry is now all on this side of the Balkans. The Shipka Pass is strongly fortified and armed with twenty-eight guns and garrisoned by a regiment of the 9th Division. Two regiments hold the Hainkoi Pass, which presents a series of formidable defences. There are few troops for the present at Drenova and Gabrova. A brigade of the 14th Division is at Tirnova. Reinforcements are moving south to strengthen the detachments holding the passes. Cavalry is also advancing against Osman Bazar. In the fighting of the 30th and 31st July, General Gourko lost three thousand men, excluding the Bulgarian loss.

The Turkish Government, alarmed by the appearance of a Russian force south of the Balkans, summoned Suleiman Pacha, with the troops which had been operating against Montenegro, and made him commander-in-chief of the army which was to defend Adrianople. The following letter, describing the new Turkish general, is from the correspondent accompanying his army :—

"ADRIANOPLE, *July* 24*th*.—The hero of the hour in European Turkey at this crisis of the country's danger is, without doubt, the victor of Montenegro, Suleiman Pacha. The difficulties thrown in the way of correspondents at Shumla following the military operations of the Commander-in-Chief are such that I naturally inferred similar restrictions would be imposed with the army of Adrianople; but I am glad to find, in an interview with Suleiman Pacha himself, this will not be the case. Fortified by a good introduction, I called upon him here, and he instantly relieved me of any other restraint than such a position would of necessity entail, and invited me to accompany him in the forthcoming operations. He was in the midst of soldiers encamped on the northern outskirts of the city near the old palace of the Sultans of Adrianople, which was until very recently the pride and boast of the place. Now it is in rapid progress of demolition, the materials as I write being carted away to aid in the fortifications around, which are fast being raised. Some fifty battalions are already collected here, the grass on the river's bank forming their bed, and the clear summer's sky above their only covering.

The General is hardly forty years old, a man of middle height, and for a wonder not inclined to corpulency, as appears to be the almost invariable effect of high command in Turkey. To look at his fair complexion, sandy beard and whiskers, and his grey eyes, one would almost imagine oneself in the presence of a migratory Scotchman bent upon amassing wealth in a foreign land, and that pure English with an unmistakable accent would proceeed from out of his mouth; but no such phenomenon, unluckily for me, occurred, and instead the conversation was carried on in French. The General told me he was hard at work incorporating the new troops, whom he found on his arrival here, with his old soldiers from Montenegro, and forwarding them up to Jeni-Zagra, near the terminus of the railway at Yamboli, where Reouf Pacha was at the moment. The news of the withdrawal from Eski-Zagra and Kezanlik, and the Shipka Pass, on the approach of the Russian advanced guard, had come in, and did not seem in the least to give cause for any anxiety, or to be unexpected by him. Various versions of the number of the enemy who had up to this moment crossed the Balkans had reached him, extending from 8,000 to 30,000, but the latter seemed to be in excess of the real figure, and was extended over a wide area. That atrocities had been committed did not admit of a doubt, but they occurred out of the main body, and were committed, it was said, by isolated bands of foraging Cossacks, who were not the easiest of troops to tame and civilize, and also by Bulgarian Christians upon their Mohammedan fellows. Nothing of the kind had occurred at Kezanlik or Eski-Zagra, and as regards his own army and the Turkish troops in general, the strongest orders of which language was capable (and that is not without meaning in the land of the Sultan) had been issued to prevent the slightest excesses of the men, who were fully aware that the eyes of all Europe were upon them. In a very few days important operations would assuredly take place, in which the army of this part would bear a foremost part. More information was given which it would be imprudent to reveal, and the General invited me to accompany him to witness the march out of camp of ten battalions which were on the point of being sent by the railway to Jeni-Zagra. More than three-fourths of the men bore unmistakable symptoms of having gone through the campaign of Montenegro; the faces of the majority, naturally embrowned with the toil of the fields, had assumed a far deeper dye, comparing strongly with those of the half-drilled recruits—much so in face, but more still in uniform; the smartness, in comparison, of the one so recently turned out of the tailor's hands rendering still more marked the utter discoloration and dilapidated appearance of the other. The original colour and material were lost to all possible recognition, and many articles of attire—especially those considered by most nations as indispensable—had been attempted to be supplied wholly or in parts by any material which came nearest to hand. The dress of the officers shared in the toil-stained and tattered appearance of the men: but in many instances not the slightest attempts at uniform were made. One officer, and a most active and indefatigable one, on the General's own staff—a German by nationality—was fain to be content with a suit of brown holland, a counterpart of which may be met with in the shop-window of any cheap, but perhaps not fashionable, tailor at 15s. 6d.

The officers' call brought this incongruity of appearance into still greater prominence—in fact, one had reason to doubt if uniform, properly understood, existed in this portion of the Turkish army—and when they in their turn had assembled their men around them to communicate the orders of the

General, the variety of knapsacks, rugs, and general impedimenta of a soldier on campaign became another source of wonderment. When we hear of pay being an almost unheard-of novelty, clothing is a secondary consideration, and can well afford to be overlooked, especially when the large majority of the men are decorated for the two campaigns in Montenegro —the unsuccessful nature of the first being far more than counterbalanced by the brilliancy of the second. They are good soldiers, and tried indeed by every hardship, extremes of weather, and the utmost amount of privation. Proud indeed the General has reason to be of them, and he can rely on their making themselves a name amongst the myriads of the Czar now beginning to pour through the Balkans. But the order to march is given, the band plays its few wild notes as a prelude to the soldiers' shout—thrice uttered by the whole as one man—of "Long live the Padishah!" and onward they go to the defence of Islam.

The massacres which followed Suleiman Pacha's first successes exceeded even those committed upon the Bulgarians in May, 1876, and have made Eski-Zagra a name which will call up memories more terrible than those of Batak.

☾ HEADQUARTERS OF SULEIMAN PACHA'S ARMY, KARABUNAR, *July 29th.*—Up to the present time no military operations have taken place, but instead we have had a feast of horrors and atrocities. Not a day passes but reports arrive of excesses of every kind, and if even a tithe of them are true the war will soon become one of extermination, and the Eastern Question will have solved itself. The villages between this little station on the Yamboli line and Eski-Zagra appear likely to become as infamous in history as those in which the Turkish name will be branded to the end of time. The passion of revenge once let loose amongst a barbarous people is not to be stayed by military mandates, no matter how severe the language in which they may be couched. It is to be hoped that the Russian Commander-in-Chief is in earnest in his desire to carry on the war in a civilized manner; and it certainly appears almost incredible to find the Turkish side professing to be horror-stricken at outrages which they have so lately been doing their utmost to palliate.

The first object I was taken to see on my arrival here was the severed head of a Bulgarian peasant which had just been brought in by a Turkish soldier who had himself performed the horrid operation in revenge for being fired at. The head was thrown into a ditch close to the station, and there remained a ghastly object enough until some charitable person covered it with earth. Next seven spies, as we at first heard, but afterwards a civil staff officer informed us they were not spies, but Bulgarian insurgents who had been charged with having blown up a railway bridge across the river here, were brought to the place of execution, which happened, much to my disgust, to be two stunted trees—the only ones growing near—adjoining the modest shed in which I happened to be quartered. None of the unfortunate beings appeared to show the least emotion as they stood surrounded by a few dozen soldiers and bullock-drivers; and a rough but ready set of volunteer Calcrafts tied the ropes to the sparse branches of the trees, slipped the knots round their necks (excepting the last, an old man, who quietly performed that duty for himself, and sat down cross-legged on the ground, his eyes shut, murmuring what appeared to be a prayer, and patiently awaiting his turn), and, hauling them up, the end came almost without a struggle. Human life in Turkey, as in all other Oriental countries, is certainly taken and lost in a different manner to our own; but I never could imagine such a scene possible as this that I most reluctantly was called upon to witness. The train just starting for Adrianople has in it the body of a Mussulman split in halves, and otherwise mutilated in the most frightful manner, which Suleiman Pacha has sent to the Consuls there as a terrible proof of what the Russians and their followers are capable. A telegram from Reouf Pacha has just been shown to me stating that the inhabitants of five villages near Eski-Zagra have been slaughtered, man, woman, and child, three hundred and forty in number, by the retreating Russians. Within the next few days I shall have an opportunity, I trust, of making inquiries from the few survivors who have made their way in a lamentable state to Jeni-Zagra, whither our headquarters are now moving. Burning villages of the Christians are to be seen marking the line of march, and a spirit of ferocity has been stirred which will make the war a byword and reproach for many a year. The whole population is flying, and can be seen in countless thousands between here and Adrianople, with their miles of bullock waggons, containing their families and household goods, their cattle and sheep in common droves and flocks toiling painfully along in a vain hope of finding rest in a peaceful country.

CHAPTER XII.

THE FIRST CHECK AT PLEVNA.

The "Army of Rustchuk"—Russian Train-Officers—A Reconnaissance on the Lom—An Unpleasant Position—Baron Krüdener's First Attack on Plevna—Carelessness of Russian Generals—Preparations for a New Attack—A Ride through the Forepost Line—General Skobeleff—A Council of War—Types of Russian Officers.

FROM following the narrative of General Gourko's brilliant but barren expedition beyond the Balkans, we return to survey the situation of military affairs between that range and the Danube, where events were occurring which were to change entirely the character and prospects of the Russian campaign.

* HEADQUARTERS 12TH CAVALRY DIVISION, HEIGHTS ABOVE LOM RIVER, *July 22nd.*—When I came back to this division yesterday, I had been absent six days, in the course of which time I had ridden over three hundred miles, had wrecked my best horse, had been to Bucharest twice, each time for only a few hours, and had never taken my clothes off. There are no pretensions to a postal service in the Russian army in Bulgaria, and the only way in which the correspondent can forward his communications is simply to act as a courier as well as a correspondent. At length, the day before yesterday, having fed the voracious maw of the telegraph wire, I was free to return for a day or two to my quarters with the advance division of this army. Quitting Sistova in the morning, I rode first for Pavlo, where on the previous day but one I had left the Imperial headquarters, my subsequent route lying over Bjela, and along the Rustchuk road till I should find somewhere or other the people I was looking for. Pavlo, where two days before there had been the Emperor's headquarters, with a division encamped around the farmyard, in which the Czar of All the Russias had pitched his tent, was now solitary, forlorn, and desolate. The headquarters were gone, and nobody was left to tell whither. A calf stood ruminating in the verandah of the Bulgarian hut under which General Ignatieff was wont to do his leisurely writing, and dogs were poking about the ground which the dinner marquee had covered. The only

relics of the Russian encampment, which had lasted for over a fortnight, were profuse straw, some bones, several dead horses, which the Russians carefully leave unburied, and an extremely unpleasant smell. I rode on to the bridge at Bjela, where, in the khan at the end of the bridge, General Timofeieff used to have his headquarters, and where I had drunk I should be afraid to say how many glasses of tea. The downs on which his division had encamped were now bare; the khan was occupied now but by a couple of very reticent telegraph clerks, who varied what used to be the standing formula of reply before the crossing of the Danube —"I haven't the faintest idea"—by the blunter "I don't know." One vaguely opined that Timofeieff might have gone Tirnova way, which I knew to be untrue. I rode on by the Rustchuk road, evening gradually coming on.

The wave of soldiers had passed and gone. I had thought the Rustchuk army was never to pass the Jantra; and now it had crossed the Jantra, and left not a detachment behind. In my haste I avoided the détour into the town of Bjela; had I gone there I should have found, as I afterwards learned, the Imperial staff housed in the pretty half-town half-village in the glen lying back from the Jantra. At Monastir it grew dark, it began to rain, and my horse fell lame. I was on a lonesome stretch of road, with fields on either side, and I saw no alternative but to strive to get some shelter among the sheaves of grain, which would also afford food for my horse, and pass the night there. But holding on a little to get on somewhat higher ground, I had the good fortune to chance on a little camp belonging to the train of two regiments of the 35th Division, which were some distance in advance. The officers were good enough to take compassion on my forlorn plight, and to ask me to spend the night with them. These train officers are invariably men of mature years; you find among them grey-haired lieutenants, men who have long since completed their term of service, and gone into the reserve; but have been called out for duty in this war. They are Russian officers of the old stamp, rough, uncultivated, illiterate, ignorant of anything but mere rudimentary soldiering, but worthy-hearted fellows, with a chronic fondness for raki, and a desire to take things as easily as possible. In the course of the evening we were joined by a venerable but gay intendant, a sprightly Hebrew, who knew a smattering of French, and who had in his waggon a store of good things, which he dispensed with great liberality. He was in charge of a drove of requisitioned cattle for the army in front—animals of the most miscellaneous kind. There were draught buffaloes and milch buffaloes, buffalo calves, and old bulls, oxen, cows, sheep, and goats. But he was hard up for fresh meat himself nevertheless, and bought a leg of mutton from a predatory Cossack, who with a leer vouched for the fact that the sheep to which the leg had belonged had been captured from the Turks. It is needless to say that the camp of the train had no night watch set, and that no military precautions of any kind were taken. Orders came for the cortége to march at two in the morning. This I regretted, for I should have to renew my journey long ere my horse could be rested. But with the officers was a Prussian, employed as armourer to one of the regiments which the train followed, and he told me I need have no concern, for notwithstanding the orders, there would be no march till daylight at the earliest. He was more than right. At eight o'clock, when I set forward, the camp of the train still lingered in the mud of the valley; the horses harnessed indeed, but the tents unstruck till the rain should have passed away.

I had left at Obertenik my division, my comrade, and my waggon; but at Obertenik now, which I reached about ten, tramping dismally on foot through the mud, and leading my lame horse, I found no cavalry division, but a small detachment of Cossacks, the escort of the headquarter staff of the Czarewitch, in command of the Rustchuk Army. He and his staff had their tents pitched in a shady garden, and in the tent of Colonel Dochtouroff, who is sous-chef of the staff, I found Prince Dolgorouki, one of the aides-de-camp of the Emperor, who had the day before brought from the headquarters of the latter to the Czarewitch some good news concerning the passage of the Balkans. With Kezanlik in Russian hands, and the Shipka Pass open, all concern regarding the passing of the Balkans may be dismissed, and with our knowledge of the whereabouts of the mass of the Turkish army, the date of the arrival of the Russians in Adrianople becomes merely a question of marching and of supplies. It must be owned that the Russians are buying their successes singularly cheap. Not a thousand lost in the crossing of the Danube. The Balkans crossed at an expenditure of certainly under a thousand more fighting men; the environs of Rustchuk reached with losses probably under three figures. What a bagatelle of sacrifice for successes so sweeping and so important! In the headquarters of the Czarewitch I failed to receive any firm assurance as to the immediate prospect of active measures against Rustchuk, and gathered, indeed, that the plan of action of the "Rustchuk Army" had not yet been definitely settled; but on this subject I will speak later.

The whole army was forward toward Rustchuk, beyond Obertenik. On the heights above Damogila, a village to the south-east of Obertenik, I saw, as I rode onward, the white tents of the 35th Division. At Trestenik, a village close to the chaussée, about six kilometres beyond Obertenik, I found the headquarters of the Archduke Vladimir, commanding the 12th Army Corps. A division of this Corps—the 12th Division—was setting out on its march from its bivouac on the plateau beside Trestenik as I rode by. It is so rare to see a Russian column march in an orderly manner, that one observed with all the greater pleasure the marked exception which General von Firck's division offered to the customary style of marching. In the infantry column no straggling was permitted on the march; the men marched at ease, and without being locked up, but in order, and at a word the whole column could have pulled itself together. When a halt was made, always in the vicinity of water, so many men per company were allowed to fall out and go to fetch water for their comrades, so there was no wild straggling around the well or the fountain, as is so often the case, with consequent loss and soiling of a fluid which is exceptionally precious just now in this part of Bulgaria. A sentry was placed on the water to preserve order, with a picquet commanded by an officer near by. As for the reserve artillery and the train of the division, it followed with the utmost regularity under the superintendence of officers specially detailed for the purpose. The vehicles were not allowed to straggle all over the road, thus blocking the way for all waggons coming in an opposite direction; they were kept to their own half of the road, the drivers were made to keep up, so that there was no loss of distance having to be made up by jerking and fatiguing trots, and the men on foot accompanying the waggons were compelled to march alongside their own vehicles instead of straggling all along and all about the line of the column. It is curious to observe the difference between divisions in respect to observance of such matters of discipline as the preservation of order on the line of march and the keeping up of an efficient circle of night watches and field guards. This 12th Division, for instance, is as smart in these respects as any German division. I noticed while passing in its rear the other day near Kriuna that where roads bisected finger-posts were set up specifying the place to which each road led. Nowhere else have I seen with the Russian armies the adoption of this simple expedient, which helps so much orderlies and provision trains, and which is universal in the German army. There are divisions through which any one may ride without challenge, and to which any force might approach within rifle shot without observation. There are others which are surrounded by a ring of sentries and picquets—too near in most instances for purposes of efficient outlook, but still guarding to some extent at least against surprise. When I give the name of the general commanding the 12th Division—Baron von Firck—a nationality is indicated which renders needless any further inquiry into the reason of the efficiency of his command; but in most cases the chief of the staff is the man who influences the state of camp and marching discipline throughout a division, which it must always be remembered is the true integer of the Russian military organization as it practically exists, the Army Corps being a thing *ad hoc*, of which this war is the first experience. I may mention one curious circumstance in the Russian army. The generals of brigade are mostly older than the generals of division. The reason is, I believe, that generals of division have been chosen because of either real or fancied efficiency; generals of brigade, having less responsibility, are not so carefully selected, and seniority rather than merit has been the principle of their appointment.

In the valley in which is situated the little wayside inn, or what once was an inn, bearing the outlandish name of Han Col Cisme, about twelve miles from Rustchuk, the 12th Division halted, and I overtook my waggon. The infantry had pushed on the cavalry a few versts, and General Driesen's headquarters were moving on to the heights where I am now writing. We are within four miles of the Danube at Pirgos, which is due north from us, and just over the crest of the slope, on the reverse side of which is our camp, is the valley of the Lom. We are rather crowded down in this corner between the Danube and the Lom. Cavalry and infantry camps are mixed up anyhow, and you might cover almost with a good-sized towel the bulk of three infantry and one cavalry divisions. A glance at the map will show that the main river Lom, the Cerni or Black Lom, entering the Danube at Rustchuk, flows down through Bulgaria in a direction nearly due north, bending to the north-east as it approaches the Danube. Along its western bank is the present position of the Russian Army of Rustchuk. It covers a broad front, although the principal concentration is near the Danube. The right flank of its cavalry is at Polomarca, a village about forty miles south of the Danube in the direction of Osman Bazar, and regiments are studded among the villages on the western bank of the Cerni Lom, all the way to Pirgos. The Beli, or White Lom, with a north-westerly course, flows into the Cerni Lom at the village of Kosova, and the triangular interval between the two rivers is occupied by detachments of cavalry belonging to the 12th and 8th Cavalry Divisions. In all, about 40,000 men are now on the Lom. This position has been gained without any fighting to speak of. There was a trivial cavalry skirmish on the height where I am now writing, and within sight of my tent door are the graves of a few dragoons who fell in clearing the crest of the Turkish troops. Two days ago there was a more serious skirmish down in the Lom Valley. There is a village called Kadikoi, about midway between the Lom and the road between Rustchuk and Shumla. There was reason to believe that Turkish troops were there in some force, and from the heights on this side the Lom, the Russians opened fire with one gun, with intent to provoke reprisals from the enemy, and so gain some idea of his strength. But the Turks were wise, or at least wily, in their generation. They replied with one gun. If the Russians had brought two into action no doubt they would have followed suit; but in the meantime a fair exchange was enough for them.

Emboldened by this seeming weakness, a couple of squadrons of Bilderling's dragoons were pushed across the Lom in the direction of Kadikoi. They advanced some distance, but not to glory. They had passed through a swarm of Circassians, lying in ambush, and suddenly the two squadrons were beset, surrounded, and assailed with great fury. It remained for them but to fight their way back, which they did with a hard hand-to-hand struggle, losing some nine men killed and twenty-one wounded. The killed were brought into camp across their horses, for the Russians will not, if they possibly can help it, leave their dead to the certain fate of being mutilated by the Turks. The Circassians followed the dragoons across the Lom, hanging on their rear, and trying to cut off detached parties; but they came a little too far. A battalion of infantry had accompanied the cavalry as far as the Lom, and had remained on this side. So when the cavalry came back thus sore beset, the infantry were ready to cover them, and the Circassians found themselves exposed to the withering rifle-fire which it has since been ascertained caused them a loss of twenty men killed and fifty wounded. Subsequent appearances indicated that Kadikoi and its vicinity had been evacuated by the Turks, and to make this certain a reconnaissance was conducted in that direction by the Archduke Vladimir himself, at the head of a squadron of dragoons, a squadron of Cossacks, and a battalion of infantry. He penetrated to Kadikoi without opposition, and found it empty and deserted; so he determined to take the opportunity that offered, and make a bold dash at the railway between Rustchuk and Shumla. His Cossacks rode on through Buzin, and struck the railway at the Guvemli station. This they burnt, and blew up with dynamite an adjacent bridge, thus effectually destroying the railway communication between Rustchuk and Shumla. Not a man was lost in this brilliant little undertaking.

There can be no doubt that the Turks, having behaved very well during their retreat so far from Sistova, and throughout this portion of Bulgaria generally, have at length given rein to their fury against the Bulgarian inhabitants of the Lom Valley. The evidence is overwhelming that this is so. I am not fond of accepting hearsay evidence in such matters, and habitually allow a good deal of margin for exaggeration. But when villages are entered with slaughtered men, women, and children lying about among the ashes of their houses; when Bulgarian husbandmen are found dead in the fields, shot apparently when labouring at their daily toil; when at the well, close to which I am writing, a Bulgarian was found desperately wounded, with the cross scored by transverse sword-cuts on his forehead; when eyewitnesses tell me all this, I am bound to believe them. There is a village called Kaceljevo, some distance up the Lom. In this village was lying Colonel Bilderling, commanding a regiment of dragoons of Arnoldi's brigade. He left the village on a reconnaissance down the river, and there were then in it about a hundred live Bulgarian villagers—men, women, and children. During his absence a detachment of Turks, whom the Bulgarians who escaped reported to have been under the command of a superior officer, entered the village. Most of the helpless inhabitants fled for refuge into the church, which is a large and handsome edifice. The door of it was broken open by order of the officer commanding the Turks, who entered and slew and spared not one of the unfortunate inmates. Not a soul who had taken refuge in the church escaped. Bilderling came back at night to find Kaceljevo empty and desolated, and its church a shamble. Then a few people who had not gone into the church, but had sought hiding-places in the gardens round the village, came in scared and trembling, and told him what had happened as far as they knew. For the rest, the spectacle in the church told its own story. My informant is Colonel Bilderling himself, and his commanding officer, the Baron Driesen, has made a report of the occurrence just as I have told it to you. I do not see what room there can be for question that this fearful story is but too true.

There have been occasional indications of an imminent battle on this front, but they have always faded away into disappointment. I think it may now be taken for certain that the Turkish troops have broken up from the Lom line, and have abandoned the cohesion with which they were credited. It may be assumed that a certain proportion have drawn in toward the fortified positions of Rustchuk—in fact we can see their camps on the slopes of the Levant Tabia—and that another portion have fallen back in another direction, probably in the direction of Shumla—it may be, however, in that of Osman Bazar. They have uniformly declined to stand, even when the pressure has not been heavy; and it cannot be said that any vigorous attempt has been made to get to close quarters with them. Simply by the *vis inertia* of the impending advance of great masses the Turks have given ground, and the line of the Lom may now be said to be clear. *Et après?* Well, I am no believer in an early siege of Rustchuk. I see no indications of a siege. I find no artillery park on this side the Danube, nor any preparations being made to bring any across. I believe that for the immediate future the military policy is simply to mask Rustchuk, and hold a force in readiness to strike wherever a blow or a demonstration may be of service in Bulgaria; to march east and give the hand to Zimmerman at Silistria, should he be threatened from Shumla; to proceed against a field force marching from Shumla against the troops masking Shumla; in fine, to be available for anything that might turn up. Just at present, were the enemy any other enemy than the Turk, a fine chance seems to offer itself to enterprising leaders of delivering a telling counter-attack athwart the line of the Russian communications. A cavalry force crossing from Silistria to Kalarash might strike into Roumania, destroy the village, and do incalculable damage, and that with but little opposition, for the Russians seem to have left Roumania strangely bare of troops. But from the Turks a raid of this kind is not to be expected, and the Russians seem to have accepted what is said to have been Prince Bismarck's advice, and put all their eggs into the basket which they have so successfully carried across the Balkans. It seems pretty certain they will carry the eggs unbroken into Adrianople. He would be a rash man who would speculate on what may result on the Russian occupation of Adrianople. This afternoon General Driesen came to our tent, and, informing us that he intended to ride along, and perhaps outside, the foremost line along the river Lom, gave us the opportunity of accompanying him. Indeed, he carried his kindness so far as to lend me a horse, my steed being *hors de combat* from overwork. It appeared that two reconnaissances were designed: one, consisting of some hussars and Cossacks and a battalion of infantry, under the command of Prince Woronzoff, was to start from Solenik, on the White Lom, and push on northward to Pizanca, on the Rustchuk-Shumla road, which it was then to follow as far as Buzin, behind Kadikoi, and as much further as the Turks would permit; the other, consisting of two squadrons of dragoons, commanded by the chief of General Driesen's staff, was to start from our camp here, and, passing through Pirgos, was to feel the Turks to the westward of the Rustchuk position, on the high ground near the river-side. A battery in front of our position here, and another above Pirgos, were to cover the latter reconnaissance and reply to any Turkish fire which might be directed against it. This is rather pottering work for the front of an army of some 70,000 strong, but it was at least better than inaction.

We rode away to the eastward over abruptly undulating downs, alternated with corn-fields, and got down into the rocky and tortuous valley of the Lom, at the beautiful village of Buzisma. The forepost line reached to the river, but did not cross it. The downs were dotted all over with field watches, and there was almost a row of sentries along the edge of the high ground overhanging the river. Behind, admirably posted, were strong picquets, composed of all three arms of the service—a squadron of cavalry, a half-battalion of infantry, and a battery of artillery constituting the complement of each. Strangely enough, there were no cavalry vedettes, and this method of outlook seems sparsely used in the Russian army. We found a good many of the Bulgarian inhabitants in the village of Buzisma. The houses were somewhat dismantled, but the harvest was gathered into the farmyards. All the live stock had been driven away by the Turks, as was to be expected. We found the inevitable Russian soldier bathing in the Lom—he would bathe although the opposite bank might have been lined by Circassians. We did not cross the river, but rode back on to our heights, and took a long, careful survey of the ground on the other side. There lay the white houses of the village of Kadikoi, which, although occupied yesterday, has not been held. Looking across the level north-eastward toward Rustchuk there loomed against the sky-line the elevated position of Said Pacha, crowned by its earthwork redoubt, and with its slope clustered thick with Turkish tents. The redoubt of Said Pacha is one of the outlying works of the Rustchuk fortified position, and directly in front of the great centre of that position the lofty plateau of the Seventh Tabia. But the scene was perfectly quiet, and there were no signs of Woronzoff's reconnaissance. So, turning our horses' heads, we rode northwards towards the chaussée along the forepost line. On the chausseé we found a Russian battery in emplacements, the gunners waiting for the order to commence firing, for from the top of the ridge opposite, on the further side of a deep, bare, and rather wide valley, a Turkish battery had come into action, firing at the Russian battery above Pirgos, which had been the original aggressor in support of a reconnaissance made by Driesen, chief of the staff. The two batteries were blazing away at each other vigorously, while behind us all the troops in the position had formed up and were waiting for orders; but no orders came. The affair was confined to a duel between the two batteries. On the slopes below the Turkish battery we, looking across the valley at our feet, could see cavalry manœuvring. Two clumps stood fast, and small parties and single horsemen moved about among the main fields without apparently any very definite purpose. My belief was that these people were Russian cavalry, operating slowly up the slopes, and feeling their way beyond the Turkish battery. Anxious to see how the dragoons were working, I rode through the infantry forepost line below our battery, and down into the valley, whence I began to mount the opposite slope with intent to join the horsemen above. But they were not our horsemen at all; they were Circassians circling about there by way of making a demonstration. I became aware of the fact that I was approaching a hostile force in no very pleasant manner. Along the slope which I was mounting, and in front of the Circassians, ran the Turkish infantry forepost line—some scattered picquets linked by a few sentries. These were hidden behind the stacked sheaves of grain, and I did not perceive that there was any such line until a fellow fired at me at a range of not beyond three hundred yards. Another followed suit, and I thought then that I had persevered quite long enough in that direction, and, having discovered my mistake, turned and galloped back down into the valley. But other Turks began to fire, and then the Russian forepost line set about replying while I was down in the dip between the two lines, and the bullets of both parties whistled clear over me. It was not so much an unsafe as an uncomfortable position, for I could not get back in the face of the Russian fire, and of course I could not go forward. I remember once being in a similar fix when travelling in Catalonia, when I chanced into the heart of a skirmish between the Royalists and the Carlists. There was no pleasure in remaining in the awkward locality, so I wriggled out literally, and reached the Russian forepost line at a spot where there was no firing, when, of course, I was promptly taken prisoner as a suspicious person apparently coming over from the enemy. By this time the force in the valley in which I had left General Driesen had come into action, and another from the other side of the river, but the fire died out when the sun went down, and no bones were broken.

The following letter presents a summary view of the situation of the Russian army in Bulgaria in the fourth week of July, and briefly mentions Baron Krüdener's first check at Plevna, the precursor of so many misfortunes, described in subsequent communications :—

* BJELA, *Jnly 23rd.*—On the 19th the Russians, sustained a severe check, if not an actual defeat, at Plevna. General Schilder, with a portion of the 9th Corps, consisting of an infantry brigade with cavalry and artillery, was sent against the place and seems to have approached it in a slovenly manner. The Turks took the offensive and repulsed the Russians with heavy loss. It is understood that Baron Krüdener, commanding the 9th Corps, will be superseded, and it is believed that the 9th and 11th Corps will be formed into a separate army under Prince Schahofskoy, to operate in the west against Widdin. Orders have been sent to the 9th Corps in the meantime to take Plevna, and tidings of the result of the new operations are now being waited for. The 4th Corps will follow the 8th Corps across the Balkans.

The Russian Army of Rustchuk has advanced to the line of the Lom River, touching the Danube at Pirgos, and is slowly wheeling on that pivot to invest that fortress. Nearly forty thousand men are now jammed into the angle between the Danube and the Lom. The Turks have abandoned the line of the Lom without fighting, and one part is believed to have retired on Rustchuk and another to have fallen back on Shumla. The Grand Duke Vladimir two days ago pushed a cavalry reconnaissance through Kadikoi, and on to the Rustchuk and Shumla Railway at Guvemli, where he cut the telegraph wires, tore up the rails, and blew up the bridge on the line with dynamite. Several isolated skirmishes have occurred, in one of which a detachment of Russian dragoons was roughly handled and lost a good many men. There was some artillery fighting near the Danube yesterday, in which a battery on the Roumanian side took part, and this morning the bombardment of Rustchuk from Giurgevo has recommenced. When the bombardment from the Bulgarian side will begin it is difficult to say. The siege train is on its way, but it crosses at Simnitza, a fearful way round. Supplies are difficult, as the base of the whole force now in Bulgaria is still Simnitza, where there still is but one bridge. An early attempt is expected to drive the Turks now around Rustchuk into their fortified defences, but the investment of the place is not yet imminent, as the progress of the troops destined for that purpose is but slow.

The headquarters of the Grand Duke Nicholas remain in Tirnova. The Czarewitch has his headquarters at Obertenik. The Emperor, with his suite, is in Bjela. The Turkish inhabitants are slowly returning to Bjela and reoccupying their houses, after having suffered terrible hardships in the woods. All report that they left their homes on a stringent order issued from Constantinople. In the Dobrudscha General Zimmermann has mastered the whole line of the Tchernavoda Kustendjie Railway after some fighting. His object is Silistria. The health of the army remains good. In the 12th Corps not two per cent. are sick.

I understand that there are no objections in the councils of the Russian headquarters to give fair consideration to propositions for peace made at the present juncture, if they are of a reasonable and satisfactory tenor; but that there can be no question as to the direct advance with all due speed on the Turkish capital if the Turks do not avert this movement by suing for terms which will give satisfaction to Russia. Neutral Powers cannot fail to recognize that the present is a favourable moment for giving strenuous advice to Turkey to be wise in time. The Bulgarian volunteers are being equipped with arms and uniform, and drilled to act as gendarmerie all over the occupied district.

* OBERTENIK, *July 26th.*—It was expected that to-day at length there would have been something of great interest to report from the Rustchuk Army. All was ready, and to-day was the day named for the decisive movement, but everything stands fast in compliance with positive orders from the superior headquarters in Tirnova. The reason for these restraining orders as regards the Rustchuk Army is not far to seek. The 11th Corps, having crossed the Danube at Simnitza, was on

the march in the direction of Shumla, and had already made progress in that direction nearly to the Upper Lom, when the mischance at Plevna to a portion of the 9th Corps arrested the advance. Prince Schahofskoy, commanding the 11th Corps, received orders to march across country from east to west, and co-operate with the 9th Corps in renewed operations against Plevna, the 9th Corps marching southward from the direction of Nicopolis. The 11th Corps was last night at Bulgareni, two days' march from Plevna. In three days, at the outside, there must be heavy fighting there.

Plevna is believed to be held by a large portion of the Turkish army of Widdin, with Osman Pacha himself in command. Now is the time for the Roumanians to make a serviceable diversion in favour of the Russians by crossing the Danube about Widdin, it would be preferable below the fortress, and threatening the Turkish communications between Widdin and Plevna. The 4th Corps will support the 8th Corps in the invasion of Turkey beyond the Balkans. In Kezanlik there are now extensive concentrations proceeding. Between that town and Eski-Zagra, which is on the Russian line of intended advance, stand five-and-twenty thousand men who have crossed the Balkans by different passes, from the Hainkoi Pass on the east to the Shipka Pass on the west. This is a mixed mass of regiments from divers corps, under the command of General Gourko. The 8th Corps has one division. The 9th is in Shipka. The other is partly through the Balkans, partly in the passes. Eski-Zagra is in Russian hands, and Yamboli is so reported also, but this is not certain. No time will be lost in pushing forward, but the delay is occasioned by the difficulty of getting artillery and supplies through the passes.

Around Rustchuk the Turks are now committing terrible atrocities in the Bulgarian villages. In Kadikoi I have myself seen the bodies of massacred men, women, and children. On the other hand, arms have been entrusted to the Bulgarian mountaineers between Tirnova and the Balkans, and on the mountains, and they are abusing badly their new liberty and their unaccustomed weapons. The Russian Cossacks get the blame of the Bulgarian outrages. Within the sphere of my observation on the foreposts about Rustchuk, the Russian troops are behaving with great self-restraint. The Turks taken red-handed in outraging and massacring are brought before a superior officer and then hanged. At Pirgos this morning a marauding Turk suffered this fate after having been tried and evidence heard last night by General Driesen. To-day direct communication by pontoon boats, not a bridge, will be opened across the Danube between Pirgos and Parapan. The Emperor remains in Bjela.

† BUCHAREST, *July 29th.*—I have just received the following from your Special Correspondent at the Russian headquarters:—"I have just come from Tirnova, where the Grand Duke's headquarters still remain. Preparations are being made there for the Emperor, whose arrival is expected shortly. Two triumphal arches had been erected, the materials for decoration being collected from the inhabitants in the following manner:—Waggons drawn by oxen and attended by police were driven through the streets, and received what contributions were forthcoming, such as carpets, coloured cloths, &c. The arrival of his Majesty is looked forward to with great interest by the Bulgarian population. The municipal organization is going on rapidly. The native police are already established with a special uniform. The Turkish inhabitants begin to take heart, and come into the town with produce from the country round. Cossacks and Bulgarian patrols bring in Turkish prisoners daily. Last Wednesday five hundred Turks were brought in from the front, amongst them several officers, under escort of the Cossacks and Bulgarian troops. The Grand Duke Nicholas examined the officers, and was surprised to learn that they had not received any pay for many months. The Russians seemed to have pushed on a little too far into the interior without sufficiently assuring their right flank, and consequently now find it necessary to rest on their oars a bit before advancing the main column further. It is probable, however, that the advance guard of Cossacks may push beyond Jeni-Zagra; but no doubt the headquarters of the Grand Duke will remain at Tirnova until the country on both sides of the Danube road of communication is thoroughly secured against the enemy. Last week the Turks evidently had the idea of cutting this communication from Plevna, where very severe fighting took place. The Turks are stated to have been nearly 30,000 strong. The Russian loss is reported very heavy. I was told at Simnitza bridge that 400 Russian wounded passed over on Thursday. Had this attempt on the part of the Turks succeeded, it would have placed the Russians in an awkward position."

The following letter describes the preparations for the second attack on Plevna, under Baron Krüdener and Prince Schahofskoy:—

* Poradim, *July 30th.*—Coming into Bjela from the foreposts in front of Rustchuk on the 27th inst., I learned of the movement against Plevna, the details of which I have already communicated by telegraph. Knowing that until the completion of that operation the movement for the investment of Rustchuk would stand arrested, and realizing of what importance it was that the right flank of the Russian advance to the Balkans should be cleared of the danger which undeniably threatened it by the concentration at Plevna of a large Turkish force flushed by the success achieved over the previous unfortunate effort to take and hold that place made by a portion of the 9th Corps, I at once determined to join the force moving on Plevna. I was indebted to General Ignatieff for a note of introduction to Prince Schahofskoy, commanding the 11th Corps, a portion of which was engaged in the operation, and my companion and myself started on the long journey in the afternoon of the 27th. We reached Pavlo the same night, and bivouacked in a Bulgarian farmyard, where milk was procurable for ourselves and fodder for our horses. As far as Pavlo the road was familiar to us, but next morning we plunged into a *terra incognita* with only the map for our guide. Of the maps of Bulgaria which I have seen all I can say is that the best are bad. They are but blind guides, and the Bulgarian peasants whom one questions as to the route have no idea either of distances or of points of the compass. They reckon by hours, and with most irritating looseness. "How far to Akcair?" "Two hours, sir." "What direction?" A wave of the hand to the right, and an indescribable howl, is the answer. You ride on for an hour, and encounter another peasant. "How far to Akcair?" "Three hours!" "What dirction?" A wild, indefinite wave of the hand to the left front, and a howl as indescribable as the previous one, is the reply of this exponent of local geography. If you desist from inquiries, and try marching by the map, you find yourself trusting to a broken reed. The most detailed map of the theatre of war is the map of the Austrian military staff; but its details are too often erroneous. It lays down a road where there is not even a cart track, and transposes villages in the most free-and-easy manner.

On all the maps is depicted a broad road, a main highway running between Plevna on the west, and the Jantra at Kosovo on the east. It was our aim to strike this main road; once on it we could no longer be in doubt as to our route. We searched for it first in Burunli. It was not there. Nobody had ever heard of it. The map made it running through the village of Akcair, but the only roads about Akcair were mere cart tracks. At Studeni, although according to the maps that village stood on it, all declared it to be a myth. We found a road leading from Studeni, and determining to follow it were comforted by the assurance of a marketender I met that Tirnova, not Plevna, was its objective. In despair I made a sort of cast, as a huntsman might whose hounds are at fault, and quite casually, in the middle of a plain, I found the road. It had been wonderfully well made for a Turkish road—a ditch cut on either side, metalling laid down on its surface, and nothing was wanting to constitute it a highway but traffic upon it. But tall grass grew through the stones upon it, and grass obscured the profile of the ditches. I do not believe that a wheeled vehicle had ever passed along it. It is a road which to all appearance has no *raison d'être*, carefully avoids the villages, and accommodates nothing and nobody. My idea is that the Turks, in some sudden spurt of ardour for keeping up with the times in matters military, had been advised that a great military road athwart Bulgaria, from Widdin to Shumla, would be a valuable work, and that accordingly the section of it between Plevna and the Jantra was taken in hand. Made, it has never been used. Farther on we found that the bridge over the Osma, the only stream the road encounters, had fallen by natural decay, and that on the other side the villagers were reaping a hay crop on the road; so we lost sight of it for miles, and only picked it up again within a few kilometres of the village in which we found Prince Schahofskoy quartered for the night, the village of Karajac Bugarski.

The 11th Corps, of which he is the chief, has had a chief share of the hard work of this campaign, with as yet but little of the glory of the fighting. The 11th Corps was the first to cross the Pruth and occupy Galatz. War was declared on the 24th April, and on the afternoon of that day a detachment of the Cossacks, attached to the 11th Corps, and led by Colonel Strukoff, streamed over the Reni road, and picqueted their horses on the heights of Barbosch. It seems a year ago, although only three months, since I called on Prince Schahofskoy to ask for permission to visit his camps round about Galatz. The corps stood long at Galatz and Braila while the invading army streamed round and over it. It made pontoons for bridges by which it was not to cross. It made batteries for the siege guns at Braila, whose gunners, not belonging to it, were to earn honour and glory by the destruction of the *Lutfi Djelil*. It made the preparations which facilitated the later crossing at Hirsova of troops belonging to another corps. It built and armed batteries at Oltenitza, and stood the brunt of the return fire from the sharpshooters and cannon of Turtukai. It constructed the siege batteries on either flank of Giurgevo, and conducted the futile and thankless bombardment of Rustchuk, about which so much ink has been wasted. Crossing the river at Simnitza, the corps marched on Tirnova, and hopes rose high in its ranks that for its soldiers no more would be the function of hewers of wood and drawers of water, but that they would cross the Balkans and see fighting and earn glory and crosses among the rose gardens of the Tundja Valley. These hopes were shattered. A day's march from Tirnova the corps was ordered to bend to the east and take up a defensive position on the line of a Turkish march from Shumla over Osman Bazar against Tirnova and the Russian communications between that place and the Danube. Well, here at least was the chance of a fight, for the Turks were reported in force at Osman Bazar, and Schahofskoy had permission to march thus far in search of an enemy. But on the 20th inst. there came to the 11th Corps the order for yet another long march. "We are the football of the army," said an angry officer to me whom I met on the road. I tried to console him by the remark that it was rather an honour than a hardship to be selected for exceptionally arduous duties; and that further, a fight clearly awaited him in this last expedition. The corps has already earned a marching reputation at least. A glance at the map will prove what splendid marching it has been to make the distance from Kosarevac, some twenty miles east of Tirnova, to the vicinity of Plevna, in six days, and that in the intense heat of the summer. In the divisional hospital of the 32nd Division, into which I looked at Bulgareni on my way to Prince Schahofskoy's headquarters, I found evidences of the severity of the long march. Several men were down with sunstroke, and there were cases of violent fever accompanied by delirium, brought on doubtless by the quick change of temperature from the burning heat of the days to the cold chills of the nights.

As I sat under the verandah of a hut talking with Prince Schahofskoy there came towards us through the dusk of the evening a form which seemed curiously familiar. There flashed through my mind the question—*Que diable êtes-vous venu faire dans cette galère?* as I instinctively rose to greet one who seemed to me no other than Colonel Frederick Marshall, erstwhile chief of the Horse Guards Blue, now one of the aides-de-camp to the Duke of Cambridge. I was wrong. It was not my gallant English friend, as good a cricketer as he is a soldier, but his Russian double. There was a good precedent for my error. Is it not told among the stalwart troopers of the Blues how, when after the Salisbury Plain manœuvres the Count Protassoff-Bachmeteff entered the Albany-street barracks in plain clothes, the guard turned out to him under the belief that it was their own colonel who was entering? At that time Count Protassoff was the colonel of the Russian Garde à Cheval as Marshall was colonel of our Horse Guards! Another curious link in the coincidence of the striking resemblance. The Wiltshire rustics have not till this day forgotten the imposing figure, clad in scarlet, and wearing a burnished helmet crowned by a golden eagle, whose splendour eclipsed all the varied glories of the foreign officers on the day of the great review at Beacon's-hill which concluded the manœuvres which were our first and last attempt at the practical imitation of real warfare. Count Protassoff is no longer chief of the Garde à Cheval, he has now the rank of major-general, and he belongs to the suite of the Emperor, but is attached to the headquarters of the 11th Corps for this expedition. To him belongs much of the merit of having introduced into the Russian army the system of regimental messes, copied from the pattern of the English system *mutatis mutandis*, of the details of which Count Protassoff made himself master during one of his visits to England. A long gossip over autumn manœuvres helped to while away the evening.

In the dead of night that extraordinary fellow General Skobeleff the younger turned up in Prince Schahofskoy's headquarters. He is the stormy petrel of the Russian army. If I were riding along a road in a given direction in expectation of seeing a fight, and if I chanced to meet young Skobeleff riding in the opposite direction, without any inquiry or any hesitation I would wheel my horse and ride in Skobeleff's tracks, in the full assurance that I was doing the best thing for myself and your readers. He is in the thick of everything. In the grey dawn of the morning of the crossing I shook hands with him on the edge of the bank of the Danube after the bayonet charge in which he had taken part. His face was black with powder, and he, general as he is, carried a soldier's rifle, with the bayonet fixed. He was in the fighting at the Shipka, and led the first column which traversed that pass. There seemed some prospect of quietude for some days on the other side of the Balkans, and the Plevna expedition offered a prospect of fighting. Skobeleff is unattached, and can rove from flower to flower, from one fighting ground to another. He is, I sometimes think, a little mad, but a man of real value in a kind of warfare such as this. It would be embarrassing if every general were a Skobeleff; but a few Skobeleffs scattered up and down through a great army have their uses. They generally end by getting shot, and earn a short memoir and a good many decorations. But I hope it will be a long time before Skobeleff meets his inevitable doom, for he is a right good fellow, and a stanch comrade. He came to us from Baron Krüdener's headquarters, with instructions that he should take the temporary command of Colonel Tutolmin's brigade of Circassian Cossacks, who have also been attached to this expedition, and execute a reconnaissance in the direction of Loftcha. He rode off in the darkness, and came back last night, after having ridden about fifty miles, with the tidings that Loftcha was held by five battalions of Turkish infantry, and its rayon infested by Circassians and Bashi-Bazouks.

On the morning of the 29th Prince Schahofskoy and his headquarters moved from Karajac Bugarski, and first went forward some distance on the direct road towards Plevna. We passed the cavalry foreposts, and advanced indeed into the vicinity of Grivica, without seeing anything of the enemy. It surprised me not a little to find ourselves faithfully followed at a very short interval by the whole of the headquarter baggage train. Now, the headquarter baggage train of a Russian general commanding an army corps and his staff is no light thing. Lord Albemarle tells us that in 1828, in the Russian column which crossed the Balkans under General Diebitsch, every general officer had his caleche. With the present Russian army, it is not alone that every general officer has his carriage —most have more than one—but the larger proportion of field officers have vehicles also. On this staff there is a baggage waggon between every two officers, and a surprising number of miscellaneous vehicles besides. The chief of the artillery has a travelling chariot drawn by four horses, driven after the manner of a four-in-hand with us. Servants swarm, and every servant contrives to find a place in or on a vehicle of some kind or other. The staff train is half a mile long if it is a yard, to say nothing of escort, marketenders, and the priest, who rides in a vehicle of his own. A train such as this must always be a great embarrassment and impediment; in an advance with favourable means of communication it is an encumbrance; in retreat, along bad roads, it must be a nuisance of the most abominable character; and fancy it following the staff beyond the foreposts! One great want in the Russian army on the march is that of a skilled and efficient field gendarmerie to regulate the trains, preserve the order of march, see that intervals are properly maintained, that ground is not lost, that straggling or irregular practices do not occur, and to clear the way of civilian traffic in front of an advancing column. Nothing could be more admirable than the manner in which these varied and important functions are performed by the German field gendarmerie, a picked corps, with numerous experienced and carefully trained officers, and the non-commissioned officers and men of which consist of stanch and trusty old soldiers who can be thoroughly depended on in every emergency. There is a field gendarmerie service in the Russian army. Its men wear a blue uniform with white aiguillettes. I saw them in considerable strength about the streets of Kischeneff: I have seen very few of them since. Now and then a field gendarme may be found jogging along with a column, but assuming no responsibility, charging himself apparently with no duty except that of getting forward, and unheeded by any one, the meanest waggoner, who in the German army would tremble at a glance from a field gendarme, taking no account of the Russian policeman in the blue coat with the white cords. There is not a single field gendarme with the headquarter train of Prince Schahofskoy. Order is not its strong point, and that it is badly superintended, or not superintended at all, is obvious from the manner in which it wandered after us on through the forepost line. It was countermarched with some precipitation when the chief turned his horse's head and rode backward within his own forepost line. Then we rode—and it followed us by a zigzag track through some very pretty country, where were numerous villages, and where haycocks stood thick in the fields, and corn-stacks in the village farmyards—to the bivouac ground in one of the tents of which I am now writing.

All night long we lay on the grass with tents struck and horses saddled, waiting for an *alerte.* It was believed that it was the intention to make the attack to-day, and that the preliminary positions were to be taken up under cover of the darkness. Fires were made up as if the army were remaining in its positions, with intent to delude the enemy, if it were not too great a compliment to pay to the Turks to suppose that they would be on the outlook for any such indications. We waited orders from General Krüdener, but they came not. About midnight two officers rode to him from Prince Schahofskoy, and brought back instructions that he meant to delay the attack, partly because some of the troops had not come up far enough, and partly to rest the whole after their long and fatiguing marching. So about four o'clock in the cold grim morning we pitched tents again, unsaddled the horses, and lay down on our cloaks for a long unbroken welcome sleep. The delay in this case I do not believe to have been dangerous. Undoubtedly the troops were sorely worn with incessant marching, and the cavalry horses were almost exhausted. One great anxiety was relieved. Reports were brought in that no more Turkish troops were marching from Plevna on Loftcha. This removed apprehension of a flank attack in force from Loftcha on the left of the Russian converging assault upon the Plevna position. Krüdener and Schahofskoy were now free to concentrate their attention on the latter place, leaving cavalry to watch Loftcha.

This morning there was a thunderstorm, which broke nearly over us, and every man had to stand to his horse to pacify him when the thunder rattled and the lightning flashed. Stampedes are by no means confined to Aldershot. We had one with a vengeance the other day on the heights of Obertenik, among the horses of the Oldenburg regiment of heavy dragoons, in Baron Driesen's division. It was brought about by a sudden thunderclap. The Russians do not picquet their cavalry horses, but merely tie their halter-ropes to a continuous cord, stretched on upright stakes. With one accord, two squadrons on the hill-top broke away, and dashed at a headlong gallop in the direction of the Turkish forepost line, which was not above four miles distant, in the direction of Rustchuk. They galloped through a battery of artillery, whose guns stood unlimbered on the crest a little farther on. The artillery horses, used to loud noises, made no attempt to stampede, but remained quietly munching their hay under the thunderstorm. The gunners caught a number of the troop horses, and the infantry forepost line secured a number more, but sixty horses got clean away, and, without slackening speed, galloped right in among the Turks, who took no measures for their restoration. Some days later an officer of the regiment, when in Kadikoi on a reconnaissance, found several of the runaway horses lying dead there. Apparently they had been overridden, and not fed at all, and so had fallen down and died. I suppose the picqueting question is by this time a weariness of the flesh, but I should like to say that, having recently seen nearly every modern system in practice, including that in use among our Indian troops, it seems to me that the practice of the Belgian cavalry is infinitely the simplest. In their stables and stationary horse-lines they have fixed picquet pegs with rings at the top. These pegs are morticed into stone, and it is beyond the power of any horse to draw them. All young horses are tied up to these, and all manner of noises are made to scare them. They struggle wildly to draw their pegs, but in vain, and after efforts more or less prolonged and energetic according to the nature of the horse, they recognize the immovable character of the picquet peg, and cease to attempt the proved impossibility. When on manœuvres a comparatively slight peg is used, and found quite effectual; the horse, having once realized that the picquet peg is not to be drawn, never tries more. It seems rather a rash experiment to lean upon such a ruse, but experience proves that it is quite safe. A Belgian cavalry officer will gather together all the most easily scared horses in his command, and give you full licence to scare them into a stampede by any expedient your ingenuity may devise. You may throw a handful of firework crackers in among them, and they will be horribly frightened, will snort and tremble all over, but will make no effort to draw the picquet pegs, although a comparatively slight effort would have the effect of doing so. The Russian Cossacks, when they turn out their horses to graze, tie one fore leg and one hind leg together; but when on picquet duty they never tether their ponies at all, but fasten the bridle over the high pommel of the saddle, and, thus secured, the Cossack pony would stand fast till he died of exhaustion. Probably it would take about a year to starve him. He is so lean, so wiry, and so thoroughly inured to privation that he must take a deal of killing. Mr. Weller calls attention to the curious physiological fact of the rarity of dead donkeys. Had Cossack ponies come within the sphere of his acute observation he would have coupled them with the donkeys.

This afternoon there has been a regular Council of War. About one o'clock the generals, staff-officers, colonels, and adjutants of the force under Prince Schahofskoy began to gather into this bivouac to receive explanations and instructions respecting the tactics of the offensive operation which is settled for to-morrow. It was a fine opportunity for observing the diverse types of Russian officers. Of these there are several schools: roughly, the old ignorant school, the young ignorant school, the old refined school, the young cultured and scientific school, and the young dashing, reckless, refined school, fluent in languages, knowing not much of the art military, but fine gallant soldiers. The representatives of the first two schools are rather boorish, give one a general impression of having been sergeants, and with few exceptions are hearty fellows with a pronounced liking for vodka, and not very particular about knives and forks. The officers of the old refined school are simply charming, full of a spontaneous courteous bonhomie which at once puts a man at his ease; fair linguists, men who have travelled, and mostly know Courts, and who are full of consideration and kindliness. I am not sure that modern soldiering is their strong point. The gentlemen of the young cultured and scientific school, with the Military Academy badge on their breasts, are very much of the type of our Engineers; a little priggish in their way, slightly mysterious over trifles, which they choose to regard as secrets, dry in manner for the most part, but when you come to know them downright good fellows, whose friendship is a privilege. It is in holiday time, or about the fag end of an adverse battle, that I should like best to meet a batch of youngsters belonging to the fifth school I have roughly designated. They rather interfere with assiduous letter-writing, but they are dear boys, and if one wishes them further sometimes, one cannot help loving them.

To-day, on the windy plain, outside the tent, were representatives of all these types: the grey-bearded, hard-faced old major who, without "protection," has fought his sturdy way up through the grades with long delays, much hard service, and many wounds. He was an ensign in the Crimea, and afterwards was forgotten for Heaven knows how many years in some odd corner in the Caucasus. He is only a major, but he has half a dozen decorations, and, please God, he will gain another to-morrow, if he has the luck to stand up. He is as hard as nails, and would as lief live on biscuit and junk as on champagne and French cookery. There is little in common between him and the tall, stately, grizzled general, an aide-de-camp of the Emperor; a man of the Court, yet who has never forsworn the camp; a man who will discuss the relative merits of Patti and Lucca, who has yachted in the Solent and shot grouse in the Highlands; who wears his decorations too, some of them earned in the forefront of the battle, others, honorary distinctions, as marks of Imperial favour. He can gallop, can this young hussar in the blue and red; he can cut the sword exercise, he can sing French songs of a somewhat improper character, he can pick up a bottle of champagne between his teeth, and holding it there let the contents run down his throat; he would give his last cigarette either to a comrade or to a stranger like myself; he has the portraits of his mother and of a French lionne of the demi-monde on his bosom, and in his secret heart he has vowed to earn the St. George to-morrow. I don't know that I quite like Lieutenant Brutokoff yet. I know the first time I met him I disliked him down to the ground. His manners

—well, he had none to speak of—and his voice was a growl, with a hoarseness in it begotten of schnapps. He did not look as if he washed copiously, and was the sort of man who might give some colour to the myth that the Russian has not yet broken himself of the custom of breakfasting off tallow candles. But he turns out a good fellow on further acquaintance, and is no niggard with his raki. There are in the throng young officers who would be a credit to any service in Europe. One, the Count Keller, not yet thirty, but a lieutenant-colonel, I became acquainted with first one bleak day on the uplands before Saitchar, when he was leading a little column, of which he had the command, against a Servian village held by a detachment of Turks, whom he drove out with skill and daring. Baron Krüdener drives up and is greeted by Prince Schahofskoy, his brother corps commander. There is a brief inverval of hand-shaking and general conversation, and then all stroll toward the farmyard of a Bulgarian cottage. The generals and leading staff officers gather close into the wide clay-floored porch, under the spreading roof, and there, standing in a group, pore over maps and discuss the plan of operations. The other officers stand in knots about the farmyard, or sit on the shafts of a cart, waiting for the detailed instructions to them which will follow the settlement of the general arrangement. The Turks are reported standing fast; their positions are known to be strong; the orders to the Russians are to succeed, cost what it may. Seldom, to alter Macaulay's line, have I promise seen of such a bloody fray. To-morrow's sun will set on smoke and fire, and all the lurid grandeur and horror of a battle-field.

CHAPTER XIII.

THE GREAT RUSSIAN REPULSE BEFORE PLEVNA.

The Russian Forces and their Leaders—The Bivouac on the Eve of Battle—Faulty Dispositions of the Russian Army—The Attack—Capture of the first Turkish Position by Schahfoskoy—Its Recapture by the Turks—Krüdener unable to advance—Disastrous Failure of the Attack—Advance of the Turks—The Bashi-Bazouks after the Battle—Retreat of the Defeated Army.

THE following letter describes the attack on Osman Pacha's position at Plevna, made by General Krüdener and Prince Schahofskoy on the 31st July, twelve days after the first Russian attempt to take that place. The whole of this letter was transmitted by telegraph, aud appeared in the *Daily News* of August 3rd:—

* PORADIM, BEFORE PLEVNA, *August* 1*st*.—The previous affair at Plevna had been the only serious reverse the Russians had encountered in the European campaign, but it had been very serious, and as an aggravation it occurred through neglect of common military precautions. When the commander of the 9th Corps proceeded against Nicopolis he made the omission of protecting his flank by not sending cavalry to occupy Plevna, then only weakly held. Afterwards an easy chance did not offer. The Turkish column from Widdin, marching too late to succour Nicopolis, turned aside and occupied Plevna. With intent to repair the blunder General Krüdener sent three regiments of infantry against Plevna and without a previous reconnaissance. These, after hard fighting, actually occupied the town. They had laid aside their cloaks and packs in the streets, and had quitted the fighting column formation, believing all was over, and were singing as they straggled along. No patrols had been pushed into the recesses of the town. No cavalry had been sent forward beyond. The whole business was slovenly to a degree. The penalty was paid. Suddenly, from a hundred windows and balconies, a vehement fire was poured into the troops straggling along the streets. They were beset on all sides, and had to retreat. One regiment left its packs where they had been taken off in the street. During the retreat, more or less precipitate, about 2,900 men were lost. One regiment lost nearly 2,000 men. The retreating troops witnessed the butchery of their wounded. On the 22nd Princo Schahofskoy received orders to leave in position at Osman Bazar two infantry brigades, and march on Plevna, right across the theatre of war from east to west, with one cavalry brigade and one infantry brigade of his corps. The 30th Division of the 4th Corps, who were crossing the river at Simnitza, en route for Tirnova, were ordered also on Plevna, to stand under Schahofskoy's orders. The 9th Corps, about and in front of Nicopolis, was ordered to co-operate in a combined movement against Plevna. The regiments which suffered in the previous affair clamoured to lead the vanguard of the renewed attack. Riding across the country from the Rustchuk front I overtook Prince Schahofskoy's headquarters, on the evening of the 28th, in the village of Karajac Bugarski, about twelve miles due east of Plevna. He had marched from the foot of the Balkans in six days. Regiments of infantry streamed through the village in the dusk amid clouds

of dust, and tramped on to take up their bivouac for the night on the downs beyond, the cavalry brigade covering the front further in advance. Reconnaissances had been pushed forward, which proved that the work in hand was no child's play. Plevna was reported to be occupied by the whole of Osman Pacha's army from Widdin, which strengthened by troops from Sophia and others coming from the late Montenegrin campaign, was in all believed to be from 35,000 to 40,000 strong. The Turkish intrenchment line ran through a series of villages lying in a semicircular order round Plevna, at a distance from it of about five miles and touching the river Vid on both flanks. A strong Turkish advance force was reported at Grivica on the road along which lay Schahofskoy's line of advance. From north to south the villages of the Turkish forepost position were as follows—Plizitza, Bukova, Radisovo, Tucenica, and Bogot. Schahofskoy was, as I have said, in the village of Karajac Bugarski. His brother corps commander, Baron Krüdener, was for the night in the village of Kalisovit, on the road from Nicopolis to Plevna, and about eight miles north-west of Schahofskoy's headquarters. As senior general Krüdener was nominally in chief command of the whole of the operations, but he acted under peremptory instructions from the Grand Duke Nicholas in Tirnova.

In the night of the 28th the younger General Skobeleff reached Prince Schahofskoy's headquarters from Tirnova, appointed to the temporary command of the Cossack brigade in the force of the Prince. He received instructions to march his brigade to the southward, and occupy, if possible, the town of Loftcha, an important position between Plevna and the Balkans—a hazardous expedition, conducted along the face of a hostile front, and likely to meet with resistance en route, and also at the point of destination. But Skobeleff galloped off with a light heart on this dangerous duty. I spent the night in the house of a very intelligent Bulgarian who had been an agent of the American Bible Society in Plevna. In answer to my remark that the Bulgarians on this side of the Balkans seemed a thriving people and not suffering severely from oppression, he stated that until 1866 Turkish rule in Bulgaria was light and tolerant. Then the Circassian settlers were introduced, and with them came lawlessness and anarchy. He attributed wholly to the Circassians the impending ruin of the Turkish power in Europe. But in quiet times the Bulgarian villagers who were wise generally found means of averting trouble from the lawless Circassians. They made regular presents—paid a sort of light tribute—to the priest of their village, who used his influence with the Circassians to avert their exactions and lawless acts. It is undeniable that for years past committees have existed among the Bulgarians in favour of insurrection and subscriptions made to this end. He himself had been president of one of these committees. This ramification coming to a head last year had alarmed the Turks and led to stern repressive measures, but from these the Bulgarians north of the Balkans had in a great measure escaped, and to the last they had remained substantially unharmed.

On the morning of the 29th Prince Schahofskoy quitted Karajac Bugarski, and made a reconnaissance along the road towards Plevna, in the direction of Grivica, where the Russians killed in the previous attempt still lie unburied. His march lay over beautiful grassy downs and through little wooded valleys. The Turks were not seen, but cannon fire was heard to the south in the direction of the march of Skobeleff on Loftcha. Retracing his steps, and bending to the southward, Schahofskoy bivouacked for the day on a plain near the village of Poradim, with a brigade of infantry in front. Another brigade marched up into line at our quarters of the previous night. The Russian front was thus widely extended, aiming at a concentric attack on the Plevna position, much in the manner practised by the Prussian Guards in retaking Le Bourget, but of course on a much larger scale, and including an attempt at wholly enveloping the enemy's position by cavalry operating on both flanks.

Such dispositions demand time, and accordingly we spent the remainder of the 29th in a pleasant but anxious inactivity in the Poradim bivouac, where hay and water were plentiful, and where the neighbouring village actually afforded wine. Patrols pushed forward, touching the Turks at Radisova, Tucenica, Bogot, and Slatina. At night Skobeleff came in with the intelligence that Loftcha and the intervening villages were strongly occupied, and the Turkish force thereabouts apparently being strengthened. About dusk began to gather near our bivouac a very sorrowful company of Bulgarian fugitives from the villages on the road between Loftcha and Plevna traversed by the Turkish troops. Women came wailing a mournful dirge for their slaughtered dead left behind in the abandoned village homes. A waggon rolled along with a weeping woman in front. Behind was stretched at length her husband, hacked, and scored, and slashed till I wondered how a spark of life yet lingered in him. One hand was half severed at the wrist, not by a sweeping sabre stroke, but as if dissection had been attempted with a blunt knife. His throat was hacked in a similar fashion. His forehead and chest were scored with transverse slashes. He was reported to be a victim of the Circassians. Further on, amid a crowd of weeping women, lay a Bulgarian in the last agonies. He had been almost scalped, and then an attempt made to cut his head off. It was not worth while bringing him along, for he must have been hopeless from the first, and he died while we stood looking on. He had come by his death at the hands of civilian Turks abiding in the same village. Fugitives narrate numerous slaughters of men, but that no women or children were touched. I am not fond of hearsay evidence, and prefer the evidence of my own senses. It is on this latter evidence that I testify to what I have written above, and also to the murders in the village of Kadikoi before Rustchuk. Still, the killing seems exceptional, and the regular Turkish troops are never accused of acts of violence. The blame is always ascribed to the Circassians and the Bashi-Bazouks.

The night between the 29th and 30th was spent with tents struck and horses saddled, waiting for the order to advance, in anticipation of the commencement of fighting at sunrise; but Baron Krüdener had determined to wait yet a day longer to perfect his dispositions and give the troops, fatigued by severe marching, some rest. The 30th was therefore spent in inaction, except that the troops were somewhat drawn forward to be within striking distance for the morrow. Tidings came that no more Turkish troops were marching from Plevna on Loftcha, which simplified matters, since fewer troops were required to watch the latter place. A general council of war was held at Poredin on the afternoon of the 30th, at which were present Baron Krüdener, Prince Schahofskoy, and the generals of division and brigades. The colonels of regiments and staff officers waited to receive instructions as to the final dispositions. It was settled that the action should begin next morning at five o'clock by a general concentric advance on the Turkish positions in front of Plevna, and that Prince Schahofskoy and the general staff should move forward at four o'clock. Several aides of the Grand Duke Nicholas arrived, and were detailed to various points to make observations, and after the battle to carry reports of the results back to Tirnova. The gravity of the task before the army was fully recognized, for reconnaissances had proved the Turks to be in greater force than was at first believed. Twenty thousand regulars had come from Widdin. The Turkish positions were known to be strong by nature, and strengthened yet further by art.

The night between the 30th and 31st was very wet, and troops did not begin to march forward before six instead of four.

The number of infantry combatants was actually about 32,000, with 160 field cannon and three brigades of cavalry. Baron Krüdener was on the right with the whole of the 31st Division in his fighting line, and three regiments of the 5th Division in reserve at Karajac Bugarski. He was to attack in two columns, a brigade in each. On the left was Schahofskoy with a brigade of the 32nd Division and a brigade of the 30th Division in fighting line. Another brigade of the 30th Division was in reserve at Pelisat. The Turkish position was convex, somewhat in horseshoe shape, but more pointed. Baron Krüdener was to attack the Turkish left flank from Grivica towards the river Vid. Schahofskoy was to assail their right from Radisovo, also towards the river Vid. On the left flank of the attack stood Skobeleff, with a brigade of Cossacks, a battalion of infantry, and a battery, to cope with the Turkish troops on the line from Plevna to Loftcha, and to hinder them from interfering with the development of Schahofskoy's attack. On the right flank stood Lascareff, with a brigade of the 9th Cavalry to guard Krüdener from a counter flank attack.

The main fault of the dispositions was that Krüdener and Schahofskoy were practically independent of each other, that the two attacks were too far apart, and without a connecting link; but the gravest evil, which did not rest with the commanders on the spot, was the weakness of the assailing force. After the previous reverse nothing should have been left to chance, and it is tempting Providence to attack the Turks in a strong defensive position with inferior numbers. The falseness of the economy stands proved to-day, when yesterday's defeat makes the Russian hold in Bulgaria extremely precarious, and must compel the withdrawal of troops from some other point where they are nearly as badly needed, to beat the Turks at Plevna; and beaten they must be, and that speedily, if the risk is to be averted lest the Russian army be forced to retire ingloriously into the Principalities.

Preparation for the infantry was to be made in regular form, but the artillery preparation loses much of its value when delivered against constructed positions spread widely. Krüdener's blunder had given the Turks time to intrench themselves, nor had they neglected the chance.

The morning was gloomy, which the Russians regarded as a favourable omen. The troops cheered vigorously as they passed the General. Physically there are no finer men in the world. In the pink of hard condition, and marching without packs, carrying only great-coat, haversack with rations, and ammunition, they seemed fit to go anywhere and do anything. Schahofskoy's right column marched over Pelisat and Sgalince. The left column headed straight for Radisovo. The artillery were pushed forward from the first, and worked independently. Marching forward, we found the cavalry foreposts on the sky-line above Pelisat, and on the sloping downs infantry deployed as they advanced, as the Russian practice is on open ground. The formation was in column of double companies, with rifle company in front of each battalion. The line and rifle companies have the same weapon, the Kranke. The rifle company is made up of marksmen whose rifles are sighted up to 1,200 yards, whereas the line is only to 600, the maximum fire-range of the Prussian infantry in the Franco-German war. Krüdener, on the right, opened the action at half-past nine, bringing a battery into fire from the ridge on the Turkish redoubt above the village of Grivica. At first it seemed as if the Turks were surprised. It was some time ere they replied, but then they did so vigorously, and gave quite as good as they got from Krüdener. The objective of Prince Schahofskoy, with whom I rode, was in the first instance Radisovo, and it behoved us therefore to bear away to the left. But before doing so we were for a short time in a position which afforded a wonderful view of the theatre of action.

Plevna is in the hollow of a valley, lying north and south. The ground which intervened between us and this valley was singularly diversified. Imagine three great solid waves with their faces set edgeways to the valley of Plevna, and therefore end on to us also. The central wave is the widest of the three, and *à cheval* of it are the main Turkish positions, of which there seem three, one behind the other. Although the broadest wave, it is not the highest. The right and left waves are both so high that one on the crest of either can look down across the intervening valleys into the positions of the central wave. But then the Turks are astride of all three waves. The crest of our wave, the ridge above Radisovo, they do not hold in force. Thus far we are fortunate; but on the most northerly wave of the three, that against which Baron Krüdener is operating, and which is broader and flatter than ours—more like a sloping plateau, if the expression is not a bull—the Turks have intrenched position behind intrenched position. Both on top of this ridge and of the central swell we can discern camps of Turks with tents all standing behind the earthworks. It is clear they don't intend to move if they can help it. Their tents stand as if they had taken a lease of the ground in perpetuity. Baron Krüdener's cannon are in action, not only in front of Grivica, which is the toe of the horseshoe, but against its northern flank also, but the return fire is so heavy that he makes no way, and for the time, at least, is fast held. We try to aid him from the crest of our ridge by bringing a battery into action against the Grivica earthwork, but the traverse of the redoubt is so high that we do no harm. We of the left column have our own business to attend to, and so we leave our casual outlook place among the plum trees and move on in the direction of Radisovo.

This village lies in a deep valley behind the southern wave or ridge of the Turkish position, and there is another ridge behind this valley. On that ridge our cannon, placed by Colonel Bischofsky, chief of Prince Schahofskoy's staff, were firing in line on the Turkish guns on the ridge beyond the valley, with fine effect. The infantry went down into the valley under this covering fire and I accompanied the column. We carried Radisovo with a trivial skirmish, for in the village there were only a handful of Bashi-Bazouks, who, standing their ground, were promptly bayonetted. The Russian infantry remained under cover of the village. I returned up the slope to our batteries. These, firing with great rapidity and accuracy, soon compelled the Turkish cannon to quit the opposite height. During the last spurt of their firing Prince Schahofskoy rode along the rear of our batteries, from the right to the left, under a fire which killed two horses in our little group. Our cannon playing on the Turkish guns on the opposite ridge quelled their fire after about half an hour's cannonade, and it was then practicable for our batteries to cross the valley passing through Radisovo and come into action in the position vacated by the Turkish guns ; and following them our infantry also descended into the hollow, and lay down in the glades about the village, and on the steep slope behind our guns in action.

Presently we had five batteries ranged along the crest of the ridge beyond Radisovo, directing a converging fire on the Turkish guns on the central wave or ridge beyond. Notwithstanding their exposed position their fire was heavy and steady. The row of cannon in action reminded me of the German batteries on the crest of Verneville on the day of Gravelotte, only that the Germans had ninety cannon engaged and we had but forty. The staff awaited the result of the preparatory cannonade on the ridge behind Radisovo. I went forward again and got up to where our batteries were in action, and there lay down. On the way I passed through Radisovo, into which were falling many Turkish shells, which flew over the ridge occupied by our cannon. It was passing strange to witness peasant villagers standing in bewildered groups in front of their houses while shells were crashing into the place, while the children played unconcernedly about the dustheaps, and enjoyed themselves without misgiving as to danger. For once Bellona was gracious to non-combatants. Not a single villager was injured by the shell fire, although several hundred shells must have fallen in the village. From my point of vantage with our batteries I could look right down into the Turkish positions. Four batteries were defending the earthwork about the little village which seemed to me to be the foremost of their fixed and constructed positions on the central ridge. It stood on a little knoll, and was well placed for searching with its fire the valleys by which it could be approached. Beyond were more, and yet more, earthworks right to the edge of the broad valley, where the roofs and church towers of Plevna sparkled in the sunshine from out a circle of verdure. The place had an aspect of serenity strangely contrasting with the turmoil of the cannon fire raging in front of it. It seemed so near that a short ride would have brought me there to breakfast, yet ere we could reach it many men were to die. Men were dropping fast around me in the battery already, for the position of the guns was greatly exposed and the Turkish practice was mostly very good.

By this time, one o'clock, our infantry had nowhere been engaged. The operations hitherto were confined to the artillery. Krüdener on the right flank had scarcely progressed at all, and his co-operation in a simultaneously combined attack on both flanks was indispensable to success. Would that Schahofskoy had but acted on a full recognition of this fact, which the obvious strength of the Turkish positions should have impressed on him. Krüdener had gained much less ground than we. He seemed little farther forward than at the commencement, whereas we were at comparatively close quarters, and within striking distance. Krüdener was behind, either because his attack was not pushed energetically, or because he was encountering obstacles with which we had not met. Now Krüdener is regarded as a slow soldier and unenergetic man. We swore at what seemed his inertness, but it was not swearing only. Schahofskoy, in his impatience, determined to act independently, and strike the Turks single-handed. If Krüdener was slow, Schahofskoy was rash. If the whole force was too small for the work, how much more so was one-half that force? Fearful was the retribution exacted for that error of judgment.

About half-past two the second period of the battle commenced. To ascertain whether the artillery had sufficiently prepared the way for the infantry to act Schahofskoy and his staff rode on to the ridge where our batteries were firing, and had to dismount precipitately under a hurricane of shell-fire which the Turkish gunners directed against the little group. A long and anxious inspection seemed to satisfy Schahofskoy and the chief of his staff that the time had come when the infantry could strike with effect. This conclusion was arrived at in the face of the fact that we of the left flank attack had but three brigades all told, one of which constituted the reserve. In other words, we were about to launch ten or twelve thousand men against commanding intrenched positions held by an immensely superior force, and no whit crushed by our preliminary artillery fire. I will now quit criticism for narrative.

Two brigades of infantry were lying down in the Radisovo valley, behind the guns; the 32nd Division—General Tchekoff's brigade—on the right, the 1st Brigade of the 30th Division on the left. The leading battalions were ordered to rise up and advance over the ridge to attack. The order was hailed with glad cheers, for the infantrymen had been chafing at their inaction, and the battalions, with a swift, swinging step, streamed forward through the glen and up the steep slope beyond, marching in company columns, the rifle companies leading. The artillery had heralded this movement with increased rapidity of fire, which was maintained to cover and aid the infantrymen when the latter had crossed the crest and were descending the slope and crossing the intervening valley to the assault of the Turkish position. Just before reaching the crest the battalions deployed into line at the double, and crossed it in this formation, breaking to pass through the intervals between the guns. The Turkish shells whistled through them as they advanced in line, and men were already down in numbers, but the long undulating line tramps steadily over the stubbles of the ridge, and crashes through the undergrowth on the descent beyond. No skirmishing line is thrown out in advance. The fighting line remains the formation for a time, till, what with impatience and what with men falling, it breaks into a ragged spray of humanity, and surges on swiftly, loosely, and with no close cohesion. The supports are close up, and run up into the fighting line independently and eagerly. It is a veritable chase of fighting men impelled by a burning desire to get forward and come to close quarters with the enemy firing at them there from behind the shelter of the epaulement.

Presently all along the face of the advancing infantrymen burst forth flaring volleys of musketry fire. The jagged line springs onward through the maize-fields, gradually assuming a concave shape. The Turkish position is neared. The roll of rifle fire is incessant, yet dominated by the fiercer and louder turmoil of the artillery above. The ammunition waggons gallop up to the cannon with fresh fuel for the fire. The guns redouble the energy of their cannonade. The crackle of the musketry fire rises into a sharp continuous peal. The clamour of the hurrahs of the fighting men comes back to us on the breeze, making the blood tingle with the excitement of the fray. A village is blazing on the left. The fell fury of the battle has entered on its maddest paroxysm. The supports that had remained behind lying just under the crest of the slope are pushed forward over the brow of the hill. The wounded begin to trickle back over the ridge. We can see the dead and the more severely wounded lying where they fall on the stubbles and amid the maize. The living wave of fighting men is pouring over them ever on and on. The gallant gunners to the right and to the left of us stand to their work with a will on the shell-swept ridge. The Turkish cannon-fire begins to waver in that earthwork over against us. More supports stream down with a louder cheer into the Russian fighting line. Suddenly the disconnected men are drawing together. We can discern the officers signalling for the concentration by the waving of their swords. The distance is about a hundred yards. There is a wild rush, headed by the colonel of one of the regiments of the 32nd Division. The Turks in the shelter trench hold their ground, and fire steadily, and with terrible effect, into the advancing forces. The colonel's horse goes down, but the colonel is on his feet in a second, and, waving his sword, leads his men forward on foot. But only for a few paces. He staggers and falls. I heard afterwards he was killed.

We can hear the tempest-gust of wrath, half howl, half yell, with which his men, bayonets at the charge, rush on to avenge him. They are over the parapet and shelter trench, and in among the Turks like an avalanche. Not many Turks get a chance to run away from the gleaming bayonets swayed by muscular Russian arms. The outer edge of the first position is won. The Russians are bad skirmishers. They despise cover, and give and take fire out in the open. They disdained to utilize against the main position the cover afforded by the parapet of this shelter trench, but pushed on in broken order up the bare slope. In places they hung a little, for the infantry fire from the Turks was very deadly, and the slope was strewn with the fallen dead and wounded; but for the most part they advanced nimbly enough. Yet it took them half an hour from the shelter trench before they again converged and made their final rush at the main earthwork. This time the Turks did not wait for the bayonet points, but with one final volley abandoned the work. We watched their huddled mass in the gardens and vineyard behind the position, cramming the narrow track between the trees to gain the shelter of their batteries in the rear of the second position.

So fell the first position of the Turks. Being a village, it afforded ample cover, and Schahofskoy would have acted wisely had he been content to hold it and strengthen it till Krüdener, on his right, should have carried the Grivica earthwork, and come up in line with him. But the Grand Cross of St. George dangled before his eyes, and tempted him to rashness. Krüdener was clearly jammed. The Turks were fighting furiously, and were in unexpected force on that broad central ridge of theirs, as well as against Krüdener. The first position in natural as in artificial strength was child's play to the grim starkness of the second on that isolated mamelon there with the batteries on the swell behind it. But Schahofskoy determined to go for it, and his troops were not the men to balk him. The word was again "Forward!" The first rush, however, was out of them. Many must have been blown. They hung a good deal in the advance, exposing themselves recklessly, and falling fast, but not progressing with much speed. It is a dangerous time when troops sullenly stand still and doggedly fire when the stationary fit is on them. Wyndham knew what it meant, and gnashed his teeth in rage over it when the fate of the Redan hung in the balance which one rush would have turned for us.

Schahofskoy kept his finger well on the throbbing pulse of battle. Just in the nick of time half his reserve brigade was thrown into the fight immediately below us, while the other half took part in the attack more on our left flank. The new blood tells at once. There is a move forward, and no more standing and craning over the fence. The Turks on the flank in the earthwork are reinforced. I had noticed some Turkish officers on horseback, standing coolly behind the bank of the vineyard that serves as a parapet to the prolongation. They ride off and speedily return, with an addition to the defending force. I can hardly say how it all happens, but all of a sudden the white smoke spurts forth all along the lip of the epaulement, and swarms of dark-clothed men are scrambling on to it. There is evidently a short but sharp struggle. Then one sees a swarm of men flying across the green stretch of the vineyard. But they don't go far, and prowl around the western and northern faces of the work, rendering its occupation very precarious. The Turkish cannon from behind drop shells into it with singular precision. As a matter of fact, the Russians carried, indeed, this the second position of the Turks, but never held it. It was all but empty for a long time, and continuous fighting took place about its flanks. About six the Turks pressed forward a heavy mass of infantry for its recapture. Schahofskoy took a bold step, sending two batteries down into the first position he had taken to keep them in check. But the Turks were not to be denied, and in spite of the most determined fighting of the Russians, had reoccupied their second position before seven.

The First Brigade of the 30th Division had early inclined to the left, in the direction where the towers and houses of Plevna were visible. It was rash, for the brigade was exposing its right flank to the Turkish cannon astride of the central ridge, but the goal of Plevna was a keen temptation. There was no thoroughfare, however. They would not give up, and they could not succeed. They charged again and again; and when they could charge no more from sheer fatigue, they stood and died, for they would not retire. The reserves came up, but only to swell the slaughter. And then the ammunition failed, for the carts had been left far behind, and all hope failed the most sanguine, as the sun sank in lurid glory behind the smoke-mantled field.

Two companies of Russian infantry did indeed work round the right flank of the Turkish works, and dodge into the town of Plevna; but it was like entering the mouth of hell. On the heights all round the cannon smoke spurted out, and the vineyard in the rear of the town was alive with Turks. They left after a very short visit, and now all hope of success anywhere was dead, nor did a chance offer to make the best of the defeat.

Schahofskoy had not a man left to cover the retreat. The Turks struck at us without stint. They had the upper hand for once, and were determined to show that they knew how to make the most of it. They advanced in swarms through the dusk on their original first position, and recaptured their three cannon the Russians had previously taken before these could be withdrawn. The Turkish shells began once more to whistle over the ridge above Radisovo and fall into the village behind, now crammed with wounded. The streams of wounded wending their painful way over the ridge were incessant. The badly wounded mostly lay where they fell. Later in the darkness a baleful sort of

Krankenträger swarmed over the battle-field in the shape of Bashi-Bazouks, who smote and spared not. Lingering there on the ridge till the moon rose, the staff could hear from down below on the still night air the cries of pain, the entreaties for mercy, and the yells of bloodthirsty fanatical triumph. It was indeed an hour to wring the sternest heart. We stayed there long to learn if it might be what troops were coming out of the Valley of the Shadow of Death below. Were there indeed any at all to come? It did not seem as if it were so. The Turks had our range before dark, and we could watch the flash of flame over against us, and then listen to the scream of the shell as it tore by us. The whizzing of rifle bullets was incessant, and the escort and the retreating wounded were often struck. A detachment of cavalry at length began to come straggling up to take over from the staff the forepost duty on the ridge, but it will give an idea of the disorganization to say that when a company was told off to cover somewhat the wounded in Radisovo, it had to be made up of the men of several regiments.

About nine o'clock the staff quitted the ridge, leaving it littered with groaning men, and moving gently lest we should tread on the prostrate wounded. We soon lost our way as we had lost our army. We could find no rest for the soles of our feet, by reason of the alarms of the Bashi-Bazouks swarming in among the scattered and retiring Russians. At length at one in the morning, having been in the saddle since six on the previous morning, we turned into a stubble-field, and, making beds of the reaped grain, Commander, Correspondent, and Cossack alike rested under the stars. But we were not even then allowed to rest. Before four an alarm came that the Bashi-Bazouks were upon us, and we had to rouse and tramp away. The only protection of the Chief of what in the morning was a fine army was now a handful of wearied Cossacks. About the Bashi-Bazouks there is worse to tell. At night they worked round into Radisovo, and, falling upon the wounded there, butchered them without mercy.

Krüdener sent word in the morning that he had lost severely, and could make no headway, and had resolved to fall back on the line of the river Osma, which falls into the Danube near Nicopolis. There had been a talk, his troops being fresh, of renewing the attack to-day with his co-operation; but it is a plain statement of fact that we have no troops to attack with. The most moderate estimate is that we have lost two regiments—say 5,000 men—out of our three brigades; a ghastly number, beating Eylau or Friedland. This takes no account of Krüdener's losses. We, too, are to retire on the

Osma river, about Bulgareni, and, to the best of our weak strength, cover the bridge at Sistova.

One cannot in this moment of hurried confusion realize all the possible results of this stroke, so rashly courted. Not a Russian soldier stands between Tirnova and the victorious Turkish army in Loftcha and Plevna. Only a weak division of the 11th Corps stands between Tirnova and the Shumla army. I look on Schahofskoy's force as wrecked, as no longer for these many days to be counted for a fighting integer. It is not ten days since the 30th Division crossed the Danube in the pride of superb condition. Now what of it is left is demoralized and shattered. So on this side of the Balkans—the 8th Corps being already committed to the mountains—there virtually remain but the 9th Corps, already roughly handled, once at Nicopolis and again previously at Plevna, one division of the 11th Corps, and the Rustchuk Army. Now if the Rustchuk Army is marched to the west against Plevna, then the Turkish Army of Rustchuk is let loose on the Russian communications to Tirnova. One cannot avoid the conclusion that the advance over the Balkans is seriously compromised. The Russian strait is so bad that the scattered detachments have been called up from out Roumania, and a Roumanian division, commanded by General Manu, which crossed a day or two ago at Nicopolis, has been called up to the line of the Osma River.

An aide-de-camp of the Grand Duke Nicholas was present at the battle, and at once started for Tirnova with the evil tidings. We are just quitting this bivouac and falling back on Bulgareni with all speed, leaving the Bulgarian villages to the tender mercies of the Turks. As I close I learn that on our left General Skobeleff was very severely handled, having lost three hundred men out of his single infantry battalion.

The following letter describes the state of the defeated Russians the night after the battle :—

Bucharest, *August 2nd.*—It was the evening of the battle of Plevna. The sun was going down behind the smoke-mantled heights, in a glow of lurid crimson. The dusk was fast settling on one of the bloodiest battle-fields of the century—closing in round the batteries whose guns were still firing, round detached parties of Russian soldiers who were doggedly maintaining the fight against the swarms of Turks who formed a ring around them, firing fiercely into their midst—round the dead and the wounded lying thick on the stubbles, on the grassy slopes, in the hollows among the maize plants and the oak copses—round the knots of wounded who had crawled for cover to the leeside of the grain stacks on the fields, and who lay there in the unspeakable agony of waiting for the inevitable doom which they knew too well was to befall them—round the groups of miscreants tramping about the battle-field intent on wreaking that doom on the defenceless wounded, and stopping ever and anon to perpetrate some barbarity. Prince Schahofskoy and his staff stood on the summit of the ridge above the village of Radisovo, which was crammed with wounded men. The fate of the battle had hung in the scale for some time, but now all hope of success had gone. There was no reserve among us in the acknowledgment that the attack had been a failure; all the concern now was to do what was possible towards minimizing the results of that failure. There was no conversation; men's hearts were too heavy for talk. We sat about on the knoll, gazing down into the pandemonium below. The General, alone and apart, paced up and down a little open space in the oak copse, gloom settled on his face. All around us the air was heavy with the low moaning of the wounded, who, having limped or been aided thus far out of the fight, had cast themselves down to gain a little relief from the agony of motion. There was not even water for them, for Radisovo is all but a waterless village, and what water trickled in a tiny rill from the fountain behind the village was struggled for eagerly by the parched and fevered wounded who crowded around it, coveting with a longing, the agony of which the reader can never know, a few drops of the precious fluid. I cannot tell when I most respect and admire the simple honest Russian soldier—whether when he is plodding along without a murmur verst after verst, under a burden just double in weight that which our soldiers carry, cheering the way as he tramps with a lusty chorus; or when, with cheers that ring with sincerity, and with an alacrity which is genuine, he presses forward into the battle; or when he is standing stubbornly confronting his enemy, conscious of being overmatched, yet never dreaming of running away; or when he is lying wounded but uncomplaining, helping his neighbour in the same plight with some trifling act of tender kindness, and waiting for what God and the Czar shall send him, with a patient, unmurmuring calm that is surely true heroism.

The darkness closed in around us, and the enemy seemed bent on following the example of the darkness. We had been on this ridge for a long time beyond the range of the enemy's batteries; but now these were advanced, and we were once more under fire. Through the darkness we could see the flashes of the cannon shots; they must be back now in the position on the knoll below—the position where four hours ago the Russian soldiers had charged home with the bayonet, and whence two hours ago the Russian cannon had been firing. A second more, and nearer and nearer came the whistle of the shells, with a swiftly gradual crescendo into a scream as they sped over us and crashed down into the village in the valley behind us; and yet nearer there was the flashing of the musketry fire in the darkness; one could watch the streaks of flame foreshortened down in the valley there, and nerves tried by a long day of foodlessness, excitement, fatigue, and exposure to sun and the chances of the battle-field, quivered under the prolonged tension of endurance, as the throbbing hum of the bullet sped through or over the straggling group. No man dared to say to that stern lowering chief, eating his heart there in the bitterness of his disappointment, that it was a bootless tempting of fortune to linger longer on this exposed spot, nor did any man care to quit for the sake of greater safety the companionship which had endured throughout the day. So we lingered on till our senses became dulled, until some dropped off into slumber, regardless of the scream of the shells and the hum of the bullets. It was a humane object which so long detained the General in a position so exposed. There was no force available to line the height and cover to ever so little extent the wounded lying on and behind it from the Bashi-Bazouks, who too certainly were prowling in the vicinity, and ever coming nearer and nearer. An attempt had, indeed, been made to get together a detachment of infantry for this purpose, and a bugler, at the General's order, persistently sounded the assembly, but the result was merely to gather a handful of stragglers from half a dozen different regiments; and although but a company was wanted, that trivial strength could not be collected, so the General, his staff, and his escort took up for the time a kind of informal forepost duty, and there we waited till the pale calm moon rose and poured the sheen of her white radiance over the battle-field. While it was yet dark there had been no cessation of the firing, both artillery and musketry, and now that heaven was holding a candle to hell, the fire waxed warmer and brisker. Up from out of it, with broken tramp, came a detachment, silent, jaded, powder-grimed. There could not have been a company all told; a lieutenant marched at its head, and it was the remnant, so far as could be gathered the sole remnant, of one of the finest regiments of the 32nd Division, that had crossed the ridge over which its débris was now listlessly trailing itself three fine battalions strong.

At length the jingle of cavalry accoutrements was heard, and a squadron of dragoons rode on to the heights, and extending in skirmishing order relieved the headquarter staff. It was a poor screen to interpose between a victorious and remorseless army and a mass of wounded men; but nothing more was available. The General had lost an army, the fragments of an army had lost their General. We turned the heads of our jaded horses, and, silent and depressed, rode down the slope across the valley and up the slope beyond. But on me fell the burden of a personal anxiety. I had missed my young friend Villiers, the artist of the *Graphic*. He had been with me till darkness on the ridge. Sorely fatigued, he had expressed a desire to go away. I had advised him to get on the slope behind the ridge, and to take some rest. But when we rode away I could nowhere find him. I quartered the slope carefully and shouted his name aloud, but without result. Recumbent men by the dozen I looked into the faces of by the moonlight, but they were all wounded soldiers. At length a Russian told me he had met Villiers some time ago in the bottom of the valley, when he had said he meant to go into Radisovo and try to be of some use among the wounded. Then he was with the doctors, and, as I trusted, would take no harm, although occasional shells were still falling in Radisovo. So, trying not to think about him, I rode on with the staff. Our pace was a slow walk, for there were wounded men everywhere, limping along the narrow pathway in front of us, prostrate on the grass by the side of it, or asleep in the very dust. Occasionally we struck detachments of infantry who had scrambled back out of the fight, and were lying on their arms in utter ignorance of the best direction in which to march. Or it might be a battery of artillery, halted in perplexing dubiety whether if they went on they might march into the bosom of the Turkish army. I believe there existed some intention that we should go for the night to a village called Bogot. But we got confused as to the road, and bewildered by the crackling spurts of musketry fire that broke out all around in the most uncomfortable fashion. Were the Turks then wholly round us, that we heard, and occasionally felt, fire as it seemed to north, to south, to east, and to west? Once such was the confusion that we were fired upon by a detachment of Russian troops, halted in equal bewilderment with ourselves, and expecting an enemy from any or every side. We made halt after halt, but there never was rest for us. A spurt of near firing would stir us, or a Cossack would ride in with intelligence that the Bashi-Bazouks were prowling near by, and through all this harassment there yet lingered with the most sanguine of us the idea that the battle would be resumed next morning, we affording an artillery support to the supposedly fresh troops of Krüdener. Where, I asked myself, is our artillery to take orders for such a purpose? We did not know where we were ourselves, much less where the army was, of which this groping, forlorn, dejected band were the headquarters. Of Krüdener's experiences or whereabouts we knew simply nothing. It was useless to despatch aides-de-camp or orderlies without being able to give them a direction in which to ride. All we knew was that ever there were wounded men about us, and that we and our horses were dead beaten.

Nature will assert herself. About one o'clock in the morning we turned aside into a field where the barley had been reaped and piled into small stacks. These we tore down, shook some sheaves out as fodder for our horses, and others as beds for ourselves, and, throwing ourselves down, fell into dead slumber. But there was no long rest for us. At three o'clock we were aroused by the tidings that the Bashi-Bazouks were close to us, and the near firing told of the accuracy of the statement. We huddled a number of wounded into and upon some carts which came up casually, and started them off, whether in the right direction or not we had no conception. Ugh, how miserably raw and chill struck the bleak morn just before the dawn! But if the rawness of the air struck to our marrow, hale and sound men as we were, what must have been the sufferings of the poor wounded, weakened by loss of blood, faint in the prostration which follows so inevitably the gunshot wound; foodless, without water, lying on the damp grass by the wayside in their blood-clotted clothes! Yet happy were they, pitiable as was their plight, in comparison with their fellows who had littered the battle-field, and had been left behind in Radisovo. The fate of the former we knew from what we had ourselves seen; of the latter, it was told to us by scared messengers that the Bashi-Bazouks had in the dead of night worked round our left flank, and had fallen upon them and butchered them in their helplessness. The horror of the news thrilled us all, but the tidings had for me a special agony of apprehension. For it was to join these wounded that Villiers was on his way when last seen, and there fell upon me the terrible fear that he had been with them when they met their cruel fate. I dared not follow out the reasoning; I recoiled from that with unutterable horror, and yet I groped around the edges of the fearful problem to which I was tethered, and could find no escape. I thought of the quiet London home under whose roof-tree I had sat and listened to a mother talk with joy and pride of an only son, of whose safety she professed to feel assured while he was with me, and there rose before me the ghastly horror of the terrible duty that must devolve upon me to plunge that home into an abyss of unspeakable woe. There remained but one hope. We had trysted to meet at the Poradim bivouac, should chance separate us. I spent the morning riding about inquiring of every one I met if my friend had been seen; the reply was ever in the negative. I reached Poradim to find the headquarters camp struck and withdrawn, and only a few lagging stragglers on the broad common. I waited there long in vain; at length the sense of another personal duty asserted itself, and with hope all but quenched in my heart, I turned my horse's head and rode away to Sistova. Travelling thence to Bucharest, I was the bearer of the bitter news to the little English coterie in the Roumanian capital, and there was cast upon it the shadow of a great sorrow, for Villiers had lived there some weeks before we crossed the Danube together, and to know him was to love him. On the evening of the day of my arrival some of us were sitting in sad conclave, trying to hope against hope, when the lad walked in among us safe and sound. He had not gone into Radisovo, having met outside it a convoy of wounded on the march, which he had accompanied, and after a night of vicissitude had followed my example, and struck for Sistova, and so on to Bucharest. I leave to the reader to imagine our joy and relief.

* Bucharest, *August 3rd.*—Compelled by two reasons, sheer physical exhaustion and the necessity for procuring another horse, *vice* the animal broken down by prolonged exertions in connection with the Plevna affair, to remain here over to-day, I regret to be compelled to speculate as to the course of events on the other side of the Danube, instead of being in the position to forward tidings of actual facts.

The battle in front of Plevna has without doubt wrought a *bouleversement* in the Russian position and prospects of a character almost unique in the history of modern warfare. How bright seemed the Russian military future this day week! Gourko stretching out his arm almost within clutching distance of Adrianople; the Czarewitch waiting but the word from Tirnova to cast a girdle of stalwart soldiers and solid earthworks around Rustchuk. Schahofskoy and Krüdener, in the full expectation of wiping out the slur of Schilder's failure at Plevna; Zimmerman swaggering at his will about Eastern Bulgaria, threatening Silistria, sending a reconnaissance in force toward Varna, and within a few marches of giving the hand to the right flank of the army of the Czarewitch, when that army should have invested Rustchuk. One bad day, or rather six hours' hard but disastrous fighting, and, lo! the scene changes; the sunshine is overcast by black clouds; the advantages of the Russians crumble like burnt-out tinder; the grim question confronts them, whether their position is not so dangerously compromised as to create disquietude for their mere safety. Devise what scheme of action they may, any and every disposition opens up a new danger. Do the broken forces of Schahofskoy and Krüdener remain unstrengthened on the line of the lower Osma, or strengthened but by the other division of the 4th Corps, with intent to cover Sistova, and the all-important single link there between Bulgaria and the Principalities—the bridge between Simnitza and the Turkish town opposite? Beaten, disorganized, and weakened, there can be no certainty that this force is able to withstand the Turks advancing in force against it, and the result of another battle that should go against the Russians would be the clearance for the Turks of the road to Sistova, and the absolute severance of the whole Russian force in Bulgaria from its base in Roumania. Do the Turks in Plevna and Loftcha prefer rather to march against Tirnova, co-operating with Mehemet Ali Pacha's army of Shumla, already known to have strong advance detachments about Osman Bazar? There is not a Russian battalion between Loftcha and Tirnova, and in the latter place there is a mere handful of the fag end of the 8th Corps, now partly in, partly through the Balkans. All the Russian force that stands between Osman Bazar and Tirnova is a weak infantry division, General Ernrot's, the 11th Division of the 11th Corps, with a cavalry brigade of the same corps. Isolated, and with its line of retreat compromised, what stand could this force be expected to make? And with Osman Pacha and Mehemet Ali shaking hands together in Tirnova, or indeed with either of them there alone, what is the plight of the 8th Corps and Gourko's people, jammed in the Balkans or dispersed in reckless raids on the farther side? Cut off from their line of retreat, it would only remain for these forces to draw together into the Balkans and hold out in the hope of succour coming in the shape of fresh troops fighting their way up from the Danube. Men aver that it is possible for Radetsky and Gourko so to hold out for a month; if so all the luckier for them. The report is here to-day that the Turks—I know not what Turks, whether from Loftcha or Osman Bazar—have already retaken Tirnova. It is eminently possible in the abstract that this is true, but I distrust the accuracy of the tidings; yet the very existence of the report is significant as indicating the general recognition of the precarious character of the Russian position.

"Ah, but," says my Russian friend, with whom I am discussing the situation, "you are ignoring the existence of the two complete army corps which constitute the Army of Rustchuk." Not so, oh Utopian strategist, not so; but pray indicate to me how you are to utilize them? Are you going to march them from east to west, reinforce with them Krüdener and Schahofskoy, and sweep on against Plevna with this overwhelming strength? I agree with you that after hard fighting and terrible loss, this force is strong enough to sweep the Turks from the Plevna position, and so relieve the pressure from the west on your line of communications, granting always that they stay in Plevna waiting for the attack. But if you had undertaken to fence on both sides a line of road of a certain extent, and if an accident smashed the palisading for a certain distance on one side of this road of yours, it seems to me that you would scarcely be carrying out your duty satisfactorily if you were to repair that gap with a slice of the palisading from the other side. And that is just what you would be doing were you to remove the Rustchuk army from its present position and march it westward to co-operate in an attack on the Plevna positions. The road from Rustchuk up the Danube would be open to a column striking out from the force now under the guns of the fortress, and marching on the bridge at Sistova, nor would anything stand between the Russian line of communications between the Danube and Tirnova, and the Turkish force now echeloned on the line between Rasgrad and Osman Bazar. Nor is this all. If the Rustchuk army be removed from its present position, the condition of Zimmerman, even now far from safe, becomes eminently precarious. He would be in the heart of a hornets' nest with no help within hail. It would be open to the Shumla army to fall upon him and smite him, aided by diversions from Silistria and Varna. You suggest that one corps of the Army of Rustchuk be left in its present position, and the other withdrawn for operations against Plevna. One might ask whether the reinforcements for Schahofskoy and Krüdener of a single corps would insure the object in view, but, granting that it would do so, picture the risks to which the other corps so forlornly left watching Rustchuk would be liable, and the contingencies were it unable to hold its ground.

The fact is that to have any assurance of safety in Bulgaria now, the Russians require there two more army corps. They are in the position of a man who is urgently pressed for five pounds, and has only about three pounds ten in his pocket, without the chance of opportune borrowing. They are borrowing, it is true. They have brought the Roumanian division under Manu up into the line of the Lom; and I hear they are pressing for the other Roumanian division now in fighting trim either to create a diversion at Widdin, or to march on Nicopolis, and cross there into the Bulgarian theatre of war. Of course there is for the present a total cessation of offensive operations on the part of the Russians on this side of the Balkans—we do not know what is happening on the other side; but probably paralysis prevails there also, and I believe that what is regarded as the least evil has been chosen, the withdrawal of troops from the Rustchuk army to operate against Plevna. The truth is, Plevna must be taken, and Osman Pacha's army must be beaten. That is an absolute *sine quâ non* to the continued stay of the Russians on the other side of the Danube. The Grand Duke Nicholas has left Bjela for the Osma, and will himself command in the pending operations, the preparations for which must consume some time.

The Russians are frank enough themselves in confessing to reverses, and I have never known them attempt to throw dust into one's eyes since the Danube was crossed. They may occasionally be silent, but they do not lie. I was surprised, therefore, knowing what I knew from personal knowledge, to hear in Bucharest yesterday on all sides that the Russians had taken Plevna. The story was told with circumstantiality, and Roumanians assured you that the news was official. I knew it must be false, and I learned later who was responsible for it. It was an invention of a high Roumanian official, its object being to stay the panic which had set in all over the Principalities with such intensity. As an instance of the panic-begotten canards, I may mention that the people asked me, as I drove into Giurgevo on the morning of the 1st, how near were the Turks; and when I reached Bucharest, alarmists were proclaiming that the Turks were already in Alexandria. The Roumanian official promulgated within his own jurisdiction the tidings of the taking of Plevna, and he also telegraphed them on to the Foreign Office in Bucharest. The permanent Under Secretary's impulse was to communicate the news to the Agence Havas and to the Roumanian representatives in other capitals. But it had occurred to him that he had better first make a few inquiries at the Russian Consulate, where Gortschakoff and Jomini are presently in residence. There he was told that he would do well to remain quiet and so the erroneous information has not been officially forwarded outside Roumania, but it has appeared in most of the Bucharest papers. It remains to be seen whether this Plevna reverse is to diminish or add to the chances of early peace. I fear the former, because the Turks will be naturally encouraged, and the military honour of the Russians will be at stake. Just before the Plevna discomfiture, I believe that the frame of mind at Bjela was eminently pacific. The truth is that, so far as regards the army, the war has lost its character of a crusade. And if the army is thus affected by the exercise of the commonest faculty of observation, its views must react on Russia, with which epistolary communication, if slow, is unrestricted. Any number of officers, many of high rank, and more than one in the personal suite of his Majesty the Emperor, have spoken to me without reserve on a topic which is of deep interest for us all. They declare themselves to have laboured under the most profound misconception as to the condition of the Bulgarian Christians. They had believed them oppressed, impoverished, impeded in the exercise of their religion, sure not for an hour of their lives, of the honour of their women, of their property. It was in this belief that they thrilled with enthusiasm for a veritable war of liberation. And, they continue, how do we actually find the Bulgarians? They live in the most perfect comfort; the Russian peasant cannot compare with them in comfort, competence, or prosperity. Personally, I may add that I should be glad if the English peasantry were at all near them in these attributes. Their grain crops stretch far and wide. Every village has its teeming herd of cattle, brood mares with foals, goats, and sheep. The houses are palaces compared with the subterranean hovels of the Roumanian and Wallachian peasants. Last year's straw is yet in their stackyards. Milk may be bought in every house. In the villages, for one mosque, there are half a dozen Christian churches. No man experiences anywhere a difficulty in getting silver for a napoleon. And the Bulgarian villager is by no means enthusiastic over his "liberation"—especially as it entails while in progress a fair chance of his having his house burnt and his throat cut by the Turkish irregulars. But while he is spared this fate, and pending the achievement of his liberation, he has as good a notion of turning an honest penny as if he were a Yankee or a Scot. He "sticks" the Russians unmercifully. So far as circumstances permit, they pay for all Bulgarian property, in the way of forage, &c., which they consume. And don't they have to pay! The Bulgarian realizes that in this matter he is the master of the situation, and lines his pocket accordingly—"puts money in his purse."

CHAPTER XIV.

SECOND PERIOD OF THE CAMPAIGN IN ASIA.

The Turn of the Tide—Defeat of General Tergukasoff at Eshek Khaliass—And of General Heimann at Zevin—Retreat of the Russian Left Wing to Zeidikan and of the Centre towards Kars—Mukhtar Pacha's Advance—Raising of the Siege of Kars—The Kurds and Circassians—Terrible Massacre at Bayazid—Relief of the Bayazid Garrison by General Tergukasoff—Battle at the Aladja Dagh—A Turkish Joan of Arc.

WE may take advantage of the interval of suspense between the second and third Russian attack upon Plevna to survey the course of events in Asia. When we last noticed them the Russians still retained the prestige of their early superiority; but we saw that the balance of military power was gradually being restored, and now we shall find that before the month of June was ended the advantage had been visibly transferred to the Turks. In the middle of June the Russians were investing Kars in the hope that its garrison might be reduced by famine. Erzeroum was threatened by the right wing of the Russian army, under General Tergukasoff, which defeated the Turks near Delibaba on the 16th of June. But from that time the fortunes of the Russians waned. They had begun the campaign with too few men; the insurrection in the Caucasus, which was aided by the Turks, necessitated a diversion of troops which might otherwise have increased their strength in Armenia, and at the same time the military authorities at Constantinople awoke to the danger to be apprehended from a continuance of their old neglect. Mukhtar Pacha received reinforcements, guns, and money, and began a series of movements by which, without fighting great battles, he gradually pushed back the enemy. On the 21st of

June he collected his forces, and defeated Tergukasoff, compelling him to fall back to Zeidikan. The most disastrous check, however, was that sustained by the Russian centre at Zevin, midway between Kars and Erzeroum, on the 25th of June. Here General Melikoff attacked superior forces occupying a very strong position under a Hungarian who bore the name of Faizi Pacha. The battle was long, and the Russian losses so great that Melikoff was compelled to retreat; Mukhtar Pacha was enabled to order a general advance, and even to raise the siege of Kars before the demoralized Russians could offer him any effectual resistance. The following letter is from the Turkish side :—

ERZEROUM, *July 5th.*—After the battle of Alaschkir, some three hours in front of Delibaba, I deemed it expedient to move towards surer lines of communication. My experience of the Soghanli Dagh camp, and the fate of my letters and despatches there, had made me somewhat less trusting than before. Besides, I noticed a somewhat unusual movement of irregular troops, Kurd and Circassian horse. Three battalions too were already moving from Delibaba towards the centre. It struck me that I could combine two objects—the despatch of my news and the chance of witnessing a movement of some kind at the centre. The Circassians were mounting, and a picturesque sight it was. The lovely mountain gorge celebrated in the annals of brigandism, where but a few days ago the Teheran courier had a desperate fight for his life, was thronged with the half-soldier half-robber Circassians. There were white-headed emirs and wild-eyed troopers with furred bonnets and various arms. There were semi-savage Kurds with preternaturally large eyes and cucumber noses, brandishing their lengthy lances, and saying things a good deal more complimentary to themselves than to the tea-drinking invaders on the snow-streaked hill beyond. Myself, my guide, and my Armenian interpreter, although we would have willingly chosen other company, took our place in the picturesque column. There were a couple of hundred of Kurd lancers; the Circassians numbered some twelve hundred. As we rode down into the Tarkbodja Valley towards the banks of the Araxes, horseman after horseman rode up beside me. They had a confused notion about an "English Pacha" who was with the army. Notwithstanding my silk turban, Asiatic scimitar, and sunburnt face, I was immediately singled out, and my opinion was asked as to whether it was likely a considerable English force would shortly arrive on the scene of action here. I replied in as oracular a fashion as possible, and rode hurriedly up to the great silk standard round which were grouped people more or less responsible for the individuals in the column. Evening was closing in as our long trailing column neared the marshy banks of the Araxes. The engineers had planted stakes from bank to bank to indicate the ford. After floundering half an hour in the sedgy borders we crossed—almost swimming our horses—and then scrambling again over the marshes beyond, got into Khorassan. I had already made myself comfortable in my oda—that is to say, the corner of the stable I shared with the horses and buffaloes. The imaum, a hadji, and a cherif had come to visit me. My partial knowledge of Arabic enabled me to talk with the imaum and the pilgrim; with the other, the cherif, I communicated through my interpreter. They all commenced cursing the Circassians. They freely expressed their opinion that these latter were sons of Sheitan. What the Padishah was thinking of when he sent such reprobates into the district they, the imaum, &c., could not imagine. Well, in the midst of all this, a Circassian horseman dashed up to the door, "The Cossacks! the Giaours! to horse!" I must say I gained my horse in a brief space. My costume was too Asiatic to permit me to linger when Cossack lances were nigh. While my horse was being saddled I rushed to the top of the house. That means I walked up an incline of thirty degrees. The inhabitants were all "on the housetop," as in old time, awaiting the advent of news, and I was there, too, with my field-glass. Every hill around had its group of watchers. All at once came a general scampering after horses, and the good Moslems, some fifty in number, marched in a body out of Khorassan. I lingered, watching the black band creeping slowly down the broken ground three miles away. A field gun came lumbering up; it halted; and then I turned bridle and retired with the entire force. It was close on midnight when a courier rode up from Khorassan to say the Cossacks had left. So we came back, but it was only for half a day. I had slept late in the afternoon, and thought all immediate hurry was over. General Kemball and his staff rode into the village. The General thought he could sleep calmly in his konak. Moussa Pacha, commanding the Circassians, was almost peremptory in his request that we all should leave at once. The enemy was close. As we had fifteen hundred horse, I suppose the enemy must have been proportionately strong. We forded the river and climbed the steep earth-banks beyond, and rode hard along the river border, halting for the night at the village of Komatsur. The sun had not risen as we mounted horse. We were moving obliquely to the Zevin position, for we were marching on Kupri Keui. Again and again we turned to look behind. As daylight came a lengthy white streak, two kilometres long, marked the blue hill-sides. The tuft-like artillery smoke was breaking out—everything showed that a serious combat had commenced. In the pale morning light the infantry columns were already passing us, and three guns went lumbering by.

ERZEROUM, *July* 12*th*.—Even at the moment when the Russian advance threatened to be rapid and decisive, when Ardahan had fallen, and the entire of the first Turkish line was broken, I do not think that public uneasiness was at so great a pitch as at this moment. Erzeroum is being prepared to withstand a siege; and extensive works of fortification are being executed at different points intervening between this and the front. The great gaps in the ramparts here, allowed to remain up to to-day, are being filled up with feverish energy. The ramparts, only a short time ago armed with a few indifferent field guns and garrison pieces of the most primitive type, now bristle with heavy Krupp artillery. The road from Trebizond is blocked with artillery convoys. Guns, both field and position, throng the way, and seriously embarrass the little commercial traffic which exists. This sudden and spasmodic activity, this hurrying up of guns—sadly needed during the last few weeks' fighting, when the artillery element may be said to have been almost entirely absent on the Turkish side—speaks eloquently of secret fears, of hostile movements recognized by the authorities, though carefully screened from the people.

Apart from the scarce-seen lines of shelter trench, visible only to the practised eye, along the marly plain and sun-scorched grass of the hill slope, and here and there a squat redoubt, easily mistaken for one of the tumulus-like houses of the country, there is little to tell of the proximity of contending armies. The Armenian peasant sits listlessly among his flocks, or plods on after the sixteen buffaloes drawing his plough. A troop of Kurd or Circassian horse comes filing through his village. He lifts his head and stares at them with the same hopeless discontent as he would at any other hostile troop that came by—as he would stare at the Cossacks, for instance, should they make their way among his mud hovels. The licence allowed to the Circassians and Kurds passes all comprehension. One could perhaps understand the policy of a Government desirous of terrorizing a rebellious population, but among True Believers and submissive Armenians and Greeks—the one desirous only of being allowed to follow their ordinary avocations in peace and tolerable security, the other willing upholders of Ottoman supremacy—it is difficult to understand why an unruly mob of undisciplined savages has been unchained. If the Sublime Porte were desirous of deliberately alienating the sentiments of its northern Anatolian subjects, it could not have taken more effective measures to effect its end. I allude especially to the Mohammedan population; and when they are forced to use language such as they have not feared to use speaking with me, a Giaour and an enemy to the Prophet, I could scarcely overrate the extent of their irritation. As regards the Christians of the province of Van, every day brings us fresh details of atrocities which rival if they do not surpass the doings in Bulgaria. Violation of female children of a tender age, wholesale pillage of villages, deliberate torture and mutilation of both sexes, are tales which have become hideously familiar to our ears.

The terrorism wrought by the irregulars is such that the authorities counsel every stranger to take with him on the shortest journey a guard of zaptiehs, lest the Kurds or the Circassians should meet him on the road. By nature the Circassian is a hardy and audacious soldier. Years of strife in the Caucasus have inured him to a life and deeds scarcely compatible with civilized usages. In exile, along the frontier of Greece and the plains of the Danube, he has been the petted protégé of the Ottoman Government, and the habits, excusable perhaps in his own country while fighting an invader, he has begun to consider as his inalienable right to practise. In his capacity as volunteer in the Turkish army, he takes fresh liberties, and the result is sad to contemplate. Still, there is some germ of good underlying all this; and though the Circassian is no match for the more disciplined Cossack, at bottom he is brave enough; and in other hands, and under different management, would be a capital soldier. With the Kurd it is different. A troop of Kurd horsemen, with their barbarous horse trappings, hair-tufted lances, and wild gestures, might easily be mistaken for a detachment of Comanche or Sioux Indians. The sausage nose and crocodile eye, the bloated face seamed with lines of brutal sensuality, bespeak the unmitigated savage, without a single grace of those barbarous virtues which often more than half redeem the child of nature in his wildest extravagances. There is a chivalry which naturally belongs to most savage races; it is totally absent in the hordes which dwell beyond the Araxes, and the unhappy Armenian Christians of the province of Van can testify by their hacked limbs and powder-blown cheeks that to be a fellow-subject of the Sultan is no protection from such neighbours when atrocities can be practised with impunity.

ERZEROUM, *July* 19*th*.—With the exception of the brilliant Russian exploit at Bayazid on Friday, military operations are in a state of entire stagnation. That the Russians have retired to close proximity with their own frontier is indubitable; why they have done so is not equally clear. Mukhtar Pacha steadily and cautiously followed up the retiring foe, keeping at a very respectful distance. Arrived at Veran Kaleh, three hours on this side of Kars, he commenced intrenching strongly, and then advanced half a day's march beyond Kars, where he remains for the present. Along the way entrenched camps are being constructed, and very large levies of irregulars are being drilled incessantly. In Erzeroum a very large force of irregular cavalry, principally volunteers from Sivas and the Syrian provinces, are mounted and getting ready to join a similar force already at the front. As I telegraphed some days ago the artillery element has been enormously increased by the advent of field and garrison guns from Trebizond; and, in fine, everything denotes a settled conviction that the real attack has yet to be made. That the Russians are only waiting the arrival of reinforcements to renew the offensive no one here doubts, and the greatest credit must be given to Mukhtar Pacha for the consummate skill he displayed in drawing the enemy on step by step to previously prepared positions, and to a battle-ground chosen by himself. Not once even did he venture to assume the offensive. He utilized the well-known, long-proved capacity for defensive warfare of the Turkish Nizams, and the Russians were forced to see that, though they might force line after line with success, with the troops available at the moment, they would ultimately arrive close to Erzeroum with such diminished forces that, as at Adrianople in the campaign of 1829, they would be impotent for further operations, far from their base, and liable to be taken in flank by the every-day increasing irregular cavalry. Between Kars and this city there are four distinct lines of defence blocking the way along the wide valley of the Araxes. One day and a half's march from Kars, the Soghanli Dagh mountains form a series of rocky ramparts unassailable in front, but somewhat apt to be turned on the Olti flank. Next comes the Zevin] and Meshingerd position, defended with such success during the recent fighting. A third line, now strongly intrenched, and armed with artillery, exists at Kupri Koi, at the junction of the Kars and Bayazid roads. Then come the huge plains of Hassan Kaleh, six hours' ride in extent, closed by the last bulwark of Erzeroum, the Deve Boyun range of hills, already long since converted into a triple line of shelter trenches and redoubts. The forcing of each of these lines would cost an enemy enormous losses, and no doubt the Russians consider it the surer and less costly plan to await the arrival of the necessary reinforcements to enable them to adopt a series of flank movements, obviating the useless loss of life inevitably consequent on a front attack.

The following letter describes a deed of treachery committed by Kurdish armed bands in the Sultan's service at Bayazid, where General Tergukasoff had left a small garrison on his advance to Delibaba. While he was fighting near the latter place about 20,000 Kurds advanced from Van and took possession of the town, the small Russian force retiring to the citadel. The relief of the beleaguered garrison so heroically effected was accomplished under the personal command of General Tergukasoff :—

ERZEROUM, *July 24th.*—The intelligence brought by each fresh arrival from Bayazid and the Persian frontier is a confirmation of the worst apprehensions entertained by the Christians here as to the fate of their co-religionists in that quarter. This evening I had an opportunity of meeting a Turkish officer who arrived from Bayazid to-day, and he tells me that the savagery and cool-blooded cruelty of the Kurds passes all bounds. I could give no better illustration of Kurd peculiarities than the story which the Turkish officer narrated to me to-day about the Bayazid affair. The Russians, thinking only of Turkish regulars, had left a slender garrison of some five hundred men in Bayazid and pushed on towards Alaschkir with their main forces, with the intention of trying to force Mukhtar's position beyond Delibaba. While engaged in this operation an enormous horde of Kurds, estimated at 22,000 horsemen, and under the influence, if not actual guidance, of Sheik Jelaledin, swept down from the Ararat chain of mountains, and surrounded the little garrison of Bayazid. The Russians retired within the walls of a mediæval building, half fortress, half palace, which occupies the summit of the hill above the platform on which Bayazid stands. Provisions were scanty, water still more so; and after a couple of days' blockade the Russians offered terms. In Bayazid at the time, apart from the twenty-two thousand Kurds, were seven regular Turkish battalions, under the command of Faik Pacha. These had arrived subsequent to the Russian failure to carry the Delibaba ridge. The Pacha willingly received the overtures of surrender, and half the entire beleaguered garrison, without arms, marched from their stronghold. Ere the regular troops could take any measures for their security, which at the time no one had any reason to doubt, the Kurd horsemen fell on the disarmed and surrendered prisoners, massacring every one without exception. On this the gates of the stronghold were closed, the remaining portion of the garrison refusing to entertain any proposition after the untoward event which had just taken place. In vain the Turkish commander of the regular forces urged on the besieged the expediency of surrendering rather than die of hunger and thirst. The Russian colonel had fallen in the first assault of the Kurds on the town, and his wife, within the beleaguered stronghold, incited the soldiery to resistance, taking her share in the defence like any of the troops. Anything was better, the Russians said, than again trusting themselves to the mercy of a faithless horde of bloodthirsty savages. And so several days went by. Water was falling short, but the besieged hit on the plan of mining towards the town, and thus establishing an unseen connection with one of the public fountains. For some time this expedient was successful, the adventurous water-seekers being almost entirely hidden from view in the depths of the subterranean opening. But in an evil day a stray Kurd observed the top of a Russian's hat protruding in an unaccountable manner from the soil. He observed, and soon guessed the truth. An ambuscade was prepared, and day after day the poor thirsty Russians had to lament one of their number, shot through the head at the gallery entrance. Twenty-six days' siege since the massacre had gone by. Provisions had long since run exceedingly short, and the besieging enemy had over and over again shouted to the caged foe the intelligence that artillery was coming up to drive them from their refuge. Just ten days ago, as if falling from the clouds, five Russian battalions, with six guns, and four thousand cavalry, attacked the Turkish force. The struggle was short. The twenty-two thousand Kurds fled at once. The regular battalions resisted bravely, but were forced to retreat, leaving over a thousand men and three guns in the assailants' hands. The long-suffering detachment in the stronghold above the town were relieved, and, after passing a night in Bayazid the Russians deliberately retired, taking with them their relieved comrades, their prisoners, captured guns, one of them of heavy calibre, and several families of the town who declared any exile preferable to further association with the mountain savages. Many maimed and cruelly mutilated townspeople were thus escorted from Bayazid; for when the Kurds and other irregulars arrived they vented their wrath on the Christians of the place, accusing them of having willingly welcomed the Russians, and proceeding to every extreme by way of punishment. My informant estimates that over twelve hundred Christians of both sexes suffered death or mutilation at the hands of the Kurds.

For some weeks past the advent of regular battalions has entirely ceased. In their place enormous numbers of irregular cavalry have been pouring in. Horsemen from Bagdad, from Sivas, from Egypt, from Africa, fill the town and suburbs with their motley squadrons. Horses have been largely requisitioned to mount them, and some thousands have already been sent to the front. A very brief period will suffice to show whether this somewhat heterogeneous gathering can be made more useful than their confrères the Circassians and Kurds.

The following letter from the Russian side treats of the causes of the Russian retrograde movement:—

Δ TIFLIS, *July* 13*th*.—It is stated now, beyond doubt, that in the presence of the Caucasian insurrection on the one hand, and the war with the Turks on the other, the Russian forces in Asia Minor are utterly insufficient for operating in the enemy's country with any chances of success for the moment. General Tergukasoff, one of the most distinguished commanders, has been compelled to retreat before the Turks towards Erivan, and is waiting now for reinforcements at Igdyr, on the Russian territory. They are marching to join him. His victories at Delibaba were of no great avail, on account of the immense disproportion of the respective number of troops, which rendered his tactical superiority useless, and deprived him not only of the hope of forcing his way to Erzeroum, but also of maintaining his position at Djadin. Moreover, reliable news having reached him that strong bodies of irregular Kurdish hordes had invested the citadel of Bayazid, the garrison of which consisted only of two battalions, he hastened back with the view to disengage that place. It would have been easy enough to scatter the savage horsemen and Bashi-Bazouks, who, more bent upon plundering than upon fighting, seldom offer serious resistance, but, unexpectedly, sixteen fresh Arabian battalions had joined them, advancing directly by Van to Bayazid, which they occupied, with the exception of its citadel. So they were prepared to receive General Tergukasoff in an excellent position with overwhelming numbers. On the other side twenty-three battalions, commanded by Ismail Pacha, pursued him closely on the road from Erzeroum to the above-named fortress, and harassed his rear, menacing thus to cut him off and to annihilate his division to the last man. In order to prevent such a catastrophe General Heimann, accompanied by the Commander-in-Chief, General Loris Melikoff, was detached from before Kars and, encountering Faizi Pacha at Zevin, attacked him without hesitation on the ridge of rocks where he had intrenched his army. Unhappily the means at hand were utterly inadequate to the task imposed upon the soldiers, and finally, General Heimann, after having experienced severe losses—some say over 3,000 men killed and wounded—was obliged to retire to the point from which he had come.

The consequence of this defeat was to render General Tergukasoff's situation more critical than ever. He had not the slightest chance of overcoming the fourfold stronger forces of his opponents, and had subsequently to avoid all general and decisive actions, even at the cost of his reputation as an able commanding officer. He was influenced, moreover, by another cause of no special military character. More than 3,000 Armenian families, to whom he had promised aid and protection in the name of the Emperor, followed his columns with all their domestic animals and movable household goods. Such an encumbrance completely tied his hands. It is true that he might have abandoned these unfortunate fugitives on the plea of hard necessity, but he felt his responsibility so deeply engaged in a moral point of view that he preferred to appear in the eyes of the world as defeated rather than dishonoured. And it was no light matter. Notwithstanding the assurance of the Porte in its diplomatic notes, nothing is more certain than the prevalence of murder, theft, violence, rape, and all sorts of indescribable outrages, in its Asiatic dominions. It makes little difference, I fancy, whether Armenian or Bulgarian throats are cut by merciless brutes, or whether an Armenian or a Bulgarian child or young girl is outraged or carried off into slavery. It is beyond doubt that the same kind of atrocities which were committed in Thrace last year are now going on, or are even being surpassed, in Armenia, where no control is likely to be exercised, and where no consuls feel called to watch events officially. When the Russians, yielding before innumerable enemies, found themselves under the necessity of rapidly retiring towards their own frontiers, thousands of bewildered Christian families joined them with all they had, imploring protection in the fear that the Turkish troops would not only rob them of everything, but would murder them after subjecting them to terrible tortures. That this fear was justified has been shown by painful experience.

The very day after General Tergukasoff retreated from a place called Suleimania five Christian villages near had been sacked and burned, and every living soul in them killed. Russian soldiers and officers found women and babes ripped up and their throats cut on the highway. From all that has been witnessed it is obvious that Turkish warfare is in no respect better than that of the Sioux Indians. What could the Russian General do in such perplexity? He acted like a man of honour and conscience, and, forming a rearguard with his brigade, conducted the Armenians, their animals, and property, without losing a cart or a horse, and without giving the enemy an opportunity of attacking him, across the Russian frontier. Then he occupied an excellent position near Igdyr, on the road to Erivan, about twenty miles distant from Bayazid, where he is to receive the necessary reinforcements. Some regiments have arrived there already; others are on their way from the north. I saw myself, three days ago, two regiments coming from Vladikawkas pass this city. Splendid, courageous-looking, and good-humoured fellows they were, who certainly are superior in aspect to the best Turkish troops that I have ever seen. Only the Syrians, not the genuine Turks, or any other Mohammedan race, are a match for them, as their officers state. Within a fortnight well-nigh 30,000 men are expected to complete the army here, some of whom are conveyed by steamers to Baku over the Caspian Sea.

The siege of Kars has been partially abandoned, and the Russian troops have retired towards Alexandropol in connection with some military plan, the execution of which, however, will depend on the arrival of fresh troops and the enemy's movements. This is all a mere question of time.

While writing these lines repeated detonations announce to the people a victory which General Tergukasoff obtained on the

10th instant at Bayazid over the Turks. After having received the reinforcements sent to meet him from Erivan, he returned without losing a moment and attacked the besiegers as soon as he could reach them. The bulk of the enemy, mounted Kurds, Arabs, and Bashi-Bazouks, fled in all directions, but the Arabian regiments resisted, and did not retreat until heavy losses had been suffered on both sides. Four field-pieces fell into the hands of the Russians, but only ninety prisoners were made. The main object, however, was the deliverance of the garrison shut up in the citadel during a blockade of sixteen days. They suffered very much from the want of water, and had to depend upon cisterns inside the fortifications. For all that, they had faith in their comrades, and were finally rewarded for their endurance. The details of the engagement are not known yet here. Notwithstanding this brilliant success, the position of the Russians is a precarious one in Armenia. The Turks there are, in fact, at least 25,000 men stronger than their adversaries. Mukhtar Pacha is just now advancing with 30,000 of his best troops on the road from Erzeroum to Kars, with the view to disengage that fortress at any cost. After his victory over General Heimann near Meshingerd he boldly crossed the Soghanli mountains, and occupied three days ago a strong position on their northern slopes. General Loris Melikoff, the Russian Commander-in-Chief, judging his army too weak to besiege Kars and resist Mukhtar Pacha simultaneously, ordered the heavy guns to be withdrawn, and suspended the bombardment, or rather the siege, of that stronghold. Then he prepared for an action in the field, and is at present encamped at Zaim, where he has decided to wait for Mukhtar Pacha's attack, till the expected reinforcements allow him to push forward again.

The general impression of this necessary retreat may not be favourable to the Russian arms and prestige, but ere long all will be set right again, and in the second part of this campaign it may be supposed that the faults committed before will be avoided, and especially the most serious one, the underrating of the enemy's means. The Russian troops continue to be in excellent spirits. Even the want of food and water under the scorching sun does not alter their disposition, and they will stand every hardship to the end with unshaken courage. The inhuman cruelties of the Turks against inoffensive persons, women, children, wounded soldiers, and prisoners, have stirred them. They are so enraged against the villanous Kurds and Bashi-Bazouks that they give no quarter to them now, and ask for none.

The following letter from the correspondent with the Russians describes a battle in which the Turks inflicted a defeat on their enemy, capturing the heights of Kizil Tepe :—

△ CAMP KURUK DERE, *August* 26*th*.—On the 25th inst. we were suddenly aroused at about three o'clock in the morning by the roar of cannon and volleys of musketry. We supposed at first that only outpost skirmishing was going on betwcen the Cossacks and Circassians, but the noise growing louder and more persistent, it soon was evident that the Turks, contrary to their usual practice, had attacked in the direction of our other camp, situated at the village of Bashkladnyklar, some eight miles off to our left. The previous evening I had expressed my apprehension of a possible sudden aggression on the part of the Turks, because I knew that a considerable number of battalions had been detached, in order to reinforce General Tergukasoff's division. As excellent spies, even without being promised any pecuniary reward and out of pure religious zeal, are not wanting among us, Mukhtar Pacha had, of course, been well informed of this state of things, and acted accordingly. Nothing, indeed, was more natural; and when I made my remarks in that sense, I wondered that what has since happened had not already taken place. The officer to whom I spoke smilingly answered that all necessary measures of precaution had been adopted, and that a Russian army was never likely to be surprised by any enemy. Well, this feeling of security has proved to be ill-founded. My fears were really far from being exaggerated.

The Turkish original position on the Aladja mountain extended from the neighbourhood of the ancient city of Ani, now dismal ruins, on the Arpa Tchai River, in the vicinity of Kars, from which fortress the supplies were drawn. The main force, however, leans its left wing on the mountain spur ending in a high hill called the Yagni, around which the fighting on the 18th had chiefly been carried on. At that time too, I had mentioned another steep hill, the Kizil Tepe (Red Hill), which, in an entirely isolated position, towers above the Kuruk Dere plateaux, almost in the very centre of the military positions, but somewhat to the left of us. On this remarkable eminence our Commander-in-Chief, General Loris Melikoff, established his headquarters on the 17th inst. It was usually occupied by a single battalion and four field-pieces, and was thus considered as almost impregnable. On account of its commanding position over the surrounding flats and undulating grounds it was well worth particular attention, especially as the camp at Bashkladnyklar, which is under the fire of its artillery, was only about two miles distant from its northern slope. When in a recent letter I ventured to assert that it was not enough now-a-days for a commanding general to enjoy the reputation of a clever and gallant officer, but that genius, or in default an imitation of such genius as Hannibal and Napoleon possessed, was indispensable for avoiding severe losses in our breech-loading warfare, I really little dreamt of lazy self-sufficient Turks being able to illustrate that truth. This, however, has happened to the extreme surprise of our generals.

It was a bright moonlight night. The mountains and plains were almost as distinctly visible as in broad daytime. Availing themselves of this circumstance, at two or three o'clock in the morning on the 25th instant, about 7,000 Turks crept stealthily, in a compact, noiseless mass, through a dark, deep ravine, without being observed by the careless Lesghian picquets and patrols, till they arrived at the very foot of the Kizil Tepe. Here deploying, they made a sudden rush, savagely yelling their "Allah-il-Allah," on the eight Russian companies which were stationed on the summit. These men, though surprised, defended themselves courageously at the point of the bayonet without yielding an inch. Hundreds of Turks who a few seconds before dashed fiercely on with the rifle in their hands fell to rise no more. At last, however, as the enemy's fast-increasing force threatened to outflank and envelop them altogether, the Russians were compelled to retreat to the camp at Bashkladnyklar, protecting and dragging away their four cannons. Here the alarm was given, and, as quickly as possible, infantry and dragoons marched to the rescue, and stormed the hill with dauntless courage, in the hope of recovering it in the way in which it had been lost. In spite of their heroic efforts, however, they were repeatedly repulsed by overwhelming numbers. The whole hill was like a beehive, thickly thronged with enemies, and had they persisted in their gallant attempt they would have all been exterminated. In the meanwhile the principal Russian forces encamped at Kuruk Dere had been roused, and battalions, squadrons, batteries, with ammunition carts and red-cross waggons behind, hastened in long columns into the field. At first a certain consternation prevailed through the camp, and, moreover, a little confusion. Orders had been issued to strike tents, pack luggage, and load everything on the numerous commissariat waggons. As the boom of the artillery thundered louder, and the sharp rattling of the breechloaders went on incessantly, I thought it best to entrust my baggage to the care of Russian honesty. No Russian soldier will, under any circumstances, allow himself to take any object not belonging to him, should he even find it in the open field, unless he is expressly permitted to do so by his superiors. After having satisfied my mind on that point, I had my horses saddled in a twinkling, and rode alone at full speed to the top of a commanding hill, where the staff officers had established an observatory. By the aid of two powerful telescopes they carefully watched the enemy's movements, and sent from time to time written messages down by orderlies to the commanding general. Here I had a comprehensive and splendid view over the whole theatre of the fighting.

Three miles from the spot where I found myself, the Kizil Tepe, or Red Hill, a dwarfy height of about 800 feet above the plain, was encircled, top and bottom, by two girdles of smoke and flames. On its rocky, bastionlike summit stood thickly crowded Turkish soldiers, under the cover of the opposite slope, and fired their rifles, aiming down into a ravine across which the Russian Tiflis regiment struggled heroically, but in vain, to reconquer the lost position. The very steep, rocky slope of the hill on that side rendered this task almost impossible. I could distinctly see how in the Turkish ranks an imaum, with turban and flowing gown, lifting his hands in fanatical ecstasy above the devoted children of the faith, seemed to be inciting them to withstand the arms of the Moscow Giaour, in Allah's and the Prophet's name. On some other parts of the battle-field Mohammedan priests were equally observed in the foremost lines, apparently animating timid recruits by fervent words of faith. One of these priests was shot. The Turks meant evidently yesterday to crush their weakened adversaries by a general attack, and so they employed all imaginable means to secure success. Many battalions, emerging by scores together, and thousands of irregular horsemen descended the mountain, and were brought at once into action. The whole long line—twelve miles—from the neighbourhood of Ani up to the Kaback Tepe, near to the road to Kars, was swarming with Mussulmans. On the summit of that eminence, situated two miles to the right of the Yagni Hill, three new battalions and clusters of cavalry appeared, with the view to outflank the Russian army, and capture their camp at Kuruk Dere. Their general advance, however, was thoroughly checked as soon as the Russian columns of combined arms, the battalions, squadrons, and batteries which left the camp here, had the necessary time to march to the enemy's encounter and to deploy before him. In the Russian order of battle the extreme left was held by two regiments of dragoons, then followed the remaining brigade of General Dewel's division, and next to it in the centre Colonel Komaroff's five valiant battalions which have seen hard work ever since Ardahan fell. Connected with them and directing its front line against the Yagni hills, the division of grenadiers operated with one of its brigades (General Cederholm) while the other remained in reserve. The extreme right was secured by three regiments of Caucasian regular Cossack cavalry and their horse artillery. Numerous troops besides protected the camp here.

It took some hours before those masses were all able to meet the enemy's lines, on account of the considerable distance which originally separated the combatants. In the meantime the now exposed camp at Bashkladnyklar was broken up. Thousands of carts and waggons transported the tents and the baggage to Kuruk Dere. The straw and dung were burnt on the spot. Again and again the Russians tried to reconquer the Kizil Tepe by storming, while shells and shrapnels were showered upon its ridge; but again and again they were repelled by the defenders, who stood, shoulder to shoulder, behind its rocky edge. On a sudden, shortly after the last assault, which was supported and followed by the play of two batteries, thick white smoke rose on the summit, and a long flame carried it to the skies. Fragments of carriages, limbs of horses and men were scattered in all directions, or flew up in the air. It was clear that stores of ammunition or a powder cart had exploded, ignited by a Russian shell. Joy and satisfaction lighted up the faces of the officers around me, and one of them made the sign of the cross. A short time afterwards, as regiment after regiment entered successively the line of battle, from the left to the right, in full array, and advanced, deployed in company columns, preceded by the usual double chain of tirailleurs, with field batteries between them, the roar of the fighting extended gradually from our left to the centre. It was, however, obvious that before the Yagni Hill the fate of the day was to be decided, because from that part of his position only the enemy might have had a chance of forcing the camp here, as it is quite open and unprotected in that direction. Yet long ere the tirailleurs there had mingled their fire with the boom of their cannon and the cracking of their shells, Colonel Komaroff's brigade in the centre was engaged in sharp infantry fighting. Steadily the Russians gained ground, and drove the Turks over the flats and the undulations till they reached the broad ravine of Subatan, at the foot of the Aladja mountain. In this narrow valley, studded at its opposite side with intrenchments and batteries, the battle came to a standstill. Had it not been for an expressly given order to abstain from advancing beyond, it is highly probable that Mukhtar Pacha's camp might have fallen into Colonel Komaroff's hands. All energy of resistance on the part of the Turks had decidedly been broken; they ceased fighting, and retired in disorder. Their dead lay in rows in the valley, and the survivors were glad to ge tout of the rifle range. In consequence of this mutual pause on different grounds, the fighting died out there at half-past one o'clock in the afternoon. Unhappily the gallant brigadier himself was twice wounded, once in his left hand, and shortly afterwards in his left side. Nevertheless, he continued to exercise his command. Prince Tchadjewadtze, the general in command of the whole cavalry, renowned as one of the ablest and most energetic leaders in the Russian army, was also wounded. A fragment of a shell struck him on the head, but not dangerously, as he is already improving and sure to recover.

While thus the struggle was going on in the centre, the grenadiers, under General Heimann's special superintendence, and led by General Cederholm, fell in with the enemy. After a brisk cannonade with smart shell and shrapnel practice the deadly rifle firing was going on in an uninterrupted line stretching two miles on either side, front against front. Like a light morning mist the smoke was wafted over the hostile forces, and prevented them from taking good aim. The Turks had evidently brought forth their picked men, several Arabian battalions, which fought with resolute stubbornness, as they are accustomed to do on all occasions, thus constituting beyond doubt the Sultan's best troops. Notwithstanding their superior numbers, and the bravery they displayed, they could not hold their ground for more than a single hour, and then were compelled to fall back to their rifle pits and intrenchments at the foot of the Yagni hills. Worn out by the want of food and water, having had all day a sun burning like a red-hot iron over their heads, both antagonists were at last satisfied to see themselves finally separated from each other by intervening hillocks. While the infantry rested, completely exhausted by the heat and the work, the cannons still thundered continuously over the whole line, but with considerably less intensity than in the morning. Finally the Turks, as I have already mentioned, moved with three fresh battalions, and over a thousand horse, down the Kaback hill on our extreme right, endeavouring to outflank the Russians there. The wild, irregular riders, in their fantastical garments, galloped down until they came unexpectedly in sight of the three Caucasian Cossack regiments. Quietly they stood in the valley, drawn in separate lines, with two batteries of horse artillery in the interstices. The Bashi-Bazouks, one after the other, as they rode on stopped their horses, fired their rifles at the enemy, who did not even reply, and turned back at full speed in order to give to their expectant comrades the dismal news that the time for plundering the Russian camp at Kuruk Dere had not come yet. They apparently judged that the Russian cavalry was more than a match for them, and in this conviction they united again in squadrons, and thought it prudent to wait, under the cover of a concealed battery, for their enemies' onset. The Russian regiments, however, warned by some shells from above that they were likely to fall into an ambush of artillery and infantry, did not stir. So the fighting ceased at four o'clock P.M. on the whole line in the same succession as it had begun, from our left to our right. The result was negative. Although the Russian troops had repulsed with great slaughter and remarkable pluck the general attack of the Turks, and had remained for four hours on the battle-field, from which they had victoriously driven the enemy, they had been, for all that, unable to wrest the principal position, the Kizil Tepe hill, out of Turkish hands. Mukhtar Pacha did not hesitate to avail himself of the advantageous position which he had obtained, and shifted to-day his whole camp down to the plain, where his soldiers are not exposed to the cold night winds as on the mountain, and find an ample supply of water. Here, as the Turks have systematically done during this war, they are intrenching themselves as strongly as possible, having one wing protected by the Kizil Tepe, and the other by the Yagni Hill. The force which the Turks brought into action consisted, according to trustworthy estimates, of thirty battalions of infantry and eight thousand irregular horsemen, with sixty cannons. The Russian army was somewhat inferior in number, but I cannot mention how much, because I am bound to refrain from giving any particulars on that subject. The losses amount in the Russian army, according to the most reliable information, to two hundred and eighty men killed and six hundred and sixty-seven wounded. As the Turks were this time the aggressors it is evident that their losses must have been more considerable. Spies and deserters affirm that they lost not less than three thousand men, and I fully believe that there is no exaggeration in this statement. Their skirmishing lines were much thicker manned than those of their adversaries, and when they retreated over the Subatan ravine, heaps of their dead and wounded covered the ground. The Russian army re-entered the camp only at ten o'clock. Here, after the work of the day, I, like everybody else, was not very agreeably surprised on seeing that all the tents had been struck, all the luggage packed on waggons, and that I had not the slightest hope of discovering my property in the dark among thousands of carriages, horses, and men, all encamped in confusion over two square miles of ground. Worn out by fatigue, I went to sleep under the cover of an immense haystack till the dry wind in the morning aroused me with shivering limbs.

The Grand Duke Michael has arrived in camp to-day, and it is probable that he will remain there until the campaign leads to a decisive result. What strikes me here is the slowness of all our military movements. This certainly does not promise well, although no serious defeat is to be apprehended with such excellent troops.

The war for Islam had produced a Turkish or rather Arabian Joan of Arc, who it appears contributed materially to the Ottoman success of August 25th.

△ CAMP KARAJAL, *August* 31*st.*—The partial success obtained on the 25th inst. by the Turks, inasmuch as they have been able to maintain their position on the Kizil Tepe, which they had conquered by a surprise due to the initiative and dashing valour of a young Arabian woman, Fatima, acting as chieftain of some Bedouin squadrons, has compelled, or rather induced, the Russians to change their camp likewise. The position at Kuruk Dere, on a plateau of a dead level, was by no means so formidably fortified as some correspondents, who never had an opportunity of seeing it, have reported. On the contrary, the undeniable fact is, that neither a lunette, nor a rifle pit, nor an intenchment of any kind had ever been formed there. The Russians, either out of military pride or with the view to allure the Turks to risk a pitched battle in the open field, have always scorned to move pickaxe or shovel for the protection of their armies. With regard to their security, they used to rely entirely on their trustworthy sharpsighted Cossacks, who with ever-watchful care are on the look-out for the enemy, and carry on an incessant patrolling along the whole line of picquets. Besides, irregular Caucasian horsemen carefully patrol the ground between the two armies, where skirmishing engagements very often follow an accidental encounter, and sometimes give rise to serious alarm. On that day, however, an unlucky star shone over the Russian destiny. The Cossacks, despite their bravery and watchfulness, were outwitted by the clever young Fatima.

A certain Moussa Pacha, formerly a general in the Russian service, who had deserted it, accompanied her. Acting in conformity with her plan, he rode with her in front of the Turkish cavalry when the assault on the Kizil Tepe had been decided on. They soon fell in with a patrol of Cossacks, who duly stopped them, asking for the password. The renegade, who had formerly received his military education with the Russians, and was thus perfectly acquainted with their field service, explained himself not only fluently in their language but gave also the password, which had evidently been betrayed to him by some bribed Mohammedan deserter. So the Cossacks, deceived in the dark, had no suspicion, and supposing the force before them to belong to their own irregulars, permitted it to advance. Then, of course, when the enemy had surrounded them, they were disarmed, made prisoners, and killed.

The following is a report of the battle of August 25th, from the correspondent with Mukhtar Pacha:—

HEADQUARTERS OF MUKHTAR PACHA, NEAR KIZIL TEPE HILL, *September 6th.*—Since the unquestionable Turkish success of the 25th August, both armies have maintained an attitude of the strictest mutual surveillance, limiting themselves to the change of encampment rendered possible on one side and necessary on the other by the capture of Kizil Tepe Hill, the Turkish objective point in the late battle. The Turkish position at the moment of Mukhtar Pacha's night attack on the Russian advanced lines on the 25th ult. occupied a series of steeply sloping terraces, descending from the summit of Aladja, 8,800 feet high, and constituting the southern slopes of the Kars valley, here opening out into the Russian plains. North in the valley-mouth, and eastward over the frontier plains, are a series of low hills rising abruptly from the rolling surface, and evidently, from their conformation and mineral structure, craters of ancient volcanoes. The hill nearest to our position, Kizil Tepe (the red summit), was for a long time a salient Russian point, occupied by the hostile army at the moment the Turkish forces commenced their march from Kars after the raising of the siege. This hill has abruptly sloping sides terminating in four irregular conical summits, amid which is a crater. It was so near to our lines that a new-comer could scarcely realize the fact that main hostile positions could possibly exist in such near propinquity. To its north, at a distance of some 5,000 yards, is the larger hill of Kuruk Dere, behind which is the village of Palderivan, up to the late battle the camping ground of the main Russian army, having its advanced detachments at Kizil Tepe. Farther off still is another hill, which, as it has not come within the sphere of late combats, has not been named. Due east of Kizil Tepe, and at about six thousand yards, is the hill of Utch Tepe (the triple summit). Until after the last engagement this hill was not occupied by either party. The Russians, seeing the Turkish advance into the plain right of Kizil Tepe, and fearing an attempt to cut the Alexandropol road, moved the bulk of their forces, partly to the plain skirting the banks of the Arpa Tchai directly on the road itself, and partly to this last-named hill. As I stood on the knoll occupied by the present Turkish headquarters, on the afternoon of the 27th ult., I could see long dark columns defiling from behind Kuruk Dere, and directing their march towards Utch Tepe. Arrived due east of our advance, these columns changed direction to the right, and numerous batteries and battalions were visible in line of battle, apparently marching against Kizil Tepe. Arrived within long cannon range, they halted. Everything was ready on our side; but a few minutes' observation showed that this display of military force was only to cover the transport waggons and stores generally to the plain behind Utch Tepe. The enemy was executing what experience has shown to be an excessively dangerous movement in face of an active enemy—a flank march. I dare say the Russians still clung to the idea which the past justified them in, that the Turks, however formidable in defensive positions, were not to be dreaded in the plain. I must chronicle my own experiences, that in the last battle the Turks, disregarding their traditional policy of a generation, went down into the plain, and not only held their own bravely against the serried attacks of a redoubtable infantry and artillery, but also captured by assault an exceedingly strong position. This departure from the past no doubt inspired the precautions we witnessed when the Russians changed front on the 27th. I don't think the Turks had the least idea of an aggressive movement when they left their old vantage ground on the hills and camped in the plain.

Winter is rapidly approaching in these latitudes and at this elevation. Ere many weeks are over no troops, much less the mongrel assembly of Southern Asiatics grouped under the standard of the redoubtable Mukhtar Pacha, could resist the keen winds that blow across the even now snow-clad range that lies at the foot of Ararat. But in the plain below, sheltered by the accentuated ridges north and south, the conditions change. Water is abundant. The cavalry horses and mule trains will be no longer served with water painfully carried in leathern *sacs* to the steep heights on which we were camped, but can drink in the abundant streams of the plain below. The failure of the Russian attempt to occupy the valley has left immense quantities of uncut corn at the disposition of the army; and the fatigue of transport has been in no small degree diminished. Since the last two battles the Turkish soldiery have gained enormously in spirit, and now I should not be surprised to see them on level ground successfully combating an equal hostile attack. Why the Russians acted as they have done remains to be explained by themselves. The Turks, as the early movements of the campaign show, expected to be overwhelmed by colossal numbers, and Mukhtar Pacha's hurried abandonment of the frontier, his leaving Kars to the doubtful issues of a siege, his subsequent retreat to Zevin, all attested the belief in the impossibility of resisting the colossal legions of the North. The Marshal himself told me at an early period of the campaign, that he had in front of him 100,000 infantry, 40,000 cavalry, and perhaps 10,000 irregulars, supported by a powerful artillery. At the time his force was little, if any, superior to half the number supposed to attack. Later on we learn that the Russians were little if at all superior in numbers, except in artillery. Why this was so, unless the Russians counted on what Napoleon I. has stigmatized as one of the gravest errors a general can make, the actual underrating of the enemy's power, moral and physical, I cannot say. The latter theory would now seem to be admissible. The Russians—accustomed to sweep from their path immense hordes of Asiatics, and encouraged by the remembrance that part of their troops had successfully resisted during two years the united military and maritime strength of four nations, during the Crimean War—counted but lightly with the Turkish army of Armenia. I will do them the justice to say that from all appearances they would not have thus counted in vain, were it not for the presence of the commander-in-chief, Ahmed Mukhtar Pacha, who has beyond question shown his immense superiority to his colleagues on the Danube. He commenced with a retreat, gradually gathering from the rear his forces as he went, and when the moment had arrived he made head against the foe, with what success history will tell. He has been the true Fabius Cunctator of the campaign. Had he at once faced the enemy at the frontier, his raw recruits, with but a slight sprinkling of veterans accustomed to defeat in Montenegro and Albania, with the historic fear of Muscovite legions before their eyes, and above all with his scant numbers, defeat was inevitable; defeat meant pursuit, and pursuit disorganization. I am not now giving my own opinion alone, but also those of the chief of the staff, an aged Hungarian officer, well known to fame, whose counsels in no small degree affected the course of operations.

I can't help wondering at the entire absence of Russian prisoners. However indifferent the enemy has shown himself on the aggressive during this year's Armenian campaign, his retreats have been masterpieces of their kind. Not a gun, not a horse, not even a wounded man has been left on the plain. Even the numerous dead were borne away, and it was a rare exception to meet the corpse of a Russian even where the dead lay thickest amid the half-mown corn-fields. This fact argues a perfection of organization, at least in one regard, which makes sensible Moslems reflect on the chapters of the drama yet unacted, and the part to be played by the Russian army of Armenia.

CHAPTER XV.

THE RUSSIAN DEADLOCK.

Survey of the Bulgarian Campaign—The Russian Mistakes—General Levitsky, Assistant Chief of the Staff—The Russian Generals—The Regimental Officers—Apprehensions of a Second Campaign—The Breech-loading Rifle and the New Tactics—Reconnaissance against Loftcha—General Skobeleff under Fire—Prospects of the Russians — A Bulgarian Winter—Supply System of the Russian Army—The Hospital Service—The Military Situation in the Middle of August—An unfortunate General—The Reinforcements—The Russian Supply System—A Ride through the Positions—Tirnova, Drenova, Gabrova.

THE month of August was spent by the Grand Duke Nicholas and his staff in preparations for a new attack on Plevna, which, made with superior forces, would, it was hoped, wipe out the memory of previous defeats, and make it possible for the Russians to resume their advance upon Adrianople. Before noticing the march of events north of the Balkans at this period, it may be useful to review the military situation as set forth in the subjoined letter, published under the heading of "The Russian Mistakes:"—

† HEADQUARTERS, ARMY BEFORE PLEVNA, *August* 19*th*.—With the news of the retreat of General Gourko from Eski-Zagra and Jeni-Zagra the campaign has come to a standstill, with results as unexpected as they are remarkable. If the Turks began the campaign with a series of blunders that were simply inexcusable, the Russians have brought it to a momentary halt, if not to a close, by two or three blunders equally grave, equally inexcusable, and from certain points of view almost equally disastrous. The first of these mistakes was the advance of General Gourko beyond Kezanlik with a force utterly inadequate to maintain itself, with the necessary consequence of defeat and retreat. This movement was made, however, by General Gourko on his own responsibility, without the orders of the Grand Duke, and his only excuse is that the movement was made before the battle of Plevna, and that at the time he expected to be almost immediately followed by at least an army corps, a mistake which, on the whole, was excusable; for nobody at that date could have supposed a Russian commander-in-chief, or a Russian chief of staff, or a Russian general capable of committing blunder number two. This was the neglect to occupy Plevna and Loftcha immediately upon advancing to Tirnova, blunder the like of which can only be found in the early stages of the American civil war, when armies were commanded by lawyers, doctors, merchants, and politicians.

Perhaps not even an American civilian general would have committed the blunder of advancing from the Danube to Philippopolis railway, with an army of fifty or sixty thousand men on his right flank, without sending something more than two or three hundred Cossacks to protect that flank, or without even sending out a cavalry reconnaissance to find out the exact whereabouts of the army that was known to be there, and to give timely warning of its approach. The imbecility displayed in this by educated military men is of that kind which simply surpasses belief and defies explanation. A glance at the map will serve to show the most unmilitary mind the absolute necessity for the Russians to strongly occupy Plevna when they advanced to Tirnova, and to seize Loftcha before they reached the passes of the Balkans. The road from Plevna to Loftcha runs parallel to that between Sistova and Gabrova, the main line of the Russian advance; and Loftcha and Plevna command all the roads from Widdin, Sofia, and Nish, where the Turks were known to have considerable forces, and the possession of those towns by the Russians would have insured the safety of their right flank and their long line of communications. The necessity of seizing these places was so evident to the most casual observer, of even the most unmilitary turn of mind, that probably not one military man in a hundred ever thought of ascertaining whether it had really been done or not. They would as soon have thought of inquiring whether the Russians were in the habit of placing outposts and sentinels, or whether the artillery had wheels. And yet this measure, rudimentary in its simplicity and necessity, was neglected by the Russian military chiefs until it was too late, with, as its result, the battle of Plevna, and the loss of seven or eight thousand of Russia's bravest soldiers as uselessly as if they had been simply led out and shot by their own comrades.

Who is responsible for this disastrous result? Evidently two men: General Krüdener, the chief of the 9th Corps, who commanded the operations on the right flank, who received the order to occupy Plevna as soon as he crossed the river, and General Levitsky, the assistant chief of staff of the Grand Duke, whose business it was to see that the Grand Duke's orders were executed. General Krüdener, occupied with the siege of Nicopolis, not only did not seize Plevna as ordered, but even withdrew the cavalry that had been sent there for that purpose to Nicopolis. As cavalry could hardly be used for the storming of redoubts, his object in doing this can scarcely be conceived. Had he even occupied Plevna immediately after the fall of Nicopolis all might have been well. Had he even sent out the cavalry to ascertain where the Turkish army was, and give warning of its advance, all might still have been well. The neglect to occupy Plevna as long as he positively knew the Turkish army was still far away would have been of slight consequence. But he did not send a single squadron to see whether that army was approaching Plevna or not, and the first detachment of his army marched into Plevna two hours after the Turks arrived there, without having thrown out a scout or an advance guard, just as though they were marching through the district of Moscow. This in the enemy's country, within ten miles of an army of fifty thousand men. But the whole responsibility in a question so important as this cannot be thrown upon General Krüdener. It is evident there must be more than one man to blame. No such important and vital measure as the occupation of Plevna and the protection of the right flank should have been or could have been left to the care of one man already occupied with an important siege.

Evidently there was somebody else who should have looked after this matter, who should have known that the order to occupy Plevna had not been executed, who should have known the reason why, and who should have repaired the neglect at once, or at least have ascertained that there was no possibility of the Turks seizing the important strategic position. That man was General Levitsky. He may be considered the executive officer of the Grand Duke's staff, who looks after details, who sees that orders are executed, who finds the best way of executing them, and who is besides, it is said, the leading spirit in the military councils for the direction of the campaign in general. General Nepokoitschitsky is old, and does not, I am told, take a very active part in affairs, so that it is Levitsky who is the real chief of the staff, and who is mainly responsible for the direction of affairs. It may not be amiss to say a word about General Levitsky here.

He is among the youngest generals of the army, and was appointed to his present high position on account of the talent he displayed in the peace manœuvres at St. Petersburg. Here, on the level plains about the capital, where every inch of the ground and every road was known to him, where the fighting was done with blank cartridges, and there were neither killed nor wounded, General Levitsky succeeded in handling an army corps very well, and usually won considerable advantage over his adversaries. Fighting a real war and handling an army of two hundred thousand men is, however, a different kind of thing from directing those peace manœuvres; and although the choice of General Levitsky for his present post may have been the one which seemed to invite the greatest chances of success, it cannot be said that it has been justified by the results. Besides the affair at Plevna, for which General Levitsky is in great part responsible, there are tactical faults in the distribution of the army for which he is answerable. The army has been, in fact, disposed of in the most unheard-of manner. Divisions, brigades, and even regiments have been cut up, parcelled out, and sent to the four points of the compass, and dispersed so far that it is doubtful whether they will ever be able to unite again during the war. The 14th Division, for instance, is an example of this. There is a part of it on the road to Osman Bazar, a part at or near Elena, a part at Khaini or Khainkin, as it is improperly called by the Russians, a part at Selvi, and a part at Tirnova—points that can have no tactical connection with each other, and which are so far apart that it is doubtful if the 14th Division, considered the best in the army, can ever be brought together again. General Dragomiroff, its commander, is left at Tirnova with a battalion or two, and his division has virtually been taken from him.

If this parcelling out continues much longer, there will be no tactical unity left, and any required force will have to be made up of fractions of battalions, regiments, and brigades, hurriedly tumbled together, without cohesion and without solidity. The fault has arisen from the assistant-chief of staff miscalculating the forces required upon given points, and then remedying the mistake in a hand-to-mouth sort of way, by seizing troops wherever he could get them—a battalion here and a regiment there—to strengthen the respective positions. Another mistake has been committed by the staff, for which General Levitsky cannot alone be held responsible. When news was received of the occupation of Plevna by the Turks, Loftcha should have been instantly seized by the Russians; and for two very good strategical reasons. In the first place, with the Turks at Loftcha, it is just as impossible for the Russians to cross the Balkans as it is with the Turks in possession of Plevna. The possession of either of these points effectually checks the Russian advance, and Loftcha, equally with Plevna, was most important for the Russians as well as the Turks.

But this is not all. A glance at the map will show that the road from Plevna to Sophia passes at no great distance from Loftcha, and that consequently, had the Russians seized Loftcha as soon as the Turks occupied Plevna, they would have threatened the Turkish line of communications, and their best line of retreat. The possession of Loftcha was almost indispensable for a successful attack upon Plevna, for it would have enabled the Russians to completely turn the Turkish positions on the south, and to have brought at least one more division—the 9th, then at Gabrova and Selvi—to the attack. In fact, the possession of Loftcha was so necessary to the Russians before attacking Plevna, that, had the Turks occupied it at the same time as Plevna, the Russians should have taken it before attacking Plevna at all. Yet a week or ten days elapsed between the seizure of Plevna and Loftcha by the Turks, and the Russian General-in-Chief never thought of profiting by the opportunity thus offered him. The best military authorities are of opinion that, as long as the present lines are occupied by the Russians, it will even yet be necessary to begin the attack upon Plevna by the capture of Loftcha. The mistake, therefore, of allowing it to be seized and fortified by the Turks is only less than that of allowing Plevna to fall into their hands. The capture o Plevna by the Turks was a surprise—caused by the most gross and culpable carelessness and stupidity, it is true—but it was still a surprise for the Russian staff. The same cannot be said of the capture of Loftcha; and the fact of their not having forestalled the Turks looks as though neither General Nepokoitchitsky nor General Levitsky understood the importance of this strategical point until it was too late.

Then, as to the battle of Plevna itself, there was displayed here an amount of carelessness, recklessness, and incapacity on the part of the Russians for which very few people were prepared; a degree of incapacity which, if it were general, and not confined to one or two officers, would simply augur that the Russians would be beaten in this war by such an enemy as the Turks, and badly beaten too. I do not think, for my own part, there is the slightest probability of such a result; but if the battle of Plevna were to be taken as a specimen of Russian military ability, then it must be confessed there would be little hope for a termination of the war favourable to the Russian arms.

Fortunately for the cause of humanity there is reason to believe that General Krüdener, who is entirely responsible for the manner in which the battle was fought, is an exception, and that no more such affairs will occur. The fact is that the battle of Plevna is as disgraceful for the Russian generals as it is glorious for the Russian soldiers. The soldiers knew their duty, and did it. It was the Russian generals who neither knew nor did theirs. The fearful losses sustained show how well the Russian soldier did his part. Those losses may be safely estimated at 8,000 in killed and wounded, out of a force of 24,000 actually engaged in the battle; that is, a loss of 33 per cent. The Prussian loss at Gravelotte, the bloodiest battle of the Franco-Prussian war, did not exceed 8 per cent., and if we wish to find a parallel for the Russian losses at Plevna we must look to some of the hardly fought battles of the American Civil War, Shiloh, Antietam, the Wilderness, with this difference, that the American troops who fought these battles were veterans, while the greater part of the Russians at Plevna had never been under fire before.

In the first place, General Krüdener hesitated and vacillated four or five days before attacking, although everything was ready, and during these four or five days the Turks were receiving reinforcements hour by hour and digging intrenchments. He assembled general councils of war during this time, composed first of all of his generals, and then of all the colonels and generals, than which a more absurd proceeding could hardly be imagined. He was wavering, undecided, irritable, and excited. When, finally, in a paroxysm of energy, he made up his mind to attack, it was already so late in the night that the different commanders did not receive the order to march until the hour named in the order for starting—that is, at five o'clock in the morning. The troops on the left wing did not get the order to start until six o'clock—that is, an hour after they should have been already on the way—and the whole army, therefore, fearful of arriving too late, had to start without breakfast, with a march of ten miles to make before going into battle.

With all General Krüdener's hesitation and caution, he does not seem to have once properly reconnoitred the Turkish positions. Had he done so he would have made his principal attack from the south, where the Turks had not fortified themselves, and from whence he might easily have turned their intrenchments. This was proved by General Skobeleff, in command of the extreme left, who actually penetrated into Plevna, and turned the Turkish position, but with a force too small to be effective. Instead of this, General Krüdener threw his army blindly against the Turkish intrenchments, like a mad bull going at a stone wall, with no other idea of taking it but the employment of pure brute force in the undirected if sublime bravery of the Russian soldier. If battles were to be fought in this way there would be no need of officers; the soldiers might do all, and the generals had better return at once to the cafés of St. Petersburg and Moscow. There was one general in this battle, the commander of the 30th Division, whose fate has been a sad one. He is an old man—one of the richest men in Russia—whose career has been a long and an honourable one, and who has been expelled from the army for—simple cowardice. He, it seems, did not appear on the field of battle at all, and nevertheless fled panic-stricken to Bulgareni, some ten miles in the rear, before halting.

It may not be amiss to say something here of the Russian army as it exists at present. In the first place all the predictions about the certain spread of sickness when once the army was over the Danube have been falsified. The health of the troops is exceptionally good, better perhaps than if they were in their barracks in Russia. This is only natural. The climate of Bulgaria is very healthy, the country considerably higher than the Danube, and rising higher and higher as it approaches the Balkans. There had been no rain of any consequence, until five days ago there was a steady downpour, which lasted two days, and rendered the roads very muddy, and filled some of the mountain streams to overflowing. The sky has now cleared again, and we shall probably have another long spell of dry weather. The hospital service is well organized, and besides the military hospital and ambulance service there is that of the Russian Red Cross, and others maintained by private societies. The sick and the wounded are therefore well cared for, and the mortality is very slight. The commissariat service seems likewise to be well managed, and I hear no complaints among the soldiers of insufficient or bad food. I have many times had occasion to try the soldiers' fare when I could not easily procure any other, and must say that, for making a good soup, the Russian soldier is unrivalled. Their rations are excellent in quality, and sufficient in quantity, and I have not heard as yet any complaints of their failing, or of the soldiers going even a single day without food.

There are complaints, I believe, about the Russian artillery. It is said the guns have not the range that was expected of them, owing either to inherent defects in the guns themselves, or the bad quality of the powder furnished. But the service of the artillery is excellent, and capable of making all that is to be made out of the guns. The horses of both artillery and cavalry are still in excellent condition, with the exception of some of the Cossack cavalry, which have been overworked. The Russian engineer service, with the famous Todleben at its head, is said to be the best in Europe. If this be true, all I can say is that the engineer service had better do something to justify its reputation. I never in my life saw roads and bridges in the condition in which they are used by the Russian army. Even the Carlists did better than this. The roads and bridges literally take care of themselves, and had the Russians had an ordinary enemy to deal with, they might meet with a disaster from this cause alone. There appears to be absolutely nobody to look after them. The Russian staff is of course in a great measure responsible for this state of things; and the Russian staff, I should say, is by no means the best in Europe. Everything that depends upon the staff is done in a careless slipshod manner that is not to be mistaken. If the head of the staff can commit such blunders as I have already pointed out, it is not to be wondered that the rest should not be up to their work. Of the troops of the line it is unnecessary to speak. The Russian soldier is beyond all praise. The officers themselves say, "Ah, if we were half as good as our soldiers, the Russian army would be the best in the world."

As to the officers of the line, the company officers and heads of regiments are undoubtedly excellent, and will compare favourably with officers of the same rank in any army in the world except the Prussian. But the same cannot generally be said of the battalion commanders, who are proverbially careless, neglectful, and indifferent. The reason for this difference is obvious, and is more or less the result of a law decreed some few years ago. By this law company officers are made more dependent on their good conduct for their positions and promotion than they formerly were, and more than is possible with regard to the heads of battalions. The command of a company may be given to a lieutenant, even when the company has its captain, should the latter show himself incapable or negligent; and as the actual command of a company brings an addition to the pay of 500 roubles, the lieutenants are very anxious to show themselves capable of commanding a company, while the captains who have companies are careful by no neglect of duty to give occasion for losing their commands and being simply attached to the regiment.

Once the captain becomes a major, however, and receives the command of a battalion, the case is different. He then has little to fear and little to hope for but his retirement and his pension. Unless he does something very bad, his battalion cannot be taken from him; and unless he has some opportunity to really distinguish himself, or unless he has powerful friends, it is difficult for him to get a regiment. The result is that he generally settles down into an apathetic, indifferent officer, who barely does his duty and no more, with nothing better to look forward to. The commanders of regiments are a better class of men. They are either those officers who distinguished themselves in the lower grades, and were promoted for bravery, a brilliant action, or great and undisputed cleverness, superior education and intelligence; or else officers from the Guard, men of good families with position, education, and fortune, generally a superior class of men. They are not often either very studious or very much given to consuming the midnight oil—at least for purposes of study, but they are brave, clever, active, and intelligent, with honour and reputation at stake, and, taken all in all, a very good class of officers.

When we come to the generals we find ourselves for the most part among a different class of men, especially if we take the older ones. The period of service of the greater part of these dates from before the Crimean war, and although there are many exceptions to this statement, they cannot upon the whole be considered a superior, or even a moderately good set of men.

They are rather below than above the average, and do not compare favourably with the class of younger officers that are growing up under them. The reason for this difference may be attributed in great part to the following circumstances: At the close of the Crimean war the feelings of the Russian people were most intensely excited against the Government and against the army, in consequence of the defeat, and the conclusion of what was universally regarded as a disgraceful and dishonourable peace. The violence of this feeling, especially against the army, may be judged by the following incident:—There was a regiment, or the remnant of a regiment, that had lost twice its number in the siege of Sebastopol, that had distinguished itself among the bravest of the brave, and when on its way home, passing through the streets of a large town shattered and broken, reduced to one-tenth of its normal number, began to play a victorious march; when the population, rich and poor, young and old, noble and peasant, rose up as one man and began to hurl stones and mud at the poor fellows, who were expecting a very different reception, to insult them with cries of "Cowards," "Runaways," and asking them why they did not play that march when before the enemy.

The popular feeling was so strong against the army that for two or three years the Government bent before it, and neglected the army; the service became unpopular, and the best and bravest of the officers who had distinguished themselves in the war, the men of good families and those who were capable of profiting by the experience gained, who had become really splendid officers in the stern ordeal of battle, became disgusted and indignant at the treatment they received, resigned their commissions, and either retired into private life or embraced civil professions. These are the men who should have been the generals of to-day. When they retired, their places were filled by men of an inferior class, whose want of means prevented their retiring into private life, or whose want of education prevented their adopting a civil profession, or whose want of sensibility made them indifferent to the contumely heaped upon them. And these are the men who are the generals of to-day. Naturally, there are among them a few who remained from a sense of duty and a love of their profession, and one of these is General Nepokoitchitsky. There are others among the younger officers who have achieved distinction since the Crimean war, either on the field of battle, as General Skobeleff; in the Cabinet, as General Levitsky; or by their writings on tactics and strategy, as General Dragomiroff; but these are few. And even of these there may be some who, like General Levitsky, will not come through the present war without damage to their laurels.

Such, then, are the generals of the Russian army of to-day. Of the sixty or seventy generals of brigade, division, and corps commanders, there is not yet one who has given any proof of extraordinary talent, who has risen enough above the level of mediocrity to attract attention, who begins to show as a figure, still less to whom all eyes are turned as the Russian Moltke of the future. General Dragomiroff is the most promising of them all, and he will undoubtedly ere long have command of a corps, and should the war continue for another campaign, as now seems probable, will certainly be at the head of an independent army. General Skobeleff, who is the most brilliant of the younger men, and who gives more promise for the future than any I have yet seen, is still too young for the command of more than a division, unless he should have some extraordinary chance of distinguishing himself, and the headquarter staff should meet with another reverse which would necessitate their taking the best man they can find without regard to age or rank. General Baron Krüdener has been relieved from the command of the army around Plevna by General Zotoff, the head of the 4th Corps, who is his senior in point of service though not in years. Krüdener still remains, I believe, in command of the 9th Corps. General Zotoff owes his present position to neither protection nor favour. He has won it solely by his sword, and something may therefore, I think, be hoped from him. He appears to be a man of resolution and energy, and it is he who will command the next attack upon Plevna, which we are expecting daily.

It may not be uninteresting here to take a glance at the plan of operations likely to be adopted on both sides. The Turkish plan is evident. It is to surround the territory now occupied by the Russians with a series of fortresses and fortified camps, then act entirely on the defensive, in which way alone they are capable of availing themselves of the splendid fighting qualities of their troops. They can play the waiting game better than the Russians, who will of course attack as soon as they receive reinforcements, and they can hope by an obstinate resistance, disputing every foot of ground and covering every square rood with trenches, to prolong the war into another campaign, if not to surround the Russians with a circle of iron which they may vainly endeavour to break. This defensive war of positions is undoubtedly the best they could have adopted. The want of military knowledge among the Turks, the utter lack of good officers, of discipline, of military skill, and the consequent impossibility of handling troops in the field, of executing manœuvres, or even tactical evolutions, makes it impossible for the Turks, even with triple numbers, to contend with the Russians in the open field. But, put a Turk in a ditch, give him a gun, a sackful of cartridges, a loaf of bread, and a jug of water, he will remain there a week or a month under the most dreadful artillery fire that can be directed against him, without flinching. He can only be dislodged by the bayonet, and with the rapidity of fire of modern arms it is very difficult to reach him with the bayonet, as the Russians found to their cost at Plevna. And it is only in this way that the splendid individual courage of the Turk can be utilized—that is, by acting on the defensive, and fighting in trenches. This is the plan the Turks have evidently adopted, and had they not allowed the Russians to seize two passes of the Balkans they might have rendered it so far successful as to inflict such fearful losses on the Russians in passing this barrier as to put the possibility of seriously threatening Constantinople out of the question. They have on one side Rustchuk, Shumla, Osman Bazar, and the Slievno Pass, all fortified and defended by troops who, however despicable they may be in the open field, are most formidable adversaries buried in trenches and rifle-pits. On the other side they have splendidly retrieved their mistakes made in not defending the passage of the Danube and Balkans by seizing Plevna and Loftcha, a masterstroke of strategy, favoured by luck and Russian stupidity, and backed up by the magnificent conduct of the Turkish troops. It checked the Russian advance as effectually as if they had recaptured the passes of the Balkans themselves with an army of a hundred thousand men. They are fortifying these places, thus completing the circle, which is only broken at Shipka and Khaini or Khainkin.

Nevertheless this plan, the best that could possibly have been adopted by the Turks, although it may retard the end, cannot avert it. In the first place no army, that is compelled to act purely on the defensive, tactically as well as strategically, can ever be victorious in the end. It is destined to be finally beaten by laws as inevitable and inexorable as that of gravitation. It is merely a question of time, numbers, and mathematics, as a glance at the present situation will show. Supposing the Turks to have three hundred thousand men here, as is claimed for them—one hundred thousand on the side of Plevna, one hundred thousand at Rustchuk, Shumla, and Osman Bazar, and one hundred thousand in the valley of the Tundja, to prevent the Russian advance. This estimate is a very liberal one for the Turks, but we can allow it for the sake of illustration. The Russians have already, in the two armies of the Grand Duke Nicholas and the Czarewitch, six army corps, without counting the two corps under the command of General Zimmerman. These six corps will give an effective force of 150,000 men, after deducting 12,000 for the Russian losses up to the present moment. With the arrival of the Guard, which counts 60,000, and three more divisions which have been mobilized, which will give a force of 40,000, the Russians will have in these two armies a force of 250,000, without counting the army of Zimmerman.

With this force at their disposal, there are two or three plans of campaign that might be adopted. In the first place, they might simply leave 75,000 men on the Plevna side, and as many on the Rustchuk and Shumla side, as mere corps of observation, and cross the Balkans with 100,000 men. If it is admitted, as it is on all hands, that the Turks cannot act with success on the offensive, 150,000 men would be enough, and more than enough, to hold the Turkish forces at Plevna and Shumla in check during the forward march of the 100,000 men towards Constantinople. As there are no positions between the Balkans and Constantinople which cannot be turned, the Turks would have no opportunity of availing themselves of the fighting qualities of their soldiers. It is true they can fortify Adrianople, but that place, situated in the midst of a broad, open plain, is not naturally a strong position, and one not easily made so by art. It would require 50,000 troops to defend it, which would only leave 50,000 for the defence of Constantinople. But in the event of such a plan being adopted by the Turks, the Russians could employ the same system I have supposed them to have employed at Plevna and Shumla; that is, they could leave a corps of observation of 25,000 men before Adrianople and attack Constantinople with 75,000, a force quite sufficient to carry it against 50,000 defenders.

This plan is not likely to be adopted by the Russians, nor is it the best one; but it is one which might be adopted as the result of a campaign conducted purely on the defensive by the Turks. The more probable plan of operations will be as follows. Leaving 100,000 men on the side of Rustchuk and Shumla to hold the Turks there in check, including the force required to hold the Shipka and Khaini Passes, they will fling 100,000 men against Plevna and Loftcha, and crush the Turkish forces there, and endeavour to annihilate and destroy them; then cross the Balkans with the same army;

beat the Turkish forces in the valley of the Tundja, before the remnants of the Plevna army, obliged to go round by Sofia, can rejoin it; then follow this beaten army, and not give it a moment of halt till it reaches the capital. An army thus pursued from the Balkans to Constantinople is not likely to make a very formidable defence; and if the pursuit were properly followed up, the attacking army would reach Constantinople long before the remnant of the Plevna army could reach it by way of Sophia. This is apparently the plan the Russians have adopted, which they are waiting to carry out, and on the rapidity of the execution of which depends the question of another campaign.

But the whole of the reinforcements which the Russians are awaiting cannot arrive before the middle of September. If they wait for the arrival of the Guards to begin putting the plan into execution, they will then at the best not have more than six weeks left in which to conclude the campaign, and they may consider themselves fortunate indeed if they have a month. Last year, it is true, the weather held up till the 1st December, and a campaign might have been prosecuted up to that time without much difficulty; but that was an exceptionally good season, and the Russians can hardly hope for so good a one this year. If the roads are not completely impassable by the middle of October, they may consider themselves indeed fortunate. But even supposing the season to hold out until the 1st November, it will be impossible for them to take Plevna, Loftcha, Rustchuk, cross the Balkans, beat the army of Suleiman Pacha, besiege and take Adrianople, and then carry the famous Kujuk Chekmejee before Constantinople, all during this campaign. Such a task might be accomplished by the Prussians, but never by the Russians with the slowness of movement that has characterized them during this war.

If the Russians await the arrival of the Guard, therefore, they are doomed to undertake a second campaign, at an expense which, in the present state of Russian finances, would be almost equivalent to national bankruptcy. There are indications that they mean to await the arrival of the Guard, and if they do it will be a mistake only equalled by that of allowing the Turks to quietly seize Plevna and Loftcha. It is only when confronted with this probability that we begin to understand the full consequences of the Turkish stroke of strategy, and the profound imbecility of the Russian generals in allowing them to execute it. A second campaign! A long, dreary winter passed in the Balkans in the snow and the mud; the army decimated by disease, exposure, and perhaps an epidemic, perhaps the plague. The long weary months of waiting, the expenditure of millions—such is the meaning of a second campaign.

The fact is, the Russians should have avoided the possibility of a second campaign at almost any risk. Permitting the Turks to occupy Plevna was a mistake; the battle of Plevna, fought in the absurd manner in which it was fought, was a mistake; but a greater mistake than either, if they permit it, will be to allow the war to drag on into a second campaign. In order to avoid this, the whole plan of action should have been changed after the battle of Plevna. They have enough troops across the Danube to take Plevna, and they had enough after the battle to do so. They had six army corps, giving an effective, as I have already said, of 150,000 men, after deducting for losses. They should have provisioned the Shipka and Khaini Passes for two months, and placed 20,000 men there to defend and hold them. They should have placed 20,000 more in front of Sistova to defend that place, and 20,000 more in Tirnova; then abandoned the whole of the line occupied by the army of the Czarewitch. This would have left them an effective of 90,000 men, which, by a rapid concentration, they could have flung against the Turkish army at Plevna and have crushed it.

It may be objected that I forget the army of Shumla, which could advance in that case, take the Russian army in the rear while attacking Plevna, and thus put it in a very dangerous position. To this I reply, that the Turks having adopted a purely defensive plan of campaign, to which they have hitherto adhered with the greatest pertinacity, there is little likelihood of their doing this. But if they did move out of their fortified camp at Shumla, this is the very best thing for the Russians, the very worst move the Turks could make. In the first place, the Russians could easily get three days' start of them, and very probably more, a time quite sufficient for the affair at Plevna. They could crush the Turkish army there, and then turn round and beat the Shumla army in its turn. If the Russians can catch this army anywhere west of the Jantra, they can simply annihilate it, providing they have first settled accounts with the Plevna army. The Turks, however strong they may be behind intrenchments, cannot stand against the Russians in the open field. The country between the Jantra and Plevna is an open rolling plain, more or less broken up, it is true, but offering no strong positions for defence, nor any capable of being rapidly fortified. If the Turks venture out here they are sure to be beaten, and this is in fact the very move the Russians have been waiting for and wishing for all along. But while wishing for and hoping for it, they have not had the courage to offer the Turks a sufficient temptation to induce them to do it. And, in fact, up to the battle of Plevna no good occasion had offered. That battle furnished the occasion, and one which the Russians should not have neglected.

Had the Turkish army come out of Shumla, it, as well as the army of Plevna, would have been crushed in two successive battles, and the war would be virtually at an end. Had it remained inactive, then the Russian army could cross the Balkans, and with the reinforcements which are already arriving, might now have been on the march to Adrianople. The Russian generals, however, after having blundered into the affair of Plevna through negligence, now run to the other extreme; and, through an excess of caution, adopt a safe and slow plan of campaign, that will prolong the war another year. They intend to crush the Turks by mere brute force and superiority of numbers, instead of by skill and generalship, even at the fearful expense of another campaign. So much for generalship. There is, of course, another view to be taken of the question. Should this plan be adopted by the Russians, a considerable portion of territory now occupied by them would have to be abandoned for a few days; and during this time the Turks might come in and massacre the population, as they invariably do wherever the Russians have passed.

The Emperor is, it is understood, very much against such a plan if it can be avoided, for this very reason. But the number of villages that would have to be abandoned are, after all, comparatively few, and the population of these might retreat into Tirnova and Sistova for a few days, where they would be quite safe until the battle would be over; and although those villages would undoubtedly be burnt, this would after all cause less misery than the prolongation of the war another year. Everything considered, therefore, the Russians seem to be managing badly; and their generals, with one of the finest armies in the world at their command, are showing neither military science nor skill. They will undoubtedly crush the Turks in the end, but it will be by mere brute force and overpowering numbers, and that too against an enemy unable to take the offensive. They began their advance as though they had no enemy at all, and since the battle of Plevna they have been acting with as much caution as though they were fighting the Prussians. What would it be if they were fighting the Prussians or even any ordinary enemy as capable as themselves of taking the offensive?

One most important fact has been made manifest by the battle of Plevna, of which the Russians must take account in the future; that is, the advantage given by modern firearms to raw undisciplined troops fighting in intrenchments on the defensive. In former days, when only two or three rounds could be fired against a bayonet charge, regular soldiers had an immense advantage over raw, undisciplined troops fighting in even the strongest positions. The rapidity of modern firearms, and the steady shower of bullets that even the rawest troops can pour against a bayonet charge or an assault, put them nearly on an equality with veterans, as long as they can fight from behind breastworks. This is a fact which the Russians left altogether out of account when they threw their masses against the Turkish intrenchments. If the Russians attack the intrenchments of Plevna in the way they did before, they are sure to be beaten. With modern firearms, a simple mob, individually brave men, without discipline and without organization, with moderately good marksmen, can hold intrenchments against even superior numbers of the best troops in the world, as long as they are only attacked in front. The thing has been done more than once, even with old-fashioned muzzle-loaders; and the Turks have shown at Plevna how easily it can be done with breech-loaders. And it stands to reason.

The knowledge that he can reload his piece, even after his enemy is within twenty paces, will give the rawest recruit a steadiness that can be obtained in no other way, and he is in a very different moral condition from the man who has discharged his weapon and knows he cannot reload it again before the cold steel will be into him. Then he has other advantages. His enemy arrives, if he arrives at all, with thinned ranks, the men out of breath after a run of half a mile or perhaps a mile, or a climb up a steep ascent. They cannot fire with the least accuracy running, and even if they stop to fire their hearts are beating with the violence of their exertions, and their hands are unsteady. They are in a very different condition from men posted in trenches with steady eyes and hands, and a rest before them upon which to take deliberate aim at an advancing foe. In my opinion, the whole system of attack upon even the simplest trenches will have to be completely changed in the future. Assaults, properly speaking, will have to be abandoned. Where such positions cannot be turned, then the attack must have recourse to the same means as the defence. Earth will have to fight earth. The attack will have to approach keeping as much under cover as the defence. They will have to take advantage of every shelter offered by the nature of the ground, and where the ground does not offer shelter, then shelter must be artificially created. The attack will likewise have to dig trenches—narrow, shallow ones—a foot or eighteen inches deep, along which they can crawl, and they must keep up a fire as incessant and well-directed as that of the defence. Strategically, they must be working on the offensive, tactically on the defensive; and not till they have arrived within a few yards of the enemy's trenches, should they think of trying the bayonet. Their progress must necessarily be slow, but it will be sure, and the loss of life will be moderate. The Russians, for instance, instead of trying to take Plevna in a single day, as they did before, if they find they cannot turn the Turkish intrenchments, should devote at least a week to it, working gradually up to each position, under cover, day after day, until the last is carried, or abandoned, as would be most likely, by its defenders.

In my opinion this is the only way trenches defended by steady troops—and there are none steadier in trenches than the Turks—can be taken without a loss of life so great as to very soon destroy an army. For be it remembered that artillery is practically powerless to dislodge troops from these deep, narrow trenches, even at the distance of a mile, which is as close as artillery dare approach without having the gunners picked off as fast as they appear; for unless the shells fall exactly in the trench they hurt nobody, and even then a shell will not hurt more than one man, or at the most two. The difficulty of hitting a trench fifteen inches wide, which in perspective is, at the distance of a mile, almost of less than an inch, may easily be imagined. General Concha, at the battle of Abarzuza, shelled the Carlist trenches three days with eighty pieces of artillery at the distance of less than a mile, and inflicted a loss of only eighty men in killed and wounded.

The fact is that the effect of modern artillery and its value have been greatly over-estimated. The moral effect of shell-fire upon raw troops is of course very great, but its material effect is very slight, and upon good troops its moral effect is, of course, nearly lost. A shell traversing a thin line of infantry may carry away a man or it may not, but it is rarely that the harm done is greater than that caused by a bullet. A shell exploding in soft ground never does any harm unless it happens to strike somebody before exploding. The French, in the late war with Germany, made a great deal of the fact that German artillery was so much superior to theirs that they were under the shell-fire of the enemy long before their artillery could reply, and yet of the losses sustained by the French in this war it has been found that not more than five per cent. were inflicted by the Prussian artillery, with all its boasted superiority. In my opinion, in the wars of Napoleon artillery was a far more effective arm on the field of battle than modern artillery with all its improvements. When fifty pieces of cannon, massed into line, belched forth a storm of grape and canister into the enemy's ranks at the distance of five hundred yards, the effect must have been very different from that of shells fired at the distance of two or three miles, and smothering themselves in the soft ground without doing anybody any harm.

The improvement in small arms has rendered the old-fashioned artillery quite out of the question, just as it has made cavalry, as cavalry, nearly useless, except for outpost and scouting duty, and rendered bayonet and cavalry charges impossible; but our highly improved modern artillery does not adequately replace the old-fashioned cannon beloved of Napoleon. At any rate, the next battle of Plevna will not be decided by artillery. Both Turks and Russians have shown how little they care for shell-fire, and besides, the Russians, it seems, can bring very few pieces to bear, owing to the peculiarity of the ground, while the Turks have not shown themselves to be very skilful in the management of their artillery. The battle will be fought almost entirely with the bullet, and it will be one of the most terrible, if not the most terrible, of the century. The Turks will fight with all the desperation given by the knowledge that they are really defending the passage of the Balkans, and that if completely victorious here they will have brought the campaign to a successful conclusion. The Russians will fight animated by a knowledge of the same facts, all the bitterness of defeat, and the desire for vengeance upon the barbarians who mutilate prisoners, wounded and dead alike.

The Turks are supposed to have 70,000 men here, and the Russians will bring to the attack at least 100,000, with which force the Turkish positions may be attacked in front, flank, and rear at the same time. If the minimum of skill and generalship is displayed by the Russian generals, more than which we cannot hope for, the result cannot be doubtful—the Turks are sure to be beaten; but if they conduct the attack with the sort of imbecile neglect which allowed the Turks to get possession of Plevna—with the hesitation, want of decision, carelessness, and disorder which marked Krüdener's attack, then I should say the Russians are sure to be beaten. Everything considered, however, I must say I think the result not doubtful. The Russian generals will display at least a minimum of military skill, and they will inflict a crushing defeat upon the Turks.

No sooner had the Russians taken breath after their severe defeat before Plevna, than General Skobeleff sought permission to do something to restore the spirit of the troops. His chief, however, would hear of nothing more than a reconnaissance, which was carried out in the manner described in the following letter :—

† HEIGHTS NEAR LOFTCHA, *August 6th.*—General Skobeleff pushed a strong reconnaissance to-day against Loftcha. Leaving the Grand Duke's headquarters three days ago he took five battalions of infantry, his own brigade of cavalry, and two batteries of horse artillery, and came out on the Selvi road half way between Selvi and Loftcha. His right wing, composed entirely of cavalry, advanced and occupied several villages encircling Loftcha, from the Plevna road to the Selvi road. He then advanced his artillery on the Selvi road to the heights a mile distant from Loftcha overlooking the town, opened fire with sixteen pieces of artillery, and pushed forward his infantry.

It was evident from the moment the heights were reached that the reconnaissance could not be turned into an attack. From fifteen to twenty thousand troops could be seen camped in and about the town, while the low hills immediately surrounding the town were strongly intrenched. There is a strong redoubt on a low hill overlooking the Plevna road, while a high, steep hill on the Selvi side is covered with trenches. There were twelve guns in position and a considerable number in reserve visible.

General Skobeleff nevertheless resolved to feel the enemy, and the hills soon resounded with the roar of artillery and the noise of shells. The Turks replied at once, and for a time there was a lively artillery fire. The Turkish artillery practice was very fair. Several shells fell near the Russian guns, but as the ground was very soft—we were planted in a vineyard—they rarely exploded, and when they did explode they only threw up the earth a little, doing no harm. General Skobeleff only lost one man by the shell-fire.

I observed the same fact on the right flank, where the cavalry advanced within point-blank range of the Turkish guns and opened fire with two small pieces of horse artillery. The Turks replied, and shells fell continually among the horses and men of the battery without doing any harm, owing to their not exploding until too deep in the ground. There was a panic on the Turkish skirmishing line at first, but they soon perceived they had only cavalry to deal with, and were not long in recovering their positions. But they did not attack, nevertheless.

In the meantime General Skobeleff had pushed forward his infantry, and my attention was soon directed to his side by a heavy fusillade. From where his guns were placed the road leads down a narrow hollow, whose sides were covered with woods, down to the foot of the steep hill which was occupied by the Turks in intrenchments. The infantry went down partly under cover of the woods, but not unperceived by the Turks, who poured a heavy fire into the woods. The Russians pushed forward, however, and in much less time than I could have thought had reached the foot of the hill. They announced their arrival with a shout, and to my surprise, knowing no attack was intended, I saw them begin to dodge up the hill two or three at a time under cover of the bushes and little hollows with which such hills are usually covered. It began to look like a real attack. The Turkish fire grew heavier and heavier, until it was one continuous roll, far more terrible than the heaviest artillery fire, because a hundred times more destructive.

It was evident from this fire that the Turks were three times as numerous as the Russians. An assault under such circumstances would be madness, and I was beginning to wonder if Skobeleff could really be madman enough to attempt it. Suddenly I saw a small party of horsemen dashing down the road within full view of the Turks, and within easy range of their fire, and perceived in a moment Skobeleff. He was mounted on a white horse, and wore a white coat, offering a splendid target for sharpshooters. As I afterwards learned, he, like myself, began to perceive that the attack was growing far too serious, in spite of his orders, and was now going forward to stop it. The soldiers were, it seems, determined on an assault, and the officers maintained, when reproached by Skobeleff, that they could not restrain them. I saw Skobeleff stop apparently to give an order, then saw him dismount, get on another horse, while the white Arabian was led back. He had received a bullet. His escort, which had been composed of six Cossacks, was now reduced to three, the others having been more or less seriously wounded, one mortally.

The fire was still raging along the Turkish intrenchments, and the Russians were still pushing forward. Skobeleff, mounting another horse, a sorrel this time, again galloped forward.

He reached the foot of the hill evidently shouting and gesticulating, while his trumpeter sounded the retreat, apparently with effect, for the skirmishers began to withdraw. Then I saw him go down, horse and man together, and I said to myself, "He has got it this time." He had had two horses killed under him at Plevna. If it is the horse only, it makes the fourth within ten days. It is impossible for him to go on in this way long without getting killed. He is fairly under the Turkish intrenchments, and within easy range of the Turkish fire, which is growing stronger and stronger. They are evidently getting reinforcements from the other side, where they are only threatened with cavalry. The roar is continuous, and rolls up and down the hollow like one continuous crash of thunder, only broken by the heavier booming of the artillery. The bullets must be falling about there like hail. It will be a miracle if Skobeleff comes out of it alive.

Here a cloud of dust and smoke gathered for a moment, and was swept away by the wind two or three minutes later. I then saw Skobeleff again on another horse, fresh as ever, coming back up the road at a trot. He had not received a scratch. The reconnaissance was now over. The troops retired as they came through the wood under the Turkish fire, which was not here very effective. The whole loss was five killed and twenty wounded on this side—rather heavy for a mere reconnaissance. Had the troops not been stopped in time, they would simply have been annihilated, as several battalions and regiments were at Plevna. It is impossible to attack the Turks in fortifications without greatly superior forces, unless the positions can be turned.

Skobeleff retired about two miles, camped, and made his report. I do not know what was its nature, but it is very evident no attack can be made on Loftcha until the Russians are ready for an attack on Plevna likewise; and no attempt can be made on Plevna until the arrival of more troops from Russia. The Turks greatly outnumber the Russians all along the right bank, and, according to all military rules, ought to attack. A successful attack upon the Russian forces before Plevna would necessitate the evacuation of Tirnova, and either the abandonment of the Shipka and Kezanlik Passes, or the isolation of the forces holding those passes. If the Turks could fight as well on the offensive as on the defensive, they would soon bring the campaign to an end, for this year at least. As seems likely, the Russians will attempt nothing against either Plevna or Loftcha for a month at least. The reconnaissance to-day can have no other object but to annoy the Turks.

When we returned to camp I fcund the Kirghiz whom Skobeleff

brought with him from Khokand sitting on the ground crying over Skobeleff's horse, which he had also brought from Khokand—a splendid animal that did eighty miles the other day without feeling it apparently, while a fine English mare Skobeleff had was completely knocked up, and had to be killed. The Kirghiz, although himself slightly wounded, had brought the horse back from under fire, and finding there was no hope of saving him, killed him, skinned him, cut off his hoofs, came into camp, sat down, and had a good cry without paying the slightest attention to his wound. He had been utterly indifferent when other horses were killed; but this one, he said, was his countryman and brother—the only thing he had to remind him of his far-away home. I saw tears rolling down the poor fellow's cheeks in a stream. He got two bullets through his clothes, one of which made a flesh wound in his arm. He likewise had two horses shot under him at Plevna.

This reconnaissance has been the most thorough and best conducted of the war. Had there been such a one pushed against Plevna before the battle the result would undoubtedly have been different.

† BETWEEN SELVI AND LOFTCHA, *August 7th.*—General Skobeleff purposely camped yesterday in dangerous positions near Loftcha in order if possible to induce the Turks to attack. The right wing, composed of cavalry, was to the left of the Selvi road, about four miles from Loftcha. What made the position tempting for the Turks to attack was that there were three roads from Loftcha, which rejoin the Selvi road about three miles behind us, making it the most natural thing for the Turks to attempt to cut us off from Selvi by turning either the right or left flank, or both.

This morning it looked as though the Turks were disposed to profit by the opportunity to undertake something against us. First a large number of troops, nearly a division, were reported moving along the road towards Plevna from Loftcha, which at first looked as though the Turks were abandoning Loftcha. A more likely explanation, however, was that this was a body of troops on its way to Plevna from the south, having stopped overnight at Loftcha. The Turks, it seems, are still concentrating at Plevna, and they are right, for there will be fought the decisive battle of the war. An hour later, information was received that a strong demonstration of cavalry and infantry was being made against our right flank, which was obliged to withdraw slowly. Two hours later, Colonel Orloff reported that a strong force of infantry and cavalry was still driving him back. As this movement, if continued, would result in our being cut off from Selvi, where there is a strong Russian force, it became necessary to withdraw, and about noon the General gave orders to march. About this time we received information that the Turks were advancing upon us by the Selvi road likewise. Although this report proved to be incorrect, Skobeleff determined to make a counter demonstration in order to give his baggage plenty of time to withdraw.

He took two cannon, protected by two squadrons of cavalry, and advanced again towards Loftcha, expecting to meet their advanced guard, to which he intended to give a warm reception. We advanced along the road without meeting anybody until we reached the position where the guns were planted yesterday. The Turks had either changed their minds or else the movement was only a stratagem. So the General planted his two guns on the same spot as yesterday, and opened fire a second time, to which the Turks instantly replied. We sent them a dozen shells by way of informing them we cared nothing for their demonstration on our right flank, and then, as the main part of the detachment had got fairly under way, we withdrew.

As we retired we saw a number of troops with a broad red band round their caps, who looked suspiciously like Turks. It was the road by which the Turks would advance in case the right wing were completely driven back, and if the rest of our army had gone on—as was possible—then these were Turks. In that case our two squadrons and two guns were completely cut off from the rest of the detachment. Our little column was tightened up, and everything made ready for a desperate stand until the rest of the detachment, warned by the roar of the cannon, should come back to our relief. The result showed how well the General had taken his dispositions for retreat. These troops proved to be our own, placed there to hold the road until we should get back.

We are camped here in a beautiful spot, awaiting events. The General proposes meantime to employ his cavalry to disperse the gathering Bashi-Bazouks, who are beginning to form in considerable numbers since the Russian defeat at Plevna.

* Bjela, *August 9th.*—I am well aware that efforts have been made to depreciate the significance and importance of the Plevna reverse. Military critics of experience and position have been inclined to make light of it, and hold the view that

the Russians might with impunity disregard Turkish forces looming ominously on both their flanks on this side of the Balkans, and pursue their advance on Adrianople regardless of their threatened communications.

I do not care to discuss the quixotry of abstract possibilities. There are rules of warfare for which experience has given warrant, and respecting which experience proves that their disregard, in nine cases out of ten, results in disaster. I formed my estimate of the results of the Plevna reverse on the battle-field. It was a forecast; and amid the groaning of the wounded and the whistling of the shells, the calm pulse demanded for a deliberate and passionless realization of the position, and its bearing on future events, is liable to fail a man; but the results have shown that I correctly estimated the significance of the reverse.

It has been said that two days after the defeated attack the Russians had so recovered their organization as to be able to renew it. It was for them of paramount importance to do so, had it been possible; but they stand waiting for the necessary reinforcements, thankful to fortune that they are not assailed in their defensive positions. My forecast of the gravity of the results of the Plevna reverse has been borne out to the letter by the Russian appreciation thereof. That reverse has altered the whole plan of the campaign.

No more reckless, if victorious, raids now. No more advances, regardless of threatening concentrations on the flanks. The Russians have virtually abandoned the expectation of pressing the war successfully across the Balkans for this year. It will suffice them if during the three months still available for fighting they can sweep Bulgaria north of the Balkans clear of the Turkish armies. The Crescent must wave over the towers of Adrianople and the waters of the Golden Horn for yet another winter. The Russians will, indeed, continue to hold the Balkan passes which they have won. A man does not throw away the keys which open the door of the treasure chamber. But the orders are to withdraw from all the trans-Balkan positions occupied, and to draw in around the Shipka Pass, this from no direct pressure of the Turkish forces beyond the Balkans, but because of the intrinsic risk always attending unsupported advances when they cease to have a definite object. Eski-Zagra has been abandoned by the retiring Russians. It is averred that there was no battle and no defeat there; that the Russians simply marched out and then the Turks marched in, and a bad time ensued for the Bulgarian portion of Eski-Zagra. Everywhere it must fare badly with the Bulgarians who, when the Russians came, cheered, and shouted, and clamoured for arms to assail the Turks wherewithal. Now they are left to the tender mercies of the Circassians and Bashi-Bazouks.

Now to speak of this side the Balkans. The paralysis brought about by the Plevna reverse still endures. The Russian attitude for the time is perfectly passive till the reinforcements arrive. Seven fresh divisions, not formed into army corps, are now on the march. Some are still in Russia, others are pressing on through Roumania. One hundred thousand men more are wanted, and are forthcoming, but they will have to be waited for. The first brigade of reinforcements is expected to cross the Danube in a few days. It is hoped that once the tide sets in a brigade will cross daily. The offensive will, no doubt, be recommenced before all the reinforcements are to hand. But a large proportion of them are indispensable for a renewed offensive. Plevna must fall, and Osman Pacha must be struck with a decisive blow. At present he can be only watched with intent to hinder further intrusion.

The Grand Duke Nicholas is in Bulgareni, in rear of the intrenched positions of Schahofskoy and Krüdener, confronting Plevna. Part of Mirsky's division stands between Tirnova and Loftcha to hinder a Turkish advance in the direction of the former important centre. Thus are stopped the gaps through which was threatened the right flank of the Russian communications, and the defensive protection is probably sufficient, but the means are utterly inadequate for a renewed offensive. It is estimated that now from sixty to seventy thousand Turks stand on the Loftcha-Plevna line, and they will take a deal of beating.

On the left flank equally a strictly defensive attitude is enforced by circumstances. There are available for holding the line from the Danube to the Balkans on this flank the two corps constituting the army of the Czarewitch, and the 1st Division of the 11th Corps, left behind by Schahofskoy when he marched on Plevna, in all about 60,000 men, necessarily attenuated over a long front, so as to leave no gap for the Turks to creep through.

The Turks are probably of about the same strength, but theirs is the advantage of choosing where to strike if they care to strike at all. Mehemet Ali Pacha may concentrate at Rustchuk or Rasgrad or Osman Bazar. The Russians must be ready to face him everywhere. They dare not take the offensive and leave tracts of unguarded flank. They are not strong enough to guard a continuous flank and take the offensive as well. There remains for them only the rôle of the strict defensive. The investment of Rustchuk must wait. The troops designed for that duty are needed elsewhere. The siege cannon are not ready if the troops were available. The River Lom still virtually constitutes the line of the Rustchuk Army, but the headquarters of the 12th Corps have been moved beyond it, from Trestenik to Kadikoi. The headquarters of the Czarewitch, with the 13th Corps about them, have advanced from Obertenik to Kaceljevo, thus confronting Rasgrad, while between Osman Bazar and Tirnova the 11th Division stands with its headquarters in Kosarevac.

Zimmerman is where he was, no further south than Trajan's Wall. It is stalemate with him. He is guarding the Dobrudscha against an enemy who does not threaten it. He cannot push forward with his thirty thousand men lest enemies from Varna and Shumla should converge upon him.

The Russian army begins to suffer in health owing in some corps to irregular rations, in others to hard marching, in all to heat; but the greatest predisposing cause is the total neglect of all sanitary precautions. They never bury dead horses or oxen, or the entrails of slaughtered cattle. They never dream seemingly of the wisdom of the latrine system. The result is a general tainting of the air, which poisons men predisposed to fall ill by reason of lassitude from over-fatigue or long abstinence from food, although men in stalwart health escape. Strangely enough, the greatest proportion of illness has manifested itself in the personnel of the Imperial suite, whose members are comparatively nursed in the downy lap of ease and fare sumptuously every day. General Ignatieff for three days was dangerously ill from a species of gastric fever, and is still confined to his room. Prince Galatzin has been equally ill from the same disorder, and is still in bed. The Emperor has five high officers known as general-adjutants on personal service about him. Of these but one is now fit for duty; the other four are ill. Nearly everybody is more or less sick, squeamish, and out of sorts. The reason is not far to seek. When I first came to Bjela it was fresh and sweet; now it has more stinks than Cologne, and the slums of Strasburg are a nosegay to it. The air is tainted thick and heavy with filth and rotting offal. Even tobacco smoke and brandy are powerless to avert nausea.

* SISTOVA, *August 10th.*—The official return of the loss at Plevna is 1,000 killed and about 4,500 wounded. The severity of the first estimate is mitigated by the coming in of individual stragglers days after the battle. It must, however, be impossible to distinguish between the killed, wounded,

and missing of such a battle, where the field remained with the enemy, and it is wiser to put the total loss at five thousand five hundred, if the official returns are to be relied on. It may be remembered that my estimate on the evening of the battle was between six and seven thousand. This was lower considerably than that of the Russians themselves, while German eye-witnesses have called it ten to eleven thousand.

The first brigade of the reinforcements is a splendid rifle brigade of four battalions. It is now at Simnitza, and will cross to-morrow. Its destination is the Plevna front. The resolution has been at last definitely taken to bridge the Danube at Pirgos also.

Between the bridge-head and Sistova the correspondent of the Agence Havas was last night assailed by a Russian soldier, who felled him with a bludgeon, filled his mouth with sand, and attempted to rob him. He was rescued by four marines, who apprehended the soldier. The correspondent is lying in the hospital at Simnitza. The soldier was punctually shot here at noon to-day. This is an isolated case of ruffianism which might occur anywhere, day or night. I have journeyed alone and unarmed among the Russian soldiers, and so far from being injured and insulted have always experienced courtesy. I do not attribute this to the fact that I am a full-sized kind of man, but to the innate docility and acquired discipline of the Russian soldier, and a single instance of ruffianism must not be allowed to tell against him.

* SISTOVA, *August 10th.*—I keep asking myself the question whether it is well or ill for the Russians that the Turks on their flanks in Bulgaria remain so fixedly in their intrenched positions instead of playing the bold and strong game of the offensive. I confess I find myself unable to answer with any degree of confidence the question which I thus put to myself. That it was well for the Russians that Osman Pacha did not take the offensive immediately after the battle of Plevna I can unhesitatingly affirm. Probably he did not lose heavily in that combat, stubborn and hard-fought as it was, and I can scarcely suppose there was much, in an abstract military sense, to prevent him from moving forward on say the 1st of August —the day on which the Russians, having pulled themselves somewhat together after the first crushing shock of the reverse, had been countermanded by their leaders from the half-effected retreat on the line of the Osma, had recovered some cohesion in the positions they had occupied previous to advancing to the attack, and were engaged in

adding by intrenchments to the strength of their foothold there.

That, although the attitude was not a cheerful one, the stout soldiers of Schahofskoy and Krüdener would have fought a hard fight, had Osman Pacha assailed them on that day, I make no doubt. The Russian soldier, so far as I have seen, may be relied upon to make a good fight of it whenever he is asked. But I cannot convince myself that, shaken by previous reverse, attenuated in strength by the losses incurred therein, and with their original great numerical inferiority, the Russian troops would have been able to hold their ground on the Trestenik-Poradim front against a determined attack made on a broad front by the whole force of Osman Pacha. Had they been broken by that attack, no practical soldier will deny that the recovery of Nicopolis would scarcely have been difficult for the Turkish general, and that there could have been not very much to prevent his grasp closing on the very neck of the Russian communications—the bridge at Sistova—if he had pursued his advantage with energy and promptitude. Between the line formed by Schahofskoy's and Krüdener's men and the bridge-head under the knoll below Sistova, there stood not a single Russian battalion.

Once beaten and broken in the Poradim-Trestenik position, it would have been impossible for the Russian troops to have so pulled themselves together as to make a stand on the line of the Osma against a renewed attack followed up briskly; it would have been exceptional good fortune and a highly creditable exploit could they have so retarded the Turkish advance as to have given time for the Russian army of Rustchuk to move from its positions on the Lom, and fall back on Sistova in time either to interpose between Osman Pacha and the bridge, or so to threaten his flank by their approach as to make him arrest his progress out of consideration for his own safety. Regarding all these things—and they must be regarded, for it is the acme of rash folly to contend that all military rules and cautions may be thrown to the wind, because of a foregone conclusion that the Turks will never take the offensive—I say then that there can be no sort of doubt it was eminently well for the Russians that Osman Pacha contented himself with despatching to Constantinople hyperbolical telegrams respecting his success, instead of following up that success by a swift and determined advance.

But this is no answer to my self-put and self-unanswered question, whether it is well or ill for the Russians that the Turks are still continuing passive in their positions. That these are too strong to be assailed the Russians confess by the maintenance on their part of a passive attitude pending the arrival of reinforcements. It is not that the ardour for the fray is quenched in them. On the contrary, they would desire nothing better than a pitched battle on each flank, if only a pitched battle could be compassed. They are confident of beating their enemy in the open field. But when that enemy firmly and respectfully declines to come out into the open, the affair assumes another aspect. If the Russians under these circumstances were to take the offensive, they would be fighting against soldiers and earthworks as well, and the task with their present strength is simply too much for them. So they are waiting while every nerve is being strained to hurry up reinforcements. The flower of the Russian army, the Guard Corps, is on the way, and Roumania is experiencing another inundation. I do not for a moment question the ability of a Russian army, even if of considerably inferior strength, to conquer a Turkish army in a battle fought out fairly in the open. Such a trial of strength, I apprehend, would be great luck for the Russians. But how unlikely is it to befall them! How impossible, rather, while standing on the defensive along a line long drawn out! The axiom that a chain is no stronger than its weakest link is true also of an army in the position I describe. Convergence is almost impracticable—wholly so, if the attacking force should strike promptly, strongly, and without affording previous indications of its intention.

And then comes the question whether the Turks are acting wisely by standing still as they are doing on what may be called the menacing defensive, instead of trying actively to improve the opportunities which undoubtedly lie open to them. No doubt they would risk much by becoming the assailants. They must know themselves better than we know them, and it may be the outcome of that knowledge that keeps them stationary in their positions, with spades as well as swords in their hands. Were they to take the offensive and succeed, great indeed would be their success. We should all say then that the game had been worth the candle. But were they to be defeated, great indeed would be the defeat and its consequences, and the world, following its time-honoured practice, would call them rash fools who had thrown away the splendid chances which Fabian tactics offered.

Well, it is certain that so far the Fabian tactics have prospered not a little. There can be little doubt that when the seven divisions now on the way to reinforce the Russian armies arrive, the Grand Duke Nicholas will have men enough at his disposal to clear Bulgaria proper before the winter—that is, Bulgaria north of the Balkans—of Turkish armies in the field. Before the time comes for going into winter quarters, Rustchuk ought almost certainly to have fallen, and probably Silistria and Widdin also; there would then remain only Shumla as a Turkish foot-hold on this side of the Balkans. But this is the full measure of the Russian expectations now, and they have to face the terrible difficulty and cost of wintering on this side the Balkans, and of renewing the campaign in the spring. They have to take note of any number of series of contingencies apart from inevitable difficulties and expenses. Pestilence may break out among their dense masses. Political complications may interfere to hamper military dispositions. There are strong indications that the war may become unpopular in Russia. In the army already nostalgia is becoming a power.

Probably few of your readers have so much as attempted to realize how terribly severe must be the strain on the resources of Russia, of her armies wintering on and across the Danube. We know something of a strain of a similar character, although our army in the Crimea was a handful compared with the Russian hosts, and we could land supplies within a few miles of its front. The army will have to be housed—it cannot abide in tents during the inclemency of a Bulgarian winter. Now, in Bulgaria the villages are few and far between; they afford the scantiest accommodation. Wood is so scarce that none is available for hutting purposes; it will not even suffice for furnishing fuel for cooking, let alone for warmth.

The crops in Bulgaria have this year been good, but much of the grain has been left unreaped on the fields, and probably on an average not above half a harvest has been garnered. Including flocks and herds, Bulgaria probably is not equal to the task of furnishing more than a month's subsistence for the Russian armies. Roumania cannot wholly supply the deficiency. The Danube is no longer a high road. The roads through the Carpathians from Transylvania and the Bukovina are impassable in winter. There must be long periods of broken weather, when communications all over the country, from the Russian base up to the army, will be wholly impracticable. If the winter is an open one, as was last winter, the Danube will not be wholly frozen over, so as to admit of traffic on the ice, while the floating ice will necessitate the removal of the bridges. The cost of maintaining for five months 300,000 men at a distance of several hundred miles from their base in Russia might well give infinite concern to the richest country in the world.

* SISTOVA, *August* 13*th.*—Two days of continual rain have so cut up the roads in Roumania as for the time almost wholly

to arrest communications and stop the march of the troops between Alexandria and Simnitza. The country is one huge morass, and the road a Slough of Despond. Therefore the reinforcements needed for a renewed attack on Plevna are greatly retarded on the march. One division crossed some days ago. Three regiments of cavalry passed yesterday. A regiment of the 2nd Division is crossing to-day, the rest of the division being in the Roumanian mud behind. The Grand Duke Nicholas sent an officer yesterday to Simnitza from the headquarters in Studen to order the reinforcements on reaching the Danube to be pushed forward on Plevna with all possible speed, directing that only half a day's halt should be allowed at Simnitza before crossing the river.

The weather has now again become rather more settled; but the rain has injured an immense quantity of stores left unprotected. I have seen a huge heap of bread sodden into mouldy pulp, and utterly useless, save to feed pigs. Some days must to all appearance elapse before you need expect any important tidings from the Plevna direction. Considerable numbers of Turkish prisoners have been crossing the Danube into Roumania during the last few days, chiefly sent down from about Tirnova, where there had been an accumulation of them.

The Grand Duke's headquarters remain at Gorny Studen, about twenty kilometres from Sistova, where he has been joined by the Emperor and the Imperial headquarters from Bjela. Studen is a mere village, affording the scantiest accommodation. I understand that for the future it is intended that the Army and the Imperial headquarters shall remain united, which seems to imply that the Emperor will encourage his soldiers by actual presence on the battle-field.

* SISTOVA, *August* 16*th*.—I am a prisoner. The Turks have not come swarming over the intrenched battalions of Krüdener and Schahofskoy out there in their bivouacs at Poradim and Trestenik, and I am no captive of the bow and spear of Osman Pacha. I am a prisoner, not of war, but of weather. Ye gods, how it rains! It has been raining hard now, with but little intermission, for three days; and when it rains on the Danube it rains in torrents. Never have I seen such rain, except at the commencement of the monsoon in Bengal, when the sky seems to open and empty on the earth in one terrific downpour the vast contents of some huge celestial reservoir. It is impossible to travel. Even if horses could act, the traveller would require to set forth

in a Boyton suit. Nevertheless, the Russian train waggons are on the move; for troops in the front must be fed, be the weather wet or dry. They come crawling over the bridge, and essay the steep hill leading from the river-side, up on to the high ground. The liquid mud at the bottom of the hill reaches to the axles. The waggons stick fast; men soaked to the marrow yell and scream, and belabour the horses, which reply by threatening to lie down in the sea of mud. Then the horses from other waggons are brought, and double and treble teams are hitched on. There is a wild scramble, and the waggons are on the level, the horses trembling and panting.

Now look at the waggons and their contents. Some are laden with sacks of bread and biscuits. These are soaked to a pulp, and brown water, thickened and coloured with the coarse flour, is streaming from the bottoms of the uncovered carts. Others carry boxes of tea. Some of these have burst because of the swelling of the tea, which has absorbed the wet; and from all a cold infusion of tea-leaves is dripping fast into the mud below. The sugar-loaves with which others are laden are slowly crumbling; "loaf" is becoming "moist" with a vengeance, and a Frenchman might rejoice in the unlimited supply of *eau sucrée* which the profuse drippings of the waggons afford. But the rain is impartial; it does not content itself with sweetening in this way the knee-deep slush; it is bent also on imparting to it a pleasant admixture of a saline character. Some carts are laden with rough salt in sacks, others with huge lumps of rock salt. The latter are stubborn. They wane, but, not so absorbent as the loaves of sugar, they do not become wholly demoralized, but retain their form. But the salt in the sacks is rapidly disappearing bodily. You may watch the rough canvas gradually collapsing as the thick dirty-white fluid oozes through the pores of it. Before the train reaches its destination I reckon that quite two-thirds of the stores it conveys will have been absolutely destroyed.

Fancy troops out in the open in such weather! Our men had a little taste of mud and rain at Dartmoor, and later in the swamps near Pirbrook, but the rain there was child's play to this. And the Russian tents are not like the stout bell-tents of the British army, while many of the Russian troops—the Cossacks for instance—have no tents at all. You may, indeed, trust in God in such weather; but it is impossible to keep your powder dry, and fighting is a physical impracticability. The reinforcements, nevertheless, under the pressure of extreme necessity, are trying to press onward through Roumania, but their progress is very slow, and their plight is pitiable. One day's good heavy rain would have been of service to the Russian army in Bulgaria. It would have purified the atmosphere, laid the dust, cooled the air, and washed away the mass of impurity which makes so noxious the purlieus of a Russian camp. With sunshine on the following day, the men would have dried their clothes, relit their fires, opened up their tents to the sun, and been not a whit the worse. But it is very different under the conditions of this continuous deluge. Everything becomes soddened; the men, hardy as they are, sink in physique, and become soddened like their belongings. Diarrhœa sets in and lapses into dysentery. The weak points of men not wholly sound are found out, and sound men become unsound. The spirits suffer, despondency and nostalgia make themselves felt. The hospitals fill up. If infectious disease once breaks out, it speads with fell rapidity.

I am not theorizing. I speak from well-remembered experience of the army of Prince Frederick Charles, engaged in the siege of Metz, in the wet autumn of 1870—and be it remembered that his army was housed in the French villages, and had a supply base at Courcelles, whither the railway brought provisions to within sound of the firing of Fort St. Jullien. It appears that rain is not common in the month of August in Roumania and Bulgaria, so that the exceptionally bad fortune of the Russians with regard to weather still pursues them. But the inhabitants concur in saying that when at this season the weather does break, the rain endures for a fortnight at a stretch, and that the weather remains unsettled throughout the month of September. In compensation October is dry and fine, and when there has been rain in the summer the winter is late in coming. Last year, in Servia snow fell in the last week of October, and by the first week in November military operations had become impossible. This rain now may give the Russians a longer term for marching and fighting later in the season.

In the meantime military operations are wholly at a standstill. Of course both sides are doing their best in the way of preparation for future work, but the pause in actual fighting for the present seems universal. With the army headquarters within an easy ride of the Danube, and with quietude reigning everywhere, a good many of the officers of the general staff are running across to Bucharest on a short visit of business or pleasure. I saw yesterday on his way back Prince Cantacuzene, who well earned a brief respite from toil and exposure by the gallantry and industry which he displayed throughout the livelong day of the disastrous fighting in front of Plevna. One may be sure there is no fighting in the wind when one sees Prince Wittgenstein for ever so short a time away from the army. There is no more eager fighting man in all the host of the Czar than this bearer of a name so well known in military annals. General Stern, the commandant of the Grand Duke's headquarters, has been to Bucharest for a day,—it may safely be reckoned more on business than on pleasure.

The Turkish quarter of Sistova is now a hospital. All the abandoned houses have been cleared out, furnished with beds and hospital appliances, and filled with wounded men as they came in from about Plevna. I have no great faith in the operating skill of the Russian surgeons. I remember that in Servia, when a difficult case occurred, there was always anxiety to have the services of Mr. MacKellar, Mr. Attwood, or Mr. Hume, the professional representatives of the British Society of the Order of St. John. But in care for their wounded the Russians surpass any nation of whose war making I have had any experience. A great proportion, by far indeed the larger proportion, of the service is voluntary, and tendered with an untiring devotion and free-handed liberality which excite the highest admiration and respect. Ladies of rank forswear comfort and the pleasures of society to come with the army and minister to the wounded. There is no *arrière pensée* in their devotion to this duty. They do not write letters to the Russian papers detailing their experiences, exalting themselves by inferential self-praise, and attitudinizing before the world as paragons of self-abnegation. If you want to know of them and their work, you must seek for them and it. They dress with the most studied plainness—I can recall other scenes where the coif of a comely "sister" has been made to assume a wonderfully coquettish aspect, and where a little flirtation was not unacceptable as the interlude to playing at nursing—and they fare very hard, without a thought of self. They tend Turkish and Russian wounded with equal care, and are zealots in their duties day and night.

One cannot say as much for the supply system of the Russian army as for its hospital arrangements. The subject of the Russian supply is extremely complicated; I have been asking about it ever since I joined the army, and I confess I don't nearly understand it yet. There is a duplex organization—a civilian and a quasi-military organization. A Jewish company, consisting of three brothers named Horovitch, are the contractors for the supply of food to the Russian army, including forage for the horses. They convey supplies, as I understand, to certain central depôts which are specified from time to time, whence the supplies are conveyed by the train carts of the respective divisions or brigades. But there is also a concurrent system of supply from the base in Russia, which is of a military character. The waggons are driven by soldiers, their movements are directed by intendants in uniform, and they are accompanied by escorts. Further, intendants go about purchasing supplies for their own divisions in the same territory where the civilian agents of the Company Horovitch are buying supplies to enable that company to fulfil its contract. This must create mischief by producing competition.

But the duplex system produces confusion as well as competition. But for the absence of red tape among the Russian officials, the realization of the fact that, if men are hungry, they must be fed, and that if cattle are wanted, and are in a neighbouring field, and there is money in the regimental treasury, or, in fact, forthcoming from any source, these cattle are to be purchased—but for this common-sense recognition of the truth that, come what will, men are not to be allowed to starve, there would have been an incalculable amount of distress. If Commissary-General Stiffneck had "declined to take the responsibility" of issuing stores on the requisition of blunt Colonel Straightforward, who saw that his men were hungry and had indented on the nearest depository of rations, and required the authority of the commissary of the brigade to which Colonel Straightforward happened to belong, and the endorsement of General Stubborn, commanding the brigade; and if the commissary of the brigade had returned Colonel Straightforward's requisition as informal because the quantity of pepper required for his regiment was miscalculated by one thirty-seventh part of an ounce, or because the salt needed was entered in the wrong column; and if General Stubborn had refused his endorsement because the commissary sent a clerk for it instead of coming himself; and if, after all formality had been complied with, Commissary-General Stiffneck had still "declined the responsibility of issue," because he had no definite authorization to dispense the stores in his possession, and insisted on a reference to the chief of the department at headquarters—then I believe that among Russian men and horses there would have been a large mortality. The Russians imitate our own army service supply system in its notorious absence of red tape in emergency, and so the soldiers do not starve. But I should not like to have the work of setting straight and systematizing the supply accounts of the campaign in which provisioning has gone on in a manner so varied and miscellaneous. Messrs. Turquand, Young, and Company would find the "European" liquidation with all its complicated ramifications the merest child's play of calculation to such a herculean task as this.

I understand that Colonel Brackenbury, R.A., who has been acting as the Military Correspondent of the *Times*, does not continue his functions, but is going home, recalled by other duties. In one sense I envy him his experiences, in another I commiserate him. He had the good luck to accompany General Gourko throughout the whole of that wonderful raid of his across the Balkans; he had the bad fortune to be unable to forward with any regularity or reasonable dispatch his narrations of the episodes of that romantic ride. It is not from Colonel Brackenbury, but from the officers whom he accompanied, that I have gathered particulars of his experiences in the Balkans. They are loud in their praise of his cheerful endurance of extraordinary hardships, his British coolness under fire, the sagacity as well as the frankness of his comments, and his hearty camaraderie. They tell me that his horse died soon after leaving Tirnova; that he made the march on a casual pony; that he had neither baggage nor supplies, neither blanket, tent, nor even macintosh; that he shared the fare of the common soldiers, black bread and apricots, and slept with them on the dew-laden grass. The Russians just now are not fond of us as a nation, but I have never found them backward in according warm appreciation to individual merit, especially when that merit is of a kind that recommends itself to the practical soldier. General Ignatieff said to me the other day that "Colonel Brackenbury had earned the respect and admiration of every officer and soldier in General Gourko's command,"—praise which I regard as a compliment to the British army. It is fortunate that Colonel Brackenbury's narrative, although delayed by circumstances impossible for him to conquer, is not lost, and it cannot fail to be a valuable contribution to our military literature.

* IMPERIAL AND ARMY HEADQUARTERS, GORNY STUDEN, *August 17th*.—The Emperor is pleasantly quartered in a good house on a slope outside the village, with his suite in tents around. The air is pure in contrast with the stenches of Bjela. The health of the suite is much improved, but General Ignatieff is still ailing, and Prince Galatzin has been obliged to leave for Karlsbad. The Emperor to-day, with the Grand Duke Nicholas, reviewed the 4th Rifle Brigade as it marched from its encampment here toward Plevna. His Majesty

seemed in excellent health and spirits. The reports as to his illness and despondency are utterly baseless. The rifle brigade he reviewed consisted of four battalions of admirable light infantry armed with Berdans. It will constitute a valuable reinforcement for the Plevna forepost work which threatens, pending serious operations, to become rather warm. The reinforcements are taking a somewhat circuitous route in order to leave the direct thoroughfare open for supplies. The Second division has camped on the downs above Akcair. The Third division is on the march about Simnitza or Sistova.

The stream of reinforcement is flowing now steadily down through Roumania. It is expected that both the Guard Corps and the Grenadier Corps, comprising the picked soldiers of Russia, will be in Bulgaria by the first week in September. The staff here calculate that 180,000 men are now actually on the march to reinforce the army. The next battle about Plevna is meant to be decisive, and hence the delay for the sake of ensuring success so far as numbers are concerned. Meanwhile General Zotoff, chief of the 4th Corps, is in command of the Russian troops holding position in front of Plevna, which is now strongly entrenched and armed with artillery. The Grand Duke in person will take the command when active operations begin.

The 4th Cavalry Division has been detached on an independent expedition, for the purpose of stopping the Turkish communication with Sophia across the Balkans, by blocking the Orkhanieh Pass, the main thoroughfare and the easiest marching route over the Balkans. It is felt here that this should have been done earlier, but if successful it will still have good results, and its value in the event of a crushing Turkish defeat at Plevna does not need to be pointed out. It would go far to make another Sedan. The expedition is obviously hazardous, and its fortunes will be watched with great interest.

The Turks at Plevna seem manifesting some intention of taking the offensive, to judge by their pushing cavalry reconnaissances in more than one direction, presumably as feelers. With one of these there was a smart skirmish on the 15th near Tucenica, a village south-east of Plevna, close to the Russian forepost line.

The Russian military authorities think there is some probability that General Zimmermann will be attacked in his position in the Dobrudscha. They have learned that the Turks have withdrawn numerous forces from Asia, and have evacuated Sukhum-Kaleh, bringing away the troops occupying it, along with large detachments of revolted Abhasians, and, having landed these troops at Varna, are concentrating them and others about Bazardjik, which certainly portends operations against General Zimmermann. The command of the sea is invaluable to the Turks, who now enjoy the advantage which substantially enabled General Diebitsch to achieve the success of 1828. General Zimmermann will be reinforced.

There was a bombardment from Giurgevo against the Rustchuk position on the 14th and 15th. It came about by reason of the construction by the Turks of new batteries facing Slobosia and Malarus, the intention being to discover the extent of their armament, and if possible destroy them. The Turkish return fire is reported to be silenced, but earthworks are not easily destroyed by a few hours' shell fire. The mills which grind meal for the Rustchuk garrison were burnt by the shell fire.

General Gourko has left Bulgaria altogether, and gone back to the Russian frontier to resume the command of his own division of the Cavalry Guard, now on the march to the seat of war. His Balkan work has materially enhanced his already high reputation as a dashing cavalry leader. General Radetsky, commanding the 8th Corps, is now in chief command at Tirnova and beyond. The weather is now fine again, and the roads are rapidly changing from mud to dust. I am informed that the recent rains have not materially affected the health of the troops.

Let me give an instance of the manly candour of the Russian military authorities. It cannot be said that my telegram narrating the Battle of Plevna was not perfectly plainspoken. It strove to tell the truth without fear or favour. I may confess to apprehensions that my plain speaking would not altogether be taken in good part, and good-natured friends have freely predicted my expulsion from the scene of operations. I have been sent for by General Nepokoitchitsky, and formally told that telegraphic instructions had been sent from the headquarters to the official newspapers in Russia, to the effect that, pending the preparation of the official report of the Plevna battle, the telegram in question was to be reprinted by them, and accepted as substantially accurate as regards details and results. It is naturally much more pleasant for a Correspondent to chronicle a triumph than the reverse, and I look forward with hope at no distant date to transmit intelligence of a Russian victory.

The following letter presents a summary view of the state of Russian military affairs in the third week in August:—

* RUSSIAN HEADQUARTERS, GORNY STUDEN, *August 22nd, morning.*— A very interesting crisis seems impending in the war, a crisis of extreme technical interest to the student of war and of momentous consequence in a general sense, whatever be its issue. The Russians since the Battle of Plevna have been tied to the defensive, and not always the successful defensive, but as they are invaders it behoves them to resume the offensive, whatever be the hazard, or stand confessed as thwarted in their scheme of invasion. The Turks are standing also substantially on the defensive, but it is a threatening defensive, with occasional and ominous strokes of the offensive. Theoretically, at least, their situation is the better one, since they have the choice of alternatives. They may strike if they consider the chances justify their striking; they may adhere to the defensive if the defensive promises better results; but appearances would indicate that they mean to take the offensive, and as the Russians are tied to this course, the question of the next few days is which side will anticipate the other in taking the offensive. A fortnight should suffice to solve the problem.

According to information on which I am entitled to rely, it is certain that the Russians will not be in an advantageous position to resume the offensive for a week, and it is certain that they will, indeed that they must, do so as soon as they are ready. What an interesting climax of a most interesting period it would be were both sides simultaneously to abandon the defensive and strike blow for blow! Only this must be considered, that the first offensive action of the Russians must necessarily be concentrated against the Turkish Plevna front, while it is in the power of the Turks to strike at the Russians simultaneously all round the edge of the broad oval now in Russian occupation in Bulgaria. It is a nervous time for the Russians till their strength increases sufficiently to put them comparatively at their ease. Any day the blow may fall and strain their resources to the utmost. The Turks by no means allow them to build on the assurance that there will be no hard fighting till the Grand Duke Nicholas gives the signal for his stout fellows to fall on. On the contrary, their attitude is actively menacing all the way round.

On the 16th there was a general reconnaissance in some force by the Turks all along the Russian left flank. From the Danube to beyond the Balkans; from under the guns of Rustchuk, from Rasgrad, from Osman-Bazar towards Bebrova, and at half-a-dozen intermediate places, the soldiers of Mehemet Ali Pacha beat up the Russian positions confronting them. There was not much hard fighting, and probably little loss on either side, but the significance of the business was that the Turks took the initiative.

From the Tundja Valley on the same day a column of Suleiman Pacha's force attempted strenuously to force the Hankoi Pass. It has been reported that success attended this effort, but I am officially assured that this was not so. A Turkish column did indeed force its way into the defile, but was there so roughly handled by the Russian artillery in position, and by a regiment of the 9th Division holding the pass, that it was compelled to retire.

A day or two later a Turkish division made a threatening demonstration from Grivica, a strong Turkish position in front of Plevna. The Turks are by no means resting after this work, now some days past. Up till now they continue to display a modified activity. They struck out from Rustchuk the day before yesterday. On the same day there was fighting, although not serious, before Osman-Bazar. I myself, riding along the Plevna front on the same day, was witness of an artillery skirmish in front of Skobeleff's position near Loftcha, where the Turks began the ball, and the Cossacks under Skobeleff's command are harassed day and night by forepost work. Now, all this may portend the close approach of the Turkish offensive. On the other hand, it may mean simply the determination of the Turkish generals so to employ the Russians all round the semicircle as to hinder concentration on any particular point. Whatever their intentions, it is certain that Turkish policy disturbs the Russian dispositions.

In a recent telegram I told you that the 2nd Division, having crossed the Danube, was massed here preparatory to marching in the Plevna direction. Suleiman Pacha is threatening to attack the Shipka Pass with forty battalions. The defenders of the Pass consist of but twenty companies under General Stoletoff, consisting of the relics of the Bulgarian Legion and three battalions of the 9th Russian Division. The 2nd Division has therefore been diverted from its intended destination, and is being marched on Selvi to relieve a brigade of the 9th Division, ordered to the Shipka. In a recent visit to the Plevna front I was surprised to find that so few reinforcements as yet had reached the Russian troops holding it. Compared with before the battle there is but the addition of the Roumanians, and the 16th Division; but to-day are crossing the Danube eight thousand reserves to fill up the gaps made by the war in the ranks of the 9th Corps which, when these join in a few days, will restore that corps to its full strength. On the other hand, Schahofskoy has marched his brigade of the 32nd Infantry Division back to his original position at Kosarevac, confronting Osman-Bazar, and he will meddle no more with the work he found so hard.

Thus on the Plevna front, when the 9th Corps gets its complement, the Russians will have two full army corps, the Fourth and Ninth—the former is nearly complete, the latter will be wholly so—at least, nominally—two Roumanian divisions of infantry and the 11th Cavalry Division. Skobeleff's detachment, consisting of a brigade of Circassian Cossacks, with some infantry and artillery, is watching Loftcha. There is to be included also the 9th Cavalry Division, and I roughly estimate the whole Russo-Roumanian force confronting Plevna at from sixty-five to seventy thousand men. In this estimate I do not include the 4th Cavalry Division, whose line of detached operation is toward the road through the Balkans from Sophia. The Russians before Plevna are unquestionably inferior in numerical strength to Osman Pacha's army.

To my thinking, the Russians have over-fortified their semicircle of environment. Roughly, they have three lines of spadework, and great indulgence in spadework, or rather in the shelter of spadework, is apt to detract from the prompt, vivacious fighting impulse in the open. The works are rough enough, and the redoubts sometimes are faultily placed on slopes leaning toward the enemy's cannon, and so needlessly exposing their interior instead of crowning the ridge, at once a better protected and more wide-ranging position. But it must be said that the troops have been very industrious, and there can be no question of their anxious eagerness to be allowed to fight again. Indeed, they do not smother their murmurs at the delay, which I do not think will be so long now as most people imagine.

The Russian authorities are greatly pleased with the appearance and apparent efficiency of the Roumanian artillery. Indeed, the Roumanian troops are everywhere now spoken of with a consideration not previously evinced. Information has reached the Russian headquarters that the Turks were organizing a sweeping massacre of Christians in the Bebrova district, between Osman-Bazar and the Balkans, and a cavalry regiment has been sent thither to afford protection.

The Russian corps, brigades, and divisions are curiously split up and intermixed. No importance is apparently attached to the cohesion of any of these integers, and the service does not seem to suffer from this dispersion. The 3rd Division now near here goes forward to Plevna. In my summary of the Plevna force I omitted the 4th Rifle Brigade, now on the march thither from here. The bulk of the reinforcements are somewhat delayed on the way from the Russian base, but the Guard Cavalry Division is expected to cross the Danube in a fortnight, and a brigade per day to follow in a steady stream.

The water is bad here. The Emperor has been slightly indisposed, but is now quite recovered.

The following two letters describe a visit to a number of the Russian positions :—

* TIRNOVA, *August 22nd.*—I had wasted some days at Sistova waiting to witness the crossing of reinforcements which never came, and at length I determined on a sort of roving cruise round the edge of the ground held by the Russians in Bulgaria, terminable at any moment by the prospect of more interesting work turning up.

In the first instance I went westward along the familiar road to the Plevna front. The position of the army there I have already treated of by telegram, and need not recapitulate. In Karajac Bugarski, which village was the headquarters of General Prince Schahofskoy two days before the battle of Plevna, I found established the headquarters of Baron Krüdener. He himself was not at home, having gone to Nicopolis to witness the crossing of the Roumanian cavalry. The chief of his staff was good enough to give me what information I wanted, and I rode on toward Poradim. The reserves, which are arriving to fill up the blanks in the ranks of the 9th Corps, will be very acceptable. One regiment in it can hardly be said to exist, having lost 2,000 men in the first discreditable mischance at Plevna, and others are very much attenuated by the hard fortune of war. All along the fall of the swell between Karajac and Poradim, the Russians have constructed continuous shelter trenches, with any number of little rifle pits in front of them. This is now nominally their third line of defence; it was their first, when on the day after the battle General Zotoff arrived, countermanded the order for the retreat on the line of the Osma, gathered what troops he could find together, and hardened his heart to stand fast. Since then he has wonderfully improved his position and gained a deal of ground, having his forepost line quite closely embracing the Turkish positions. The utility of this will be found when the next battle comes to be fought.

On the 31st July most of the troops under Schahofskoy's command had to march some ten miles before they reached striking distance of the enemy, and although good soldiers will fight under any conditions, however untoward, a wise commander will ever try to bring his men into action as fresh as possible, and, moreover, to let them have their breakfasts before they begin to fight—a precaution which, I understand, was neglected throughout the troops under Schahofskoy's command. It may be said that to see that the men had their breakfasts is scarcely the duty of a general in command of an army, and that if the regimental chiefs are good for anything they must be good enough for seeing to this. I know no better regimental chiefs in the wide world than those of the German army, but nevertheless in his orders issued the evening before Gravelotte Prince Frederick Charles did not omit to ordain that his men should not go into action with empty bellies. "The — corps, quitting its bivouac at — o'clock, will march over — to — and will there halt and cook its food, marching forward on — at — o'clock." I quote from memory the exact form of the order, leaving blank the details; but the Crown Prince's orders at Sedan contained similar instructions, and everywhere the Germans recognized that it is not the Englishman alone who "fights best on a full stomach."

As I rode down into Poradim past the yard where the forlorn staff of Schahofskoy gathered for orders and consultation on the morning after the battle, I passed some companies of the 30th Division tramping down towards the big kettles by the side of the brook, to obtain each man his portion of soup. The companies did not muster strong, for the regiment belonged to that brigade of the division which suffered heaviest at Plevna. I feel very deeply for poor General Powzanoff, the general who then commanded this division, and has suffered disgrace and discredit since for his conduct in the battle. It is an unhappy story, and I prefer avoiding details, but this I would aver with some confidence, that it was not cowardice which prompted General Powzanoff's withdrawal from the field of battle. I believe that he lost his head, but not that his heart failed him. He came into our tent on the afternoon before the battle, and having introduced himself, spoke in a very soldier-like manner of the impending battle. I remember his last remark as he left us: "I hope God will give us all strength to do our duty as beseems Russian soldiers." He is an old man, he had never seen war in earnest before, they took both his brigades out of his hands, and I suppose he went to pieces. The story goes that the Grand Duke sent him away with a fine mixture of arbitrary assumption of profound medical knowledge and of genuine kindly feeling for a soldier in misfortune. "I observe that you are very ill, and that there is no chance of your recovering your health without returning to Russia." "But, your Imperial Highness, I am not ill at all. I never was better in my life!" "Allow me, please, to know better. I can see you are ailing seriously, and I must recommend you to recover your health in the bosom of your family." Such is reported to have been the dialogue.

With the war correspondent the aphorism *omne ignotum pro magnifico* undergoes a modification into *omne invisum pro parvo.* He finds human nature too strong for him, and undervalues that of which he himself has not had the good fortune to have been the eye-witness. There were war correspondents with the Russian army who opined that the battle of Plevna was but a "check"—not a reverse. I remember having heard a funny story reported as having been told by a quaint old Scotch divine. Noah, having embarked his cargo, was engaged in navigating his bark when he was accosted in a friendly and affable manner by the Devil, paddling around in a canoe on the surface of the flood. The point of the story lay in the terms of his Satanic Majesty's greeting to the aquatic patriarch. "Moist weather, Mr. Noah!" were the words which the Scotch parson put in the mouth of Lucifer, and they describe the Flood about as accurately as the term "a check" characterizes the defeat of Plevna. But be it what you will, it will not be through the default of correspondents that the next Battle of Plevna is not described in full detail in probably every land boasting a newspaper. Several congregated prematurely, others came later, but still too early, and Poradim is almost as strongly garrisoned by correspondents as by soldiers.

General Zotoff, who has command of the whole Army of Plevna, has his headquarters there. I had not the advantage of making the general's acquaintance, and, therefore, cannot say whether his leading characteristic appears to be wiliness; but there is one indication that such is the case. The field telegraph wire from the great headquarters in Gorny Studen terminates in Karajac Bugarski, and has not been carried on to Poradim, whither from the previous place all telegrams have to be sent by Cossacks. The electric telegraph is a nuisance always, but is, perhaps, the worst of all nuisances when it communicates between an anxious headquarter and an outlying general. Despatches arrive just as he is dining, messages come even while he is enjoying slumber. Tchernaieff used to say at Deligrad that if any kind friend would abolish the telegraph wire between Belgrade and him he would give a year of his life. But if a general in command elects to be cut off from direct communication with the chief headquarters, there seems no reason why he should neglect to be thus on rapport with the several headquarters of the divisions under his command. I have said that the telegraph is a nuisance, as I suppose not a few of your readers have reason to know. It is an instrument in warfare worth many rifles and sabres. But here is this Plevna army with its headquarters unconnected by wire with a single subsidiary headquarters. It is wearisome to speak even in terms of comparison—ever odious—of the German army as contrasted with the Russian army, but at least I may urge that the German army is the Russian model, and I cannot resist the impulse to say that I have seen a telegram expedited from the headquarters of a Prussian general ten minutes after they were fixed at the end of a twenty-mile march, the setting up of the field-telegraph having kept pace practically with the march of the troops. Every Russian division has a telegraph train attached to it, whose drums contain a hundred versts of wire, yet the Czarewitch was days at Obertenik on the road to Rustchuk, without telegraph communication with the Imperial headquarters at Bjela, barely fifteen miles in his rear.

In the Plevna Army I found a strong belief existing that there would be no Russian action for a fortnight at least. I have since heard that the term named may probably be shortened, but if I were to venture my own individual opinion it would be to the effect that quite a fortnight will elapse before there is fighting at Plevna, if the initiative is permitted to remain with the Russians. I believe that twelve heavy siege guns are about to be brought up—whether for defence or for offence I know not. I only know that about Plevna I have seen nothing to bombard with as the term is distinguishable from the term to shell. If the Russians are to begin bombarding field works with heavy siege guns, the Turks may show a front before Plevna till you in England are cooking your Christmas puddings, and longer. The road to Plevna is in through the back door, while a continuous rat-tat is being kept up on the front door.

Of the strength of the Plevna force I have this morning sent you an estimate, which is, perhaps, on second thoughts, somewhat overstated. One may speculate in vain as to the thoughts of Uriah the Hittite when he found himself placed in the fore part of the battle, since he has left us no record of his emotions; but I imagine they must not have differed materially from those now felt by the Roumanian cavalry division in the singularly hazardous excursion across the River Vid, on which by order they have embarked. In a very short time, as a sententious Russian put it to me, the Roumanian cavalry will be either heroes or mincemeat.

Poradim was very drowsy when I left it late in the afternoon, to ride eastward through Bulgareni, to the head-quarters at Gorny Studen, there to gather some details concerning a movement of which a hint had reached me. In a previous letter I tried to describe the devious course of the river Osma about Bulgareni. On the main chaussée (conventionally) running east and west, the bridge over the river had gone, and a long détour had been necessary to reach a high peaked stoné bridge crossing the river a little to the north-west of Bulgareni. As I rode across this bridge on the morning after the battle, when a surging mass of vehicles was struggling for the precedence of single file, it struck me how disastrous would have been the result had the Turks pursued. The river Osma, although narrow, is a deep trench, seldom fordable, and this bridge, eight feet wide at the most, and with a very lofty and difficult pitch, was the sole means of crossing it in Schahofskoy's rear. Bulgareni is not twenty miles from Sistova, and a couple of pontoons might have been brought in a few hours—there are plenty of surplus ones on the Danube now. But such a precaution at facilitating the means of retreat, should retreat be necessary, did not appear to have occurred to anybody, and the neglect might have produced a catastrophe equal in its degree, as it would have been similar in character, to the concluding scenes of the tragedies of the Beresina and Königgrätz.

With other men, other counsels, is no unfair assumption, and I certainly anticipated that, to ease the passage of supplies, and facilitate the march of reinforcements, to say nothing of wise precaution, there would by this time have been other means of crossing the Osma at Bulgareni than the old high-keyed bridge. But the anticipation was not justified, although three weeks have elapsed since the battle was fought. The approaches have indeed been dug for two additional bridges, and the military carpenters are chopping away at the massive obsolete structures intended as central piers, and gradually taking such form as enables one to judge that the woodwork of bridges is in preparation. On my return journey, travelling towards Gorny Studen, I suffered for the belief I had dared to cherish that it was impossible but that the Russians should have repaired the bridge on the main chaussée on the main line of march from the headquarters of concentration to the headquarters of operation. I would not cross the old stone bridge, and rode straight into the heart of the deceitful peninsula. There were troops around the villages studding its fertile bosom—it was not possible that they had been marched round by the stone bridge to reach these camping grounds! But when I gained the bank of the Osma, opposite the gap in the hills through which the chaussée route strikes away eastward to Gorny Studen, I found no bridge ready. The men were working at one cumbrous, primitive affair, which will probably be ready in a few days—a commencement had just been made on a second bridge. Such is the progress achieved during three weeks of so-called preparation for another attack on Plevna! Too disgusted to go back, I swam my riding horse across the ugly, sullen Osma; but my waggon had ignominiously to return, and effect the crossing at the original stone bridge.

At Gorny Studen this morning, I was told that Suleiman Pacha is threatening the Shipka Pass, and that the 2nd Division, under the command of Prince Imeretinski, had been sent away to release from Selvi reinforcements for the scanty body of defenders—only about some twenty companies—with which General Stoletoff was holding the Pass. It would be eminently worth while to be there if the threatened attack should actually be made, and I determined to start at once; but, on the other hand, I was cautioned that I would do well to be back at Gorny Studen by the 27th inst., if I wished to witness still more important operations from their commencement. My only hope then was that if there was to be fighting at the Shipka, it should occur on the only day which I had available for witnessing it—the 24th, since it would be necessary for me to quit the Balkans on my return journey to Gorny Studen on the 25th. It was rather a forlorn hope on which to set out on a four days' ride; but then I have never been beyond Tirnova, and a man who is interested in this war ought to see the Shipka Pass simply as the gratification of a legitimate curiosity.

My companions and myself, leaving Gorny Studen this morning before the heat of the day acquired its full intensity, struck almost due south by mere cart tracks linking together the pretty villages in the leafy hollows. No prettier country can well be imagined. It undulates fantastically, and presents continual surprises of diversified surface; but everywhere trees are dotted singly or in clumps, which gives the scene a park-like aspect. There are no soldiers anywhere, save an occasional post of some half-dozen men encamped in a clump of trees on the outskirts of a village, and peace and plenty reign without alloy. On the threshing-floors in their farmyards, the peasants—if peasant is indeed the proper term for a man who owns land, and cattle, and horses—are winnowing the barley-grain from the straw by the time-honoured plan of driving a team of ponies round and round over the straw. Some use the fore-carriage of an ox-waggon with a mass of weighted branches trailing behind; but the ponies are most common in this actual "treading of" the threshing-floor. It is clear that the sufferings under which the Bulgarians north of the Balkans professed to labour at the hands of the Turks could not have been of a kind affecting their material prosperity, for we find them as the Turks left them, wealthy in agricultural possessions beyond any farmer-peasantry of whom I have any cognisance.

The beautiful and romantic Zavrada Pass, which constitutes a natural approach of surpassing grandeur to Tirnova—that surely most picturesque of all towns—can never lose its charm. The combination of water, rock, and foliage is perfect, and every turn in the winding road affords a fresh joy. But while we felt the beauty of the scene, we felt, too, how different from now were the auspices under which we first traversed that pass. We were with the cortége of the Grand Duke when he rode into Tirnova amid the plaudits and the glad weeping of a population beside themselves with joy. Flowers were showered down from the windows, and strewed his path; priests and girls struggled for the honour of kissing his hand. To be with the Russians in Tirnova then was to be a welcome guest, for every door stood open. The strains of triumphal music swept along the quaint narrow streets, and the precipices, amid which the town hangs rather than is built, sent back a melodious echo.

How strong the contrast now! The road up the steep into the town was blocked by a double row of vehicles, one driven by weary and somewhat irritable Russian soldiers, the other by sullen Bulgarians, who have found out with great alacrity that they have rights since the Russians came, and are not only no longer subservient, but even in a tentative way inclined to be uncivil if they can but harden their nerves. The place was never clean, but it is fouler now than ever. Above the entrance stands, gaunt and ugly, the skeleton of a triumphal arch, to which no more clings the last shred of decoration: it looked like the gallows mourning the abolition of capital punishment. The narrow street was a disheartening chaos of vehicles, whose horses scrambled about over the filthy stones; of miserable fugitives squatting listlessly wherever they could find a corner, or trying to push through with their donkeys laden with clothes and children; of Bulgarian civilians foolishly drunk and reeling about over the stones, amid the jeers of the Russian soldiers; of limp Bulgarian lads in uniform, of whom the Russians will persist in trying to make soldiers, a service for which they lack alike heart and stamina; of time-worn men of the original Bulgarian Legion, who having come somehow out of the pandemonium of Eski-Zagra with uncut throats, have drifted back hither demoralized and disgusted; of German-Jew chapmen, selling everything from bad champagne to rubbishing boots; of marketenders seeking shops whereat to replenish their waggons, and of Bulgarian priests walking about in long petticoats.

I went to the house to which on my previous visit I had been welcomed with open arms, and now found some difficulty in getting in—I think, indeed, that I should have been refused altogether had I not recalled to the memory of the landlady the fact that I paid well for my previous entertainment. As for my horses, the only place I could find for them was a wretched subterranean stable under a loathsome khan—a stable reached by successive tiers of rotten and foul stone steps, and when there neither hay nor corn was to be had for them; they had to be fed on bread. It was too late to call on General Radetzky or General Dragomiroff, who I had been told had been both resident in the place. All I could learn was that a mass of troops had marched off the day before in the direction of Gabrova, and that further detachments had gone on later.

* GABROVA, *August 23rd.*—I was heartily glad at an early hour this morning to say adieu to the smells and vermin of Tirnova. It was unpleasant riding for the first mile, but soon we cleared the purlieus of standing camps, and leaving the picturesquely impracticable town behind, entered on the sublime defile by the side of the Jantra, under the shadow of great impending precipices. Presently we quitted the Jantra, no more to see it till we reached the vicinity of Gabrova, and we threaded glen after glen, climbed steep after steep, passed through sweetly-situated village after village, all embowered in foliage, till we reached the Valley of the Drenova, and suddenly found ourselves looking down into the snug-lying town of Drenova. We abandoned for most part of the way the chaussée, with its clouds of dust and long trains of rattling provision waggons, and rode by the narrow hill tracks, which at once shortened the way and made it pleasanter. We rode through thick woods, where dense foliage shaded from the blistering sun-rays, by wimpling streams on which were gurgling mill-races,

and then came the cool splash of the water over the mill-wheel and the scent of the balsams and the thyme from the miller's garden, fringed by willows whose tresses laved themselves in the stream. We rode through verdant meadows, our horses' hoofs whisking aside the rich lush-grass, by babbling fountains, where from the face of a hoary wall which the Romans might have built, but on which the Turks have carved an inscription, springs a crystal jet of clear water, transparent as glass, cold as ice, grateful alike to the parched throat and the burning temples. We skirted vineyards where the heavy masses of dark green foliage but half screened the pale green clusters of grapes just beginning to soften into ripeness, by orchards over whose walls the plum-branches nodded heavy with yellow and purple globes, by detached farm-steadings, each one the habitation of several families, united to each other by the ties of relationship.

The ride would have been an unadulterated pleasure but for the heat and the miserable fugitives. Let me speak first of the minor detraction from our enjoyment. I may claim to know something of heat. I have been in the Red Sea in July. I have ridden with Sir Richard Temple across the parched *maidans* of Bengal in the month of May, when the thermometer in the dead of night never fell below 106, and when two indigo planters betted among themselves which of the two of us would the earlier succumb to sunstroke. I know how the Nepaul Terai reeks in the hot season, and I know the hot closeness of a Highland glen in August; but for fierce, cruel, blazing, burning, scorching heat, I have never felt anything to compare with the last ten days in Bulgaria. Somehow, ragingly hot as it is, the heat does not enervate one greatly, for it is a dry heat; but it melts one, it burns one, it so blisters the face that the skin of it becomes painful to the touch. As I write, I look across at my companion, and I can compare him, so far as colour goes, to nothing so truly as a boiled lobster; he returns the compliment with the aggravation that the boiled lobster I resemble in tint must have been boiled in a decoction of burnt sienna.

And now let me speak of those unfortunate creatures who, warned by the fate of their neighbours, have hurried across the Balkans to escape the fell retribution of the Turks. It is not for me now to inquire closely whether when Gourko's Cossacks were in their villages and Leuchtenberg's dragoons clanked along their streets, these Bulgarians were themselves full of nothing save the milk of human kindness toward—or should I say against?—their Turkish co-inhabitants, against whom the current of the fortune of war seemed to be setting so swiftly and steadily. Let us take them as we find them. The whole road from Tirnova to Gabrova, but perhaps more especially between Drenova and Gabrova, seemed one great picnic; but it was an inexpressibly mournful picnic. My artist companion revelled in the picturesqueness of the vivid colours of the women's dresses, but he had no heart to sketch the bivouacs in their profound misery. We were the witnesses not of a few handsful of casual flightlings, but of the general exodus of the inhabitants of a whole territory. There were peasants, but there were also families of a better class—families whose women dressed, not in Turkish trousers, in gaudy-patterned petticoats, and bodices of all the hues of the rainbow, but as the Englishwoman of to-day dresses. There were women to whom you felt it not quite the thing to speak without an introduction, and whose habitation was under a tree; whose means of conveyance was a donkey, on which they sat with a child in front of them, and another clinging behind them. Many had no means of conveyance at all save what God had given them, and one saw women plodding painfully, carrying children in their arms, whom they tried to shade with parasols, poor fond things—the tender folly of motherhood, when homes were blazing behind them, and misery about them and before them.

In Servia last year I had witnessed scenes which faintly foreshadowed those of to-day; but as I rode along, what rose to my mind most vividly were the woeful stories of our own British women in the terrible times of the great Mutiny, when there passed away, all in a moment, the accustomed care for tatties, and punkahs, and thermantodotes, and darkened rooms, and all the manifold appliances of Anglo-Indian civilization; and there suddenly confronted them—and they rose to the occasion—the stern task of striving, under the burning sun, to save the lives of their dear ones. Most of the better-class fugitives told me that they had fled from Kezanlik; but, indeed, the whole population of the southern slope of the Balkans have crossed the ridge, and are now drifting slowly down the northern slope. Many are stationary. They are waiting events. They are not the victims of panic, to whom assurance will only come when a sight of the Danube is attained. They are flying before a near, a tangible, and a fearful danger, but they hail any indication of a prospect of safety for them in returning. The march of troops to-day, of which I shall presently speak, has arrested the flight of great masses of the fugitives. It has done more. I passed a goodly number actually tramping back in the wake of the column. They believed in the safety of Russian bayonets. But then it must be said that most of these came from the villages on this side of the Shipka Pass.

The aspect of Drenova made me long for time to linger over its quaintnesses. It is as picturesque as is Tirnova, but quite in a different style. It owes little of its picturesqueness to its situation. But the houses ! They are almost without exception built with fronts of dark wood, elaborately carved and projecting storey over storey, till the third tier is reached, with outward sloping shutter flaps on the ground floor; in the storeys above, massively grated windows, cut in the woodwork. What adds so much to the effect of houses so built is that along the face of many are carried trailing vine boughs, laden with rich clusters of fruit, which dangle in front of the windows, and give a charming freshness to the street. The architecture has a curious resemblance to that of many houses in the principal street in the Native town of Bombay, and the resemblance is heightened by the circumstance that several of the houses have their fronts rudely but brilliantly painted in fanciful and allegorical designs, chiefly of figures of a wildly impossible type in the present circumscribed condition of the animal kingdom.

I can do what it has never previously been in my power to do in respect to any place of public entertainment in Bulgaria. I can recommend the khan of Drenova as reasonably clean and fairly comfortable. Only it was full—crammed to the ceiling with fugitive families who could afford to pay for a room, or part of a room, pending events. But it was a great thing to get hay and corn for the horses, and a seat or cushion in a passage while we ate the soup and roast fowl which a pretty Bulgarian cook prepared for us. The road from Drenova to Gabrova, although a fair specimen of engineering skill, must be hard work for horses drawing vehicles. But we could not feel for the horses, for admiring the wonderful surprises of the scenery. The only road I know to compare to it in this respect is the route up into the Black Forest from Hausich, on the great Baden plain, to Freiburg, near the ridge where the waters of the Kinsig, flowing into the Rhine, and of the Danube, spring from two fountains not ten paces apart on the slope above St. Georges. During our journey we had seen but few soldiers. Certainly the Russians had left scanty supports between Tirnova and the "twenty companies" of whom my valued informant in Gorny Studen had spoken as constituting for the time the sole garrison of the Shipka Pass fortifications. But in a deep gulley about six miles from Gabrova, we came on the reserve artillery train of two brigades of the 8th Army Corps. The waggons were being dragged up the steep singly by spare teams of horses located there for the purpose.

We descended once more into the Valley of the Jantra, and in a meadow about two miles from Tirnova we found two infantry battalions just recommencing their march after a short halt. Their colonel rode to the rear to give some directions as to the ambulance waggons following, and I recognized an old friend. The first time I met Colonel Duhonin, chief of the 55th, the Podolsk Regiment, was at Jilava, near Bucharest, when he was engaged in paying his men; the second time was on the Turkish bank of the Danube, on the morning of the crossing from Simnitza to Sistova. The blood was then flowing down the blade of his drawn sword from a bayonet wound in the right wrist, which he had received in leading the assault on the height above the ridge. He had wrapped it up, and said nothing about it, but retained his place at the head of his regiment, and now I was pleased to see the Cross of St. George on his broad breast.

Colonel Duhonin and we rode on together into Gabrova, and he told me about the dispositions. The Russians were paying the penalty, in forced marching in broiling weather, of disregarding eventualities. They had determined to hold the Balkan passes they had won—a wise determination, but they had neglected to have troops within easy distance in case they were threatened. Now, Suleiman Pacha is in Kezanlik and looking very grimly at the Shipka, and it is found necessary to reinforce "at the double" the "twenty companies" holding the pass. The 2nd Division had been diverted to Selvi, to relieve a brigade of the 9th Division and be handy for Loftcha. To reinforce the garrison of the Shipka there has been hastily gathered together the 2nd Brigade of the 14th Division—Dragomiroff's—of the 8th Corps, the 2nd Brigade of the 9th Division—Mirsky's—of the same corps, and the sorely reduced Rifle Brigade, which has been across the Balkans with General Gourko, and has earned splendid renown, and suffered fearful losses in a dozen fights from Hainkoi to Karabunar. The first brigade named is commanded by General Petroceni, the second by General Derozinski, and the chief of the gallant riflemen is General Tzwilzinski. Petroceni's brigade has been gathered partly from about Elena, partly from the villages below Tirnova, and Colonel Duhonin told me so fast and steadfastly had his men marched that they had neither slept nor cooked for two days and two nights. And yet the stalwart fellows were not nearly beaten, but took the road again at a swinging pace and with a hearty chorus. They were marching without knapsacks and without baggage; they had abandoned everything by the way that no delay should occur in their obedience to the peremptory and urgent summons. The colonel was much troubled because his men had insisted in giving away their bread to the hungry refugees, and he did not know where they were to find more. But he has a kind heart himself. At a short halt some refugee women begged him and his officers to take their children and educate them in Russia, where there were not Turks. "All in good time," was his reply. "We are going to fight now. When the Czar wills that we go home to Russia, then we may think of your children. God knows we are thinking of our own now."

As the column tramped through Gabrova the people gave bouquets of sweet flowers and wild thyme to the soldiers, and crowded on the flanks with copious supplies of water. Duhonin and his men went on. I have stayed for the night in the town, where I am told are General Radetzky, commanding the 8th Corps, and General Dragomiroff, commanding the 14th Division; but I have been unable to find either. Most of the houses in Gabrova have been emptied of furniture to facilitate the quick flight of the inhabitants. I am in quite a mansion, but it contains not so much as a rug.

* GABROVA, *August 24th, Evening*.—Since I wrote the above, I have visited the Shipka Pass, and seen a battle. There is no time to write letters which the telegraph will supersede, and the necessity for reaching an available wire compels me to arrest at this point my intended ride round the Russian positions.

The following letter from another correspondent gives further details respecting the situation before Plevna and elsewhere.

† HEADQUARTERS OF THE ARMY BEFORE PLEVNA. PORADIM, *August 23rd*.—The mistake made by the Russians after the Battle of Plevna in not concentrating the whole army against Plevna, and taking it, is already beginning to produce its result. The Turks have been receiving reinforcements more rapidly and in greater numbers than the Russians, and are beginning to take the offensive all along the line. News was received here two days ago that large Turkish forces were concentrating in the valley of the Tundja against the Shipka Pass; and an order was immediately sent by the Grand Duke for the Shipka Pass to be reinforced. I am not allowed to say whence these reinforcements were taken, but the fact seems to be that this movement on the part of the Turks was not calculated upon, and was not provided for.

To-day news has arrived that the Turks are driving the Russians back on the road between Osman Bazar and Tirnova, though it is not yet stated whether anything like a decisive battle has taken place there. Simultaneously with this, the information has arrived that 30,000 men under Suleiman Pacha, already spoken of as concentrating before Shipka, had attacked the Russian positions in the Pass with great vigour and resolution, and that this attack had been repulsed three times, after a struggle, with great losses on both sides. It is not known here whether the reinforcements sent off reached in time to take part in the battle, and the Russian position is now so critical everywhere that I do not mention how many troops there were to defend the Shipka Pass.

Not only have the Turks been taking the offensive at Osman Bazar and Shipka, but it has also been reported here that the Russians have sustained a defeat somewhere near Rasgrad, or somewhere between there and Rustchuk, the details of which are unknown here. For two days there has been considerable firing on our advanced posts, as though the Turks were preparing to take the offensive, and great movements of Turkish troops have taken place about Plevna. The day before yesterday artillery was moved out on the high road from Plevna towards Sistova and Nicopolis, together with ammunition trains and large numbers of infantry, as though they were preparing to attack; and the Russians have been on the alert, expecting an attack at any moment. However, no attack has taken place here up to the present, but to-day we hear the thunder of artillery on the right, between the Russian right wing and Nicopolis, where the Roumanians are holding the line; and to conclude all, a strong Turkish detachment has marched out on the road from Loftcha towards Selvi, evidently with the intention of attacking that place. This movement is so serious that General Zotoff has sent a detachment under General Skobeleff from his left wing to take this Turkish force on the flank, and force it to draw back on the right in that disadvantageous position. I am also obliged to avoid mentioning the strength of this detachment.

Reinforcements are arriving very slowly, and although it is known that three out of four divisions have crossed the Danube since the Battle of Plevna, I have not yet been able to ascertain where they have gone, nor can I see any indications of the Russians taking the offensive for a long time yet. What object there may be for thus remaining apathetically on the defensive when they have such imperative reasons for pushing on the war to a rapid conclusion, I cannot imagine, but mismanagement in some quarter is evidently at the bottom of it. It is not likely that the Turkish offensive will produce any great result. I do not believe in the capacity of the Turks to direct an army on the offensive, but always have acknowledged the cohesion of the Turkish troops when fighting behind entrenchments. The mistake made by the Russians after the Battle of Plevna was in not continuing the attack on that place. They should have garrisoned the two Balkan passes and Tirnova and Sistova, abandoned the whole line occupied by the army of the Czarewitch, and then, by rapidly concentrating both armies against Plevna, have crushed it at a blow. They had six army corps even then across the Danube. Of these corps five have scarcely been under fire. Only one, the 9th, has severely suffered; but this corps would have amply sufficed for the defence of Sistova. The other five army corps will give an effective of 125,000 combatants, of which 40,000 might have been used for the defence of the Balkan passes and Tirnova, leaving 85,000 men who would have been concentrated against Plevna, and at that time would have sufficed to take it. Had the Turkish army at Shumla moved across the Jantra to attack the Russian army in the rear it would have been too late, for the Russians would have had time to crush Plevna, and then turn round and crush the Shumla Army in its turn on the open glacis west of the Jantra. Two hard-fought battles would have rapidly crushed both the Turkish armies in succession. There would then have been nothing but the army of Suleiman Pacha south of the Balkans to prevent the onward march, which the Russians could have easily undertaken with the reinforcements now arriving. The result of not adopting this plan will evidently be a second campaign, the winter passed in Bulgaria and the Balkans amidst snow and mud, and the loss by sickness of half the army, and the expenditure of millions.

August 23rd, Evening.—The cannonade heard to-day on our right wing does not seem to have been on the side of the Roumanians. I can only account for it in this way. Three or four days ago General Zotoff sent a strong detachment of cavalry round behind Plevna to reconnoitre the country, burn any stores that might fall into their hands, and destroy bridges and the telegraph. This detachment crossed the road between Loftcha and Plevna. It must be somewhere behind Plevna now, working round towards the right wing. This cavalry may have engaged the Turks somewhere, which would account for the cannonade we have heard.

Russian public feeling is showing itself very much dissatisfied with the military operations. The Russian papers, while admitting the courage of the soldiers generally, speak with contempt of their generals, and include them all in one universal condemnation.

It has been announced that the reconnaissance made by General Skobeleff against Loftcha some days ago, an account of which I have already sent you by telegraph, was an attack in which Skobeleff was repulsed with the loss of four hundred men. The fact is, the affair was merely a reconnaissance. Skobeleff had orders not to attack under any circumstances, and his loss was five men killed and twenty-five wounded. Skobeleff reported that a division and a half would be required to take the place, whereas he had only five battalions, and expected that orders would be given to take Loftcha. Indeed, this was the original intention of the Russian Commander-in-Chief, but a sudden spell of rainy weather caused delay in the attack, and when the roads became passable the offensive was taken up by the Turks everywhere. This induced the Russian Commander-in-Chief to postpone the attack upon Loftcha for the present. I may remark that in the great battle at Plevna Skobeleff, who had the command of the extreme left wing, actually penetrated into the town, and in spite of this fact was the only general who succeeded in carrying off all his wounded, not losing a single man.

CHAPTER XVI.

THE FIGHTING IN THE SHIPKA PASS.

Suleiman Pacha's Determined Attack—Hurried March of Russian Reinforcements—The Shipka Position, its Strength and its Weakness—The Bulgarian Legion under Fire—The Russians all but Surrounded—The Critical Moment—Arrival of Russian Reinforcements—The Rifle Brigade—General Radetzky—The Russians Resuming the Offensive—A Fight in a Wood—General Dragomiroff—Repulse of the Turks—Anxiety at Head-Quarters—The Aides-de-Camp Outstripped—The Emperor and the Correspondent—A Turkish View of the Fighting.

THE third Russian attack on Plevna, delayed by the slowness with which reinforcements arrived, was destined not to take place before a series of most determined attempts had been made by Suleiman Pacha, who commanded the Ottoman troops south of the Balkans, to break through the Russian defences of the Shipka Pass. It was a serious question for the Russians whether, with the troops at their disposal, they could at the same time keep at bay the Shumla Army under Mehemet Ali Pacha, on their left, prepare a new assault upon Osman Pacha at Plevna, and resist the efforts of Suleiman Pacha in the Balkans. The following letter, the whole of which was transmitted by telegraph, describes a visit to the Shipka Pass and a hard-fought battle there, the cause of the abandonment of the tour round the Russian positions, of which a description was given in one of the letters comprised in the preceding chapter:—

* SHIPKA PASS, *August 24th.*—On the morning of the 22nd I was informed at the Imperial headquarters at Gorny Studen that Suleiman Pacha, with an army of forty battalions, having been foiled in an attempt to force the Hainkoi Pass, was now threatening the Shipka. Acting on the maxim given by Prince Frederick Charles to his officers, I at once rode in the direction of the cannon thunder.

In reality Suleiman Pacha had already on the 19th occupied the village of Shipka, and had commenced an attack on the 21st on the Russian positions at the head of the Pass. Fighting has lasted almost continually from then until now, and it is only about an hour ago that an apparently decisive result was obtained. I had been advised at headquarters to overtake the 2nd Division, commanded by Prince Imeretinski, which had been dispatched from Gorny Studen to strengthen the extremely weak force left in the redoubts of the Pass; but later I had learned that the division had been diverted to Selvi to fill the blank left there by the earlier march of the brigade of the 9th Division that had been in position there, to strengthen the Shipka garrison. The 2nd Division at Selvi will also be available for its share in the impending attack on the Plevna-Loftcha line still held by Osman Pacha. I also learned at Tirnova that General Radetzky, commanding the 8th Corps, and General Dragomiroff, commanding the 14th Division of that corps, had gone forward to Gabrova with hurriedly gathered reinforcements for the hard-pressed people in the Shipka Pass.

All the way from Tirnova to Gabrova the country was one vast melancholy encampment, and the road one continuous mournful procession of miserable fugitive families from Kezanlik and the villages on the southern slopes of the Balkans, where the Turks had regained their fell sway of rapine and murder on the withdrawal of General Gourko's force. Most had fled so hurriedly as to have left everything behind, and the abject misery of the women of the better class in the squalid encampments is not to be described.

On the evening of the 23rd, near Gabrova, I overtook the Podolsk Regiment of the 2nd Brigade of the 14th Division. The Colonel told me that his regiment had been so hurriedly pressed forward that his men had not cooked or slept for two days and two nights, and he knew not when they would do either. He marched straight on through Gabrova. I stayed there for the night. In Gabrova I was told that the fighting had been raging in the Shipka Pass for three days, and that the Turks continued to push their attacks with extraordinary pertinacity and determination. In the dead of night came rumbling over the stony streets long convoys of ambulance waggons laden with wounded men, and another of empty ammunition waggons, both indications of serious work the day before.

Before daylight this morning the sound of the renewed cannonade came down the passes, and along the quaint old street of Gabrova, where the townspeople collected in anxious groups, and whispered with pale lips. It had volumes of terrible significance for them, that sullen booming of cannon up in the Shipka there, not three hours' march from their doors. While the Russians stood their ground there the pale citizens were safe; but let them be worsted, and three short hours would see the leaders of the swarms of murderous Circassians riding down the old main street, with its projecting fronts, and its resemblance to Cairo. For the Russians to be worsted meant letting loose a horde of savages on that vast aggregate of fugitives who were camped in every field, and beneath every tree, from Gabrova to Drenova. For the Bulgarians, then, each moment was an agony of suspense. Nor is it easy to realize how deeply the Russian chiefs must have felt the sense of responsibility weighing upon them. A leader may see his soldiers falling around him. They go down in fair fight. They die, so to speak, in the way of business; but to know that on their staunchness and skill hang the lives of countless women and tender babes must be terrible. Yet how glorious to realize and be equal to the burden of responsibility! I am sure the Russian soldiers fought none the less stoutly because for two days before they reached the scene of action they had been marching with pitying hearts and cheering words through the miserable fugitives cowering along their path. I saw the noble-hearted fellows empty their havresacks of bread into the laps of the starving Bulgarian women and children, although the act left themselves foodless, without a guess when they should eat next. I saw them with infinite patience groping into corners of recondite pockets, fish out the poor coppers which they had been saving for schnapps and tobacco, or perchance to take home to their young ones in the humble cabin in far-off Russia, and bestow them instead on the gaunt children of the fugitives, with some expression of rough jocularity which was but a cloak for a tear and a blessing.

Leaving Gabrova in the pale half-light of the moon and of the dawn, we made forward along the beautiful romantic valley of the Jantra, through beech forests interspersed with clearings around tiny villages. Here we passed a long column of Cossacks, each man with a led horse. These were the horses on which the advanced guard of the Rifle Brigade was hurried forward last night, reaching the ridge and coming into action just in the nick of time to avert a very serious, if not disastrous result. The roar of cannon high above us—it seemed in the very clouds—swelled louder and louder in volume as we drew nearer, and wounded men were already trickling to the rear, a sure sign that the fighting had been warm and close from its very commencement.

Suddenly the road left the Jantra valley, and bending sharp to the left, struck up the mountain side. There was no cessation in the steep ascent for about five kilometres. The road was extremely tortuous, having to twist, and turn, and wriggle to take advantage of any available ground. But although in places terribly steep it was quite practicable for vehicles, being broad and smooth. This is the road which the Russian pioneers have constructed during the Russian occupation, and so long as this road remains undestroyed, to cross the Balkans in peace time will be little greater exertion than to drive from Blairgowrie to Braemar. Patches of the old track remain. It must have been no road at all, but a simple avalanche of boulders hurled miscellaneously over fixed jagged rocks. About five kilometres from the bottom stands on the hill face a hut used by the Turks as custom-house and guard-house. It was on a knoll about this where the Russians of Mirsky's original advance first came into action against the Turks on a hillock higher up, on which stands a dismantled little khan. On that occasion the Grand Duke Nicholas the younger commanded a detachment. He is perhaps the most practical soldier, in his steady faith in the wisdom of getting to close quarters with the enemy, of all the many soldier members of the great Imperial House.

At the custom house we passed a provision train. At the Khan was the dressing place of the third line, whither, after having had their wounds bound up in the field, came such soldiers as were able to walk. Although a steady evacuation further to the rear had been practised, this place and its vicinity were thronged with the severely wounded men, among whom was an extraordinary proportion of officers. Two colonels were brought in while I passed. The Shipka will be known as par excellence the officers' battle of the war.

On my way to the scene of action, and while surveying it before following closely the movement of the troops engaged, I was much impressed by the peculiarity of the ground. The Shipka Pass is not a pass at all in the proper sense of the term. There is no gorge, no defile; there is no spot where 300 men could make a new Thermopylæ; no deep-scored trench as in the Kyber Pass, where an army might be annihilated without coming to grips with its adversary. It has its name simply because at this point there happens to be a section of the Balkans of less than the average height, the surface of which, from the Jantra Valley on the north to the Tundja Valley on the south, is sufficiently continuous, although having an extremely broken and serrated contour, to afford a foothold for a practicable track, for the Balkans generally present a wild jumble of mountain and glen, neither having any continuity. Under such circumstances, such a crossing-place as the Shipka Pass affords is a godsend, although under other circumstances a road over it would be regarded as impossible. What was a mere track is now a really good and practicable, although steep, high road. The ground on either side of the ridge is depressed sometimes into shallow hollows, sometimes into cavernous gorges; but these lateral depressions are broken, and have no continuity, otherwise they would clearly afford a better track for a road than the high ground above.

The highest peak is flanked on either side behind the lateral depressions by a mountainous spur higher than itself, and therefore commanding it, and having as well the command of the ridge behind. The higher one, that is to say, the westmost of these two spurs, can rake the road leading up to the Russian positions. These spurs break off abruptly and precipitously on their northern edge, and therefore afford no access into the valley north of the Balkans. Their sole use to the Turks, therefore, was in affording positions whence to flank the central Shipka ridge. It is possible also for troops to descend from them, struggle through the intervening glens, and climbing the steep slopes of the Shipka ridge, give the hand to each other on the road which runs along its backbone to its summit. This done, the Shipka position would of course be turned, but the advantage would be of little avail till the road had been opened by carrying the fortified positions on it. Without the command of the road an enemy might indeed send bands down the road on to which he had scrambled, into the lower country about Gabrova, to burn and plunder, but I repeat that the road over the Shipka constitutes for an army the only practicable line of communication in this section of the Balkans.

Much has been said of the strength of the Shipka position. In these opinions I do not concur. It seems to me that unless strongly held with wide extending arms of defence, it is easy to be attacked and very difficult to be held with any security. The strength of a position does not depend wholly on its elevation or even on the difficulties of access to a direct attack, but on the clear range around it which its fire can sweep, and its ability to concentrate its fire on critical points. Herein lies the defect of the Shipka as a defensive position. It cannot search with its fire the jumble of lateral valleys and reverse slopes which hem it in. A brigade of light infantry might mass in a hollow within one hundred yards of the Russian first position without exposing itself to the artillery fire of that position.

The troops engaged in to-day's battle were as follows:—The Bulgarians and a regiment of the 1st Brigade of the 9th Division under General Stoletoff; the 2nd Brigade of the 9th Division, under General Derozinsky; the Rifle Brigade under General Tzwilzwinski. The 2nd Brigade of the 14th Division, commanded by General Petroceni, arrived at nine in the morning, brought up by the commander of the division, General Dragomiroff, the whole force being under the chief command of General Radetzky, commanding the 8th Corps, which is composed of the 9th and 14th Divisions, in all twenty battalions, which if full would give an aggregate of about seventeen thousand men; but every regiment engaged had already fought, and lost. The Tirailleurs and Bulgarians shared the fortunes and misfortunes of General Gourko. The 14th Division fought hard in crossing the Danube. The stones of the Shipka had already been splashed with the blood of Mirsky's gallant fellows of the 9th Division. I set down the total strength as not above thirteen thousand.

The operations had commenced at daybreak. An attack was made on the Turkish commanding position on the Russian right flank, by the Tirailleur Brigade and the Brianski Regiment of the 9th Division. Almost at the same moment the Turks from that position renewed their turning effort, extending their left with intent to push across the intervening deep valley and gain the top ridge of the ground in the rear of the Russian positions, and so hem in the Russian forces. These simultaneous attacks met in the valley separating the parallel ridges held by the Russians and Turks. The fighting became at once fierce and stubborn. I had been told about eight o'clock that in half an hour the Turks would be driven back. When I reached the crest of the Russian ridge I was forced to confess I saw no immediate prospect of this. A furious infantry fire was raging in the valley between our bare central ridge and the Turkish higher wooded ridge. The bareness of our slope brought it about that our men went down into battle without cover, blistered by the Turkish infantry fire from their wooded slope, and by the shell fire of the mountain batteries on the summit. The Russian battery in the first position confronting the Turkish summit fired, but at rare intervals. It is true it is waste of ammunition to shower shells into trees, but the Turkish battery on the sky line unquestionably afforded a mark, and it would have been worth while to throw a few shells to help to cover with their moral effect the advance of our infantry. I fancy there was a long period when the battery was short of ammunition. The road is so exposed that fetching ammunition was extremely dangerous. The Turks had detachments of marksmen detailed with seemingly no other duty than to sweep the Russian road at the exposed points of its course, and, indeed, to fire at everything and everybody exposed on the Russian ridge. To see anything and to attain shelter from the rifle fire were incompatible objects.

I went up on to the sky line once and sat down to study the interesting scene below, and my white cap-cover in an instant drew fire from half a dozen rifles. We were all under rifle fire continually the whole day, from the commencement of the action till the Turkish position was finally carried. From staff officers who had been on the ground during the whole period of operations I received details of the forces engaged and the character of the fighting on the previous days.

The Turks began the attack on the 21st, pushing on directly up the steeps above the village of Shipka. The Russian garrison in the works of the pass then consisted of the Bulgarian Legion and one regiment of the 9th Division, both weakened by previous hard fighting, and probably reckoning little more than three thousand bayonets, with about forty cannon. No supports were nearer than Tirnova, a distance of forty miles,—a grave omission. The garrison fought hard and hindered the Turks from gaining any material advantage.

though the latter forced the outer line of the Russian shelter trenches on the slopes below the position of Mount St. Nicholas, the highest peak of the Shipka crossing. The Russians had laid mines in front of their trenches, which were exploded just as the head of the Turkish assaulting parties were massed above them, and it is reported that a large number of Moslems were blown up into the air in fragments. The loss to the Russians on the first day's attack was but two hundred, chiefly of the Bulgarian Legion. On the second day, the 22nd, the fighting was not heavy, the Turks being engaged in making a wide turning movement on the right and left flanks of the Russian position, and these attacks were next day developed with great fierceness and pertinacity.

Yesterday the Turks assailed the Russian position on the front and flanks, and drove in the defenders from their outlying ground. The radical defects of the position became painfully apparent—its narrowness, its exposure, its liability to be outflanked and isolated. Fortunately reinforcements had arrived, which averted the mischief which had otherwise, to my thinking, imminently impended. Stoletoff hit his hardest, and a right good fighting man he is, full of energy and force after four long days of intense mental and physical strain; but he could not perform impossibilities with thirty thousand men thundering on his front and flanks. But there had come to him, swiftly marching from Selvi, a brigade of the 9th Division, commanded by another valiant soldier, General Derozinski, and this timely succour had been of material value to Stoletoff. The fight lasted all day, and at length, as the sun grew lower, the Turks had so worked round on both the Russian flanks that it seemed as though the claws of the crab were about momentarily to close behind the Russians, and that the Turkish columns climbing either face of the Russian ridge would give a hand to each other on the road in the rear of the Russian position.

The moment was dramatic with an intensity to which the tameness of civilian life can furnish no parallel. The two Russian generals, expecting momentarily to be environed, had sent, between the closing claws of the crab, a last telegram to the Czar, telling what they expected, how they had tried to prevent it, and how that, please God, driven into their positions and beset, they would hold these till reinforcements should arrive. At all events, they and their men would hold their ground to the last drop of their blood.

It was six o'clock; there was a lull in the fighting, of which the Russians could take no advantage, since the reserves were all engaged. The grimed, sun-blistered men were beaten out with heat, fatigue, hunger, and thirst. There had been no cooking for three days, and there was no water within the Russian lines. The poor fellows lay panting on the bare ridge, reckless that it was swept by the Turkish rifle fire. Others doggedly fought on down among the rocks, forced to give ground, but doing so grimly and sourly. The cliffs and valleys send back the triumphant Turkish shouts of "Allah il Allah!"

The two Russian generals were on the peak which the first position half encloses. Their glasses anxiously scanned the visible glimpses of the steep brown road leading up there from the Jantra valley, through thick copses of sombre green, and yet more sombre dark rock. Stoletoff cries aloud in sudden access of excitement, clutches his brother general by the arm, and points down the pass. The head of a long black column was plainly visible against the reddish-brown bed of the road. "Now God be thanked!" says Stoletoff, solemnly. Both generals bare their heads. The troops spring to their feet. They descry the long black serpent coiling up the brown road. Through the green copses a glint of sunshine flashes, banishes the sombreness, and dances on the glittering bayonets.

Such a gust of Russian cheers whirls and eddies among the mountain tops that the Turkish war cries are wholly drowned in the glad welcome which the Russian soldiers sent to the comrades coming to help them. Some time elapses. The head of the column draws near the Karaula, and is on the little plateau in front of the khan. But they are mounted men. The horses are easily discernible. Has Radetzky, then, been so left to himself, or so hard pushed, that he has sent cavalry to cope with infantry among the precipices of the Balkans? Be they what they may, they carry a tongue that can speak, for on the projection to the right of the khan a mountain battery has just come into action against the Turkish artillery on the wooded ridge, by the occupation of which the Turks are flanking the right of the Russian position. There are no riders on the horses now, and they are on their way down hill. But a column of Russian infantry are on the swift tramp uphill till they get within firing distance of the Turks on the right, and then they break, scatter, and from behind every stone and bush spurt white jets of smoke.

It is a battalion of the Rifle Brigade, hurried up on Cossack ponies, the brigade itself is not three kilometres behind, and it is a rifle brigade that needs no more fighting in the Balkans to link its name with the great mountain chain. It is the same rifle brigade which followed General Gourko in his victorious advance and chequered retreat. The brigade has marched fifty-five kilometres straight on end without cooking or sleeping, and now is in action without so much as a breathing halt. Such is the stuff of which thorough good soldiers are made. Their general, the gallant Radetzky, accompanies them, and pushes an attack on the enemy's position on that wooded ridge on the Russian right. But Radetzky, who himself brought up the tirailleurs, and so at the least reckoning saved the day, marches on up the road with his staff at his back, runs the triple gauntlet of the Turkish rifle fire, and joins the other two generals on the peak hard by the batteries of the first position. As senior and highest officer present, he at once took command, complimenting General Stoletoff, whom he relieved, on the excellence of his dispositions and stubbornness of defence.

In the night the renewed attempt to carry the Turkish positions threatening the right flank might well have been spared. But it was felt that there was no safety, far less elbow-room, for the Russians, until the Turks should be driven off that dominating wooded ridge looming so ugly on the right flank. The left flank, which the Turks assailed the previous day, was now comparatively safe. So to-day's fighting began at daybreak with a renewed attack of the Russians on the position specified. The Bulgarian peasant boys displayed singular gallantry in the same work as that in which the despised Indian bheestie has so often done good service to our soldiers, by going down into the actual battle, right into the first line, with stone crocks full of water for the fighting men. This water was fetched from far in the rear, along a bullet-swept road,—for there is no water on the position itself. One lad had his crock smashed by a bullet as he passed me, and he wept, not for joy at his fortunate escape, but for sorrow at the loss of the article which enabled him to be of service.

The fighting hung very much in the valley, and the reinforcements of the 9th Division sent down effected not much perceptible good. About nine Dragomiroff arrived with two regiments of the 2nd Brigade of his own division. The Podolsk Regiment, he left in reserve near the khan; with the Jitomer Regiment, he marched up the road to the first position. There was no alternative but to traverse that fearfully-dangerous road, for the lower broken ground on its left was impracticable, and reported besides to be swarming with Bashi-Bazouks. The Jitomer men lost heavily while making this promenade, and having reached the peak, found no safe shelter, for the Turkish rifle fire was coming from two quarters simultaneously. So the infantry were stowed away till wanted in the ditch of the redoubt. Radetzky and his staff remained on the slope of the peak, and here Dragomiroff joined, and was welcomed by his chief.

The firing in the valley waxed and waned fitfully as the morning wore on to near noon. The Turks were very strongly established in their wooded position, and there was an evident intention on their part to work round their left and edge in across the narrowed throat of the valley towards our rear. About eleven the firing in the valley swelled in volume. It was almost wholly musketry fire, be it remembered. Taking off my white hat I crept up to the edge of the ridge and looked down upon the scene below. The Russians had their tirailleurs in among the trees of the Turkish slope, leaving the bare ground behind strewn with killed and wounded. The ambulance men were behaving admirably, picking up the wounded under the hottest fire, and indeed not a few were themselves among the wounded. As to the progress of the Russians in the wood little could be seen, the cover was so thick, but it was clear that the battle waged to and fro, now the Russians, now the Turks, gaining ground. Occasionally the Russians at some point would be hurled clean back out of the wood altogether, and with my glass I could mark the Turks following them eagerly to its edge, and lying down while pouring out a galling fire. It seemed an even match; the Turks and Russians alike accepted valiantly the chances of battle. The Russian tirailleurs, finely-trained skirmishers, looked out dexterously for cover, and the Turks displayed fine skirmishing ability, but the soldiers of the Brianski line regiment were not so good at finding cover. There was clearly no thought among them of quailing, but they stood up in the open as I have seen our Guards do in a sham fight, and took what came. As a natural result, this fine regiment showed the greatest proportion of casualties.

There is something terrible in a fight in a wood. You can see nothing save an occasional flash of dark colour among the sombre foliage, and the white clouds of smoke rising above it like soap bubbles. Hoarse cries come back to you on the wind from out the mysterious inferno. How is it to go? Are the strong-backed Muscovites, with these ready bayonet points of theirs, to end the long drawn out fight with one short, impetuous, irresistible rush; or are the more lissom Turks to drive their northern adversaries out of the wood backwards into the fire-blistered open? Who can tell?

The fire rages still. The mad clamour of the battle still surges up around into the serene blue heavens. Wounded men come staggering out from among the swarthy trunks and sit down in a heap, or crawl on to the ambulance men. I leave the edge of the ridge soon after eleven, and pick my way up towards the peak, on the slope of which the generals and staff are surveying the scene. The bullets here are singing like a nest of angry wasps. One bullet strikes on the right knee General Dragomiroff, who has been standing calmly in the face of the fire, looking down upon the battle. One of the best generals in the Russian army is *hors de combat*. He is as brave as he is skilful. He never so much as takes his spectacles off, but when we have borne him into comparative shelter quietly sits down, and, ripping up his trouser-leg, binds a handkerchief round the wound. Surgeons gather round him; but, like the true soldier he is, he says he will take his turn when it comes. He is carried further out of the line of fire, his boot removed, and the limb bandaged. Then he is placed on a stretcher, and is borne away. The last words on the noble soldier's lips are a fervent wish for good fortune to the arms of the Czar.

The Tirailleurs and Brianski Regiment were not making headway in their difficult enterprise of attacking direct in front the steep Turkish slope, with its advantage of wooded cover, although they have foiled the efforts of the Turks to work round by their own left into our rear. We can see on the sky-line the Turkish reinforcements as they come up out of the valley by the road close to their mountain battery, on the bare spot near the edge of their left flank. It is determined at twelve o'clock to deliver a counter flank attack on the right edge of the Turkish ridge, simultaneously with a renewed strenuous attack of the Tirailleurs and the Brianski men from below. The two battalions of the Jitomer Regiment, each leaving one company behind as supports, emerge from the partial shelter of the peak of the Russian first position, and march in company columns across the more level grass land at the head of the intervening valley. They have no great dip to traverse, and their way is good marching ground, but the Turkish mountain guns, from the battery high up on the wooded peak of the Turkish position, are ready for them, as also is the Turkish infantry on the Turkish right edge of the ridge. The fire sweeps through them, and many a gallant fellow dyes the grass with his blood. But the battalions press steadily on, and dash into the wood at the double. The Russian artillery had done its best to prepare the way, for their battery on the peak had fired hard while they were crossing over, and a reserve battery near the khan down below had come into action. But now the artillery had to cease, for there was danger in blind firing into the wood when our men were in it. The arbitrement had to be left to rifle and bayonet.

The crisis of the battle had now arrived. It remained for us but to gaze into the perplexing mystery of forest, and to hope fervently. The fighting of the infantry on the Turkish front and flank lasted for a long hour, and raged with great fury, but it was clear that the Russians were gradually gaining ground. The Turks were seen withdrawing their battery of mountain guns near their right flank, a sure sign that danger menaced it if it stayed longer. Then the left battery followed their example, a sure sign too that the Tirailleurs and Brianskis were gaining the ridge on the Turkish left also. There remained but the central peak of the Turkish position. That carried, the ridge was ours, and our right flank would be set free from the dangerous pressure on it.

The fight was on the balance. The Russians as they stood could all but succeed, but not quite. It was an intensely exciting period, and Radetzky was equal to the occasion. I have mentioned that the Jitomer battalions had left two companies in reserve when they marched out from behind the peak. Radetzky realized that fortune was not unkind; but that she needed just a little more wooing. He himself took one of these companies; the Colonel of the Jitomer Regiment placed himself at the head of the other; and thus led, the two companies set forward to throw themselves into the fray. Military critics will say that the chief of an army corps should not be at the head of a company. The abstract truth of the criticism may be owned; but there are times when specific advantages outweigh conventional and general objections; and a brave leader, with a cool head, may be left to judge for himself if the opportunity has come to commit an error that he may gain a victory. To be headed by the General in command would have inspired the least spirited troops. The soldiers of the Czar want no adventitious encouragement to stimulate in them the ardour for the fray. The Jitomers had been chafing at their inaction, but it was clear that the leadership of their chief thrilled them with increased zeal. Their ringing cheers rose high above the rattle of musketry as they dashed across the grassy slope at the head of the valley, and precipitated themselves into the wood.

Fortune, thus energetically wooed, yielded. There was a concentric rush on the peak. Its rude breastworks were surmounted; there was some hot bayonet work, and then a tremendous volley of Russian hurrahs told that the Turkish ridge was cleared and the position won. This was at two o'clock to the moment. The Turk, if unspeakable, is also irrepressible. All day he had fought with stubborn valour, and would not yet own himself beaten. He came on again out of the valley beyond his late ridge, and strove to retake it; but the Russian soldiers are not fond of relinquishing positions earned by the price of blood, and the Turks were repulsed. By three o'clock they had abandoned the effort for the time, and the fire hereabouts had all but died out.

Radetzky now came back to the peak of his first position, panting, but content. He had fought a good fight and won it. Now he determined to strike while the iron was hot, and attempt to recover the outlying positions in his front towards Shipka, on which the Turks had encroached on the first day of the fighting. The Podolsk Regiment was called up from reserve, and went down to the attack under cover of a heavy fire of artillery from the Russian batteries around and beyond the position on Mount St. Nicholas. This attack also was partly successful, and Radetzky increased his elbow-room in front as well as on the flank. The Turks will no doubt renew the attack to-morrow with fresh troops, probably both in front and on the flanks. They are reported as pressing on through the narrow and difficult pass on the east of the Shipka, and leading down into Triavna. But I know that the Grand Duke has ordered a brigade to that point, with more troops to follow. I know that reinforcements are streaming on to the Shipka position. As I write, the 1st Brigade of the 14th Division is arriving. Radetzky has broken up the dangerous pressure on his flanks. He means to hold the ridge whence he has expelled the Turks, and he certainly ought to be able to hold it. All danger is not yet over, but the atmosphere looks so much clearer that I think myself safe in leaving here to despatch this long telegram, notwithstanding that the Turks are recommencing their efforts to regain the lost position.

The Turkish troops engaged were nearly all Nizams—trained regulars, who fought admirably. There are very few Turkish prisoners. One avers that Suleiman Pacha has one hundred thousand men, which must be an exaggeration, even if they included the swarms of Circassians and Bashi-Bazouks collected to ravage the country north of the Balkans. I put down the Russian loss to-day at over 1,500 killed and wounded—a large proportion of the small force engaged. The Turks lost perhaps fewer to-day, but in the previous days, when they were attacked, they must have suffered heavily.

During the fighting I spent some time with the surgeons working in the most advanced positions, and should like to bear testimony to their admirable devotion to duty and their skilled dexterity. In their eagerness to assist the wounded, the Russian surgeons somehow neglect the axiom that their quarters should be in a sheltered spot; but indeed on all the ridge it was hard to find a sheltered spot. The Turkish bullets whistled over and through the little group. Indeed, one patient received a fresh wound while the earlier one was being dressed; but the surgeons pursued their duties with a noble courage and disregard of risk. Their kind attention to the wounded, and their attention to trifles—such as supplying water, laving burning faces, and administering restoratives—filled me with admiration. As I leave the position at six o'clock comparative quietude reigns.

* Russian Headquarters, Gorny Studen, *August 25th.*—Riding backward from Shipka through the night, I passed masses of reinforcements, artillery and infantry, hurying forward to Shipka. It would be improper to specify their strength, but it is such as ought to secure the safety of the all-important position. Riding hard all night long, and to-day also, without either rest or food, I was fortunate enough to reach the headquarters here in advance of any of the aides-de-camp whom the Grand Duke had sent to the fighting region to report the progress of events. All news previously reaching the headquarters had come by telegraph, and chiefs hard pressed by fighting functions, have no leisure to telegraph copiously.

Having communicated some details to the officers of my acquaintance on the Imperial staff, General Ignatieff acquainted the Emperor with my arrival, and His Majesty did me the honour to desire that he should hear what I had to tell from my own lips. The concern of the Emperor was not less strongly evinced than was his thorough conversance with the military art, and the promptitude with which he comprehended my details was more, I fear, owing to the trained skill of his perception than to my lucidity. He expressed an anxious desire that every effort should be made to supply his noble soldiers with the food they so much needed, and expressed great gratification when I was able to tell him I had seen camp kettles bubbling even amid the whiz of bullets. The simplicity of His Majesty's habit of life is apparent at a glance. He carries no luxury with him, and I have seen a subaltern's tent at Wimbledon far more sumptuously accoutred than the campaigning residence of the Czar of All the Russias. His Majesty desired that, on leaving him, I should go to his brother, the Grand Duke commanding-in-chief.

Answering the questions of His Imperial Highness was like going through a competitive examination. He was fully master of the subject, and if I had not taken pains in gathering my facts from a wide area, I should have felt extremely foolish. As it was, I was able to draw for the Grand Duke a plan of the operations, and to illustrate my unskilful draughtsmanship by verbal explanations which I trust His Imperial Highness found of some value. He had received telegrams to-day from General Radetzky to the effect that, as I had anticipated, the Turks had renewed the combat with great energy this morning, and that hard fighting was raging, the flanks as well as the front being threatened.

I expected no less; but none the less do I hold to my impression that Radetzky, having so far widened his area to the right and left yesterday as to prevent the dominance thence of the Shipka position, will be able now to hold his ground against all comers, especially with the reinforcements arriving. I take it for granted that he utilized last night by making such dispositions as shall prevent the Turks from regaining the positions from which he yesterday drove them. It is a military axiom that it is easier to hold a position than to carry it. The Grand Duke had received a telegram that General Petroceni, the gallant chief of the 2nd Brigade, 14th Division, was this morning in action. Another telegram from Gabrova from General Stoletoff told that General Radetzky had ordered that fine officer to take his Bulgarians down into Gabrova for a little rest after five days' continuous fighting, with no food save dry bread. It is a good sign that they can be spared. The Bulgarian Legion has proved that the despised Bulgarians can fight like lions.

* BUCHAREST, *August 26th.*—Information follows me here that the fighting at the Shipka Pass is still raging, having been again renewed to-day, but that Radetzky continues to hold his own. It is now a question of endurance, and the Turks may add to the difficulties of the Russian position by taking the offensive on the left and right flanks. Indeed, Mehemet Ali Pacha has already been striking out against the Czarewitch; but I adhere to my impression that the Shipka Pass, as now held by Radetzky, is safe, and that unless Suleiman Pacha can run a column through another pass, regarding the practicability or the contrary of which I know

nothing, he will wreck his army by thus dashing it continually against the rock of Shipka.

The subjoined letter, dated a day later than that commencing on page 407, is from another Correspondent, who arrived subsequently to the departure of the writer of the previous despatch:—

† SHIPKA PASS, *August 25th.*—The fight is still raging here with unabated fury. The arrival of Radetzky with reinforcements saved the situation for the moment and drove back the Turks, who were on the point of seizing the Pass; but the Russian position is still most critical. The Turks had not only turned both the Russian flanks by seizing Berdek on the left and the mountains on the right, but had constructed a redoubt and planted a battery on the right which commands the road leading up to the Pass. This gives them possession of the ridge running parallel to that up which the road winds, one thousand five hundred yards distant as the crow flies. The redoubt enfilades the road in several places, and the Turkish infantry, by extending along this ridge, which is thickly wooded, can practically render the road impassable.

How true this is may be judged by the fact that it was on this road that General Dragomiroff was wounded, and that to-day General Petroceni, the commander of the 1st Brigade of the 9th Division of the 8th Corps, was killed on this road, fully a mile on our side of the summit of the Pass, by a bullet which traversed his lungs, killing him almost instantly. Men are picked off by the Turkish skirmishers two miles behind the Pass, where the road is exposed, and even where the road passes on the other side of the ridge the men are killed and wounded by the bullets dropping over from random firing. Men are killed and wounded all round the point where I found Radetzky and his staff to-day, although sheltered behind the brow of the ridge, which rose thirty to fifty feet above them. It will be seen, therefore, that the Russian position still remains most critical, in spite of the arrival of reinforcements. General Radetzky, indeed, informed the commandant of Gabrova the day after his arrival that he had better warn the inhabitants to be ready to fly at a moment's notice. The fact is that until the Turkish redoubt spoken of is taken it is impossible to say what will be the result of the Turkish attack on the Shipka Pass. The road up to the Shipka would have already been rendered impassable but for the fact that the Turks have been so busy defending the redoubt that they have not yet had time to turn it to its proper use by shelling the Shipka road from the battery at the foot.

General Radetzky had no sooner arrived than he began making dispositions in earnest. From the highest point of the Pass there is a high short narrow ridge extending to the right at nearly right angles to the road. At a distance of half a mile it rises into a sharp peak, which is crowned by a Russian redoubt, effectually protecting the Russian batteries from that side. Half a mile farther, or perhaps less, the ridge rises into another peak, which, with the first one, forms a perfect saddle-back. This peak is crowned by the Turkish redoubt, already spoken of, and it is the head of the ridge mentioned which curves round on our right until parallel with the road, thus enabling the Turkish infantry to command it.

The Russian commander should have occupied this second peak, and would undoubtedly have done so had he had enough men, but he only had one regiment, three thousand men, and the débris of the Bulgarian Legion—only enough to defend the direct approaches to the Pass. It is true that another regiment was sent from Selvi to reinforce him as soon as it was known that the Turks were preparing to attack, but it was then too late, as the Turks seem to have occupied this position the first day. Besides, it was soon demonstrated that two regiments were required to protect the direct approaches against Suleiman's violent onset.

The two peaks occupied by the Russian and Turkish redoubts are thickly wooded, as well as the connecting ridge between. General Radetzky advanced his troops along this ridge under cover of the woods, and opened fire on the redoubt with two or three batteries. He at the same time sent troops across the deep hollow from the road to take the Turkish redoubt on the Gabrova side, by advancing up the steep mountain flank. Soon a terrible musketry-fire told that the troops were in contact, and the attack fairly begun; and for hours the mountains re-echoed with the continuous roll of musketry and the thunder of cannon.

The Russians advanced like Indians under cover of the trees, which were, however, too small to afford good shelter, firing as they went. In a short time they had reached within fifty yards of the redoubt. Here they found obstacles which for the moment were quite insurmountable. The Turks had cut down the trees around the redoubt, making an abattis over which the Russians found it almost impossible to pass. They gathered around the edge under cover of the trees, and suddenly made a rush for it, but were driven back with fearful loss. The soldiers became entangled in the masses of brushwood, trunks, and limbs of the trees over which they were obliged to scramble, while the Turks poured in a terrible fire upon them at this short distance, and mowed them down like grass. Of the first assault launched against the redoubt I am afraid very few got back under cover to tell the tale. It was very evident that the assault under such conditions could not succeed. Only one battalion had been sent to attack. The force was insufficient, and of this one company sent to the assault was nearly destroyed. Reinforcements were sent by Radetzky. The attack began again, but dispositions were made to place a large force in such positions that it could pour a heavy fire into the redoubt to cover the assault until the assaulters were almost up to the parapet.

This attack seemed almost on the point of success, for the colonel in command, whose name I forget, said that if reserves were given to him he could take it. The officer in command of the reserves let them go; but they were nevertheless repulsed. Then Radetzky mounted and rode to the ground, followed by part of his staff. The chief of the staff, General Dimitriofsky, on foot, bareheaded, and supported by two men, with an expression of extreme suffering on his face, had put himself at the head of a battalion to lead the assault. A shell had struck the ground beside him, covering him with earth, knocking him down, and rendering him senseless for a few minutes. The attack still went on. The fire became terrible. From among the trees rose a large column of smoke, marking the place of the Turkish redoubt, which was dimly seen through it, while the thick woods were full of the roll of the Russian musketry fire.

The Russians advanced steadily. They rushed over, or through, the abattis; they even got into the battery, and actually held it for a few seconds, but were driven out again. They surrounded the place on all sides, pouring into it a terrible fire, but were again driven back. In the meantime the Turks, to support the defence, began to attack in front and rear. Musketry and artillery were heard coming up from towards Shipka mingling with the nearer din around the redoubt in a most sinister way. The wounded came trooping steadily back with wounds in their heads, arms, and bodies. Some were on litters. One was carried by his companions. Some were limping along by themselves, presenting a most pitiable spectacle, covered with dust, smoke-begrimed, haggard, wretched. I don't know yet what are the losses, but they must be very heavy, for the fight continued until late at night. The wounded were coming back steadily all the time. Besides these were the poor fellows, too severely wounded to be moved, who will probably fall into the hands of the Turks, to be murdered, tortured, and mutilated.

To sum up, the attack has been unsuccessful. Reinforcements are arriving, and the fight will probably be continued to-morrow.

* SISTOVA, *August 27th.*—Fighting is still going on upon the flanks of the Shipka Pass positions, but Radetzky continues to maintain his ground, although his losses are serious.

If I remember rightly, Richie Moniplies, in the "Fortunes of Nigel," tore his cloak in his endeavours to conceal the rents in his clothing covered by that garment. That is what has very nearly happened to the Russians. The military leaders, in their early burst of success, gained possession of a certain area of Bulgaria. To that area they have clung pertinaciously. They had only so many men to hold the ground in Bulgaria pending the arrival of reinforcements, rendered necessary by the unexpected development of the Turkish fighting strength, and these they have disposed round the edge of the area occupied after the manner of a fence. Now the strength of the fence is only equal to the weakest portion of it, and realizing this, and dreading Turkish attacks from right and left on Tirnova, they kept thereabouts a body of troops belonging to the 8th Corps, available to strengthen any weak position that might be threatened. There was reason in this, but it was a very dangerous experiment to leave a handful of men to hold the all-important Shipka position beyond easy hailing distance of support. When Suleiman Pacha took the village of Shipka there was not a Russian soldier between the handful on the exposed Shipka position and Tirnova, forty miles away. Reinforcements arrived in the nick of time, but, as explained in my telegram, the safety of the Shipka position was an affair of minutes, and if the Turks had struck all round the Russian area simultaneously, either the Shipka position must have been left to its fate, or some other section of the fence line must have been seriously endangered.

I think it would have been better policy if the principle of protecting the area once occupied had been abandoned, and the idea of using the Russian forces as a palisade had been abandoned also. They should have been concentrated into one or two central positions, say one strong army at Gorny Studen, another at Tirnova, with a strong detachment thrown forward into Gabrova to answer the menace of the Shipka Pass position. A mobile army at Gorny Studen could have struck right or left at the Turkish forces showing themselves in the open, just as in 1814 Napoleon struck out at Schwarzenberg and Blucher. The aim of the Russian army ought not to be to hem the Turkish armies in defensive positions, but to tempt them to adventure into the open, and then in pitched battles conquer them, in accordance with the invariable precedent. I think, however, that the crisis is virtually past, for let us hope that tinkering tactics have been abandoned. The arrival of reinforcements, now flowing in in a steady stream, should enable the Grand Duke to breathe more freely.

I hold to my conviction that the Shipka is safe, and that thus is defeated the great strategic scheme of the Turkish leaders to hem the Russians within the large *tête-de-pont* in Bulgaria with the ultimate intent of driving them over the Danube. How narrow was the escape of the Shipka need not be now closely inquired into, nor what would have been the consequences if the Russians had lost their hold of that critically important point. The next few days will be full of interest. These past I shall expect the Russians to take the initiative in a vigorous offensive policy on both flanks, and so relieve themselves from the existing pressure, and having done so, pursue their design of sweeping Bulgaria proper clear of the Turkish armies in the field. It behoves the Grand Duke to rely with greater confidence on the unquestionable excellence of his troops as acting fighting men, not alone as mere pieces of palisading, and to pursue a bold and vigorous line of action, even at some risk. The Balkan passes need not be held by strong garrisons, if troops are maintained within easy hail, say at Gabrova, to ensure the safety of the Shipka; at Elena to do the same office by the Hainkoi. The rôle of invader is vigorous, offensive action, not inactive defence. The spirit and condition of the Russian soldiers are high and satisfactory. They may be relied on to fight a good fight. Let them have their innings.

General Dragomiroff has telegraphed to the Emperor that in six weeks he expects to be fit for duty again.

Colonel Wellesley returns to the Imperial headquarters to-day.

* GABROVA, *August* 31*st*.—This day week I despatched you a telegram describing the long and obdurate fighting in the Shipka Pass up to that date, the 24th instant, and said that the Turks would certainly renew strenuously their effort to attain the object for which Suleiman Pacha had already expended so much blood. I nevertheless was impressed with the conviction that Radetzky firmly held the position. So strong was that conviction, that I thought the circumstance justified me in quitting the scene of action for the purpose of reaching the telegraph base.

It was a serious thing for a Military Correspondent to adventure such a prediction while as yet the fighting zeal of the Turks remained unbroken, and in making it I was conscious of the responsibility I incurred to your readers. Since the despatch of my message I have reason to believe that telegrams, giving quite another colour to the course of events, have been transmitted to England, but never in my experience have sensational telegrams availed to alter stern facts. I have to-day visited the Shipka Pass to find my prediction amply verified. All is now quiet there. Radetzky has been left in comparative peace ever since the desperate fighting of Saturday last. So far from his position being impinged on it has been extended. There are no Turks now on his left. The wooded mountain on his right wing, which he cleared of the Turks on the 24th, he had to quit for want of water, and the Turks came back. But now again the Turks have abandoned that position, and solitude reigns among the trees under which furious fighting raged. You may walk along the road from the khan in the rear of Radetzky's position right along to the final peak of the Balkans on Mount St. Nicholas, and thence down into the shelter-trenches, without once hearing the whistle of a bullet, where once the air vibrated with the hum of them.

The truth is that Suleiman Pacha has had enough for the time of the Shipka Pass. For five days he beat out the brains of his gallant stubborn soldiers against its defences and its defenders. Let no man after Shipka venture to assert that the Turkish soldiers are only good men behind earthworks. I respect a fine soldier wherever I find him, be he Greek or Jew, Gentile or Barbarian, and the irrepressible dash and obdurate indomitable valour of the Turkish troops, in assaulting day after day this Shipka position, may claim to rank with any evidence of soldierhood with which I am acquainted. But their valour proved unavailing. Suleiman Pacha has abandoned the attempt, and marched away from the neighbourhood of Shipka. Some say that he is still in Kezanlik; others that he is searching for another pass. My own belief is that he is engaged in trying to re-organize his shattered forces. Five thousand Turkish corpses fester in the blazing sunshine between the Shipka village and the fringes of Mount St. Nicholas. All his Montenegrin soldiers have been removed. There remain still formally confronting the Russians a few battalions of Egyptians, with some cannon on the heights, and a few more miscellaneous battalions in Shipka.

The Imperial and Grand Ducal headquarters were singularly

pessimist. "The Shipka smells very bad," was a remark made to me in several quarters as I passed the day before yesterday. But yesterday, between here and Drenova, I met General Nepokoitchitsky on his way back to Gorny Studen. He had come to choose new positions—an ominous errand; but he found the old ones available and satisfactory, and went back relieved.

This morning a large mass of superfluous reinforcements, which had been hurried up to make a fight of it all the way from Shipka to Tirnova, had the Pass been forced, started on their march back whence they came. The tendency of the Russian military authorities is always to extremes. The danger the Russian fortunes underwent at the Shipka Pass, owing almost wholly to the folly of leaving unsupported a handful of men to hold that Pass, was so great that when the storm burst and the peril was realized, every available man, down to the brigade guarding the Emperor, was hurried pell-mell towards the position, where there was only standing room for a limited number of men. The 2nd Division has to-day returned whence it came. It is the same with the detachment of the 11th Division. Radetzky still has all the 14th Division, a brigade of the 9th Division, the Tirailleurs, the Bulgarians, and a detachment of foot Cossacks, with strong artillery, to hold the Pass against all comers.

It is not a pleasant position. All the water is brought from a spring near the foot of the ascent. For lack of wood most of the cooking is done down by the Jantra, and the food is brought up in great kettles. The effluvium from the unburied dead and the unsanitary camp taints the freshness of the mountain atmosphere. All the troops bivouac. Radetzky inhabits a domicile which is a place between a bower and a cavern. He says that the Turks made upwards of one hundred distinct attacks. God willing, says the stout old chief, he can and will stay there, come Turk or devil, till he gets relieved. The Russian loss during the fighting is set down at eight hundred killed and two thousand eight hundred and odd wounded. The figures are official. I should have thought the number considerably greater.

Now that this danger is averted, it behoves the Russians to do something more than merely move their troops to and fro to block the Turkish onslaughts. For the assailed, the policy of passive defence is a foolish and fatal policy, but it is simply the *reductio ad absurdum* of an invasion; nor is it probable that the Turks for their part, although they have not been successful at the Shipka, will fall in with a prolonged period of mutual inactivity.

The following letter describing the fighting in the Shipka Pass is from the Correspondent with the Turks :—

"ADRIANOPLE, *August* 26*th*.—The Shipka Pass is being most obstinately defended, and, notwithstanding the utmost bravery which Suleiman Pacha's troops have shown, victory as yet has been withheld, although on one occasion it has been almost within his grasp. His bold method of pushing his enemy hard after striking a blow, instead of losing half its value by pausing to recover himself, has brought him at one bound, as it were, to within 500 yards of the Russians. The Balkan road runs through the village of Shipka (now almost burnt to the ground), and creeps along and along the bare mountain, on the summit of which is the chief Russian position. The highest point nearest this, as well as every ridge before reaching it, is thickly entrenched by the Turks, and it will be impossible for an enemy of ten times his strength to attempt to make a descent. The mountains to the right and left, both of which are wooded, and form excellent cover to the attacking parties, have batteries established upon them, altogether numbering sixteen guns; those on the right (three batteries), being of higher elevation, effectually command the Russian side before them, where the Balkan road runs at their feet. The left has not such an advantage, and the ascent from the bottom of the defile is exceedingly precipitous, and almost inaccessible.

On Thursday and Friday last the severest fighting which Suleiman's army has had occurred—the first day's fighting being on the right—and towards the close of the day the Russians were actually forced to beat a retreat, and the Turks gained momentary possession of a trench. By some strange error they were not properly supported, and had in their turn to retire, to the intense mortification of their commander, who, it is said, had fully determined that the battle should be won before the day closed. On Friday a change of tactics occurred, and the firing was entirely on the left, and went briskly on the whole day, without any advantage, however, excepting the loss it has inflicted on the already weakened garrison. Your Correspondent on the other side will doubtless have given you correct information of the numerical strength of the Russians before us. We hear they do not exceed 7,000 men, with twelve or sixteen guns, but these are all heavy Krupps, whilst we have only at present brought up sixteen mountain pieces. Suleiman's army is variously estimated at from 30,000 to 50,000 men—a happy medium may or may not represent the correct figures. Who knows? I doubt if the general himself could say, in its present condition, with fighting going on vigorously on all sides, and a large extent of country to defend. An army more suited to the task before it, or a general more fitted to the command in mountain warfare, there could not be.

The telegraph will have informed you whether the Muscovite is still master of the Balkans; if not, he will have a hard time of it on the other side, for Osman Pacha is not far distant. As to the poor peasantry, God help them! Those on our side are in a pitiable state, but how much worse must they be if the Turks descend upon them. It must not be supposed that the Russians, even if they lost their position on the stony ridge above referred to, could not hold those adjoining, although at a lower elevation; still, they are regular forts, and will stand a very strong attack. By threatening to cut off their retreat we may—should the first position fall—hear of surrender, but unless the Russian general is extremely unfortunate, he will make a hard fight until ample reinforcements arrive.

The entire Turkish system of care for the wounded is in a most lamentable state, and were it not for the English doctors, the condition of things would be incredible; hundreds of wounded, even as it is, have to shift for themselves, whilst the English ambulance is crowded with the poor soldiers in dreadful suffering, waiting their turn for relief. In the hospital, or rather houses, of Kezanlik, there are at this moment no less than 800 wounded left to the care of two Turkish surgeons.

August 26th.—Matters looked rather differently in Suleiman's camp on Saturday. A lull in the din of battle had taken place, that hot, drowsy morning, and for a few hours the unwonted silence was almost unbroken, occasional shells only being exchanged as mere matters of courtesy. Just when the general himself, and not a few of his soldiers, were snatching a welcome doze on the plain at the Pass foot, the whirr of a shell aimed near headquarters broke the pleasant stillness. As if to prove there was no mistake about it, another and another fell; but this time aimed apparently directly at a long train of covered bullock waggons toiling slowly across the plain, freighted with the wounded from the left Turkish position, where their losses had been particularly heavy. A white flag with the crescent was carried at the head of this sad procession, but justice must be done to the Russians on this occasion against wilfully firing on it, for the small size of the flag prevented its being easily distinguishable at the distance from which they fired, their batteries on the main

Balkan road to the spot in question being not much less than 4,000 yards off. Two bullock waggons were broken by the frantic efforts of the drivers to get away. The shelling went on even after the string of waggons had passed from view at such a pace as few bullocks ever went before. The Russians could hardly have seen the fall of their shells, owing to the proximity of the foot of the mountain, and it may charitably be supposed that they imagined some battalions of troops were massed at the place in reserve.

It transpired afterwards that the Turkish troops on the left had met with a check, and had retired precipitately from a position which they had succeeded in occupying, and the Russians, wishing, no doubt, to make the most of the occasion, had lost no time in endeavouring to increase what threatened to be a panic with their foe on this side. Suleiman awoke to the sense of danger, and promptly ordered three batteries of his heaviest field artillery and three battalions of troops to form line across the plain at the mouth of the Pass, so as to ensure the Russians a warm reception if they should have had the temerity to advance. His precautions were well taken, and he has since continued them as a precautionary measure against any contingency.

The English Societies of the Red Crescent have established themselves in conjunction with one of the Turkish ambulances and the Surgeon-in-Chief of the army, on the roadside, in a shady place, with a clear stream of water running beside it, and 5,000 yards from the nearest Russian battery. The number of wounded increases daily, and by an arrangement easy to understand, the Turkish surgeons have taken in hand the slighter cases, leaving the heavier ones and amputations entirely to their English *confrères*. A Turkish officer of rank was dangerously wounded a day or two since, and instantly placed himself under the care of the Englishmen in preference to his own countrymen. The fact is worth noting, and is by no means an isolated instance of the same kind. The opinion of Dr. Leslie Hume and Dr. Sandwith, who are in charge (Dr. Attwood doing good service in directing the hospital arrangements at Adrianople), from the numbers passing through their hands, from those whose wounds are dressed in other quarters, and from what they can learn, is that there have been at least 6,000 in killed and wounded up to the afternoon of the 26th—a heavy price to pay for the positions gained, but as nothing in comparison to the importance of establishing the foothold he has obtained from which to drive out the Russians. The enemy's losses cannot fall far short of the same total.

The night of Saturday will not soon be forgotten by either side as that of the heaviest and most prolonged of any previous fighting,. It commenced at nine o'clock with a sharp rifle fire on the Turkish left, and proved to be a night attack by the Russians on a battery which had been effecting great damage in the trenches on the face of the main Russian centre or rock position. The flash of the Turkish rifles as they met the ascending Russians could be easily distinguished, sparkling through the trees, from the plain, and their vividness and frequency showed only too well how hotly the contest was proceeding. Hour after hour passed thus with varying success, and it was not until six in the morning that silence reigned again, and the news circulated throughout the camp that severe as had been the Russian attempt, it had been resolutely held at bay, and by a greatly inferior numerical force, without the advantage which the Russians had of drawing upon their immediate reserves to an almost unlimited extent. The losses on both sides must have been enormous, for the firing did not cease for one moment in its violence throughout the night. The Turkish loss was heavier, owing to a sad error in the regular troops imagining, in the obscurity of the night, that the dismounted Circassians and Bashi-Bazouks were Russians; a mistake natural enough as regards the former, excepting that they are not always to be met with in the front, at least when fighting is going on; in their turn they fired into the regulars also.

It is subject of remark that during the whole night the Turkish batteries on the right did absolutely nothing to help matters by way of diversion, as they might easily have done by shelling the Russian batteries in the front and such of their enemy's troops as were within range. The position was held unsupported, and the glory of its defence is alone due to its own scanty battalions, and their slight reserves. With the heavy losses which Suleiman's army has now sustained, and notwithstanding the admirable manner in which they fight, it is somewhat doubtful if any general attack will be made for a few days. The Russians, with their telegraphic communications open from the positions themselves to their main body, can call up, as they evidently have already been compelled to do, any amount of reinforcements on the instant, whereas those of the Turks are far behind.

CHAPTER XVII.

THE THIRD ATTACK ON PLEVNA.

Sortie by Osman Pacha in Force—Capture of Loftcha by Imeretinsky and Skobeleff—Dispositions for the Attack on Plevna—The Four Days' Cannonade—The Infantry Attack—The Mameleon Redoubt South-East of Plevna—Gallant Advance of the Russians—Arrival of Turkish Reinforcements—Repulse of the Russians—Turkish Attack on the Radisovo Ridge—Counter Attack by Krüdener and Kriloff and its Repulse—Skobeleff's Attack on the Double Redoubt on the Loftcha Road—Capture of the Redoubt—Six Turkish Attacks for its Recovery—The Redoubt Recaptured—Skobeleff returning from the Battle—Capture of the Grivica Redoubt by the Roumanians—General Failure of the Third Russian Attack on Plevna.

By the end of the month of August the Russians were looking forward to a new attack on Plevna as an event near at hand. Their preparations, however, were not completed, and on the last day of that month Osman Pacha anticipated the blow by making a sortie in considerable force against the Russian positions. He was repulsed with loss. Four days afterwards the Russians gained an important success by wresting the town of Loftcha from the Turks. The long-expected attack on Plevna was commenced on the 7th of September by a cannonade, and was succeeded on the 11th by the infantry assault by which the Russians hoped to restore the fortunes of the campaign. The following letter gives a summary view of military affairs at the end of August:—

* Gorny Studen, *September* 1*st*.—Following upon his recent short visit to the Imperial headquarters here, Prince Charles of Roumania has been appointed to the chief command of the Russo-Roumanian Army before Plevna. General Zotoff takes the post of second in command. Yesterday Osman Pacha inaugurated the new appointment by assuming the offensive, and directed a serious and well-sustained attack against the Russian left centre, almost directly in front of Poradim.

At six o'clock in the morning a large force of Turkish cavalry advanced beyond the Turkish foreposts between Radisovo and Grivica, and drove in the Russian advanced posts on the line between the villages of Pelisat and Sgalince. This done, at eight o'clock the Turkish leader developed a regular attack in force in a direction already prepared by his cavalry. The Turkish infantry engaged were estimated by the Russians at 25,000 men, with more than a proportionate quantity of artillery. The Russian force engaged consisted of three regiments of the 16th Division, which was not engaged in the previous Plevna battle, and two battalions of the 30th Division in reserve, which division took part in the battle of the 30th July. The Uhlans and Hussars of the 4th Cavalry Division arrived in time to be of some service.

The Turkish attack was in some degree a surprise. General Zotoff was away from Poradim, making a formal visit to Prince Charles, and in his absence nobody was in a position to make comprehensive dispositions, but he returned in time to take the direction of affairs before the fighting was over. It was stubborn, and in places desperate. The village of Sgalince, and the hollow near it, the weak point in the Russian defence, four times changed hands, but they are stated to have ultimately remained in possession of the Russians. The Turkish attack then was thus far repulsed, but the previous forepost line of the Russians was not wholly recovered, and the Turks have thus established an indentation on the semicircle of the Russian environment. The Russians state their loss in the day's fighting at 800 killed and wounded, which figures indicate the seriousness of the affair.

To-day the Turks are reported to be remaining quiet. There is every indication that within the next few days the Plevna district will be the scene of momentous events. If Osman Pacha is working on a plan, a strong blow at the Russian centre, such as that delivered yesterday, can have no other result than to precipitate the long postponed crisis. I may mention a curious belief current among the less well-informed officers of the Russian army, that Osman Pacha is no other than Marshal Bazaine.

The return of the 2nd Division from the reserve position behind the Shipka to Selvi was very opportune. Yesterday there was lively work on the Russian left flank also. Early in the morning a Turkish force, consisting, according to the Russian reports, of eight battalions of infantry and four squadrons of cavalry, advanced from Rustchuk to the village of Kadikoi, between the Black and White Loms, and the scene of previous fighting detailed in my letters from the Rustchuk army. Kadikoi was occupied only by a Cossack regiment of the 12th Division, which withdrew in the face of superior force, and the Turks occupied it. Later in the day, however, they were attacked by the Ukraine infantry regiment of the

12th Division, which, the Archduke Vladimir reports, drove them out and forced them to retire under the guns of the Rustchuk position.

Commencing on Thursday, and continuing yesterday, there was general fighting along the front of the centre and right flank army of the Czarewitch from Nisova on the White Lom southward over Solenik, Gagovo, Sultankoi, Popkoi, Mehemedkoi, and beyond, in front of Osman Bazar. Here it is believed Mehemet Ali Pacha was personally in command. Great masses of Turks everywhere drove in the Russian forepost line. An important battle is imminent, but the tactics of the Turks resemble those of the combatants in the American civil war. When they gain any ground they sit and fortify themselves in it by entrenchments before moving to acquire any more. There is obvious caution in this policy. The Russians have abandoned the Popkoi position, after having entrenched themselves in it. The reason is stated to be the discovery of its ineligibility as being commanded by higher ground within cannon range. The new position is behind the old one. I have not learned whether the Turks have occupied the Popkoi position. A parlementaire from Mehemet Ali Pacha on the subject of the treatment of the wounded and the Bulgarian civil population has been here. He is singularly incoherent as to the objects of his mission, has no definite proposals to make, and there are suspicions that in reality he is a spy. On some subjects he is charmingly frank. Speaking to him of the Bashi-Bazouks the Grand Duke called them "wild beasts." "Oh," said the envoy, "I am not expected to defend them. I always take an escort myself when I must pass through their camp."

The Emperor presents to Radetzky a sword set with diamonds and inscription engraved upon it, "For the defence of the Shipka Pass."

The new week promises to be bloody. Summer wanes, and decisive results become every day of more importance to the Russians, for there are indications not to be disregarded—financial, political, and social—which point against the probability of the continuance of the war into another campaign.

The following is a fuller account of Osman Pacha's sortie by an eye-witness:—

† PORADIM, *August* 31*st*.—Another Battle of Plevna has just been fought. The Turks this morning at eight o'clock made a furious attack on the Russian positions here, which resulted in one of the most hardly fought combats of the war.

The Turks some time ago made some feeble reconnaissances, which resulted in one or two slight cavalry skirmishes, a most unusual thing for the Turks, and about the time the attack was made on the Shipka they made a demonstration here which kept us on the alert, but which resulted in nothing else. It seemed so certain that the Turks would not attack here, and it was so evident that the Russians were not ready to resume the offensive for some days, perhaps for some weeks, that most of the Correspondents had gone away in despair. I had saddled my horse to follow their example, when, about eight o'clock, my ear caught a dull, scarcely audible thumping that sounded more like a horse stamping at flies than the booming of artillery. Artillery it proved to be nevertheless, for in a few minutes it grew louder and clearer; and looking towards the line of low hills in the direction of Plevna, some four miles distant, we saw several columns of white smoke rising behind them, showing where the artillery was already hard at work. The indistinctness of the sound was caused by a slight breeze blowing towards Plevna—for the distance from Poradim to our extreme front is scarcely five miles. Was the attack real or feigned? and would not the real battle take place on our right wing, formed by the Roumanian troops? were the questions which occurred to everybody.

The co-operation between the Russians and Roumanians, I may remark, is not very good. A few days ago General Zotoff changed the position of the troops of the right wing, which movement left the regiment of the Roumanians quite exposed. He informed the commander of the regiment of this fact, requesting him to make a corresponding movement, to which the Roumanian colonel replied that he had no orders to receive from General Zotoff. In like manner the Roumanians, contrary to the wishes of the Russian Commander-in-Chief, insisted upon finding another crossing of the Danube, and have crossed at the mouth of the Isker with two divisions, where they are so far away from the Russian army that they are beyond the reach of help from the Russians in case of a sudden attack by the Turks. The Turks have really enough troops to make a demonstration against Zotoff, and at the same time, by a sudden movement, to fall upon the Roumanians at the mouth of the Isker, and drive them into the Danube. General Zotoff could not of course know whether he was threatened with a real or only a feigned attack until it would be too late to help the Roumanians.

When the battle began this morning everybody was of opinion

that it would prove to be only a demonstration here on our centre, and that we should soon hear of something very serious on our right wing. What made an attack here seem still more improbable was that two days ago it was reported that Osman Pacha had sent 20,000 men from Plevna to Loftcha, either to attack Skobeleff on the Selvi road, or to reinforce Suleiman Pacha by way of Trojan. I waited a few minutes to hear whether there were any reports of an attack on either wing, and what report would be made from the front. The report from the front was a long time coming; so long that I grew impatient, and mounting, rode to the left wing, some three miles distant, in order to see for myself what the attack might mean.

As I rode out towards Pelisat I met great crowds of Bulgarian refugees, some of whom had fled from the Turkish advance in front of the Russian lines, others from the village of Pelisat itself, where there would probably be hard fighting in case of a battle. The whole population had put all their movable effects into waggons and carts, with the women and children, and were driving their live stock before them. The country behind the Russian lines everywhere, I may remark, is covered with refugees camped in waggons, and in hastily-constructed straw huts. They retreat with the Russians, and again move forward with them, showing unabated confidence when the Russians make even a slight movement in advance.

In a few minutes I had passed over the level plain between Poradim and Pelisat, a plain planted with Indian corn and vines. The ambulance waggons were already coming back with wounded. The vine hills between Pelisat and Sgalince were covered with clouds of smoke, which rose up in great white flecked balls that rolled off and disappeared in the direction of Plevna, while the deep savage roar of small-arms mingled with the thunder of artillery in a way which showed that if the Turks were making a demonstration it was a very violent one, to say the least of it.

Just to the right of Pelisat was a Russian battery throwing shells that went skimming along over the hill that rose beyond, and exploded out of sight, right in the direction of a Russian redoubt which I knew was about a mile in front of Pelisat. This was a most alarming circumstance. If the Russians were shelling their own redoubt it could only be by a fearful mistake, or else because the Turks had taken it, in which case our left wing must have already been driven back on Pelisat, and in danger of being turned. But strange to say, there were very few balls falling here, while the fight seemed to grow more terrible towards the centre in the direction of Sgalince.

Full of anxiety, I galloped forward to the hill just to the left of Pelisat, which promised a view of what was going on at the front. I found a squadron of dragoons hovering just behind the crest of this hill, and with half-a-dozen officers on the top watching the progress of events. I was now on the extreme Russian left and, as I soon ascertained, on the extreme front likewise. In front and beyond Pelisat the ground rose in a lazy incline for a distance of a mile. About the point where the Russian redoubt stood, which was not, however, visible, a mile and a-half to the right, was the village of Sgalince, the Russian centre, before which was another redoubt, and a series of trenches. Forward towards Plevna the ground still rose higher, so that the Russian positions were and are commanded by the positions taken by the Turks in their forward movement. The disadvantage cannot be avoided by the Russians without falling back several miles. The Russian redoubt a mile in front of Pelisat had been taken by the Turks early in the fight. The Russian left wing had been driven back on Pelisat, in front of which trenches had been dug and lined with troops.

The battle began to look like a serious one indeed. It had been raging more than an hour since we heard the first gun fired, and in that time the redoubt had been taken by the Turks, retaken by the Russians, and retaken again by the Turks. This accounted for the strange firing of the battery in the centre in the direction of Sgalince to the right of Pelisat, which was still blazing away, sending its shells screaming along the ground as they rose with the hill before us and exploded beyond.

I had not been at my new standpoint more than five minutes, when the crest of the hill, a mile in front, suddenly grew black as with a line of ink drawn across the sky. What was it? We applied our glasses, and soon made it out to be the enemy who had just crowned the hill after taking the redoubt behind, and was now preparing for an assault on the Russian centre. Their presence there showed that the redoubt must have been again captured by the Turks, though for a minute we could not make out whether they were infantry or cavalry. In less than a minute they began to descend the hill right in our direction, as though determined to drive our left out of Pelisat, and turn it. The battery to the right of the village now limbered up, and retreated back on the plain about a quarter of a mile, and again took up position. My own position, with a handful of cavalry behind the hill, now became rather disagreeable. If we were pressed back on the plain we could see nothing. If we remained where we were there was an extreme probability of being cut off and obliged to make a wide circuit to rejoin the army, not to speak of the probability of being directly in the line of fire. In less than five minutes the Turks began to descend the hill in our direction, not with a rush, but leisurely, and without firing, not in masses nor lines, but scattered and diffused. They came down about half-way in this manner, the Russian artillery tearing up the groups among them all the time in the most savage manner.

I was just beginning to think of the expediency of clearing out when there was a change. The Russian infantry fire, which had for the last five minutes been very heavy about Sgalince, now began to roll along the hill-crest in our direction, and the Turks, who were just coming into range, began to drop rapidly. I do not know whether the Turks originally intended to attack our left or not, but the fact is that there was a change in the direction of the attack. The advance now veered to the left, and went at the Russian trenches on the crest of the hills, half way between Pelisat and Sgalince, with a shout, opening fire at the same time. When they descended into the little hollow and were lost to sight for a time, while the Russian trenches flamed and smoked, a storm of balls was poured into the advancing Turks. This lasted from fifteen to twenty minutes, during which time a fearful loss of life must have occurred. Then we saw them begin to withdraw, as they went carrying off the wounded. But they had not yet had enough.

Encouraged by their success in taking the redoubt, and believing they could also take this line, they had no sooner withdrawn from the Russian fire than they formed and went at it again. They dived down into the Valley of Death to struggle there amid smoke and fire, a death struggle of giants; for there is nothing to choose between Russian and Turk on the score of bravery. Many bodies of Turks were found within ten feet of the Russian trenches. The little slope, on the crest of which the trenches were situated, was literally covered with dead. I counted seven on a space of not more than ten feet square. The battle here was terrible, but the Turks were again repulsed, and again they retreated up the hill. It will hardly be believed that they went at it again; and yet they did so. To us who had watched the two preceding assaults it seemed madness, because we could see that the Russian fire never slackened an instant, and that the Russian line never wavered, while we knew the Russian reserves were waiting behind ready to fall in at the least sign of wavering.

The scene of carnage was again repeated, but it only lasted a moment. The Turks, completely broken, withdrew, sullenly firing, and taking time to carry off their wounded and many of their dead. Still they held the redoubt, upon which they fell back apparently with the intention of holding it; but they were not allowed to remain long there. The attack on the redoubt in the Russian centre had been equally unsuccessful with that on the Russian trenches on the left. The Russians pursued them with a murderous fire, and then six companies went at them with the bayonet and swept them out of the redoubt like a whirlwind. At four o'clock the Turks were in retreat everywhere. The Russians occupied the whole of their first positions, besides pursuing the Turks a short distance with cavalry. The Russians were about 20,000. Their loss is estimated at 500, and the Turkish loss at 2,000 killed and wounded.

† PORADIM, *September* 1*st*.—I rode over the battle-field when the affair was over. The Sanitary Corps had already carried off the wounded, both Russian and Turkish; but the Turks left very few of the latter, and only about 300 dead on the field. Their losses could be better judged by the number of knapsacks left on the ground, which was strewn with them. The Russians had already begun to assemble and bury their dead. They were laid out in rows, Russians and Turks side by side.

From the Russian point of view I look upon the whole system of fighting in fortifications as a mistake. It would have been much better for General Zotoff to have retreated upon the Bulgarians, and drawn the Turks out into the open country, where their want of military science, good officers, and the impossibility of executing manœuvres on the field of battle, would have put them at a great disadvantage with the well-drilled Russian troops. The Russians have always been wanting the Turks to come out and fight in the open field, yet they entrench themselves in such a manner that the Turks have no temptation to come out, and find it impossible to do so when they try. If the Russians wish to fight them in the open field they should offer temptations to them to come out in the open field, and not meet them everywhere with fortifications. We have no news from Skobeleff, who may have been attacked yesterday likewise. The Turkish wounded say that an attack was meditated all along the line. Skobeleff is on the Selvi road, half way between that place and Loftcha.

On the ground between the left redoubt and Pelisat the Russian and Turkish dead were lying side by side. This ground had been fought over twice. The little hollow breaks through the crest of the hill of Sgalince and curves to the left in the direction of Pelisat for a distance of a quarter of a mile. It was along the brow of the low banks of Pelisat, by the side of the hollow, that the Russian trenches had been dug, among low brushwood two or three feet high, which partially hid them. It was here that the battle had raged hottest. Here, half way between Pelisat and Sgalince, the Turkish attack was made with the greatest violence and persistence. The Turkish dead were lying here so close to the trenches that they might have shaken hands with the Russians lying inside. It was certainly a desperate attack and a desperate resistance; but had the Turks even carried these trenches, as seemed possible, they would have been driven out by the Russian reserves lying in wait behind. The Turks, I observed, fired comparatively little, for what reason I know not, and they evidently hoped to win the day with the bayonet alone. It was in this little hollow I saw the Turks descend three times.

Everything considered, the attack seems to have been well directed. It was made so suddenly, and with such violence, that the Russian redoubt was taken almost by surprise. The first time it was in fact taken almost before General Zotoff knew the attack had begun; but I look upon both the attack and the defence as useless expenditure of blood. The capture of these positions would have been of comparatively little importance to the Turks, unless they had followed it up by an attack on the positions behind Poradim, which General Zotoff has fortified as his second line of defence, and they did not bring forward enough troops to have followed up the advantage had they gained one. They should have attacked with fifty thousand men instead of twenty thousand; or, better still, have attacked the Roumanians while only making a strong demonstration against General Zotoff, which everybody thought they would do.

* GORNY STUDEN, *September 4th.*—The Russians yesterday succeeded in defeating the Turkish force holding Loftcha, and driving it from a defensive position west of the place. The Russian force engaged consisted of the 2nd Division and a rifle brigade which had returned from Gabrova, marching ninety kilometres, one brigade of the 3rd Division, and Skobeleff's Brigade of Circassians Cossacks. None of the Russian troops, except the last brigade, had been previously

engaged, and their strength may be reckoned at about 22,000 men. The Turks cannot be estimated at more than 7,000.

Skobeleff on the previous evening marched from Kakrind, his previous defensive position, and carried a position on the north-east of Loftcha, which rendered the place virtually untenable. In the night, therefore, the Turks fell back on the fortified range of heights behind the town, and there awaited the attack. This was begun with artillery at sunrise, and the Russians' advance was so conducted that their artillery, passing south of Loftcha, took up a position enfilading the range of heights held by the Turks, and also cut off their retreat into the Balkans over the Trojan. Nevertheless the Turks resisted stubbornly, and were only driven out by hard infantry fighting, which lasted till near sundown.

The Russians underwent several repulses before they were finally successful. The Turks tried to retire upon Plevna; but Skobeleff's Cossack horse artillery stopped the way, and they went away due west, pursued by Skobeleff's Cossacks and part of the Imperial escort.

The following letter was written on the evening before the commencement of the third attack on Plevna:—

PORADIM, *September 6th.*—Leaving Gorny Studen yesterday morning, the headquarters of the Grand Duke went on to the village of Radenica, a few kilometres behind this place, where they now remain. Coming on to Poradim I found here Prince Charles of Roumania in chief command of the whole Army of Plevna, with his staff and escort. Here also was General Zotoff, who has the nominal position of chief of staff to the Prince. To-day Prince Charles paid a lengthened visit to the Grand Duke Nicholas, and the final arrangements were perfected. To-morrow morning at dawn of day a momentous battle will commence, but it will last more than one day.

Riding out this afternoon in the direction of Bogot, I found the troops advancing everywhere. The mistake of the last battle will not be committed of having troops half exhausted by a long march before attaining striking distance. The whole force, except the reserves, to-night bivouac close up to the forepost line. The scene was singularly impressive. Here a long column of cavalry, with dancing pennons, wound up the gentle green slope of the downs. Here a whole regiment stood in dense black square waiting for the command to march. Here another deployed into line swept briskly forward, with bayonets flashing in the sunshine. As the soldiers returned the greeting of the general they cheered lustily. In that cheer lingered no undernote of the sentiment conveyed in the greeting of the Roman gladiators. Battery after battery passed onward, the rattle of the wheels muffled by the grassy carpet. Slowly and with infinite labour the ox-trains lumbered forward, drawing the big siege-guns and their ammunition on the way to the prepared position whence to-morrow the huge projectiles will whistle into the Grivica redoubt. The hospital waggons, empty now, were pouring forward by the score. To-morrow night will see them full enough, for, to quote King Henry of Navarre, "Never saw I promise yet of such a bloody fray."

The following is an enumeration of the troops on the ground, with my estimate of their strength:—The 9th Corps, Baron Krüdener, comprising the 5th and 31st Divisions, 18,000 men. The 4th Corps, General Kriloff, containing the 16th and 30th Divisions, 20,000 men. One Brigade of the 2nd Division, Prince Imeretinsky, 6,000 men. One Brigade of the 3rd Division, 6,000 men. One Rifle Brigade, 3,000 men. The 1st Roumanian Division, Colonel George Angelescu, 14,000 men. The 2nd Roumanian Division, 14,000 men, Colonel Alexander Angelescu. In all say 80,000 infantry. The following are the cavalry details:—The 4th Cavalry Division, 2,000 sabres. The 9th Cavalry Division, 2,000. One Brigade of the 11th Cavalry Division, 1,000. One Brigade of Circassian Cossacks, 1,000. A portion of the Imperial escort, 200. The 1st Roumanian Division, 2,000; the 2nd Roumanian Division, 2,000. Total of cavalry, say 10,000. In all a compact and well-equipped army of about 90,000 men, with 250 field guns and 20 siege guns of 15 centimetre, an army the greater part of which had already been under fire, although this circumstance goes for but little with Russian soldiers. The Roumanians have not previously been seriously engaged, but are in fine condition and good heart, and seasoned by long camping and marching. The general in command of them under Prince Charles is General Cernat, previously War Minister, an officer with a high reputation for organization.

The arrangements for to-morrow do not appear of a complicated character. There has been a talk of elaborate strategy and of turning movements, passing both north and south of Plevna and falling on the rear of Osman Pacha. Some indication of a turning movement was suggested when Prince Imeretinsky took Loftcha, but the suggestion was deceptive. The course of attack promises to be almost identical with that pursued on the previous occasion. I have explained, I fear *usque ad nauseam*, that the Turkish positions were roughly in the form of a horseshoe, the convexity pointing toward the east, and the town of Plevna standing about the centre of the base. The Russians have been environing this horseshoe leaving the base open. To-night they simply move up closer, and to-morrow they will attack on the line of environment straight to their own front. Grivica stands in the toe of the horseshoe, and opposite the horseshoe is the Russo-Roumanian centre, in the rear of which is the place where I now write.

Here are fixed for the day the army headquarters, and here Prince Charles will probably be joined by the Grand Duke Nicholas with his staff. The Russians have the ground to the left, the ground of Schahofskoy in the previous battle. The Roumanians have the section of the environment to the right of the centre, being the ground on which Krüdener fought so stubbornly, although ineffectually, on the 30th of July. The front of each section is of about equal extent. The Turkish positions opposite the Roumanian section are the stronger both by nature and art. But there are but 28,000 Roumanians to 50,000 Russians. It seems logically to follow that the function of the Roumanians is intended to be chiefly of a demonstrative character. They will doubtless assail the Turkish positions opposite to them, and take advantage of opportunities should such offer. But they will do good service if they, to use a technical term, "hold" the Turks confronting them while the centre and left are delivering blow upon blow on the weaker sections of the Turkish front opposite them.

It cannot, indeed, be said that Grivica is a weak point, but it will not be quite so strong as it is now, after siege cannon have battered its earthworks for several hours. Opposite to it stands the Russian 5th Division, which will fall on after the artillery preparation. The line is prolonged toward the left flank by the 31st Division. On the downs above Sgalince and Pelisat, where General Krüdener, commanding the 9th Corps, made up by the two divisions just named, will have his headquarters, the alignment is yet further prolonged by the 30th Division and the 16th Division, reaching from the touch of the 31st Division to Bogot, where the 16th Division is chiefly massed, and where General Kriloff, commanding the 4th Corps, will have his headquarters. Prince Imeretinsky, from Loftcha, has detached one brigade south to Trojan to guard against trouble from that region, and to-day has marched north along the chaussée in the direction of Plevna with three brigades, viz., one brigade of the 2nd Division, one brigade of the 3rd Division, and the Tirailleur Brigade.

Of the details of his dispositions I am unaware, except that he touches General Kriloff near Bogot, and that his force is *à cheval* of the Chaussée, and constitutes the Russians' extreme left flank, which is very strong either for direct attack or for outflanking the Turkish position.

* NEAR RADISOVO, *September 7th.*—General Zotoff left Poradim last night, and spent the night in personally seeing to the disposition of the troops, returning no more to Poradim.

From no point is it possible to witness the whole of a battle extending over so wide an extent of front, and it remains for a Correspondent to choose the locality he considers likely to be most interesting. General Zotoff overnight had named to me as a rendezvous-place for the morning the heights between Sgalince and Pelisat, and thither, in the first instance, setting forward while it was yet dark, I directed my way. The morning was cold, but fine, with no clammy drizzle as on the morning of the previous battle. There was a weird impressiveness in the period of waiting up there among the long grass, watching the east for the light wherewithal to begin the fell game of battle. There had been a sharp frost during the night, and as the sun began to rise the whole surface of the earth was covered with a dense frost fog, which hung until dispelled by the sun's rays. About Pelisat I found the light brigade of the 4th Cavalry Division standing in reserve, along with a regiment of the Roumanian infantry and some Roumanian militia. I followed the road from Pelisat to Plevna in the direction of Radisovo along the high ground which had constituted the line of Schahofskoy's advance. We were on a broad saddle with undulations on either side of us. On the road we passed several battalions of the 30th and 5th Divisions, who had been working all night making battery emplacements for big guns, and were now going back towards Pelisat to constitute the reserve. We found ourselves just in the rear of the line of our batteries. On the slopes on our right were twelve of the big guns. On the slope on the other side were eight more, singularly close to the village of Grivica. In position in front of the great guns were the field batteries. The two on the right fired against the Grivica redoubt above the village. Three more were blazing away at what, in my narrative of the previous battle, I called the first Turkish position on the lower central ridge in front of Plevna.

The firing began about half-past six, it being now eight. There was no artillery firing apparent elsewhere than from the batteries whose position I have described. In the hollows in front, behind, and on the flanks of the batteries, were stowed away the infantry of the 5th and 31st Divisions, constituting the 9th Corps. Radisovo on our left front, held by the Turks yesterday, was reported evacuated overnight by them, and we had batteries, not indeed quite on the height before it, where in the previous battles Schahofskoy's cannon stood and fired so long, but on the slope to the right of it, almost in in a line with, but retired from the height I have named. The firing waxes and wanes. A few of the siege guns on the right which can get sight of the towers of Plevna down the long hollow are pitching shells in that direction, and the field guns fire in gusts and then are almost still. The indomitable Grivica redoubt now fires, now is still with an almost comical nonchalance. Now and then a man is wounded in the batteries in our immediate front, but as yet the work is child's play, and the work of the day can hardly be said to have begun.

Affairs not progressing rapidly here, we rode away due south across the fields behind the Radisovo hills and valley to Tucenica. Mounting the slope beyond we looked back north-west toward the reserve on the slope of the height behind Radisovo, and observed there a large mass of infantry and artillery belonging to the Turkish division; while above them on the ridge a battery was in action. Radisovo itself we could not see, because it stands imbedded in a curious fold of the valley. Whether it was held by the Turks or not we could not tell. We saw a few horsemen moving about, but whether Russian or Turkish patrols it was impossible to see on this slope. No mass of troops was visible, nor any artillery. A column of infantry and artillery was marching through Tucenica on the southward to Bogot, and this we followed, although it took us somewhat further away from Plevna, because by going towards Bogot it would be possible to learn what, if anything, was doing on our left flank. So far as regards the right opposite Grivica there was as yet nothing save artillery fire. On the plateau above Bogot troops stood ready to march. They were in battle array, and although their uniforms were sombre, still they made an imposing show. As we came up the slope by Bogot we passed a battalion of the 9th Division, an isolated battalion, marching down toward Tucenica, followed by a sotnia of wild-looking Kubanski Cossacks.

Putting our horses to feed in a deserted farmyard, we moved up through the massed troops, horse, foot and artillery, toward where the staff of General Zotoff stood on the hilltop. As we tramped Skobeleff dashed past us at the head of a sotnia of Circassian Cossacks with whom he had been making a reconnaissance along the Loftcha-Plevna chaussée, and was on the way back to make a report. Prince Imeretinsky, fresh from his victory at Loftcha, was here above Botok, and his regiments were tramping down the slope, steadily up the hill, and down the slope again, on their way over Tucenica towards the ridge about Radisovo. After a brief halt we followed the great column, a curious mixture of regiments of the 2nd Division, the 11th Division, and even the 12th Division, and followed on to the height behind Radisovo, the spot where Schahofskoy delayed awhile to enable Krüdener to come up in co-operation.

The battle had as yet hung fire, but now it was certainly warming. Our cannon, great and small, on the Russian right flank, where we had been in the morning, were firing furiously, whether still against Grivica or not we could not as yet tell. Another battery on the left of us, above Radisovo, was shelling what was called the Turkish first position. The well-remembered scene lay stretched before me. The village of Radisovo at my feet, where the wounded died at the hands of the Bashi-Bazouks, the ridge above so swept erstwhile by the Turkish shells that I had to dismount, with now once again its slope occupied by masses of Russian infantry, the white smoke hanging in the valley and on the low central ridge behind, the further ridge crowned with the Turkish camps, the towers of Plevna down among the green trees in the valley behind the town where the Russian dead lay so thickly. It was much the old thing. We were working round on our left flank, but there was that indomitable Grivica redoubt blazing away as hard as ever.

There seemed no hurry. We sat down contentedly on the slope above the village and looked down into the place so peaceful-seeming there with its low roofs amid the setting of greenery. How history repeats itself! Here again are the shells crashing into Radisovo or exploding against the slope on which we rest. Here again are Russian infantry men lying down on the reverse slope beyond Radisovo, waiting for the word to cross the crest and sally down into that valley already littered with so many Russian dead. Here again are the Russian guns on that crest belching their thunder against the Turkish positions. Still through all this turmoil, as through the last, the white towers and sparkling roofs of Plevna smile serenely in the sunshine.

We lie here hour after hour and watch the scene. It is impossible to tell the progress of the fight, for it makes no progress. Still hour after hour the batteries which first opened in the morning blaze away. The batteries on the crest above

Radisovo fire steadily if less swiftly. The battery on our left hand more slowly still. The Turkish shells burst with great clouds of smoke and dust on the crest on the reverse slope and village of Radisovo. The Grivica redoubt holds its own with its fire. Nowhere does the Turkish artillery seem in the least degree dominated. The village of Radisovo is blazing at our feet. It has at length caught fire after so many hair-breadth escapes. The sun sinks, and the situation remains unaltered. Scarcely a rifle has been fired to-day, all the work done has been with artillery, and the Russian loss is a mere handful. Probably the Turkish is not much greater. In every material sense Plevna is as far off being taken as ever. The Russians are taking two bites at a cherry. Will they do it at two?

* BEFORE PLEVNA, *September 8th.*—When the fighting, or rather cannonade, recommenced this morning, it was not easy at first sight to recognize that the Russians had gained any advantage by their profuse powder-burning of the day before. Last night the parapet of the Grivica redoubt had seemed a good deal jagged by the Russian shell fire; but, under cover of night, all its defects had been made good, and it looked as trim as if never a shot had been fired at it. But the Russians had been at work also during the night. They had gained a large slice of ground in the direction of Grivica, that is, their working parties had been pushed forward in the fortunate darkness, and a battery of siege guns had been built and armed on an elevation comparatively close to and overhanging Grivica village, and within easy battery range of the irrepressible redoubt.

As soon as the sun rose that battery came into action against the redoubt, supported by isolated big guns. Away to the right, and further to the rear on the left in rear of the advanced battery, the original battery of siege guns sent its fire sweeping down the valley and over traversing undulations into what in the previous battle was called the Turkish first position, the redoubt and entrenched village in the central swell. This position was also receiving the fire of two or three batteries of field guns stationed on the heights beyond Radisovo, the height where Schahofskoy's cannon stood so long. The redoubt could not reply to the siege battery, the range of the latter being too long, so it accepted punishment from that quarter, and pounded away in reply to the field batteries on the ridge. The practice was not good. I don't fancy there were ten casualties on that ridge throughout the day.

The Russian siege battery firing into the Grivica Redoubt made admirable practice: shell after shell, as I sat watching through my glass, burst in the parapet or went slap into the redoubt. Every now and then the guns were silent for ten minutes or so at a time, and sanguine people began to think that the stubborn defence had been abandoned, and that the defenders had departed bag and baggage. But when the Turk is in a place and means to stop there, he is a difficult customer to dislodge. The pause had been but a short interval to repair damages, and presently the Grivica gun-fire would recommence in its old jaunty fashion. It is not the key to the position, but its reduction would be a valuable gain; and instead of spreading their fire as they have done, the Russians should have concentrated upon it the whole weight of their bombardment, and made it untenable by dint of a hailstorm of shells. As it is they may bombard it for a week, sacrifice a brigade of infantry, and then after all not succeed in taking it. The assault was intended to have been begun yesterday afternoon at five, but the Russian clock is always more or less slow, and it came to pass that, owing to late starting and delays by the way, the troops were not quite all in position by the appointed time, and so the attack was postponed. Everywhere now the infantry are in position waiting for the word.

The scene from my commanding elevation is singularly interesting. Behind every swell, in the hollow of every depression, lying down behind the screen of Indian corn, are soldiers, some far away out beyond the batteries, and the Russian shells and Turkish shells whistle over their heads without disturbing them. Others are snugly stowed to the right and left of the batteries, lying on the reverse slopes so as to be clear of the hostile shells. All round the edge of the horizon, from the River Vid on the north, to the Loftcha-Plevna road on the south, rises up against the pale blue sky the white smoke of the cannon-fire. The Turkish horseshoe is girdled by a cincture of cannon-fire and armed men; but the Turk hardens his heart and gives back shell for shell, as in the impending fight he will return cheer for cheer, rifle-shot for rifle-shot, and bayonet-stab for bayonet-stab.

It is a curiously lazy moment for a Correspondent. After he has written down dry facts he has little to record. A regiment rises out of one hollow and marches through the tall Indian corn to another hollow, which is thought a better place. The villagers of Grivica down there in the hollow between the batteries, with shells interminably whistling over their heads, are actually engaged treading out their barley, on the primitive threshing floor of hardened mud, the men shaking the straw, the women driving the ponies in the endless round. Stoicism, or fatalism, or indifference, or despair, which are we to call it? Old Baron Krüdener, with his staff about him, looks down on the scene from behind the battery overhanging Grivica. The veteran has slept upon the field, and there is a look on his face that would indicate that he is no longer the victim of peremptory commands to do what his personal judgment condemns.

Some Roumanian guns are firing steadily into the Grivica Redoubt from the position at the corner of the wood on Krüdener's right, but it is a long range, and the shells are falling short of the redoubt on to the slope more to the left instead. Going down into a little valley and ascending then a little hill we find ourselves in the rear of the Russian great battery of the right flank, a battery containing twelve siege guns. The emplacement in which these are lodged is rough enough, but strong. The guns are fired en barbette. The battery has three faces: One armed with six guns looks down the valley towards Plevna and gives its fire to the redoubt and fortified village known as the Turkish first position. The centre face with three guns looks toward a Turkish redoubt behind the Grivica Redoubt, and connecting it with the great Plitzitza position on the due north flank of Plevna. The right face, armed with three guns, looks across at the Grivica Redoubt itself.

There are those among the spectators who think that Osman Pacha has virtually evacuated the position, and has left to hold it only a few thousand men with guns of position. To my thinking this view is utterly fallacious. The Turks are to-day developing a wider range of artillery fire than they did on that dreadful day when Schahofskoy and Krüdener in vain dashed against their positions. The Turks are adepts in marking time. They fire no harder than they find necessary. They are firing now steadily and deliberately in reply to a fire which, to all appearance, is not materially injuring them. If needful they could, I think, fire harder. Let the word be given to attack with infantry, and I venture to predict for the attacking Russians a mighty warm reception.

I note the Turkish camps on their most northernly ridge full of men all the way back from the Grivica Redoubt to the Plitzitza scarped height. On the central swell, I can see masses of their infantry men lying in the hollows, having turned out for the sake of safety from the shell-scourged redoubts. Leaving the great battery I ride round more to the left and more forward, coming over the level and descending a little way down the slope into the shell-fire. The theatre of the defence, and a large portion of the offence, the whole, indeed, of its right and centre, lie displayed before me. Directly opposite me is the Grivica Redoubt. Almost directly to the left of me is Plevna. Almost directly on the right is the Russian great battery. On my left front there are the Turkish positions—the main positions in fact before Plevna—those positions assailed by Schahofskoy on the 30th July. Their guns by this time are in full action, for the plot thickens towards noon. The Russian infantry has been pushed forward in skirmishing order, a tirailleur leading them, and the Archangel and Uglaskosky regiments following through the maize fields on the centre swell, driving back the outlying Turks. The artillery follow them, and come into action at short range against a Turkish redoubt. The Russians have now three lines of fire—the first, the field guns down in the maize; the second, also field guns, on the lower undulation behind at medium range; and the great cannon behind. The Turkish return fire, chiefly directed at the Russian first line of artillery, is very heavy. The ground is ploughed in all directions with their shells. Hardly any harm is done. The infantry lie quiet in the hollows along the fields; the gunners take their chance among the maize, and the enemy's shells mostly fly over them. Indeed, it is open to doubt whether the aim of the Turkish fire be not partly to search the reverse slopes.

For an hour and more there was very little change in the aspect of affairs hereabouts, so I moved still farther to our left to the crest of the range beyond and above Radisovo, where Schahofskoy's cannon stood so long. When I first arrived the crest was one array of field batteries, and the firing was very heavy, the Turkish shells doing great damage among the gunners, and falling behind among the infantry on the reverse slopes, and in Radisovo. But between two and three o'clock the guns advanced from the crest down the slope towards the Turkish positions, and continued to fire somewhat slackly at this shortened range. The fire of the guns on the left of this range of batteries must have reached into Plevna, and the reply came not alone from the Turkish batteries of the outer redoubts, but also from the cannon on the flanks of the town.

This despatch leaves the field at five o'clock. There are no indications of the assault to-day, and I believe it will not be commenced till to-morrow afternoon, although a redoubt may be earlier assaulted. The cincture of Russian cannon is drawing close round the Turkish positions; but the test will be not with cannon, but with prowess of men with arms in their hands. The Emperor, Prince Charles, and the Grand Duke were all on the battle-field both yesterday and to-day. The losses are much heavier to-day than yesterday.

* BEFORE PLEVNA, *September 9th.*—The attack by the column of Prince Imeretinsky's command, headed by General Skobeleff, from the Russian left flank beyond the Loftcha-Plevna road, against one of the redoubts on the south-western side of Plevna, was witnessed and has been chronicled by one of my colleagues. It was being prepared for when my despatch of yesterday left the field, and the result proved the truth of my belief that so far from the Turks having entirely abandoned the Plevna position, they are there in force, and mean to resist to the bitter end. There was heavy artillery fire during most of the night, for the Russians were determined to give no respite to the Turkish gunners in the redoubts. Last night and this morning there have been occasional spurts of infantry fire as well on the front of the horseshoe. As I begin to write, at nine A.M., there is evidence that the situation is materially changed from where my narrative yesterday left it.

The Roumanian batteries on the Russian right have been pushed forward more against the Grivica Redoubt, which is now assailed with cannon-fire from north-east and south. A battery has come right out into the open in front of the redoubt, and is maintaining its position there very obstinately in spite of the fire of the redoubt, which, now materially reduced, seems concentrated upon it. The Russian advanced batteries of what may be called the centre are still in the maize fields, and the heights in front of Radisovo is firing steadilv into what I have all along called the first Turkish position on the broad low central swell. They are very close up, but between them and the Turkish position is a broad sloping natural glacis affording no cover for attacking infantry, and the fire of the redoubt continues so strong that an assault on it would entail, if not sure failure, at least certain terrible loss. The Russian infantry is hidden everywhere around the concave, but is in readiness for the attack when the proper time is judged to have arrived. The siege guns in the Russian great battery have ceased firing, except those on the face looking towards Grivica, the range being somewhat uncertain. The firing on both sides is extremely languid, save occasional spurts. Apparently both are tired out. There is no use in staying here any longer. We go along to the ridge above and beyond Radisovo, and survey the scene from the exact spot where Schahofskoy stood and witnessed the early successes and final discomfiture of his men. We are now quite on the right flank front of the redoubt constituting the first Turkish position, and, looking across the valley, once strewn with Russian corpses, can see with a glass the Turkish gunners going coolly about their work amid the bursting of shells. Plevna lies on our left front. There comes now no Turkish fire on to the ridge where we stand, hot place as it was yesterday. The Russians have infantry massed on its reverse slope, waiting for the attack. They keep their guns silent just here, although the batteries on the same ridge to the right and left give and take.

Surveying the scene leisurely, I can discern how much stronger than at the time of the last battle Plevna is now. On the south and south-west of the town are several wholly new redoubts. There is one very large one on a detached knoll due south of the town, and on the long wooded ridge stretching up from it towards the Vid there is quite a chain of redoubts linked together by a covered way, and making a good line of Turkish cover on their right flank, and indeed partly in their rear as far as the river Vid. It was against the farthest of these redoubts that General Skobeleff went last night. Through the glass I can see little knots of Russian soldiers among the trees, and a few Turkish soldiers out on the stubble behind the works. These new redoubts command also the Loftcha-Selvi road, and they cover the side road coming into Plevna from out of the valley of the Vid, which otherwise might be utilized in a turning movement. On this southern face of which I speak are three strong redoubts connected by a covered way, with battery emplacements at intervals and rows of shelter-trenches. In front, on the central swell, I discern eight separate redoubts, besides a line of defence on the downs immediately covering the town of Plevna, and this is wholly exclusive of the great northern ridge. Its summit and slopes are one great entrenched camp, studded with redoubts and battery emplacements. The longer one looks at the place the more thoroughly does one come to feel the toughness of the work taken in hand by the Russians. The position must be attacked as a whole and taken as a whole. Granted that the northern ridge is taken and occupied in its integrity, the position of the central swell is not materially impaired. Suppose a lodgment effected on the central swell, that lodgment would be commanded by the northern ridge and the redoubts on the south of the town. All that is wanted to make the Turkish position virtually impregnable was the occupation and fortification of the ridge in front of Radisovo, that ridge on the exposed crest of which I am now writing. Probably this was not undertaken owing to a conviction that the force available was not strong enough to hold so wide an area.

Where is the Turkish force, be it great or small? I sweep the scene with my glass, and the only living things visible are the gunners on the slopes under the entrenched camps. But there are no moving figures around them; no soldier treads the brown sward between the redoubts; and yet it is said that in the entrenched camps on the northern ridge alone are quite 30,000 Turks, and I venture to aver that let the Russian infantry advance and very soon from the edge of the shelter-trenches and redoubts would burst out white jets of musketry fire. Toward the afternoon the cannon-firing has been much heavier than in the early part of the day. There has been some forepost skirmishing fire. The field-guns were within 800 paces of the Turkish redoubts, which as night fell offered great temptation to the Turkish infantry. In the afternoon a battery was constructed on the height above Radisovo. This battery will be armed in the night with six or eight siege cannon from the great battery, and the fire of these will fall at a short range on the first Turkish position. All the preparations are being made for the assault to-morrow. Krüdener moved at dusk to the Radisovo height with the 31st Division, to be closer for the assault upon the Turkish first position. Everything portends for to-morrow a bloody day.

* BEFORE PLEVNA, *September 10th.*—Still this long drawn-out artillery duel continues, and it is still doubtful whether the assault will be made to-day. In my telegram yesterday I mentioned a movement forward to the height before Radisovo of a portion of the siege guns of the Russian great battery, and of three regiments of the 31st Division. There was no cessation of cannon-fire until after nightfall, but after my message left the field occurred several interesting episodes. The Grand Duke, with Prince Charles and General Zotoff, came forward into the line of the batteries on and upon either side of the prolongation of the ridge on which stands the Grivica Redoubt, in order to watch the effect of the infantry fire against the Turkish gunners working the cannon of the redoubt. Already indeed the Roumanian infantry had occupied a species of natural shelter-trench in front of their advanced battery, and had been doing their best to pick off the Turkish gunners; but much effect had not been apparent. A couple of companies of Russian infantry, just as the sun was sinking, quitted some brushwood about half up the slope between the village of Grivica and the redoubt. They had lain in this brushwood all day. They advanced in skirmishing order

up the slope towards the redoubt, firing as they advanced. They got up pretty close, and were not without hopes of entering the redoubt without much opposition. The impression had prevailed that the Turks were evacuating the redoubt, and the officers thought that they had seen the Turkish guns going back from out of the redoubt towards the entrenched camp. A Cossack officer with nine men left the advancing skirmishers, and pushed on towards the glacis. They got within a hundred yards of the foot of it, but then there confronted them a row of Turkish rifle muzzles, and a row of Turkish heads above the crest of the shelter-trench, a little way in front of the outward slope of the parapet of the redoubt. The Cossack did not, under these circumstances, think it advisable to persevere, and retired on his supports, who remained where they were until nightfall, exchanging a desultory fire with the Turkish skirmishers in the shelter-trench. During the night there were several outbursts of infantry fire, but none of importance.

This morning, the field guns in the valley against the Turkish first position in the central swell are moved somewhat farther forward, and the field guns which were yesterday on the heights in front of Radisovo, have given up that position to the siege guns, and have themselves moved forward down the slope, where they are now in action against the southern flank of the Turkish first position at a very short range; but the cannonade languishes. The time would seem to have come for delivering the assault, if it ever is to be delivered; but I understand that once again there is a postponement. The Turks are to have another day of shell-fire, and then to-morrow, reckoned as an auspicious day, as it is the Emperor's name-day, the great effort with the infantry is to be made. It may be worth noting that the bombardment began on the anniversary of the Emperor's coronation. It is a dull day. We look, for instance, to vary the monotony, to Prince Tcherkasky, who has abandoned for a time the reorganization of Bulgaria. He is riding about the field at the head of a train of ambulance waggons, anxious to discover the best place at which to station them. Yesterday I advised him to go to Imeretinsky, on our left flank, and there he found a harvest. To-day I ventured to suggest to him that he will do well to place his vehicles on the heights behind Radisovo, as one of Krüdener's divisions will there be in his front under fire. He rides on in the direction indicated, unmindful that that part of the road he must traverse is swept by the Turkish shell-fire.

It was very monotonous here, and I ventured once more on the height in front of Radisovo, although, owing to the removal thither of some siege suns, the return fire from the Turks made that position far from an elysium of safety. I found on the reserve slope three of Krüdener's regiments; on the crest itself, the General of Artillery, with his staff, sitting down to save exposure. On our left, nearer Plevna, was the siege battery, sending shells right over the Turkish central swell into the entrenched camp on the northern ridge; while at our feet, on the slope, and also in front of the Turkish first position on the central swell, the Russian field-guns were firing at the redoubt. The Artillery-General told me that in it there had been four guns yesterday which had been dismounted, and that during the night four more had been brought up into it, which were now replying. They were making sad and slow work of it in the midst of the hurricane of shells poured into the redoubt, and every now and then many minutes elapsed when the fire therefrom was altogether silent, and when it seemed that the redoubt had been silenced. But the Turk dies hard; and ever after a pause came back a shell or two. The central ridge was being heavily bombarded by the Russian field batteries to the left of the great gun battery, and was answering with spirit, aided by the guns in the redoubt. Due south of Plevna the Russian batteries on the ridge were also firing at the church of Plevna, which had been converted into a powder magazine. From this summit it was clear that the Russian fire was gradually beating down the fire of the Turks. The Roumanians on the right flank had worked very far round, so as to reach behind Rahovo, and the cannon of their right attack were now shelling the Turkish entrenched camp on the northern ridge, which the siege guns beside us were also pounding into. Imeretinsky was thundering on our left flank, although he did not appear to have got any closer than when Skobeleff went for the redoubt the evening before last. The day wore away with no further incident.

To-night the Emperor and the Grand Duke sleep in Poradim, so as to be near at hand for to-morrow's work. If nothing unforeseen occurs, the assault will be made ere to-morrow's sun sets. It is time Plevna was over and done with, for the Czarewitch has been compelled to fall back from the line of the Lom. To-night it rains and thunders.

The following letter, describing Skobeleff's attack upon the Turkish redoubt, is from another Correspondent:—

† Before Plevna, *Saturday*, *September 8th.*—This attack upon

Plevna resembles a siege more than anything else. So far there does not seem to have been a single shot exchanged by the infantry. After a hard day's work yesterday the big battery of twelve siege guns opened fire this morning at daybreak, and has been pounding away ever since until now, twelve o'clock. I observe a considerable escâpe of gas from the heavy steel guns of 13 centimètres calibre, of which there are four. Behind this battery is an observatory, consisting of a ladder about 60 feet high, sustained by ropes, on the top of which is generally a soldier with a field-glass, watching the result of the firing. The position of this man when a shell comes along, as it does every now and then, threatening to cut the ladder in two and bring him down with a rush, must be very disagreeable.

The Roumanian batteries away to the right can be heard pounding away on their side, and from our position in the big batteries smoke can be seen to the left overlooking Radisovo, where the Russian guns are blazing away in exactly the same position they were in yesterday; and although yesterday evening the necessity of advancing the batteries nearer the Turkish positions was admitted on all hands, we found this morning on looking at the position that nothing of the kind had been done. The fire of the Turkish redoubt of Grivica does not seem to have slackened in the least, in spite of the number of shells thrown into it yesterday; and although we can see the earth flying into the air in the middle of the redoubt, and now and then pieces of the parapet are carried away, the Turkish guns reply to the Russian as regularly as clockwork. Whatever loss may have been inflicted upon them in men, certainly we do not seem to have succeeded in dismounting any of their guns. It is very probable that the Turks have not many men in the redoubt, but they are hidden in the trenches and low places in the ground outside, and beyond that, a few only are kept in the redoubt for the management of the guns, who as fast as they are killed are replaced by others. Were it otherwise, if the Turks kept the redoubt full of men, the loss would be terrible, for an enormous number of shells have been thrown into it by the Russians and Roumanians.

Part of the guns of the big battery are fired upon this redoubt, part on the entrenched camp away to the left of the redoubt overlooking Plevna, and part on the Turkish batteries in the hollow between Grivica and Plevna. The fire of these batteries is less steady, more irregular, and not so well sustained as yesterday. It is probable that some of the guns have been dismounted. The firing, nevertheless, is still kept up. I must say I do not believe much in the effect of this artillery fire. There were to be mounted altogether four hundred guns bearing upon the Turkish positions; but, so far, not more than one hundred or a hundred and twenty seem to have been brought into position; and, as far as may be judged, the effect to the present moment has been very slight. They will have to come to much closer quarters than at present before the artillery fire can be made to tell.

If on the Russian right and centre the attack maintains its character of a siege, such is not the case on the left, where General Zotoff has ordered an advance. Leaving the big siege battery about noon, which was slowly pounding away with sledge-hammer blows on the Grivica redoubt and the lower batteries, I rode along the line to the left, passing behind the whole series of batteries, from the centre past Radisovo, almost to the Loftcha road. We found a battery behind Radisovo, throwing shells into one of the Turkish redoubts in front of the town. No embankments had been thrown up here, but the guns simply placed in line along the brown hill, were worked very rapidly, and I observed that there was no escape of gas from the breeches of these guns. This battery was behind, and to the left of Radisovo, on the ridge which runs parallel to the little hollow which goes down through Plevna from Grivica. In front of Radisovo is another ridge running parallel to this, and on this ridge was placed one more Russian battery, while the side opposite to the Turks was covered with infantry lying behind cover on the crest. This battery was also pouring a well-sustained fire into the lower Turkish redoubts before Plevna.

We passed behind the battery, proceeded farther to the left, where the hillside was covered with cornfields, vineyards, and a number of trees, threw ourselves down under the shade of the trees to lunch with the aid of some delicious grapes just ripe, and watch the battle from this point. Plevna was quite visible, and we could have been little more than two miles distant from it. And far down before us, distant about a mile, was a line of troops still lying under cover of the ridge, apparently waiting for the moment to begin the attack. These troops could not have been more than a mile from Plevna, and from our standpoint seemed not more than two or three hundred yards from the town.

The view from here is exceedingly fine. Down in what seemed a narrow valley or gorge, we could perceive the town of Plevna, with its masses of green foliage, from which rose the slender spires of two or three minarets. On the mountain behind Plevna, some distance above the town, we could distinguish two redoubts on the other side of the Loftcha road, from which rose two columns of smoke. Behind and above these redoubts were high wooded mountains extending round towards the right. On the other side of this valley is a ridge beginning behind Plevna, and extending to the right as far as Grivica. It is on this ridge that the principal Turkish defences are built—two entrenched camps and two or three redoubts, the last of which, behind Grivica, is the one against which Krüdener's forces were broken, and against which the Roumanian batteries, and part of the heavy siege batteries, are now playing. From the hills all around rose columns and columns of white smoke, and there was not an instant when these hills were not echoing with the thunder of a hundred and fifty guns, Turkish and Russian, that were roaring at each other.

Then again on our left, on a ridge this side of the Loftcha road, at a distance of a mile and a half or two miles, was another Russian battery pounding away at some invisible foe on the other side. The sun is hot, and a veil of smoke hangs over hill, valley, and mountain, which often makes it difficult to distinguish with certainty anything but a sudden flash of fire and a huge ball of white smoke that rises from each discharge of the line described by the Russian and Roumanian positions round Plevna, which begins opposite Bukova, extending nearly parallel with the Sistova road until beyond Grivica, then curving round past Radisovo until within two miles of Plevna, nearly on the Loftcha road, then extending along the Loftcha road on the ridge as far as opposite Krishine. The line thus described is exactly in the form of a reaping-hook, with the point opposite Bukova, the middle of the curve opposite Grivica, the junction of the handle close into Plevna, and the end of the handle at Krishine. The point nearest Plevna, it will be perceived, is near the Loftcha road, at the junction of the handle with the blade.

We had not been in our position under the trees more than ten minutes when we were evidently perceived by a look-out in one of the Turkish redoubts below Radisovo, and probably believing that the Indian cornfield by the side of us, interspersed here and there with trees, was very likely filled with troops, they began to shell us. After they had thrown three shells, all of which fell within twenty yards of us, and the last considerably nearer, we thought it was time to decamp, and withdrew behind the ridge, where a considerable number of soldiers were lying. We finished our lunch under the shade of another tree in a less advantageous position for sight-seeing, and when I again mounted the top of the ridge I was surprised to see two more Russian batteries far down the ridge, in the direction of Plevna, just to the right of the spot where we had seen the Russian troops previously. These batteries were now within a mile of Plevna, and were shelling one of the redoubts behind Plevna in a corner formed by the course of the Sofia road. Columns of white smoke were rising to the sky, and the sharp whip-like cracks of these field pieces were mingling angrily with the dull heavy roar of the siege guns in the big battery above. I pushed down through the vineyards and cornfields and trees farther and farther towards the Loftcha road, following the ridge down to where it ends in the deep narrow ravine running almost parallel to the Loftcha road.

I had here climbed up into a tree to get a better view of the situation, when a Cossack came and informed us that there was something more interesting going on on our left, that the Russians were advancing there, with "hurrahs." We went back across the ridge a short distance and saw what it was. The Russians under Imeretinsky and Skobeleff, the same who took Loftcha the other day, were advancing rapidly along the ridge bordering on the Loftcha road towards Plevna. The Loftcha road, before entering Plevna, passes over the high round of a hill covered with trees, which are not so thick, however, as to be called a wood. The summit of this hill is about a mile and a half distant from the Turkish redoubts in the bend of the Sofia road. The Russians were advancing over this mountain in loose order, with cavalry ahead, for we saw a number of horsemen making their way through the trees, and a few minutes later perceived a couple of squadrons of dragoons advancing along the Loftcha road, cautiously treading their way as they went. They were already over the top of the hill, probably half a mile, when we saw the dragoons, in skirmishing line, turn their horses' heads back, and begin firing as they slowly retired. Then there was considerable firing from the skirmishing line on both sides, although I could not distinguish the Turks from the Russians among the trees. Then the Turks began throwing shells towards where the dragoons were massed under the trees. They must have been able to see these dragoons, for the shells fell directly in the line. Each successive shell fell closer and closer, so that the dragoons began to shift their position.

This lasted perhaps twenty minutes. Then from the whole side of the mountain began to be heard the rattle of small-arms, which grew heavier and heavier, and the mountain and trees were soon covered with clouds of thin blue smoke. It was the infantry arriving in line and beginning the attack. The Turks were posted in the trees at the foot of this mountain, and probably half a mile in front of the redoubt, and replied to the Russian fire with vigour. The Russians gradually advanced down the side of the mountain through the trees, driving back the Turks, part of whom seemed to retire upon Plevna, but the greater part upon the redoubt. The Russians pushed down to almost the bottom of the hill, and we saw the Turks retreating up the smooth slope leading towards the redoubt by hundreds, and from the redoubt itself began to be poured forth a heavy fire upon the Russians on the opposite slope. The Russians pushed down steadily nevertheless in loose order, firing as they came; but as they neared the foot of the slope the Turkish fire became terrible. From the parapets of the redoubt poured forth a steady wave of flame, and the redoubt itself was soon hidden in the thick fog of white smoke that rose over it. The roar of this tremendous fire was simply fearful. I do not remember to have ever heard anything like it, or to have ever seen in any battle anything like so well-sustained a fire.

This also lasted about twenty minutes. Then the Russian skirmishing line, which had already reached the foot of the slope, began to withdraw, and in a few minutes they had retired to a position half way up the slope, where they halted, and the slackening of the fire told that for the moment the attack upon the redoubt, if attack it was, had failed. We now saw the Turks coming down again from the redoubt, and re-entering the trees at the foot of the slope where the Russians had been, and likewise those who had retreated towards Plevna seemed to come out again, for we saw them in the maize fields, just on the other side of the ravine between us and them, pushing along as though they would turn the right of the Russian attack. This was impossible, because the infantry on our side were lying close behind the ridge, and would have effectually prevented any movement of this kind.

During all the time this fight lasted our batteries, which I have already spoken of as having advanced so far down towards Plevna, were quite silent; why I cannot understand, for just at this moment when the attack was going on they should have concentrated their whole fire upon the redoubt, and I cannot understand why the infantry, which was lying in masses near these batteries, did not take part in the attack. The whole burden was on the left column advancing by the Loftcha road, nor was there any attack made anywhere else at the same time, nor on any other of the Turkish positions.

The artillery fire had ceased everywhere. Everybody seemed to be waiting the result of this attack. This was just the very way to make the attack a failure, even if it had any chances of success, for the whole army to stand still and look idly on while one small detachment was trying to attack the redoubt. It is a very strange proceeding. Not a single shot was fired at the small body of skirmishers who came out from Plevna, and annoyed the right of the attack, although they were within easy range both of the artillery and infantry.

The attack had begun about five, too late in the day to accomplish anything if the capture of the redoubt had been intended. This was probably not hoped for to-day. The Russians remained in the positions to which they had withdrawn on the slope of the mountain, and the Turks began to swarm out of the redoubt down to the foot of the slope. They were evidently attacking in their turn, and bent upon driving the Russians back to the point which they had originally occupied in the morning. Although it was not light enough to see, I imagine that the Russians had already been strengthening their positions by digging, for they now poured a fire from the line they had occupied, which in steadiness and fury was only equalled by the Turks from their redoubt. The Turks had already advanced a considerable way up the slope before the Russians opened fire, and they did not stand a moment under it. They retreated through the trees, and again up the slope to the redoubt, hotly pursued by the Russians, who followed them to the foot of the slope.

The fire on both sides was now dreadful, and the Russians seem to have received a considerable number of reinforcements, for their advance was far more steady and swift, more self-confident than the previous one had been. They swept down into the little hollow between the opposite slopes, and then poured a terrible fire on the Turkish redoubt from behind the trees, and under cover of the banks, stones, earth, and anything they could find to shelter themselves. This time the attack was moreover supported by our batteries on the right, which now advanced still nearer Plevna, and concentrated their fire on the Turkish redoubt.

At the time the Russians were advancing down the hill, the whole valley was filled with smoke. The town of Plevna, as well as the Turkish redoubts and even part of the wood where the Russians were, had become invisible. The sun was now just setting behind a mass of clouds, but it was seen for a few minutes like a fiery blood-shot eye, which tinged the smoke hanging over everything with the colour of blood. Then it suddenly disappeared behind the mountain, and darkness settled down over the scene. The fire continued for some few minutes longer, and from the redoubt, as from the foot of the slope and the foot of the mountains, sprang forth thousands upon thousands of jets of flame like fireflies. Then the fire suddenly ceased. The fight for the night was over. The Russians remained in their positions at the foot of the slope which leads up to the redoubt, about a quarter of a mile from the parapet. It could not have been their hope or intention to advance any farther.

To-day's attack was begun too late to have carried the redoubt, unless it could have been done by a simple assault with the bayonet—a manner of attack which, I think, the Russians have abandoned against the trenches held by the Turks. They will probably dig trenches here in the night so as to shelter themselves from the fire of the redoubt, and then either work gradually up to the redoubt by means of shallow trenches, which could be dug very rapidly, and which would enable them to reach the parapet in the day, or, choosing a favourable moment to-morrow morning, make a rush for it. Of the two plans, the former, in my opinion, has the better chance of success. The distance from the Russian positions to the redoubt is probably something over a quarter of a mile, up a smooth even slope, where there is not cover for a rabbit. The glacis is a quarter of a mile, or perhaps a little more, in extent. The loss of an assaulting column rushing up over this glacis under the fire the Turks poured out of the redoubt yesterday, would be something terrible. If the Turks stood to their positions and fired with anything like precision, not one man would probably reach the parapets; but then it is also possible that the defenders of the redoubt, seeing the Russians close, would lose their presence of mind, and fire wildly over the heads of the assaulting party.

I now retired from the position which I had occupied during the whole fight; and although it was almost dark, and I did not think I could be seen from the Turkish redoubt, I soon found out my mistake. I and my comrade had not been under cover for more than three or four minutes, when a shell was fired at us, which passed over our heads, and exploded not more than forty feet before us, exactly in the road which we were following. As there was no battery anywhere near here, and no Russian troops either, the shot could only have been fired at us, and it was the last fired by that redoubt this evening.

We made our way back to the top of the plateau behind

Radisovo, but the night now became so dark that it was impossible to find one's way across the fields. There was no water here for our horses but that contained in a muddy, stinking pool, which, however, they drank greedily. For ourselves, we obtained a drink from an ambulance, and then, coming upon a heap of unthrashed wheat, we gave a few bundles of it to our horses, and made the rest into a bed and a house for the night. The greater part of this telegram was written here in the fields by the light of a spluttering candle blown about by the wind. All around us we see the flickering of lights and camp fires in the distance, and every now and then flashes of fire in the direction of the battery of Russian siege guns, or the Turkish redoubt at Grivica, followed by a dull booming like thunder, show that here neither Turk nor Russian is asleep.

† LEFT WING, NEAR THE LOFTCHA ROAD, *Sept. 9th*, 9 A.M.—The night passed off quietly enough. About ten o'clock there was a sudden outburst of musketry fire, which lasted a few minutes, and which was probably a false alarm on the part of the Russians or Turks. Then, again, we were awakened about twelve o'clock by loud cheering away somewhere on our left. I jumped up and looked about me. All was darkness, with here and there in the distance a smouldering camp fire burning dimly. There was no other light but that of the stars, and intermittent flashes now and then on the horizon that seemed like sheet lightning, followed by a heavy boom that in the stillness of the night made the air vibrate strangely. I lay down again, and went to sleep.

This morning the artillery fire began at daybreak all along the line, but in a desultory manner. Just before sunrise there was a sharp musketry fire somewhere down before Radisovo, which lasted perhaps twenty minutes, then ceased. Shortly after sunrise the fusillade began again with violence towards the Loftcha road, but it seemed to come from considerably behind where it should have been, if it were a renewal of the attack of yesterday. The Turks were shelling this place so hotly, probably under the supposition that the trees and Indian corn concealed Russian troops, that I had to decamp. I retired to a point next the ridge, where I still had an excellent view of the two Turkish redoubts in the bend of the Sophia road, the positions where the attack occurred yesterday, and the whole length of the ridge, behind which lies the Loftcha road. I then perceived that, so far from renewing the attack this morning, the Russians had withdrawn in the night from the foot of the slope which leads up to the Turkish redoubt, and were back on the summit of the low woody mountain or hill whence they had attacked yesterday.

This hill or ridge, as it seems from here, is cut in two by a depression of considerable depth, through which passes the Loftcha road. The Russians on their side of the road were not long perceiving that the Turks were on the other occupying the place, where I saw the dragoons first advancing yesterday. Imeretinsky's artillery is where it was yesterday, about a mile back from the present Russian position on the hill, and fully two and a half miles from the redoubts which he was attacking yesterday, and which cannot be even visible to his artillerymen.

Imeretinsky does not seem to have brought a single gun nearer to the attack than this point. The Russians seem to be very much afraid of losing their artillery. I have already spoken of the unaccountable conduct of their artillery in stopping fire upon the Turkish redoubts when the attack began, and when it ought to have been hottest. I can so far find no excuse for this inaction unless they suddenly ran short of ammunition at that critical moment, for the Russians were never so near the redoubt as to make it necessary for the artillery to cease firing. The attack was not sustained by the artillery, and was begun far too late in the day to succeed. The five o'clock attack, as I said, was led by Skobeleff. When I arrived at my new standpoint, there was a lively artillery fight going on between Imeretinsky and the Turkish batteries which had advanced during the night on the hill on the other side of the Loftcha road. Suddenly there arose in front of the hill against the black thunder-cloud which hung over it an immense pyramid of flame, that seemed to rend the sky to the zenith. Then followed a long volume of smoke that rose white as snow against the blackness of the cloud. Then there came a series of startling reports all in a second, as though a battery of a hundred guns had been fired. Then there arose on the Russian hill a long, loud shout. They had exploded a Turkish magazine.

I now learned from an officer here on observation, who was sending reports to General Kriloff every few minutes of the progress of events, that Skobeleff was on the ridge before me, and I was about starting to join him, when the sudden din and uproar of battle, like a thunder-clap, held me spell-bound with admiration. The crest of this ridge suddenly began to vomit flame and smoke. Above this ridge, far higher up, were balls of flames that flashed and disappeared, each leaving a small round fleece of white smoke. The Turkish shrapnel exploding over the heads of the Russians was deafening; and the heavy booming of the distant siege guns slowly pounding away at short regular intervals, as though keeping time, produced a sublime effect. The Turks were in their turn attacking the Russians from the other side, and the Russians had evidently reserved their fire until the Turks were very near, which accounted for the sudden furious outburst. "That Skobeleff," said the officer near me, "how he is giving it to them!" and three or four Cossacks watching with intense excitement depicted on their faces, expressed their satisfaction, convinced that he was there in the middle of the fight, with that charmed life of his, ordering and directing.

In the meantime the Turkish skirmishers coming from Plevna pushed along our side of the ridge on the other side of the deep ravine, as though going to take Skobeleff in the rear. To-day our artillery seems to be more wide-awake than yesterday, for a battery now came galloping down through the vines and corn, and unlimbering in a moment, began shelling these skirmishers, while the Turkish redoubt instantly opened on this new battery. The latter, however, paid no attention to the redoubt, but concentrated its whole fire on the skirmishers, and, as it was taking them in rear and flank, they soon began to retire. The Turkish shells fired from the redoubt all passed over the battery and exploded in a little hollow behind, about fifty yards to the right of where we were, and all nearly on the same spot. The Turks never seem to correct their aim. In a few minutes the fire began to slacken, and two or three minutes later a loud shout swept along the ridge before us, followed by prolonged cheering. The Turks were evidently beaten back. Then the fire ceased, but the shouting continued, going farther and farther away. Skobeleff was evidently going at the flying Turks with the bayonet. Now the fighting is over for the present, but the big guns are still pounding away on our right.

The great infantry assault was made by the Russians on the 11th of September, the fifth day of the bombardment. The following letter, the whole of which was transmitted by telegraph, describes the operations directed against the redoubts of the first and second Turkish positions, and the redoubt on the detached mamelon south-east of the town, considered by the Russians to be the weakest point of the Turkish line of defence:—

* BEFORE PLEVNA, *Tuesday*, *September* 11*th*.—I have to record the events of to-day, the results of which it is not possible dispassionately to estimate with the din of battle still ringing in one's ears.

To-day was the fifth day of the bombardment. After the thunder of last night the morning broke with rain, which settled down into a dense mist through which objects were invisible at a distance of one hundred yards. We lost our way several times in riding from the place where we had snatched a few hours' sleep to our old position of the day before on the heights in front of Radisovo, which exposed position the Artillery-General of the 9th Corps, Colonel Wellesley, a Prussian Correspondent, and myself, had all to ourselves.

Affairs did not seem much altered since yesterday. About 10 A.M. the fog lifted somewhat, and let us have a partial view of the scene before us. The guns of the redoubt of the Turkish first position on the central swell still replied to the fire of the Russian batteries in the valley to the east of it. The Grivica Redoubt was still alive, although its fire could not be called brisk. To our left, near the Loftcha-Plevna road, there were occasional bursts of infantry fire, but these were very intermittent, and always died out after a few minutes. The Turks were visible out in the open between their first and second positions, on the central swell, toiling away at spade work under the shell-fire of the Russian batteries. The Russian siege-gun battery near us was occasionally firing over the central swell at the entrenched camps on the northern ridge of the Turkish position, and occasionally throwing shells into the town of Plevna.

Soon after ten almost total silence prevailed, only a single report echoing sullenly among the heights at rare intervals. There grew somehow upon one the impression that this was but the calm before the storm. Of this lull the Turks jauntily took advantage to come out from behind the parapets of the earthworks and stroll about the glacis with the utmost nonchalance. Everybody spoke in whispers, as if afraid or loth to break the universal unnatural stillness, interrupted only feebly by the far-off cannonade and musketry fire of Imeretinsky, round on the extreme left, near the Valley of the Vid. The drizzling fog came down again, and veiled alike friend and foe.

At eleven precisely, a furious musketry fire suddenly burst out on our left. We could judge that it came from the soldiers pushing their way out of the gap through which passes the Loftcha-Plevna road, but the fog hid everything from us. Only the sound told us that the attack must be on the redoubt on the summit of the isolated mamelon south-east of the town of Plevna. It was impossible to see twenty yards in front of one. Everywhere the cannon opened a heavy fire, and their smoke made the obscurity denser. It must be the assault at last, and, alas! it is invisible. Louder and louder swells the roll of the hidden musketry. We reckon that Skobeleff must be at work down there on our left, but we can hardly discern each other as we lie upon the crest of the ridge. We are in the thick of the din, but we might as well have no eyes. It is the most mysterious, weird situation possible to conceive. It is impossible to tell how the fighting is going. The musketry fire seems to advance but little, but its roll unquestionably swells in volume. The hiddenness of the whole thing is intensely torturing. The thick air above us, as we are lying down, is torn by the whistle of bullets, and the yell and scream of shells. In vain we chafe for the merest glimpse down into the hollow on our left. The thick waves of fog and smoke swathe everything as with a huge dingy pall. The Artillery-General is almost mad with irritation at his inability to see anything. We can do nothing, however, but possess our souls in patience; but as the minutes wear on, we can discern by ear that the Russians must be gaining ground. It seems to us here at one moment, to judge by the sound of the firing and of the cheering, that they had actually carried the redoubt on the summit of the isolated mamelon. Will they then assail the redoubts of the central swell, or make a dash for the town of Plevna, or do both? It must be a terrible time for the Turks thus assailed by invisible foes, and in ignorance whence the next blow is to be struck and where it is to fall. So far as I can make out, they seem to be reserving their fire till their foes come to close quarters. As for the Russians, although they are firing heavily as they advance, it must be firing at random. It is certain that they can see no enemy. In one sense the fog is an advantage for them, because by it they are being somewhat spared in the rush forward. But the sound of their firing must indicate some mark to their enemies, and in the obscurity the directness of their advance must be impaired. The Turks make little response to the furious shell fire of the Russian batteries on their positions, perhaps because many of their guns have been dismounted, or because they are short of ammunition, or because they feel that it would be in a great measure labour lost in the thick fog. We know nothing, save that the air is full of noise and of missiles, that we are a prey to a suspense which would be insupportable were it not that it must be endured.

About twelve the fog begins to lift, almost as dramatically as it fell. We can see the line of the Turkish northern heights, but the intervening valley is full of dense white smoke. Then presently we get a glimpse into, as it were, the interstices of smoke, and discern the Russian field batteries in the valley, blazing away with all their might at the Turkish first and second positions on the central swell, but the fog and smoke still obstinately hang round and above those positions themselves, and utterly obscure for the time the region of the attack on our left.

At one moment it seems as if the roll of the Russian musketry fire were wavering and receding. Then the sound swells again. There is an evident rally, and the noise moves forward. Just for a moment in the break of the smoke I get a glimpse through the obscurity at the Turkish second position on the central swell, and note that its cannon, disregarding the Russian fire poured into it, are firing hard in the direction of the hostile musketry fire. So mysterious is the situation that a Russian officer sitting by us starts the theory that it is an attack not by the Russians at all, but by the Turks; and it is certainly impossible to adduce any evidence to the contrary. We can make nothing of it, and are fain, in the language of Lord Dundreary, to give it up.

One thing is certain now, as the time passes on, that if the sound of firing be any indication, the infantry fighting has a tendency to retrograde from the Turkish front. It is coming nearer and nearer to us, and if it indeed be an attack on the part of the Turks they are storming the western verge of the ridge on which we lie. In utter desperation we abandon our position, walk westward along the ridge farther to our left, and nearer to the fighting just above the western edge of the village of Radisovo, exactly along the space held by Schahofskoy's staff as forepost line on the night of the 30th July. I found several batteries of Russian field artillery of the 31st Division in steady action against the first and second Turkish position on the central swell, and only a little to the right and rear of the infantry men still engaged in desultory fighting, as evidenced by the maintenance of a dropping fire.

The colonel in command of the battery told us with an assumption of indifference, which I am sure was feigned, that the fighting dying out was merely forepost work, to clear the way for the grand assault against the redoubt on the isolated mamelon, which was to be made in the afternoon. He may, indeed, have believed what he said, but another tale was told, when for an instant a sharp eddy of wind blew fog and smoke away from the mamelon and slopes leading up. There was no fighting there now, but with my glass I could discern the Russian dead and wounded lying about sadly thick. As for the Turks, some of them were dispersed at random, in among the wounded on the slopes. We could divine their fell purpose. Successive bodies of Turks were streaming down the slope of the mamelon against the huddled mass of Russians retiring seemingly on their shelter-trenches athwart the mouth of the road ravine and ascending the slopes to our immediate right. There could be but one inference, that the Russian infantry had unsuccessfully assailed the mamelon redoubt, and that its garrison was taking the counter offensive. It was also clear that Skobeleff had attacked the redoubt and covered way due east from the isolated mamelon. My artillery friend stated further that all the four-pounders of his division had been sent to the left on towards the Sophia road with intent, he believed, to hinder the Turks from any attempt to retreat in that direction; an attempt which did not seem to be probable. It was edifying to witness the composure with which those soldiers of the battery who were off duty slept steadily while the cannon were being fired close to their ears, and while the shells were whistling over their heads.

Anxious to command the position a little more fully, we went yet farther to the left on the extreme westward peak of the Radisovo ridge, and thence, since the fog had now in a great measure cleared away, we looked down upon the whole scene. A regiment of the 16th Division was languidly plying its musketry fire down the valley traversed by the Loftcha-Plevna road, and appeared to have half a mind to emerge therefrom for the purpose of attacking again the redoubt on the isolated mamelon. But the place was scored by the Turkish shelter-trenches, and the Turks there blazed away, steadily but not ardently. Near to us the skirmishers of a brigade of the 30th Division were dodging their way down to the base of the south-eastern face of the mamelon. This was at two o'clock, and for nearly two hours little forepost affairs of no consequence went on.

Evening.—I spent the greater portion of the afternoon in and about the battery on the height directly in front of Radisovo. This battery was on the extreme left of Krüdener's position, and points its fire partly against the redoubts of the first and second Turkish positions and partly against the redoubt on the detached mamelon south-east of the town. It was this last redoubt which the Russian chiefs clearly considered the weakest point of the Turkish position. The heavy firing at eleven o'clock on our left, which the artillery colonel told me had been mere forepost work, was in reality an assault on this redoubt by three regiments of the 4th Corps, pushed home in the fog right up to the Turkish shelter-trenches outside the ditch of the redoubt. In spite of the spirit with which the attack was made it failed, and Kriloff's men had to fall back up the valley traversed by the Loftcha-Plevna road, and on to the slopes over against the Turkish redoubt. I also learned that a curious order had been given to all the artillery to fire each alternate hour hard and gently.

It was observable from this elevation that the Roumanian cannon on our right had actually passed by the Grivica Redoubt still held by the Turks, and had come into action against the redoubts on the central swell, with the two guns left in the Grivica Redoubt as armament, firing into their rear. This was gallant but inexplicable till one learned that the redoubt and the entrenched camp behind it were full of Turkish infantry. To anticipate, let me state that these at sundown compelled the Roumanian guns to retire in a line with the village of Grivica. At half-past three all the Russian batteries began to fire with great swiftness, and continued till it was necessary for the gunners to hold their hand, lest the missiles should fall among the Russian stormers once more assaulting the redoubt on the detached mamelon of which I have already spoken.

At four o'clock a mass of infantry in loose order, preceded by a skirmishing line, and followed by supports and reserves, came up out of the chaussée valley, drove the Turks out of their shelter-trenches at the foot of the mamelon, and pressed on vivaciously up its southern slope. This was a Brigade, or thereabouts, of the 16th Division. Simultaneously, down the slopes of the heights which are a prolongation of that on which we stood, another Brigade advanced. This one belonged to the 30th Division. The Brigade crossed the intervening valley at full speed, and began to advance up the south-eastern and eastern sections of the slope of the mamelon, while on the lower slopes they hung somewhat, and it seemed did not quite like the work cut out for them. They extended to the right under shelter, and then after a moment's lingering the skirmishing line dashed out of shelter and began swiftly to ascend the wide natural glacis lying below the redoubt. This glacis was already dotted with the dead of the morning.

The mass deploying steadily, followed the skirmishers, with the supports behind them, the reserves lying down under shelter behind. At that moment the shell-fire from the guns of the first and second Turkish positions crashed in among the advancing Russians. From tier above tier of continuous shelter-trenches lining the outside of the ditch of the redoubt streamed a torrent of musketry fire from the Turkish infantry lining them. Still the Russians laboured doggedly onwards and upwards in the teeth of these impediments. But the slope was steep, and the ground slippery from the drizzling rain. Just at this moment we descried at first a slender column, then heavier, on the edge of the reverse slope of the mamelon, making for the redoubt from the direction opposite to the Russian advance. This proved to be Turkish reinforcements coming up to strengthen the garrison of the redoubt. To deal with this new enemy on the right flank, the Russians with great promptitude threw back their right, the soldiers lying down and firing into the advancing Turks, while the mass, with which the supports had by this time mingled, pressed on towards the Turkish shelter-trenches outside the redoubt.

Here for the first time came ringing back to us, through the thick moist air, the volleys of Russian cheers. That the leaders with that cheer actually gained the first Turkish shelter-trench, I can testify from my own eyesight. For about five minutes the fate of the redoubt hung in the balance. Then, tortured by the fire on the front and flank, the Russians began to fall back, at first slowly, but presently at a run. The reserves took no part in the attack.

The Russians had fallen fast as they advanced. Perhaps they fell faster as they retired. The Turkish infantry promptly followed up their advantage, sallying out with flaming volleys down the slope after the Russians, and driving them to the shelter of their own trenches, over ground studded with Russian dead and wounded. The second assault was thus, like the first, a failure; and as the dusk was coming on I anticipated no more fighting for the day, and was walking back out of the exposed battery to find my horse and ride to such shelter as the battle-field affords. The Turkish infantry, regardless of the fire of the Russian batteries, were streaming into their redoubts for night duty. The artillery fire was gradually waning. Suddenly it swelled again. Yet another desperate effort, followed hard on the last, was in course of being made, on that stubborn isolated redoubt there.

The troops engaged were three fresh regiments drawn from the same divisions as those composing the previous attacking force. The previous attack from the opening to the finish had occupied just half an hour. This one was disposed of in the gloaming in a similar manner after twenty minutes. The mamelon redoubt of the Turkish Plevna position remains intact.

The Emperor with the Grand Duke was on the battle-field till nine o'clock. Of the Russian losses I know no details, but they must have been heavy. Many of the wounded cannot be removed. The weather is abominable. There was about sundown hard fighting around the Grivica Redoubt, and it is reported to have been taken.

September 12th, morning.—The Emperor returned to headquarters here late last night. The battle-field of the last five days is silent this morning. There is a talk of submitting the Turkish Plevna position to a regular siege, sapping up to the redoubts, while a close blockage is instituted, with intent to starve Osman Pacha's army. The villages enclosed within his lines are full of supplies for the simple wants of the Turkish soldiers, and the fields groan with heavy crops of maize. The losses this morning are spoken of here as about 5,000 to 6,000, but there are no details. The Grivica Redoubt was taken yesterday after sundown.

The Emperor this morning has gone back to the battle-field to visit his soldiers.

The subjoined letter, in which the same great battle is described by another Correspondent, relates chiefly to Kriloff's repulse, and to Skobeleff's capture of the double redoubt, with his subsequent repulse after a terrible struggle and with enormous losses:—

†LEFT WING, LOFTCHA ROAD, *September 12th.*—I was with General Zotoff when the battle of Tuesday began. It was eleven o'clock. The General and his staff were on the ridge behind Radisovo. They had just lunched. A moderate artillery fire was going on, and the General had informed me that the attack would begin between two and three o'clock, when suddenly a lively fire was heard on the skirmish line away to the left in the direction of the Loftcha road, followed by a heavy fusillade, which soon swept the road to the foot of the Radisovo ridge, and streamed up its crest nearly to Radisovo itself.

Everybody was surprised. General Zotoff looked at his watch and said, "It's not yet time. What can it be?" Mounting my horse I rode down the ridge behind Radisovo, where the fire seemed raging hottest, to try and make out what was going on. For some time it was impossible to ascertain whether the Turks or Russians were attacking. The fog and smoke were so thick that nothing could be seen. It was only by the fusillade that the progress of the fight could be judged. For nearly an hour General Zotoff did not learn what it was or how it had begun. As the time for the Russian attack had been fixed for between two and three o'clock, it was soon evident that it must be a Turkish attack, and as I afterwards ascertained, it began in this wise:

Skobeleff and Imeretinsky, in order to begin the attack on their side upon the redoubt, had to advance their troops on to the hill immediately fronting the redoubts in the bend of the Sophia road. It was from this hill that the attack had been made upon Skobeleff four days before, and the hill had since been abandoned by the Turks except a few skirmishers. Skobeleff advanced at eleven o'clock to take possession of this hill. The Turks immediately opened fire upon him. This was the beginning of it. I have not yet been able to learn whether the Turks meant a general attack upon the whole Russian line, or whether it was a sudden movement caused by Skobeleff's advance. At any rate, the Turkish attack spread from the Loftcha road over Plevna, and up the Radisovo ridge, a position which has already been described. In the middle of this ridge is a low hill or hump. From this point down to the end of the ridge, which is scarcely a mile from Plevna, the Russians had planted twenty-eight guns, the greater part of which were not more than 1,000 or 1,200 yards from the Turkish redoubts and trenches, and were a continual menace and danger to the Turks. It seems that they had suddenly decided to try and carry the Radisovo ridge, and the attack here was directed principally against the hump or hill already spoken of, opposite one of their own redoubts. It was impossible, owing to the fog and smoke, to see the position of the combatants on either side. The fight lasted until nearly two o'clock. The Turks made three attacks upon Skobeleff, which were successfully repulsed, and two on the Radisovo ridge.

The three fights with Skobeleff were short, quick, and sharp, neither lasting more than five or ten minutes. This was owing to Skobeleff's manner of defence. He ordered his troops to reserve their fire until the Turks came within a hundred yards, then to open upon them a sudden and terrible fusillade against which no troops could stand. This drove them back almost immediately. Three times they came to the charge, and three times were they repulsed in the same sudden and furious manner.

The two attacks upon the Radisovo ridge lasted longer, and

appeared to be repulsed with less ease. Not until about two o'clock did the fire die away, showing that the fight for the moment was over. Then the fog lifted slightly, and the position on both sides could be seen. The Turks in the trenches down towards Plevna were trying occasional shots, distinguished by little puffs of smoke, with masses here and there in the redoubts showing with an occasional shot from their cannon that they had been repulsed with heavy loss—how much it is impossible to state, but as the loss of the Russians fighting under cover, was more than five hundred, that of the Turks must have been between two and three thousand. The three days' artillery fire had evidently done them, however, very little harm, and it showed how strong they felt themselves to risk a repulse, knowing to a certainty that it would be followed almost immediately by a Russian attack. Indeed, in my opinion, this repulse did more to prepare the way for the Russian attack than the whole three days' artillery fire had done. They had suffered severely, and must have been more or less discouraged and demoralized, as troops, even the best, always are at such a moment. It was most favourable, therefore, for the Russian attack, which was begun almost immediately, so that the fire had hardly ceased half an hour when it began again with unexampled fury.

I took my stand on the old position near the Loftcha road, between Krüdener's left and Skobeleff's right, from which point I had as good a view as could be obtained for the fog and smoke at the bottom of the Radisovo ridge. Immediately to the right of Plevna, where Kriloff commanded, and round the redoubts in the bend of the Sophia road, where Skobeleff was attacking, the fog was so thick that the greater part of the time I could only follow the attack by the sound and the smoke. Most of what I now relate I saw with my own eyes, and part I have learned from Skobeleff himself, and the officers who took part in the combat.

It has been said that nobody ever saw a battle. The soldier is too much excited with the passions of the fight as well as enveloped in smoke to see far around him. The general is too far away from the actual conflict, too much busied with the news arriving from different parts of the field, and with giving orders, to see the battle, although he knows it better than any one. It is only the Correspondent who is daring enough to take and hold a good position who really sees a battle; but to-day, owing to the dense fog, no Correspondent can say he saw more than an occasional scene or episode in this terrible struggle. At most he could only hear and follow by the dense volume of smoke, and thickening fog changing its colour, the crash of musketry and the thunder of artillery. Here is what I saw.

A little to my right, where General Kriloff attacked the redoubts down near Plevna, invisible from the point where my colleague took his stand, the fire had been raging with fury for nearly two hours, a steady, continuous roll and crash, intermingled with the louder thunder of cannon, which filled the air with the uproar of the bullets and shells. During all this time there was little to be seen along the crest of the Radisovo ridge, where the Russian guns could be perceived at work, with figures flitting round them, dimly seen through the smoke, strangely magnified by the intervention of the fog, until the gunners appeared like giants, and the guns themselves, enlarged and distorted by the same medium, appeared like huge uncouth monsters, from whose throats at every instant leaped forth globes of flame. There were moments when these flashes seemed to light up everything around them. Then the guns and gunners appeared for an instant with fearful distinctness, red and lurid, as though tinged with blood. Then they sank back again in shadowy indistinctness. The uproar of the battle rose and swelled until it became fearful to hear—like the continuous roar of an angry sea beating against a rock-bound coast, combined with that of a thunderstorm, with the strange unearthly sounds heard on board a ship when labouring in a gale.

This terrible storm of battle continued without ceasing for nearly two hours. The Russian guns were pouring their fire into the redoubt, and the Russian infantry into the trenches, while the attacking columns were advancing cautiously under cover of the smoke and fog and standing corn to get a position as near as possible before making the final rush. At about five o'clock the smoke lifted again, carried away by a gust of wind. At this moment I saw before the redoubt, down near Plevna, a mass of Russian soldiers rise up in a field of Indian corn, and push forward with a shout. The Turkish fire just then seemed to have been dominated, nearly silenced, by the terrible storm of shot and shell poured in by the Russians. The moment seemed favourable for the assault. Either the Turks were abandoning these redoubts or they were lying behind the parapet awaiting the attack. Which was it? we asked. The question was soon answered. The Russian shout had scarcely died away when there flashed along the parapet of the redoubt a stream of fire that swayed backwards and forwards, while the smoke rose over the redoubt in one heavy white mass. One continuous crash filled the air with bullets, from which to the spectator looking on it did not seem possible for even a rabbit to escape.

Into this storm of bullets plunged the Russians, with a shout as though of joy, and then disappeared into a little hollow, and for the moment were lost to view. Then they emerged again, disappeared in the low ground at the foot of the glacis, rushing onward as though the bullets were but paper pellets; but, alas! sadly diminished in number. Would it be possible for them to reach the parapet? Was it possible for flesh and blood to break that circle of fire? To me it seemed utterly out of the question. Did but one bullet in ten find its billet, not one of these gallant fellows would return through that cornfield. While waiting to see them emerge from this little hollow, my excitement was so great, my hand trembled so, that I could not hold the field-glass to my eyes, and for the moment was obliged to trust my naked vision. They were evidently very near the redoubt. A rush might do it. Victory was almost within their grasp, but they required a fresh accession of strength; a rush of new men from behind; another wave coming forward with new impetus to carry the first up over the glacis; a second wave, and perhaps a third, each bringing new impulsion, new strength. I looked for this wave of reserves. I looked to see if reinforcements were coming up—if the General was doing anything to help the gallant fellows struggling there against that circle of fire.

I looked in vain. My heart sank within me, for I saw that all this bravery, all this loss of life, would be useless. While these poor fellows were madly fighting their lives away by hundreds in a desperate struggle—when the victory was trembling in the balance—not a man was sent to help them. They were left to die overwhelmed, broken, vanquished. It was sublime, and was pitiful. I see a few of them struggle up the glacis one by one. They drop. They are not followed, and here they come again, a confused mass of human beings rushing madly back across that cornfield, less than half of those who went forward. When this disorderly remnant was seen flying back—broken, destroyed—two more battalions were sent to pick them up, and carry them back to the assault. Two more battalions! they might as well have sent a corporal and two more men. Two more regiments were what was required, and they should have been sent at the moment when that mass of men rose up in the cornfield, and went on with a cheer. The new troops would have reached the glacis just as the assault began to waver, would have carried the hesitating mass onward, and all would have gone into the redoubt together. Instead of this, General Kriloff sent two battalions, and that when it was too late. The poor fellows went over the hill singing gaily, and disappeared in the fog and smoke. I could have cried for pity, for I knew that most of them went uselessly to simple slaughter. It was impossible for these fresh battalions to renew the assault with the slightest chance of success. These two battalions, like the rest, were doomed to almost certain destruction.

The fog again settled down over the redoubt, hiding Turks and Russians alike. I could tell by that fearful rifle-fire that they were going at it again, and I turned away. Soon the cessation of firing told that it was all over; but the second attack was more easily repulsed than the first, and I perceived likewise that the whole Russian attack made from the Radisovo ridge by Krüdener and Kriloff was repulsed all along the line. It was inevitable; I foresaw it from the first. The mistake was made and repeated continually by the Russians of sending too few men against such positions, according to old rules made before breech-loading days. In those days a fixed number of men were considered enough to carry a position, and sending more was only increasing the chances of loss without increasing the chances of success; but the number required to carry a position defended by breech-loaders is about four or five times as great as against muzzle-loaders—a fact which the Russians have not yet learned, but which is all the more important when the breech-loaders are in the hands of soldiers like the Turks.

I will now relate the events which occurred on the Russian extreme left, commanded by Prince Imeretinsky and General Skobeleff. Here the attack was conducted in a very different manner. While the battle was raging in front and to the right of me, it raged with no less fury round the redoubts and on the other side of the Loftcha road, but up to the moment of the second repulse of Kriloff, Skobeleff had not yet made his assault. He had well prepared the ground, however. At four o'clock he had brought down twenty pieces of artillery to the spur of the ridge overlooking Plevna. Not more than a thousand yards distant from the redoubt I saw an immense volume of smoke rising, and heard a terrible thunder, which was not more than five or six hundred yards away on my left. It was evident that Skobeleff, risking his artillery in this advanced position, was determined to make a desperate effort to capture the redoubt in front of him.

I have already described the positions here, and now only need refer to them to make the description understood. The redoubt Skobeleff was attacking was a double redoubt in the bend of the Loftcha road down near Plevna. He had advanced his troops down the slope of the mountain to within easy range. As the Turks immediately opened fire upon him from the redoubt he returned the fire with steadiness and precision, putting his men under cover as much as possible, his cannon pouring a steady stream of shell and canister into the redoubt as well. In fact he worked his cannon so much that several pieces have been spoiled. He had evidently determined to risk everything to capture this redoubt, and if Plevna were not taken it would not be his fault. For three hours he kept up this fire, and just after Kriloff's second repulse, the Turkish fire having somewhat relaxed, dominated by the Russian, he thought the moment had come for making the assault.

He had four regiments of the line, and four battalions of sharpshooters. Still keeping up his murderous fire, he formed under its cover two regiments in the little hollow at the foot of the low hill on which was built the redoubt, together with two battalions of sharpshooters, not more than twelve hundred yards from the scarp. Then placing himself in the best position for watching the result, he ceased fire and ordered the advance. He ordered the assaulting party not to fire, and they rushed forward with their guns on their shoulders, with music playing and banners flying, and disappeared in the fog and smoke. Skobeleff is the only general who places himself near enough to feel the pulse of a battle. The advancing column was indistinctly seen, a dark mass in the fog and smoke. Feeling, as it were, every throb of the battle, he saw this line begin to waver and hesitate. Upon the instant he hurled forward a rival regiment to support, and again watched the result. This new force carried the mass farther on with its momentum, but the Turkish redoubt flamed and smoked, and poured forth such a torrent of bullets that the line was again shaken. Skobeleff stood in this shower of balls unhurt. All his escort were killed or wounded, even to the little Kirghiz, who received a bullet in the shoulder. Again he saw the line hesitate and waver, and he flung his fourth and last regiment, the Libansky, on the glacis. Again this new wave carried the preceding ones forward, until they were almost on the scarp; but that deadly shower of bullets poured upon them; men dropped by hundreds, and the result still remained doubtful. The line once more wavered and hesitated. Not a moment was to be lost, if the redoubt was to be carried.

Skobeleff had now only two battalions of sharpshooters left, the best in his detachments. Putting himself at the head of these, he dashed forward on horseback. He picked up the stragglers; he reached the wavering, fluctuating mass, and gave it the inspiration of his own courage and instruction. He picked the whole mass up and carried it forward with a rush and a cheer. The whole redoubt was a mass of flame and smoke, from which screams, shouts, and cries of agony and defiance arose, with the deep-mouthed bellowing of the cannon, and above all the steady, awful crash of that deadly rifle-fire. Skobeleff's sword was cut in two in the middle. Then a moment later, when just on the point of leaping the ditch, horse and man rolled together to the ground, the horse dead or wounded, the rider untouched. Skobeleff sprang to his feet with a shout, then with a formidable, savage yell the whole mass of men streamed over the ditch, over the scarp and counter-scarp, over the parapet, and swept into the redoubt like a hurricane. Their bayonets made short work of the Turks still remaining. Then a joyous cheer told that the redoubt was captured, and that at last one of the defences of Plevna was in the hands of the Russians.

Having seen as much as I have seen of the Turkish infantry fire from behind trenches and walls, I thought it was beyond flesh and blood to break it,—a belief which had been strengthened by Kriloff's repulse, which I had just witnessed. Skobeleff proved the contrary, but at what a sacrifice! In that short rush of a few hundred yards, three thousand men had been left on the hill-side on the glacis, the scarp, and the ditch—one-fourth of his whole force. I believe that Skobeleff looks upon such attacks upon such positions as almost criminal, and disapproved highly the whole plan of attack on Plevna; but he believes that if an attack is to be made it can only be done in this manner, and that, although the loss of men may be great, it is better that the loss should be incurred and the victory won, than half the loss with a certainty of defeat. Skobeleff seems to be the only one among the Russian generals who has studied the American war with profit. He knows it by heart, and it will be seen by those who have studied the great civil war, that in this assault Skobeleff followed the plan of the American generals on both sides when attempting to carry such positions, to follow up the assaulting column with fresh troops without waiting for the first column to be repulsed. If the position proves too strong for the first column, then reinforcements are at hand before they have time to break and run.

Skobeleff had the redoubt. The question now was how to hold

it. It was dominated by the redoubt of Krishine on the left already spoken of. It was exposed at the Plevna side to the fire of the sharpshooters, and to the Turkish forces in the wood bordering on the Sophia road, and open to the fire of the entrenched camp. There was a cross fire coming from three different points. At daylight next morning the Turks opened fire from all sides. The distance from the redoubt at Krishine had of course been accurately measured, and the guns dropped shells into the redoubt with the utmost precision on the exposed sides. The back of the redoubt was a solid rock on which it was impossible to erect a parapet. All the earth had been used for the construction of the parapets on the other side. It was evident that the position was untenable unless the entrenched camp on the other side of the Plevna and the Krishine Redoubt could be taken. Skobeleff renewed his demand for reinforcements made the evening before. Although his losses had been great, the spirit of his troops was so good that with another regiment he was willing to undertake to capture the redoubt and the entrenched camp, or he would undertake to hold the positions until something could be attempted in some other quarter. Could one or two more positions be carried during Wednesday, say the Krishine Redoubt, and one entrenched camp on the same ridge as the Grivica Redoubt, the fall of Plevna might be considered certain. At sunrise the Turks began an attack upon the captured redoubt, and the storm of battle again raged with fury here while all was quiet everywhere else. The desperate attack of the Turks was repulsed. Another attack was made and another repulse, and this continued all day long, until the Turks had attacked and been beaten five successive times.

The Russian losses were becoming fearful. General Skobeleff had lost, he thinks, 2,000 men in attacking the redoubt. By the afternoon he had lost 3,000 more in holding it, while his battalions shrivelled up and shrank away as if by magic. One battalion of sharpshooters had been reduced to 160 men. A company which had been 150 was now forty. An immense proportion of officers were killed, or wounded only. Only one commander of a regiment is alive; scarcely a head of a battalion is left. Two officers of the staff are killed, one of whom was Verastchagine, brother of the great artist. Another brother was wounded. General Dobrovolsky, commander of sharpshooters, was killed. One officer was blown to pieces by the explosion of a caisson. Captain Kurapatkin, chief of the staff, standing beside this officer, had his hair singed and suffered a severe contusion. Only General

Skobeleff himself remained untouched. He seems to bear a charmed life. He visited the redoubt three or four times during the day, encouraging the soldiers, telling them help would soon arrive; Plevna would soon be taken; victory would soon crown their efforts; telling them it was the final decisive blow struck for their country; for the honour and glory of the Russian arms; and they always replied with the same cheery shouts, while their numbers were dwindling away by hundreds. He again and again sent for reinforcements, and again and again informed the Commander-in-Chief that the position was untenable. The afternoon wore away and no reinforcements came.

General Levitsky, as I have been informed, formally refused reinforcements, either because he thought the position, in spite of General Skobeleff's representations, was tenable, or because he had no reinforcements to give. General Kriloff, on his own responsibility, sent the remnant of a regiment which had attacked the redoubt, which I saw rush forward and then back through the Indian cornfield. Of the 2,500 there were barely 1,000 left, so it was utterly incapable of going into action that day, and even this regiment arrived too late. General Skobeleff had left the redoubt at four o'clock to go to his tent on a woody hill opposite. He had been there scarcely an hour when he was informed that the Turks were again attacking the right flank on the Loftcha road immediately above Plevna. He galloped forward to see, and was met by an orderly with the news that the Turks were also attacking the redoubt a sixth time. He dashed forward towards the redoubt in hopes of reaching it in time, but was met by a stream of his own men flying back. They were exhausted by forty-eight hours' incessant fighting, and were worn out, hungry, and dying of thirst and fatigue. Owing to the inactivity of the Russians during the day, the Turks had been enabled to collect an overwhelming force, which had made one last desperate effort and had succeeded in driving Skobeleff's force out. One bastion was held till the last by a young officer, whose name I regret I have forgotten, with a handful of men. They refused to fly, and were slaughtered to the last man.

It was just after this that I met General Skobeleff, the first time that day. He was in a fearful state of excitement and fury. His uniform was covered with mud and filth; his sword broken; his Cross of St. George twisted round on his shoulder; his face black with powder and smoke; his eyes haggard and blood-shot, and his voice quite gone. He spoke in a hoarse whisper. I never before saw such a picture of battle as he presented. I saw him again in his tent at night. He was quite calm and collected. He said, "I have done my best; I could do no more. My detachment is half destroyed; my regiments do not exist; I have no officers left; they sent me no reinforcements, and I have lost three guns." They were three of the four guns which he placed in the redoubt upon taking it, only one of which his retreating troops had been able to carry off. "Why did they refuse you reinforcements?" I asked. "Who was to blame?" "I blame nobody," he replied. "It is the will of God."

† BUCHAREST, *September 14th.*—I left the battle-field before Plevna at noon yesterday. The two redoubts taken by General Skobeleff on Monday evening were held by him for twenty-four hours. During Tuesday the Turks made six attacks, and finally, about six o'clock in the evening, drove him out. He lost three cannon which he had placed in the redoubt. He asked for reinforcements several times, but General Levitsky refused them, thinking Skobeleff had enough men to hold the redoubt. Finally, General Kriloff, on his own responsibility, sent the remnant of a regiment which had attacked the lower redoubt near Plevna, and whose effective strength was reduced to 1,000 men utterly unfit to go into battle. Even this regiment arrived a few minutes too late, and another regiment sent from the Headquarter Staff to reinforce him arrived when Skobeleff had already retreated. The loss of this redoubt is disastrous for the Russian attack, as it seems that the Russians in possession of these two redoubts and the Grivica Redoubt had counted upon recommencing the offensive immediately. This is now impossible until the arrival of reinforcements. When I left the battle-field all was quiet except a light artillery fire. The Russians are still in possession of the Grivica Redoubt, which was under a continual heavy fire from the Turks. This redoubt was visited by Colonel Wellesley, who says it is heaped full of dead Russians and Roumanians.

The campaign against Plevna has been a severe one for Correspondents. A Correspondent, the brother of the famous artist, Verastchagine, has been killed. The great artist himself, as is well known, is seriously wounded. Two more Correspondents—one representing the *Scotsman*, and the other the *St. Petersburg Exchange Gazette*—have been wounded; while others—nearly all—come back seriously ill, or completely knocked up. A Correspondent of the *Times* has succumbed to the unhealthy weather. The day the attack began on Plevna he was for several hours at the point of death, but happily now is out of danger. Lieutenant von Huhn, a Prussian Military Correspondent for a German paper, has just returned very ill. Severe though the campaign has been to Correspondents, it has not been so fatal as that of Servia, in which, out of twenty who were at the front, three were killed and one wounded.

The following letter describes the taking of the Grivica Redoubt:—

* BUCHAREST, *September 14th.*—A friend whom I left at the Plevna front has been kind enough to forward to me the following particulars of a later date than my last despatch covered. He writes from Poradim on the evening of the 12th:—

As you may remember, when we rode to the rear last night, we saw no reason to doubt that the Grivica Redoubt was still in Turkish hands, knowing as we did that the assault made upon it at three o'clock had been repulsed, and we set down the smoke rising round below it to an attempt on the part of the Turks to drive back the Roumanian artillery which had passed the redoubt, and were in action absolutely in its front. In reality, however, the Grivica Redoubt fell last night before the determined bravery of the Roumanians. I forward you detailed information concerning the protracted struggle.

It appears that at half-past two P.M. the redoubt was attacked by two Roumanian brigades, each consisting of four battalions, and three battalions of Russians. The Roumanians attacked from the east and south-east, the Russians from the south and south-west. The attack was made in the following manner:—First a line of skirmishers, with men carrying scaling ladders, gabions, and fascines among them. The latter had their rifles slung on their backs, and were ordered in no case to fire, but merely to run forward, fill up the ditch, and place their ladders behind. Then followed the second line in company column formation for the attack, followed by the third line to support the assault.

At half-past two P.M. the attack was made by the Roumanians, and it is said that by some mistake the Russians arrived half an hour too late. Be that as it may, the assault was repulsed, and all retired except two companies of infantry, which rallied, and, keeping under cover, maintained a brisk fire against the work.

At half-past five the attack was renewed by a battalion of the Roumanian Militia, followed by two Russian battalions of the 17th and 18th Regiments. The redoubt was then carried, and the Turks withdrew to the other redoubt, a little to the north of the captured work. But it was soon apparent that the redoubt could not be held without reinforcements, and three Roumanian battalions, with a battery of artillery, were ordered forward. They lost their way, however, in the fog, and were thus precluded from rendering the required assistance, consequently when the Turks returned to the attack the allies were driven out.

The third assault soon followed, and the work was finally captured at seven P.M. Four guns and a standard were the trophies of the feat of arms. More than once during the night did the Turks advance with shouts of "Allah!" but no serious attack was made. Thus, to my surprise, when I reached the Plevna Valley this morning, I beheld a flag-staff up, defiantly exposing the Roumanian flag, in that hitherto dreaded Grivica Redoubt. I was given to understand that preparations were in progress for an attack on the Turkish entrenched camp on the Turkish northern ridge about 2,000 metres west of the Grivica Redoubt.

I found the village of Grivica full of ambulance waggons and wounded-bearers, and in a line running from the top of the hill in front of the redoubt down into the valley in front of the village was a line of field batteries just coming into action. In the rear of the village, and also lying down the slope of the hill, was a line of Roumanian infantry under the shelter of the cover-trenches; and in their rear again was a reserve of field batteries. The infantry force in this advanced line amounted in all to about 4,000 Roumanian troops.

By this time it was past ten o'clock. As the position we occupied yesterday on the height above Radisovo had the double advantage of the best view of any assault on the entrenched camp oppôsite, and also of anything occurring on the Russian left flank nearer Plevna, I rode thither, passing under a very heavy cross fire as I traversed the valley and the way between the Turkish and Russian batteries. Reaching the Russian positions, I rode along the reverse slope of the Radisovo height until I came behind our old observatory of yesterday, and I remounted the ridge to find our old friend Krüdener's left flank battery still in position. Just before I arrived a shell from this battery had caused a great explosion in the redoubt forming the second Turkish position on the central swell, much to my intense regret that I was not in time to see this fortunate shot. Having satisfied myself that I might safely push on a little nearer Plevna without missing the attack on the Turkish entrenched camp opposite, I made my way still farther to the left to the tree beneath which we yesterday witnessed the Russian unsuccessful assaults on the Turkish mamelon redoubt. The guns of Imeretinsky and Skobeleff, which half encircle the western half of the valley, were pounding away as yesterday, but did not appear to have made much advance, if any. There soon, however, became visible a long line of fitful puffs of bluish smoke out of the wood which faces the covered way connecting the two redoubts covering the town towards the south-west. This rifle fire was speedily answered by a line of Turkish fire from behind the covered way, as well as a hot fire from some shelter trenches in the middle of the valley which separated the combatants.

Having watched this apparently harmless duel for some time, we came under the notice of the Turkish skirmishers in the valley too closely to render it advisable to remain here any longer. I therefore remounted and returned east along the reverse flank of the Radisovo height, with intent to cross the valley, and, if possible, get into the Grivica Redoubt. On my way every now and then I had a glimpse of the slowly progressing, or indeed almost stationary, attack on the Turkish entrenched camp opposite. I descended the slope into the valley, crossed it, and made my way up through the village of Grivica towards the redoubt. On mounting the plateau above I soon found myself under cover of the transverse hillock running down into the valley from the height above, and sheltered behind it from the fire of the Turkish camp were massed a few battalions of Roumanians, with a battery or two, constituting the reserves intended to support the attack on the entrenched camp.

I was here told that it would be impossible to ride up into the redoubt, for as soon as I left the covered way by the hillock I should come on to an open gap between it and the redoubt, which is continually swept by two Turkish guns. Intent on persevering, I observed a short way off a ditch running up the hill in the direction of the redoubt. This I determined to avail myself of as far as it reached, and leaving my horse, I commenced my way up the ditch, which was filled with Roumanian infantry. After meandering about in all directions I found that the ditch soon ended in a cul-de-sac. Between me and the redoubt, a distance of about six hundred yards, there was a small Roumanian battery, and for this I ran at speed, the ground I traversed being literally strewn with dead Roumanians and Russians. The fire seemed to become heavier as I neared the battery, which, however, I reached in safety. There was nothing for it now but to commence running again as soon as I had caught my breath in the little battery. The Roumanian officers squatting in the entrance of the redoubt shouted to me to run in their direction. This I did, and was thankful when, in rushing in among them, and picking my way through the dead, they pulled me down to the ground and made me squat beside them for security against the continuous shower of lead.

I had now time to look about me, and examine the work. It has a ditch all round it, and the parapets are high and thick. The only entrance, curiously enough, is a narrow opening facing to the south, it having been constructed for defence towards the north. Presently I asked leave to enter the redoubt, which was granted with the advice to make a bolt of it, as there was a dangerous corner to pass. This I did, and pray I may be spared ever again witnessing the sight which met my eyes.

The interior of this large work was piled up not only with dead, but with wounded, forming one ghastly undistinguishable mass of dead and living bodies, the wounded being as little heeded as the dead. The fire had hindered the doctors from coming up to attend to the wounded, and the same cause had kept back the wounded-bearers. There were not even comrades to moisten the lips of their wretched fellow-soldiers, or give them a word of consolation. There they lie writhing and groaning. I think some attempt might have been made, at whatever risk, to aid these poor fellows, for they were the gallant men who twenty-four hours before had so valiantly and successfully struggled for the conquest of that long uncaptured redoubt, and it was sad now to see them dying without any attempt being made to attend to them.

I could fill pages with a description of this harrowing scene and others near it which I witnessed, but the task would be equally a strain on my own nerves and on those of your readers. I am aware that Colonel Wellesley, the English military attaché, having visited this redoubt and witnessed the spectacle it presented, spoke of it to a Roumanian officer, who explained that the doctors were obliged to take cases in the order of their occurrence, and since the Roumanians had suffered not a little two days before, the doctors had still not been released from their attention upon those early cases.

In the centre of the redoubt is a kind of traverse and a curious covered corridor runs around it. In this I imagine the Turks sought protection from the shells which fell into it unintermittently for so many days before its capture. An incessant rain of bullets poured over the work as I made my way over the bodies on the ground. I was naturally deeply interested to know whence the Turks were firing, and having reached the parapet I crawled up, and taking off my cap, peeped over. To my immense astonishment I saw another Turkish redoubt not more than two hundred and fifty yards from us, to the north-west, from which this fire was being maintained. The Roumanians, it appears, had failed to capture this redoubt yesterday; but it is absolutely necessary that they should become masters of it, as their position is rendered almost untenable by its remaining in the hands of the Turks. The fire had not diminished as I returned from the redoubt down hill towards the village, and the Correspondent of the *Scotsman*, who had joined me, was struck by a bullet on the ankle, which luckily did little harm, only grazing the ankle bone.

We rested a little behind the hillock where the Roumanian reserves were lying, and then pushed back in order to see what progress was being made, towards the Turkish entrenched camp. We had scarcely left the Roumanians when a tremendous Turkish shrapnell fire, which searched most thoroughly the reverse slope of the hill where they were, was opened against them, and maintained until they were compelled slightly to change their position, and the skirmish line had also to fall back. Since by this time it was 6 P.M., I knew that the attack had been abandoned for that day, and therefore returned to quarters.

The Russians estimate their losses on the 11th at 125 officers and 5,000 men. I estimate the Grivica losses at about 1,500 killed and wounded.

* BUCHAREST, *September 17th.*—It is incomprehensible to me that nobody in England appears to realize that the third Battle of Plevna was in effect fought out on Tuesday, the 11th inst., and that the Russian failure was then consummated in virtue of the defeat of the successive Russian assaults on the redoubt crowning the mamelon to the south-east of the town.

These assaults, categorically described by me, were the important and crucial events of the day. The mamelon redoubt is the key to the position. The Russians were free to choose their own time for the attack. It was open to them to make the attack with the strength which seemed to them most appropriate. They attacked three times during the day, and failed. Can the hope, then, be strong, that it is possible for them ever to succeed?

The Russian official telegrams are by no means joyous documents, as assuredly they would have been had any substantial success been won. The Russians were definitely thwarted, and finally paralyzed on the 11th instant.

I find, nevertheless, the English journals up to the 15th instant so utterly ignoring the reality as to write of the Russian partial successes. The Russians have lost before Plevna this time more than 20,000 men. For the first time in my knowledge has the work overwhelmed the Russian medical and sanitary staff, and great numbers of the wounded are literally rotting and festering unfed, their wounds undressed, their cleanliness disregarded. As for the Roumanian army, its surgical arrangements are utterly inadequate. The surgeons make no concealment of the grim fact that a wounded man's time for being looked at comes on an average two days after he has been struck.

The Russo-Roumanian army has abandoned now even the pretence of prosecuting the attempt against Plevna, and has fallen back into the positions occupied before the commencement of the bombardment. The field artillery remain still in some of the positions of the bombardment. The intention is announced of a third renewal of the attempt in a fortnight with the arrival of the Guard. I have great doubts whether another attempt will be made on Plevna, and very much stronger doubts whether such an attempt, if made, can succeed.

The Turks are better soldiers individually than the Russians. Of that, after seeing not a few battles, I stand assured. The strategy of both, perhaps, is equally bad; but as regards both major and minor tactics the Turks are simply immeasurably superior. The Turks are better armed than the Russians, both in great and small arms. The Turks have engineers who can design admirable defensive positions. The Russian engineers seem incapable of repairing a hole in a bridge. The Turks seem as well provisioned as the Russians. The Turks are flushed with success. The Russians are depressed by failure after failure.

Nor is this all that impairs the Russian soldiers' dash, for that it is becoming impaired my reluctant personal observation of the war can testify. There is no braver man alive than the Russian soldier, but a brave soldier cannot continually face more than the fair chances of war. The Russian soldier is called on to face these, and dangers in addition which appeal with infinitely greater intensity of horror to his imagination. He knows that if he but receives a bullet in the ankle joint when he is in the front of an unsuccessful attack, the chances are even that he will die a death of torture, humiliation, and mutilation. No moral courage, no mental hardihood, can stand against this horrible consciousness, and in the attack on the 11th I distinctly observed his reluctance to begin the storming part of the attack.

CHAPTER XVIII.

THE SECOND DEADLOCK IN BULGARIA.

Tone of feeling at the Russian Head-Quarters—The New Plan of Operations against Plevna—Kriloff's movement on the Turkish Line of Supply—General Kriloff's Failure—Entrance of Convoys into Plevna—An Expedition in the Black Sea—Renewed Fighting in the Shipka Pass—Great Attack by Suleiman Pacha—Failure of the Turks and subsequent Panic in their Army—The Russian Army of the Lom—Retrograde Movement of the Czarewitch—Battle of Cairkoi—Retreat and Dismissal of Mehemet Ali Pacha—A Reconnaissance of the Turkish Positions—The Military Situation in Bulgaria—Public Feeling at Constantinople.

THE failure of the third attack on Plevna profoundly discouraged the Russian Army, from the Commander-in-Chief to the private, and lowered immensely the estimation in which the military power of the empire had previously been held in Europe. The Emperor, however, on this occasion showed the tenacity of his family. He ordered up very large reinforcements and prepared for a winter campaign. The following is a letter from the Russian Headquarters, written six days after the defeat:—

† GORNY STUDEN, *September* 19*th*.—I find the feeling here not so gloomy as I had expected. Military men acknowledge that they have been beaten, but as much by their own errors as by the bravery of the Turks, and there is not the slightest sign of hesitation, or weakening of the determination to fight it out. The idea of peace is not entertained. Everybody feels that it is a death struggle in which Turkey or Russia must go to the ground irretrievably, and the final issue is not doubted for an instant. Although the struggle must be hard, and may be long, Russia must ultimately crush her adversary, it is held, if only by mere brute force, in default of science, skill, and generalship.

Every preparation is being made for a winter campaign. A military railway from Fratesti to Simnitza is to be constructed, which will, it is hoped, be ready by the end of October, but I predict not before Christmas. Steam ice-boats have been ordered in view of the freezing of the Danube, with intent to keep the river open. A contract has been taken for warm clothing and housing for the troops during the winter campaign. Everything indicates the Russian determination to carry on the war to the end. Anybody knowing the feeling, not only of the Russian nation but of the army, knows that no other policy is possible; but the men on whom lies the responsibility for that mismanagement of the campaign which has so complicated the future may expect a stern reckoning. General Ignatieff is just now under a cloud. The generals who have muddled the war now complain that he did not give them to understand that the Turks would fight so hard, and misled them as to the number of men needed to make a successful invasion. As well might they say that they did not know the Turks were going to shoot with bullets. All the facts about the Turks were common property before the war; their war-strength, their bull-dog courage behind earthworks, their tenacity, their ferocity. Only one element was left out of the calculation—the profound incapacity of some of the Russian generals.

The Roumanians yesterday again attacked the redoubt from which a fire is so steadily maintained on the Grivica Redoubt. After displaying much gallantry they had to abandon the attempt. It is said that they will renew it, and there is certainly plenty of fight in Prince Charles's gallant young army, but in my opinion little chance of success unless they work up to the hostile redoubt by sap.

It was foreseen that a long time must elapse before the Russian Army would be in a position to renew its attack upon Osman Pacha with any chance of success. General Todleben, the engineer who, twenty-three years before, had defended Sebastopol with so much skill, was sent for, to advise upon the best means of effecting the reduction of Plevna. The following letters describe the state of affairs before Plevna towards the end of September:—

† Sgalince (before Plevna), *September 23rd.*—The position of affairs has little changed here. The attack on Plevna has settled into a siege. Since the day when Skobeleff was driven from the redoubts he had captured there has been no fighting

of serious consequence. The Roumanians, however, have persisted in making attempts against the second Grivica Redoubt. They are now steadily pushing forward by flying sap. The Russians mean to pursue the same tactics on their side as soon as they can get spades and shovels. The head-quarter staff have succeeded in understanding that these implements are occasionally useful in war, and have ordered a supply of them. If everything goes well, that supply may be expected in a month or six weeks, and then the siege may begin in earnest, provided the Roumanians, who have shovels, have not already taken the place. Regular approaches and the cutting off of the supplies are the means now adopted for the reduction of Plevna. This course was as open on the 1st of August as on the 1st of October.

General Kriloff, who now commands the cavalry, is in the rear of Plevna on the Sophia road for the purpose of cutting off the Turkish supplies. As the Turks have few cavalry, and that not good, General Kriloff should have it all his own way. The country is open, well adapted for cavalry movements, and an active leader with cavalry and horse artillery should make the passage of convoys difficult. As the Turks must have more than 60,000 men in the Plevna position, the question of supplies must be an urgent one with them, unless, as has been alleged, they have accumulated them for several months. This seems improbable, and the magazines surely must require replenishing. There has been no news from General Kriloff since he left, but distant cannon-fire was heard to-day coming from far behind Plevna, which would indicate that he is at work.

News has been received here that more Turkish forces are coming from Sophia. As they can only be Mustaphis, not Nizams, it is hoped that Kriloff will meet and drive them back; though, if there be really a possibility of starving out Plevna, it might be better to let these additional mouths to feed come in, and confine attention to the destruction of trains. Prince Charles remains at Poradim; General Zotoff's headquarters are at Sgalince. The general staff is at Gorny Studen. News has just been received of Hifzi Pacha's arrival at Plevna with a small escort. It is supposed that he avoided Kriloff by taking the by-ways. The approaching Turkish forces are at Lucovatz. General Kriloff is somewhere between that place and Teliche. Lascaroff must have joined Kriloff ere now. I should have stated that Kriloff passed round the north of Plevna, starting from the Roumanian right. If Hifzi's arrival means that the Turks are taking the offensive, it will probably be against Loftcha.

† VERBICA, *September 24th.*—The Roumanians are advancing steadily against the second Grivica Redoubt by trenches. They are now only eighty yards from it, the distance between the two redoubts being about 250 yards. Their fighting spirit and cheerful endurance of hardships are admirable. This redoubt taken, there is another about half a mile distant. Then two, or perhaps three, entrenched camps along the northern ridge, whose western termination is an elevated position overhanging the River Vid. The Turks are not pushing counter saps, and if the assault be delivered with resolution the redoubt should certainly fall.

Great volumes of cannon smoke were seen about Loftcha yesterday, indicating fighting there, but up to midnight General Zotoff had no news from that quarter, or from General Kriloff. I am now starting to join General Kriloff behind Plevna, on the Sophia road.

† ETROPOL, NEAR SOPHIA ROAD, IN REAR OF PLEVNA, *September 25th.*—The Russian attempt to cut off Turkish supplies so far has not been successful. In spite of a large force of cavalry and artillery we have here, the Turks have succeeded in pushing two convoys through under our very nose. The first was a convoy of about 2,000 waggons, accompanied by reinforcements for Plevna, consisting of ten tabors of infantry, one battery of artillery, and three regiments of cavalry.

General Kriloff, who is in command here, did not discover them until they had arrived at Teliche, where he went to attack them. He found them already entrenched with guns in position and mounted in a battery. An artillery fight ensued which lasted all day, with no result, Kriloff being unable, of course, to attack so large a force of infantry with his cavalry. That night he retired to the previous position he occupied at Dubnik, on the Sophia road, and nearer Plevna. Next day the Turks advanced upon Dubnik, and attacked him in turn. Another artillery fight ensued, which lasted all day. Towards evening, however, two columns of infantry came out of Plevna, and taking Kriloff in the rear obliged him to withdraw, thus leaving the road open for the passage of the reinforcements and convoy. He retired upon Tristenik, while General Lascaroff, who had only then succeeded in forming a junction with Kriloff, was obliged to retreat further back across the Loftcha road to Bogot. The Turks, therefore, passed the convoy without the loss of a single waggon.

The whole affair was very feebly managed, partly, I believe, because General Kriloff's instructions were unsuited to the force under his command. He was told to hold the Sophia road at

Dubnik, a thing which was manifestly impossible against infantry, especially at a point so near Plevna, where he could be attacked in the rear. A general in command of such detachments should have no definite instructions except to do as much harm as possible to the enemy, choosing his own time and place. Convoys should be attacked forty or fifty miles beyond Plevna, and the attack kept up if necessary until under the very guns of the place. In a running fight of this kind, extending over forty or fifty miles, even with a convoy protected by infantry, the greater part of the carriages would be smashed by the artillery, the draught horses and oxen killed, and the drivers frightened away. As the Turks have little cavalry, and that only of the very poorest kind, the Russian cavalry can range the whole district between Plevna, Widdin, the Danube, and the Balkans with impunity, the country being so open that there is not the slightest danger of being cut off by infantry. General Kriloff is not a cavalry man at all, and he handles cavalry as if it were infantry, is afraid of being cut off, and thinks he must keep his communications open, forgetting that cavalry in such an open country as this can only be cut off by cavalry, of which the Turks have none worth speaking of. The Bashi-Bazouks and Circassians never attempt to make a stand even against one-fourth of their numbers. General Kriloff, instead of retiring upon Tristenik to keep his communications open, should, on the contrary, have cut loose from the Roumanian right wing, and advanced on the Sophia road to the Balkans with half his forces to meet the next convoy, while the other half might have moved in the direction of Widdin to meet supplies coming from there. In this way only can cavalry be made useful here.

Upon retiring, Kriloff left two regiments of Cossacks at Etropol to watch the Sophia road, and another convoy slipped through the fingers of this detachment yesterday. Etropol is too far from the Sophia road, in the first place. Then they did not place outposts sufficiently advanced to give warning in time. This convoy, besides, did not come along the Sophia road, but on another alongside it, which we have only lately discovered. By the time we received information of its coming and had reached the scene of action, the convoy was almost under the guns of a protected bridge on the Sophia road over the river Vid.

Had we charged even then we might have captured the greater part of the convoy, as it was only protected by cavalry that ran away. We waited several minutes for the artillery to come up, and then the officer in charge lost about fifteen minutes in writing a report to General Kriloff, to say that he meant to attack. By this time the convoy for the most part had got safely over the Vid, either by the bridge or by a ford, so that the report was superfluous. We threw a few shells at them, to which the guns protecting the bridge instantly answered. Then, as it was quite dark, we retired to Etropol, our whole spoil being a pair of oxen.

Evidently things must be managed better than this if the Turkish supplies are to be cut off.

† TRISTENIK, *September 26th.* — Upon returning here this morning we found General Kriloff gone with his whole detachment to Kreza, over the Isker. It seems that a reconnaissance he sent to Mahaleta yesterday reported that there is a Turkish officer, high in rank, at Kreza, organizing a force of cavalry from the Circassian villages in the neighbourhood, and likewise obtaining recruits for the infantry. Kriloff has gone off there in hopes of taking the officer prisoner and stopping the recruiting business. The whole force at his command is hardly necessary for this, and this is not the way to prevent the arrival of supplies along the Sophia road. It is raining fearfully, and the population of several abandoned villages is camped around Tristenik in the mud, presenting a sad spectacle.

† VERBICA, ROUMANIAN HEADQUARTERS, *September 26th, evening.* —The Roumanians are pushing forward their works against the second redoubt with a perseverance and a pluck worthy all praise, and which is the more remarkable as the Russians are doing absolutely nothing on their side. The rain is continuous, the mud in the trenches is fearful, and it is very cold besides, but officers and men alike stick to their posts in spite of this with a pluck and resolution which excites my admiration. They evidently mean to take the second redoubt, or have a desperate try at it. They are now within sixty yards with their third parallel, and they are just beginning the fourth parallel, which they mean to push within thirty yards of the redoubt before giving assault. At this short distance the terrible Turkish fire is reduced to a minimum, as the Turks will not be able to fire more than two rounds before they come to the bayonet. The Roumanian soldiers seem to be stout fellows, and I think they are sure to get this redoubt. Were the Russians advancing as rapidly on their side Plevna would fall before two weeks. But from all I can make out the Russians are completely at sea. They seem to have no plan, no idea, no head, and not to know what to do next.

They are waiting for reinforcements, which are arriving slowly, and which, when they are all here, will hardly more than cover the losses by battle and by sickness during the last two months. I think history offers no such example of a splendid army in such an utterly helpless condition. The Roumanian generals are showing far more pluck and energy.

The Turks are pushing no counter works against the Roumanian advance, and apparently content themselves with repairing the damages caused by the Roumanian artillery. There is a possibility that they have mined the redoubt, and mean to blow it up when driven out.

Their defeat before Plevna had not relaxed the firmness with which the Russians held the Shipka Pass, by which they hoped one day to re-enter Roumelia. The two next following letters are from the Turkish side, the first relating to a most determined attack made by Suleiman Pacha on the 17th of September:—

"SHIPKA PASS, *September 19th.*—The attempt to carry the formidable Russian positions in the Shipka Pass has for the moment proved unsuccessful. Fort St. Nicholas, the high rock frowning upon the mouth of the pass, which to the Czar and Sultan is of equal importance, had an exceedingly narrow escape of changing owners on the 17th instant. At one time, indeed, soon after the attack commenced, which was shortly before daybreak ("the darkest hour before the dawn" being well chosen as best for all night attacks), it was fully believed that it had fallen. Had the attacking force been supported by the efforts of those upon whom devolved the duty of co-operation, all might have been well with the Turks, and the standard of the Prophet have again assumed its place on the entire range of forts, at present forming so insuperable an obstacle to the capture of the now celebrated pass.

Suleiman Pacha has waited until he has succeeded in forming as handy an army as any of his brother generals can boast of, and, from all that can be gathered, it is no fault of his that he is not at this moment crowned with the success which the plan he had formed appears fully to warrant. The causes have not yet been fully ascertained, but there can be no doubt it was in no way his intention to dream of capturing the Russian positions by a direct attack upon the principal one of them. A threatening demonstration on some or one of the chain of forts in the rear of Fort St. Nicholas and parallel with the main road through the pass, might stand a very fair chance of success, and this would appear to have been intended on the present occasion.

The troops told off to commence the attack (nearly 3,000 in number) did their duty admirably, and succeeded in obtaining a firm foothold upon the rocky fort, a considerable portion of which soon fell into their possession. Exposed for hour after hour to a galling fire on their front and on both flanks, it is marvellous how they stood their ground so long, seeing, even with their then advantage in point of numbers over the enemy in their immediate front, that they could not, unless a diversion were made in their behalf, hope to maintain their ground, even if the entire fort fell into their possession. Upon whose shoulders the blame rests (and certainly Suleiman himself ought to be freed from it) is not an easy matter to ascertain. The only reason which can be assigned for the failure is that the points chosen by the right and left attack were found to be too strong; still, to capture them was one matter, but to make an important auxiliary movement is a far easier one.

Very feeble flank attempts were made by the generals to whom the duty was assigned, and scarcely credible accounts have been bruited about of the inefficiency, and even absence altogether from the fight, of the officers with these troops. The action lasted until nearly mid-day, when the unsupported troops in the centre, having no hope of co-operation from east or west, and having actually seen a large body of the enemy rapidly coming up to attack them, were very properly ordered to retire. Disappointed and galled as they were, it was not to be wondered at that they fled in disorder down the side of the steep rock, which it had cost them so much to gain; and great is Suleiman Pacha's good fortune that the fear occasioned by their flight did not communicate itself to the rest of his army. A useless sacrifice of life and limb is alone the result of the day's work; about 1,000 were killed, wounded, and missing, and there is scant hope of the Turks finding the latter taken prisoners, the bayonet having been actively employed during the retreat.

We shall doubtless not have to wait long before the next attack is made, as the weather in the Balkan range will soon be breaking. When that movement is commenced, it will, at the least, be with the knowledge of why the present attack failed; and costly as has been the acquirement of that knowledge, it may in the end save disasters still greater.

(SHIPKA PASS, *September 22nd.*—After a defeat, the next

thing naturally to be expected is a panic among the troops to whom the fortune of war has been unfavourable. Such was the case on the night of Tuesday last, when, from some unknown cause—possibly owing to the soughing of the wind, which had risen high as the sun went down, and predisposed the nerves of the picquets to believe every crackling branch a Russian footstep—the alarm was given, and the greatest excitement prevailed amongst the horde of irregulars who form the rear in advance and the van in retreat of Suleiman Pacha's numerous army. They cared not to wait until the cause could be ascertained—the fact of the alarm being given was enough, and the Russians might be on their heels. At every step as they rushed pell-mell down (generally laden with the booty they had succeeded in plundering on the march), they added to the confusion, especially amongst the swarms of camp-followers, and the great numbers of Bulgarian peasants who are enforcedly employed in the transport service. .

It was not for more than an hour after the panic had arisen that any signs of its being allayed could be observed, though the admirable conduct of the regular troops in calmly taking up their assigned positions should have put to the blush even such poltroons as those who had been the first to fly. A little reflection might soon have convinced the most chicken-hearted of Bashi-Bazouks, with his waist stuck full of an armoury of pistols and daggers, that something more than a few stray shots would herald the Russian advance. He did not, however, give himself the time for thinking, but joined his comrades in the rush to the rear, till he discovered himself to be alone and without a following, even of the class who are to be found with all armies in the field.

Somethiug ought to be done to efface both Monday's misfortune and Tuesday's disgrace, or the morale of a large portion of this army will be seriously deteriorated. Upwards of a month has elapsed since Suleiman Pacha occupied the heights which have given him such a powerful advantage over the Russians, who are cooped up in the rock and the earthworks behind which lie across the pass, and yet nothing has been effected towards the capture of what has now become a veritable stronghold. His telegrams have announced the closing of every inlet of the besieged with the exception of the main road from Gabrova; and why this is not attempted to be blocked whilst a sufficient portion of the army keeps the garrison at bay, is by no means apparent. Suleiman's next step is looked for with the liveliest interest, as upon it depends the continuance of that confidence which hi good name has hitherto inspired, and a change of generals is not always attended with advantage in an army situated as is that of the Balkans.

Ten thousand men is a very moderate estimate of the number placed *hors de combat* since the 20th August saw the Russians retiring to their rocky fortress before the onward march of the hitherto victorious Turks, and what is the result beyond the infliction of perhaps a similar loss on their enemy, who has had time to display his skill, and has effectively done so, in marvellously strengthening his previously weak defences? The fighting going on as I write in the main army near Bjela cannot fail to have its effect here, and a victory on the north may in an instant do for Suleiman what a month has not enabled him to effect.

The sweeping condemnation at Philippopolis of between three and four hundred unfortunate Bulgarian insurgents—taken with arms and without—may strike terror to the hearts of those of the Sultan's subjects of that nationality who remain faithful or are wavering in their allegiance, but it certainly strikes one as a ruthless display of what may be expected if the Crescent again shines over this unhappy land.

The failure to take the Pass on the 17th was the more annoying as Suleiman Pacha, anticipating the issue of the struggle, had telegraphed to the Seraskier that he had captured Fort St. Nicholas, and the good news had been transmitted by the Porte to all its Ambassadors at Foreign Courts.

The duties which had been assigned by the force of circumstances to the army under the Czarewitch, designated at its formation the Army of Rustchuk, had from the first, as we have seen, a defensive character. This force had to guard a line extending from the Danube to the foot of the Balkans, and prevent the interference of the Turkish Army of Shumla with the Russian line of communication with Tirnova, or with the operations about Plevna. The line was moved backwards and forwards from time to time, but it was never broken through. Early in September, the Czarewitch had taken up a position between the Kara Lom and the Ak Lom, which rendered it possible for the Turks to make a turning movement, as his line extended from Elena through Djulin to Cairkoi, leaving the country between Cairkoi and the Kara Lom open to the enemy. It was therefore decided to fall back, and, instead of Schahofskoy advancing to join the Czarewitch, the latter relied upon his own forces. At this time the Turks were preparing for a forward movement, and when the Czarewitch fell back, the Turks followed up, engaging his rearguard at Karahassankoi, Popkoi, Opaka, and Kaceljevo. These affairs were all treated as great victories by the Turkish reports, but they were regarded in the Russian camp as of comparatively small importance, so far as their strategic results were concerned. Many losses were sustained on both sides, with no compensating result. The Porte, however, considered that Mehemet Ali ought to be able to do more than he had done, and under its pressing orders he fought the Battle of Cairkoi, on September 21st, and having failed, retreated on the 24th. This failure cost him his command. To an English Correspondent at Varna he said, "he had been dismissed because he had refused to break his neck against a stone wall." He has since stated that he had only 40,000 men at his disposal.

+ Headquarters of the Army of the Czarewitch, Dolny Monastir, *October* 1*st*.—A whole week has passed since the unsuccessful attack of the Turks on the Russian positions at Cairkoi, and they have made no other offensive movements. It has long been apparent to me, as I have frequently hinted in previous despatches, that the army of Mehemet Ali is comparatively small. It has shown itself only at one point at a time, and although occasionally ostentatiously displaying tents on hill tops, and executing manœuvres in plains in sight of the Russian positions, it has nevertheless failed to give me any impression of large numbers. At headquarters it is believed to consist of 40,000 men, but this number is cercertainly exaggerated.

Within the past two or three days the enemy has renewed the tactics he has diligently practised since the withdrawal of the army of the Czarewitch from the Banicka Lom, and, after having made vigorous but unsuccessful attempts to turn the left of the 11th Corps at Cairkoi, he has disappeared quickly from the positions he held one week ago. According to the reports of our scouts, he has re-crossed the Lom, and is now concentrated near Kaceljevo. The Russian outposts are now at Polomarca, Opaka, Ablava, Ostrica, and Strobko, all along the west bank of the Lom, occupying very nearly the same positions as they held before the retrograde movement.

It will be remembered that the army of the Czarewitch withdrew after three battles along the line, in each of which the Turkish losses were very great, and the Russian comparatively little, because our troops had the advantage of holding good defensive positions in cover, and only attacked the Turks in order to follow up a repulse. At the Battle of Cairkoi the Turkish loss was over three thousand, increasing the sum total of dead and wounded since the attack on our line a month ago to between nine and ten thousand men. This loss is evidently too great for the resources of Mehemet Ali, and he has found himself obliged to evacuate the territory he had gained with so much difficulty, for the same reason that the Russians withdrew,—namely, a lack of corps to hold the entire line.

We now have before us the rather serious spectacle of two armies occupying a line sixty miles long, which neither has force enough to hold against an advance of the other. The all-important *rôle* of the army of the Czarewitch has been to cover the line of communications to the Balkans, and to keep the Danube from Sistova downwards. Events have proved that the advance beyond the Jantra was useless, since it was delayed until the Turks recovered from the panic which the crossing of the Danube caused among them. By assuming the offensive the Russians have gained nothing whatever. The positions along the Bjela-Rustchuk chaussée (high road) are strongly fortified, and Bjela itself may be said to be impregnable. It will be understood that the Jantra is far in the rear of the actual positions held by the army of the Czarewitch, for his advance posts are from fifteen to twenty miles to the eastward of the river, and his corps are concentrated at about two-thirds that distance toward Rustchuk and Rasgrad.

In the upper valley of the Lom no advance has yet been made. The weather continues clear and cool. Snow lies on the summits of the Balkans. The roads are hard and dry again, and the effects of the recent severe attack have vanished.

+KARA VERBOVKA, *October 4th.*—The sudden and unexpected withdrawal of Turkish forces across the river Lom, which began on Sunday, opposite the right wing of the 13th Corps and the left of the 11th, is as inexplicable as it is complete and positive. The tactics of Mehemet Ali, since his brisk and successful aggressive movement a month since, have been to keep in sight at some point of his line a sufficient force to make it seem evident that an attack was meditated, and, by quickly moving this force from one side to the other of the semicircle occupied, he has kept the attention of the Russians alive along the whole line. There is no question of the truth of the statement, made in my last despatch, that both armies, although continually making demonstrations more or less important, have found themselves much too weak in numbers to undertake a serious attack. Neither army has force enough to defend its line if the enemy made an attack in earnest. On this account the campaign of the Rustchuk armies has been a succession of small battles and lively skirmishes, resulting in considerable total loss for both sides, and without the least final advantage to either in positions gained or territory occupied.

Several times in previous despatches I have mentioned the rapidity with which a strong Turkish force would disappear from the hills along the Banicka Lom. By successive similar sudden movements, the whole Turkish army has in three days completely vanished from before us. On Monday the Cossacks found the camps about Sinankoi deserted, and the enemy completely withdrawn from the territory between the Banicka Lom and the Lom. On Tuesday morning, at five o'clock, the great camps about Kaceljevo, where the enemy was discovered strongly fortified and concentrated from positions on either side held the day before, were quiet, and to all appearances no movement was meditated. Two hours later not a soldier was visible, only a few Circassian outposts and Bashi-Bazouks. In the afternoon the whole army paraded along the road leading over the hill to Kadikoi, with music playing, drums beating, and colours flying in full sight of the Russian outposts. They left strongly entrenched positions directly along the east bank of the Lom from Kadikoi southward to Popkoi, evacuating the heights still farther south around the village of Cerkovna, where the battle took place ten days ago, and leaving every foot of the ground which they have occupied during the past month. They posted themselves somewhere to the eastward, as much lost to the Russians as if they were a hundred miles away.

It is a curious, if not a ridiculous, system of warfare where the outpost and scouting service is conducted with so little enterprise that a force of 20,000 of the enemy can disappear and be entirely lost for several days, when they have, in reality, only retired a few miles, and have posted themselves in new positions like the old one. This is, nevertheless, an event of very common occurrence with the Rustchuk armies, and sometimes during several days neither force will feel the other. The conformation of the ground is well adapted to the easy concealment of small camps, and even of the movements of troops, for the country is undulating, and everywhere there are large tracts of a small growth of oak trees, crossed by frequent paths, and practicable for cavalry and light artillery.

I have just returned to Kara Verbovka from a reconnaissance made to discover the whereabouts of the enemy. This is a village situated on the Lom, nearly opposite Kaceljevo, which occupies a narrow little valley half a mile east of the river. For two days this has been neutral ground, and small bands of Turkish marauders have been scouring the valley for meagre plunder. With a small force of cavalry under the command of Prince Manueloff and Baron Kaulbars, we left the village, where we had assembled under cover of a dense mist, and defiled into the green valley of the Lom. A cold rain, which had drenched us all night, continued at intervals as we began our march, and the fog gradually disappeared as we descended the slope, disclosing the whole landscape, the hillsides across the valley, and the dotted rows of straw huts which the Turks build wherever they pass a day. Not a living thing was visible in the valley, not a sign was there of an occupied camp. A regiment of hussars was sent along the road to Opaka and Polomarca, while Cossacks and lancers took possession of the village of Kaceljevo and surrounding heights. Two Bashi-Bazouks were captured, who reported that the enemy were 35,000 strong in the immediate vicinity of Kaceljevo. Therefore we proceeded with some caution. Arriving at the summit of a hill to the east of the village, we found strong batteries, freshly made; an outpost camp just deserted, with garments and utensils left behind in hasty flight; and still farther on a large deserted camp, with artillery hidden in the bushes.

Two miles beyond the village we came out on an open field, and there lay before us a panorama of the whole Turkish encampment miles away, extending along the farther side of the valley on the east branch of the Lom, around Solenik and Kostankza, in front of Pizanca, Turlak and Esirdje. We could count seven distinct camps, with great droves of cattle feeding on the adjacent hillsides, and far away on the horizon two or three isolated rows of large square tents. There seemed to be very little artillery, but considerable regular cavalry, and a force perhaps of 15,000 infantry, who were mostly Egyptians. From the hill, and just across a valley dividing us from the Turkish camp, could be seen, lying flat in the furze, a strong detachment of infantry ready to welcome us. A few Cossacks dashed down into the valley and exchanged some shots with the outposts. The cattle were hurriedly driven away as the lances of our three squadrons bristled on the hill-top, and there was a stir of preparation visible in the camps, but we only looked on until dusk, and then retired. Meantime, the hussars on our right had found a small camp, and charged down upon it, capturing a number of horses and cattle, and killing a score of Bashi-Bazouks and Circassians. They report the enemy strong at Karahassankoi and Sadina. The result of the reconnaissance is to prove that the whole Turkish force, retired along the line of railway between Rasgrad and Rustchuk, is strongly concentrated at several points, especially near Kadikoi, and has now re-occupied almost the same line as that held before the advance of a month ago.

The cold storm continues, and the roads are impassable for artillery. If there be an engagement of importance it must take place in the immediate vicinity of Rustchuk, but I doubt if the Turkish army will attack for some time, as it has evidently chosen strongly defensive positions with the intention of discontinuing its attempts to break through the Czarewitch's forces.

+ HEADQUARTERS OF THE ARMY OF THE CZAREWITCH, DOLNY MONASTIR, *October 3rd.*—We are still playing at the old game of hide and seek on a large scale, and the oft-repeated story of the sudden disappearance of the Turks is again told at headquarters, and commented on with more gravity than it is possible for any one to command who appreciates the ludicrous side of the situation. Imagine two large armies, forty or fifty thousand strong, losing each other every day or two! It is a farce which, if it were not serious, would be in the highest degree ridiculous. A long irregular line from the Danube to Tirnova is held by opposing forces, neither of which thinks itself strong enough to make a serious attempt to break the line of the other, but both manœuvre about on the hills, wearying the soldiers in rapid marches, and wasting them in small engagements which result in considerable loss of life, but in no advantage to either side. I doubt if there has ever been such a grand farce enacted since the invention of gunpowder.

Even the advance of the army of Mehemet Ali a month ago I have ceased to regard as a serious attempt to break the line of the Czarewitch's army. Beginning at Karahassankoi, where General Leonoff on the left and centre of the position, and Baron Kaulbars at Haidarkoi on the right, made a most gallant resistance, which was rivalled by the defence of Ablava and Kadikoi a few days later, the advance was unchecked by the least opposition, and had the Turks made their appearance on the hillsides along the Jantra I have not the slightest doubt but they would have easily taken Bjela and probably reached Pavlo, only a few hours from Gorny Studen. What is more, it is evident to every one who knows the positions that at any time within two or three weeks after the attack on Kara-hassankoi it was an easy matter to break the line at almost any point. Mehemet Ali did not follow up his advantages; he sauntered across to the Banicka Lom, saw plainly the Russian organization very much broken up, and knew that the force was very much weakened by the drafts from Plevna; nevertheless, he paused lazily in the sunny grain fields along the plateau east of the Banicka Lom, and let his enemy recover and pull himself together again, and stand on the defensive concentrated in a little half circle scarcely ten miles across.

One must come to one of two conclusions—either there was very bad generalship on the Turkish side, which the well-directed attack partly disproves, or the advance was only a demonstration on a large scale. For my own part, I am much inclined to cling to the latter opinion, considering the facilities the Turks have for knowing the numbers and dispositions of the Russian forces, and the superiority of tactics of the Turkish generals, proved by their skilful manœuvring in the face of the enemy. Of the generalship on the Russian side it is unnecessary to speak, for it is a matter of universal comment and criticism, and I need only refer to the descriptions of the different movements which I have sent from time to time by telegraph, and let every one judge for himself.

Here on the field it is with the brave, patient private soldier that one must sympathize the most. Armed with a rifle which has a range a third shorter than the Turkish weapon, he is obliged to stand fire for a long time before he can return a shot. Ordered to march squarely into a rain of bullets without any cover, he never for a moment hesitates longer than to cross himself, but is off cheerfully, and enthusiastically convinced that he is serving God and his country when he is fighting the Turk. Wounded, he still goes on until he falls, and then never loses his pluck even to the last. What a pitiable sight it is to see the long trains of ox-carts of the rudest description, their octagonal wheels grinding, screeching, and jolting over the rough roads a mile and a half an hour, every one with two or three wounded men whose groans almost drown the squeaking of the axles. A soldier is wounded at the front. Possibly he gets attention from the courageous attendants of the Red Cross under fire, and then is carried by his comrades miles to the rear and is put into one of these torture carts, to be pounded and jolted for three days until he reaches a hospital.

While I relate the experience of almost every soldier wounded at a distance from the main hospitals, I do not intend to imply that as far as it goes the ambulance service is defective; the trouble is that it doesn't begin to go half far enough, but is on the same cumbersome scale as the supply trains, with far too little force to properly attend to the wounded which come to the rear after any large battle, and a certain ease and deliberation of movement which is agonizing to one accustomed to see the duties of the ambulance corps attended to with enthusiastic promptitude. It is in human nature to get careless of the life and callous to the sufferings of the wounded if it be impossible properly to attend to them. Those who have no anæsthetics to give get accustomed to the groans of the unfortunates, and without being aware of it become hard-hearted, and to the outsider appear even cruel. This is the experience of every one. I must say that I have seen more to horrify me in the treatment of the wounded here than ever before, and in every case there was a good reason for the neglect. But no one will pardon a neglect which is the result of lack of hospital supplies on a field where all other supplies are over-abundant.

One thing the private soldier certainly has, and that is food, and plenty of it, and of excellent quality; but the clothing is scanty for this cold season that has so suddenly come upon us. In the summer the soldiers wore their coarse white shirts as blouses and carried their coats in their knapsacks. Now the sacks are light, and everything is put on to resist the cold. The thin linen shelter-tents are only an apology for sleeping under the sky; wind and rain penetrate everywhere; boots torn and thin after months of almost constant marching become soaked and full of mud, and the long days and longer nights are spent in fruitless attempts to get dry. The private soldier rarely solaces himself with a good grumble, the recognized prerogative of all soldiers, but stands patiently and takes it as he takes the fire of the Turks, as he toiled along the dusty tracks in the intense heat of summer—always without a word. Supplies of clothing are already on the way here, the bootmakers are busy on all sides making up the leather which arrived a few days ago, and before winter fairly sets in every one will be comfortably clothed.

Side by side with the men in the ranks, sharing with them all their hardships, having scarcely greater comforts and luxuries, are the officers of the line, most of them intelligent and even cultivated men, who have all the merits of the private soldier. They are the strong buttresses of the army, and deserve every sympathy and encouragement. Often, very often, I have seen a detachment left in a position by itself with only the officers of the line to direct its movements. On one occasion a squadron of cavalry held the wing of a position. It was fiercely attacked by an overwhelming force of infantry. Without a word from the staff, the line officers took charge of the whole left wing and saved the day. Compare the life of the gallant colonels and brigadiers who sleep night after night at the forepost, personally superintending every detail of placing the vedettes and protecting the front, with the existence of the generals, so far away that they learn of a battle after it has been lost, drinking champagne to the sound of music,—and the sympathies must go with those who do the work. Perhaps in this descending scale of merit in the Russian Army is to be found the reason why the front of the line is not better protected, why the Turks get lost to us now and then, and why a severe fight results only in loss of life and not in any change of position.

The long line of the Czarewitch's army has been exposed to attack constantly for months. From the headquarters, whenever a battle occurs, a member of the staff is sent away post haste to advise and assist the general in command at the point in question, and the position is considered safe, I suppose, because this combination of practical and theoretical knowledge must necessarily cover all possible turns and crooks of military science. It is true that such a line has been difficult to keep with a force so limited. It has been about fifty miles long, with scarcely as many thousand men to hold it; but notwithstanding unaccountable movements and wild manœuvres the line has been kept to the present time, and half of the original plan of the Russians has succeeded. Of course this plan was to make two walls of men from the river to the Balkans, in order to permit the safe passage of troops towards Adrianople. Both armies on the flanks were to be strictly defensive ones, and the active force was to be over the Balkans.

The *naïveté* of this plan of campaign is apparent, and Plevna has proved how much easier it was to draw the lines of these walls on the map than to build them and keep them unbroken. No one could imagine the fierceness of the fire from the breech-loading rifles, which is far hotter than any ever before experienced by soldiers. From a thin skirmish line of Turks comes a pelting of bullets that in muzzle-loading times a regimental line in close order could never equal. A successful charge is a physical impossibility. To look ahead a little, I venture to say that no one in the Russian Army can think of the winter campaign with complacency. Forage is already short. After a day's rain the roads are ankle-deep with mud, and it is difficult to get about on horseback, almost impossible with wheels. Fuel is not over-abundant. Thus far we have burned the fences about the houses and the timbers of the houses themselves. In cold weather, in a territory already pretty well scoured of every scrap of straw and hay, and with absolutely nothing to support life, a good day's ride in fine weather from the base of supplies, life will be a constant struggle. The cold wind from the Balkans is now a great discomfort and a source of much sickness. Yet the soldiers look remarkably strong and may support the rigours of winter with the same remarkable endurance which they have shown in the heat of summer. But there is all the difference in the world between a close warm room in a hut in Russia with the thermometer below zero, and the same temperature in Bulgaria in a shaky cabin or a thin tent.

DAMOGILO, *October 7th.*—The same officer who proposed a plan for the taking of the grand redoubt in Plevna, by loading a cannon with St. George's crosses, and firing them into the enclosure, has suggested that it might have been well to advertise for the Turkish armies of the past few weeks, for they have been most of the time quite lost to us. But we have found them now, and are likely to keep track of them in the future, because it looks very much as if they intend to stay where they are, considering they have behind them the line of the Rustchuk-Varna railway. Without stopping to discuss the Cossack, whom I regard as the most ineffective cavalryman in the world for scouting service, I will briefly refer to the topography of the country, in order to make clear the position of both armies, if not partly to account for the ease with which the Turkish camps disappear like soap-bubbles in the very face of the Russian forces.

The valley of the Lom is broad and open, with the river winding about in a fertile interval between very high hills, for the most part covered with a dense growth of scrub oak, quite impassable except by frequent cart paths, which cross them in all directions. The valley is much broader, and the hills are higher on the upper part of the river towards Popkoi, while near Rustchuk the river runs between steep cliffs in a gorge-like bed. It is a stream scarcely more than a rod wide, while both of its branches—the Banicka Lom and the Beli Lom—are rivulets a yard or two broad only, and are crossed at frequent intervals by bridges and fords. West of the Lom and the Banicka Lom the hills are broad and flat-topped, with little wood, and the Tirnova-Rustchuk chaussée runs along the summits in a straight line north-east to Rustchuk.

From this chaussée one can overlook the whole country, and the Russian camps are all visible, nestled in the grain fields near the villages.

East of the Lom the country is quite similar in character, but more broken by small valleys, and near Rasgrad is much wooded. Between the Lom and Banicka Lom is a plateau of irregular horseshoe form, full of villages, interrupted by frequent deep valleys; but in general terms a high plateau. This was entirely occupied by the Turks in their recent advance, but they penetrated among the hills farther west at only one or two points, and confined their demonstrations to the positions along this line. The small ridges with the patches of woodland formed a succession of screens, behind which it was easy to manœuvre large forces without their being seen by the enemy, and the network of roads, more or less good, made concentration at different points an easy matter. There were the two armies facing one another across a valley perhaps half a mile wide; the foreposts kept up an almost constant guerilla fight; several attacks were made of more or less importance; and then suddenly nothing remained on the hill-tops but empty straw huts and bush shelters; and the Cossacks leisurely wandered off to find where the Turks were gone.

But for the fact that the Circassians are about as dangerous to the Turks as they are to the Russians, they would be excellent soldiers, for they protect the front quite perfectly. As it is they are quite as likely to shoot the Turkish officers for the sake of booty as they are the Cossacks. An officer who came to Popskoi with a flag of truce begged for a large sheet to display when he returned to the lines, and had a Cossack sent on in advance to announce his arrival, for he was in great fear of his own foreposts, declaring they were quite sure to shoot him if he did not take great precautions.

When on Tuesday last the right wing of the Rustchuk army was seen marching along the hills across the Lom, to the music of drum and bands, with colours flying and arms flashing in the sunlight, it seemed very much like bravado, and was a fitting flourish at the end of an aggressive campaign of a month without a result. Word came in that there was no one in the valley of the Lom, so a reconnaissance was planned, and the order was given for three regiments of cavalry to assemble in the little village Kara Verbovka, on the west bank of the river, on Wednesday evening. I was invited to accompany the expedition, which was commanded by Prince Manueloff and Baron Kaulbars. The result of the reconnaissance I have announced by telegram, but the details of the expedition and of the trip across the river to send the despatch to Bucharest, are worth mentioning.

As we left the corps headquarters at dusk on the evening named it was warm and agreeable. We looked forward to a pleasant picknicing between the lines of the two armies, and trotted away—a few Cossacks, two officers, myself and servant—towards the village, passing the Russian positions along the Banicka Lom at about nine o'clock. We had a couple of Bulgars for guides who, although born and brought up in the neighbourhood, knew nothing of the country, and lost us entirely before we reached the top of the hills across the river. On we went, always ascending, and it began to rain drearily long before we got to the summit of the range. At last we ran across a deserted Turkish battery with plenty of wood lying about, built a fire, lay down in the ditch and slept an hour, and woke up to find that the rain had extinguished the fire. We knew that the Turks always build huts wherever they camp, so we searched in the darkness until we found some bush shelters, crawled under them, and slept until daybreak, completely drenched by the cold rain, which flooded the ground and entered the hut in a dozen streams.

A dense fog covered the earth, hiding the landscape completely, and after building a fire with straw dried with the heat of our bodies and warming ourselves thoroughly, we started away through the mist and rain to find the village, and at last came to the rendezvous just before the regiments assembled there. When we came into the village there was not a living thing in sight; the fog canopy made the silence most oppressive, and we listened in vain for a sound. A most mournful sight was this village, full of pretty little Turkish cottages half hidden among the trees. The doors standing wide open, the paper windows all broken, the furniture destroyed, and the gardens trampled, with not so much as a stray dog to bark at the approach of a stranger. There had been plenty of marauders about, so we searched the village thoroughly, and the Cossacks found a couple of Bashi-Bazouks hidden away in the fields near by. Both had Peabody-Martini rifles, were tall, square-shouldered fellows, well dressed in the ordinary Turkish peasant's costume, and carried a great quantity of ammunition. The thought naturally occurred to me that they would be immediately shot, but they were treated with marked gentleness, interrogated at length, and sent away to the rear. I was told that no officer was willing to take the responsibility of ordering the execution of men in cold blood, yet I believe that no other people in the world would have let these fellows off, for they were simply murderers caught with their arms in their hands. In all probability they will be set free, as they don't wear any uniform, and will find their way back to the Turkish lines again. It is said that a great many have done this, and I cannot doubt it.

When the fog lifted we filed down the gentle slope into the valley of the Lom, and crossed the river by a ford, then quickly up the hill to the village of Kaceljevo, near at hand, which was quite as lifeless as the one we had just left. Here the Cossacks, who are supposed to know the way always, took the wrong path and delayed the advance an hour or more, for they were to go forward in the centre, the Lancers on the left and the Hussars on the right. At last we climbed the great hill back of the town, and had the whole country for miles around under us like a map. To the south was the great mountain near Karahassankoi, and beyond, a glimpse of distant Popskoi in the intervale; east in the horizon was the ridge where the railway runs; north, the hills about Rutschuk; and west, the valley of the Lom, and the summits far beyond. Cruising about in the low oak-trees on the hill-top we came suddenly upon a deserted battery, and a camp near by, evidently just left, for, notwithstanding the recent rain, dry clothing was lying about, and quantities of utensils were strewn along the road. Equipments left behind showed that regular cavalry had occupied the post, and scattered clothing of Bulgar women proved that the marauders had made this their headquarters as well. The Bashi-Bazouks had told us that the hills about Solenik were covered with camps, so we were not surprised to see from the east side of the summit white tents all along across the valley of the Beli Lom.

We approached until we could see the uniforms of the soldiers in the camps, and the only unusual movement there was when the Cossacks came out in full sight, and then we saw the Turks driving away over the hills the great herds of cattle which were feeding on the slopes. There were but few soldiers in the camps, but a cautious advance to the edge of the hill overlooking Solenik showed the infantry lying in the edge of the furze to receive us. Of course we could not attack. The Cossacks went down and had a brush with the Circassians in the edge of the valley, and when darkness came on we retired and met the Hussars, who had been successful in breaking up a camp they had found, killing twenty-five Bashi-Bazouks and Circassians, and not losing a man.

In the rain and darkness we found our way near midnight to the positions again, having made an advance in the twenty-four hours of only about twenty-five miles from headquarters. When we came near the spot where we left our luggage the day before, we two separated from the force and went to the camp, expecting to find some one to welcome us. Not a tent, not a soldier was there; all had disappeared during the day, having been ordered off to some position we were unable to discover. It was midnight; we had neither eaten nor drunk since the evening of the day before, for no one carried rations on the expedition on account of the heavy roads and the necessity of going light weight. There was nothing to do but to stable the horses in a ruined house and turn in there ourselves and sleep. The next day, before taking the despatch and letters I was about to send to Bucharest, we made an effort of a few hours to find the spot where we had left our luggage; but after having fasted forty-two hours I gave up the search and rode for Batin, arriving towards dark. Leaving our horses in the village, we had a mile and a half to walk to the Danube, and landed at last on the island a mile above the new bridge an hour after sunset. We knew there was a path across the island where the bridge is being built, so we fought our way through the tangled undergrowth in the rain and darkness until we reached the muddy track and followed it northwards until it came plump into the Danube on the other side. Not a boat was to be found, not a soldier was within hail. At last we found some Bulgars, who guided us to a camp of marines, who kindly set us over the stream, and we were landed in the marshes, three or four miles from the solid land, where the lights of Petrosani twinkled in the distance.

A brisk cold wind drove across the marsh, and the rain ceased for a time, but it was as dark as a pocket. On we trudged, scarcely able to walk after our excursion, stumbling about over the track, at times knee-deep in the muddy water, and after great difficulty reached the lagoon which separates the marsh from the high land. To find the bridge was a problem which we only solved after a half-hour's blind search, and at the other side of the bridge was a not over-intelligent soldier, who was with difficulty persuaded to let us pass. At two in the morning we were sound asleep on the floor of a dirty little Greek restaurant, with Russians, Greeks, Moldavians, and Bulgars singing choruses over the cheap wine, and filling the room with vile smoke.

I have given a meagre description of a trip in Bulgaria in bad weather to show what the difficulties are, and how it is quite out of the power of any one to make even a short journey except at great personal discomfort, and with no little fatigue. It seems as if our picnic days are over now. Sleeping in a tent in the hot weather was rather to be avoided, but now even this miserable shelter is welcome. Bulgar houses, which we shunned as we would the pest, on account of the myriads of insects that swarm within the walls, we now look upon as a luxurious refuge from the damp, chill atmosphere. To give a brief resumé of the new positions: The Russians are now concentrated nearer the Danube than before, opposite the strong force of Turks at Kadikoi, a village about ten miles from Rustchuk. The line still lies along the Banicka Lom, but cavalry occupies the whole territory west of the Lom. The positions of the Russian right are about fifteen miles from those of the Turkish left, along the railway near Rasgrad, while the 12th Corps and part of the 13th are in the immediate neighbourhood of the Lom, near Rustchuk. The 11th Corps has not greatly changed its positions during the past two weeks.

In the following letter, a Correspondent who had followed the campaign from its commencement reviews the errors and failures of the Russian generals.

† BUCHAREST, *Oct. 15th.*—The rain has been pouring down for a week—steadily, persistently, obstinately, with scarcely a respite; the sun has not looked out once; the sky is a dark grey spongy blanket, hung low down over our heads, which is dripping, running over, and discharging itself in bucketfuls. The weather god has positively taken sides with the Turks, and having delayed the opening of the campaign for more than a month, now seems determined to bring it to a close a month or six weeks earlier than was to be expected. For should this weather continue the campaign is at an end, and nothing can be done but wait for the ground to freeze and a fall of snow, when possibly a winter campaign may be attempted. There is still hope that this may not be the case, that the rain may cease, and that we may yet have a month, and perhaps even six weeks, during which something may be done. Everything therefore depends upon the weather, and the prospect is not encouraging. The results of the campaign so far, may be summed up as follows:—The Russians have crossed the Danube, they have taken the fortress of Nicopolis, and they have lost 50,000 men in killed and wounded.

For a campaign undertaken with such high hopes, with everything requisite to bring it to a victorious conclusion except military talent—begun with two most important operations brilliantly and successfully carried out, this is a result as unexpected as it is discouraging. For be it remembered that the only real conquests of the campaign, the passage of the

Danube and the capture of Nicopolis, were made with a loss of less than three thousand; and we have absolutely nothing to show in exchange for the rest of this immense loss of 47,000 men. Had the Russians sat quietly down after the capture of Nicopolis and not moved a foot, or had they gone to sleep and slept all summer, they would have been in exactly the same position they are in to-day, and they would have been 47,000 men richer; that is, nearly one-third of the force with which they first crossed the Danube at Sistova. One-third of the army lost and nothing to show for it but three defeats —such is the result of General Levitsky's military science—Levitsky, the Moltke of Russia.

There is another point worth noting in reference to this campaign, which is that the two great Russian successes, the passage of the Danube and the passage of the Balkans, were accomplished by a lucky chance, in which good luck and Turkish incapacity counted for a good deal more than Russian skill and generalship. At Sistova, as General Dragomiroff very truly remarked, the Turks were asleep; at Shipka they were unprepared. If we look, on the other hand, at the successes of the Turks, we see that they have been accomplished, first, by a splendid stroke of strategy; second, by the most desperate valour; third, by consummate skill in engineering. The Russian successes were the result of chance and unforeseen circumstances; the Turkish victories, on the contrary, were won by downright good generalship, military skill, and science—elements which may be calculated, estimated, and counted upon in the future.

These are the facts, let Generals Levitsky and Nepokoitchitsky digest them as they may. Their excuse is, I believe, that they had not enough troops, and that they did not know the Turks were so strong. The excuse is a very feeble one. In the first place, the Russian mobilisation began and the Russian staff was formed last November, five months before the declaration of war, seven months before the fighting actually began. Where were their spies during all this time, and why did they not have correct information with regard to the force, armaments, organization, and numbers of the Turks? And if they had not enough troops there were plenty more, and the Emperor was ready to give them had they been asked for. Again, why did they not know of the march of Osman Pacha from Widdin to Plevna? There was a month during which Osman Pacha was marching upon Plevna, and Generals Levitsky and Nepokoitchitsky never knew it and never found it out. Why did they not know, and why did they not find it out? And having given such proofs of incapacity as these, why do they not, if they have any patriotism left, resign and go home? These are questions which not only the Russian people but the Russian army is asking, without receiving any satisfactory answer.

It is true that the Russians began the war with an insufficient number of troops—that is, with an insufficient number to take Constantinople, or even to reach the capital, and I am willing to admit that it is doubtful whether they had enough to take Adrianople, though I am convinced they had enough in the beginning to have crossed the Balkans and occupied the country to the very gates of that place. But from saying they have not enough troops to take Constantinople to the assertion that they have not enough to take Plevna there is an immense difference. It is a difference the importance of which the headquarter staff have probably not even perceived. It simply means this—that they began a war with the avowed intention of capturing Constantinople with a force which they find, after having been increased by half, is still too weak to capture an unfortified village twenty miles from the Danube. For although Plevna is fortified now, it was not fortified when the march on Constantinople was begun.

Such a mistake, such a miscalculation, avowed and acknowledged, and even offered as an excuse, is a confession of imbecility beyond what even could have been expected. The Russians had across the Danube at the time of the last attack upon Plevna, including the Roumanians, about 200,000 men. If this force is not capable of taking Plevna, what force, it may be asked, will be required over the Danube before a sufficient number of troops can be sent against Plevna to ensure its capture? What force will be required to cross the Balkans? How many more troops must we have to take Adrianople? And, above all, what force will be required to reach Constantinople? Evidently, at this rate we shall soon be into the millions; and if the Emperor means to prosecute the war with the present headquarter staff, he had better call out two million men at once.

It may not be without interest here to take another glance at the last Battle of Plevna, and see what military lessons can be drawn from it. In the first place, the lesson already taught by the previous affair, which was only too clear to anybody who had eyes to see—the madness of attacking trenches defended by breechloaders by assault—has been enforced and confirmed, and the Russian generals have at last learned it at an expense of 15,000 more men. But there are other things which they may learn from it which they ought to have learned in school. In the first place they should know that artillery fire, to be effective against such positions, should be directed, not against earth, but against men. Now, the four days during which the Russians shelled the Turkish positions they never once advanced their infantry. The consequence was, that the Turks were not obliged to advance theirs. They kept their troops stowed comfortably out of the way of the shells, and only put them forward when they saw the Russians were preparing for the assault. Naturally the Russian shell-fire did them very little harm, and for all the effect it had upon the result, they might as well have made the assault the first day. The Russian infantry should have been advanced as if to attack; this would have compelled the Turkish infantry to occupy their trenches, where they would have been exposed to the fire of the Russian shrapnel. I do not believe much in modern artillery anyhow, except where the fire of a large number of guns can be concentrated on a small space; but if it is to be of any use at all, it must be by directing it against men and not heaps of earth.

With the recapture of the redoubts taken by Skobeleff the attack upon Plevna ended. Up to that moment, there was still a hope that the attack might be continued, and that success might finally crown so many heroic efforts. The Russians had taken three strong positions; could they get two or three more equally important, Plevna would inevitably be theirs. There seems to have been some idea of renewing the attack, for Skobeleff, I am told, on Wednesday afternoon was requested to hold his position a few hours longer, even after he had reported several times that the place was untenable. Only a few hours longer! When men were going down by the hundreds, and companies and battalions under the terrible fire of the Turks were shrivelling up like green leaves in a furnace flame.

The melancholy part of it is, that generals who send men by the thousand to perish under fire have themselves no idea of what fire is. They have no grip of the battle, no feel of the fire, and they have no other way of discovering that a position is untenable, or a line of resistance too strong, but in seeing their soldiers in flight after having performed perhaps prodigies of heroism and of valour. So Skobeleff was requested to wait a few hours, while the headquarter staff would reflect on the situation. The situation was as follows:—The redoubts taken by Skobeleff were untenable, but they, as well as the redoubt of Grivica, offered a foothold from which the other positions might have been attacked with success. Skobeleff asked for reinforcements, but not to hold the redoubt, for so far as the redoubt was tenable he had enough troops to hold it as long as it could be held. He asked for troops to continue the attack upon the redoubt of Krishine, or upon the entrenched camp on the other side of Plevna, or he would undertake to hold the place while something was attempted on some other point; only whatever was to be done would have to be done quickly. But the morning wore away with the continued attacks of the Turks, continually repulsed and continually renewed, and the whole Russian army lay quiet all day long and watched that heroic struggle and did nothing. This inactivity of the Russians allowed the Turks to finally concentrate in the evening an overwhelming force against Skobeleff and to overpower him. The headquarter staff could not make up its mind what to do, and while meditating on the subject the redoubts were lost.

It is true, as I have already stated, that General Kriloff took the responsibility of sending a regiment which had made the unsuccessful assault of the day before, and which was reduced from 2,600 to 1,000 men, a regiment utterly unfit to go into action; and even it arrived too late. It is likewise true that a fresh regiment was sent, which arrived an hour after the redoubts were lost, and thus just in time to assure the retreat. But sending these regiments, even had they arrived in time, was a mistake. They would, of course, have enabled Skobeleff to hold the redoubts a few hours longer; but this would only have resulted in a still greater loss of men, without any object. Unless it was intended to continue the attack from this side, the redoubts should have been abandoned as soon as the attack failed on other points, for holding them these twenty-four hours resulted in a loss of some 4,000 men. If, on the contrary, it was intended to continue the attack from this side, then a division, and not a regiment, should have been sent to Skobeleff. The whole plan of attack was a mistake; but there is little doubt that the attack, having been begun, might have been, and should have been, continued the next morning. The line of defence had been broken in two places. Had the Russians concentrated all their strength on these two points early next morning, and renewed the assault with vigour, they would, in my opinion, have carried the place. Their loss would have been fearful, but the army of Osman Pacha would have been destroyed, and the way would have been open to Adrianople. As it is, 15,000 men have been lost, and, because they have been lost, the Russians are not quite so near Adrianople as they were before.

All the mistakes of the campaign have been repeated in miniature in the attack upon Plevna, with a fidelity which shows how little the headquarter staff have profited from previous blunders. Their first intention was to await the arrival of the Guard before beginning the attack, and unless they had adopted the plan I had already sketched out, of abandoning the line of the Jantra, and making a rapid concentration of the whole force of both armies upon Plevna, this was the only possible thing to do; for to attack Plevna with less than one hundred thousand men was simply folly. Suddenly it occurred to them, that if they waited for the arrival of the Guard they would be thrown into another campaign. This was a consideration that might have occurred to them at first, and which should have necessitated a complete change in the whole plan of campaign. When it finally did occur to them, it resulted in a spasmodic fit of energy and this last attack upon Plevna. But instead of bringing together a force sufficient for the purpose, that is, a hundred thousand men, they hurriedly scrape together what they could without interfering with the army of the Czarewitch, and make the attack with 65,000 bayonets in the forlorn hope of taking Plevna, and thus being able to reach Adrianople this year.

It was a forlorn hope only, and not even General Levitsky believed in success. It was a plan that did not merit success, and it was only the unexpected valour of the Roumanians—an element nobody had counted upon, the sublime bravery of the Russian soldier, and the splendid dash and generalship of Skobeleff, that ever made the result doubtful for a moment. I know that the forces brought up during this last attack have been estimated at a hundred thousand, but I also know that the estimate is greatly exaggerated. I know that the whole force of General Zotoff, up to the time of the arrival of the 2nd and 3rd Divisions, did not amount to 30,000 men; that these two divisions between them, after the loss incurred by the second in the affair of Loftcha, did not add an effective of more than 15,000 men, thus making the Russian force 45,000. As to the Roumanians, I know that their army is estimated at 32,000 men—on paper: but, when you deduct from this the cavalry, the sick, the men detached for guarding communications and for various other duties, and last, but not least, the difference between the complement on paper and the actual number of bayonets, their effective did not give more than 20,000—or 65,000 bayonets in all.

The attack, therefore, was made in the first place with an insufficient number of troops, for the Turks had an equal or perhaps a greater number. But the question is not in war to have a numerical superiority upon every point, but to have it upon one or two important points. An inferior force, skilfully handled, will often suffice to beat a much superior force, and the Russians who had, when we consider the advantages of the position held by the Turks, an inferior force or power, should have endeavoured to make up for this by concentration against one or two points, only making at the same time demonstrations on the whole line. This would have given them the required numerical superiority on the given points. In a conversation I had with Skobeleff before the battle, he agreed with me that the plan of a general attack was a mistake, and the result proved it. Had the attack been confined to the Grivica redoubt and the redoubts on the Loftcha road, and demonstrations made by Krüdener and Kriloff, instead of those furious attacks, repulsed in such a bloody manner, the loss incurred by Krüdener and Kriloff would have been avoided, and the 9th and 4th Corps would have been fresh for the renewal of the attack next day on the points of the Turkish line which gave way.

The plan of a general attack was in short the reproduction in miniature of the general plan of the campaign,—instead of concentration, the distribution of forces already too small. That the Russian staff should have adhered to this plan, and should still adhere to it after the repeated disasters of Plevna, shows that they are simply incapable of profiting by the lessons of the war, and that the Russians, with one of the best armies in the world, will be beaten as long as the present staff remains in command, by what may be technically considered one of the worst.

In my opinion there are, besides the plan of a siege and starvation, two ways of taking such a place as Plevna. The first is the plan of an assault, made with about three times as many men as the Russians had in the last affair, that is about 120,000, and handled in the manner of Skobeleff by hurling them against the positions, brigade after brigade, until by mere force of momentum and bravery they sweep everything before them like the waves of a rapidly rising sea. The loss to be incurred in such a plan is fearful, but the loss of the enemy would be greater still, for the reason that wherever there is a crossing of bayonets, the beaten side must be simply annihilated. Had the Russians attacked Plevna in this manner, they would have lost 30,000 men, but the army of Osman Pacha would have been destroyed. Not 5,000 would have escaped to tell the tale.

The other plan is more slow, and perhaps not more sure, but it requires a far smaller force for its execution. It is that of advancing by means of flying saps—narrow shallow trenches, rapidly constructed under cover of night, or a heavy rifle fire. A man can, with a shovel in ordinary ground, and stimulated by an enemy's fire, put himself under cover in three minutes, and he will make himself a comfortable rifle-pit in five. Give the Russian army shovels, and they will dig their way into Plevna in a week at the outside. The trouble is, that while in the Roumanian army every two men out of three have shovels, in the Russian army there are only five hundred shovels to the division, or about one to every twenty men, and this in a war against the Turks, which the whole military history of the Russians might have taught them was destined from the first to become a war of sieges, a kind of war in which the shovel plays a no less important *rôle* than the rifle! This plan I have every reason to believe was under discussion, and had to be laid aside owing to the want of shovels.

So far it must be acknowledged that the Turkish generals have shown far more skill in the conduct of the campaign than the Russian. Their plan consists simply in placing their soldiers in trenches and supplying them with cartridges, bread, and rice. But true generalship after all consists, not in carrying out a theoretical plan by a theoretical army, but in adapting existing means to required ends. In this, which is really the highest kind of generalship, the Turks have excelled; and they have taught a bitter lesson to the French generals, who during the late war with Germany showed their incapacity, and not only their incapacity, but their unwillingness, to fight with anything but the army of their dreams.

I have spoken of Russian generals in a previous letter, and I may add another reason to the ones I then gave for the want of capacity and talent displayed among them. In the first place, all those high in command are very old men. They are men who studied the military art forty and even fifty years ago, since which time the science of war has undergone most important changes and developments—a revolution, in short. In addition to this, they are men who, for the most part, never look in a book, and who rarely read a newspaper, and appear to be utterly oblivious of the march of progress and of science, especially in the military art. Their whole lives may be said to have been passed in one occupation; their whole minds, whatever they ever had, concentrated on one object, and that one of the most trivial to which the human mind can descend—card-playing. They have done nothing else, thought of nothing else, for years. Their minds have rusted until they are as dull, as heavy, and as incapable of receiving new impressions as the veriest clodhopper. Called from their card-tables by the trumpet of war, they rise, rub their eyes, look round them completely bewildered, and are as thoroughly out of the current of modern war as if they had been asleep for forty years. Not even Rip van Winkle, with his rusty gun dropping to pieces after his long sleep, was more bewildered and lost than the majority of these poor old generals suddenly thrown into the campaign at the heads of their brigades, divisions, and corps.

It may be asked why the Emperor does not send these old dotards back to their card-tables, and replace them by younger men and men of talent, of which, after all, the Russian army is not destitute. Well, in the first place, there is the tradition, according to which no functionary must be removed or disgraced as long as it can be helped—from some absurd idea that the prestige of the Government would suffer. The Government would be acknowledging its own fallibility. The result is that the Government, instead of renouncing, assumes the responsibility of all the stupidity, of all the idiocy, all the perversity, and all the dishonesty of the functionary. Then it must be confessed, the kind heart of the Emperor has much to do in retaining these old incapables in their positions. He cannot bear the idea of depriving an old, and as he considers a faithful, public servant of his position, and thus disgracing him, and so unconsciously prefers to sacrifice the lives of thousands of brave fellows to this misplaced feeling of kindness.

One more fact while I am on the subject, illustrative of the way things are managed in the Russian army, for which the headquarter staff must be held responsible. At the time of Suleiman Pacha's attack upon the Shipka Pass, although the pass had then been in the hands of the Russians for something like six weeks, the plan of the pass and positions had not been made. This is a fact which, for military men, speaks volumes. And yet such men as these have dared to take the direction and command of an army of 300,000 men. It is simply madness.

The following letter treats of the posture of military and political affairs in October, as seen from a Turkish point of view:—

:: CONSTANTINOPLE, *October 7th.*—It was officially announced on Wednesday that Suleiman Pacha is to replace Mehemet Ali as the Serdar Ekrem, or Commander-in-Chief. Every one has been trying to guess the reason why Suleiman is thus honoured. That Mehemet Ali would be removed has been considered probable for several days. He has not shown himself specially active, nor displayed remarkable military ability, and no doubt failed signally in the action of the 21st ult. Above all he is of Giaour origin; and unless he could have been uniformly successful, he was pretty sure to arouse the jealousy of the generals under him. But that Suleiman should be his successor is difficult to understand.

Suleiman is not a coward, nor is he destitute of energy. But his previous services are not of a kind one would have thought to warrant his promotion to the most important post in the Turkish army. In Montenegro he showed himself altogether incapable of defeating an army much smaller than his own. When he was recalled, and sent to oppose General Gourko, he pushed on rapidly to the front, and made the successive attempts to force the Shipka Pass, which your readers know so well. But both in Montenegro and in the Shipka his one great rule in war seems to have been to pound away at whatever opposed him, whether an army or a stone wall. If the war between Russia and Turkey is to be conducted on the pounding principle, and each party is ready to sacrifice any number of men, provided that the enemy can be made to lose at least an equal number, there can be little doubt, I fancy, which army will soonest be exhausted. In Montenegro and at the Shipka, Suleiman can hardly have lost less than 40,000 men, and these beyond a doubt among the best soldiers which the Sultan possesses—war, in fact, under him, has been mere butchery.

Notwithstanding the successes of the Turks at Plevna, the depression in the capital during the past fortnight has been very great. It is noticed as a significant fact, that Turkish consolidés have fallen whenever there has been a report of a Turkish victory, and have risen when on the contrary the telegraph has given us news of a Turkish defeat. It is not merely that the Christians of the capital—Greeks, Armenians and Bulgarians alike—have no stomach for the war, that was to be expected; nor is it only that the stoppage of commerce with Russia has put an end to the Black Sea trade, upon which a considerable portion of the population of the capital lives; that the increased taxes upon an impoverished people have brought thousands to the verge of starvation; that the large mass of Government officials—most of whom are Turks—have been unpaid for months, and have had all of them to submit to very large reductions in their salaries; that the issue of caimé, or paper money, has reduced the earnings of boatmen, porters, and day-labourers generally to nearly half what it was before the war; and that native merchants, as well as foreigners, can get no money out of the Government for goods which they have supplied.

These are the incidents, in great part the natural incidents, of war; and, provided the war should be successful, would be borne usually by a people as inevitable ills worth bearing for the sake of the benefits which were to be derived from the struggle. But among the Turks themselves there is the feeling that the war, beyond preventing their immediate destruction, or causing a lessening of their territory, can only be disastrous. As one of the most thoughtful among the Turks said a few days ago:—"We know that Europe will never allow us to increase our territory, no matter what our success. Servia, Roumania, Montenegro, and Greece, can never again be added to Turkey, be our success what it may. The struggle, too, is between us and the rest of the inhabitants of the Empire. We have to supply all the fighting men; and the thousands who have already been killed are a terrible drain on the fighting population of the Empire."

The Turks themselves feel that it is, to say the least, very improbable that at the end of the war they will be in a better position, even though they win, than they were before the war began. England, it is clear, or nearly so, is not going to help them, and every victory they gain is so much loss merely to preserve the *status quo* of their country before the war. They, too, have an inkling, I fancy, of what M. Thiers meant when he said, that he had more dread of Russia defeated than of Russia defeating. Let me say also, in passing, as I have often said before, that none of the inhabitants of European Turkey wish to call Russia master. The argument I have often used from the analogy of the hatred of Greece towards Russia is sound—that if the Christians of the Empire were decently governed, or, better still, governed themselves, they would be hostile to Russia too. Roumania and Servia are the tools, willing or unwilling, of Russia, because their dread of being absorbed by Turkey overcomes their dread of being annexed by Russia. Take away the first, as Europe did for Greece, and the latter becomes at once prominent. Russia defeated means Russia making the war one of life or death, and playing the game of sacrificing man for man.

Turks know that by Russia warfare has always been conducted with an almost wanton disregard of life, and that she has always shown herself a dogged and an obstinate enemy. If the war is to be conducted through one, or two, or three more campaigns, such as that which is now drawing to a close, while the drain of men upon Russia will be terrible, it will be proportionately very much greater upon the Turks. Russia, bankrupt, will even then only be in the condition in which Turkey has been for the last two years. Unless, therefore, Europe interferes, the endurance of Russia is likely to be far greater than that of Turkey, and the terms which will be exacted by her heavier than those which she would have required had the war been finished this autumn. Such, I believe are the opinions of the most thoughtful among the Turks, among whom I would class the Sultan himself, who is reputed to have been always opposed to the war, and who deeply feels the enormous sacrifices which have already had to be made, and the small amount of benefits which can be derived therefrom.

Yesterday's Turkish papers announce that the Government has decided to call out all the remaining reserves which have not yet been summoned. Most of us were under the impression that this had already been done, but it is asserted that there are yet 160,000 men who can be added to the army. The redifs or militia have long been called out, including a large body of men who have served their terms in the army. Those who remain, the mustafez, and who are said to form so large a body, are the Landsturm or last reserve. When it is remembered that the Turkish army comprises the whole of the male Moslem population between certain ages, it may be understood how terrible is the drain upon the population of which I have spoken. That which makes the matter worse, not only for the Turks, but for the country, is that while the Christian villages may have a redundant population, or may at least be able to spare a considerable number of men, nearly the whole male population of hundreds of Moslem villages has thus been taken away. Harvests are neglected, cultivation is at a standstill, and the deepest distress prevails in many places, because the whole of the bread-winners are away.

In estimating the surprises of the war, the fact should be taken into account that the failure of the Turks in putting down the insurrection in Bosnia and Herzegovina, in fighting with Montenegro, and to a less extent in fighting with Servia, was a failure with Turks drawn mainly from European Turkey. With the exception of a not very large detachment from the district round about Beyrout, the Turkish army eighteen months ago was hardly recruited at all from Asiatic Turkey. After the beginning of the war with Russia, Asia Minor, Syria, and Egypt were drawn upon for a supply of men. The Egyptians may be dismissed, since by all accounts they are worth little as soldiers, even during a summer campaign, and in winter will probably be worth still less.

The men from Asia Minor are not merely the best soldiers

Turkey can produce, but form as good material for making soldiers as any in the world. Many of them are mountaineers, all of them have been inured to hardship, and have, indeed, known little else. Most of them come from the occupations of the country rather than from those of towns, and even those who have lived in the towns have been porters or boatmen, or camel-drivers, or engaged in some other out-of-door occupation, which has helped to make them strong and hardy. The great majority are agriculturists, and as shepherds or farm labourers have been used to roughing it. They have moreover all been trained more or less to the use of arms. The result of their previous training is, that men who have not been put into uniform before have been converted into fair soldiers after a few days' drill, and when sent to the front have proved cool soldiers and good shots. The very want of success which the Turks everywhere encounter when brought face to face in business with keen Arabs or Greeks or Armenians, has driven the Turks, or kept them, to the land and to occupations which are the best training for such soldiers as the Turkish Government has need of. The result has been that the successes gained lately have been such as could not have been foreseen by those who judged only from the failures I have mentioned. The mountaineers of Anatolia and Armenia have done that which their co-religionists from European Turkey entirely failed to do. These men will, I apprehend, stand a winter as well as Russians. What the Syrians and Egyptians will be able to do remains to be seen.

We are now in the midst of the month of Ramazan. One of the five precepts of the Mohammedan religion is the keeping of this month as a fast. It is kept strictly except, I believe, by soldiers, who are permitted by Moslem law to disregard it. The Turkish day consists of the evening and the morning; in other words, lasts from sunrise to the following sunset. During this period in the whole of the month of Ramazan no true believer either eats, drinks, or smokes. The result is that a very much smaller amount of business is transacted during this month than during any other of the year. Eating commences at sunset, and is usually followed by a certain amount of festivity, after which come a few hours' sleep. In the Turkish quarters, two hours before daylight, the rattle of harsh drums, accompanied by harsher voices, and the sound of nondescript instruments, awakes the faithful to the fact that the time has come to eat enough to last them until sunset. This meal is concluded just before the sunrise gun, and then the faithful again betake themselves to sleep. Practically they are good for nothing in the way of work during the rest of the day.

This fact is recognized, and in the public offices and in the law courts there is a general suspension of business, as Turkish officials, like other mortals, are incapable of work upon an empty stomach. In justice, however, to the poorer class of of Turks, I ought to add that they manage to do a fair share of hard work, even during Ramazan. I have seen wood-cutters whom either good will or necessity has compelled to work during these days, notwithstanding the fact that they could not even take a draught of water, while the perspiration was streaming from every pore. It was impossible not to feel kindly towards these poor fellows as they asked, time after time, how the day was proceeding, and as at the last they rolled up their cigarettes and got their matches ready to have their longed-for smoke the instant the twelve o'clock gun (Turkish time) announced that the sun had sunk below the horizon.

Yesterday morning, at about ten o'clock, four very loud and almost simultaneous explosions greatly alarmed the inhabitants of this city and the vicinity, and all sorts of rumours were immediately afloat as to the cause. The utmost excitement prevailed, crowds of people congregated in almost every street, and many of them were pale with terror. The explosions were caused by a very alarming accident which took place at the Government powder-mills at Zeitounlik (the Place of Olives), close to Makrikeny, about five miles from the capital. Four pug-mills situated near to each other blew up at almost the same instant through the explosion of some grains of powder while the stone used in working the powder was turning. The four mills were in a moment destroyed, and a great number of lives, variously estimated at from 50 to 200, were lost. It is impossible as yet to ascertain the precise number, but I fear that the latter is more likely to be nearer the truth. A great quantity of machinery and powder was destroyed, though the Turkish Government estimates the loss at only £10,000, and says that it feels confident that the loss can be repaired within a fortnight at the latest. The Imperial cartridge manufactory is close by the scene of the explosion, and had that building also blown up the loss to the Government at the present moment would have been almost irreparable.

The greatest promptitude was exhibited in hurrying to the rescue of the sufferers. The medical staff of the Stafford-house Committee instantly proceeded to the scene of the accident. The Government has already given orders for the immediate reconstruction of the mills, and the wounded have been taken under the Sultan's protection, whatever that may imply, and are to be cared for at the expense of the State. Great anxiety was manifested amongst the British colony on the accident becoming known, as several Englishmen in the Ottoman service are employed in the neighbourhood. Only one Englishman, however, was near the spot at the time, and he was not seriously wounded. The sufferers are mostly Mussulmans and Armenians. I happened to be on the Marmora at the time, and not more than three miles from the mills, which are on the sea shore. My attention was suddenly aroused by a sound which startled all on board the small steamer by which I was a passenger, for we took it to be an explosion on board. This was almost immediately followed by another, and then again by two others in rapid succession. Men and women ran to and fro in an excited state for an instant, half expecting to find themselves blown up. Some of the passengers on the bridge had, however, seen the explosion on shore, and the word was at once passed that the powder factory had blown up. We then all saw a huge pear-shaped mass of smoke shooting up into the sky, and knew that we were safe. I learn at the last moment from a medical man who had just returned from the spot, and who was there yesterday shortly after the accident, that there were probably not less than 150 persons killed. Though he was among the first to arrive after the accident, many bodies had already been hurried into hastily prepared graves, and at one containing Armenians a service was being as hastily read over by an Armenian priest.

The following letter, which appeared yesterday in the *Stamboul*, is from Ali Suavi Effendi, who is at the head of the chief Turkish college here:—

"I have received many letters. Some ask me to preach in the Mosque of Sheik Zadé-Bachi; others to give my appreciation of the situation. I am going, therefore, to give you my appreciation on this subject, because next week may witness great events. All my appreciations of European policy may be summed up in the following words. [The italics are in the orginal] :—*The source of every political evil, of every crime, is the English Government.* Those who can understand this phrase will have no difficulty to overcome. In Europe there is no policy, there is no justice, there is no humanity. These words I have not taken from any book, nor from the newspapers. I have studied the events, and it is the events themselves that have inspired me. Neither must it be believed that I thus expressed myself against my friends who are in Europe, and who can have no knowledge of what I write. While I was in Europe I told them, "You don't know; you don't understand." Many men read, but few understand. Find me ten men able to understand, and all the difficulties will disappear. To make the English understand their ignorance would benefit everybody, but especially the Ottomans. This is why I don't give up my correspondence with Englishmen. They say, "England ought to help us; she has not done so, and she will not do so." What do these words mean? Where is England, and what is she? I have studied England; therefore I know well that all the evils from which the world suffers come from the English Government. I believe that if England reforms herself the world will equally reform itself. If the English, cause of every ill, were really bad people, I would not trouble about them; they are good enough; but the reason why they are the tools of Russia is ignorance. England cannot make war, for she possesses nothing. England possesses altogether 12,000 cavalry; she has only 6,000 horses. England does not possess more than fifty ironclads; seven only can make war. Her mines of coal and of iron, &c., are used up. The manufactories of England are cut out by those of Brussels. England is henceforth a porter (hamal), who, in order to live, must carry goods and merchandise from one to another. Why has England fallen so low? England has plunged herself into the abyss of debt in order to aggrandize Russia. England has attempted the dismemberment of Turkey and of three other States in favour of Russia and of herself. England has undergone very material losses. The knowledge which I possess upon these attempts is drawn from English official documents. If these documents had attracted your attention you would have comprehended too. These documents are printed, but you and the English don't understand. If ignorance were blotted out from England the blood of thousands of men, leaving thousands of orphans and widows, would not have been shed, and milliards would not have been added to the national debt. . . . . It is necessary to say that our conduct, if it does service to the Ottoman Empire, will also render service to the rest of the world—that is to say, with our wish to put the whole world in order. . . . There are Englishmen who work with us. In consequence, and in order to make you understand what I have said in the beginning of my letter—to wit, that every evil springs from England, and that if she does not take care she will end by ruining herself, both to the profit of Russia, and in order to show the ignorance of those who lend their ears to her declarations—I intend to give lectures, as I have already done, at Galata Serai. You must, therefore, attentively read and understand these lessons."

The only importance which can be attached to this letter arises from the fact that it comes from the Director of the Imperial Lyceum. Even the last paragraph is not so absurd as it seems.

While the Russian army had done so little to distinguish itself either in Europe or Asia, and the small Black Sea fleet could not venture to put to sea, many feats of individual officers showed what might be expected of the Navy under more favourable circumstances. The expedition described in the following letter, most merciful in its object, was made at a time when fast and powerful Turkish ironclads held unchallenged possession of the Black Sea.

SEBASTOPOL, *September* 11*th*.—I returned yesterday from the expedition which I told you the *Vesta* and *Vladimir* were about to undertake. The result has been most successful, and at the same time bloodless. Considering the danger of the voyage, and the skill with which Captain Baranoff has executed it, I think it will be allowed to equal anything in the history of blockade running.

We left Sebastopol at midnight yesterday week, the *Vesta* leading as senior. Every light had been carefully covered, and even the port-holes of our cabins plastered over with felt, so as to exclude any possibility of a gleam of light discovering our whereabouts to the enemy. Our vessel was painted a bluish grey, so like the colour of the sea that at a hundred yards it was barely distinguishable. In this phantom guise, on one of the darkest nights that can be imagined, we glided in silence into the open sea, the only sounds being the steady throb of our screw, and about every ten minutes the call of the officer on watch to the men stationed in the foretop. This call, which for eight days and nights has never ceased, will long remain impressed on my memory. "Foretop, keep a good look-out," still rang in my ears, as last night, for the first time during a week, I slept for more than an hour at a time.

When clear of the land the captain informed us of our destination, which was Kertch. This port has not been entered since the war began, and though, of course, the movements of the Turkish fleet are only to be conjectured from telegrams, the captain told me he fully expected to have a battle before arriving, for several ironclads were supposed to be in that part of the Black Sea. As the day broke the lovely south coast stood out in all its grandeur. At sunrise we were rushing past Aloupka Castle, whose towers and terraces, flooded in light, contrasted well with the surrounding scenery. Here man has exhausted his ingenuity in rearing a fabric unique and unrivalled; but even this grandest effort of human genius, situated as it is, serves only to mark how insignificant is the work of our hands when compared with that of nature. Towering in the background of the castle, Ai Petri looks down from a height of 4,500 feet, and seems in its rugged majesty to frown at the toy which the vanity of man has carved for its footstool. On past Orianda, Livadia, Yalta, and Massandra, the *Vesta* and her consort sped. At breakfast time we were half-way on our journey, and as the sun was sinking I had the pleasure of congratulating the captain on having successfully accomplished the first step of the expedition, and on our being the first Russian steamer that had entered Kertch since the war broke out.

As the captain told me he should only land for his orders I did not go on shore, and in a few hours the throbbing of the screw and the call to the foretop brought me on deck to find that we were once more on the sullen Euxine. The captain now explained to me the object of the expedition. A large number of wounded men were at a place called Gagri, not far from Sukhum-Kaleh, and the admiral had asked Baranoff if he would endeavour to embark them and convey them to Novorosiska where there was an hospital. The odds were considerably against our ever getting there, much less returning, but brave men do not calculate odds when their comrades are in want of help. If the whole Turkish fleet had been known to be at anchor in Gagri Bay, Baranoff would only have altered his plans, but not his course. His plans at present were to proceed direct to Gagri, to offer battle to any single ironclad he met; and if attacked by several, to endeavour to escape, failing which he should take to the boats and blow the *Vesta* up. Fortune favours the brave, and after thirty hours of excitement we dropped anchor in Gagri Bay.

"Heaven grant we may find all ready for us," was the prayer of the captain as the armed boats left for the shore, a prayer which from the desolate appearance of the place, and the fact that not a soul was visible, I feared would not be granted. As we neared the shore the sign manual of the Turk was plainly to be distinguished. Every house had been burnt to the ground, a few dogs, a cat, and a Cossack boy inhabited or rather perambulated the ruins; the Anglo-Indian telegraph had been torn down for at least a mile on the southern side of the town, and no signs of our being expected were to be found. About half-a-mile to the north a Russian telegraph officer was engaged in arranging communication with Europe, and he told us there were neither wounded nor unwounded soldiers nearer than Gadahout, a coast village about half-way between Gagri and Sukhum-Kaleh; so, after spending some hours in the vain hope that news would arrive, our captain recalled the boats, and we steamed on to Gadahout, before which interesting village we dropped anchor about half-an-hour previous to sunset.

I will now mention two of the officers of the *Vesta*, whose names, if the war continues, will be public property. The second in command on board the *Vesta* is Prince Galitzin Galovkin. This officer, who is of immense size and strength, is the inheritor of more than one princely title and has also a large fortune. When the war broke out he rejoined the navy and was appointed to his present position. His escape from death during the late battle is almost miraculous, and his coolness and courage from beginning to end of that trying five hours were as remarkable as his escape.

At about 10 p.m. on Thursday night lights in front of us and at sea were visible, and we prepared for action. The Prince, as second in command, had determined if an expedition with the torpedo boats became necessary to take the command of it, and now, to all appearance, the hour was come, for even the phosphoric light, indicative of some immense body moving rapidly, was plainly visible, and the order to prepare the torpedo launches went forth. With as little noise as possible these small boats, with their heroic crews, were in the water, and with the Prince as leader they had left for what was very probably a fatal task. As I stood on the bridge trying to make out the arrangement of the expedition, I could hear Galitzin's voice giving his orders as coolly as if he were superintending the capture of a shoal of herrings or sprats, instead of conducting a forlorn hope against perhaps several monster ironclads. The boats had scarcely left the side when the sky darkened and a storm arose. The captain at once recalled the expedition, and under cover of what was now a small tempest we ploughed onward in safety, and for ought I or any one else can tell, we may have passed within 100 yards of the whole Turkish fleet. Next to Prince Galitzin on this expedition should be mentioned the torpedo officer, Eugene Romanovitch, a youth in years, and when off duty the leader in everything savouring of fun and mischief. He speaks English, and we have fraternized greatly.

As soon as we had anchored I went on shore with the Prince, our crew, of course, being armed. On landing the only signs of life were some miserable-looking curs picnicking on horse bones and sheepskins. Bullock carts, empty boxes, old clothes, &c., were strewed in every direction, but what had been the fate of their owners, or who those owners were, was left to our imagination. A few yards from the wharf a felucca, about thirty feet long, was anchored, but in our anxiety to land we postponed to ourselves the pleasure of visiting it, more especially as we believed the village to be in Russian possession. The houses were only about 100 yards from the shore, and to these we now approached. At the entrance to the main street we found a Russian soldier, who at first we thought was wounded, as he could not speak, and looked dreadfully ill. It happily appeared afterwards that he had only lost the use of his tongue, and not the member itself. We then proceeded to call at several of the houses, but found no one at home; and as it was now getting dark, and we had to visit the felucca, the Prince gave the order to retire. As we were pulling to the felucca we heard firing—first, a few straggling shots, and then a fusillade—but concluding it was some skirmish inland we took no notice, and boarded our prize from both sides. On going below we found it freighted with firearms, and amongst them some very nice repeating rifles of the Winchester system. As it was now nearly dark, the captain recalled us and at once put to sea, steering direct for Constantinople. I asked him his reasons, and he told me he felt sure that no ironclads would be looking for him in that direction, and that if he was seen his course would perhaps prevent his being interfered with, the Turks not having yet realized the consummate impudence of these little cruisers.

The captain's clever plan met with complete success, and having given all the ironclads the slip, at about one a.m., he headed again for Gadahout, having determined to make a descent with all the boats and search the place thoroughly. At six a.m. we were at anchor, and now the scene was exciting. A mitrailleuse was mounted in the launch, and about 100 sailors, commanded by Prince Galitzin, were ready. The captain's boy, Terracuta, a fine lad of fifteen, was armed to the teeth, and giggling with joy as I tumbled into the launch alongside of him, and I verily believe there was not a man left on board who was not hoping that reinforcements would soon be needed. As we approached the shore a few men appeared, at first in rather a hostile attitude; but soon perceiving that we were Russians a wild hurrah was given, and in an instant from behind every rock and bush, men who, for the last few minutes had been covering us with their rifles, rushed down to the beach, and the scene as we landed could not easily be described. It appeared that the day before, only some hours previous to our arrival, a Turkish steamer painted grey like ourselves, and doubtless one of the ironclads in search of us, had put into Gadahout Bay, but had left almost immediately. The small Russian detachment, seeing another grey steamer accompanied by a black one arriving about sunset, naturally concluded that it was the Turkish vessel returned with a reinforcement, and consequently when they saw we were landing they all hid themselves. I asked one soldier to show me where he had been hidden, and he took me to a ruined house next door to one I had entered the night before with two sailors. I asked him if he had seen me before. He grinned, did that ingenuous youth, and answered, "kakniett," which may be rendered "rather." The shots we had heard were fired at us, for it turned out that the felucca was their prize first, and their feelings became too strong for them when they saw what they thought was the Moslem boarding it. We were now informed by the officer that if we returned to Gagri we should find the troops and the wounded all ready for us; so after transferring on board their wounded—I think about half a dozen, and a Turkish prisoner, who evidently found himself in clover—we returned to Gagri, towing the felucca with us for the purpose of utilizing it for the transport of the wounded, &c.

We anchored in Gagri Bay about noon, and now a change had indeed taken place. The martial strains of a band were heard, and on landing we found a force of about 2,000 of as fine-looking fellows as one could wish to see. The shore, which yesterday was desolate, to-day teemed with life; herds of oxen, bullock carts, native conveyances of every description, groups of mountaineers in their picturesque dresses and gipsy-like encampments were visible as far as the eye could reach. The commanding officer had everything ready, not only for the embarkation of about 100 wounded men, but also for that of a battalion of about 600 men, whom the general required transport for as far as Taopse, a march of ten days through the mountain passes, but only about twelve hours by sea. Our captain was quite alive to the danger of crowded decks, but with the usual celerity and silence boats arrive and depart, the mountains of heavy baggage melt away from the landing place, a long file of wounded are carefully accommodated in the felucca which has been forced up against the ricketty old wharf, and in about four hours from the time we anchored every man was on board, and even the commissariat department had sent the beef and other necessaries for the troops. There remains now only to embark the General Shalkoonikoff, who was coming with us, and we had to proceed to a place some twelve miles further up the coast to meet him.

The signalman on one of the highest posts on shore now announced the smoke of a steamer to the north of us and the masts of another to the south. With the pleasant prospect of being rammed behind and before, we slipped out of Gagri Bay and were soon enveloped in our usual gloom. About ten p.m. Prince Galitzin went on shore at a place called Sandripsh for the General, and having returned shortly with his Excellency, we steamed on for Taopse, arriving about six in the morning, when the disembarking of the troops was carried out with the same admirable ease that distinguished the embarkation. I have had a great deal of experience in embarking and disembarking troops in peace and war time, and in almost all parts of our dominion, but I never saw anything to equal the rapidity and ease with which the Russian overcomes apparently insurmountable difficulties. It must be remembered also that a Russian soldier carries a heavier weight than ours; that he is a larger man, and consequently takes up more space in a boat; and, finally, that the camp equipage of 600 men in its lightest marching order is about as vast as that of an English division under similar circumstances. We left Taopse early in the day, and at sunset steamed into Novorosiska, where the General and the wounded were landed. After this, the work of the gallant little cruisers having been so successfully accomplished, we passed for the last time into the open sea, and challenged the blockade of the powerful navy of Turkey by sweeping it from the Caucasus to Sebastopol, and from thence to Odessa.

It may be interesting to the admiral in command of the ironclads to learn that the little *Vesta* and her consort have during the last 200 hours steamed over 1,807 miles of the Black Sea, and during that time they have only twice entered a port—Gagri, Taopse, and Gadahout being open roadsteads. Having observed frequent mention of the Russian Black Sea fleet in English papers, and as many of your readers may be under the impression that such a force exists, I will describe it—three old cargo-boats of the Russian Steam Navigation Company and the Emperor's yacht: none of these are plated or defended by armour, and with the exception of the yacht they might almost serve as launches to Turkey's powerful ironclads. Their want of armour is, however, balanced by the devoted courage of the officers and men, and though it can hardly be expected that they will be able to continue to defy with impunity the monster ironclads everywhere on the look-out for them, I think it by no means improbable that before they are sent to the bottom the navy of Turkey may have still further proof that the race is not always to the swift, or the battle to the strong, and that the little cargo-boats of the company will again challenge with success tho much vaunted blockade and supremacy of the Black Sea.

CHAPTER XIX.

CRISIS OF THE CAMPAIGN IN ASIA.

The Camp of Mukhtar Pacha—The Turkish Soldier at Prayer—Two Notable Deserters—The Russian Camp—Arrival of Reinforcements—The Battle of October 2nd—Capture of the Great Yagni—Russian Mistakes—Renewal of the Fighting—Preparations for a Grand Attack—General Lazareff's Great Flanking March—The Field Telegraph—The Battle of Aladja Dagh—Complete Overthrow and Flight of Mukhtar Pacha—Large Capture of Prisoners and Guns—Condition of Kars.

HAVING driven the Russians from all the posts they had occupied between Kars and Erzeroum on the one line, and Bayazid and Erzeroum on the other,—having reduced the main body of the Russian army to a defensive position before Alexandropol and compelled its left wing to stand helplessly by while one of the least competent of Turkish commanders actually crossed the Russian frontier in the direction of Erivan, —Mukhtar Pacha had reached the measure of his allotted success. From this time his arrangements began to lose the impress of his former prudence, although weeks were to elapse before their character was to be brought to a decisive test, and to be exposed by his utter and irreparable defeat. The following letters show the course of military events until the Turkish Army was broken in pieces almost under the walls of Kars :—

HEADQUARTERS, ARMY OF MUKHTAR PACHA, *Sept. 17th.*—Now that Ramazan has arrived, people seem more intent on their religion than on their military exercises. I don't mean to say that the latter are neglected. Mukhtar Pacha, as rigid a

Moslem as exists in the Sultan's dominions, is too good a soldier to allow that. But the interval is well taken up with the prolonged prayers which at this season seem to make the Turkish soldier forget his empty stomach, his parched throat, and unlighted cigarette. Whatever may be said of the Turks, they are in their way a strictly religious people, and scrupulous to the last degree in adhering to the external forms of their worship.

At this austere season, from the moment the dawn colours the eastern sky until the Ramazan gun booms out into the evening air, not a morsel of food crosses the lips of the soldiers, not even a drop of water, and over and over again, when, seeing the wistful eye of a trooper turned towards my lighted chibouk, I have proffered my tobacco pouch, it has been motioned away with a self-denial worthy of an eremite of the wilderness. And each of the many times a day as the long-dawn, wailing cry of the Muezzin rises above the murmur of the camp, soldiers are to be seen hurrying eagerly to prayer as to a banquet, and unhappy seems the man on duty who cannot join the seried rows of worshippers who, in company, sometimes in battalion, face toward Mecca and follow the orisons and genuflexious of the Imaum who stands before their centre. Each man takes his place in the ranks, his hands hanging close by his sides. Then he lifts them to his ears, as if to shut out all worldly sounds. Then he lays them on his knees, and bowing his head forward seems lost in contemplation. After a few seconds he sinks to his knees, and leans back upon his heels, and then bowing with his forehead to the earth, exclaims, or rather chants, "Allah Akhbar" (God is great). Three times he thus bows and chants, and then he stands up, bowing forward, chanting three times "La Allah il Allah" (there is no God but God). The remainder of the somewhat tedious prayers which follow consists principally, as far as I can make out, of long verses of the "Koran."

In all his simple religious exercises the Turkish soldier is devoutness and attention itself, and it is perhaps most in privacy that this is most apparent. I have frequently come unexpectedly upon some rugged soldier in one of the wild, lonely ravines that gash the hillsides around, standing before the ragged overcoat which served him for a praying carpet, and going through his rather active religious motions with a zeal which would do credit to the most self-conscious Pharisee. The stranger who for the first time witnesses the united prayer of Turkish soldiers in camp is considerably puzzled by the selection of heterogeneous articles brought forward to the place of worship, when the Muezzin's call has concluded. Religious custom requires that each man be provided with a praying carpet of one description or another, and that he take off his shoes as well. One man brings a jagged sheep-skin, another a goat-hide, a third the saddle-cloth of his horse, a fourth, mayhap, his jacket; every one has something or another on which he may kneel. To see some hundred men thus hurrying to the spot where the blue-robed, white-turbaned Imaum stands, a stranger to their ways might be easily led to imagine them so many persons eager to dispose of superfluous garments, and taking advantage of the fortuitous presence of a dealer of Israeltish nationality.

The Russians, too, have been lately celebrating national festivals. On the 9th ult. we were startled by the thunder of cannon from Karajal, the fortified hill on which their right flank rests. The Marshal's long brass telescope was at once put in position, and every field-glass was directed against the frowning heights along which the heavy white smoke-clouds clung in the morning air. We looked in vain for the little secondary smoke-bursts that should have indicated exploding shells. In our advanced positions men ran to their arms and the parapets were black with eager, puzzled soldiers. It was only a salute of twenty-one guns in honour of the anniversary of the Czar's coronation. "May Allah destroy him," was the appropriate Moslem exclamation, when after due search in a Russian military calendar the cause of the salute was discovered and conveyed to the soldiery. Three or four days after another blank salute sent us again to our almanack. This time it was an Imperial birthday, that of the Emperor or Czarewitch, I forget which. Whichever it was, the object of the salute had the same Turkish good wishes as on the former occasion. Sometimes we have a light cavalry skirmish out in the plain, and on such occasions a good deal of artillery fire is apt to take place as the combatants come within range of the guns on either side. As a rule some five or six men are killed and twice as many wounded. Rarely does the affair go further.

Three days ago Said Bey, a nephew of the celebrated Schamyl, of Caucasian memory, got knocked over in one of these desultory fights. He lies in his tent shot through the breast. Dr. Casson, an English surgeon out here, tells me he has but little chance of life. Occasionally the monotony of camp life is stirred by the arrival of a deserter, usually a Pole or a Mahommedan Circassian, or a Tartar. The advent of one of these last has begun to cease to charm. At first their arrival was hailed as a sign of great things and a wholesale desertion of the similar element in the opposing army. However, as it seems that quite as many go over from our side as come to us from the opposite, and as the gravest doubts are entertained about the genuineness of the sentiment prompting the change of sides, we begin to look rather coldly on these allies, and to receive with a certain amount of scepticism the wonderful and oft-repeated stories of Russian discontent and demoralization they bring us.

I have, however, met with a couple of genuine deserters, and that, too, of no inconsiderable rank. One is a Mohammedan Circassian, who, when the Servian war broke out, held the position of aide-de-camp to the Emperor of Russia. A staff officer in the camp here, and who had been for many years one of the Turkish military attachés at St. Petersburg, told me he had there been intimate with this Circassian, who had on more than one occasion assured him that in case of war he would take the earliest opportunity of changing sides. He has kept his word, and I see him often in the tent of the état-major, with his splendid uniform of the Russian Circassian Guard—a long tunic of fine white cloth, heavily laced with silver—his belt, sword sheath and hilt, as well as the various pouches and secondary articles such persons think fit to hang around their persons, of magnificently wrought and enamelled silver and gold. The second of these more notable deserters is a person of much greater importance. It is but a few days since he arrived at headquarters, where I saw him in the tent of Mukhtar Pacha. He is called Eeyoub Aga, and comes from the neighbourhood of Erivan. At home his rank is little short of princely. He commands the fighting men of 6,000 families. His brother was a cavalry divisional general in the Russian army, and was killed, or died (as Mukhtar Pacha told me in a significant manner), shortly before the defection of his brother. This Eeyoub Aga passed over to the Turks at Bayazid and thence came on here. He is a tall, gaunt man, with an expression of face very much reminding me of the late Tulu Moussa (bearded Moses), the Persian bandit chief, about whom I have had occasion to write some time since. As a reward for his change of side, Eeyoub Aga has been decorated by the Marshal with the Medjidie of a high class, and has had three other orders given him for his uncle and nephews.

The Polish deserters to the Turkish army are few and far between, notwithstanding the measures taken by their compatriots here to attract them. I dare say it is not generally known that a "Polish Legion" exists as a component part of the Turkish army of Armenia. We have one of forty men, nineteen of whom are cavalry, the rest infantry. The history of the formation of this body, designed at its inception to be the nucleus of an imposing force, is curious enough. The men, principally residents in Constantinople, volunteered for the Army of the Danube. Among them was a considerable sprinkling of ex-Austrian and Russian officers, who undertook, by the distribution of Polish revolutionary proclamations, to cause the wholesale desertion of the Polish element in the regiments opposed to them, and subsequently to organize these deserters into a Turko-Polish Legion. For some inscrutable reason the Constantinople authorities decided on inducing this handful of adventurers to come here. They were told that immense numbers of prisoners had been taken, among them several thousand Poles, who were at Trebizond, awaiting officers to organize them. The forty Poles and their two officers at once abandoned the Danube mission and hurried away to Armenia. At Trebizond they were fêted by the inhabitants, and informed that the Polish prisoners and deserters were still at Baiburt. At Baiburt the future legion was believed to be at Erzeroum, and at Erzeroum the authorities had good reason to think that the mass of the prisoners were still at headquarters. Thus the gentlemen composing the unfortunate "nucleus" were led on step by step to the heart of Armenia, where they still remain.

Such is the tale as told to me by the two officers commanding the cavalry and infantry sections of the "nucleus," and confirmed by the statements of their men. They took part in the battles of the 18th and 25th of August, in the latter of which the infantry lost one man killed, and two wounded. Since their advent here they have been busy scattering lithographed revolutionary documents about the field in every locality where Russo-Polish troops might be apt to meet with them, the only fruit secured up to the present being two rather dilapidated-looking Poles, who would in any case probably have taken the first opportunity of coming over. Of course the whole story about the immense band of prisoners awaiting organization was a fable, not a single prisoner of any kind having been taken by the Turks up to that moment. Indeed, from the commencement of the campaign here up to to-day the entire number of prisoners would not exceed a dozen. The Polish nucleus is now on the point of breaking up. The men are dissatisfied with their food, and with their treatment generally. They declare they originally volunteered for the Danube, and only undertook to do exceptional "organizing duty" here during three months. The time has elapsed, and they declare they will disband unless Government keeps to its original promises.

What the next move of the contending armies on the frontier will be is hard to say. Neither party shows the least inclination to make a move—at least at the centre. But from either flank come rumours of proximate action. Mukhtar Pacha told me he was informed that the Russians were gradually sending off their heavy baggage from Ardahan; and it is a fact that their troops no longer occupy the town itself, confining themselves to the two commanding forts of Emir Oghlou and Ramazan Oghlou, the capture of which at the commencement of the campaign secured for them the speedy possession of the place itself. Considerable Turkish forces, partly drawn from the Erzeroum garrison, are gradually drawing in that direction, and action of one kind or another seems probable.

The following letter is from the Correspondent in the Russian camp:—

△ CAMP KARAJAL, *September 27th.*—A more dismal place than that in which our headquarters are established cannot be easily imagined. Death itself must lose its horrors for people condemned to vegetate in such a spot, and so it is not difficult to explain why our officers and men long for a murderous battle, in the hope of getting away from this life-wearying site. Instead of pondering here over the achievements which we should be able to accomplish if we had only 20,000 men and 100 cannon more, we ought to try our strength in turning and storming Mukhtar Pacha's position at once. Then we should have a chance of conquering good winter quarters in Erzeroum. There is obviously plenty of room for daring strategy. At all events it seems, at the worst, to be less disadvantageous, and more honourable even, to recede before the Turks, after having experienced a loss of some 3,000 men in a determined assault, than before the cold season, with perhaps double that loss. Moreover, defeat is unavoidable in the second case, whereas in the first, if our men have but pluck and our leaders ability, we have more chances of success than of discomfiture.

We are not so weak now as we were months ago, when General Heimann dashed his head against the rocks of Zevin. Two complete divisions have reinforced us since. At first the 40th arrived, and now we have also the Moscow Grenadiers, the last battalions of which joined our army only three days ago. These new troops are composed of keen-looking, well-armed, and well-accoutred young men, who, provided they are skilfully conducted, and have not their courage wasted in pitiful skirmishing engagements, are certainly capable of turning the Turks out of any position accessible to human feet. Yesterday His Imperial Highness the Grand Duke Michael paraded them and bade them welcome. He was highly satisfied with the inspection and had reason to congratulate their leaders as well as himself, for they are a body of first-rate soldiers.

Everybody is now inclined to predict that a sharp stroke at Mukhtar Pacha's position is near at hand. The Pacha himself seems to be of a similar opinion. He was very busy on Monday about the Kizil Tepe entrenchments, examining them closely and ordering the construction of additional earthworks. I don't doubt that something has been planned here, but I am also led to suppose that nothing definitive has been fixed. As an excuse for the continual frittering away of time, it is alleged that the new chief of staff, General Gurtchine, of whose skill and energy great things are reported, is obliged to study the situation, and to review the links of the complicated chain with which our army is trying to fetter its opponent. What has been done during the course of this summer was little more than a groping in the dark with regard to the enemy's strength and resources, the final knowledge of which has been bought by bitter experience. It may be that the Bulgarian campaign is still absorbing the main interest and solicitude of the Russian Government. For all that it cannot be denied that a decisively victorious campaign here would bring the Russians more easily to Constantinople through Asia Minor than through the Danubian and Balkan stronghold. In Armenia, moreover, Russia has prospects of indemnifying herself for her enormous sacrifices in men and money; but she scorns the chance of acquiring substantial advantages in the hope of rehabilitating her military fame in the European theatre of war. We are thus confined to an otherwise incomprehensible inactivity. We are spellbound to the most objectionable place on earth. The fighting which has gone on has never had a very serious character. The losses sustained during the whole present campaign in dead and wounded do not amount to more than 5,000 men—that is to say, they are of less importance than those of a single day's battle before Plevna. Our soldiers have not been earnestly put to the test yet, although they enjoy the renown of being the very best in all Russia.

In the following letter, the same Correspondent with the

Russians describes the first battle of Aladja Dagh, the prelude to the memorable battles of October 14th and 15th :—

△ CAMP KARAJAL, *October 4th.*—Although exceptionally fatigued through riding all day on horseback, without anything but a dry biscuit, I shall endeavour to give a full and accurate account of the battle which was fought on the 2nd inst. and the following day around the Aladja mountain, and which is likely to be renewed every hour.

After long waiting for reinforcements, these at last arrived in the shape of the first division of the Moscow Grenadiers, sixteen battalions, each full 1,000 men strong, together with forty-eight field-pieces, and two regiments of cavalry. After almost equally long deliberations it was decided to make a general attack on Mukhtar Pacha's position on the Aladja mountain and its dependencies of spurs and isolated hills, forming—from the Arpa Tchai river, in the neighbourhood of Ani, to Kars—a continuity of natural strongholds, entrenchments, and batteries. The day before yesterday was fixed for its commencement. Although deep secrecy had apparently been kept among the superior generals on the subject, enough of the plan of operations transpired beforehand to leave no doubt about the general features of the impending operations. Everybody in the camp knew what was about to go on, to the great astonishment of our staff. At last they became aware that a man of certain consideration, who was in the habit of sneaking through the camps, without professing to follow any honest vocation or business, had disappeared on the very eve of the day of action. Though no conclusive proof of his guilt has hitherto been brought forward, public opinion adjudges him guilty of being a Turkish spy. He has not returned since, warned perhaps by a bad presentiment or some accomplice.

The general plan of operations was as follows :—General Sholkowaikoff, who, in the absence of General Dewel, is in command of the 40th Division on our left, was ordered to turn the Aladja Dagh from Ani with five battalions and a battery. He was expected to reach its summit, and, descending from it, to fall on Mukhtar Pacha's rear. A brigade of the same division was to keep the enemy at bay on his right wing, assisted by a heavy battery established there some days before, which, as a mere demonstration, had to cannonade the Kisil Tepe. Here no assault was premeditated, and the object was only to draw the enemy's attention to this point, important for him, but not for the Russians. To General Heimann, with the Circassian Division of Grenadiers, was entrusted the task of closing in with the enemy's centre and main force, so as to prevent him from withdrawing his troops from Subatan, in order to reinforce other positions which we intended to take, if possible. To his right, the first division of the Moscow Grenadiers, at General Loris Melikoff's direct disposal, had to act against the Yagni hills. I believe I have stated already in my former letters that Great Yagni, situated about ten miles from our camp, is a very regular conical hill, with a plateau at the top, towering 750 feet over the plains and smooth undulations stretching from Kurukdere to Kars. A direct assault on that hill, which on former occasions had cost the Russians a good deal of blood, was now considered as likely to lead to no good result, and in consequence its capture did not enter into the original disposition.

The real and most important point, according to the views of our staff, against which all our efforts had to be concentrated, was Little Yagni, an entirely isolated, bulky elevation, with a comparatively extensive platform on the top. Though of considerably less height than its namesake, its sides are quite as steep, while a rocky crest, very much like that of the Kizil Tepe, borders its extended summit. This, however, does not consist of a uniform level, but is separated by an intervening flat depression, so as to form three distinct terraces, of which the southern one is about 200 feet higher than the northern. This hill, situated at a distance of about nine miles from Kars and two from the Great Yagni, completely stops the road from Kurukdere to that fortress. It is very probable that the information upon which it had not only been strongly fortified and garrisoned by Turkish infantry, but was also armed with twenty cannon of heavy calibre, was received from spies. The honour of taking by assault this commanding point was conferred upon the 2nd Brigade of the Moscow Grenadiers, under Major-General Count Grabbe, and eight battalions detached from Ardahan for that purpose, under General Komaroff. This gallant officer, who had been slightly wounded on the 25th of August, has since recovered. His fellow-sufferer, General Tshadtchewadze, wounded on the same day, had also reassumed his command of our whole cavalry. Three battalions, which, as a rule, garrison the fortress of Alexandropol, had also been ordered to Karajal, to cover the camp and headquarters, and to form the reserve of the 2nd Brigade of the 70th Division, which, as I have stated above, had nothing to do but to check an improbable offensive movement of the Turks against our left wing opposite the Kizil and the Yagni Tepes.

The general object apparently was to carry out a complete turning movement on both hostile wings, either to surround Mukhtar Pacha entirely or to cut off his communication with Kars. Could this have been effectually managed, no doubt he would have been compelled to surrender with his army within a few days, for, his supplies of ammunition and provisions being in danger of immediate exhaustion, he must either have broken through the Russian lines, or tried to make his way with disbanded troops across the Russian territory, in the hope of joining his comrade, Ismael Hakki Pacha, who is still entrenched before Igdyr.

After this explanation, let me come to the events which I witnessed in following General Loris Melikoff's staff. The troops ordered for the advance started from their camps at eight o'clock in the evening of the 1st inst. At three o'clock precisely the next morning we followed, riding at a moderate speed, to the south-west on a country track over the vast plain. Our way was lit by the waning moon and countless stars shining with intense brilliancy. A cold wind made our trip by no means pleasant, as it brought the temperature near to the freezing-point. The staff consisted of about fifty persons—general officers, aides-de-camp, and servants—escorted by three sotnias of Cossacks from the Caucasus, not armed with lances, but accoutred and dressed like genuine Circassians. The ground, in appearance almost level, is in fact cut through at intervals by a few rocky ravines, between which lie long-stretching undulations rising gradually towards the south. After two hours and a half of wearisome riding, we arrived at dawn of day at an eminence some 150 feet above the flat-topped ridge of the rising ground called the Kaback Tepe (Pumpkin Hill).

Hitherto no reports of firearms had reached us. But from the top of this commanding point, at half-past five, sharp and general firing suddenly struck our ear. To our right and left the roar of the cannons, and the sharp, dry, knocking, rattling of the musketry came down, sounding in the distance like the noise produced by the work of some hundred road-makers, breaking flint-stones in a re-echoing hall. The principal object of attack, the Little Yagni, rising now clear in sight, frowned over the plains of Kars like an impregnable fortress. Its summit was surrounded with breastworks, ditches, rifle-pits, and blinded batteries. The Moscow Grenadiers and the Ardahan Division were already supposed to be at work. I say supposed, because in fact they were not. On seeing from the Kaback Tepe some forty guns firing with a range of three miles, at earthworks which were prudently left empty by the Turks, it seemed to me that the attack lacked the character which was likely to secure victory. Had the infantry been led immediately to the assault in tirailleur lines before the dawn of day, without firing a single round they would have carried that hill, I am sure, within half an hour. In the way the attack was conducted it was obvious that the enemy, who, judging by the number of his tents, had there about 3,000 men, had time to bring all his available means to the defences.

I have not the slightest doubt that the twelve hours' cannonading did no harm whatever to the earthworks, and inflicted only trifling losses on the garrison, for they had for the most part retired to the sides of the hill that were out of range. To our left, the impetuous General Heimann had already hurled his division in skirmishing lines against the Aladja mountain, and its southern continuation, the Awly-yer hill, separated from it by the upper part of the Subatan ravine. The incessant sharp volleys gave evidence that the Turkish main force had been concentrated there. It was soon clear also that a direct assault on those rocky steeps and terraces, strengthened by numerous entrenchments and stone barricades, had no better chance of succeeding to-day than on previous occasions. Within the first half an hour it was clear that the carefully elaborated plan of operations again combined all the faults of previous tactics, magnified, moreover, by the absence of that dash which, at the beginning of the present campaign, was characteristic of this army.

Some one seems to have suggested, and brought others to believe, that in this breech-loading time an assault by infantry is obsolete and unnecessary, and that all war might, with less effusion of blood, be just as well, or better, done by the artillery alone. Such, unhappily, seems to be the erroneous idea at headquarters. Yet, of all the shells, which I have had the opportunity of watching here, fired on our own or on the Turkish side, not a single one caused damage worth the pains and the powder. When they burst in the earth it was at such a depth that their weak charges were unable to overcome its resistance, and, consequently, the fragments did not fly off. They only exploded properly when the shell happened to strike on a rock or other hard substance. I have not even heard that a single one of our soldiers has been killed by the famous shrapnels, which, at all events, are much more efficacious than simple grenades. At ridiculous distances of above three miles they, too, are likely to produce little more than an innocent shower of leaden drops. Anyhow, artillery alone is not capable of dislodging such stubborn soldiers as the Turks are from the bottom of their deep rifle-pits. Further discussion on the subject would be preposterous, in the face of a series of experiments which are everywhere conclusive in favour of my assertion.

Our cannon still boomed at the rocks and the earth, while masses of infantry were either idling as reserves in the depressions of the ground, or were employed in a disastrous but useless skirmishing with the enemy. For hours each tirailleur lay behind a heap of stones, which he had previously piled up for his shelter, and took a deliberate aim at some similarly protected adversary. Such fighting only kills and wounds, without the hope of a useful result. At six o'clock in the morning this state of things was on both wings as clear as the rising sun, whose rays gilded the glorious white crown of Mount Ararat. In the centre before us stood, three miles off, cutting the blue sky with its regular conical profile, Great Yagni. It covered the front of Mukhtar Pacha's centre and left wing, commanding the plain before them, and enjoyed the reputation of impregnability, since at different times various Russian assaults on its steep slopes had been repulsed with considerable loss. From its foot to its top it was covered with rifle-pits and ditches in three superposed rows, cut in conformity with the configuration of the ground in projecting and re-entering angles.

The prospects of success there appeared, indeed, so very poor, that it was considered by the Russian staff useless to attempt the conquest of that natural fortress. Therefore only a demonstration, supported by a brigade and two batteries, was intended against it, calculated to distract the enemy's attention from the more serious attacks on the Little Yagni. On examining through our glasses the greater hill, we found that its garrison was exceedingly feeble. The breastworks on its base and its middle were not manned at all, and even the fortifications bordering the top plateau were only very insufficiently armed, as was proved by the spasmodic and unconnected rifle firing and the apparent absence of cannon. On learning this General Loris Melikoff ordered a general assault on the hill. From three sides the troops advanced merrily in skirmishing lines, with supports and reserves, cheering as they passed their commanding General, who spoke to them some encouraging words. The cannons, redoubling their firing, flung shrapnel after shrapnel to the top. An hour afterwards the whole hill was swarming with grenadiers, who steadily climbed up its steeps, despite the frantic firing of its defenders. At eight o'clock the Turkish battalion on the summit of the Great Yagni had ceased to exist. Our men had entirely occupied the impregnable hill, and were waving joyously their caps and muskets.

While this was being accomplished, the indifferent cannonading on the right, between our batteries and those on the Little Yagni, was still going on. It might have continued for a century, and nothing would have come of it. As soon as it became evident that the men on the top of Great Yagni were genuine Russians and not Turks, as some of us still supposed, the staff rode off in order to inspect the conquered position, and to decide the further course of operations now possible through so brilliant a beginning. The hill was rather too steep for our horses, and we rode round it to the right, over the plain two miles wide which separates it from Little Yagni. What in the world had we to do with that Little Yagni? Had it been blocked up after the defeat of Mukhtar Pacha's main army, its defenders must have surrendered within three days from want of water. The opinions on that point were unanimous among all the officers. The task of shutting in the garrison of Kars—at the utmost 6,000 men—ought to have been entrusted to a single brigade, which might have occupied and fortified the heights contiguous to Great Yagni, and opposite to Little Yagni. When our staff passed by, one of our infantry regiments had already been deployed in skirmishing order, and was engaged with that garrison. Besides, strong bodies of our numerous cavalry, commanding that plain, challenged in vain the Turkish irregular horsemen. All their ferocious Circassians, disgusted on account of their receiving neither pay nor food, had left Mukhtar's camp in a wholesale desertion a fortnight ago. Only worthless, cowardly Kurds remained for the sake of murder and plundering.

All of a sudden the Turkish heavy battery on the top of Little Yagni changed its mark. Cutting the air with portentous howling, a well-aimed shell struck in the very midst of the squad of Cossacks forming our vanguard, throwing the earth high up. A horse with empty saddle sprang about bewildered, but his stunned rider, recovering his senses, caught him, quickly mounted, and joined his troop at a gallop. Old General Loris Melikoff, keeping his horse in the same steady pace as before, did not seem to care for such trifles as shells and the stray rifle-bullets humming around us. Taking the lead of his staff, with his green Mohammedan standard embroidered with red inscriptions in Arabic letters flying before him, he gave an example of cold-blooded courage to his officers. Almost immediately a shell whizzed by and struck the ground, bursting some twenty yards behind our party.

Then came another and another, all passing over us, till at last one fell only five yards off the very centre of our crowd. The officers, huddling together nevertheless, received the noisy failure with a scornful hurrah.

A few seconds more, and another big shell burst right amidst our staff, perhaps only one yard behind General Loris Melikoff's horse. Earth and small stones flew about. For an instant, as the foremost part of the crowd disappeared in the dust, I thought the commanding General killed. He, however, rode quietly on and smiled, as a somewhat fainter hurrah accompanied the bursting of the iron monster. It had grazed the right side of Lieutenant Petroff's face, and the pressure of the air made him deaf on that side. His cheek became swollen, and severe headache ensued. This was the only accident we had to complain of. No other officer was wounded or contused. Some of the horses, however, were scratched or bruised a little by the earth and the pebbles. The shell itself produced no effect in the middle of such a crowd of horsemen, and the fragments found their grave on the spot where they intended to dig ours. A few minutes afterwards we were out of dangerous range.

As we wheeled round into the valley, 400 yards wide, which separates Great Yagni from the bulk of the Aladja Mountain, two regiments of cavalry dashed at full speed into the plain, where the Turkish battalions from Kars were engaged with our skirmishers. Of course, I expected that they would sweep like an avalanche over that dry, level ground, and cut down in a gallant charge the enemy's scattered soldiers. As far as I could see no such thing happened. The cautious warriors, when the bullets began to tell on them, lost much of their pluck, and placing their confidence rather in their muskets than their broadswords, indulged in a skirmishing entertainment. Afterwards I heard of their achievements, and how they had slain hundreds of Nizams and Bashi-Bazouks, but I had not the good fortune to see this feat of arms. Presently, four Red-Cross men carried a man on a litter to the ambulance in the rear. We went up to the patient and discovered that he was not, as we thought, a Russian, but a wounded Turk. All our soldiers are well acquainted with the fact that the Turks kill, torture, and mutilate every Russian prisoner, yet they cannot murder in stupid, fanatic hatred, a helpless suffering wretch, although the inexorable law of retaliation seems to demand it. All the Turkish prisoners, some 140—wounded and unwounded—were kindly treated and well attended to in my presence. At the time when we had reached about the middle of the valley, from which a road, cut in zigzags, leads to the summit of Great Yagni, Victory turned her smiling face towards the Russian commander, but he disdained the opportunity, and listened to General Heimann's opinion.

Opposite Great Yagni runs a high barren ridge, sloping gradually upward to a flat-topped summit called the Awly-Yer, which is severed from the Aladja Mountain by the Subatan ravine, about two miles above the village of Hadji Veli Koi. This commanding point—the most important of the whole Turkish position, and subsequently well fortified—was literally inaccessible from the plain at the foot of the Aladja, towards which it falls off some 1,500 feet in a succession of steep gradients and perpendicular rocks. At its base the Turks had concentrated their main force; and Mukhtar, relying on the strength of Great Yagni, had neglected to occupy with the necessary troops the summit of the Awly-Yer. This fact had been ascertained by our cavalry patrols. Two squadrons of Cossacks had even remained for two hours at Veli Koi, a village situated to the south of that elevation, right across Mukhtar's only line of retreat, where they met not a single Turkish soldier. The Pacha, moreover, was utterly unable to send a sufficient force quickly enough to the Awly-Yer, because he was closely pressed in front by the 2nd Brigade of the Caucasian Grenadiers, under Major-General von Schack, a Prussian by birth and education. Six of our battalions had just descended the Great Yagni, six others were near at hand, and had they been momentarily withdrawn from the superfluous attack on the Little Yagni, it is probable that they would have taken the Awly-Yer almost without loss from the side of its totally unoccupied southern ridge. Possibly such movements did not enter the original plan; but plans are worthless when the fighting has once begun, and all depends on the capacity to seize favourable opportunity.

It seems that General Loris Melikoff asked an officer whether he knew the road to Vezin Koi. The Awly-Yer was obviously the only tactical object worth storming at any cost; it was the magic point from which the fate of the day was suspended by a thread. Its occupation by the Russians would have unavoidably led to the destruction of Mukhtar Pacha's entire army. Its very key, the Great Yagni, was already in our hands. At this moment, unhappily, General Heimann, in an interview with Loris Melikoff, was pleased to assert formally that his troops, advancing from the Subatan plain, were quite able to finish taking the Awly-Yer, as they had done with the Great Yagni, and that, therefore, our available force might be advantageously employed against the Little Yagni and the garrison of Kars. This strange opinion prevailed. General Loris Melikoff's genius was impaired by pernicious advice. His whole staff recognized it, but nobody ventured to utter an objection. General Heimann, of course, did not take the Awly-Yer as he had promised, in his sanguine fashion, but was, on the contrary, repulsed with considerable loss; while the three brigades ordered to assail the Little Yagni had no better chance. Even had we had a reserve of 50,000 men more they too would never have succeeded in the attempt of taking those fortifications and works by assaulting them. This was conspicuous enough at nine o'clock in the morning, and the wisest plan would have been then to withdraw the troops, for the opportunity had been missed.

The staff turned its back to the Awly-Yer, and followed the zigzags of the road which the Turks had recently made for the convenience of the garrison on the summit of the Great Yagni. Company after company, as they passed us descending, cheered the commanding General, who wished them good luck. On the hillside, as we went up, lay a young grenadier, moaning as he tried to lift his head and rest on his elbow to answer the questions and receive the consolations of the General. Overcome, however, by weakness and pain, he fell back and shut his eyes, while the blood still gushed from the wound in his side. Higher up a dead Turk, stretched across the narrow track on his face, compelled us to make a circuit. On reaching at last the level top of Great Yagni a ghastly sight struck our eyes. All the pits and ditches around were filled with the corpses of Turks. The dead were almost all shot through the head, because the remaining parts of their bodies had been sheltered by the parapets. Here they lay as they fell, on their backs or faces, side by side, or one above the other. A negro with grinning teeth hung right across a white soldier, and his long arms stretched out over the rocky abyss. Some preserved the ferocious expression which they had borne when still alive, and lay with clenched fists and distorted limbs; others, calm and quiet, looked like stone. In a pit, opposite each other, sat two softas. Though in the uniform of soldiers, they were easily recognized as religious students by the white muslin band tied around their fezzes. One had his skull laid open by a shell fragment, the other was shot through the temple. Both had obviously been killed by the same shrapnel. Some hundred dead bodies encumbered the trenches; others lay strewn over the hillside.

When we came to the top the Russians had already buried their own killed, and had removed all the wounded and prisoners. About 140 Turks had been taken alive. We learnt from a soldier that the famous Kara Fatima, the Turkish heroine, had met with a fatal end. They said that she lay in one of the captured tents, shot through the heart. Together with an officer I sought her all over the hill, but I did not find her; but some asserted that, on the persistent entreaty of the Turkish prisoners, she had been buried immediately by compassionate Russian soldiers. The number of tents on the hill justified the supposition that it had only been defended by about 450 men. Two Turkish officers were among the dead. One stood still upright in the trenches, leaning over the breastwork, with his right arm stretched out as if in the action of firing a revolver. The other, a stout, obese fellow, lay on his back before his own tent. He had been killed before he had time to get on his coat, which he had slung over his huge shoulders.

We had a magnificent look-out from the Great Yagni over the whole field of battle. Kars, a grey heap of stones, uninviting like the remainder of this melancholy country, rose in sight. From one of its northern detached works—I believe Fort Mouchlis—a monster cannon thundered at intervals, sending its shots in the direction of the Little Yagni. The troops were still wasting their forces against well-armed natural strongholds, when it would have been a comparatively easy thing to cut the army off from their supplies. I cannot account for the persistence with which our General always engages the enemy's whole front line, with the result that we are everywhere too weak, and have nowhere strong reserves at hand which alone are likely to secure victory at the favourable moment. So the battle, very similar to previous ones which had been fought on the same ground, was protracted from hour to hour to no purpose. It was the accustomed style of tirailleur engagements at respectable distances, without moving, accompanied by the annoying but harmless noise of 200 cannon. We descended the Great Yagni on the opposite side, resting at an eminence at its foot. As I knew beforehand that nothing would come of our supreme efforts, because the same causes must necessarily bring about the same results, the same faults the same failures, I did not wonder when General Heimann asked for reinforcements, while the Little Yagni blunder neutralized about 16,000 men.

At last, in the afternoon, the smoke of cannons was seen on the ridge of the Aladja Dagh itself. It came from General Sholkownikoff's brigade, which had thus succeeded in threatening the rear of Mukhtar Pacha's camp near Subatan; and, in the case of his discomfiture, was ready to prevent his escape across that mountain. Mukhtar's very existence was threatened by this dangerous turning movement. As he, however, does not lack experience with regard to unexpected surprises in the mountains, to which he had been accustomed during his prolonged struggle with the Montenegrins, he was able to parry the stroke with remarkable skill and success. It may be, too, that he knew, through the instrumentality of his spies, the whole Russian plan. Only so can it be explained that he paid little attention to the important Great Yagni position, while he covered the Little Yagni with men and guns in profusion. As he was also well acquainted with the fact that General Sholkownikoff's movement had no serious purport, and was meant to be a mere demonstration, he not only took no heed of it, but planned a counter-action which was likely to compel a less circumspect adversary to surrender. As it was, however, General Sholkownikoff retired without losing a prisoner.

The day came to an end, and with it the battle. Weary after a sleepless night, the members of the staff sat down and talked together, or endeavoured to slumber a little with the earth as a mattress, and the rocks as pillows. We had nothing to eat and drink, but nobody was very hungry, because of the fatigue and nervous excitement. Waiting for a result, but despairing of success, we were longing for an end, when, on a sudden, a well-known howl broke the air above us. A second afterwards, a smash and crack amidst our browsing horses and yawning Cossacks announced that we were within range of the enemy's guns. A few minutes elapsed, and there was another howl and another smash and burst. These shots came from the invisible summit of the Little Yagni, at least four miles off. Everybody thought it wise to retreat from so inhospitable a spot. The whole army was ordered to bivouac that night on the positions which had been conquered or occupied during the day, in order to renew the battle on the following morning. Not admiring this plan, I left the staff, and made my way back to the Karajal camp. The poor staff officers, a polite and interesting body of princes, counts, barons, generals, and colonels, made themselves as comfortable as possible in the cold air, on the hard, stony ground, without shelter, water, and fuel. Moreover, the poor horses had not been watered for the last twenty-four hours. There is not a drop of water to be found for ten miles around Great Yagni, with the exception of the Subatan streamlet still in Mukhtar's grasp.

General Loris Melikoff sent two battalions as a garrison to Great Yagni, ordering them and the sappers to strengthen the entrenchments with additional earthworks. In case of need, two divisions were near at hand to support the troops on its summit. I could not but suppose that, despite all hindrances, the Russians would keep their dearly bought conquest at any cost. The water question was a very serious one indeed, especially as the road on the other side was exposed to the Turkish firing. Still we had plenty of beasts of burden, including thousands of camels, especially fitted for this sort of transport. On the following morning, the 3rd instant, I rode to the Karajal observatory, to examine the battle-field of the previous day on our left wing, which I had not seen yet. There the Grand Duke, his son, and his brilliant staff, with the field-telegraph office at their immediate disposal, had been waiting some hours. Hitherto nothing remarkable had occurred. The outposts of the 40th Division, under General Lazareff's able command, had had a little indifferent skirmishing at the Kizil Tepe.

At half-past two o'clock, P.M., I saw through my field-glass three strong lines of Turkish tirailleurs, one behind the other, advancing, rifles in hand, at a quick pace. They occupied a front of at least three miles in length, were preceded by two batteries, and followed by compact supports and reserves, all arranged in perfect order. The whole force must have consisted of about 15,000 men, having their right wing covered by the Kizil Tepe. It was obviously their intention to make a desperate attack on the Karajal camp, and they seem to have supposed that the whole Russian forces had been brought over to our right wing. They were the more led to believe this as on the previous day no signs of troops had been shown here. General Lazareff, with the 40th Division, backed by a regiment of the garrison of Alexandropol and numerous horsemen, lay in ambush for them during the course of that day. The Russians were quite prepared to receive the assaulting foe. Their soldiers lay in rows concealed in the folds of the ground, or behind pyramidal heaps of loose stones. Ostensibly, only two battalions and a battery, together with some cavalry, leaving the Karajal position, marched to the fight. The Turks, encouraged by this apparent weakness, hastened their steps. Their batteries galloped ahead, and opened a brisk shell-fire on those of the Russians, who replied steadily with only eight guns. At the same time, the Kizil Tepe flung shell after shell at all moving objects on the field—ammunition carts, Red Cross waggons, cavalry, herds, and labourers—fortunately without hurting anything but the soil. The skirmishers, too, rattled away while the Turkish infantry drew nearer and nearer, without firing a round. They dived down into the ravines and reappeared, always resolutely advancing against the Russian cannons, which had in the meanwhile been reinforced by another battery of eight pieces. Although both were exposed to the bullets, they made no preparations for limbering up, but continued their slow firing. The Turkish batteries were soon silenced by the advance of their own men, who masked them.

Then at last the enemy saw the sunbeams dancing on the levelled rifle barrels peeping behind stones and sods. Now, at once, he began firing with frantic rapidity, but did not slacken his moving ahead. Only stray shots from sharpshooters answered the challenge. Finally, however, the Russians lost their temper, and, returning the fire volley for volley, showed a line of battle of no less extent and power than that of their adversaries. Then they rose together and faced the shower of lead, advancing and firing, firing and advancing, line after line, running from cover to cover, but always moving ahead, right down on the enemy. Every soldier seemed to believe that the Grand Duke's eyes were especially fixed on him. It was refreshing to see how this division, in contrast with the monotonous unproductive skirmishing of their comrades on the previous day, went on without a moment's hesitation, with admirable and matchless courage. The Turks became demoralized by this unexpected resistance, supported by forces quite equal to theirs. Their advance was checked, and came to a standstill. Soon they retrograded slowly, but always firing. It was of no avail. They were driven back irresistibly from undulation to undulation, till at last they turned their backs and ran, seeking shelter behind their pits and breastworks. But again and again the Russians followed and dislodged them at a rush with the bayonet, compelling them to recede, either step by step or in short runs. The Turks became, from minute to minute, more disheartened. Soon they had had enough of the game, and shortly after nightfall were in precipitous flight towards their fortified camp around Subatan, at the foot of the Aladja Dagh. General Lazareff pursued them fast, even through the dark. His lanterns were the incessant sparkling of the long line of firing rifles, and the occasional broad flash of the cannons. When he had lost sight and feeling of the frightened enemy in that pitch-dark night, the firing died gradually out, and the slaughter came to an end.

The Turks, completely routed, took refuge behind their entrenchments, while the Russians, after having thrown up breastworks and pits, passed the night on the ground they had so gallantly conquered. Their losses were severe. The 40th

Division had nearly 700 killed and wounded in this three hours' fighting, whereas the Turks had left about 400 dead on that part of the field which the Russians chose to occupy. I was at a loss to understand why General Heimann, who commanded to the right of General Lazareff, did not assist him. Two regiments of cavalry could have outflanked and annihilated the scattered enemy at the proper moment. Be this as it may, I have not yet witnessed here a more judiciously combined and a more brilliantly conducted affair than that of the afternoon of the 3rd instant. It was carried on in the true military style. Careful plans and brave troops concurred in bringing it to a very satisfactory result. It is to be regretted that the time was too short for a full display of the General's abilities and his soldier's courage, as otherwise I do not doubt the camp at Subatan and the Kizil Tepe would both have been taken. On both sides there was no interminable, never-progressing cannonading, no timid skirmishing. The guns did not fire a minute longer than was necessary to introduce the action, and the tirailleurs, with most laudable pluck, were eager to settle the question of victory or defeat at once. Every single man had visibly made up his mind either to die or to conquer.

General Lazareff must be proclaimed the hero of the battle, and the Grand Duke was highly gratified with this striking proof of his ability. For the 4th a general renewed assault on the Little Yagni was announced. This seemed incredible after the bitter experiments on the 2nd. Luckily the rumour has not been confirmed by events. As the staff had not returned yet, I presumed that something important was in view. I at first intended to ride directly to the foot of the Great Yagni, but learned that our headquarters had been transferred to the Kaback Tepe. Everybody in the camp laboured under the belief that the Great Yagni had, once for all, remained in the possession of the Russian troops, and that the line of communication of the Turkish Army with Kars had been efficaciously interrupted. My astonishment was, therefore, equal to my disappointment on being informed at the Kaback Tepe bivouac that the Great Yagni hill and all the surrounding valuable positions, which the Russians had conquered on the 2nd with so considerable an effusion of blood, had been finally given up on the plea that it was difficult, if not impossible, to provide the troops and animals there with water. It is true that both had undergone, during the last two days, extreme hardships and privations. On the other hand, however, it would be difficult to deny that the inconvenience might have been mitigated easily enough, as thousands of carriages and beasts of burden, camels and others, in the Commissariat Service, are at the General's disposal. The Turks, moreover, had made, two months since, the necessary arrangement for the proper sustenance of their garrison on the summit of the Great Yagni. What they had managed to overcome the Russians might have overcome too. I don't know why the system of digging Abyssinian wells has never been tried in this barren country, where water must be found at a certain depth. The rich cold springs spouting out of the Kurukdere ravine indicate the presence of large supplies, filtered down from the high mountains all around. The question, anyhow, is worth an attempt.

At the Kaback Tepe a little shelling and skirmishing was going on without visible effect. Mukhtar Pacha stood triumphantly with his staff on the top of the Great Yagni, which he was allowed to occupy without spending a single drop of his soldiers' blood. He has, after a narrow escape, due only to unaccountable blunders, the right to boast that he has succeeded in stopping the Russian advance. The Russian staff has since returned home to headquarters. Whether another effort will be made on the Turks, whether it will be more wisely planned and conducted than the previous ones, and arrive at any substantial result, nobody can tell yet. Bad weather has now set in, the troops have been withdrawn to their former quarters, with the exception of General Count Grabbe's brigade, which is still waiting on the Kaback Tepe for further orders. I believe that something grand is projected, and then only it will be decided whether the actual campaign will come to a premature conclusion or not. Should, however, the previous very conspicuous faults be repeated, I cannot anticipate much glory and success.

The system of scattering all available troops, say 60,000 men, over a length of eighteen miles, cannot but lead to discomfiture in tactics as well as strategy. No sufficient reserves are at hand, and, if they were, would be too far off to act immediately on the enemy's weak point. Two such points were discovered in the course of the late battle: Vezinkoi and the rear of the Aladja position, where General Skolkownikoff operated. Both advantages if followed up would have led, no doubt, to an entire victory. Where was the *coup d'œil?* Where were the reserves? Why was the pluck shown on the next day by General Lazareff only? No concentrated action of artillery, no sweeping dash of the cavalry on the broad plain, and, for all that, heavy losses. We had, according to the latest accounts, 3,360 men *hors de combat*, among them 960 killed and 2,400 wounded. We lost only two prisoners. Fifty-four officers were wounded, a small and insignificant proportion compared with the loss of men as the result of other engagements. One colonel of the artillery has been killed. Whether other officers were killed and how many, I have not ascertained yet. Spies and deserters, whose accounts, however, are subject to suspicion because they want to procure a flattering reception for themselves, declare the losses of the Turks to amount to about 8,000 men. Two hundred and forty of their prisoners are in our hands. Reinforcements are again demanded, but only locally.

The experience of the fighting on the 2nd and 3rd of October was not, however, lost. It was resolved by General Melikoff to attack the Awly-Yer (the Acolias Hill of the Russians, the Evliatepisse of the Turkish despatches, and the Olya Tepe of many maps), indicated in the preceding letter of our Correspondent as the real key to the Turkish position, and to prepare for that operation by sending General Lazareff to the rear of Mukhtar Pacha's left. With this object General Lazareff accomplished a march of forty miles by the ruins of Ani, until he had reached the heights of Orlok, thus out-flanking the Turks. On the 14th of October General Lazareff attacked the Turkish left in the rear, compelling it to fall back in the direction of Kars and Vezinkoi. This done, it was decided on the next day to assail in front the positions of Ahmed Mukhtar Pacha, of which the fortified hill of Acolias formed the key. After preparing the way by a well-directed cannonade, the Russians advanced to the assault. In the afternoon General Heimann, with three regiments and a battalion of riflemen, made a brilliant attack upon Mount Acolias, which he succeeded in carrying. By the Russian occupation of this position, Ahmed Mukhtar Pacha's army was cut in two. That part of his army which retreated in the direction of Kars was attacked by the troops under General Lazareff and subsequently pursued by General Heimann. Towards five o'clock in the afternoon the whole Turkish Army was completely defeated, leaving an enormous number of killed, seven thousand prisoners, and four guns. The three Turkish divisions forming the Turkish right wing were entirely surrounded and driven out of their positions on the Aladja Dagh with great loss, and at eight o'clock in the evening were compelled to surrender. Thirty-two guns and an immense quantity of war material were captured. Ahmed Mukhtar fled to Kars.

The following letter from the Correspondent at the Russian headquarters describes the preparations for the battle of the 15th of October :—

△ CAMP KARAJAL, *October* 13*th*.—Since the 2nd instant continuous fighting has been going on here. After the sanguinary engagement at Subatan on the 3rd, however, the encounters have not been of a serious character, and are, on either side, mere demonstrations, intended to draw the enemy's attention from the real object of operations. In opposition to our former inactivity during the best part of the season, due chiefly to the insufficient number of troops, a busy military spirit now prevails in our army, and judicious combinations are on the point of being carried into effect with the view of outwitting Mukhtar Pacha; though it certainly must be admitted that he is not the man to be circumvented by ordinary means, especially while he sticks with unshaken tenacity to his stronghold on the rocks. Still one crushing power is brought forth against him, which to counterbalance is a difficult task even for a great genius—overwhelming numbers.

Mukhtar Pacha's once considerable host is fast melting away, because his Government are bending the bow of enduring patience, peculiar to their enthralled populations, to the point of breaking it. The Circassians, unable to find anything worth plundering in the locality with which to sustain themselves and their horses, constrained by hunger, have long ago left the camp in crowd. The mustafiz and redifs, most of them men who were the only support of their families, have either openly done the same, or, asking for a short leave of absence, on the plea of fetching their own provisions, have never again returned. The Turks, besides, it is well known, can endure anything but cold, which is likely to tell severely on them in a fortnight hence. If, as is probable, this reckless system of compelling the army to provide for its wants at the expense of the country where it is quartered should be continued, it is easy to foresee that their resistance must very soon crumble to pieces. Still the Russian Commander-in-Chief is not at all willing to leave things as they are and to entrust to fate or General Winter the reduction of the Turkish forces. Although the attack on the 3rd instant may be called in a certain sense a failure, inasmuch as the routing and dislodging of Mukhtar Pacha did not directly follow, as had been confidently hoped by our leading strategists, yet that battle and the following series of engagements have led to a state of things synonymous with victory.

The total losses of Mukhtar Pacha are estimated by spies at above 8,000 men, owing particularly to the several desperate assaults on General Sholkownikoff's brigade, which had occupied the summit of Mount Aladja, in the rear of his very headquarters, and to the discomfiture inflicted on him by General Lazareff before Subatan on the 3rd. During the night between the 9th and 10th instant the Mushir secretly withdrew from his fortified advanced position in the plain, together with the Kizil Tepe and Great Yagni hills, and retired to his former entrenched encampments, half way up the Aladja. It may be that the turning movement which the dashing General Lazareff, with twenty-six battalions, forty-eight field-pieces, and six regiments of cavalry, is directing from the south-east on Mukhtar's line of communication with Kars, and eventually Erzeroum, has induced him to concentrate his scattered and diminished troops. On the other hand, it can hardly be supposed that he had been fully informed by his spies, never paid as they are, of that hazardous, but certainly very daring and efficient operation, on the date of his retreat, when it was in its very beginning, and even if he knew of it he may have considered it as a mere cavalry raid.

The startling fact that a field-telegraph line has been established without interruption from the Karajal headquarters to General Lazareff's division, following him all along his circuitous march of at least forty miles through a mountainous, hostile country, completely in the rear of the actual Turkish position, gives ample proof of the fact that the Pacha is ignorant of that double-edged move on this great chessboard. The telegraphic communication was indeed once interrupted, and much anxiety was felt about it, but within two hours it was re-established. The wind, and not malicious Turks, had thrown down some of the poles. This inference seems correct, therefore, that the Pacha's hasty retreat was rather prompted by the comparatively enormous losses he had sustained, either from the relentless fighting during the week previous to his withdrawal, or from wholesale desertions, than by General Lazareff's intrepid interposition. Had his valuable Circassian scouts not disappeared, driven away in despair and disgust, they would have assuredly succeeded in fathoming the Russian design, or at least in destroying the telegraph line, which now enables a simultaneous movement of our two columns to be carried out, the object of which is to envelop Mukhtar Pacha and compel him either to starve on his barren cold summits or to surrender. Should General Lazareff, whose whereabouts is still kept secret, be directed to attack and occupy the Orlok summit and Vezinkoi, while we assail the same points from this side of the mountains, victory is probable, and Mukhtar Pacha will then have to fight for his existence. If, on the contrary, these operations should turn out to be only a sort of affected strategy, without being followed by a tactical decisive stroke, nothing can come out of it but a retreat in the mud when the impending bad weather sets in here.

I hope that this time General Lazareff's movements will not be arrested or impaired by half-measure instructions, which render success impossible. Should the Mushir, despite his circumspection and general sharpsightedness, be caught in the meshes of the extensive strategic network thrown around him, the siege of Kars and the loss of Armenia might be the consequence. At all events, the Pacha's prospects are bad—worse indeed than they have ever been before. The task of extricating himself out of his internal and external difficulties, without yielding his ground, is worthy of the highest military talent, and, if successfully accomplished, would be a title to glory for him. I have, however, full faith in General Lazareff's ability, courage, and resources.

The Kizil Tepe, on the conquest of which Mukhtar Pacha, on the 25th of August, based a claim of victory, is now again in Russian hands. The entrenchments there are all of very neat and careful workmanship, and prove the peculiar aptitude of the Turks, or their advisers, for this branch of warfare. Their guns—withdrawn, of course, before the surrender—had all been placed in deep cuttings, and covered in with double crossed rows of strong timber, with a thick bed of earth on the top. How the Russian artillerists could dream of dismantling such blindages and dismounting the guns by firing at them from their favourite distance of three or four miles, one is at a loss to understand. The Russian staff, it seems, has come at last to a better knowledge of the tactical importance of the Great Yagni, and is now determined to keep it. Since the day before yesterday a redoubt has been erected at its foot opposite the Awly-Yer summit, and has been armed with cannon of heavy calibre for the purpose of bombarding the enemy's camps night and day. I hear them firing now. Mukhtar Pacha, deeply disappointed at the constant progress of the Russian earthworks, which proves on the Grand Duke's part a firm resolution to maintain his hold there, had recourse to a desperate assault. Before daybreak this morning he marched out six battalions of volunteers, supported by reserves and artillery, and hurled them against the Great Yagni. This brigade stealthily advanced towards the new redoubt, and would have surprised and taken it but for an accident. The Russians, inconceivably careless as they sometimes are, had not only neglected their outpost service, but had not even a squad of Cossacks at hand for scouting and other useful purposes. But, fortunately for them, at the very moment of the Turkish attack, two other battalions arrived which had been told off to relieve those on working duty. So three battalions instead of one were able to act. Posted partly behind the entrenchments, they received the assailants with a well-aimed, quick fire, and compelled them, after an hour's fighting, to retire in disorder, charging them with the bayonet. General von Schack states that, had he had at his disposal a regiment of cavalry, he would have annihilated them to the last man. The Russian losses amount to only twenty-four men killed and wounded. The Turks left 123 corpses on the field, and may, in consequence, be estimated to have lost some 400 men. Such engagements and tactical movements are only the prelude to what is expected to take place when General Lazareff shall have reached his destination, the Orlok summits or Vezinkoi. Then we hope the question of our invading or not invading Armenia will be definitely settled. His horses are much fatigued by their long and difficult journey across those mountains, and it is on these grounds that he is advancing slowly. To-morrow, or the day after to-morrow, however, we confidently expect a result. Whether it will involve a great decisive battle, or will lead only to a series of minor engagements, or to Mukhtar's retreat without his accepting the challenge, will soon be decided.

P.S.—I have just spoken to one of the Turkish wounded prisoners, a captain, aged about 45, who was taken this morning before the Great Yagni Hill. His name is Osman, and he is a native of Adrianople, which place he left six years ago. He was struck on the thigh by a fragment of stone, and suffered at first great pain. Now he feels a good deal better, owing to the excellent medical treatment and the careful attendance he is enjoying. As I know Adrianople well, I had no difficulty in getting into his confidence. His statement is as follows:—The Mushir had for a time made up his mind to remain where he was around Subatan during the coming winter, and had ordered for that purpose the erection of earth huts for the troops, which were being built.

On seeing, however, the fast increasing number of Russians threatening his flanks and rear, he thought it advisable to concentrate his forces by retiring to the summits of the Aladja, and abandoning all his advanced positions in the plain. Mukhtar is well aware of General Lazareff's turning movement, and has detached to meet him the Ferik (Lieutenant-General) Selim Pacha, with fifteen battalions, who is now occupied in fortifying the Orlok Mountain and Vezinkoi. The Pacha's decision as to his eventual retreat to Kars will depend upon the issue of the expected battle. The Turkish lieutenant-colonel commanding the column of attack to-day has likewise been wounded, but was carried out of the turmoil by some of his soldiers.

The following is a description by the same Correspondent of the great Battle of Aladja Dagh, which at length decisively and irrevocably determined the character of the campaign in Armenia. It is followed by another account of the same battle by the Special Correspondent with the Turks.

△ CAMP KARAJAL, *October* 17*th.*—Mukhtar Pacha's army has ceased to exist. I can state this truth on personal knowledge of the operations by which the dissolution of the Turkish force has been accomplished before my own eyes. The Ottoman General, who had proudly kept his position for months on the almost inaccessible mountains and hills opposite Kurukdere, has been shattered against his own rocks.

I stated in my last letter from Karajal that General Lazareff, at the head of 27 battalions, 40 guns, and six regiments of cavalry, had directed a turning movement against Mukhtar Pacha's rear with the view of cutting him off from Kars and Erzeroum, and crushing him thus, once for all, between the two principal portions of our army. His march across the mountains was, of course, somewhat hampered by his cannons and military train, which compelled him to seek and follow a rather circuitous carriage road. He was at first guided by the Arpa Tchai River down to Kotchiran. From here he passed over to Dighur, where he left two battalions, and then, wheeling round to the north-west, he chose for his mark the Orlok Hill and Vezinkoi. This village, strongly entrenched, secured Mukhtar's position and his communications with Kars. I stated in my last letter that the Mushir, on hearing of General Lazareff's serious movement, detached Selim Pacha with fifteen battalions to meet him. It seems, however, that he had reinforced a few days later these troops with another division, entrusting the whole corps to the command of his lieutenant, Raschid Pacha, President of the Military Council, and now our prisoner.

Mukhtar's obvious intent was to weigh with all his available forces on General Lazareff, trying to crush him or to compel him to retreat whence he came, and then fall on the other fraction of our army here. That he had this idea is ascertained by the unanimous evidence of the prisoners, and it is, moreover, in accordance with common sense. General Lazareff, however, had in the meantime occupied on the 13th the Oghur Hill, after a sharp engagement. Then he telegraphed to the Grand Duke's headquarters that Mukhtar was before him with superior forces, and he urged, therefore, that from our side a simultaneous attack might be directed against the Turkish lines. This message reached here precisely at three o'clock on the morning of the 14th. The Commander-in-Chief at once complied with Lazareff's request. I have already pointed out the remarkable circumstance that a field telegraph had been established with laudable celerity and regularity throughout the length of that circuitous line of operations. Although it was only protected by Cossack picquets, it had never been interrupted but once, by a mere accident, and for two hours.

Our whole strategic plan was suspended on that thin wire. On its strength depended the fate of this campaign in Armenia, because it alone rendered an harmonious tactical action possible which secured success, and without which we could not hope to dislodge the enemy from his strongholds. The Pacha, ignoring either this state of things, or, in his Turkish prejudice against all innovations, scorning that peculiarly useful modern contrivance, laid no stress on its establishment. He found out subsequently that that wire was in fact around his neck ready to strangle him at a moment's notice. And so it did. The battle on the 2nd instant was, it seems, the most efficient practical lesson taught to our strategists. They recognized at last their former capital faults and blunders, both with regard to general conception and to tactical details. Generals Obruteneff and Gurstchin were yet experimenting on the 2nd instant, when, in reference to the available force, their plan was too complicated and extended. The visible good effect of General Sholkownikoff's turning movement then rendered it obvious in which direction it was best to act. So that operation was again performed, but judiciously on a larger scale, and aiming at more important points.

We had no unnecessary trouble, bloodshed, and neutralizing of our forces before the impregnable Little Yagni Hill. We had not abandoned again the Great Yagni, the guardian bastion of Mukhtar's front, but kept and fortified it. We did not rely on Mohammedan cavalry scouts for the security of our army and the watching of the enemy's doings, but closed him in with two divisions, which established a solid curtain of infantry double posts, with guards and regulars patrolling before their encampments. It was at last universally acknowledged that the Awly-Yer Hill was the enemy's centre pivot, and that the Great Yagni was doubtless the key to his position. Its possession alone enabled us to attack that all-important point. I have already stated in my last letter how stupid it was on the part of the Turks to evacuate it. General Heimann was charged to carry the Awly-Yer at any cost, and had for that purpose the gallant division of the Caucasian Grenadiers and 56 cannon at his disposal. The Moscow Grenadiers, posted on his left, received orders to refrain from acting until that hill was taken. They formed the reserve, and observed the enemy's movements on the Aladja Dagh. Opposite this mountain a heavy battery of 24-pounders had since the 12th bombarded the enemy's camp there night and day, at intervals of fifteen minutes, in order to disturb it and harass the Turks. Our right wing was covered by the Ardahan Brigade, under General Komaroff, and some regiments of cavalry, which were intended to check the garrison of Kars, and that of the Little Yagni.

Early in the morning of the 15th, at about five o'clock, his Imperial Highness the Grand Duke and General Loris Melikoff left with their staffs the Karajal camp, and proceeded to the environs of Subatan, where the Moscow Division of Grenadiers had their position. I was not ready to accompany them, not having been informed in time of the news concerning General Lazareff's message and the subsequent intentions, thus I was only able to start about two hours later together with the Russian Consul, Mr. Obermüller, who formerly exercised his functions in Erzeroum. We rode over the well-known plain, stretching from the Karajal hills to the Aladja Dagh, towards Subatan. We had no time to spare, for sharp firing at the Awly-Yer attracted our attention. There, I well knew, the fate of the day would be decided, and therefore we were determined to reach that point as quickly as possible. Distances here, though they appear insignificant, are in fact enormous, because objects for estimating them, such as trees, houses, &c., are utterly wanting. One sees a hill before him of apparently small size, and is thus inclined to judge it only a walk of an hour from the point of observation, but on trying the distance one finds that it takes three or four hours' fast riding to reach it. Then the little hillock turns out to be a bulky cluster of plateaus and summits of some miles in extent.

We followed the foot of the Aladja. The guns placed on its terraces flung from time to time some shells at our reserves and the heavy battery, without doing any harm. None the less they became somewhat annoying on account of their disagreeable howl and the dry crack of their bursting. The Awly-Yer, which soon stood threatening before us, had a more serious, warlike aspect than its big neighbour. It was encircled by two broad rings of white smoke—one around its basis, produced by the incessant firing of fifty-six cannons, and the other, on its summit, by the musketry and artillery of the Turks, and the bursting Russian projectiles. This time the Russian gunners behaved well. They had placed their pieces at the reasonable distance of 1,800 yards, and laying aside the inefficient shells, concentrated a shrapnel shower on that part of the enemy's front which had been selected to be assailed by the storming battalions. Balls of white smoke, waving for awhile in the calm air like balloons, indicated that the terrible messengers of death and destruction had burst at the proper point for sending fragments and bullets among the lines of the defenders.

I observed how at once the musketry ceased after the bursting on a certain spot, and only a few minutes afterwards it began again, when living men had replaced the dead and wounded. Three strong columns of Grenadiers lay in clusters on the steepest parts of the northern side of the hill, as though riveted to it. They were waiting there for final orders, in comparative security, because the Turks behind the breast-works were unable to hit them. The latter could not venture to stoop forward for that purpose without the risk of being shot immediately by the Russian artillerymen or tirailleurs. In this manner the fighting continued for three mortal hours, and had apparently come to a standstill. Already the suspicion rose in my mind that this engagement, like the former ones which I had the opportunity of witnessing, would end without any other result than that of mere slaughter. We thought it convenient to rest awhile, and had some breakfast. Its principal ingredient was the Russian black rye bread, which is hard enough to be used instead of cannon-balls in case of need.

The fighting on all other points than the Awly-Yer was insignificant. The Aladja and the Little Yagni continued their indifferent cannonading, aiming at random. All my attention was of course drawn to the Awly-Yer, where perhaps the future destiny of the Turkish Empire was at stake. Seeing no advance, I thought that General Heimann might again have failed to understand the full importance of the task entrusted to him. Why did those Grenadiers not move, although sure to be badly dealt with if they finally had to retire before the enemy's pursuit? It was a moment of anxiety and disappointment. The idea that Mukhtar had evidently neglected to fortify and garrison that hill with the utmost care, was, however, somewhat comforting. Then, on a sudden, three Turkish cannons boomed to our left beyond the Subatan streamlet and ravine, which separate the Awly-Yer from the Aladja. From this mountain descended, towards the Awly-Yer, a strong line of Turkish tirailleurs, coming obviously to the rescue of that hard-pressed position. But before they could even cross the ravine their advance was arrested by a Russian line which compelled them to withdraw. At the same time the three columns of Russian grenadiers told off for the assault on the Awly-Yer moved onward up that hill.

We were in our saddles in a twinkling, and galloped ahead, with the view of witnessing this supreme achievement. A rocky ravine, however, with perpendicular borders, only visible when about ten yards off its margin, checked our speed, and compelled us to make a circuit. Finally, we found a path leading down and up again. There we discovered the naked bodies of apparently Russian soldiers in an advanced state of decay. They were not mutilated or disfigured. Unluckily, we had at that moment no leisure to ascertain whether other victims of Turkish brutality lay unburied on that dismal spot; so we hurried on. Then, again, large tracts of the dry grass which uniformly covers the fields and pastures were burning before us, ignited by the Turkish shells. Our horses snorted, frightened by the approach of the flames, but we forced the animals through. The black Grenadiers swarmed on all sides over the yellow hill. Steadily they climbed towards the summit, always firing, in face of the desperate resistance of the Turks, who disappeared in the smoke. Onward the Russians stormed, crowding more and more together as they approached the cone, towards the enemy, while their batteries covered the top level with shells and shrapnels. When we passed one of them, a colonel ceased firing, and said with proud satisfaction:—"Go and look at the work we have done up there. I think we have served them well." At that moment repeated hurrahs sounded through the air, and the Grenadiers jumped in crowds over the enemy's ditches and parapets. Then the baffled Turks, relinquishing all hope, ran for their lives, pursued by bullets and bayonets.

The formidable redoubt was at last taken by that gallant onslaught. When we arrived at the foot of the steep, shell after shell was still fired at the middle part by a Turkish battery on the slope of the Aladja next to the Awly-Yer, and by cannons on the top of a commanding mountain opposite it, bursting behind and before us. But when all our men had arrived at the summit, that firing stopped on a sudden, and the terrible hill which, ten minutes before, was all fire, smoke, and noise, was once more silent. To our right we saw General Heimann riding to the top with his staff. We reached it about the same time as he, and I believe I was the first to have the honour of congratulating him on so brilliant a victory. General Heimann, losing no time, paraded his soldiers, and ordered immediately a sharp pursuit, which was carried out in a clever manner. They met with only a feeble resistance on the part of the Turks, who hastily withdrew in disorder.

The next fortified plateau to the south-west, situated just before that of Vezinkoi, was also stormed within an hour. In the meantime we saw the white smoke rise on the opposite side of that village. There General Lazareff assailed the enemy from his rear, and barred his retreat to Kars. The batteries also closed in with the scattered Turks wherever they perceived them, and covered them with a hailstorm of projectiles. The vanquished foe tried to rally and escape in all directions, but found no issue, and was soon close hedged in by infantry, artillery, and cavalry. Here it is said that Mukhtar himself was wounded in the hand, and sought for attendance and shelter in Kars, abandoning thus his doomed army. In truth, however, he had not received a scratch. He had commanded the battle from the summit of a mountain, the name of which I do not remember just now, next to the east of the Awly-Yer, from which a couple of guns still continued to molest us. I saw him there through my field-glass, together with General Kemball, if I am not mistaken. When the Awly-Yer was conquered by the Russians, those gentlemen disappeared, and had a narrow escape to Kars, by availing themselves of the opening between us and General Lazareff.

Another party of Turks—the bulk of the garrison of the Awly-Yer and its environs—were pursued through a pretty large valley, which is formed by the upper part of the Subatan streamlet and its tributaries. The battle had been won in a brilliant style, but yet the trophies had not been counted, and still separate Turkish brigades on the Aladja and the Little Yagni made a show of resistance. The parapets and ditches of the Awly-Yer redoubt looked indeed very much like those of the Great Yagni twelve days before, after it had just been stormed. Rows of dead Turks, some horribly disfigured by shell fragments, were to be seen upon the earthworks and at the bottom of the ditches. Some were literally torn to pieces by the shrapnels. I think most of them were killed by the artillery, which indeed had done its duty this time. An officer of high rank lay dead on his back in the ditch. He was a pacha or colonel, perhaps; but it could not be made out because the soldiers had stripped him of his overcoat and boots. The contracted brow and the fierce expression of his lips proved that he had met with a sudden death. His fine Arab horse lay dead by his side. Very few wounded remained on the field when we came up.

I don't think that the Russians have sustained great losses by that assault, because, in the first place, the shrapnels had told terribly on the Turks, and had greatly diminished their number and demoralized them before the storming began; and, in the second place, the hill itself was too steep to permit them to fire over the earthworks with good effect. Most of their rifle shots were aimed too high. The inside of the redoubt, comprising the whole natural platform of the hill, was ploughed with shells, and strewn with their fragments and bullets flattened on the stones. Three Krupp guns, with the manufacturer's name on them, together with their carriages and ammunition, were captured there. One of them had its right wheel broken by a shell, but the other two were in serviceable condition, so the Russian officers tried their range at the fugitives. The first shot, however, fired without the necessary elevation, nearly fell among a column of their own soldiers.

The Turks are evidently not in want of rifle ammunition yet. About a railway truckload of cartridges, partly in their original boxes, partly in loose heaps, or strewn singly over the ground, might have afforded the means for annihilating a whole army. Some empty two-wheeled bullock-carts and tents, almost in rags, constituted the remainder of the booty. The tents were immediately cut into strips by the Russian soldiers, who wrapped them around their feet as an excellent substitute for stockings. Lines of cavalry, with their horse artillery, now trotted up between us and the Great Yagni, riding towards Kars, in order to cut off the enemy's retreat. It was now four o'clock; the weather was fine and rather hot; but notwithstanding my curiosity I resisted the temptation to follow up the advancing columns to Vezinkoi, where General Lazareff, descending from the Orlok Mountain, had begun a decisive attack. The day before he had already repulsed a reconnaissance directed against him by Raschid Pacha. To him and to General Heimann—especially to the latter—the prominent part of this day's glory is due. The Emperor will perhaps create him Count of Awly-Yer—at least he has deserved such a distinction.

On riding back to the Karajal camp, I had the good fortune to witness a sharp engagement between the Moscow Grenadiers and the Turks in the Aladja Dagh. The Grand Duke, who observed that attack from the heavy battery, which was now useless and silent, had ordered another regiment to the advance. The Turks answered with spasmodic cannon and rifle firing, but were gradually driven from terrace to terrace beyond their camp to the summit of the mountain. About half-past four they gave up further resistance, and retired to the opposite side, leaving everything they had in the hands of the Russians, with the exception of some of their guns. They hovered there in the wilderness for a while, without water, food, fuel, or shelter, and then despairing, surrendered at about half-past eight the same evening. They denied that they had cannons, but they had, and it is likely that they have hidden them in the recesses of the Aladja. Hitherto the Russians have had no time to seek for them, but they will do so, I hope, before the snow is likely to cover that mountain. Thus well-nigh the entire Turkish host had been swept away.

Unfortunately, the garrison of the Little Yagni, watching their time, when everybody's attention was drawn to Vezinkoi, escaped with stores, cannons, and ammunition to Kars. This, I regret to say, was the fault of our cavalry, which did nothing to prevent the retreat, on the plea of its being dark already, else it would have been literally impossible for the Turks to slip through our lines, as the hill is surrounded on all sides by dry and level ground. Colonel Kavalinsky, chief of the staff of the cavalry, reported at nine o'clock to the Grand Duke that seven pachas, thirty-six cannons, and twenty-six battalions had surrendered and laid down their arms. On the following day also many prisoners and some guns were captured. The exact number of the enemy's loss has not been recorded yet, but, at all events its total will amount to nearly three-quarters of its original strength. That is to say, his entire army has been scattered, destroyed, or captured. Among the captives we had the doubtful honour of seeing here at the Karajal camp the seven pachas and some colonels. We remarked among them Raschid Pacha, Lieutenant-General and President of the

Military Council; Hussein Kyazim Pacha, chief of Mukhtar's staff; Mustafa Pacha, and the so-called Madjar Omer Pacha. The last-named, a genuine Russian by birth, educated in a military school at St. Petersburg, and a former Russian officer, took an active part in the Hungarian revolution in 1849, and, coming over to Turkey with Kossuth and the other refugees, embraced Islamism. Thenceforward he distinguished himself as a fervent adherent of the Prophet. As years have elapsed since that time he has nothing to fear from the resentment of his countrymen, and will be considered and treated like the other Turkish generals. By the Grand Duke's orders each of these gentlemen received a good deal of money for his travelling expenses.

The Russian losses are about 50 officers and 1,600 men killed and wounded, numbers quite insignificant as compared with the result of the battle. The consequences are uncertain yet, but some hope that Kars may be induced to surrender is still entertained, and negotiations for that purpose are said to be going on. I do not believe, however, that the Turkish commander there is inclined to give the fortress over without fighting for it. In the meantime General Heimann is marching across the Soghanli Dagh (Onion Mountain), towards Erzeroum, the garrison of which is exceedingly feeble. Should, as there can be little doubt, General Lazareff be sharp and lucky enough to shut out Ismail Pacha from Erzeroum, and crush him between his own force and that of Tergukasoff, that fortress cannot then be defended. Its chief source of weakness, as I have said, is its extent. It requires an army of at least 50,000 men to garrison its numerous detached forts, and the central enceinte. The Russians, therefore, must make it their principal object to prevent all succour of men and material from entering the city, and then it cannot fail to succumb to a general escalade. If even Dervish Pacha should advance with the greatest imaginable despatch from Batoum viâ Trebizond, he cannot reach Erzeroum before General Heimann. It is true that the weather, which is as bad as possible, there being continuous rain, may prove a more serious hindrance to the progress of the Russians than all the Turkish forces together. The Battle of Aladja Dagh will, of course, redound to the honour of his Imperial Highness the Grand Duke Michael in the Russian annals. We hardly expected so brilliant a victory after the series of inconceivable blunders committed since the opening of the campaign. The camp is being removed from here to Wladi Kars, but very slowly, because the means of transport are insufficient.

The following letters are from the Correspondent who had been with Mukhtar Pacha throughout the campaign, and who, besides witnessing, may be said to have shared the defeat of that commander. For some of the details, which only the Staff could know, the Correspondent was indebted to the General himself:—

ERZEROUM, *October 24th.*—The tide of fortune has turned, and I find myself here part of the crowd that fled in disorder before the Russian attack of the 14th and 15th inst. It was a terrible disaster for the Turkish arms, all the more so that sanguine expectations were entertained as to the power of resistance of the Ottoman Army acting on the defensive. To understand the catastrophe it is necessary to go back a couple of weeks. We, that is the Correspondents of European journals, tried in vain to telegraph the situation. We were met by that passive resistance which characterizes the Ottoman Government. A telegram had first to be translated into Turkish at the headquarters, and modified at will by the young staff officers who had a smattering of French. Even then the authorities at Stamboul often took exception to the mild messages sent; but it was only three weeks after that the Correspondent was notified that, by "order of the superior authority," his message of such and such a date was intercepted. Over and over again, when the crisis was imminent, I tried to communicate the fact by telegraph. All to no purpose. No one who has not lived in countries like this can imagine the systematic obstruction which mars the best efforts of a Correspondent.

I have already telegraphed viâ Syra some details of the initial fighting in the plain north of the Turkish positions on the Aladja mountains. During three days fierce attacks were made by the Russians on the two hills—the Greater and Lesser Yagni, which block the passage to Kars. We estimated the Russian loss at 12,000 hors de combat on the occasion. This was on the 2nd, 3rd, and 4th of October. Then came a pause. Turkish officers told me confidentially the day on which we were to enter Gumri (Alexandropol), and soldiers ate their maigre pilaff all the more cheerfully, thinking over the flesh pots that awaited them beyond the Arpa Tchai. The capture of Kizil Tepe and our advance into the plain had filled every one with hope; but dark was the disappointment which followed the order of the 8th to abandon the hard-won heights, and retire to our old bleak quarters on the slopes of Aladja. Mukhtar Pacha's spies had brought him intelligence of the arrival of heavy Russian reinforcements, and others were said to be en route for the camp. Our position was deemed too extended to resist a serious attack from superior numbers; and hence the order to retire. It was ten o'clock on a bleak stormy night, and after the Marshal's tent had been already struck, that the rest of us at headquarters were notified that a move was necessary. Even General Kemball had no earlier warning. I myself, at half-past ten, wrote, at the dictation of a staff officer, the note which warned him to get ready. The camp fires still blazed in the plain, though the troops were already marching for their new quarters. Not a musket shot announced that the enemy's outposts had cognizance of the retreat; and, on the whole, as regards secrecy, the retrograde movement was admirably conducted. Not so, however, from the point of view of order. It has rarely been my chance to witness such utter confusion. No one seemed to know where the new position was. I met battalions stumbling about in the Cimmerian darkness of the mountain side, commanding officers demanding in vain whither they should conduct the men. I found Dr. Casson and his ambulance in a state of hopeless despair. The train of rude ox-carts sent to transport the wounded and hospital material had disappeared in the darkness. The tents were still standing, and Dr. Casson and his young colleague, ill with typhoid, were literally "left alone." The Doctor prayed me, as I, too, rode by in hopeless search of the new headquarters, to send him back his arabas; but as at least five hundred of these vehicles were groaning and creaking over the Cyclopean rock masses, I was soon obliged to give up my search. I rode on up the slopes of Mount Aladja, meeting everywhere parties of troops and transport waggons, every one asking every one else where they were supposed to go. After three hours of weary search I resigned myself to destiny, and, dismounting from my horse, lay down on the scanty grass, crisp with hoar frost. I tried to sleep in vain—people stumbled over me in the dark. Bewildered soldiers roused me a hundred times to ask the way, and camels and mules groaned and grumbled around me all the livelong night. When dawn came stealing over the ghostly summit of Ararat, I looked around. Headquarters were established half a mile off, but as yet no tents had been pitched. I found the Marshal eating his breakfast outside his tent door. The staff officers were wandering about looking for their tents, mislaid during the night. Mine was nowhere to be found, so I camped under shelter of a rock. There I indited the telegram which I hope has reached you. I took the precaution of sending three simultaneously. One I got translated into Turkish and sent from the camp. Another I sent by special messenger to Kars, to be forwarded to a friend in Erzeroum, and thence to London; and a third I sent by courier to Trebizond and Syra, to be thence sent on. From old experience I know what Turkish translations are, especially when made by an interested staff officer expressly told off to take the sting out of unfavourable messages. Consequently I didn't rely much on my camp despatch. Viâ Erzeroum I had better hopes, as an intelligent agent there would at once perceive the gist of my message and re-establish its meaning when translated into French.

On the morning of the 9th October it was evident, from the movements of the Russian patrols, that they were infinitely astonished at our nocturnal retreat. They couldn't apparently understand the thing, and their manœuvres showed they were fearful of a stratagem. Towards eight o'clock the entire Russian Army was in movement, advancing straight towards us. Seven squadrons of Cossacks, preceded by a long line of cavalry skirmishers, came first, closely followed by an ominous-looking line of batteries. It was a moment of intense anxiety for us. We believed the enemy was about to make a general assault. The Cossacks entered Subatan, a village we had held previously, in front of our centre. Five minutes after eight guns were in position on the ridge above the village. Hadji Veli, another village to the left, was next occupied, and simultaneously a column of infantry scaled the isolated hill of Kizil Tepe, the capture of which had earned for Mukhtar Pacha the title of "Ghazi," or "Victorious," conferred by the Sultan, together with a sabre of honour, a decoration in diamonds, and a present of two horses from the Imperial stables. About eleven o'clock the entire Russian line had advanced close under our positions, and the eight guns at Subatan opened fire. We sent out three battalions in skirmishing order to check the advance. A battery of Krupps took up its position on a rocky knoll and replied to the Russian fire. At one P.M. the infantry were engaged, and five Russian batteries added their fire to that first in action. The Russian batteries are of eight guns each, and the forty-eight pieces thus brought forward, formed in semicircle, literally deluged our advanced line with projectiles, especially directed against the Turkish batteries. Fortunately for the Turkish gunners, the enemy's fire was execrable. The vast majority of the shells burst two or three hundred yards short or over. Now and then a shell burst almost on the Turkish guns, but these were the exceptions. The musketry fire, extending over a line of about three miles, for nearly all our force was engaged at this hour, was violent in the extreme, especially on the Turkish side, where the soldiers plied their Martini-Peabody rifles with an absurd rapidity. The enemy's fire was much more deliberate, and I noticed their officers galloping to and fro to check any excessive outbreak of musketry fire which might occur. Long after sunset the scintillations of rifle-fire continued, emphasized by the broad gleam of the artillery.

After much reflection I am still unable to make out since what was the object of this engagement. We had abandoned deliberately certain positions, and certainly we did not try to retake them. Neither did the Russians seem disposed to push their occupation farther up the Aladja. We lost nearly one thousand hors de combat on that day, and it was pitiable to see the state of the wounded. In the Turkish Army here there is absolutely no provision made for carrying the wounded off the field. Those who can limp away struggle on often for hours seeking help, and those more severely hit often rest forty-eight hours on the field. I had been unable to find my tent, and was obliged to bivouac a second night on the hill-side. All night long moaning crowds of wounded came issuing out of the darkness like troubled phantoms, asking feebly for the "basta bane" (the ambulance). No one knew where it was, and the miserable sufferers went on groaning and complaining into the darkness. I afterwards discovered that the ambulances were just three miles away on our left flank. I venture to say that not one of those poor fellows found relief that night, and all of them must have passed the long cold night, like myself, freezing amid the rocks.

On the 10th all was still. Not a shot from either side, except from one large position gun which the Russians had established on Kizil Tepe, and from which they threw occasional shells against the redoubt on Lakiridgi Tepe, a conical hill on our extreme right. Large masses of Russian troops moved over the plain by Kaback Tepe, ultimately occupying the greater Yagni hill; and long columns were seen defiling towards our right, marching in the direction of the ruined city of Ani, on the banks of the Arpa Tchai River. These latter subsequently disappeared, and we were at a loss to account for their destination. In the afternoon the Marshal and his staff rode to the summit of Aladja to reconnoitre; but nothing could be made out. The 11th passed without incident save the continued shelling of Lakiridgi Tepe by the heavy gun on Kizil Tepe. On the 13th the Russians made a reconnaissance towards Kars, and some heavy firing took place in that direction. The enemy was evidently trying how far he could venture without drawing us from our positions; and the knowledge thus they gained proved fatal in the end. Mukhtar Pacha was evidently resolved, *coûte-qui-coûte*, to stand on the defensive. Towards sunset the same evening we were most disagreeably surprised by the range of two siege guns placed in position near Subatan. The headquarters were concealed from view behind a rocky ledge, from the crest of which the Marshal was in the habit of observing the plain with a large telescope. I was sitting at my tent door, for by this time I had managed to find a tent. A loud whirring noise attracted my attention, and next moment a sixteen-centimètre shell burst with a crash not twenty yards from the General and his staff. The range was enormous. From the flash of the gun till the arrival of the shell seventeen seconds elapsed. The enemy's guns were at a distance of seven thousand yards, and, besides, our position was some eight hundred feet above the plain. As a first shot at an unknown distance, the correctness of the aim was remarkable in the extreme. Shell after shell followed in rapid succession, some directed against headquarters, the position of which must have been indicated by spies, as the tents were hidden behind rocks, and some against the fortified hill of Evliatepessi, on our extreme left. All night long this shelling continued; and for my personal safety I was obliged to pack up and move to the ambulance, situated, as I have said before, some three miles to the left. This was a fortunate move for me, as it gave me an opportunity of witnessing the turning movement of the enemy, which resulted in our total defeat. Dr. Casson's ambulance was pitched in a narrow gorge close by the Turkish one. A troop of Arab horse watched the plain below and guarded the ravine which ran close by. It was midnight as I established myself in the tent kindly given me by the doctor. He seemed very uneasy about his wounded. The ambulance flags flying beside the tents were about as big as an ordinary pocket-handkerchief, and there was every reason to fear that they might not be visible to the artillerists below. It was decided to move from this dangerous spot higher up the hill; and accordingly next morning the change was effected. The tents we pitched on the brow of the long slope of Aladja stretching towards Kars, whence we commanded a view of both plains, north and south.

To render the battles of the 14th and 15th instant intelligible a slight description of the ground is necessary. Aladja is a mountain 8,800 feet in height, its base of an elongated oval form, running east and west. The summit, of a conical form, is towards the south-eastern extremity of the oval. At the same point it throws out a large spur to the southward. Both the summit and this spur were strongly entrenched, and occupied by eight or ten battalions and some batteries of field artillery. The bulk of the Turkish forces occupied the lower portions of the northern slope, and numbered from thirty-five to forty thousand regular troops. On the extreme right (east) is a flat-topped hill, named Lakiridgi Tepe, and on the left a similar one, Evliatepessi (the Awlis Hill), which, as will be seen later on, played an important part in the fighting. To the north of Aladja is an immense plain, the mouth of the Kars Valley. To the east of this plain are the isolated hills of Karajal, Kizil Tepe, and Utch Tepe, all three in the possession of the enemy at the commencement of the fighting. Towards Kars, that is westward, the plain is bounded by two hills, the greater and lesser Yagni. The greater Yagni is midway between Evliatepessi and the lesser Yagni, and, as I have already stated, was occupied by the Russians after our retrograde movement of the 8th instant. The other two hills were in our hands, and strongly entrenched. Continuing the line formed by these three hills, to the south of the western extremity of Aladja are three similar isolated hills, one exactly opposite the long end of the Aladja oval. Then comes a large plain-like valley, and beyond, at some eight miles distance, a chain of mountains, gradually lessening in height towards Kars, and slightly oblique to Aladja.

I passed the 14th in comparative tranquillity, watching the huge shells from the Russian guns of position burst on the devoted crest of Evliatepessi and in the Marshal's group of tents. The enemy's troops were swarming below—moving incessantly. The insects of a disturbed ant-hill could not have shown greater activity. Far out in the long dreamy plain, where distance seemed annihilated by the glassy atmosphere, the Cossacks trooped and trained towards the wide opening between the Yagni hills, evidently watching the Kars valley lest any unforeseen advent of reinforcements might derange the storm about to burst on us. It was half-past two in the afternoon as, field-glass in hand, I strolled leisurely on the hill-crest above the ambulance. The eye ranged far and wide over a tract of plain on either side, which it would be a long day's journey to traverse. The boom of a gun from one of the mamelons to the south of Aladja attracted my attention. "Some stray Cossacks," I said to myself, and I turned my glass to the northern plain. Another boom, and another, and then the long rattle of musketry. This time my accustomed eye perceived the long white line of drifting vapour which nothing but constant practice could distinguish from the mist lines of these lofty hills. Another look, and slender creeping lines were visible on the distant slopes. Here was the explanation of the disappearance of the Russian reinforcements. The enemy, having made a long détour from the camp of Karajal, turning our right flank by Ani and Dighur, had marched parallel to the rear of our position, and were actually attacking the rear of our left flank. The Marshal and his staff were already on the hill whence proceeded the cannonade. The Russians had occupied a lofty hill to the north-west, where they had placed a couple of batteries. Some Turkish battalions despatched across the valley were furiously assailing the flank of the enemy's line of march, and the latter were replying from their upper positions. It was easy to distinguish the lines of fire. The Turks, as usual, plied their Martini-Peabody rifles with a zeal that streaked the hill with one snowy line of palpitating smoke. The Russians, as usual, fired with deliberation. I could almost count the rifle shots on their side, though the force they deployed was fully equal to that of the attack. The enemy's artillery was principally engaged shelling Turkish forces further on towards what turned out to be the objective point. Till near sunset the combat continued, the Russian columns still streaming onward, apparently heedless of the serried volleys and file-firing of their adversaries. The Turks, who it seemed numbered eight battalions, together with seven despatched from Bayazid, and three squadrons of irregular cavalry, finding themselves worsted, commenced retiring towards the extremity of the hill range next Kars. The sun set redly beyond the distant summits, and with its rays the fire of the combatants died out.

The Russians had advanced half way from the higher hill whence they had commenced to the final conical hill which terminated abruptly in the flat valley. Mukhtar Pacha, deeming the day's fighting over, turned rein and rode with his staff over the long slopes leading to his headquarters. I, too, was tired. I turned my horse to graze, and, lying down on the scant yellow grass, gazed on the scene of conflict. A quarter of an hour passed, and streaks of fire were seen issuing from the point to which the Russians had advanced. I couldn't make it out at first. Little by little these streaks increased in number, and the terminal hill seemed all ablaze with bursting projectiles. But there was no sound of artillery. The enemy was bombarding the position with Congreve rockets. The fire was so rapid that the sky was all ablaze. At least sixty per minute were discharged. To me they seemed to burst much too high to do any execution unless the heads were charged with bullets. Then I saw long lines of flickering fire go up the hill, parallel to the crest of flame that crowned the crest. Half a dozen times these fiery lines approached and recoiled. Then they mingled; then came a pause. Rocket and musketry fire ceased. I judged that the Russians had taken the hill. Turkish officers laughed at me; told me the position was impregnable; but I retired to my tent with sad misgivings. I ordered everything to be packed, and the horses saddled ready for any contingency. I said to myself, if the enemy has captured that hill, they are between us and Kars, and to-morrow's dawn must see a desperate conflict. I couldn't sleep. I went to the tent of Dr. Casson, where he watched beside his sick colleague. We talked over the immediate prospects. He was very uneasy. I told him I believed a retreat was imminent, and that should the Russians have captured the terminal hill behind us, we should have to retreat on the morrow over a slender strip of ground swept by the enemy's fire. While we were speaking two battalions went by in the dark, followed by long trains of waggons. Then came artillery fourgons and pack mules, and long lines of baggage camels succeeded. It was a procession without end. Long into the night the cavalcade passed us by. It was evident a retreat had commenced, and yet no orders for the ambulance had arrived. Dr. Casson called up the officer attached to the ambulance, and sent him with his dragoman to headquarters to know what should be done. In half an hour the man returned to say that the headquarters had shifted its place under the incessant shell-fire of the two heavy guns in the plain, and that it now occupied the place of the commissariat department already retiring. Mules were being waited for to bear off the baggage of the officers, and then the staff would retire. Timely notice would be given. We waited on through the dreary hours of the night. No one could sleep, for it was evident a crisis was imminent. Night hung darkly over the long weird mountain slopes. Not a star was visible in the inky expanse above. All was still, save the faint jingling of the artillery horses going by, and when from time to time the thundering roll of the Russian heavy guns followed the lightning-like flash in the plain below, and the heavy shells went screaming hoarsely to Evliatepessi, and the former site of the staff.

I had retired to my tent and sunk into an uneasy slumber. A thundering detonation roused me. A heavy shell had burst within twenty yards of my tent. I sprang to my feet and rushed from the tent. The white smoke was still curling upwards from the frosty turf, torn into a black circle by the shell. Another projectile whistled over my head and burst against the rocks beyond. Every one in the ambulance was astir. We were being deliberately shelled. Dr. Casson, half dressed, was having his sick and wounded carried on litters higher up the mountain, out of range of the 16-centimetre projectiles. His colleague, the young volunteer doctor, was prostrate after the reaction of a severe typhoid attack. I had leaped to horse as the second projectile burst, and never shall I forget that poor feeble young man lying among the bare, bleak rocks in the grey mountain air, as I galloped by. If the Russians fired deliberately on the ambulance, it was a piece of atrocity. I can scarce believe it was so. For four days the ambulance was in the same place and was respected, although well in range of the heavy guns. On the morning in question the ambulances were still in the same place, but the ridiculously small flags against which I had remonstrated the day before, hung heavily against the masts. It may be that the officers and gunners of the battery were relieved, and that the new comers were unaware of the nature of our camp. If not, the thing was a piece of unparalleled barbarism.

Seeing that the projectiles continued to fall within the ambulance, I rode hurriedly away to get out of range. Mukhtar Pacha, accompanied by General Sir Arnold Kemball, came sweeping by. I rode after them, and together we mounted the steep hill at the western extremity of Aladja. A battalion already occupied the heights, sheltering behind some scanty earthworks. The Marshal sat under cover of a parapet and ate his frugal breakfast. Already in the plain below, to the east towards Subatan, the enemy was swarming in thousands, and still the heavy guns fired incessantly on Evliatepessi. Twenty times the ground on the top of this unfortunate hill was ploughed up in a manner to render it difficult to understand how any troops could exist within the crowning redoubt. It was seven o'clock when the Russian attack developed itself. Some ten battalions were seen advancing between the two deep ravines which seam the plain. In advance came two batteries of eight guns each, a third in reserve. At half-past seven the artillery opened fire on Evliatepessi, the shells falling with an accuracy which contrasted strongly with previous artillery fire. The two heavy guns near Hadji Veli continued their terrible fire, each shell falling right in the middle of the redoubt. On Evliatepessi, an isolated hill blocking the road between the two ravines, the shells rained incessantly. Behind the Russian guns the attacking force opened out, and presently took the advance of the guns. At the same time another column, with one battery, passed between the assailed position and the greater Yagni Hill, attacking at right angles to the main force. At half-past nine the first musketry fire was heard, and from that moment the dull roar of small arms was continuous. The entire plateau on the summit of Evliatepessi was one cloud of dense white smoke, which reeled and palpitated with bursting shells and the fire of the three guns of the defence. Four battalions—some two thousand men—held the trenches below the crest. The Russian columns crept nearer and nearer, and the artillery was close enough to be under musketry fire. At last came a moment when the gradually lessening fire of the defence showed how fatally the Russian fire was telling. Mukhtar Pacha ordered up a battery from the rear to sweep the front of the hill with its fire.

The critical moment had arrived. We had at least twenty battalions in the old positions and on the summits of Aladja. The hill attacked, Evliatepessi, commanded the line of retreat: this once lost, the forces on Aladja were cut off. Seeing the gradually lessening fire of Evliatepessi, and deeming its capture inevitable, as we had not a single battalion to send to its relief, I determined to leave the hill where the General and his staff were placed, and seek safer quarters. I rode across the stony plain towards Sivritepe, a triple hill to the rear, strongly intrenched and armed with artillery. As I rode towards this point, I noticed that the enemy, from the positions in rear of our left, where they had established themselves on the preceding evening, were already firing on the road yet cumbered with waggons and mules. I turned to the right to get out of range of the shells, and there in the plain met an enormous crowd of Bashi-Bazouks on horseback, Circassians, Kurds, and Arabs. They were brandishing their lances, whirling their matchlock guns, and otherwise conducting themselves in a seemingly warlike manner. I halted among them on the ridge which divides the Kars plain at this point. At one o'clock the Russians carried Evliatepessi by assault, after four hours and a half of infantry combat. At this juncture the Marshal left the hill on which he had stood since morning. Scarce five minutes elapsed after the capture of Evliatepessi, when the Russian field batteries, covered by a cloud of Cossacks, dashed forward between the captured position and the greater Yagni Hill. The fire of the two or three batteries thus brought into action swept obliquely the only line of retreat left to the Aladja troops; and at the same moment the

Russians established in rear of our left flank opened fire. The line of retreat was all but impassable. Lingering convoys still struggled over the stony surface; and a couple of battalions, with a haste scarcely dignified, were making for Sivritepe. I must here state that through all the confusion which followed, Mukhtar Pacha bore himself like a true soldier, retiring only when his soldiers left him no other choice. The irregular cavalry, principally composed of Arabs from Orfa and Aleppo, fled in disorder as the first shells burst over them, retiring *pêle-mêle* behind Sivritepe.

At this juncture the Russians made a general advance in front by Evliatepessi, and on our right flank from the positions won on the preceding evening. There was no further resistance. The battalions occupying the forts on Sivritepe fled in disorder. As I looked on them from a distance, I could scarce believe it was infantry I saw in such a disordered crowd. I supposed for the moment the fugitives were spectators or else Bashi-Bazouks. A few minutes undeceived me. They were Nizams, the infantry of the line. Nearer and nearer advanced the Russian batteries in front and flank. I left the commanding ridge of the plain on which I stood, and made for our last position, the hill of Vezinkoi, not far from Kars. This is an isolated hill in the plain, and takes its name from a ruined Armenian village close under its brow. Here, around a large water reservoir, were accumulated the waggons, mules, and camels of the commissariat sent off the night before from Aladja. Some four thousand irregular cavalry and panic-stricken infantry were mixed up with the ox-waggons and camels. It was a scene of utter confusion. A reserve battalion of regular troops, deployed in open order with fixed bayonets, prevented the runaways from flying to Kars. Nearer and nearer thundered the Russian guns, and each detonation thrilled the disorganized mass with terror. It was only by a stratagem I got through the blocking line of infantry. The road to Kars was cumbered with ox-waggons, baggage, mules, and what was supposed to be their escort. All were running at full speed. The oxen galloped like horses. The mules careered madly; and often when their burdens slipped from their backs, the frightened conductors went on, not daring to lose time in picking up their charge. The panic was complete. A mile farther on was a line of infantry with levelled rifles, threatening all runaways; and, as I myself saw, firing repeatedly on those who sought to get off by a side movement. It was with the greatest difficulty I got through this second line.

As I neared Kars the guns of the lower forts were firing on

bands of fugitive cavalry. At first I believed it was on adventurous Cossacks, and my belief was strengthened on seeing sabres flashing in the setting sun, plied amid the hurrying crowd. The idea crossed my mind that the confused column of fugitives had been assailed by the enemy's cavalry. My field-glass, however, showed me the red fezzes of the cavaliers, and I rode on a hundred paces, and was abreast with the cavalry. A revolver was thrust into my face, and I was commanded to turn again to the field of battle. It was the Colonel Hussein Bey who thus threatened me. He is a man of considerable animal courage, if I can believe the stories which reach me; but on this occasion seemed to have lost his head altogether. "Colonel," I said in French, "don't you know me? I am an Englishman and a newspaper correspondent." "I don't care who you are; it is perfectly equal to me," he said; "turn, or I blow your brains out." A dozen bayonets were at my breast, as many soldiers struck my horse with their musket butts. Of course I turned. It was not a time for explanation. Still, I turned again, and remembering that Hussein Bey had received English hospitality for seven years, I added, "Colonel, you will have reason to remember this. Your coward troops are flying before the Russians, and you wish to force me back into the panic-stricken crowd." Same answer as before—and, knowing from hearsay the temper of the man, I said no more, but went on into the dire tumult where Kurd lancer and Arab cavalry were mixed together in hopeless confusion. An officer, a major, came dashing by carrying despatches. He was one of Mukhtar Pacha's aides-de-camp. I appealed to him. A few explanatory words followed with the colonel. "Pass, English correspondent," he said; "one of those people who come to earn money in our country." Some bitter words rose to my lips, but in view of the situation I held my tongue and rode on towards Kars. At the gate was a double guard. "No one enters here," was the word. "Where is the Pacha?" I demanded furiously, utterly worn out with imbecile Turkish foolery. The word Pacha is enough to bring most Moslems to their knees, and I was shown into a neighbouring fort, where a half-blind old man, who scarcely looked at me, told me I might go. Colonel Hussein Bey, five minutes after our meeting, fled for his life. When he bullied me he had no idea the Russian battalions were so near.

The confusion within Kars was indescribable. I believe that if the enemy had assaulted at that moment the town was his without even the semblance of a struggle. A heavy slumber, consequent on the weary watching of preceding nights, followed. At dawn I was on foot. Patrols lined the narrow streets, seeking to collect the scattered soldiery. The Marshal dared not show himself in the streets. Some even said he was killed. By midday I had made up my mind. It was evident that Kars was about to be besieged, and that not a moment was to be lost if I wished to escape. Long before daybreak on the following morning I was on my way, accompanied by my old companion, M. Le May, of the Paris *Temps*. Before I leave Kars I must mention the parting words of Dr. Casson, who remained behind to take care of his sick colleague. "Will you," he said, "thank the Stafford House Committee for their aid?—but I wish you to say that the supplies sent by Colonel Loyd-Lindsay were by far the most practical and best selected of any I have received." The doctor seemed to take the idea of the siege lightly enough. He had something to do, and that seemed for him an all-sufficing reason. For just the same reason, and because a blockade in Kars would have left me with all the news for myself, and without occupation for the readers of the *Daily News*, I resolved on an immediate retreat. I chose a trusty Moslem guide, who looked upon every Russian as a son of Sheitan. "On my head and my eyes be it," he said, "if I do not bring you through the Russian lines." Before daylight, away over the hills towards the opening of the Olti valley. Every kilometre the anxious question was heard, "Have you met the Cossacks?" Answer —"There is cavalry ahead, we don't know what they are." Three hours' ride and a long gorge opens away towards the flat of the Kars valley. Horsemen dot the plain. "Cossacks!" every one exclaimed, and we hurry away, *ventre à terre*, hotly pursued. Three men are hard at my heels. Seeing the crescents glittering on the pursuers' housings, "Selam alik," I said, turning rein. "Ou alikoum el Selam," was the reply. They were Circassians, as much on the look-out for the Russians as myself. To say that we were fatigued would be nought. For fourteen hours and a half we toiled over rocky summits, for we dared not go down into the plain below. I made the last couple of miles on foot, amid a storm of thunder and sleet and rain. I staggered into the village of Bashkoi, beyond the village of Hadja Kaké. The latter is the important village of the district, but we dare not halt there for fear of the Cossacks, who, the villagers told us, were sure to come that evening for forage. I was announced in the village as the "English Pacha," and the best hovel of the place was put at my disposal. The poor Kurd villagers (who, by the way, under other circumstances, would have complacently cut one's throat) swarmed round me for protection and information. I was tired to death with my fourteen hours' ride, but I managed by the light of the blazing fire logs to indite the copy from which this letter is written. The pen had dropped from my hand, I was utterly overcome with weariness, when loud noises were heard outside. Every one was afoot grasping his arms. My impression was that we were surprised by the enemy's cavalry. I rushed towards the door. Judge of my surprise—I almost upset Mukhtar Pacha himself. Behind him stalked General Sir Arnold Kemball, as grave us usual "What, you here?" the Marshal said. "Your Excellency," I replied, "I am a fugitive, before the bad weather and the fortune of war." The night was glacial. A great fire of pine logs from the Soghanli Dagh blazed on the primitive hearth.

How strange was that night. Some cold meat was produced and a kettle of tea was made. A general silence pervaded the *oda*. No one wished to be the first to speak. It was the respect one naturally pays to misfortune. Mukhtar Pacha turned to me abruptly and said, "What do you think of the enemy's artillery fire during the battle?" "Excellency," I said, and I felt a little shy about giving my true opinion, "I think the Russian artillery fire was very good indeed." "Yes," said the Marshal, "that was the grand point where they beat us. It was the old story of France and Prussia. Two days before the battle I sent spies into the Russian camp. They told me that one hundred and thirty young officers had arrived. I don't know to what nationality they belonged, but to them I attribute the excellence of the fire which beat us." The Marshal paused, and then with a smile he said to me, "This is the second time you have seen me beaten. You remember Verbitza?" I certainly did remember Verbitza, in Herzegovina, when the Montenegrins almost destroyed the Turkish army. "Excellency," I ventured to ask, "what may be our losses in the late fight?" The Marshal replied immediately, "We have lost twelve thousand prisoners; the loss in killed and wounded I don't know." Since then I have learned our losses. Over twelve thousand infantry prisoners, five thousand killed and wounded. Twenty-five guns captured, with seven Pachas, named as follows:—Hadji Rechid Pacha, commanding 1st Division; Hassan Pacha, Chief of Staff; Omer Pacha, General of Division, 3rd Division; Shefket Pacha, commanding 2nd Division; Nadjeb Pacha, General of Brigade; Mustapha Pacha, Division General; Omer Pacha, Hungarian Brigade General. At dawn we continued our dreary retreat over the dark mountain slopes, where the poor wearied soldiers had slept all night long amid the wet grass. Two thousand eight hundred men constituted the remnant of the army of Kars. Eleven thousand men had been left at Kars, with the few field pieces remaining; and we were retiring with what was left of the army in the field, dragging ten mountain guns over the muddy ways. I left Mukhtar Pacha with his scanty force on the slopes of the Soghanli Dagh. He seemed to hope to be able to effect a junction with Ismail Pacha coming from Bayazid. Meantime, all is panic here. The waggons for Trebizond are so laden with fugitive women that no place is left for men.

ERZEROUM, *November 3rd.*—I am not a Turk, and yet I can't help echoing the talk of a good many Mussulmans here. "Why were we defeated at Aladja?" they ask. That, I take it, is a question few could answer, perhaps not even the Commander-in-Chief. I know the General intimately. He excuses his want of success by the runaway conduct of his soldiers. "I could see no reason for their flight," he said to me on the memorable evening when, at the village of Bashkoi, we sat together all the night long. Yet it seems pretty simple. The Russians were numerous; our flank was turned; and nothing remained but retreat. For me, as well as for many other spectators, the question was why the retreat was commenced only at ten o'clock P.M. And then, why were the baggage and artillery horses sent away? One would have said, under such peculiar circumstances as surrounded that total defeat, why not send off that which was most precious, the army first, and afterwards the sacks of corn of the *Idaret* (Commissariat). It matters but little now why all this was not done. There are other considerations still more important. I have already described the fight as I saw it, standing side by side with the Commander-in-Chief; and afterwards as I saw it from a point which, from prudential reasons, I thought it best to occupy, when the critical moment had arrived, and when nothing but desperation could have retained a general on such ground as Mukhtar Pacha occupied that day. Now that all is comparatively over, and that the Russians are at the very gates of Erzeroum, people begin to find fault with Ghazi (Victorious) Mukhtar Pacha. They ask why, during the decisive combat, were the battalions of our army left behind on the summit of Aladja. Why did we lose seven generals and forty-two pieces of artillery—not twenty-five, as I wrote in my last letter, not wishing to exceed the possible loss? All this is incomprehensible for the moment. The fact remains, that of an army of eighty-five battalions and some seventy-two guns, we have only straggling, disorganized troops and stray cannon. No one can say what was the idea of the Commander-in-Chief. It is to be hoped he had an idea; at present, however, all is obscure. Together with the remnant of the army, 2,800 men and ten mountain guns, we fled from Kars. I left the General at Yenikoi, a village not far from the celebrated field of Khorumdusi. It was a sad wet day. The long white fog-clouds veiled the surrounding hills, and the wretched, barefooted soldiers, drenched to the skin, came straggling in, no one knowing where to go for his quarters. The Russians might have been close on our heels for aught any one knew to the contrary; and yet the Turkish troops were *pêle-mêle* in the village, without an idea of defensive preparations. It didn't matter much, perhaps. Two thousand eight hundred men more or less couldn't be of great importance in such a struggle.

I found the Marshal occupying my old quarters in the Konak, or principal house of the village. He was tranquil and composed as ever. The idea of "Kismet" never deserted him. I came to ask an order for some house in which I could remain for a couple of hours to dry my soaked garments and partake of a little food. The troops filled nearly every available hovel, and I was more than delighted when an aide-de-camp found me a kind of hay-loft where I could eat the thick sour milk and leathery bread which was the only food obtainable. Knowing the free-and-easy proceedings of the troops, the inhabitants had hidden away everything in the shape of eatables, save that which they could not deny, their every-day food. It was three o'clock in the afternoon as I mounted my horse amid a downpour of rain. General Sir Arnold Kemball and his aide-de-camp rode by, telling me they were en route for a village twenty miles farther on. Two hours' weary stumbling over mountain gullies, and along the banks of a flooded river, brought me to the village of Kara Urgau. Not a soul was left in the place, and amid the falling shades of night I pushed on to Zevin. There every one was packing up, and I was glad to find shelter in a kind of aboriginal hut, and luxuriate on a supper of sour milk and honeycomb. Then two days' ride to Erzeroum. Meantime Mukhtar Pacha retained his position at Yenikoi, sending two aides-de-camp to discover the whereabouts of Ismail Pacha retreating from Bayazid. They brought back word that the latter General, who on the 24th had left of Zeidikan, was menaced by a considerable Russian force coming from the north. A slight encounter took place, and Ismail succeeded in reaching Kuprikoi, uniting his eight thousand men with the three battalions at that place. On the 28th, Mukhtar, ascertaining that the Russians were advancing in force over the plateau of Khorumdusi, retreated with all his force to the plain of Hassan Kaleh. The same night his rear-guard was assailed, and he was forced to fall back on the position of Deve-Boyun (the Camel's-neck Defile), the last line covering Erzeroum. On the morning of the 29th the Russians were camped in the plain at the village of Khoredjuka, within cannon-shot of the guns of position in the Turkish redoubts. Only yesterday I counted their tents, and saw the Cossacks roving over the plain within three hours' march of Erzeroum.

At the commencement of the campaign I gave a *résumé* of the Turkish lines of defence. To show the present situation I recapitulate briefly. After Kars and its positions further east—those of Aladja, the scene of the terrible fighting and defeat on the 15th—come three distinct positions, where an army can make head against considerably superior forces—Khorumdusi (the scene of Mukhtar's victory), a plateau adjoining the village of Zevin, and two long days' march from Erzeroum, the lines of Kuprikoi, commanding the junction of the Bayazid, Kars, and Erzeroum roads, and the Deve-Boyun heights covering the last pass leading to the capital of Armenia. We were driven from Aladja; we fled past Khorumdusi, and we abandoned Kuprikoi for want of sufficient men to defend it. The enemy is at the very gates of Erzeroum. Deve-Boyun once lost, Erzeroum must soon go with it. The population of the town, Mussulmans as well as Christians, say plainly they don't want a bombardment, and will make no defence. The army, such as it is, some fifteen thousand demoralized soldiers, with a crowd of motley Bashi-Bazouks from Bayazid and Toprakaleh, cannot shut itself up here. That would be to leave the whole of Armenia in the invaders' hands, and to entail its own inevitable surrender. Hence the energy with which the all-important pass is being fortified. The one spare field battery has been sent from Erzeroum, and is being distributed among the different redoubts. Some batteries of mountain guns make a fair show at advanced points, and the hill-sides are being furrowed with intrenchments. The pass of Deve-Boyun is a narrow valley, leading due east from Erzeroum to the wide plain of Hassan Kaleh, the latter an old-fashioned Turkish town, near which are the fountains of the Araxes. The pass is skirted by rounded hills, and near its eastern extremity is crossed by a ridge which constitutes the second line of defence. Then comes a deep, precipitous ravine, and immediately beyond another ridge. On this is situated the headquarters of the army. It is the link between the hills which form the first and principal lines. Opposite its centre, slightly to the left, is a long hill, crowned by a steeply bounded plateau, narrow like the hill itself. It is strongly intrenched, and forms the centre of the defence. To its right are two conical hills, somewhat oblique to the front, on which are two redoubts, armed with guns of position, and occupied by several battalions. To the left of the long hill is a rounded mamelon, projecting spur-like from the lofty mountains which fringe the plain. From this mamelon long trenches extend further east, intended to secure our left flank. In front of all run two rivulets, which, uniting, form one of the tributaries of the Araxes. In case of need, a large portion of the front could be inundated by blocking the course of these streams. From every point of view the line is exceedingly strong, and, unless I am much mistaken, the Russians will not try to carry it by direct attack. But it has its weak points, which, to my mind, are fatal. To the north is the valley of Olti, parallel to the pass; to the south, another similar valley coming from the direction of Bayazid, and both debouching into the plain before Erzeroum. These valleys are separated from the plain of Hassan Kaleh by lofty mountains, at this season heavily covered with snow. By either of the valleys the enemy can turn the formidable barrier in their path; and our latest intelligence informs us that they are doing so. During my visit to the positions of Deve-Boyun yesterday, I had a conversation with Faizi Pacha, chief of the staff. He admitted the danger of the situation, while informing me that both these avenues of attack were occupied by our troops. "We hope too," he said, "to be able to link these forces on our flank with the centre." I am afraid, however, that the scanty Turkish army, fronted as it is by a formidable Russian force camped within cannon-shot on the plain in front, can scarcely afford the necessary troops to guard the lateral avenues. Conscious of this weakness, we are taking measures to inundate the opening of the Olti valley at a point close to the city named Giurji Boghas, close to the village of Hindsk. The Cossacks, coming by way of Olti and Nahriman, are already reported within view of these new defences. Then, again, there is the road leading from the Olti valley to Baiburt, by which, without the necessity of striking a blow, the enemy can cut our communications with Trebizond and the Black Sea coast. It is probably with a view of hindering this movement, for which a few squadrons of cavalry alone would suffice, that the long-promised reinforcements, if they really exist, have, as we are told, arrested their march at Baiburt. Meantime, with our fourteen or fifteen thousand men, the sum of the united fragments of Mukhtar's and Ismail's armies, we await our fate. In Erzeroum a panic prevails. A large number of persons refuse to open their shops, all business is at a standstill, and every day hundreds of women crowd the waggons going to Erzingan and Trebizond.

CHAPTER XX.

INVESTMENT OF PLEVNA AND FALL OF KARS.

Arrival of the Guard before Plevna—Completion of Divisions from the Reserve—General Gourko on the Orkanieh-Plevna Road—Capture of Gorny Dubnik, Teliche and Dolny Dubnik—Completion of the Investment—Osman Pacha's Position—Turkish Prisoners of War—Condition of Kars—Artillery Attack on the Fortress—Capture of Fort Hafiz Pacha—Summons to surrender—Defiant Refusal—Grand Assault on Kars—Capture of the Fortress and Garrison, Guns and Stores—Rejoicings at Plevna.

THE failure of the third attack on Plevna had convinced the Grand Duke Nicholas that he had no longer anything to hope from a repetition of those headlong front attacks upon earthworks in which, until that time, all the art of his staff had consisted, while it was only too evident that the tremendous losses sustained before Plevna were seriously affecting the *morale* of the soldiers. It was therefore resolved to call for the aid of the skilful officer of engineers who had designed the defence of Sebastopol, and also to await the arrival of the new troops who were by this time well on their way. Whether the necessity of completing the investment of Plevna was foreseen when General Todleben was sent for is uncertain, but it was recognized soon after he arrived in the camp, when also the weekly appearance of new troops promised to furnish before long the means of completing the blockade. Osman Pacha, having repulsed the last and greatest attack upon his position, showed himself anxious for the despatch of supplies and reinforcements. General Kriloff, as we have already seen, had been sent with a strong body of cavalry to guard the road from Orkhanieh to Plevna, but proved lamentably unequal to the task. On the 21st September Ahmed Hifzi Pacha set out from Orkhanieh with a convoy of fifteen battalions, a battery of eight guns, and a long train loaded with provisions and ammunition. The train advanced slowly, but Kriloff so little understood what he had to do that it entered Plevna without the loss of a single waggon, Kriloff taking credit in his report for not having lost a man in opposing its progress. A second convoy reached Osman Pacha in like manner, as a third would have done, had not the Roumanians interfered and captured it. An end, however, was soon to be put to these displays of Russian helplessness. The Guard had arrived, and the ranks of the battalions which had fought during the summer had been filled up. General Gourko, who since his retreat to the Shipka Pass had not been actively employed, now received orders to assume the command of a strong cavalry force, and to take possession of the Orkhanieh road. His arrival on the scene was the signal for activity of a most productive kind. The first intimation of his advent was the announcement that he had captured the position of Gorny Dubnik, the centre of the principal Turkish defences on the Orkhanieh road. The place was strongly intrenched with a large redoubt of four hundred yards, flanked by two smaller works. It was held by twelve battalions of Turks, and was attacked by twenty-four battalions, with sixty-four guns, and a regiment of cavalry. The fighting lasted from six A.M. to six P.M., when the Turks hoisted the white flag; five of their battalions escaped to Plevna, while seven surrendered. This success cost the Russians 154 officers and 3,000 men. On the same day a division of the Guards sent against Teliche, a fortified position west of Gorny Dubnik, suffered a severe repulse. Teliche, however, was captured on the 29th of October, when five battalions surrendered after a feeble resistance. On the 1st of November, Dolny Dubnik, east of Gorny Dubnik, was taken. It was held by 5,000 Turks under a Pacha, and was fairly intrenched, but when General Gourko advanced against it with a division and a half and sixty-four guns, and opened a cannonade, followed by rifle firing, the Turks, having the road to Plevna open to them, abandoned the place, General Gourko not losing a man. With the occupation of Dolny Dubnik, the road from Plevna to Sofia through Orkhanieh was closed, and the investment of Plevna was regarded as complete. The Russian cavalry now made excursions over a large extent of country south of Plevna, capturing the Turks' supplies, who since the loss of the road to Plevna had been counting on an army of relief to be formed at Orkhanieh. They took Teteven, near Orkhanieh, and Vratza, and then Etropol, within ten miles of Orkhanieh itself. The following letters relate to these transactions :—

† BUCHAREST, *October 26th.*—The news has just been received here of the fight on the Sofia road. The Turks had fortified a position there between Gorny Dubnik and Teliche, and it was here, it will be remembered, that General Kriloff tried to stop Chefket Pacha's convoy by attacking a fortified position with cavalry and artillery instead of the convoy itself. The Turks have evidently been trying to reopen their communications by establishing a number of small forts along the Sofia road. This was one of them, and as it was probably too near the Russian line to be convenient they took it, as they will undoubtedly take any others there may be this side of the Balkans. The Russians have 3,000 prisoners, one regiment of cavalry, and four guns. The fighting, it is said, was hard, and the Russian losses considerable.

A Russian officer just returned from the positions before Plevna gives me the following account of affairs there. It is untrue that the Turks have succeeded in getting any supplies of provisions into Plevna lately. No convoy has succeeded in getting through since about the time that General Gourko took command of the cavalry. The investment of Plevna has been complete now for about a week; that is, an investment with the aid of infantry. As fast as the soldiers of the Imperial Guard arrived they took up their position on the Russian left, where General Skobeleff stands with the 16th Division, continuing the line of investment over the Loftcha road, on to the Sofia road, and further round as fast as the troops arrived.

There is a large force of infantry on and near this road, and the line is continued from here to the Roumanian right by the Russian and Roumanian cavalry under the command of General Gourko. The investment is therefore complete, and it is evident from the manner in which it has been done, and from so much infantry being sent behind Plevna, that the Russian plan looks farther than merely obliging Osman Pacha to withdraw from Plevna. In fact, if it were merely a question of stopping supplies, a large force of cavalry under General Gourko would have sufficed. It is true he could not have prevented the arrival of reinforcements, but with his artillery he could always smash the waggons, kill the horses of the train, and destroy the supplies, even if he could not capture them. Infantry was, therefore, not absolutely necessary on the other side of Plevna, and that such a strong force has been sent seems to point to the intention of the Russians not only to starve out Osman Pacha, but to cut off his retreat likewise. It is impossible to ascertain for exactly how long Plevna is provisioned, and it is probable that the Turks themselves do not know; but it is evident that, unless their supplies are sufficient for the whole winter, Ghazi Osman Pacha will soon be in a most critical position, one resembling somewhat that of Bazaine at Metz. We may suppose that Osman will show more patriotism, more generalship, and especially more tenacity than Bazaine; but it is evident that unless he has a much larger supply of provisions than is believed, he will soon be in a bad way.

The Russians are receiving reinforcements every day, and there is every appearance that they intend to surround Plevna as the Germans did Paris with a series of works, through which Osman will find as much difficulty in breaking as General Trochu did with the German intrenchments around Paris. Osman will have to fight his way out or surrender sooner or later, for the Russians will soon have enough troops to complete the investment by infantry, and make a circle of resistance as solid as that of the Germans around Paris. The only question is for how long is Osman Pacha supplied with provisions. As the Turks have had all summer in which to store up provisions in Plevna, there is really no good reason, except Turkish improvidence, why they should not have enough to last them until next spring; but there is every reason to believe that they have not so much. My informant thinks that the fact of the Turks having sent fifteen or twenty thousand men as reinforcements into Plevna some weeks ago, is evidence that they do not fear running short of supplies. But this by no means follows. In the first place, the reinforcements escorted large convoys of supplies, which would not have got through without an escort. Then, besides, the Turks could not know that a complete investment would be attempted, and may have hoped to prevent it. The arrival of these reinforcements, therefore, is no proof that there are plenty of provisions in Plevna. The appearances are that Osman will attempt to force out his way through the Russian lines sooner or later, and that the attempt will end in a disaster as complete as that of Mukhtar Pacha.

I must say, now that the question of a second campaign is resolutely faced, the prospect is more hopeful for the Russians than at any time since General Krüdener's defeat in July.

† BUCHAREST, *October 28th.*—The battle at Gorny Dubnik seems to have been a more serious affair as regards fighting than I could at first have supposed. When General Kriloff was there there was only a small earthwork, which the Turks appeared to have constructed in haste as a sufficient obstacle to cavalry, but one that would not have stopped a strong force more than a few minutes. The Turks must have strengthened and reinforced it since then. It is situated near the road in the middle of a plain, on a very slight eminence, and possesses no natural advantages of position. As the Turks have established a line of these posts to keep open the road, they cannot put a large number of troops in any one of them without weakening the army in Plevna. They probably had five or six thousand men here, yet the Russians acknowledge a loss of twenty-five hundred men, which shows the terrible effects of breech-loading arms properly handled. Nevertheless the Russians took it, and as they surrounded the place before attacking it no part of the garrison could escape. All were either killed or taken prisoners.

As the Russians report that two thousand prisoners were taken, the Turkish loss would probably be between three and four thousand killed. The result of the affair is to show that the Turks cannot keep the road open by this system of small detached forts. There has been a rumour here that the Turks have recaptured part of the positions; but this I do not credit. The Turks could not have a large force near there, and, as there are two divisions of the Guard over the River Vid, it is not likely that the Turks could have recaptured anything from them.

† BOGOT, *November 4th.*—The belief here that Plevna cannot hold out more than a few days longer is very strong. No supplies have reached the place for more than a month, and it is invested by a circle of earthworks manned by forces that are growing stronger every day with the arrival of troops from Russia.

The question now is, What will Osman Pacha do? It is pretty certain that he has no great amount of supplies, that his troops are suffering severe privations from hunger and cold, and that much depression and discontent prevail is evident from the number of deserters who come in daily. The easy surrender of Teliche after five hours of artillery fire is an ominous event which points to the same conclusion—that is, a scarcity of provisions. They probably never thought that the Russians could completely invest Plevna, or only thought so lately, as was shown by their feeble attempt to keep open communications by building a line of small detached forts. Osman Pacha has no hope of relief from outside, and if he is as short of supplies as is believed here, he must ere long choose between surrendering at discretion or cutting his way through the Russian lines.

The Russians seem to think he will surrender, but I for my part have no doubt he will attempt to cut his way out. Whichever he chooses, the result will be a disaster to the Turkish arms. He can undoubtedly succeed in escaping with part of his army, if he does not allow his troops to become too much weakened by hunger before making the attempt; but he will lose his artillery, which may not after all be worth much, as a great deal of it is disabled; and will lose more than half his army. His effective is now estimated at 45,000 men. After deducting for losses and sickness, if he reached Sofia with 20,000 he would be lucky; for it should be remembered that the Russians hold not only one point on the Sofia road but the whole road up to the summit of the Orkhanieh Pass, which is practicable, it seems, for an army. He will have to break through three lines of intrenchments, and although his troops are good in defending trenches, they are not so good in attacking them. If the Turks in trenches can repulse the Russians, the latter can much more easily repulse the Turks under the same circumstances.

The Russian lines are completely connected by a telegraph encircling the place, so that the Russians can concentrate immediately upon the point of the circle that is attacked. This is further facilitated by the peculiarity of the ground, which enables the Russians to see every part of the Turkish positions from some point in the Russian lines. Any concentration of the Turkish troops can therefore be seen and the numbers estimated, unless such concentration be made at night. Even then the exact numbers could be seen at daylight, as soon as the movement began, so that it is impossible for Osman Pacha to gain time by making feints. He will simply have to gather his troops together during the night, and throw them in a mass upon some point of the Russian lines at daylight, and get through. The result can hardly be less than disastrous, though less so, perhaps, than capitulation.

Much speculation is indulged in as to the direction in which Osman Pacha will try to break through. It seems more than likely he will attempt it by the Widdin road, where the

Russian line is weakest; but although this appears his greatest chance of success, perhaps that success, if attained, would be of little use; for while one half of the Russian army pursued him, the other half could cross the Balkans, and crush Chefket's small force at Sofia. Osman Pacha's object upon getting out should be to effect a junction with either Chefket, Reouf, or Suleiman, which would be impossible if he broke through on the Widdin side. The Sofia road and the line from the Loftcha road are held by the Guard. The Loftcha road is held by Skobeleff, on ground which he has fought over twice. The passage cannot be effected except by the most desperate fighting and the most fearful losses. Should he attempt on the east to effect a junction with Suleiman, he would, supposing he succeeded in breaking through the Russian lines and earthworks, still have with the remnant of his army to meet the Army of the Jantra with the Grand Duke Nicholas on his back. Everything considered, I think Osman Pacha's chances are bad, unless he has three or four months' supply of provisions. Nevertheless, skill and energy might do wonders, if seconded by incapacity and stupidity on the other side. At any rate, the result of this Plevna campaign must be a great military event, and one of the highest interest. The weather is fairly good. There is rain and sunshine every day. The sky is clear nearly every night; the weather is warm; the roads are moderately good. Three days of rain or three days of sunshine would make them very bad or very good. There has been ten days of cold weather, during which the troops suffered severely, but now they are not badly off. The season of sickness has not yet begun, nor will it until the weather finally breaks up. This may not be until the first of December. Even then, should we be favoured by extreme cold and snow instead of rain, the health of the army would not suffer much.

The Russian reserve system seems to be working very well. General Skobeleff tells me his division, which suffered so severely in Krüdener's defeat, and which also lost heavily at Pelisat and in the last Plevna affair, numbers 11,500 men. Little is doing here in the way of bombardment. Three or four times only during the day a great crash breaks against the sky, and comes rolling back to us in muffled thunder. It is caused by one hundred to three hundred guns speaking in unison, and concentrated upon a single spot. General Todleben has had all the distances divided into small sections. There are about four hundred guns in position around Plevna. From one hundred to all the four hundred can be concentrated on any point of the Turkish positions; and whenever the Turkish reserves or any masses of troops can be detected anywhere, the guns are directed upon that spot, and a simultaneous fire is ordered by telegraph. For two or three hundred shells to fall in a small space, within a few seconds of each other, is fearful. This is the only way modern artillery can be made effective. The fire is sometimes concentrated on the redoubts, sometimes on the town in the same way. Had the artillery been handled in this way when assaulting the redoubts, it would have been useful. As no assault is intended now, it does little good, except when masses of troops are caught.

The Emperor arrived here yesterday, and went to Dorny Dubnik, on the Sofia road, accompanied by the Grand Duke Nicholas. They are to return to-morrow.

+ Bogot, *November 4th, Evening.*—Three detachments of prisoners passed through here to-day, counting in all perhaps 5,000 men. They were captured at the recent engagement on the Sofia road. One batch of officers came under a special guard, and bivouacked here for the night. There are 250 of them, including some who are said to be pachas, and one Englishman, who insists that he is a surgeon, but who is generally believed to have been an officer. His name I could not learn. Many of the officers are mounted. Some have pack horses, with quantities of effects. All are well dressed, and have no lack of warm clothing. They have plenty of money, which they spend freely for bread and tobacco, and seem, on the whole, to be gratified with their fortune, which has brought them into the hands of the Russians. The soldiers are comfortably clothed, and appear well-fed and healthy. These prisoners will be sent to Sistova, as was the batch of 3,000 which passed here two or three days ago. A very small escort accompanies them—almost ridiculously small, in fact—but they are quiet, and manifest no disposition to cause trouble.

† Dolny Dubnik, *November 6th.*—The Turks abandoned this place, lost the position they held on the Sofia road, and retreated into Plevna without firing a shot. The Russians were making dispositions to surround and capture the place as they did at Gorny Dubnik and Teliche. The Turks, seeing this, evacuated it at midnight. When the Russians advanced the next morning they did not find a soul.

It was the best thing the Turks could do, as it was evident the position could not be held. The capture of this place has enabled the Russians to shorten their line of investment considerably. Their line has now been drawn right round the Turkish works everywhere, and the investment is more complete and effective than I had thought, as every part is occupied by infantry, no part being left to cavalry. From Grivica round to the Loftcha road the line is just where it was at the moment of giving the assault at the last attack on Plevna. The artillery occupies the ridge before Radisovo, with the guns extended down the line towards the Loftcha road to not more than a mile from Plevna. On the Loftcha road General Skobeleff is not as far advanced as he was at the time he made his assault. The Turks, taking advantage of the moment after the battle when the Russians had withdrawn, and warned that they were not invulnerable here, have constructed four new redoubts, so that Skobeleff now, instead of three redoubts, has seven before him. When Skobeleff first attacked here, when Krüdener was defeated, he found no defences at all, and he entered Plevna but with only one battalion. His line is now considerably in front of a village called Brestovec. From here the line extends to the Vid. It then crosses the Sofia road about a mile from the bridge over the Vid. From here it passes parallel to the river until just below Opanes, where it again crosses the Vid, and curves round to the Grivica redoubt, about a mile in front of Grivica. The Russian line of investment is thirty miles long. The Turkish position measures from the Grivica redoubt to the bridge over the Vid eight miles; from the Krishine redoubt to the Bukova redoubt is about five miles. The line is is of an irregular, oval shape, with a circumference of about twenty miles.

With the force the Russians have here now, 120,000 men, they can fill two lines of continuous trenches around the whole line of investment as full as it is convenient for men to lie in trenches. It will be seen, therefore, that Osman Pacha is surrounded by a circle which it will not be easy to break through. As to the supply of provisions, accounts continue to be contradictory, but since my last telegram a herd of about five or six thousand head of cattle, whose existence was not known before, has been discovered, by having been driven out to feed on the hills. Other indications point to the probability that Osman may hold out thirty or forty days yet, though not longer. His army is already on short rations, however. Ten soldiers receive two and a half pounds of meat daily between them, and the supply of corn and flour is not thought to be great. At any rate, whether Osman has supplies for one month or for three, the result must be the same in the end. He will have to surrender or cut his way out, either of which will be such a disaster for the Turkish arms that Russia will be enabled to bring the war to a rapid conclusion. Turkey can never raise such another army as that of Osman Pacha, and the loss of this army is now only a question of some weeks more or less. The Russians will stay here till Plevna falls, and we think we already see the beginning of the end.

The soldiers have built for themselves very comfortable huts all along the line of positions, and although they will undoubtedly suffer in case of a rainy winter, they will be able to keep up the investment with ease. As to supplies, the army on the west side of the Vid can live on the country between the Danube and the Balkans nearly up to the Servian frontier by means of their cavalry. The country is rich in Indian corn, wheat, barley, hay, and straw. On the other side, they will be supplied from Roumania, and this can be done with ease. Everything considered, the Russian prospects are brighter than they have been since last July, and everybody feels it. The change of feeling since I was here last is very great Much of this cheerfulness is, I believe, owing to the fact that such men as Todleben, Gourko, Skobeleff, and Imeritinsky have come to the front, and, although not forming part of the staff, have active parts in the direction of the war. But the great fact is that Osman is caught in his own net and cannot escape.

The inherent weakness of an army such as the Turkish, that can only act on the defensive, now becomes glaringly evident. If Osman's army could manœuvre on the field of battle; if it had discipline, good officers, tactical education, enabling Osman to handle it as an army should be handled, he would not undoubtedly allow his communications to be cut and himself to be shut up like a monster spider in his own web. He would have retired from Plevna before it was too late, have refused battle against superior numbers, but have hovered on the Russian right flank ready to strike at a favourable moment—a continual menace to the Russian communications. The enemy could never cross the Balkans as long as this army remained anywhere between Plevna and Widdin; and with its back to the Balkans it could always have defied attack, as easily as at Plevna. Such might have been the development of the campaign if Osman Pacha's army were like a European one, capable of acting on the offensive, of manœuvring in the open country, of executing rapid movements, of striking swift, heavy blows. As it is, his troops can only sit in the trenches and shoot until they are all starved out like wild beasts.

By the beginning of November the Russian army had not only been joined by all the new corps which had been summoned from Russia, but all the battalions before Plevna had been brought up to their full strength. Their girdle of investment was tightened by the Russians whenever any ground was to be gained. The following letter describes a struggle which grew out of a successful attempt in this direction made by General Skobeleff:—

† GENERAL SKOBELEFF'S HEADQUARTERS, BRESTOVEC, LOFTCHA ROAD, *November 10th.*—The monotony of the last few days has at last been broken by an affair which, although not of very great importance, has nevertheless kept us employed for the last twenty-four hours. As might be expected, the break in the monotony of our existence came from Skobeleff, who is one of those restless spirits that cannot keep quiet. However, he had very good cause for action in the present case.

I have already described the Russian line of investment, mentioning with the rest Skobeleff occupying his old positions on the Loftcha road. This is the only point on the line where the Russians do not hold the same ground as at the moment of the assault. After the battle of Plevna it was thought unsafe to remain here, and Skobeleff was ordered to fall back on Tucenica, completely abandoning the Loftcha road, and placing an impassable ravine, which runs parallel to the road about a quarter of a mile distant from it, between him and the Turks. When he again advanced to occupy his old positions he found, as I have already stated, that the Turks had considerably advanced theirs, and had constructed four new redoubts. He succeeded, however, in occupying Brestovec, on the left of the road, and in constructing a redoubt in front and on the left of the village, and the line of trenches across the road to the ravine already mentioned. The Brestovec redoubt is just opposite the Turkish Krishine redoubt, from which it is distant about 1,300 yards. But this Brestovec redoubt forms a kind of angle projecting into the Turkish lines, and was somewhat exposed and dangerous. It became necessary to strengthen the Russian line. This could be done by seizing the small wooded hill immediately in front of the right wing between the Loftcha road and the ravine already spoken of.

It was most unfortunate for the Russians that these positions were ever abandoned, for they are about as high as the Krishine redoubt, they completely command Plevna, and the two redoubts captured by Skobeleff in the last affair, and fortified, would have rendered the Russian positions here much stronger than they can now be made. The Turks have now constructed a strong redoubt on the summit of the hill between the Krishine redoubt and the Loftcha road, the very spot where Skobeleff planted two batteries during the last affair. It was not the hill with the redoubt which Skobeleff resolved to capture, but one between the Loftcha road and the ravine. It was defended by trenches, and held by about fourteen tabors, perhaps 7,000 men, though Todleben believed there were a great many more, as the position was most important. The combined movement was arranged with General Gourko, who was to open fire all along the line, and likewise advance and occupy the position in front of him towards the bridge over the Vid, in order to shorten his line likewise. The weather, which for several days had been very fine, became foggy last night, and a thick heavy fog hung over us all day yesterday, reminding me very much of the day we last attacked Plevna; but the fog was neither so wet nor so cold. It was so thick that one could not see more than fifty feet.

The attack was fixed for five o'clock. By that time it was so dark that nothing could be seen more than five feet off. Skobeleff reviewed his troops that were destined for the attack—the battalion of sharpshooters. He then got down from his horse, went about among the men, talked to them, told them, especially the under-officers, just what they were to do, and finished by informing them he would lead the assault in person. This regiment, I may remark, was one which attacked and carried these same heights during the last affair of Plevna on the second day of the bombardment. The regiment, having taken these heights, slipped out of the hands of its officers, and pursued the Turks to the foot of the glacis of the redoubt afterwards captured by Skobeleff, with the result that two-thirds of the regiment were destroyed. The regiment is now full again with reserves that have come up. It was the recollection of this event that decided Skobeleff to lead the attack himself. It was important that the men should be stopped at the right moment and at the right place, and that the intrenchments which he intended to throw up should be properly laid, as a little mistake easily made might end disastrously. It was not, therefore, mere bravado which made him decide to lead the assault himself.

At half-past four he mounted his horse, put himself at the head of his troops, and disappeared in the fog. At five o'clock the fog began to turn dark, showing the approach of night. The Turks must have thought there would be little call for further vigilance that day. On the approach of darkness the roar of eighty guns was heard that vomited splashes of flame upon the murky fog, and then were silent. Then came the scream of eighty shells seeking their destination in the obscurity. Then there was the crash of the infantry fire along the whole line except on the point of the attack, for it was Skobeleff's design to use the fog for cover and take the Turks by surprise. The infantry fire rolled along in front of Brestovec, where I had taken my station, and soon the bullets began singing overhead, telling that the Turks were replying; but we could hear as yet little firing on the right wing, where the attack was to take place. Finally, after about a quarter of an hour, there were two or three volleys in this direction, followed by a Russian shout, and we knew the position was carried.

As it turned out, the Turks were surprised, and did not discover the approach of the Russians until they were within one hundred yards. By the time they had seized their arms and fired two rounds, the Russians were on them with the bayonet, and it was all over. In a moment those who did not fly were bayoneted. The attack was led by two companies of sharpshooters, followed closely by the 9th Battalion and the Vladimirsky regiment. Every man was provided with a shovel, and immediately began making trenches, as indicated by Skobeleff. In a very few minutes they were under cover from a heavy but ill-directed fire poured into them from the next hill, not distant more than 250 yards. Skobeleff stayed until about ten o'clock, when he thought the men had made the place secure, and returned to Brestovec to supper. He had scarcely washed when the fire broke out again with fury on the right flank. Skobeleff mounted again, disappeared in the darkness and fog, and did not return till this morning. He found the Turks making a desperate attempt to recapture the position, and arrived on the ground in the nick of time, as some confusion had ensued, for the reserves, who lost their way in the fog, coming in the wrong direction, got fired into from their own side. There was also a report that Skobeleff was killed, which discouraged the troops. He arrived in the middle of the Turkish assault, one fellow having leaped into the trench with the cry of "Allah!" where he was bayoneted. The attack was repulsed, but the Turks made a second and third one, and each time were driven back with ease.

The position, if not taken within the next twenty-four hours, may be considered secure. The Russian loss was comparatively small, only 250 killed and wounded, among whom were two or three officers, one being Captain Dombrowsky, of the sharpshooters, of whom Skobeleff speaks in the highest terms.

The Turkish loss, of course, was much heavier, as the Russians were under cover almost immediately on getting possession of the hill, and lost less than a hundred in the assault itself. The weather is fine again to-day.

BUCHAREST, *November* 11*th*, *Night*.—A Russian success is reported here to-day—the occupation of Vratza by General Gourko. This victory is evidently of some importance. Vratza, or Vraca, as spelt on the Austrian map, is situated some fifty kilometres west of Plevna, and although only occupied by 1,500 Turks, mostly irregulars, still formed a considerable depôt of ammunition and provisions, which, I hear, are now safely in the hands of the Russians. The loss on the Russian side is reported small.

+ HEADQUARTERS OF GENERAL SKOBELEFF, BRESTOVEC, *November* 10*th*.—This village has been in Russian hands only three or four days, and even now is in the ragged edge of the Turkish infantry fire from the rifle-pits in front of the Krishine redoubt which crowns the summit of the smooth hill to the north. Stray shells make the empty houses re-echo with a musical prolongation of the noise of the whizzing bits, and the singing of the Peabody-Martini bullets is heard at short intervals day and night through. The village is not an agreeable place of residence, for it occupies a little valley only a few hundred yards from the Turkish works, and the dip seems to be just at the right angle to pick up all the odd bits of lead and iron that come anywhere in this direction. The casualties are perhaps more numerous here than in the trenches, on account of the peculiar conformation of the ground; but, then, to be anywhere in the neighbourhood of General Skobeleff is always to be in dangerous quarters. The trenches run along the northern edge of the village, behind the garden hedges, and out across the open slope to the left, into a battery on the hill directly opposite the Krishine redoubt. The former position was back on the Loftcha road, but a young officer of the 16th Division saw a good opportunity of flanking the Turks who held this point three or four days ago, and with a hundred men drove them out of the place, and occupied their lines himself. This village, by the way, is just where the village of Krishine is marked on the Austrian map, a half-mile north-west of the hill where the Loftcha road descends into the valley towards Plevna. This new position of General Skobeleff not only brings him nearer to the Turks, but shortens the line of investment materially. There is a certain green hill to the north of the line, thinly wooded, and not over five hundred paces from the battery on the Loftcha road;

on the slope of this hill has been stationed the advanced picquets of the Turks, who have made it at times decidedly uncomfortable for passers between the battery and this village, and have sent a multitude of compliments in this direction. General Skobeleff has been meditating for some days the capture of this territory, and it was decided to attempt the advance last evening, in conjunction with a forward movement of General Gourko on the left.

We had been basking in the warm sunshine for a day or two, and had begun to believe that it was the real Indian summer after all, but yesterday morning the sun rose pale and feeble, no warmth penetrated the thick curtain of fog that clung to the earth, and as the day advanced the mist grew more and more dense, until, by the middle of the afternoon, it was impossible to see the distance of a hundred yards. All the forenoon the troops were moving in small detachments toward the place of concentration near the Loftcha road, and every-one knew that an attack was arranged for five o'clock in the afternoon. The fog effectually concealed the hostile lines from one another, and the batteries were silent. To us who were waiting this silence was ominous, for it was broken by the muffled tramp of men and words of command as the detachments went away into the fog. At three o'clock the ragged red and yellow flag was taken from its place by the side of the door of the low mud hovel occupied by General Skobeleff, and the staff assembled to inspect the troops and to accompany the General, who was to conduct the attack in person. It was a most picturesque and romantic cavalcade that filed out of the yard and followed the young leader out to certain danger and possible death. General Skobeleff, alike heedless of cold and damp and whizzing missiles, was the only one who was not bundled up in overcoat and capuchon. He led the way through the narrow alleys of the village, mounted on a white horse—the soldiers look for the white horse as much as for their beloved commander—confident, cheerful, inspiriting to look upon. Behind him a motley retinue; Circassians with long surtout and silver-mounted harness and weapons; blonde youths already scarred and covered with decorations, correspondents in civil dress, Cossacks half hidden in their grey-coats and hoods, and in the middle of the group a picturesque Circassian on a white horse, bearing the tattered banner, quite like an old crusader, with his quaint arms and curious dress. The flag, too, is quite mediæval in appearance, and completed the illusion to perfection. It is a square silk banner, fastened to a Cossack's lance, and has on the one side the white cross of St. George, and on the other the letters M.C. (Michael Skobeleff), and the date 1875, in yellow on a red ground. The tattered silk was carried through the Khokand campaign, and has fluttered in all the hard fights which have made the young General so famous. We went on, losing our way a dozen times, and at last reached the spot where the troops were massed near an encampment of straw huts, all drawn up in order, with arms in hands and with spades to intrench the ground they were about to take; stretcher-bearers in a group at the rear, a suggestive but unpleasant sight; a battery of mitrailleuses bundled up like so many human beings to keep out the damp, and in front of the troops, the little body of picked men, each with his shovel, his rations, and plenty of ammunition, who were to make the first rush across, use the bayonet, and then throw it aside for the spade, and endeavour to cover in time to resist the attack of the returning Turks.

It was a dramatic and intensely impressive scene, these square masses of earnest men, every one with his eyes fixed on the face of the General, who passed before them all with the customary greeting, which was answered with a will like one voice from the battalion, in turn. Against the background of grey mists which had now settled down so thick that objects were not visible the length of a company front, came out the forms of men and horses in exaggerated relief, and made wonderfully picturesque the groups and masses of expectant soldiers. General Skobeleff dismounted and told the men just what he expected of them—that they were not to storm the works of Plevna, but only to run forward and take the piece of ground they knew perfectly well in front of the road, and to hold it until they had works thrown up. He cautioned them, as many were young soldiers sent out from the reserves to fill the great gaps in the ranks, not to advance too far, but to mind exactly what the officers told them. He would be with them himself, and would direct the movements personally. Surely a finer lot of men never went into a fight; young, healthy, devoted, and confident, every face wore an expression that was a proof of courage and earnestness and even religious zeal. As we stood there the darkness rapidly increased, and it was nearly five o'clock as the troops moved forward at quick pace in front of the General and staff. As the men passed they all received encouraging words, and they went by smiling at the good-natured chaff from the General, who called to them by name, remarked on their new boots, which he said were like those of a Spanish don, and told the musicians they would play a waltz in the new redoubts on the morrow.

The perfect confidence of the soldiers, inspired by the presence of the man whom they regard as a protector, infallible leader, and beloved friend at the same time, made the success of the undertaking assured, and as they went down over the hill to the trenches, to await the opening salvo of artillery, we took our place—a little knot of non-combatants—in the trenches on the hill alongside the battery which was to give the signal for the assault. The hot breath of sixteen field pieces scorched our faces as the opening salvo shook the heavy air, then came a cheer on the right, just down in the hollow, and the singing of bullets filled the air over our heads. We were seated in the trench of the picquet line, and when the bullets began to chip off the twigs on the top of the breastwork, and plump into the earth at our feet, we began to look about us to see what we were depending on for support. Only a thin line of men were lying against the dirt, rifle in hand, anxiously trying to see some object in front to shoot at. An officer came along and extinguished all the fires, and kept cautioning and encouraging the men, ordering them to stop firing and to watch. The musketry rattled and roared in the hollow and off on the green hill on the right, and sounded like the surging of a storm. The battery alongside kept banging away, deafening us, and blinding us with the flash. In the dense fog every noise was magnified, and as the shells screamed past us and exploded with a sharp, ringing sound behind us in the village, it seemed as if they were ten times the ordinary size. The darkness was impenetrable, An officer or a couple of stretcher-bearers loomed up occasionally through the fog, and dodged and jumped into the ditch as the leaden shower came over us. Down below in the hollow we could see no flash, only from that darkness came a hot spitting of lead that made it almost certain death to face. The fog began to condense and gather on the ground, and the cold increased, and still the battle roared, and rose and fell, ceased and began again. At last it was evident from the firing that the position was taken, and we retired to the village to the music of the shells and bullets, and up to our little camp as quickly as possible, for we were anxious for men and horses. We found all safe, but tent and waggon riddled with bullets, and only one soldier's horse limping with a wound. We put the waggon in such shelter as we could easily find behind a straw stack, and awaited the next burst of battle, which we knew was sure to come. At a quarter-past ten it broke again, and the same fiendish noise and rattle went on as before, and the bullets and shells kept singing about our ears for a long half-hour, and all was silent, with an occasional cannon report, until daybreak, when we were awakened by a new peal of artillery, and had the same continuous rattle of bullets among the twigs. Then we learned the details of the occupation of the ridge, which have reached the public long before this by telegraph.

As I write the popping of rifles is heard on the ridge, for the Turks do not seem satisfied with the loss of the position, and make frequent but ineffectual attempts to regain it. A visit to the ground gained showed me what they had done in the few hours of darkness. An irregular zigzag trench runs across the hill to the further side toward the Tucenica ravine, where there is a square battery for the Gatling guns. Along the trenches and among the trees there is no sign of the struggle. The sights of a battle-field are only horrible after the affair is over, and it was a relief to find no dead man, no wounded man, no marks of a scuffle or a bayonet fight, even on the ground where the struggle had taken place. Now we are waiting the final result, and occupy our time in skirmishing about between the shelter and the fire for tea and food, and spend the moments of lull in the shower of bullets in arranging for the next burst of the lead mine. The penetration of the Peabody-Martini bullet is simply remarkable. At the distance of two thousand yards from the Turkish lines I have dug them out of a foot of solid earth of a threshing-floor. At the distance we are now from those who hold the rifles nothing short of a thick earthwork will stop them, for they skip merrily through the roofs of the houses and through the mud fences, and bury themselves deep in the earth. During the fight which has just taken place I have heard for the first time the new falconets at work. In a telegram I spoke of the use of these demi-cannon, as I called them for want of a better word. They are simply short rifles of about ·80 bore, breech-loading, and carrying a ball heavy enough to penetrate an ordinary breastwork and kill the man behind it at 250 yards. The report sounds more like the bursting of a small shell in the lines than like a gun, for it is just between the rifle and cannon report in volume. A telescopic rifle, with a good marksman to use it, would do more damage to the Turks than a thousand of the falconets, and put a stop to all circulation of soldiers in the open opposite the Russian lines.

I have given the notes of one day at Skobeleff's camp and headquarters. This is the treat he generally gives his visitors. The General himself is asleep on a stretcher in the trenches, and will not come up again until the occupation of the ridge is a settled fact, and there is no more danger of the Turks retaking it. It is no wonder that the soldiers of such a general fight well.

+ HEADQUARTERS, DOLNY DUBNIK, *November* 16*th*.—The position here remains unchanged. Since the seizure of the Green Hill by Skobeleff, already described in a previous telegram, no important movement has been undertaken by the Russians. The Turks have made three attacks upon Skobeleff's position on three successive nights, but were each time repulsed with heavy loss. The defence of this new position is most successful and brilliant, and the position itself is of more importance than I was at first disposed to acknowledge. Skobeleff remains night after night in the trenches, and has succeeded in pushing his lines up to within one hundred yards of the Turks. They are indeed so close to each other that scarcely a night passes without heavy firing. Fire is opened all along the line upon the slightest alarm. At the same time that Skobeleff advanced, the Guards pushed forward to a position directly under the Krishine redoubt, where the outposts now are, and the line extends back over the hills to near the bridge over the Vid. The village of Krishine remains neutral ground. Two days later the Roumanians and Guards advanced to within rifle-shot of the bridge.

The circle of investment is now drawn as close as can be without actually besieging the Turkish positions. Nevertheless, in only two places, at the Grivica redoubt and on Skobeleff's position, are they within speaking distance of each other. There has been very little artillery fire during the last two days, and Todleben seems to have abandoned his plan of concentrated volley firing upon specified points, and only puts it in practice once in forty-eight hours. Deserters coming in from the front of Plevna report that the soldiers receive three-quarters of a pound of bread daily, and a small piece of meat twice a week. They complain bitterly of the privations to which they are subjected.

At the same time that a million and a half of Turkish rations were captured at Vraca the families of several Bashi-Bazouks and seamen were taken. They passed through here yesterday, escorted by Lancers and Guards, on their way to Plevna, whither they are sent as a retaliatory measure for the Bulgarians who are driven from Plevna. They were looking very miserable, but were transported in ox-waggons filled with straw. They were treated here with the greatest kindness by the officers, who took them to their quarters, and gave them food and even money, in spite of the fact that one of the women shot a Russian sergeant in the streets of Vraca some time after the occupation. It seems like a severe measure as regards the women and children, but in all such cases the measure depends for its justification on its success. The *lex talionis* is a hard law. Nevertheless, it may prevent more suffering than it causes if it stops the Turks from driving Bulgarian women and children from their homes.

The weather still continues fine. There has been no rain since the 1st of the month, and if we are to judge by appearances it may still hold fine another month. Nothing new has transpired relating to the amount of supplies Osman has. It is believed he will be able to hold out for another month. The Russian troops are in excellent health, and, indeed, the weather is so fine that the officers who have indoor quarters prefer dining in the open air. There has been no attack to relieve Osman by a force coming from Sofia. There has been no fighting since the fall of Teliche, and the Turks have not shown themselves on this side the Balkans. Bulgarian spies have latterly reported that forces are on the march from Sofia estimated variously from 15,000 to 40,000 men, but these reports have little credit here. As the Russian cavalry is considerably advanced, we should have timely warning of their approach should any attempt be made.

The army of the Czarewitch had little occupation, besides that of making reconnaissances in the latter part of October and the first half of November. In one of these Prince Sergius Leuchtenberg, third son of the Grand Duchess Marie, sister of the Czar, was killed. He was attached to the staff of the Czarewitch, and had participated in several of the battles along the Lom, on every occasion showing himself courageous even to recklessness. He was out with his troops when a ball struck him in the forehead, death being instantaneous.

Before noting the rapid and critical development of the campaign in Asia, we may glance at the effect which the recent successes had produced in the Turkish capital :—

: : CONSTANTINOPLE, *November 9th.*—A movement has been going on in the capital during the last week about which I have found it difficult to get at the truth. Some of the mosques have been placarded with denunciations of Mahmoud Damat, the brother-in-law of the Sultan, attributing to him the misfortunes of the war, and charging him with having sold his country to Russia. All sorts of rumours have been current about him. Two days ago it was asserted that he had been poisoned.

Yesterday the Turkish newspapers stated that he had had a fit of apoplexy. I have reason to know, however, that he is well, and that if he has had any fit it must have been of a mild character. There is evidence, however, of dissension among the Pachas which may lead in a few days to important events. Hitherto Mahmoud Damat's influence at the palace has been sufficiently great to keep his enemies in check, but his deserved unpopularity is, I think, at last likely to bring about his downfall. He is unpopular alike with the Pachas and the people, and would no doubt have been got rid of long since but for the personal influence of the Sultan. The favour of the Sovereign, however, has, I believe, now been withdrawn, and Mahmoud may be considered in disgrace.

The outcry against Mahmoud is only one of the phases of the movement of which I have spoken. The party of Murad has been stirring, and on Friday and Saturday last the Government took the precaution of surrounding the Palace of Cheragan, where the late Sultan is confined, with soldiers. This movement is attributed to the Young Turkey party, though it is difficult to see what they would be at. There is no doubt a party, but I believe a very small one, in favour of Republicanism, of the meaning of which, except that it is government without a Sultan, they probably know nothing, and it may be well that some of the Pachas who are out may have been willing to use some of the hot-brained fanatics to get rid of the Sultan and the Pachas who are in, and take their places. It would be absurd to suppose that there was any patriotism in wishing to return to Murad. The present Sultan has done nothing which ought to make the Turks discontented with him, while Murad still continues in weak health. Another explanation attributes the movement in favour of Murad entirely to Mahmoud Damat, the theory being that it is of his creation, in order to gain the credit of himself bringing it to the notice of the Sovereign, and of showing him that he, Mahmoud, is still the only man who can render his seat on the throne secure.

It is fair to regard these signs of dissatisfaction and dissension as the result of the Turkish defeats in Asia Minor and about Plevna. The depression among the Turks of all classes is really very great, and is given expression to on every hand Notwithstanding that telegrams have been issued by Government concealing the real facts, the truth has none the less become known. Perhaps even the constant repetition of warnings to the newspapers that they will be suspended, the last of which appeared only yesterday, if they publish "false news," that is, news unpleasant to the Turks, or, in the words of the communication, "of a nature to trouble men's minds," makes the public believe the news to be worse than it actually is. Twice a week we receive our English papers, and a larger section of the receive community the newspapers of Athens. It is unnecessary to say that the latter represent nothing in a favourable light for the Turks, and yet it is from them rather than from the Turkish papers under a strict censorship that the general impression of the progress of the war is derived. Not only is the war going against the Turks, not only do they see a large amount of destitution, misery, and poverty in the capital and in the provinces, but most of them have come to understand that in spite of the bravery of their soldiers Turkey can gain nothing by the war which she has undertaken. I have spoken in previous letters of the enormous drain upon the Turkish population which the war has made, and I mentioned a fortnight ago that the last reserves have been called out. These men have been arriving during the last week, and yesterday I saw some hundreds of the latest arrivals drawn up in line to be marched up to the Seraskierate or War Department to obtain their uniforms and to be drilled. It was a sad sight. There could hardly have been a man among them under forty years of age, probably hardly a man who was not the father of a family or the supporter of one. But while such a sight to a European was sad, the effect could not be otherwise than depressing to a Turk. He knows that the chances against his winning have always been great, and are perhaps now greater than ever. But the more thoughtful among them know a fact which makes them more despondent still; that every month of war, whether they win or lose, is weighting them the more heavily in their struggle with the Christian races of the empire. For Europe the Eastern Question may mean a struggle simply between Russia and Turkey. The Turks know well that when the present war is over the silent, inevitable struggle which has been going on during the last thirty years for wealth, education, and supremacy must be resumed, and resumed with largely diminished numbers on the side of the Turks. In short, in this war the Turks have everything to lose and nothing to win, the greatest success that they can hope for being to lessen the terms which Russia will exact. The result of this knowledge is to increase the party in favour of peace, at the head of which is the Sultan himself. In a country where one set of Pachas is perpetually intriguing against another, and where defeat by the opposing party usually means banishment, there will always be a party which will encourage the outcry for prolonging the war, if the Pachas who are in attempt to make peace. Still, in spite of them, the peace party is growing stronger, and is daily increased by the belief, which M. Thiers also entertained, that the longer the war lasts the more exacting will be the terms of peace.

It was announced yesterday that the Porte, in consequence of urgent requests, has consented to allow neutral vessels still remaining in the Sea of Azof to pass through the Black Sea, the Bosphorus, and the Dardanelles, to the Archipelago, on the sole condition of stopping to sell their cargoes in Constantinople, when such cargoes consist of grain. Whether there are any neutral vessels now in the Sea of Azof may, I believe, be reasonably doubted. This much, however, is certain—that several vessels have left Constantinople with the connivance of the Government, have run the blockade, if one may speak of running a blockade where the permission of the blockaders is given; have returned with Russian cargoes to the Bosphorus, and have, of course, not been molested by the authorities. This is in Constantinople a matter of notoriety; the names of the vessels are known to everybody who cares to make inquiries, and the motives of the special permission given to their charterers are freely spoken of. The fact possesses this importance—that permission being granted to vessels under the Greek flag, a similar permission ought to be granted to English and other foreign vessels. Indeed, if any English vessel should be caught in attempting to run the blockade, the fact of permission having been granted to certain vessels raises the entire question of the existence of the blockade.

The two Geshoffs have now been in prison at Philippopolis over seventy days. Up to the present hour they have neither been interrogated nor subjected to any form of trial. No charge whatever has been communicated to them or to anybody else, except, possibly, Mr. Layard. It seems now that their detention has been further increased by a difference between the civil and military governors. Ibrahim Pacha, the military governor, has, however, now been removed; and a telegram has, it is stated, been sent by the Grand Vizier to bring the prisoners to Constantinople. After this they are to be exiled; why or wherefore, except that they are wealthy and influential Bulgarians who have not bribed sufficiently high, nobody can tell.

After his rapid flight from the battle-field of Aladja Dagh and from Kars, described by a correspondent in the preceding chapter, Mukhtar Pacha effected a junction with the forces of Kurd

Ismail Pacha, commanding the right wing of his army at Kuprikoi. Although this place had been fortified with a view to such danger as that which had now emerged, it was not deemed prudent to stay there; and the retreat of the united forces was continued through Hassan Kaleh to the Deve-Boyun heights covering Erzeroum, at a distance of six miles east of the city. There, thanks to the foresight of Mukhtar Pacha's Chief of the Staff, Faiza Pacha (a Hungarian named Kohlman), a strong position had been prepared; and there the army rested until the 4th of November, when General Heimann, who had been joined by General Tergukasoff, carried the position by assault after nine hours' fighting. The Turks lost forty-two guns, including guns of position and the whole of their field artillery.

The following letter describes the storming of the formidable Deve-Boyun position east of Erzeroum by the Russians under General Heimann:—

ERZEROUM, *November 5th.*—When I closed my last letter by saying that I thought the position of Deve-Boyun impregnable when attacked in front, and that in all likelihood the enemy would in preference try a turning movement, I little calculated on Russian *élan* and the dogged obstinacy of their attack. Yesterday they attacked us frankly in front, and took all our positions, after a hard day's fighting. The third and last barrier has been passed, and at the moment I write the Russian siege guns are being pointed on the town. We have been summoned to surrender, and Mukhtar Pacha's reply, as I telegraph to-night, is that he will defend the town while a single man remains.

The Russians, following up the disastrous retreat from Kars, had camped in the plain of Hassan Kaleh, at the village of Khoredjuka, about an hour and a quarter from the Turkish positions at Deve-Boyun. At this last-mentioned point the mountains girding the Hassan Kaleh plain on the north and south close in, forming a narrow pass leading to Erzeroum immediately beyond. From its peculiar form, and the curve which it describes, it has been named the "Camel's Neck." Its eastern entrance is guarded by three military positions, which on the occasion of the battle constituted our centre, right, and left. The centre is a long hill crowned by a narrow plateau strongly intrenched, and was defended by sixteen field-guns. The right, at the other side of a shallow valley, giving access to the pass, consisted of two conical hills, one dominating the other; behind them obliquely were two other mamelons occupied militarily. The right was commanded by Ismail Pacha, Vali of Erzeroum, and for some time past commanding the army corps of the right at Bayazid. The left of the position of Deve-Boyun consisted of a rounded hill, a spur thrown off by the higher mountains on that side. It was crowned by a redoubt, and lines of trenches stretched further west along the slopes of the adjoining hills. Thus the position, slightly concave towards the front, commanded all access to the pass. Its entire length was some three hours' march. To defend it we had an army of about 15,000 men. This consisted of 2,800 men, the remnant of the Army of Kars, which accompanied Mukhtar Pacha in his flight from that town; of 1,500 picked up at Kuprikoi; of 4,500 from Ismail Pacha's army, retiring from Bayazid; of stragglers who came up; of troops from the garrison, and of four battalions arrived from Trebizond. Faizi Pacha, an old Hungarian officer, chief of the staff, worked hard at the defences.

It was believed that the Russians would never dare attack in front the tremendous heights which fronted them. Our only care was the guarding of the valleys by which our flank could be turned. The Russians, with a rare ability, seem to have calculated on the general situation, the demoralized condition of the army, and the want of artillery which must necessarily have followed the capture of the forty-two guns at the battle of Aladja, took the bull by the horns, and stormed the position. The French courier coming from Persia had passed through the Russian lines on the previous evening, and had brought word that all the Russian generals were present, and with them the French military attaché, General de Courcey. This led us to imagine that something serious was pending, but all the same we never dreamt of the audacious *coup* in store for us. Bashi-Bazouks and Arabs from Orfa and Aleppo flaunted their tawdry rags in the muddy streets of Erzeroum, and universal confidence reigned throughout the town. At last the day of combat arrived. On Sunday, November 4th, the Russians launched their entire force against Deve-Boyun. This consisted of forty-eight battalions. (I give the statement of Mukhtar Pacha, commanding-in-chief the Turkish army.) Between eight and nine in the morning the long dark Russian lines were seen opening out in the wide dim plain that stretches away to Hassan Kaleh. The Russians are so given to an almost perpetual military movement that not much attention was attracted by the long lines of infantry in the plain. I had seen the same thing so often from the heights of Aladja that I turned away my field-glass, convinced that it was only a Sunday parade. Later on I found out my mistake. Gradually the long black parallel lines crept closer, so quietly that if one were not observing attentively, the shortening of the distance might pass for an optical illusion. But the Turkish gunners had more accustomed eyes, and the long white curdled smoke-cloud that breaks from the central battery announces that the fight has begun. Gun after gun puffs out without any apparent impression on the menacing lines. In fact, they are at long range, and at best Turkish artillery fire is far from excellent. Not so the enemy's artillery fire. Shell after shell is planted in our midst with a precision which recalls the battle of Aladja. "I don't believe," said one old Moslem officer at my side, "that Russian officers direct those guns; they are English or they are Prussian." I had seen the changed character of the artillery fire when the Russians drove us from before Kars backwards on the Soghanli Dagh. The Marshal himself, Mukhtar Pacha, called my attention to this extreme accuracy of fire, as he had done on a former occasion when the Russians stormed Evliatepessi Hill. An attack on the centre seems evident, but yet the Turks make no movement. Every one is at his post, and an ominous silence broods along the line, save when from the right the heavy guns thunder out at intervals. Suddenly the Russians open right and left, directing their dividing forces outside our extreme flanks; on one side towards the glens leading to the valley of Olti, on the other to the flank of the mountains south of Erzeroum. A stubborn resistance follows, for the Turks have had time to march battalions to the threatened points. All day long the dull roar of musketry reached us from the lateral valleys. On the left, Mehemet Ali Pacha, the bravest soldier in the Army of Anatolia, holds his ground. At the centre, Moussa Pacha, a Circassian chief, commands; on the right, two Pachas have already fallen, Rufat Pacha and Hakif Pacha. Hussein Pacha, the old artillery commander, takes their place, and the fight goes on. It is evident the Russians are getting the worst of it, for their fire begins to recoil along the dun hill slopes on both right and left flank. I believed it was a Turkish victory, and that we were sure of at least a month's fighting before Erzeroum could be even menaced.

It was three o'clock in the afternoon when we saw the enemy on both flanks retiring, to rally out of cannon-shot of our positions. During the side attacks the Russian artillery was hard plied, and of eighteen guns at our centre fourteen were dismounted or useless. Then a sudden inspiration seemed to seize the Russian General. His rallied battalions were hurled against the long hill which formed our left centre. Arrived at its base, a steep slope screens the assaulting columns from the fire of the defenders. Russian reserves are pouring steadily forward. The artillery of the attack continues its deadly fire. The Turks on the long hill waver —they fly. The Russians are already on the plateau. Mukhtar Pacha, with several battalions, dashes at once to the critical point. Too late! The officers of the battalions fall dead, and flight ensues. The centre is carried. "I remained there," said the Marshal to me afterwards; "I wished to die." But people came round him, and he was carried away. Then came a hurried retreat on Erzeroum. The darkness only saved the army from annihilation or capture. We lost forty-two field-guns and pieces of position, and about 4,500 men killed, wounded, and prisoners. The Marshal himself admits 1,000 killed. We are for the moment blocked in Erzeroum. To the Russian summons to surrender, the Marshal, after demanding twenty-four hours' grace, replied that while a stone of the fortress remained erect he would hold Erzeroum. We have 12,000 troops in garrison, much provisions, and plenty of ammunition. It is from the plain west of the town that we fear assault. I write these lines hurriedly, just before the departure of an unexpected Consular courier, as welcome as unforeseen. The Cossacks already rove over the Erzeroum plain, and it may be this will be my last letter from the Turkish lines. Whether the Russians will let me write remains to be seen.

November 10*th.*—Yesterday at three o'clock A.M., the Russians surprised Azizieh Fort, which was retaken by the Turks after severe fighting, continuing all day.

The Russians are advancing along the mountains south of the plain to interrupt our communications with Trebizond. Heavy cannonading from forts and rampart continues. Orders from Constantinople forbid newspaper telegrams. To-morrow the town will probably be completely invested. The losses on both sides are exceedingly heavy. The population undoubtedly wishes to surrender.

On the night of the 9th of November, two battalions of the Elizabethpol Regiment surprised Mount Azizieh, which overlooks Erzeroum on the east, and which was defended by three great redans. They took 500 men and 20 officers prisoners, spiked

20 guns, and then retired, as Fort Medjidieh, commanding Azizieh, rendered the position untenable. The Russian loss was about 400. The attack was intended to have a far more important character, but according to General Heimann's official report several columns of the attacking force lost their way in the darkness, and thus the principal operation fell through.

On the night of the 12th of November another attack was made, but without success, and the Russian commander then determined to wait for reinforcements, in the meantime sending his cavalry out to cut off the communications of the city.

General Melikoff, who had convinced himself that the fortress of Kars might be captured by a skilful use of the means at his disposal, had remained before that city, removing his headquarters to Veran Kaleh, and kept up a lively cannonade against that place. On the 28th of October the correspondent with the Russians there wrote—

△ CAMP BOYUK TEKME, BEFORE KARS, *October 28th.*—Since the headquarters were removed from the Karajal Hills, subsequently to the battle on the 15th, fifty miles off and nine miles to the south-west of Kars, I have not had the opportunity of telegraphing or writing. We have no telegraph office yet at our disposal, and several days may still elapse before one is likely to be established anywhere near. My own transfer to this place was connected with much trouble. As I was unable to load my big tent and sundry luggage on a single pack-horse, I was obliged to apply for a bullock-cart. It was not an easy thing to obtain one, though it was understood that I should pay for it as liberally as possible. Only after urgent entreaty the governor of the conquered country, a good-natured old general, condescended to allow me the accommodation. Before obtaining it we lived at the Karajal camp as though we were out of the world. Officers passing occasionally knew either nothing about what was going on at the front, or narrated impossible events the coinage of their own fancy.

The removal of the Turkish prisoners was the last act performed in the great drama of the 15th instant. Now the curtain is lowered, but on the stage a new play is prepared—the siege of Kars and the attack on Erzeroum. Meanwhile, let me relate an episode of the victory of the 15th. General Gubski, the able and scientific head of the artillery before the Awli-Yer, on advancing after the storming of the hill towards Vezinkoi, was stunned by a rifle bullet, which grazed the top of his forehead, without wounding him. He fell senseless from his horse, but recovered half an hour afterwards, and then continued his duties incommoded only by a slight headache. A few minutes later, while in conversation with General Heimann and the young Prince Mirsky, a Turkish shell burst right between the party, covering them all over with earth, which filled their overcoat pockets; but not one of the three was even scratched by the fragments of the projectile.

On the 22nd I was gratified at last by obtaining the much-desired bullock-cart, on which the bulk of my household goods were placed. This two-wheeled vehicle has a close resemblance to those used by the Aryans in their migrations towards the West thousands of years ago. The axle-tree, turning round with the block-wheels, supports two long beams, joining at the fore part at a sharp angle with the thole for the bullocks by means of a wooden bolt. The bottom of this triangular construction is formed by three cross-beams and some hurdle-work. This primitive machine ploughs through the muddy country at the rate of two miles an hour. For all that I was as glad to hire it as though I had obtained a Pullman saloon. The journey was far from being a pleasant one. We reached at first Subatan, still distinguished by its solitary poplar tree, the branches of which have been badly dealt with by the bullets. At nightfall we reached Hadji Veli Koi. Both villages have witnessed a series of sanguinary engagements, and their lanes have been reddened with human blood. Now they lay in ruins deserted by the inhabitants. Only three or four of the larger semi-subterranean houses have been spared for the benefit of the military authorities. who make use of them as post stations, hospitals, or depôts. All the remaining huts have been destroyed by pulling down the timber supporting their flat roofs, which is indiscriminately used as fuel by the soldiers encamped here. The Turkish peasants have thus literally lost everything which they could not manage to take away in their carts. Only the rough cyclopean black walls and the excavations give evidence that people lived here a fortnight ago in comparative security, under the protection of their own soldiery. We found piteous accommodation there for the night in one of their hospital tents which had just been pitched, and underneath which the cold wind blew in. On the following day we passed slowly over the late battle-field, having on our right the Awli-Yer Hill, and on our left the hill from the summit of which Mukhtar Pacha had witnessed the discomfiture of his army. Here and there we met with the carcases of dead horses, or a still unburied corpse. All these places, which some days ago re-echoed with the roar of battle, were calm enough now. Only endless strings of bullock-carts and horse-waggons, conveying the Russian camp implements, moved towards Vezinkoi. Three heavy 24-pounders were equally on their way to Kars; each of them was dragged along over the steep track by a team of twenty-two buffaloes, while numerous vehicles conveyed their ammunition and paraphernalia. These formidable engines of war throw their projectiles a distance of six miles. They will be brought to bear against Kars, in the hope that the inhabitants will finally impress upon the military authorities the necessity of surrendering that fortress. I don't suppose that the fanatics inside care much about their hovels being knocked over. As I have heard since, they have not the slightest doubt of Ismail Pacha joining Mukhtar with 30,000 men somewhere, and of their coming quickly to the rescue of the beleaguered city. They may be grossly mistaken in their calculations. Independently of the fact that Mukhtar's troops are demoralized and very weak in numbers, Ismail too is not in a position to make a bold resistance. When he heard the news of the battle on the 15th, he took, on the 20th inst., to flight, pursued by sixteen battalions under General Tergukasoff's command. In his disorderly haste he has in the first place left about 4,500 of his sick and wounded behind, entrusting them to the generosity of his adversary, perhaps with the cunning view of hampering him. In the second place, hundreds of his soldiers desert daily, and others throw away their arms, ammunition, and knapsacks, with which the road to Erzeroum is strewn. These facts do not speak much for the efficiency of his forces, should he even be lucky enough to reach Mukhtar or Erzeroum before the Russians. In case, however, the two Pachas should succeed in entering Erzeroum with their hosts, by one way or another, the Russian generals will most probably fail to take this important place by surprise, and then, as they have no heavy guns at their command, their situation may become awkward when the cold weather sets in, which we expect from day to day. While writing, I am informed that Generals Heimann and Tergukasoff effected their junction yesterday at Kuprikoi, only about twenty-five miles distant from Erzeroum, and are now pursuing Mukhtar and Ismail Pacha. The Turkish generals are not now capable of resisting the Russians an instant in the open field, but the danger is that they may find shelter, food, provisions, arms, ammunition, and new courage within the walls of Erzeroum, till Ali Pacha from Batoum, and reinforcements from Constantinople, come up *viâ* Trebizond.

As to my further journey to headquarters, I have little of interest to narrate. The succession of dreary hills and tablelands, all uniformly carpeted with withered grass, bore a repulsive aspect, and the carcases of horses and bullocks were far from giving the landscape a touch of the picturesque. Moreover the whole scenery was veiled in mist, and the temperature was not quite intertropical. We reached Vezinkoi, on the heights of which Generals Heimann and Lazareff had met on the day of the memorable battle with their victorious troops. Here a camp was established belonging to a brigade ordered to invest Kars on this side. The plateau behind, and the rocky conical hill close by, vomited no more iron and lead from their numerous intrenchments, which one by one had been stormed with irresistible pluck on the 15th inst. On examining those formidable positions I could not help thinking that if the Turks had shown their ordinary stubbornness it would have been doubtful whether the Russians, with their comparatively small attacking forces, could have carried the day. As I am well acquainted with the environs of Plevna, I can say that here was a more difficult piece of work to be achieved than on those soft, sloping hills. Stupid pride had ruffled Ghazi Mukhtar, or he would have retired from his useless position on the Aladja, from which winter would have driven him anyhow, and would have kept the plateaux of Vezinkoi only, with a firm hold on Kars. He might still have been the Ghazi, whom he is no longer but in name. In fact, the Turks were demoralized by the belief current among them that they were surrounded by a force of 100,000 men. In magnifying thus their enemy's numbers they fought with a faint heart, and ran much quicker than they ought. Their wounded and dead cannot be therefore so very numerous as was at first supposed, and some of the gallant cavalry charges mentioned in the official report, especially those on the troops retreating from the Little Yagni, did not at all bear the epic character attributed to them. As to the number of prisoners, either at first gross exaggeration was indulged in by the staff officers, or most of the captured Turks ran away again, hidden by the darkness. Now it is avowed that only seven thousand were taken alive. Vezinkoi had some thirty Greek families among its population. These descendants of Xenophon's deserted or captured soldiers, perhaps, were driven away by their Turkish fellow-citizens some months ago, and their houses destroyed.

We rested here but a few hours, waiting for the carts, and then moved on again over the hills and table-lands bordering the plains of Kars, some 1,000 feet below. That fortress, looming at the foot of the opposite range of mountains, was rendered conspicuous by the sunlight which had managed to pierce the heavy clouds. The town has a semi-amphitheatrical site between two spurs, on the slopes of which the cubiform black houses are clustered. The difficulty of attacking it in a regular way consists chiefly in the rocky ground before the forts, which does not permit sapping, unless with sandbags. About nightfall we reached, three miles to the west of Vezinkoi, the small Turkish village of Teknely, where we sought and found hospitality under the roof of the head man. The spacious dwelling-room, vaulted with heavy timber, was separated from the stables by a railing only and its higher floor. A cheerful fire blazing in the chimney had an alluring aspect, and promised us a comfortable rest after our tiresome journey in the dull, drizzling atmosphere. We—that is to say, a consul, a volunteer captain, a rich proprietor and marshal of the nobility of Kazan, and myself—congratulated ourselves on having met with this rather unexpected good fortune. I stretched my aching bones on the carpet which the obliging Turkish landlord had spread over the floor. But lo! a frightful deception was in store for us. The fear of having one's throat cut while slumbering, and being thrown into the deep well inside the house, vanished when legions of vermin began crawling over our bodies. The feeling of comfort disappeared as by enchantment, and gave place to that of utter disappointment. Then a Turkish woman, decently veiled with an old towel, rushed in bewildered, crying for assistance. On inquiry it soon turned out that a stack of straw belonging to her absent husband had been partly pilfered by passing teamsters and Armenian irregulars, for the benefit of their hungry horses. We settled the dispute as well as we could, and it was agreed that the unwelcome customers should be liable to pay the price of the straw, in conformity with the regulations of the Grand Duke on that head. On the whole, the damage done before our interference was not so important as the excited lady endeavoured to make us believe. We returned to our hotbed of parasitical insects, where Cossacks, Armenians, and Turks had already gone to rest, and slept the sleep of the just, despite the countless legions of vermin. With us sleep was out of the question. We were indeed glad to leave at dawn of day this intolerable cavern of torture. The people there had assured us that the headquarters were only six miles beyond Teknely. So we entrusted our luggage to the care of an irregular Armenian rider, and adopted a quicker pace for our horses. We passed another Russian camp and depôt, and a little later the ruins of an Armenian village, which had been utterly destroyed by the Turks. Whether its population had been murdered or not we could not ascertain, as nobody living was visible on that dismal spot. We rode on, up and down, for miles. Ascending a slope in a straight line, in order to avoid the circuitous carriage road, my horse jumped suddenly over a muddy, suspicious-looking rivulet, instead of walking through it, as I expected him to do. Being thus taken by surprise, I was thrown off the saddle on my back. On recovering my senses I found my head comfortably lodged on the soft turf just between two fragments of rock, each of which was only a few inches from my temples. I was neither hurt, nor stunned, nor bruised, and therefore, knotting the broken bridle together, I followed my companions, who had believed me dead. The six miles were gradually lengthened to no less than twenty-five, and only late in the evening did we arrive at the headquarters, established on the Kars River around the village of Boyuk Tekme. The carts, of course, could not follow us up such a dstance, and the consequence was that I was compelled to pass another luckless night on the floor of a suttler's tent, covered with my rough felt capot. On the following day the carts arrived, and I was thus enabled to set myself up again.

The camp here is now complete, with the exception of the most essential thing for a newspaper correspondent, the European telegraph. Every day they say that to-morrow the line is sure to be established, but when the to-morrow has become to-day no signs of activity in that direction can be made out. I believe that this untoward delay is caused by the want of the necessary poles, which must be fetched from the wooded mountains between Tiflis and Alexandropol. Time is of no value in Russia. The grand-ducal camp here stretches on both sides of the Kars Tchai, a river which is on the average thirty yards wide and one in depth. Here the watering of the animals and the supply for the men is easy enough, but the drawback is likely to be fever and diarrhœa on account of the pools of stagnant water which here and there are spread over the valley, and have all the appearance of breeding foul and unhealthy miasma. It is true that the heat is over now, and the pestilential exhalations are less to be feared; nevertheless, the sun has a good deal of power occasionally. Despite of all that has been said about the rigour of an Armenian winter, I find the climate here much milder and more genial than that of Bulgaria, notwithstanding our 5,500 feet of altitude.

The commander of Kars has, as usual, been summoned to surrender. The Council of War which was thereupon held returned a negative answer. Before the garrison rejected the Russian proposal a Turkish colonel of artillery, a certain Hussein Bey, who had been trained for eight years at Woolwich, visited, with his aide-de-camp, our headquarters, and was politely received. His object, however, was not to sign a capitulation, but only to obtain as much information as possible about our strength and doings. The blockade of Kars is a very effective one. Some Turks tried to get through our lines, but the endeavour was frustrated by vigilant Cossacks. The day before yesterday two English doctors, too, one of whom had just recovered from typhoid fever, were escorted to our camp. On the eve of being shut up for perhaps many months in Kars, they thought it practicable to proceed under a flag of truce to Erzeroum, where they had left their depôt, baggage, and two of their colleagues. The Russian outposts, of course, stopped them and conducted them to our headquarters. Here they presented their passports, and expressed the desire to return home. In compliance with this reasonable request they were guarded, and then conveyed to Tiflis at the expense of the Russian Government. They were very civilly treated here by the officers. Some, however, gave vent to a certain bitterness of feeling, complaining of the English public having sent scores of Red Cross expeditions to the murderous Turks, but none to Russia. I explained that the barbarous and miserably provided Turks were more in need of medical attendance than the well-organized and civilized Russians. The fact is, that every Cossack here is better clad, fed, paid, and attended to than any Turkish captain.

Our three long rifled 24-pounders bombard slowly the city of Kars at a very respectable distance, which renders an answer impossible.

Very bad weather has set in just now. The cold rain is furiously beating against my tent; but, notwithstanding, I hear the heavy boom of our guns cannonading Kars.

On the 4th of November the same correspondent wrote:—

Δ CAMP, BOYUK TEKME, *November 4th.*—The iron band around Kars is so tightly drawn that no living being can go out or in without being challenged and stopped. Every day Turks and Armenians, trying to break the blockade, are arrested and escorted to headquarters, in order to undergo a close examination as to their identity and their movements. On questioning them, their invariable answer is that they know nothing whatever about anything; but gradually, either frightened by threats of being shot as spies, or inveigled by offers of money and sundry presents, they begin to talk. At first they are timid and incoherent, but soon, giving course to their fancy, they state things beyond the limits of all probability. We made thus, shortly after the battle, a doubtful acquisition. A young man, calling himself Osman Bey, has deserted the Prophet's colours, and has declared his readiness to become again a Christian. The Russians are enchanted at having made so distinguished a convert. The young man, however, is simply the son of an English doctor in Pera. An artillery fire is kept up night and day by a battery of long-range 24-pounders established near the village of Matzera, in the neighbourhood of the Little Yagni. Hitherto nothing is known with regard to the effects of this bombardment, which, however, will assume more formidable proportions after the arrival of the siege train from Alexandropol. We only know that the inhabitants, as well as the garrison of Kars, are disposed to capitulate, if things should go adverse for the Turkish arms at Erzeroum.

One of the most important consequences of the victory of Aladja Dagh will certainly be the reaction which it is sure to produce in the eastern parts of the Caucasian mountains, where about two months ago a fraction of the population took to arms, and rose against the Russian Government, allured by childish promises which the Stamboul rulers held out to them through the instrumentality of the son of the famous Sheikh Schamyl. Emissaries and letters had been sent to the Kabardians, Lesghians, and Daghestanies, stating, with a power of imagination worthy of the Thousand and One Nights, that in the first place half a million of victorious Ottoman soldiers were on the eve of invading Russia, and of marching to their assistance, and in the second that some fifty camels, loaded with gold, were ready to cross the frontier with the view of enriching every one of the valiant mountaineers. This appeal to the greed of the people was indeed opportune, for without it we may fairly doubt whether their chivalrous propensities and religious zeal would have been raised to the boiling point. What had they to complain of? They pay no taxes, are permitted to bear arms, and nobody ever thought of interfering with their religion. They may erect mosques, study the Koran in their own schools, perform their religious duties, and marry as many wives as they think fit for their domestic convenience. The only obligation imposed upon them in exchange for so many immunities and absolute personal freedom is to recruit among themselves, in accordance with their warlike instincts, a limited number of irregular horsemen as a contingent to the Russian army in case of a war. These volunteers are not called out at their own expense, but receive abundant rations and a monthly pay of thirty roubles. Moreover, all legitimate booty which they chance to make—as cattle and stores belonging to the enemy—are either bought of them in hard cash by the Government, or they are at liberty to sell them wherever they think best. In truth, no people in the world are better off than these Mohammedan Caucasians. In addition to all this, they are prevented from carrying on the sanguinary and ruinous feuds with neighbouring tribes which formerly not only led to the destruction of a vast amount of property, but sometimes to the extirpation of whole tribes, as a consequence of the terrible law of retaliation. They are intelligent and shrewd enough, however, to understand that, after the battle on the 15th of October, the camel loads of gold may be considered to have vanished for ever. No gold, no Circassians, is a proverb the truth of which Ghazi Mukhtar Pacha was enabled to test when his Caucasian horsemen left him by wholesale desertion, in spite of their boundless fanaticism. That the Turkish prisoners made on the 15th ult. were partly escorted by a Lesghian irregular regiment was a stroke of refined policy on the part of the Russian authorities which cannot fail to give ocular evidence of the discomfiture of the host which was so confidently expected to assist in the deliverance of the Caucasians from the yoke of the infidels. As after the failure of an insurtionary movement discontented populations are disposed to keep the peace for a long time, the troops employed there will soon be available.

For Kars, however, a critical period was approaching. As soon as General Melikoff found that Hussein Hami Pacha would not surrender, he determined to commence artillery operations against the south-east front of the fortress. On the 4th of November his long-range guns opened fire from Magardik. On the 5th, the Russian army marched from Karajal to Vezinkoi. On its way it was attacked by ten Turkish battalions issuing forth from Fort Hafiz Pacha. The Turks were repulsed, and the Russians, following up their advantage, entered the fort after its defenders and effectually disabled its guns. When the Russian siege batteries were completed, they extended from the Kars Tchai, near Komadsoi, to the foot of the hills near Vezinkoi, and brought a concentrated force to bear upon the southern and eastern faces of Kars. The object of General Melikoff was so to harass and dispirit the men as to prepare the way for an assault, and we know now that in this he succeeded, for just before the catastrophe Hussein Hami Pacha telegraphed to Mukhtar Pacha at Erzeroum that his men were so cowed and dispirited that he feared the fortress would fall at the first assault. Orders were issued from the Russian headquarters for attacking Kars on November 13th, but the weather had made the ground slippery, and the operation was postponed, only however for four days, as the following telegram from the correspondent with General Melikoff shows :—

△ Veran Kaleh, *November 18th*, 6 p.m.—I have just returned from Kars with intelligence of one of the greatest and most difficult military feats ever accomplished—viz., the storming of a fortress, not only of very considerable natural strength, but also constructed by skilful European engineers, English and Prussian, after the best modern principles; a fortress armed with more than 300 Krupp and other heavy guns.

Kars is ours. In a single night it fell into the hands of about 15,000 Russians, who with irresistible courage climbed the steep rocks, the ramparts, and walls, and drove an equal number of desperately fighting Turks in a headlong flight over their ditches and parapets, compelling them to die or surrender.

All the nice inferences drawn as to the impossibility of storming even small intrenchments defended by breechloaders have proved to be incorrect. The nine forts of Kars, its citadel, and numerous batteries and redoubts, did not withstand a single night the onslaught of spirited young troops, for so at least were the Moscow Grenadiers and the 40th Division.

Such an important event cannot, of course, be described at once in all its particulars, and especially by a fatigued correspondent, with his fingers as cold and stiff as icicles. The escalade had been originally fixed for the 13th instant, but was postponed owing to the bad weather until last night. In deep secrecy the columns assumed their appointed positions. General Lazereff, with the 40th Division, commanded the right wing, and attacked the Hafiz Pacha Fort, crowning a steep rocky height. General Count Grabbe, with a regiment of Moscow Grenadiers and a regiment of the 39th Division, assailed in the centre the Khanli Tabia, Suwarri Tabia, the Towers, and the Citadel, while the Ardahan brigade and another regiment of Moscow Grenadiers, under Generals Roop and Komaroff, assailed positions further to the left at half-past eight o'clock yesterday evening.

The engagement began in the centre. The chivalrous Count Grabbe led the foremost of his brigade in storming Khanli Tabia, and fell dead, pierced by a bullet. Captain Kwadmicki, of the 39th Regiment, jumped first on the rather too short ladder, and entered the terrible. redoubt at 11. His sword was clean cut out of his hand, and his clothes pierced. Hoaene, a large massive redoubt, surrendered early in the morning, then the three towers. The Citadel and Fort Suwarri were carried at the same time as Khanli Fort. Hafiz Pacha Fort was taken, and in the morning Karadagh. The other forts, especially Tekmash and Arab-Tabia resisted till eight this morning, then 40 battalions fled towards Erzeroum, but were overtaken by dragoons and the Orenburg Cossacks, and laid down their arms, and were brought back as prisoners.

The whole fortress and city, with 300 cannons, stores, ammunition, hard cash, &c., fell almost intact into our hands. The Turks lost 5,000 killed and wounded and 10,000 prisoners, and many flags. The Russian loss was about 2,700. The soldiers made but a trifling booty, and spared peaceful citizens, women, and children. This I state as an eye witness.

General Loris Melikoff directed the battle throughout. The Grand Duke was present also. The former entered the town at 11 o'clock A.M. to-day.

△ VERAN KALEH, *November 20th, Evening.*—Yesterday the Grand Duke Michael made his solemn entry into Kars, and received the homage of the inhabitants. He then proceeded to the citadel, where he entertained his officers at breakfast. Afterwards he visited Forts Hafiz and Kanli. The Grand Duke thanked the troops in the name of the Emperor, passing in review several battalions, and the artillery paraded before the conquered fortifications.

It is ascertained now that the garrison was above 20,000 strong, Only 18,000 Russians were employed in the attack. The town is full of Turkish sick and wounded, in a filthy and neglected condition. Medical assistance is sadly wanted. Typhoid fever is spreading. The cold is intense.

To-morrow the staff will go to Kars. Tartars and other mounted militiamen are still pillaging unchecked, but order will be restored to-day. Great difficulties are experienced with the numerous Turkish sick and the prisoners.

Thus fell the great Ottoman stronghold in Asia. The event made a deep impression upon Europe. It raised the military capacity of the Russians, and at the same time exposed the want of resources of the Turks. In the army before Plevna it was hailed with great rejoicings, for it excited the hope that after so many months of reverses and hardships the good fortune of the western army of Bulgaria might not be less than that of the Army of the Caucasus.

Woodfall & Kinder, Printers, Milford Lane, Strand, London, W.C.

1090368R1

Printed in Great Britain by
Amazon.co.uk, Ltd.,
Marston Gate.